ANNUAL REVIEW OF
SOCIOLOGY

ANNUAL REVIEW OF SOCIOLOGY

VOLUME 22, 1996

JOHN HAGAN, *Editor*
University of Toronto

KAREN S. COOK, *Associate Editor*
Duke University

http://annurev.org   science@annurev.org   415-493-4400

ANNUAL REVIEWS INC.   4139 EL CAMINO WAY   P.O. BOX 10139   PALO ALTO, CALIFORNIA 94303-0139

ANNUAL REVIEWS INC.
Palo Alto, California, USA

International Standard Serial Number: 0360-0572
International Standard Book Number: 0-8243-2222-3
Library of Congress Catalog Card Number: 75-648500

Annual Review and publication titles are registered trademarks of Annual Reviews Inc.

♾ The paper used in this publication meets the minimum requirements of American
National Standard for Information Sciences—Permanence of Paper for Printed Library
Materials, ANSI Z39.48-1984.

Annual Reviews Inc. and the Editors of its publications assume no responsibility for the
statements expressed by the contributors to this *Review*.

TYPESET BY TECHBOOKS, FAIRFAX, VA
PRINTED AND BOUND IN THE UNITED STATES OF AMERICA

PREFACE

The *Annual Review of Sociology* is more than a record of the changes in a dynamic discipline, it is an instrument and participant in these changes. To further advance this purpose, the *Annual Review of Sociology* has become the first of the 26 volumes produced by Annual Reviews Inc. to be published electronically as well as on paper. The electronic version of Volume 22 of the *Review* appeared on-line on June 1, 1996, three months prior to its August print publication.

To access this and subsequent volumes of the *Annual Review of Sociology* on the Internet, you can now type "http//www/annurev.org/soc/home.htm" and access a wealth of sociological research materials: abstracts of all *ARS* articles for the past 12 years, full text of all articles published in *ARS* from 1993 to 1996, over 80 bibliographies, as well as an address book into which every visitor is invited to enter his or her name, address, and e-mail address. Any scholar on-line can search the database, read or print out abstracts, order and download articles, or purchase any journal published by Annual Reviews.

We invite our readers to visit the *Annual Review of Sociology On-Line* and to offer us suggestions or comments for making the material more useful to sociologists. We expect to continue to offer *ARS* in permanent form in bound volumes for the indefinite future, but the electronic availability of our chapters months in advance of paper publication will, we hope, be a real service to our readers.

Seymour Martin Lipset's prefatory chapter is an especially appropriate introduction for this volume's entry into the electronic age. Lipset continues to offer profound insights into a changing social world, and his essay chronicles the extraordinary breadth of this contribution. The chapters that follow continue the theme of change, with essays on feminist research methods, changing gender relations and divisions in household labor, categorical data analysis and experimental surveys, cross-national and comparative research, computer networks and corporate interlocks, mass media, postcommunism and market transitions.

The Editors

Annual Review of Sociology
Volume 22 (1996)

CONTENTS

vii   CONTENTS (*Continued*)

RELATED ARTICLES IN OTHER *ANNUAL REVIEWS*

From the *Annual Review of Anthropology*, Volume 25 (1996)

The Anthropology of Cities: Imagining and Theorizing the City, S. Low

Anthropological Perspectives on Hazards and Disasters, A. Oliver-Smith

The Construction of Urban Poverty and Homelessness in the New Global Economy, I. Susser

From the *Annual Review of Psychology*, Volume 47 (1996)

The Design and Analysis of Social-Interaction Research, DA Kenny

Stereotypes, JL Hilton and W von Hippel

Teams in Organizations: Recent Research on Performance and Effectiveness, RA Guzzo and MW Dickson

The Social Structure of Schooling, SM Dornbusch, KL Glasgow, I-C Lin

From the *Annual Review of Public Health*, Volume 17 (1996)

Benefit-Cost Analysis in Public Health, LB Lave and SV Hoshi

Pervasive Media Violence, S Schooler and JA Flora

Racial Differences in Health: Not Just Black and White, but Shades of Gray, M Lillie-Blanton, PE Parsons, J Gayle, A Dievler

Population and Women's Reproductive Health: An International Perspective, K Miller and A Rosenfield

Health and Unemployment, D Dooley, J Fielding, L Levi

Annu. Rev. Sociol. 1996. 22:1–27

STEADY WORK: An Academic Memoir[1]

Seymour Martin Lipset

Public Policy Institute, George Mason University, Fairfax, Virginia 22030

KEY WORDS: socialism, exceptionalism, politics, social mobility, oligarchy

To Robert K. Merton, without whom it never could have happened

---

Some years ago at a cocktail party in Washington, I approached General Colin Powell, then still head of the Joint Chiefs, and told him that he and I had a lot in common. The General, who did not know me, reacted with a quizzical look. I commented that we were both born in Harlem, moved when quite young to the Bronx, and went to and graduated from City College. I did not add what was more relevant, that he joined the ROTC, the Reserve Officers Training Corps, while I joined the youth section of the Trotskyists, then known as the Young People's Socialist League, Fourth International. Our different behaviors after entering City College determined much of our later life, although the General exhibited more consistency in his career than I did in politics. He remained with the military until retirement. I left the Trotskyists within a year after joining them in 1940, although I remained active in various left socialist groups for a number of years. I served, among other things, as the national chairman of the Youth Section of the Socialist Party, also known as the Young People's Socialist League, or YIPSILS. My final resignation from socialist organizations occurred around 1960 when I quit the Socialist Party, which had become a futile organization. Intellectually I moved a considerable distance, from believing in Marxism-Leninism-Trotskyism to a moderate form of democratic socialism and finally to a middle-of-the-road position, as a centrist, or as some would say, a conservative Democrat. In recent decades, leftist critics of my writings and subsequent politics have placed me in that category known as neoconservative.

My parents were both born in Czarist Russia in Minsk and Pinsk. My mother, Lena, came to America as a young child in 1907. Her parents, who died before I was born, in the 1918 flu epidemic, were religious Jews. She was a seamstress

---

[1] I am indebted for this title to Irving Howe, who used it for a book of his essays.

0360-0572/96/0815-0001$08.00

before she married, and she kept a kosher home afterwards. My father, Max, arrived as a young adult in 1911. He had apprenticed as a printer (compositor) in Russia. Shortly before he died in 1945, he told me of his experiences in Russia. The most noteworthy related to his membership in the printers' union in Kiev. Since the Russian printers, while supporting the Social Democratic party, refused to ally themselves with the Bolsheviks or Mensheviks, major leaders of both factions spent time at union meetings to win support. He told me Stalin came to a small one in Kiev. When I asked my father how he could remember Stalin, since he was almost unknown at the time, my father responded that he could because Stalin was different. All the others, Bolsheviks and Mensheviks, discussed Marxist theory and revolutionary tactics. Stalin, however, talked about organizational structure and efficiency. He told the printers they would gain more economically by working with the Bolsheviks.

The two strands, Judaism and Marxism, that concerned my parents clearly had an impact on me. I joined both Jewish and socialist organizations as a teenager, and some of my earliest research dealt with printer unionism. As noted above, I spent many years in socialist groups until my mid-thirties, largely ignoring Jewish issues and activities. My first and late wife, Elsie, whom I married in 1945, although also a socialist, was much more of a dedicated Jew than I in the early years of our marriage. Starting with the Six Day War in 1967, I became very active in campus-related Jewish groups. I have written many articles and pamphlets, edited one book and coauthored another, dealing with Jewish subjects. And I have remained committed to politics as a scholarly vocation and as my main avocation.

The substance of my academic career flows in many ways from my early and continuing political interests. As a Trotskyist or socialist from high school through graduate school, I became interested in three questions. The biggest one was—why had the Bolshevik revolution in the Soviet Union led to an oppressive, exploitative society? The groups with which I was affiliated, the Socialists and the Trotskyists, had no doubt but that the Soviet Union was a more oppressive system than any in the democratic capitalist world. They recognized that the Soviet Union was a totalitarian tyranny. They also believed that the Communist parties of the world, including the American one, were almost totally controlled by Moscow and served the interests of the ruling class of that country, not those of American workers or workers anywhere. The big question was, therefore, how did a revolution, led by people who had come out of the socialist movement, which had been dedicated to reducing inequality and making the world more free, result in totalitarianism?

The second question that concerned me was: Why had the democratic social-ist movement, the Second International, the social democrats, failed to adhere to policies that would further socialism? By "furthering socialism," I mean the coming to power in industrial countries of socialist parties who would make their countries more egalitarian, more democratic, and less economically oppressive by enhancing the role of the state in the economy as well as by changing political practices. The social democrats seemed to pursue policies inimical to their coming to full power and enacting socialism. Essentially, the social democrats were following compromising and nonrevolutionary policies that prevented them from gaining the support of the workers and other socioeconomically inferior members of the population. When elected, they did not carry out programs that would contribute to the destruction of capitalism. Left socialist critics like myself were pure rationalists. We believed the correct policies would have prevented the Nazis from coming to power in Germany or Franco from winning in Spain, or would have enabled the socialists to win office in various countries. The issue for us was why the democratic socialist parties had failed to follow a correct Marxist line; we asked what had led them to be compromisers, reformists, and advocates of the middle way?

The third political question that interested me greatly was why the United States had never had a major socialist party. The United States is the only industrialized country that has never developed an electorally viable socialist or social democratic party or powerful labor movement. An American Socialist party was founded at the turn of the century; the greatest proportion it ever received of the vote for president was 6%, and that in only one year, 1912. It was not able to win an election in a political unit larger than a city. It failed to secure the support of the trade union movement. The American Federation of Labor, the AF of L, always opposed socialism and efforts to create a labor party. The third question, therefore, was Sombart's old one: "Why no socialism in the United States?"

Attempting to answer these questions was to inform much of my academic career. That career, I should note, took root in sociology as a result of a discussion I had in 1941 with a then-Trotskyist colleague, Peter Rossi. As a student at City College I had first decided to take a science degree in order to qualify as a dentist. That incongruous objective, given my political interests, was dictated by the fact that the only member of my family who made out well during the Great Depression was an uncle who was a dentist and who had never married. Securing a good income was particularly important because my father, who was a printer, was employed irregularly for most of the 1930s. My family was able to survive economically because he worked occasionally as a "substitute." That is, he could be employed on a day-to-day basis when printers were in more demand, as before Christmas, although he was unemployed most of the year. On occasion we were forced to go on home relief, as welfare was known then. But we also depended on largess from my uncle Bill, the dentist. He was my mother's brother, and various members of my mother's family decided that this asset, namely my uncle's practice, should be kept in the family. I was the oldest male and it was therefore incumbent on me to study dentistry.[2]

Fortunately for my prospective clients, I decided after one year at City that dentistry was not for me, and I shifted to history. This decision was changed when Peter Rossi came to me and said that we should major in sociology. I asked why, and his answer was that the graduate program related to undergraduate sociology was social work. And social workers, who deal with people in economic trouble, would always be in demand, assuming, as he and I did, that the depression with massive unemployment would recur after the war. This made sense to me, and we both became sociology majors.

Various experiences as an undergraduate reinforced my political interests and beliefs. I had occasional difficulties with some of the Stalinist teachers, particularly in the English department, but I will not elaborate on that here other than to say I believed they deliberately downgraded me for my political commitments. As many alumni of the City College radical movements have written, the political groups spent much of their time in what were known as the alcoves. The alcoves were partitioned areas off the large cafeteria of the college. Different groups used different alcoves. Alcove One was inhabited by the anti-Stalinist leftists, that is, the Trotskyists, the socialists, the anarchists, and Zionist socialists. Its noteworthy alumni include people like Daniel Bell, Irving Kristol, Irving Howe, Nathan Glazer, Philip Selznick, and many others. Alcove Two, right next door, was the Stalinist hangout. I had frequent arguments with some of them. Alcove Three was inhabited by the right wing Zionists, the followers of Jabotinsky. Beyond Alcove Three not much attention was paid to politics.

The student radicals of the 1930s and early 1940s, at least at City College, took study and reading seriously. We were particularly dedicated to the Marxist classics and to securing a knowledge of comparative politics. We read and discussed Marx and Engels, Lenin and Trotsky. We also studied the political events that led to the Russian Revolution, the triumph of fascism in Italy, of Nazism in Germany, the Spanish Civil War, the experience of Popular Fronts in various parts of Europe as well as American politics. The Marxist critics of reformism, from Lenin onwards, had no good explanation of why various socialist leaders or parties had "betrayed" the revolution, other than that they somehow came to represent the interests of the petty-bourgeoisie, of the middle class, rather than

---

[2]Knowing this would have delighted Trotsky. He once described the American Socialist party, which he did not respect, as a party of dentists.

the proletariat. The critical commentary tended to be moralistic rather than sociological.

For some of us in Alcove One, one book changed this: *Political Parties* by Robert Michels. Michels had been a German social democrat and sociologist. He became interested in trying to understand why his political party, the Social Democratic party of Germany, the largest and most important socialist party in the world before the great war, had become bureaucratized and was not, as he understood it, internally democratic. Michels was a protege of Max Weber, who had urged him to study party organizations and machines. His book, published in 1911, focused on the German Social Democrats. The German party and, he argued, all other parties as well were and necessarily had to be dominated by an oligarchy. Parties competed with each other for electoral support in the larger polity, but within their own organization there was, Michels argued, no democracy. Policy was set from the top; new leaders were chosen by the existing elite.

The bulk of *Political Parties* was devoted to explaining why oligarchy is inherent, not only in the nature of large-scale organizations, but also in the characteristics of the masses, of the rank and file. Michels basically argued that voluntary organizations like parties or trade unions, professional bodies, veteran groups, and the like have a one-party internal structure. The paid officials, the leaders and bureaucracy, control access to relevant information, dominate the press of the organization, have a near monopoly on political skills, and can therefore overwhelm opposition, which is inevitably less well organized and politically incompetent. In any case the membership lacks the interest, knowledge, and skills to take part in internal politics and to counter the leadership. Given the privileged position of the union leaders or party bureaucracies, it followed that they are not in the same economic class as the membership, that the organization's policies reflect the position of the higher status and more powerful officials, not of the rank and file.

Political Parties was brought to the attention of Alcove One by Philip Selznick, who was a few years older than me. Selznick was the first among us to go on to graduate school, studying sociology at Columbia where he worked with Robert Merton, who had just arrived at Columbia as an assistant professor. Selznick had become the leader of a small group within a secessionist Trotskyist party, the Workers Party. The Party had rejected Trotsky's argument that in spite of Stalinism the Soviet Union was still a workers' state, albeit a "degenerated" one, which should be defended by left-wing groups. Selznick went further to proclaim a major heresy, namely, the rejection of Bolshevism and of Leninism. He argued that Stalinism was rooted in Leninism. He founded a small anti-Bolshevik faction with about 25 members, known as the Shermanites, after his party name, Philip Sherman. It did not last long within the Trotskyists. The group published a small magazine, *Enquiry.* Its one "adult" adherent was Dwight MacDonald. But it included a high percentage of eventually distinguished scholars and writers: Gertrude Jaeger, Gertrude Himmelfarb, Irving Kristol, Martin Diamond, Herbert Garfinkle, Peter Rossi, William Peterson, and others.

Political Parties was an eye opener to me and to others. It seemed to explain two of our questions—why the Soviet Union had become a dictatorship after the Russian revolution, and why the social democratic parties were so inept at fighting for socialism. Michels, in effect, said that there was a ruling stratum within all parties and that if a socialist party came to power it would reproduce within the larger polity the kind of hierarchical political system that existed inside the party. He concluded his book by saying that while socialists may triumph, that is, capture office, socialism never would. He argued that since the socialists were ideologically more concerned with extending democracy in Germany and other European countries than was any other party, the fact that they, even though extreme democrats, were authoritarian internally demonstrated that democracy was impossible. (I came to disagree substantially with this conclusion, recognizing that competing parties that offer a choice defines democracy, even though the internal structure of subordinate groups representing interests and values are oligarchic, but that recognition occurred later.)

The Russian Bolsheviks had a party structure more elite controlled than that of the German Social Democrats. Because they operated in a dictatorial regime, it was understandable that on coming to power, the Bolsheviks created a repressive system. And since the oligarchs of social democratic parties, like all dominant strata, were largely concerned with maintaining and extending their power, status, and privileges, it was also understandable that the parties they controlled would not be revolutionary, that they would not be interested either in really extending the participation of the masses. Michels' theory of the "iron law of oligarchy" went a long way to accounting both for Stalinism and the failures of the Social Democracy.

Exposure to these political and intellectual ideas helped liberate me from Leninist or Trotskyist beliefs and contributed to my decision to follow in Selznick's footsteps and study sociology in graduate school. But to be honest, I must report that the actions were largely a result of fortuitous circumstances. I graduated from City College in 1943 in the middle of World War II. I received a draft deferment in 1942 that lasted for close to a year to enable me to graduate. As it turned out, when I was given a physical examination by Selective Service I was deferred for being severely nearsighted. Given this rejection, I had to do something else. The sociology department at City College offered me a teaching fellowship. A condition for the fellowship was to be registered as a graduate student, so I applied to Columbia, which was a mile away, and went there.

Political developments in Canada at the time affected my interests since they bore on the question of "Why no socialism in the United States." The Canadian social democratic party, then known as the Cooperative Commonwealth Federation, or CCF, had taken off electorally during the war. It had been formed in the depths of the depression in 1933 and had a fair amount of early electoral success, winning about a dozen members in parliament, largely from western Canada, particularly in the provinces of Saskatchewan and British Columbia. In a 1943 provincial election in Ontario, Canada's wealthiest and most populous province, the CCF was a close second, missing being first by two legislative seats. This development was naturally of considerable interest to American socialists. For the first time in North America a socialist party had gained significant electoral strength. I began to read everything I could find on the CCF and attended a national convention in Montreal.

I visited Columbia for the first time in the fall of 1943 and, on the strong advice of Phil Selznick, met with Robert Merton. Merton was to become the most important intellectual influence on me in my academic career. In talking to him on this first visit, I told him that two topics interested me as possibilities for my PhD dissertation. This was a fairly unusual statement from a novice, who had not taken any graduate courses. I recall Merton looking somewhat puzzled. The topics I described to him were studies of the CCF and of the political system of my father's union, the International Typographical Union (ITU). My interest in the latter was not to reaffirm a family tie, although that tie had enabled me to learn the about ITU's unique (for unions) internal politics. It was the only labor organization to have an institutionalized competitive party system with turnover in office. And, therefore, it challenged Michels's "iron law of oligarchy." I went on to do both "theses." When I finished the work on the Typographical Union, which appeared as *Union Democracy* (1953), I went into Merton's office with a copy of the manuscript under my arm and told him: "Here's my second dissertation." He, of course, had no recollection of the conversation we had had ten years earlier.

My interest in the CCF, which was the beginning of a lifelong concern with Canadian society and politics, stemmed, as noted, from the issue of why there was no socialism in the United States. I had assumed at the time (although I now know better) that Canada, particularly English Canada, is very similar sociologically to the United States. Hence, if Canada could develop an important socialist movement, so presumably could the United States. I thought it should be possible to learn about the conditions that could produce a socialist movement in this country by finding out how this had happened in Canada.

When I finished my graduate work at Columbia, I received a fellowship from the Social Science Research Council to go to Saskatchewan where the CCF had elected a government in 1944, to study the party and the government. The research enabled me to learn a great deal about Canada, about social science methods, and about the United States. Perhaps the most important lesson, as I have reiterated many times since, is that the best way to learn about your own country is to go abroad and discover the ways that behavior, practices, and institutions you take for granted at home are different elsewhere.

Most of the political analysis in my work on Saskatchewan helped to explain the occurrence in the midwest of populism and other forms of agrarian radicalism on both sides of the US-Canadian border in the late nineteenth and first half of the twentieth century. The analysis did not, however, contribute to solving the "why no socialism in the United States" puzzle. The one answer suggested by the Canadian-American comparison was a political science argument, namely that the parliamentary system, which characterizes Canada and other Commonwealth countries, is much more conducive to the formation of third parties than is the direct national election of the chief executive required by the American Constitution.

Comparing different, yet similar, outcomes in Saskatchewan and the neighboring Republican state of North Dakota was especially useful. North Dakota has been governed by Republicans and Saskatchewan by a third party of social democrats. The Non-Partisan League, which had secured control of North Dakota in 1918 after winning the Republican primaries, held office in the state during the 1930s and was basically a social democratic group with a state program very much like that of the CCF in Saskatchewan. It, however, functioned within the Republican party. In comparing the history of radical groups on both sides of the border, the evidence suggested that the major differentiating factor has been the variation in electoral systems. Choosing presidents in a national vote undermines third parties' efforts, while parliamentary single district elections are much more encouraging to such. In the former, the American, multiparty coalitions are impossible, and those who wanted to sustain a third party are pressured to support the "lesser evil" of the two major parties, not to "waste their vote." In Canada, which follows the British parliamentary system, the electorate can vote only for a member of the House of Commons or provicial legislature. Hence if third party sentiment is strong in a given constituency, that party is a viable choice, even if it is weak nationally. Prime ministers are chosen by the House of Commons, and a small party can affect that decision when no one party has a majority. A four-member independent labor-left group led by the future leader of the CCF, VS Woodsworth, was able to do so in 1925 and so secured important policy concessions for their votes.

The thesis that the presidential system severely discourages third parties in the United States was advanced by a major Socialist party leader, Morris Hillquit, before World War I, and by Norman Thomas, the perennial Socialist candidate for President, on a number of latter occasions. The Canadian-American comparison, and particularly the Saskatchewan-North Dakota one, seemed to reinforce the argument strongly. Added to the wasted vote thesis is the impact that the less-disciplined American congressional parties have on encouraging factions to work inside the old parties. This is made possible by a popularly elected chief executive who holds office regardless of support in Congress, and by employing a primary nomination system that permits diverse groups to compete for popular backing within the two major coalitions.

More important than the conclusion about the impact of the electoral system was my formulating an understanding of the relationship between what is now referred to as civic society, or the role of mediating institutions, grass roots or voluntary associations, and the development of and institutionalization of democracy. My first published article, which appeared in 1947 in the *Canadian Journal of Economics and Political Science*, dealt with the topic, as did my subsequent work on the Typographical Union and democracy in unions and other private governments. Saskatchewan sensitized me to the relationship as I began to realize that this intensely politically active area, with a population of 800,000, had at least 125,000 positions in community organizations and government that had to be filled. Public positions included many rural municipalities, which were smaller units than counties in the United States, and thousands of school and library boards. Communal groups were comprised of a variety of farm organizations, such as cooperative elevators which stored grain, telephone companies which were locally owned and controlled, coop stores which existed in every community, hospitals which were controlled by the local residents, and the like. Questionnaire data indicated that the same people served in a number of local posts. These community activists were involved in politics, and they could create new social movements and parties. Here was Tocqueville's description and analysis of the role of voluntary associations in the United States in the 1830s still operative in North America in 1945 and, as I was to learn later, also among printers. Saskatchewan and the Typographical Union had strong civil societies.

The decision to study the CCF not only bore on my political interests, it also reflected my concerns for class analysis and the study of social movements. Much of *Agrarian Socialism* deals with the processes of class formation, of the ways a class becomes organized and conscious of its collective interests. The study also was intended as a contribution to organizational sociology, to indicate the ways bureaucratic interests and expertise affect policy. This concern was linked to Michels' and Weber's theories of organization. Methodologically, the Saskatchewan study was an example of what Paul Lazarsfeld called "deviant case" analysis, the specification of new variables and hypotheses to account for exceptions to a general rule. Clearly responsive to my desire to further the socialist cause, the book presents a bridge to the study of what would eventually to become my major substantive and political interest, democracy. It is an empirical analysis of the political consequences of a vibrant civil society, a topic that formed the main theme of *Union Democracy* and which informs my current work on democratic systems.

My second major study, the analysis of the political system of the International Typographical Union, had two sources. One, of course, was my father. He had been a lifelong member of the union since he had arrived in New York from Russia before World War I. He would occasionally take me to union meetings which were held every month in a New York high school. More significant, or more important intellectually, as a stimulus to me to study the ITU, was Michels' *Political Parties*. Michels had argued that all large-scale voluntary associations like unions and parties have a one-party system, are controlled by a self-cooptating oligarchy. The academic literature on the governance of trade unions in America and elsewhere basically agreed, emphasizing the absence of organized opposition in unions (though it should be noted, not in American parties). Uncontested elections and conventions controlled by almost permanent officers have meant relatively little in the determination of policy in most unions. However, if this was true for the bulk of the union movement, it was not for the Typographical Union.

That organization, as those who have read *Union Democracy* know, had an institutionalized two-party system. All elections were contested, both local and national. The role of the opposition within the ITU was like that of political antagonists in the larger polity, that is, to present alternative programs and to criticize the activities of incumbent administrations. Members could have an impact on policy as well as help determine who became officers by choosing between two opposition slates. Here was a living system that illustrated Joseph Schumpeter's conception of democracy, a system in which the rank and file, or the electorate, can select between competing elites, basically opposing parties. The research was conducted in collaboration with two sociology graduate students, Martin Trow, who was involved from the start, and James S. Coleman, who joined in the later stages of the study. Coleman also wrote his dissertation, which I supervised, using data from the study.

Union Democracy is an analysis of the social conditions for democracy within private governments. But much of what has been written about democracy in national polities, an important topic in recent years, is dealt with in *Union*

Democracy. We emphasized the role of what is now called civil society, a myriad of mediating institutions between the top of the organization or society and the rank and file of citizenry, in stimulating and sustaining opposition. Surprisingly, a true civil society existed within the Typographical Union. The printing industry had produced an occupational community that subsumed many voluntary associations. Using survey data, we were able to show that printers were led to seek out each other's company for two reasons: (*a*) many of them worked nights or evenings and therefore had to see people who were on the same job shift as themselves, and (*b*) the marginal status of printers, on the border between the (white collar) middle and (manual) working class, also pressed them to interact with each other off the job. These resulted in the creation of an occupational community of many clubs and organizations of printers. In New York, there was a baseball league, bowling groups, veterans organizations, ethnic associations, and various social groups. The occupational community of wheat farmers that I described in Saskatchewan clearly had parallels within the printing industry. To extend our hypotheses we looked at printers' unions in other countries. While the party system of the ITU was unique, printing unions elsewhere tended to be more democratic than the rest of the labor movements and were involved in occupational communities.

Michels' theoretical perspective formed the guiding framework for the study, for the analysis of a deviant case, of an exception to the "iron law of oligarchy." The Typographical Union did not have an oligarchy. Its leaders could be, and were, voted out of office. We consciously dealt with it methodologically as a deviant case, and, as Paul Lazarsfeld suggested, this meant that the theoretical model had to be modified or amplified. What made the ITU different from other unions was institutionalized opposition, a functioning two-party system. Support for the union parties were linked to fixed cleavages—ideological, ethnic, religious, and economic subgroups within the industry. In subsequent writings on democracy, I have occasionally referred to material in the book; I regret that, because it came out in the 1950s and dealt with unions, its theoretical generalizations, particularly its emphasis on subgroups, on civil society, have not in the main fed into the literature on democracy that has appeared in the past two decades.

Following *Union Democracy* my next major work was a series of studies of social mobility in the United States and other countries, some of which I conducted with my friend at Berkeley, Reinhard Bendix, and Hans Zetterberg, a Swedish sociologist who taught for some years at Columbia when I was on its graduate faculty during the early 1950s. My interest in social mobility stemmed to some considerable degree from the "why no socialism" question. A friend, William Peterson, wrote an article in *Commentary* in 1954 dealing with the issue. He argued that the main reason for the absence of a strong socialist movement was that the United States had a higher rate of mass social mobility than did European societies, that in an open society it was much more difficult to organize a radical, class-conscious party than in more highly stratified, less open, societies.

I knew the literature on social mobility because I was teaching a course on stratification at Columbia at the time. One of the major works available in English, published in 1928, was a book by Pitirim Sorokin, *Social Mobility*. Sorokin, who hailed from Russia and knew many languages, reported on hundreds, if not thousands, of small studies, some dating back to the nineteenth century. He documented considerable social mobility, upward movement into the dominant strata as well as into the middle classes, in many countries. It seemed that the comparative image of Europe as a more closed postfeudal society, in contrast to the United States as a more open one with considerable mobility, was untrue. This conclusion was reinforced by the findings of another friend, Natalie Rogoff, who was then at the Bureau of Applied Social Research at Columbia, comparing mobility in France and the United States based on national survey data. She reported that there was very little difference in the mobility rates in the two countries, particularly when people were classified dichotomously as manual/nonmanual, middle class/working class.

What, then, was the difference between the stratification systems of the United States and the European countries? Basically, they had varying class values. The American ideology stressed those of an open society—achievement, upward mobility, getting ahead for all. Most of Europe, however, was postfeudal. Its social class structures had emphasized social status as a relatively permanent characteristic linked to family origin and occupation. In Germany and Sweden, people were addressed by their occupational title. The Continental countries had different words to address those who were higher and lower than the speaker. Class, or status identity, therefore, has continued to be a much more explicit part of European social structure than in the United States. But the differences in status structure, though affecting class identity and propensity for class politics, presumably did not yield varying rates of social mobility on the mass level.

One of our principal assumptions, derived in part from Thorstein Veblen, was that regardless of how societies perceive class, as rigid or open, people are motivated to try to move up. Even in a status-bound society, those who are lower class regard being socially inferior as a negative factor, as punishment, and will seek to improve their situation if the economy and other structures allow. Conversely, since the factors related to class or status position, such as intelligence, education, and achievement motivation, are not fixed inherited characteristics, some will lose position and will wind up beneath the status of their parents. Hence many will rise or fall in all societies. What most determines varying national rates is the degree of expansion or contraction of stratified positions, mainly economic ones. Hence Europe during the Industrial Revolution necessarily experienced high rates of mobility. A society could emphasize status differentiation and still be quite open.

These assumptions underlay the conclusions that Rogoff and I wrote in an article in *Commentary,* stating that varying national rates of upward or downward mobility do not account for class consciousness or the lack of it. What does help to explain it is the value system of societies, and we noted that ideological egalitarianism characterized the United States. Following Tocqueville, we emphasized that Americans believed in equality of opportunity and of respect, that people should be treated equally. Such values helped prevent the formation of class-conscious political movements in America. Conversely, in European postfeudal societies, social class, with its emphasis on deference and superiority, was an explicit part of the social landscape and made it much easier to form class-conscious parties.

I left Columbia in 1955, where I had become an associate professor, for a year at the Center for Advanced Study in the Behavioral Sciences at Stanford. I did not return. It is hard to explain why I gave up the opportunity to remain permanently in what I considered to be the greatest center of sociology, to work with the three scholars I most respected—Merton, Lazarsfeld, and Lynd. The answer, which I once shared with Lazarsfeld, was that my very respect, admiration, for them was inhibiting. I was intimidated by the thought that they were in a position to evaluate my every action. Whatever I knew as a sociologist I learned from them. I entered Columbia as a political activist, I left as a scholar. What they had taught me was to respect facts, research findings, especially when they challenged my beliefs, and to think "multivariately," to understand the complexity of society, to think through the need to hold variables constant, doing the mental equivalent of a regression analysis. Wherever I went thereafter, I would always be a product of Columbia sociology in that intellectually glorious revolutionary decade.

I moved to the University of California at Berkeley in 1956. I continued to work on stratification and social mobility, often collaborating with Reinhard Bendix. We completed a reader in stratification, *Class, Status and Power,* which had considerable influence. We also pulled together various articles, some based on original research in California, others on secondary analysis of survey data from different countries, and on the published literature, and produced a book by Bendix and myself, *Social Mobility in Industrial Society* (1959). The work was basically a series of related essays, some by me and some in collaboration with Bendix and Zetterberg.

At Berkeley I chaired a group of social scientists, mainly political scientists and sociologists, but also some economists, who were interested in issues of political, economic, and social development in Third World countries. A number had been working in Africa, Asia, and Latin America. My personal interest was in the conditions for political modernization and democracy. These activities led to my appointment as Director of the University's Institute of International Studies, which helped support and coordinate comparative and area research.

My work on democracy, which had begun with *Union Democracy* (1953) and was continued subsequently with *The First New Nation* (1963), extended in a curious way some of my earlier efforts as a young socialist at comparative political analysis. I used to give lectures on the reasons for the failure of the revolution and the socialist movement in different countries. I discussed why the Nazis triumphed in Germany, the Francoists in Spain, why the British Labour party failed to inaugurate socialism, and so forth. This concern for the failure of social democracy or the conditions for the success of socialism was in a sense transmuted into analyses of the transition to democracy in comparative perspective, a subject that continues to be a major interest. My most important book on the subject is *Political Man: The Social Basis of Politics,* which appeared in 1960. *Political Man* basically is a comparative study of the democratic order. In it, I reported my effort at a quantitative analysis of the factors differentiating democratic countries from undemocratic ones; this was first published as an article in the *American Political Science Review* (1959). The quantitative methods employed were primitive by contemporary standards, simply arithmetic and percentages. Still, I was able to document that the emergence and spread of democracy were related to socioeconomic development, to changing occupational and class structures, to higher per capita income, to widespread diffusion of education, to social homogeneity, and other factors. The book takes off from Aristotle, from his generalization that democracy is most likely to be found in polities with a large middle class. Inegalitarian countries are more disposed to be either oligarchies or tyrannies, i.e. old fashioned dictatorships or modern totalitarian systems.

Political Man was intended to demonstrate the utility of sociological approaches to politics, not only to democracy. Thus it also includes a lengthy analysis of the relation of different forms of legitimacy to types of governance, as well as of studies of partisan and ideological choices and of levels of electoral participation. It was originally planned as a reprint of various articles I had written in the late 1950s, but the editors at Doubleday suggested making it a more integrated book by rewriting these, which I did. For over a decade, the book became the text in political sociology, sold over 400,000 copies, and was translated in 20 languages, including Vietnamese, Bengali, Serbo-Croatian,

Burmese, and Hungarian. It received the book award of the American Sociological Association, then called the MacIver Prize.

Considering what I might do to further contribute to the analysis of sociopolitical development, I noted that the study of development did not involve just
looking at the so-called developing countries of the Third World, since the
industrialized nations necessarily had once been developing countries. This
generalization, of course, includes the United States. As a member of the Program Committee for the then forthcoming 1962 World Congress of Sociology,
I proposed that we emphasize development, in both historical and comparative perspective. I agreed to organize a session on the developed nations, in
which I would report on the United States. This meant looking, on one hand,
at how it had changed from the eighteenth century on, and, on the other, how
it differs from other contemporary developed democratic countries. What are
the variables that have made for different patterns of governance and class
relations?

The book that came out of this project, *The First New Nation: The United
States in Historical and Comparative Perspective* (1962), was a National Book
Award finalist. It begins with the early United States and examines the role of
George Washington and others of the Founders, as well as structural factors, in
determining the organizing principles of the new nation. It sought to deal with
Tocqueville's question of why the United States became the first institutionalized mass democracy. In reading through the literature on this early period, I
became interested in and fascinated with George Washington, who I concluded
was one of the most underestimated figures in American history. This may be
a curious observation to make about the man recognized as the father of our
country, the leader of the revolution, the first president, but I believe it is true.
Washington is perceived by Americans as a two-dimensional picture on the
wall, not as a vibrant living person who made major decisions and showed real
intelligence when so doing.

I emphasized in the early part of the book that Washington understood the
problems of new nationhood and new democracy, particularly of legitimacy. A
new nation by definition is low in legitimacy, has a weak title to rule. To establish
the principle that incumbents should turn over office if they lose an election is
not easy. Democratic rules of the game have to be institutionalized. As I read the
record, Washington consciously recognized many of these considerations. He
understood that his prestige, what might be called his charisma, had to be used
to legitimate the new polity. He, therefore, deliberately stood above the fray.
Although he was sympathetic to the Hamiltonians, he did not enter publicly
into controversy—hence, the debates, the political struggles could go on under
him. Washington, in effect, legitimated the new polity. He also, then, set an

important precedent in retiring from the presidency without being defeated. The first contested election, that of 1796, could take place under his aegis.

Democracy in the United States benefited greatly from antistatist and egalitarian revolutionary ideology. The American creed is sometimes referred to as classical liberalism, or libertarianism, emphasizing laissez-faire and suspicion of the power of the state as well as equality of respect and opportunity. This ideology led to the system of checks and balances, designed as Madison put it, to have part of government limit the power of other parts in order to prevent a popular tyranny, and to the insistence on a bill of rights to constrain the power of the central government. These developments occurred at a time when unified monarchical power, mercantilism, and aristocracy prevailed elsewhere.

Other sections of *The First New Nation* deal with contemporary variations by comparing the United States with other economically developed democratic countries, with the predominantly English speaking nations—Canada, Australia and Britain—and also with Germany and France. To do so I tried to use a modified format of Talcott Parsons' pattern variables. These are dichotomies for classifying social action. I characterized countries as stressing egalitarianism or elitism, specificity or diffuseness, particularism or universalism, and other such polarities. I rank-ordered the four predominantly English speaking countries on these polarities and then attempted to relate their values to their political styles and institutions. These cultural differences, of course, stem from varying histories and structures—from having been new nations or not, experiences of revolution, of sustaining monarchy, of continuing aristocracy, and of different types of religion, e.g. voluntary, predominantly Protestant, congregational and sectarian denominations in the United States, or hierarchically organized state-related churches in the other countries.

Religion was to become a major component of my efforts at comparative country analysis. America is the most religious and moralistic nation in the developed world. These attributes flow in large part from the country's unique Protestant sectarianism and ideological commitments. Given this background, it is not surprising that Americans are also both very patriotic and pacific and can be very critical of their society's institutions and leaders. Europeans, who take their national identity from common historical traditions, not ideologies, and are reared in a state church tradition, have been unable to understand the American response to Watergate or the sexual peccadilloes of politicians.

I decided that if I was to deal with political development I should have some Third World area competence, and so in the early sixties I started studying Spanish. But as leftist student protest, endemic in Latin America, began to grow, with its denunciation of the role of the United States abroad, including its scholars, I dropped the project. It did, however, have two products, one, a small book in Spanish on student politics, *Estudiantes universitarios y politica en el tercer Mundo* (1965), and an edited volume (with Aldo Solari) which appeared in English and Spanish, *Elites in Latin America* (1967), in which I discuss the role of values in economic development.

In 1965, I moved to Harvard University to become the George Markham Professor of Government and Sociology. Again, it is hard to explain the move, particularly in a line or two. My best recollection is that I felt I had become overly involved in Berkeley academic politics and administration as the Director of the Institute of International Studies and as a close adviser of the President of the University, Clark Kerr. Moving to Harvard seemed a way out.

Following *The First New Nation,* and continuing in a Parsonian mode, I and my Norwegian friend Stein Rokkan edited a book of papers presented at a conference held in the mid-sixties by the Research Committee on Political Sociology, of the International Political Science and Sociology Associations, which we had organized and led. The conference dealt with the ways that political cleavages and elections affect parties in various countries. Rokkan and I then wrote a long article, introductory to a book reporting on the papers of the conference called *Party Systems and Voter Alignments* (1967). In it we tried to systematize the emergence and institutionalization of the cleavages that underlay democracy in European polities. We noted cleavages stemming from the national revolution, the conflicts between the periphery and the center, e.g. ethnic, linguistic, and economic groups located in outlying regions and the national center. Cleavages also flowed from church-state tensions, a land-industry division between the landed elite and the growing bourgeois class, and—the eventually overriding one, derivative from the industrial revolution—the class struggle between capitalists and workers. We tried to tie this analysis to Parson's analytical approach. This introductory essay has been important in establishing the linkage of parties to cleavages in democratic polities. It received the Leon Epstein prize in Comparative Politics from the American Political Science Association and is frequently cited in research dealing with the new party systems of emerging democracies in former Communist and Third World countries. I have added to the theory a new cross-cutting "postindustrial" cleavage between the better educated, concerned for an improved quality of life, e.g. environmentalists, and the materialist strata, both workers and owners, concerned with increased production, derived from D Bell and R Inglehart.

A few years later, I put together a book of essays mainly written in the 1960s, called *Revolution and Counterrevolution* (1970). The articles followed up on themes formulated in *Political Man* and *The First New Nation.* The first section is an effort to show how history and sociology may contribute to each other's analytic framework. Another seeks to tie together, in theoretical terms, the approaches to stratification of Marx, Durkheim, and Weber. The relationship of religion to politics is also analyzed.

Following this work, I returned to another topic treated in *Political Man*— the politics of intellectuals. I tried to explain why American intellectuals were on the left politically. A political science colleague and friend, Everett Ladd, and I used the opportunity presented by a massive study of American faculty conducted by Clark Kerr's Commission on Higher Education to undertake a comprehensive analysis of the outlook of American faculty. The Kerr Commission had gathered 60,000 questionnaires from what was initially a random sample. I had taken part in planning the research, together with Martin Trow. Trow was interested in analyzing educational behavior, I in the politics. Given a sample of 60,000, it was possible to test many hypotheses about variations in attitudes and activities, particularly the factors related to the liberal left emphasis of academics. One of the most interesting findings, documented in *The Divided Academy: Professors and Politics* (1975), reiterating conclusions of earlier studies, is that the more research oriented, the more successful, the more recognized, the more creative an academic is, the more likely he is to be on the left. Conversely, faculty who are primarily teachers and/or who are at the least prestigious institutions are the most conservative.

Explanations for these seemingly anomalous results that inverted class analysis among intellectuals had actually been presented earlier by Thorstein Veblen in a 1919 article, by Joseph Schumpeter in some essays on intellectuals in politics in the forties, and by Paul Lazarsfeld and Wagner Thielens in their book *The Academic Mind* in the mid-fifties. These scholars suggested that intellectual creativity involves rejection of what has been the intellectual status quo, what has been taught. Veblen explicitly argued that innovation in science is an act of rebellion. Hence, those people who are most innovative and most creative were also most likely to be on the left, at least in the context of American politics (they could be on the right in leftist dominated polities). The finding that the established intellectuals are more radical than the less prestigious countered the assumptions of left-wing scholars and writers, who wanted to believe, particularly in the activist sixties, that the successful are sellouts.

Creativity is not the only source of leftism. Friederich Hayek wrote in 1949 that as he traveled around the faculty clubs of America, he found the dominant tone was socialist, by which he, of course, meant supportive of the welfare state. And though an archsupporter of free enterprise and laissez faire, he reported that the socialists in academia were smarter than his cothinkers. Hayek's explanation for this finding was selective recruitment. He believed that a study of a cohort of young people over time would reveal that the brightest on the right would choose occupations that support the system, particularly business and the free professions. Conversely those critical of business or other established activities would prefer intellectual and nonprofit pursuits. The data from the Carnegie survey of 1969, as well as various studies of student values, basically confirm Hayek. Undergraduates who plan to go into academia or other forms of public service are much more to the left than those who look forward to business careers or, for that matter, other monetarily rewarding occupations, such as the free professions or engineering.

The politics of academe and intellectuals continued to inform a major part of my research agenda through much of the seventies. Ladd and I published two monographs in 1973, in addition to *The Divided Academy, Professors, Unions and American Higher Education* and *Academics, Politics and the 1972 Election.* We also conducted two national surveys of faculty in 1975 and 1977, the results of which were published in two series of articles in *The Chronicle of Higher Education.* My concern over the politicization of the American university was also reflected in various writings on student politics. The most important of these is *Rebellion in the University* (1972). The book is historical, noting the role of students as the shock troops of protest and rebellion through much of western history. It also deals with the content of the protest of the 1960s and with the characteristics of the protesters. It is congruent in many ways to the analyses of the politics of academe or professors.

The "Why No Socialism in the US?" issue remained of central interest to me. In 1974, I signed a contract to write a book that would explore the question. Over the decade of the seventies, I wrote a rough draft of over 700 pages, which sought to evaluate all the hypotheses in the literature from the Marxist fathers through latter day socialist and communist writers, and from the many social scientists and historians who have dealt with the subject. Essentially, I reiterated with abundant supporting evidence that the major factors fall into two categories: sociological, or the antistatist and egalitarian value system and egalitarian social relations that negate proposals to enlarge state power and prevent class consciousness; and political, or the constitutional elements that determine the Presidential system and the electoral framework, which serve to undermine third party efforts.

Curiously, however, I was unable to bring myself to finish the book. I could not understand this, since as my vita will attest, I have not been reluctant to finish and put whatever I am working on into print. In fact, I mined the manuscript for many articles, including one of almost book size length (170 pages), "Why No Socialism in the United States?" in *Sources of Contemporary Radicalism* (1977), ed. S Bialer & S Sluzar. Together with John Laslett, I edited *Failure of a Dream? Essays in the History of American Socialism* (1974), which includes a number of my articles and comments. In other essays, I applied the analytic schema and variables used to explain socialist failure in America to the variations in left politics across the Atlantic. These included "Industrial Proletariat in Comparative Perspective" (1981) and my presidential address to the American Political Science Association, "Radicalism or Reformism: The Sources of Working-Class Politics" (1983).

I can note that together with Gary Marks, a former student and now a distinguished political scientist, I have turned to finally completing the book. Other than the passage of time and the end of Stalinism with the demise of the Soviet Union, there has been one major development in my thinking, which may have unlocked my inhibitions. I realized in 1995 that one of the major factors I have emphasized, the electoral system, is not as important as I had thought. I owe this insight to Ross Perot, although it could and should have come from earlier third party or independent presidential candidacies. Perot secured 19% of the vote in the 1992 election, and he has maintained that level of support in trial heats in opinion polls through early 1996. He is, of course, far from being a socialist. Other nonsocialists, Theodore Roosevelt in 1912, Robert LaFollette in 1924, George Wallace in 1968, John Anderson in 1980, in addition to Perot in 1992, have received a larger vote than any Socialist nominee ever attained. Eugene Debs secured 6% in 1912, and 3% in 1920. Norman Thomas in six campaigns between 1928 and 1948 never won more than 2%, and that during the depths of the depression in 1932. Clearly, sizable minorities of Americans have been willing to "waste" their ballots by voting for a third party protest candidate, but not if he is a socialist. The direct election of the chief executive undoubtedly does serve to inhibit the emergence and institutionalization of national third parties, as EE Schattschneider contended, but it has not prevented the occasional expression of large-scale protest against both major parties. However, Americans, regardless of how they feel about the political system, have never used statist socialism as a vehicle for the expression of their discontent.

The conclusion that socialists could not overcome the deep-rooted American antipathy to statism is reinforced by the behavior of the labor movement. During the high point of American socialism, in the years before World War I, the party could not win the support of organized labor, which was also antistate. The American Federation of Labor was not meek or conservative. Its record of strikes and violence surpassed almost all European unions; its ideology was syndicalist, for workers' independent power, against support from the government. Its leader for 40 years, Samuel Gompers, when asked his politics, once replied, "I guess, two-thirds anarchist." And the revolutionary labor movement, the Industrial Workers of the World, the IWW, the Wobblies, were explicitly anarcho-syndicalist, not socialist.

Removing the electoral system as a major explanation for socialist weakness leaves value and class systems, ideological equalitarianism, meritocracy, and antistatism. These form the heart of Tocqueville's discussion of American exceptionalism. And presumably they will constitute the core of the forthcoming book on socialist efforts in America.

To demonstrate that I have not been committed solely to the analysis of left-wing outliers, I can report that I have had a parallel, if less dedicated, interest in right-wing movements. This was first exhibited in an article on "The Radical Right" (1955), followed up by two lengthy ones in a collection *The Radical Right*, edited by Daniel Bell (1955, 1963). These dealt with the social roots of Coughlin's movement in the 1930s, and of McCarthyism and the John Birch Society in the 1950s and early 1960s, and stressed their traditionalist and populist antielitist character.

While I was working on the last of these articles, the Anti-Defamation League approached me to conduct a major study of anti-Semitism in the United States, which they were prepared to fund. I was not interested in this, since I did not think anti-Semitism was a serious problem in the United States. I suggested, however, that I would like to take on a broader subject, right-wing extremism. ADL agreed and I recruited a close friend, Earl Raab, to collaborate on a book, *The Politics of Unreason* (1970, 1978), which dealt with the subject historically from the end of the eighteenth century to the 1970s. We emphasized two sources: Protestant sectarian moralism—though Catholics, who had been targets of bigotry, came into the support picture in the 1930s and later; and status insecurity derivative from mobility, both upwards, more prevalent in prosperous times, and downward, during recessions or depressions. The book was awarded the Gunnar Myrdal Prize. Two chapters in *Political Man* dealt with the right, asserting that fascism has three forms, right or traditionalist, e.g. Franco's Spain; centrist (Nazi); and left (Peron); and that the lower less-educated strata have a greater propensity to support authoritarian movements. These chapters have occasioned much discussion and criticism, largely from the left.

My wife Elsie became a victim of a rare form of cancer in the late 1960s that required recurrent lung operations. She had never liked living in the cold and austere New England climate. Thus when an offer to move to Stanford in 1975 as the Caroline S.G. Munro Professor of Political Science and Sociology and Senior Fellow at the Hoover Institution came up, I accepted. We spent twelve happy years there before she died.

I have written articles addressed to the debates over the content of sociology. In a book of essays, entitled *Conflict and Consensus* (1983), I sought to counter the assumptions presented by some critics of established sociology that the discipline overemphasizes consensus in society, thereby reflecting a conservative orientation. In my evaluations, I have stressed the connections between conflict and consensus and noted that some of those criticized for being overly consensual, like Talcott Parsons, have in fact been as much concerned with conflict as with the alternative polarity. Societies necessarily have both, i.e., they must contain mechanisms to sustain conflict and consensus. Marx, himself, stressed the presence of stabilizing elements in all complex societies. The book also includes the Lipset-Rokkan essay on "Party Systems and Voter Alignments." In the early 1980s, William Schneider, who had been a student of mine at Harvard, and I dealt with various tensions, sources of conflict, in American life in *The Confidence Gap* (1983, 1987). We documented the decline of confidence in American institutions, particularly business, government, and labor, from hundreds of opinion polls, and we sought to explain it. The book is both statistical and historical/political. We noted the importance of the rise of television in reporting bad news, which is what all news sources report. Television, however, does this more effectively, because news reported in pictures ("you are there") seems less open to journalistic bias than when it appears in print. The gap, which started during the Vietnam War period, has continued to the present, and as I have noted in a mid-1990s article, there is more malaise, popular discontent, than at any time since pollsters began to monitor the phenomenon.

I returned in the late 1980s to the effort started at Berkeley, to report and specify the conditions for institutionalized competitive politics, particularly in emerging democracies. In collaboration with two former students, Larry Diamond and Juan Linz, who have done most of the work, I edited three commissioned volumes on democratic transitions. Following a conceptual scheme we laid out in *Democracy in Developing Countries* (1988, 1989), area experts reported on the conditions that have affected the success or failure of democratic transitions in many nations in Africa, Asia, and Latin America. Some reports were updated in 1995 in *Politics in Developing Countries*, which described ten nations across the three continents and included a long theoretical and synthesizing introduction. I have elaborated on my 1960 essay on the social requisites of democracy, with two journal articles, "A Comparative Analysis of the Social Requisites of Democracy" (1993) and "The Social Requisites of Democracy Revisited" (1994). The latter was given as the presidential address to the American Sociological Association. The first was written with two students, KR Seong and J Torres.

Some years after Elsie's death, I married Sydnee Guyer. We spent a very good year at the Russell Sage Foundation in New York during 1988. Although a fourth generation San Franciscan, Sydnee, whose career had been in public relations and television production, preferred the cultural life of New York and the East Coast. Since I was approaching the retirement age at Stanford, I began looking for a position in the East. George Mason University, located just outside Washington, made me an excellent offer in their new Institute of Public Policy, which I accepted. I am also affiliated with the Woodrow Wilson Center for International Scholars and the Progressive Policy Institute as a Senior Scholar. Here were to be my first experiences of direct exposure to the Washington scene, while I retained my affiliation to Stanford's Hoover Institution, where I spend summers. Both Sydnee and I like Washington.

My most comprehensive effort at dealing with the response to democracy in historical and comparative perspective appeared in 1995 in a four-volume *Encyclopedia of Democracy*. The set, which I edited, contains more than 400 articles by over 200 authors, including an analytical introduction and four other articles by me. The *Encyclopedia* reports on important democratic figures, events in most countries, and major experiences. They also summarize the theoretical literature.

During the 1990s, I published three books that reflect efforts to come to terms with American exceptionalism. The first one, *Continental Divide: the Institutions and Values of the United States and Canada*, continues themes presented in *The First New Nation*. It seeks to understand the United States by looking at it in comparison with Canada. As I stress, two nations came out of the American Revolution: Canada the country of the counterrevolution, and the United States the country of the revolution. The northern nation is much more statist, Tory (noblesse oblige), communitarian, elitist, group-oriented, and deferential. The southern is much more individualistic, antistatist, antielitist, supportive of laissez-faire, and less obedient. Two countries on the same continent, with most people speaking the same language, vary considerably in outcomes such as church attendance, crime rates, divorce statistics, legal systems, party systems, electoral participation, strength of labor organizations, welfare and health policies, and many others. Canada is much more of a social democratic welfare-oriented country, with a greater emphasis on family and personal security. The United States is more committed to competitive meritocratic values, institutions, and behavior. My continuing work on Canada received the Gold Medal of the International Council for Canadian Studies.

The second book of the 1990s, *Jews and the New American Scene* (1995), in collaboration with Earl Raab, seeks to analyze the American Jewish community as it is today. It notes, as I have in earlier articles, that American Jewry reflects the exceptional and unique characteristics of the United States and differs in systematic ways from Jewry in other countries, where the dominant Christian denomination is more hierarchical and state-related. Raab and I emphasize that the melting pot, i.e. assimilation, continues to characterize the relationship of ethnoreligious groups to the larger American society, exemplified in the extremely high intermarriage rate of Jews, Catholics, and almost every other ethnic group with the exception of African Americans. The melting pot is melting as never before. Assimilation has been inherent in the welcome America has given to the Jews, evident in George Washington's letter to a synagogue in 1791 in which he stated that Jews were not tolerated in America, that they *were* Americans. The book also reports on the extraordinary success of Jews in the intellectual, political, and business worlds, which demonstrates the openness of the society. And I can report that my writings on American Jewry received the first Marshall Sklare Prize of the Jewish Social Studies Association.

Writing a book on American Jewry helps to cap off my deep interests and participation in the Jewish community. I served over the years as President of the American Professors for Peace in the Middle East, as Chairperson of the National Advisory Board of the National Hillel Foundation, as Chairperson of the Faculty Council of the United Jewish Appeal, and as Co-Chairperson of the Executive Committee of the International Center for Peace in the Middle East, headquartered in Tel Aviv. I also have been involved in research activities for the major Jewish defense organizations and the Wilstein Institute for Jewish Policy Research.

My participation in Jewish activities has not meant a lessening of concern for American politics. I have been active in Democratic party politics with two moderate or centrist groups, the Coalition for a Democratic Majority (CDM), which I co-chaired in the seventies, and the Democratic Leadership Council (DLC), which I have served as a Senior Scholar in its think tank, the Progressive Policy Institute (PPI), and for some years as President of the Institute support group, the Progressive Foundation.

Finally, as 1996 opens, I have published a new book, *American Exceptionalism: A Double-Edged Sword,* which seeks to pull together much of my research and thinking about the ways in which the United States differs from other countries. The term "American exceptionalism" was coined by Alexis de Tocqueville and has meant that the country is qualitatively different from Europe. It still is, though perhaps in some new as well as old ways. The reference in the title to a double-edged sword reflects the fact that while American exceptionalism means that America is better than other countries on some criteria, it is also worse on various other criteria. The United States has the lowest rate of voting, the highest crime rate, and the most unequal distribution of income among developed countries, but also the most open educational system, the greatest emphasis on equality of respect, the highest rate of mobility into elite positions, and the greatest guarantee of personal rights. It has the least government, the lowest taxes, less welfare and health benefits, a weak trade union movement, and no social democratic party.

Although *American Exceptionalism* is not a book about politics, it argues that the nation's libertarian organizing principles, its ideological identity, go far in explaining both the absence of a socialist party and the fact that the Republican party is the *only* major antistatist libertarian party in the industrialized world. In 1906, HG Wells wrote that two parties were missing in America; there was no conservative, i.e. Tory, noblesse oblige, statist, communitarian party, and no socialist party either. Both American parties, he argued, were (classically) liberal, libertarian in modern parlance. The depression of the 1930s had shifted American politics toward the left; postwar prosperity pressed it back to its traditional values. Perhaps the greatest incongruity that I seek to explain is that America is the most meritocratic nation, open to talent from all strata in elite positions, and yet has the most unequal distribution of income in the developed world. For my explanation, read the book.

A British sociological reviewer of my work once described it as the sociology of a patriot. By this he meant that I think the United States is a great and effective country. I do, in spite of the fact, as I emphasize in *American Exceptionalism,* that there is much in it that no decent person could feel positive about, particularly the state of race relations (which merits a long chapter in the *Exceptionalism* book), the high violence rate, and the changes in sexual morality, e.g. the growth in illegitimacy. But it is important to note that many positive and negative elements are interrelated, e.g., the emphasis on achievement, on getting ahead, is linked to the high crime rate. Populist elements are related to the low rate of voting turnout. A higher percentage of the relevant age cohort has attended school than in other countries; today the United States leads in graduate enrollment. Yet mass, more open, education has helped to produce lower quality outcomes than that reached in the elite-oriented segments of school systems found in some other European and Asian cultures which prepare a minority of students for university.

I have moved around in my academic career, and the changes have affected my research agenda. My position at George Mason University has given me new insights on Washington politics, which should be reflected in future writings. This article is obviously not a comprehensive report on my intellectual activity. I have had to leave untouched the more recent parts of it, for reasons of time and space. Writing this has whetted my appetite for discussing the way the world around me has affected my actions. This article is only an introduction. I look forward to writing a longer memoir, in which I report on my relations with my Columbia mentors as well as my colleagues in the profession. I have known most of the leading political scientists and sociologists since World War II. I will tell how the disciplines and university world changed during the past half-century. I am particularly interested in discussing my relations with my students, many of whom have become leaders in political science and sociology. Two of my Stanford political science colleagues who studied the impact of dissertation advisors reported that students who worked with me were more productive, published more, than others. My propensity to publish has seemingly an impact on those working with me. I also hope to discuss my relationships with my wives, Elsie and Sydnee, and children, David, Daniel, and Cici. They have added zest to my life.

Literature Cited

A complete list of the "Publications of Seymour Martin Lipset epigraph from 1947 to 1991 may be found in 1992 *Reexamining Democracy: Essays in Honor of Seymour Martin Lipset,* ed. G Marks, L Diamond, pp. 332–55. Newberry Park, CA: Sage. Publications from the end of 1991 to 1996 are listed below.

Books by SM Lipset
The Power of Jewish Education. 1994. Boston/Los Angeles: The Wilstein Inst.
(with Raab E). 1995. *Jews and the New American Scene.* Cambridge: Harvard Univ. Press
1996. *American Exceptionalism: A Double Edged Sword.* New York: Norton
Edited Books
(with Diamond L, Linz J). 1995. *Politics in Developed Countries: Comparing Experiences with Democracy.* Boulder: Rienner
Encyclopedia of Democracy. 4 Vols. 1995. Washington, DC/London: Congr. Q. Press/Routledge
Articles by SM Lipset
(with Clark T). Are social classes dying? 1991. *Int. Sociol.* 6:397–410
Affirmative action and the American creed. 1992. *Wilson Q.* 16:52–62
Political correctness, historically speaking. 1992. *Educ. Rec.* Winter:5–11
Labor pains. 1992. *The New Democr.* May:14–17
Political ethics and voter unease? 1992. *The Public Perspect.* 3(July/Aug):8–10
Compromise needed in Pretoria. 1992. *Times Lit. Suppl.* Sept. 20:9–10
Equal chances versus equal results. 1992. *Ann. Acad. Polit. Soc. Sci.* 523:63–74
Two americas, two value systems: blacks and whites. 1992. *The Tocqueville Rev.* 13(1):137–77

Polls don't lie, people do. 1992. *New York Times,* Sept. 10:A23
The politics of the United States. 1992. In *Oxford Companion to Politics of the World.* New York: Oxford Univ. Press
Canada and the United States compared. 1992. In *Canada,* ed. M Watkins. New York: Facts on File
(with Jalali R). 1992. Racial and ethnic tensions: a global perspective. *Polit. Sci. Q.* 107(4):137–58
Conditions of the democratic order and social change: a comparative discussion. 1992. In *Studies in Human Society: Democracy and Modernity,* ed. SN Eisenstadt, 4:1–14. New York: Brill
Introduction. 1992. *Rebellion in the University,* pp. ix-xxxv. New Brunswick, NJ: Transaction
(with Schram M). 1993. Foreword: interpreting the 1992 election. In *Mandate For Change,* ed. A From, W Marshall, pp. xix-xxviii. New York: Berkeley Books
Roosevelt redux for Democrats. 1993. *Wall Street J.* Jan. 21:A14
The significance of the 1992 election. 1993. *PS: Polit. Sci.* 26:7–16
Reflections on capitalism, socialism and democracy. 1993. *J. Democr.* 4:43–55
Roosevelt and Clinton. 1993. *Society* 30:73–76
The sources of political correctness on American campuses. 1993. In *The Imperiled Academy,* ed. H Dickman, pp. 71–96. New Brunswick, NJ: Transaction
Culture and economic behavior: a commentary. 1993. *J. Labor Econ.* 11:S330–47
Canadian studies in the United States: a summary. 1993. In *Canadian Studies in the U.S.: Inventory and Prospect,* ed. J Jockel, W Metcalfe, K Gould, pp. 397–416. Washington, DC: Assoc. Can. Stud. in the US

(with Seong K-R, Torres JC). 1993. A comparative analysis of the social requisites of democracy. *Int. Soc. Sci. J.* 45:155–75

How the left failed. 1993. *Times Lit. Suppl.* May 21:10–11

(with Kash DE). 1993. Steps toward smooth transitions. *The Washington Post* May 23: C7

Politics of the United States. 1993. In *The Oxford Companion to Politics of the World,* ed. J Krieger et al, pp. 936–43. New York: Oxford Univ. Press

The (Perot) Phenomenon. 1993. *The New Democrat* 5:14–16

(with Clark TN, Rempel M). 1993. The declining political significance of social class. *Int. Sociol.* 8:293–316

Juan Linz: student-colleague-friend. 1993. In *Politics, Society and Democracy: Comparative Studies,* ed. A Stepan, H Chehabi, 4:1–9. Boulder, CO: Westview

A contrarian view. 1993. *The Public Perspect.* 5(Nov/Dec):6

Un approccio storico e comparativo all'opera d: Ostrogorsld. 1993. In *Contro I Partiti: Saggi sul Siero di Moisei Ostrogorski,* ed. G Orsina, pp. 13/25. Rome: Edizione Boria

(with Hayes J). 1993\1994. Individualism: a double-edged sword. *The Responsive Community* 4:69–81

The social requisites of democracy revisited. 1994. *Am. Sociol. Rev.* 59:1–22

(with Bence G). 1994. Anticipations of the failure of communism. *Polit. Soc.* 23:169–210

State of American sociology. 1994. *Sociol. Forum* 9:199–220

American exceptionalism—Japanese uniqueness. 1994. In *Comparing Nations: Concepts, Strategies, Substances,* ed. M Dogan, A Kazancigil, pp. 153–212. Oxford, UK/Cambridge, MA: Blackwells

Social studies. 1994. *Times Lit. Suppl.* March 18:24

Some thoughts on the past, present and future of American Jewry. 1994. *Contemp. Jewry* 15:171–81

American values in comparative perspective. 1994. *The Transatlantic Forum,* pp. 13–23. Queenstown, MD: The Wye Cent. Aspen Inst., Belmont Eur. Policy Cent., The Progress. Policy Inst.

In defense of the research university. 1994. In *The Research University in a Time of Discontent,* ed. JR Cole, EG Barber, SR Graubard, pp. 219–25. Baltimore: Johns Hopkins Univ. Press

American democracy in comparative perspective. 1994. In *A New Moment in the Americas,* ed. RS Leiken, pp. 1–13. New Brunswick, NJ: Transaction

Why didn't we anticipate the failure of communism? 1994. In *Legends of the Collapse of Marxism,* ed. JH Moore, pp. 234–55. Fairfax, VA: George Mason Univ. Press

Remarks. 1994. In *Aaron Wildavsky 1930–1993,* pp. 31–34. Berkeley: Inst. Gov. Stud.

Juan Linz: student-colleague-friend. 1995. In *Essays in Honor of Juan J. Linz: Politics, Society and Democracy: Comparative Studies,* ed. HE. Chehabi, A Stepan, pp. 3–11. Boulder, CO: Westview

Trade union exceptionalism: The United States and Canada. 1995. *Ann. Am. Acad. Polit. Soc. Sci.* 538:115–30

The political profile of American Jewry. 1995. In *Terms of Survivals: The Jewish World Since 1945,* ed. RS Wistrich, pp. 147–67. London/New York: Routledge

Malaise and resiliency in America. 1995. *J. Democr.* 6:5–18

(with Hayes JW). 1995. Social roots of U.S. protectionism. In *Trade, Liberalization in the Western Hemisphere,* ed. I Cohen, pp. 471–502. Washington, DC: Econ. Comm. Latin Am.

An interview with Seymour Martin Lipset. 1995. *The New Fed.* July/Aug:8–10

Genes are not the answer. 1995. *Times Lit. Suppl.* Sept. 22:10

Introduction. 1995. In *The Encyclopedia of Democracy* ed. SM Lipset, I:iv-ixxvi. Washington, DC: Congr. Q. Press

(with Diamond L). 1995. Colonialism. In *The Encyclopedia of Democracy,* ed. SM Lipset, 1:262–67. Washington, DC: Congr. Q. Press

Economic development. 1995. In *The Encyclopedia of Democracy,* ed. SM Lipset, 2:350–56. Washington, DC: Congr. Q. Press

Legitimacy. 1995. In *The Encyclopedia of Democracy,* ed. SM Lipset, 3:747–51. Washington, DC: Congr. Q. Press

(with Diamond L, Linz J). 1995. Introduction: what makes for democracy? In *Politics in Developing Countries,* ed. L Diamond, J Linz, SM Lipset, pp. 1–66. Boulder, CO: Rienner

The politics of american social policy, past and future: comment. 1996. In *Individual and Social Responsibility,* ed. VK Fuchs, pp. 336–40. Chicago: Univ. Chicago Press

What are parties for? 1996. *J. Democr.* 7:169–75

Annu. Rev. Sociol. 1996. 22:29–50

TALKING BACK TO SOCIOLOGY: Distinctive Contributions of Feminist Methodology

Marjorie L. DeVault

Department of Sociology, Syracuse University, Syracuse, New York 13244

KEY WORDS: feminism, gender, research, methodology, epistemology

ABSTRACT

This essay characterizes "feminist methodology" as a field of inquiry rooted in feminist activism and in feminists' critiques of the standard procedures of social science. Feminist methodologists do not use or prescribe any single research method; rather, they are united through various efforts to include women's lives and concerns in accounts of society, to minimize the harms of research, and to support changes that will improve women's status. Recent writing on feminist methodology has addressed the uses of qualitative and quantitative research tools, possibilities and problems of research relations, epistemologies for feminist research, and strategies for developing more inclusive methodologies.

INTRODUCTION

Nearly every writer on the topic agrees that there is no single feminist method, yet there is a substantial literature on "feminist methodology" representing a diverse community of sociologists in lively and sometimes contentious dialogue. This community, and the very idea of "feminist sociology," are products of the "second-wave"[1] women's movement that began in the 1960s and early 1970s,

---

[1] Scholars refer to the women's movement of the 1960s as the "second wave," to distinguish it from the earlier period of feminist organizing in the nineteenth century. The earlier wave also brought women into the universities and produced a significant body of work by feminist scholars; Reinharz's (1992) survey of feminist research includes these forerunners in order to emphasize the continuity of feminist concerns and strategies.

29

and has grown and differentiated in the years since through specialization, conflict, institutionalization, and cooptation (Ferree & Martin 1995, Roby 1992).

Many would agree that a method, consciousness raising, was at the heart of this women's movement. In various settings, small groups of women began to talk together, analyze, and act. The method of consciousness raising was fundamentally empirical; it provided a systematic mode of inquiry that challenged received knowledge and allowed women to learn from one another (Allen 1973, Combahee River Collective 1982). Whether caucusing within established organizations or building new connections, women who became feminists began to see an alternative basis for knowledge and authority in a newly discovered community of women and "women's experience." Subsequent developments would reveal the complex fragilities and resiliencies of this construction, which Donna Haraway characterizes as "a fiction and fact of the most crucial, political kind" (1985:65).

Though the women's movement began outside the university, feminists in nearly every discipline soon began to apply its methods to their context and work, embarking on a collective project of critique and transformation. They pointed to the omission and distortion of women's experiences in mainstream social science, the tendency to universalize the experience of men (and relatively privileged women), and the use of science to control women, whether through medicine and psychiatry, or through social scientific theories of family, work, sexuality, and deviance (Glazer-Malbin & Waehrer 1971, Millman & Kanter 1975). Scholars of African descent produced a complementary literature on racist and gender bias in scholarship during this period (Ladner 1971, Jackson 1973)—stimulated in part by "expert" opinion that blamed women for the ostensible deficiencies of African-American families.

Over the last 25 years, academic feminists have created new cross-disciplinary audiences for work based on these feminist critiques as well as new curricula, journals, conferences, and organizations to support and disseminate the work (Kramarae & Spender 1992, McDermott 1994). Referring to this history is the beginning of my answer to questions about the distinctiveness of feminist writings on research methodology. I mean to suggest that learning the history of feminist scholarship—and recognizing its roots in the women's movement—are key to understanding it.

Feminist sociologists are committed to both feminism and social science, and they use the tools of the discipline to "talk back" to sociology in a spirited critique aimed at improving the ways we know society. In the discussion that follows, I characterize feminist methodology as a field of inquiry united by membership in these overlapping research communities—bound together not by agreement about answers but by shared commitments to questions. Then I

examine recent work and questions currently on the agenda for feminist methodologists. I focus on sociological work, but I also draw from other disciplines
where these have been especially influential in sociology.

FEMINISM, FEMINIST RESEARCH, AND FEMINIST METHODOLOGY

"Feminism" is a movement, and a set of beliefs, that problematize gender
inequality. Feminists believe that women have been subordinated through men's
greater power, variously expressed in different arenas. They value women's
lives and concerns, and work to improve women's status. While this kind of
definition is broadly inclusive, it is also misleadingly simple. There are many
feminisms, with different emphases and aims. Jane Mansbridge (1995) suggests
that despite this variation, feminists are united by a sense of accountability to a
movement that is best conceived as a changing and contested discourse. In any
occupation or organization, feminists make decisions about how to respond to
institutional contexts that sometimes welcome and sometimes resist feminist
insights; they consider how to use their resources (both material and intellectual)
to further their feminist goals, and which demands of their institution should
be resisted in the name of feminism. Thus, feminist methodology will not be
found in some stable orthodoxy but in an evolving dialogue.

I wish to draw a distinction in this essay between "feminist research" and
"feminist methodology." I understand "feminist research" as a broader category including any empirical study that incorporates or develops the insights of
feminism. Feminist studies may use standard research methods, or they may
involve explicit attention to methodological critique and innovation. I would
like to reserve the term "feminist methodology" for explicitly methodological
discussion that emerges from the feminist critique. I follow philosopher Sandra
Harding's (1987) suggestion that we distinguish between "methods" (i.e., particular tools for research), "methodology" (theorizing about research practice),
and "epistemology" (the study of how and what we can know). For the most
part, feminist researchers have modified, rather than invented, research methods; however, feminist researchers have produced a distinctive body of writing
about research practice and epistemology, and that is where I locate "feminist
methodology."

SECOND-WAVE WRITING ON METHODOLOGY

Feminist sociologists of the second wave began immediately to think skep-
tically about existing research methods (see Reinharz 1985 on "feminist distrust") and to search for alternatives. By 1983, there was a substantial body

of literature (Reinharz, Bombyk & Wright 1983). The focus on methodology gained momentum during that decade, and when philosopher Sandra Harding edited an interdisciplinary anthology (1987) that illustrated feminist methods with exemplary work, sociologists were well represented; as authors of four of ten substantive chapters, they included Marcia Millman and Rosabeth Moss Kanter, Joyce Ladner, Dorothy E Smith, and Bonnie Thornton Dill.

Two overviews of feminist research methods that have been especially influential in sociology (Cook & Fonow 1986, Reinharz 1992) also adopted the strategy of collecting exemplars of feminist research and looking for common features. These writers drew on the work of scholars who had been developing particular feminist approaches in some detail. These included adaptations of survey and experimental methods (Eichler 1988), interview research (Oakley 1981), inductive fieldwork (Reinharz 1983), marxist and ethnomethodological approaches (Smith 1987, Stanley & Wise 1983/93), phenomenology (Leveque-Lopman 1988), action/participatory research (Mies 1983, Maguire 1987), oral history (Personal Narratives Group 1989, Gluck & Patai 1991), and others. More recent additions to the list include feminist versions of experimental ethnography (*Inscriptions* 1988), and methods based on poststructuralist insights (Lather 1991, Game 1991, Ingraham 1994).

The range of approaches mentioned here reflects the fact that feminist researchers are located throughout the discipline. Shulamit Reinharz (1992) holds that feminists have used (and modified) every available research method; and her comprehensive review includes studies across the full range. The pluralism in this kind of definition is attractive to many feminists for several reasons, not least of which is a well-developed sense of the dangers of "ranking," whether of oppressions or methods. By insisting on diversity, this approach avoids needless division and leaves open the future strategies that feminist researchers might want to adopt. But the continuing proliferation of writing on feminist methodology suggests a strongly felt sense of difference from standard practice.

WHAT IS FEMINIST METHODOLOGY?

I locate the distinctiveness of feminist methodology in shared commitment to three goals:

1. Feminists seek a methodology that will do the work of "excavation," shifting the focus of standard practice from men's concerns in order to reveal the locations and perspectives of (all) women. The aim of much feminist research has been to "bring women in," that is, to find what has been ignored, censored, and suppressed, and to reveal both the diversity of actual women's lives and the ideological mechanisms that have made so many of those lives invisible. A key method for doing so—drawn in part from the legacy of consciousness raising—

has involved work with the personal testimony of individual women (Anderson et al 1990). However, it would be misleading to equate feminist responses to this methodological demand with qualitative methods, for two reasons. First, some feminists argue that quantitative techniques can also perform the work of "making visible" and are sometimes necessary or more compelling than personal testimony (Sprague & Zimmerman 1993). In addition, qualitative methods practiced in nonfeminist ways can easily reproduce the mainstream failure to notice women and their concerns. What makes a qualitative or a quantitative approach feminist is a commitment to finding women and their concerns. The point is not only to know about women, but to provide a fuller and more accurate account of society by including them (Nielsen 1990).

Often, feminist researchers use this strategy to find "voices" for themselves, or for women who share experiences that have been meaningful for them (Stanley & Wise 1979). But the commitment to excavation and inclusion makes feminist researchers accountable for considering women whose experiences are different as well. Negotiating the tension between investigating experiences with intense personal meaning and casting wider nets has been a continuing challenge. Western, Euro-American feminists have been roundly criticized (rightly, I believe) for too often presenting investigations of particular groups of women's lives in terms that are falsely universalized (Dill 1979, Baca Zinn et al 1986). But the call for excavation makes feminist researchers accountable to recognize and correct such mistakes, and one strand in feminist methodological work involves sustained attempts to move beyond these incomplete and limiting analyses.

2. Feminists seek a science that minimizes harm and control in the research process. In response to the observation that researchers have often exploited or harmed women participants, and that scientific knowledge has sustained systematic oppressions of women, feminist methodologists have searched for practices that will minimize harm to women and limit negative consequences (Nebraska Feminist Collective 1983, 1988). Such concerns enter nonfeminist research discussions as well. What marks the feminist discourse is not only a particular concern for women's welfare, but particular sources for research strategies. Feminist researchers have drawn, more or less consciously, on the work of grass-roots and professional women's organizations to develop inclusive procedures and less hierarchical structures (Strobel 1995). Feminists have written of many experiments in leveling hierarchies of power and control in research relations, and they continue to debate whether and when such leveling is possible and how much should be demanded of feminist researchers.

3. Feminists seek a methodology that will support research of value to women, leading to social change or action beneficial to women. This criterion for

feminist research is mentioned in virtually every discussion; by implication, authors point to many kinds of change that could satisfy this call, from changing theory or bringing new topics into the discipline, to consciousness raising or decolonization (for the researcher, the reader, or participants in the research), to producing data that will stimulate or support political action or policy decisions. The concern with change, like the call for research that does no harm, is shared by researchers working in other critical traditions. What makes practice distinctively feminist is its relevance to change in women's lives or in the systems of social organization that control women. Reviewing accounts of change accomplished through participatory research studies, Patricia Maguire (1987) notes that inequities in the benefits of projects are often obscured by gender-neutral language. Researchers had reported, for example, that "villagers" had increased access to resources when closer inspection revealed that male villagers had been the primary beneficiaries and the women left out.

Accomplishing change through feminist research and assessing whether it has occurred are, of course, quite difficult, and relatively little writing addresses these problems. (For some notable exceptions, however, see accounts of feminist participatory research in Maguire 1987, Mies 1983, 1991; of policy-oriented work in Spalter-Roth & Hartmann 1991; and of activist work in Gordon 1993.) Too often, I believe, the call for change functions as a slogan in writing on feminist methodology, and authors make assumptions about change without sufficient examination of their own implicit theories of social change.

Together, these criteria for feminist methodology provide the outline for a possible alternative to the distanced, distorting, and dispassionately objective procedures of much social research. Whether the goals implied in these criteria are fully achievable is debatable (Acker, Barry & Esseveld 1983) but probably less important than whether they are useful in redirecting research practice to produce better knowledge. My intention in this section has been to claim a distinctiveness for feminist methodology without giving it a fixed definition: I mean to suggest that it must always have an open and "provisional" character (Mohanty 1991:15), but that it is nonetheless a "strikingly cumulative" (Reinharz 1992:246) discourse, held together by core commitments to addressing particular problems in the standard practice of social research and by a common history of learning through activism that provides much of its energy and insight.

RECENT EMPHASES IN FEMINIST METHODOLOGY

The 1990s have been a period of energy and growth in feminist methodology. Discussions have ranged through technical, ethical, and representational issues to the fundamental questions of how and what researchers claim to know.

The Great Divide: Qualitative and Quantitative Approaches

Like outsiders to this body of writing, feminist methodologists themselves often rely on competing or simply unarticulated assumptions about what does (or should) hold this body of work together, and those working to develop feminist methodology sometimes seem to write at cross-purposes. This seems especially true in writing on feminist uses of "qualitative" and "quantitative" methods (see, for example, Cancian 1992, Risman, Sprague & Howard 1993, Cancian 1993). Like scholars in the discipline at large, feminist methodologists sometimes have difficulty communicating across this rather artificial distinction.

Many feminist researchers suggest that qualitative methods fit especially well with feminist goals. Indeed, some feminist researchers who work with qualitative methods seem to claim that these methods are more feminist than others (Mies 1991, Cancian 1993, and Kasper 1994 are possible examples), and some autobiographical accounts (longer ones such as Reinharz 1979 as well as brief asides, as in Stacey 1988 or Gorelick 1989) fuel this notion by recounting frustrations with training in dominant methods and subsequent uses of qualitative approaches.

However, Joey Sprague and Mary Zimmerman (1993) suggest that feminists have made major contributions by finding concepts and practices that resist "dualisms," and they urge resistance to the qualitative-quantitative division. Similarly, Mary Maynard and June Purvis, editors of a recent British anthology (1994), decry the tendency to associate feminist research so strongly with qualitative tools. Implicitly invoking the importance of uncovering hidden experiences, Liz Kelly, Sheila Burton, and Linda Regan (1994) question the presumption that women who participate in research will be more likely to share sensitive material in face-to-face interviews than via less personal survey techniques. Lynn Weber Cannon, Elizabeth Higginbotham, and Marianne LA Leung (1988) point out that small-scale qualitative projects may be more likely than quantitative studies to reproduce race and class biases of the discipline by including only participants who are relatively available to researchers. Others emphasize the consequences of research in urging that feminists not give up quantitative methods and their positivist foundations. Those focusing on policy issues point out that "hard" data are often most convincing outside the university (Spalter-Roth & Hartmann 1991). And Uma Narayan (1989) points out, from the perspective of a nonwestern feminist, that positivism is not always a problem, and certainly not the only one, in research in nonwestern nations. Religion and cultural tradition often contribute to women's oppression, and positivist science can be a force for liberation (and this seems true for western societies as well).

Still, research methods seem to be labeled feminist more often by researchers working in interpretive traditions of sociology. Those working with survey techniques or doing secondary analysis of large data sets, though they may label their projects feminist, are more likely to stress that their methods are those of a rigorous and mostly conventional social science. Explicit discussion of how feminism might modify quantitative practice seems relatively difficult to find.

One common approach to feminist quantitative work involves correcting gender and other cultural biases in standard procedure. Christine Oppong's (1982) work on household studies in nonwestern societies and Margrit Eichler's handbook *Nonsexist Research Methods* (1988) serve as relatively early examples. Both authors point to the many ways that standard survey techniques build in unnoticed assumptions about gender and culture. Those working with survey data have begun to alter survey design and analytic procedures to lessen or eliminate these sources of bias. However, attention to sexism in research procedure probably often depends on the presence of feminists within research teams, where they are usually more likely than others to call attention to these biases. In addition, these refinements are typically discussed as technical responses to social changes, so that connections to feminist theorizing and activism are obscured. One recent exception is Michael D Smith's (1994) discussion of feminist strategies for improving survey data on violence against women; he notes that while these improvements have begun to appear in other projects, they originated and have been most consistently implemented in feminist studies.

Of course, quantitative research always involves interpretation, and many researchers bring feminist theoretical insights to bear on quantitative research design and findings (Risman 1993). Some have begun to write more explicitly about how they have used feminist interpretive frameworks. Roberta Spalter-Roth and Heidi I Hartmann (1991), for example, argue that effective feminist policy research requires a feminist standpoint as well as conventional tools such as cost-benefit analysis. They reject "hegemonic views that see *only one* public interest" (44, emphasis in original), and they adapt the tools of policy research to evaluate the costs and benefits of various policies for women. (See also Steinberg, as cited in Reinharz 1992:91–92.)

Many feminists advocate combining quantitative and qualitative tools, often through collaboration with other researchers. Several European scholars have written about feminist cross-national studies, which often required that participants consider varying national histories of social research and different perspectives on the value of qualitative and quantitative approaches (Windebank 1992, Cockburn 1992, Millar 1992). Susan Greenhalgh and Jiali Li (1995) argue for combining demography with ethnography, in an examination of imbalanced sex ratios that point to generations of "missing girls" in several Chinese villages. They advocate collaboration on political as well as intellectual grounds, suggesting that feminist critique may have negative consequences for demographers, who need continuing access to large data sets controlled by nations and organizations that often seek to deflect criticism. They believe feminists working in other traditions have much to contribute theoretically and often have "more political space" (605) in which to offer critical interpretations of demographic findings.

One further possible bridge between the qualitative and quantitative "branches" of feminist methodology may lie in analyses of statistics as they are constructed and used in particular organizational settings. Dorothy Smith (1990a) suggests examining statistics as textual parts of a "ruling apparatus" that coordinates social relations. She examines data on gender and mental illness, for example, not as evidence of "real" differences, but as pointers toward the management of gendered responses to stress through different social services (see also Waring 1988, Dixon-Mueller 1991, and Hill 1993 on statistical accounts of women's work). Several chapters in Liz Stanley's collection of research conducted at Manchester University (1990a) provide suggestive examples of work based on a similar strategy (Farran 1990, Pugh 1990, Stanley 1990b). While quantitative researchers are surely aware of these underpinnings of their data, the technical practices of that research community require at some point a suspension of discussion of these issues. Analyses that hold them in view offer possibilities for bringing feminist issues more fully into the quantitative traditions of the discipline.

Research Relations: Possibilities and Problems

Feminists have been attracted to interview and ethnographic research partly because these methods offer possibilities for direct interaction with participants. Because these methods have been so widely used, there is now a great deal of feminist writing that documents in increasing detail the various ways that women (and less frequently, men—see Stanko 1994) interact in field research situations. Much of the earlier writing was based on the idea that women's shared interests and concerns would provide resources for dismantling the hierarchies, fictions, and avoidances of research based on positivist frameworks; the argument was that women could talk together more freely and reciprocally, using shared experience as a resource for interpretation (e.g. Oakley 1981, DeVault 1990). More recent writing has provided correctives to early statements that may have mistakenly portrayed feminist research as "rather comfortable and cosy" (Maynard & Purvis 1994). Some researchers have critiqued the notion that women enjoy the advantages of "insiders" when they study other women: Catherine Kohler Riessman (1987) argues that "gender is not enough" to produce easy rapport, and Josephine Beoku-Betts (1994) shows that "Black is not enough" in a discussion of fieldwork among Gullah women in the Sea Islands of the southeastern United States (see also Zavella 1993 on "insider dilemmas" in research with Chicana informants, Phoenix 1994, DeVault 1995). Diane Reay (1995) discusses "the fallacy of easy access," and Pamela Cotterill (1992) complains that the feminist literature celebrating woman-to-woman interviewing did not prepare her for difficult questions regarding the boundaries between research and friendship relations.

Writing on interview research and ethnography has also focused on ethical issues and the potential for misrepresentation. The close relations that are possible seem to pose heightened dangers of exploitation, which led Judith Stacey to ask, "Can there be a feminist ethnography?" (1988), and much writing has been focused on the "dilemmas" of feminist fieldwork (Frontiers 1993). Reay and Cotterill both question the ethics of aggressively pursuing participation in interview research, and ethnographers are much concerned with "imbalances of power" (Scanlon 1993).

These writings have certainly put to rest the myth of "hygienic research" (Stanley & Wise 1983/93:114-15) by discussing in some detail the complexity of face-to-face research encounters. Strategies for confronting these dilemmas have been developed at several levels, through revisions of practice, choices based on ethical considerations, and experiments with representation. At the level of fieldwork practice, for example, Rosalind Edwards (1990) argues for acknowledging racial differences quite explicitly in order to facilitate more honest disclosure, and others have advocated methods for reviewing data with informants in order to resolve—or highlight—disagreements and contradictions (Billson 1991, Personal Narratives Group 1989, Gluck & Patai 1991, Bauer 1993, Skeggs 1994). Some writers, emphasizing the moral dilemmas of the fieldworker's relative freedom and control, have suggested that feminist fieldwork should include special efforts to give something back to participants (Scanlon 1993), or strategies for working with local groups to make change (Park 1992, Gordon 1993). A Lynn Bolles (1993) suggests that one valuable role for western feminists working in other parts of the world is to support indigenous research. Some feminist researchers argue that representational questions pose fundamental moral/ethical dilemmas; they seek solutions in writing strategies (Opie 1992; Rofel 1993; Wheatley 1994a,b, and response by Stacey 1994).

Feminists have written extensively on these dilemmas as they arise in face-to-face research methods, but of course concerns about exploitation and misrepresentation come into play whenever data come from human informants, no matter how distant the process of collection may be from analysis. Some wonder if feminists have overemphasized potential problems of power, producing "excessive demands" (Reinharz 1993) on feminist researchers. The focus on problems of exploitation has produced an association of qualitative feminist methodology with special ethical demands that sometimes seems to obscure other aspects of its distinctiveness. Although these discussions have been lively and productive, one risk is that they may require a moral purity in feminist (or perhaps in women's) qualitative research that is simply unattainable, while leaving similar questions relatively unnoticed in discussions of other research traditions.

Knowledge Claims: Feminist Epistemology

Although the initial feminist critique focused primarily on bias in the application of dominant methods, philosopher Sandra Harding (1986) contends that even this "empiricist" critique tends to subvert the notion of objectivity, since it points to knowledge as social product, and to influences of the knower on what is produced. Moving beyond this kind of critique has brought new questions. If the ground for feminist work is not the distance and dispassion of "objectivity," what will be the basis for legitimate authority? Part of the answer has been to embrace the apparent opposite, subjectivity, and to center inquiry around women's experiences and feelings (Jaggar 1989). However, the turn to subjectivity has been only part of the answer feminists have begun to develop (though it is sometimes mistakenly taken as the defining characteristic of feminist method). As Loraine Gelsthorpe (1992) points out, feminist methodologists have refused to choose between subjectivity and analytic rigor; they seek methods that can incorporate, or at least do not deny, subjectivity. Thus, for those working on feminist methodologies, theorizing links between experience and knowledge has been a central concern.

Many sociologists have taken up some version of what have come to be called "standpoint" approaches (e.g. Reinharz 1983, Stanley & Wise 1983–1993, Smith 1987, Collins 1990). Dorothy Smith's is probably the most widely known and fully developed version of this project within sociology. Her writings over two decades (collected in Smith 1987, 1990a,b) record a long struggle to change a positivist sociology that is organized not only by men's concerns but by the demands of "ruling." (Ramazanoglu 1989 recounts a similar struggle.) Smith's aim is not merely to uncover or give testimony about experience but to make a place for it in analysis that will be focused differently and serve different interests. The feminist sociologist, in her formulation, must refuse to put aside her experience and, indeed, must make her bodily existence and activity a "starting point" for inquiry. From this beginning, the inquiry points toward an analysis of the social context for experience, the relations of ruling that organize daily life and connect all members of a society in systematic interactions.

Smith developed the approach primarily through examples from her life as a single mother, showing how she moved between the grounded activities of raising children and the abstractions of her academic work. She suggests that most women live some version of this movement between particularity and the extra-local projects of management and administration, whether through work as caregivers or in other subordinate positions in the social division of labor. Further, she argues that these positions—where social life is being "put together" from actual, embodied activity—provide a point of entry to investigation that is superior to the starting points derived from abstract theorizing. The argument is not that women know better by virtue of occupying these positions, but that the work accomplished there must be part of any adequate account of social organization.

Many others have taken up the notion of attention to women's experience (though not all have followed Smith's call to look beyond experience in the analysis), and this work has stimulated much discussion of the concepts of "standpoint" and "experience." The notion that some positions provide a "better view" of social organization or a preferred site from which to "start thought" (Harding 1991) seems to accord some knowers an "epistemic privilege" associated with their identities. However, critics point out that identity is not automatically associated with superior insight, and the sociological literature on insider-outsider dynamics certainly calls into question any easy assumption about the consequences for research of particular identities, which are always relative, crosscut by other differences, and often situational and contingent. Another view emphasizes how taking a standpoint invokes the particular experiences associated with some location in society; critics suggest that the idea of "women's standpoint" puts in place an account of experience that fits for only some women. They argue that analyses like Smith's risk emphasizing concerns of white (Collins 1992) or heterosexual women (Ingraham 1994). Smith responds (1992) that theorizing standpoint in either of these ways misses her intention: Rather than calling up a particular identity or set of experiences, the injunction to start inquiry from women's experience is a way of pointing the feminist researcher to material sites where people live their lives, so that "anyone's experience, however various, could become a beginning-place [for] inquiry" (90).

The notion of "women's experience" has been productive for feminist scholars, but it has also become a richly contested concept. Some critics of the emphasis on experience—often those feminists working in quantitative or marxist traditions—point out that individual views are always partial and often distorted by ideology, so that a woman's own testimony may simply reflect the biases of the larger society (Gorelick 1991, Risman 1993). Those influenced by poststructuralist theory argue further that experience always arises in language and discourse (Scott 1991), and that women's testimony will always be marked by language and desire (Clough 1993; see also reply by Smith 1993 and Clough's response).

Those working empirically with approaches that make room for experience address these points in several different ways. Smith contends that women's "bifurcated" consciousness encompasses both the knowledge required to participate in social relations, organized largely through ideological processes, and the often incompletely articulated knowledge that comes from activity. She calls for explicit analysis of how women's activities are connected to the interests of "ruling" (especially Smith 1990a), and how the ideological processes of ruling shape, without fully determining, women's accounts of their experience.[2] Frigga Haug and her colleagues (1987) use "memory-work"—the collective, critical analysis of written memories—to investigate the social and ideological underpinnings of subjectivity in a somewhat different way, more focused on the societal construction of gendered selves. Patricia Hill Collins (1990) develops an epistemology that builds on processes of knowledge creation in African-American communities, where dialogue, caring, and personal accountability are central. She emphasizes that perspectives are always located and claims only a "partial truth" for the knowledge produced from a particular standpoint; she points out that knowledge that is admittedly partial is more trustworthy than partial knowledge presented as generally true. Liz Stanley and Sue Wise (1983/93) also suggest that different standpoints will produce different knowledges, and they accept as a consequence that knowledge claims will be based on a "fractured foundationalism."

These different stances among researchers working in different ways with women's perspectives point to varying epistemological ambitions across the range of feminist methodology. Like other scholars, feminists are considering the consequences for empirical work of the postmodern challenge to objectivity and a science based on a single narrative. Some have embraced a postmodern position that welcomes multiple versions of truth, and these have begun to write about alternative bases for assessing knowledge claims (Richardson 1993, Lather 1993). Others hold that empirical investigation should provide accurate accounts of a social world that can be known in common and should be assessed on that basis (these include feminist empiricists like Risman 1993; those following Smith 1992, whose investigations focus on "actual" social practices; and some who seek an intermediate position).

Kum-Kum Bhavnani (1993) suggests that researchers can strive for what she calls "feminist objectivity." She draws on the writings of feminist philosophers of science who propose replacing traditional constructions of objectivity with more durable claims to "situated knowledge" (Haraway 1988) or a "strong"

---

[2]Studies following Smith in this line of work are collected in Campbell & Manicom 1995.

(Harding 1992) or "dynamic" (Keller 1985) objectivity. Moving the suggestions of these writers to the terrain of empirical work, Bhavnani proposes that the process of producing knowledge should always be visible; the feminist researcher should find ways of recognizing and revealing to audiences the micropolitics of the research situation and should take responsibility for representing those who participate in ways that do not reproduce harmful stereotypes. In addition, researchers claiming feminist objectivity must be attentive to differences and to the limits of their knowledge claims. Echoing some of these themes, Collins (1990) proposes that a feminist Afro-centric epistemology would measure knowledge against concrete experience, test it through dialogue, and judge it in relation to an ethic of personal accountability.

Such emerging feminist formulations repudiate the traditional version of objectivity that requires a separation of knower and known. Out of skepticism for accounts that seem to have no grounded basis (but turn out to be anchored to dominant interests), feminists suggest making the researcher visible in any product of research. This call for visibility involves viewing the self, in Susan Krieger's (1991) terms, as resource rather than contaminant. Precisely how to use and locate the self most effectively remains unresolved. However, the demand for accountability can be seen as the rationale for experiments with autobiographical and dialogic modes of presenting research (e.g. Orr 1990, Kondo 1990, Ellis 1993, Linden 1993) as well as a thread that connects them to projects that are more traditional in format. (The feminist practice of identifying authors by their full names—which I have followed here despite editorial policy—can also be understood as a technical modification that helps to make particular researchers more "visible" in feminist texts.)

Another theme emerging in feminist epistemology involves shifting focus from individual knowers to the perspectives of groups or communities. This shift in focus should perhaps represent a reminder rather than a new idea, since the "experience" so valued in early feminist consciousness raising was in fact a collective construction. The reminder has come from feminists too often ignored in the feminisms that are most visible; this work is discussed below.

Shifting the Center (Again)

It is ironic that writing on feminist methodology has so rarely incorporated the perspectives of women from underrepresented groups and nations (and their male allies), even as these writers have become more central to feminist theory. Though attention to racial/ethnic differences and joint strategies for combating racism have had a continuing presence in second-wave activism and writing (Moraga & Anzaldúa 1981, Bulkin, Pratt & Smith 1984), these efforts have typically been contentious and difficult, and contributions of women from underrepresented groups have too often been ignored or appropriated.

Women from these groups continue to mount pointed challenges to emerging orthodoxies that ignore their perspectives.

From the beginning of the women's studies movement, African-American feminist scholars have had a keen sense of the need to establish an autonomous presence. A landmark anthology (Hull, Bell Scott & Smith 1982) stressed the precarious position of Black women in society and higher education, the knowledge gaps that result from their absence, and the importance of knowledge creation in Black women's communities; these themes continue to be central to "women of color" or "Third World" feminism. The editors predicted that Black women's studies would "come into its own" in the 1980s but noted that this movement was only beginning. They saw "far too few courses and far too few Black women employed in institutions" (xxvii-xxviii) and commented that "the majority of white women teachers and administrators have barely begun the process of self-examination which must precede productive action to change this situation" (xxviii).

The 1980s were indeed a time of putting these issues on the agenda. White feminists like Elizabeth Spelman (1982) wrote compellingly on the problems of false universalization; theorists began re-envisioning the concepts and strategies of their feminisms (e.g. Harding 1991); and feminists writing on research relations became more attentive to ethnic and cultural differences (as discussed above). More importantly, new writing from "third world feminism" combined work by social scientists and creative writers to offer new conceptualizations of identity, building more fundamental critiques of the disciplines and modeling evocative writing strategies (Anzaldúa 1990a, Mohanty, Russo & Torres 1991). Social scientists began to consider strategies for empirical investigation that could be aligned with these perspectives.

Patricia Hill Collins' *Black Feminist Thought* (1990), while usually considered a work of theory, also treats methodological issues; the book concludes with an extended discussion of epistemology, and the entire text illustrates an approach to knowledge production that draws from and builds upon the "subjugated knowledge" shared within communities of African-American women. Chela Sandoval (1991) also draws lessons from the strategies of particular communities—the activist communities of what she calls "US third world feminism"—and finds in the everyday resistances of women of color a "method" (applicable beyond formal research, but certainly relevant there) of differential, oppositional consciousness. She advocates a "self-conscious mobility" that would allow feminists to enact opposition more fluidly, "between and among" possible identities and tactics (14). While adopting some strategies like those of Collins, Sandoval also emphasizes multiple identities and coalition across cultural communities.

Himani Bannerji (1995) extends marxist and feminist "standpoint" methods, arguing that gender, race/ethnicity, and nationality are always part of the organization of social activity, so that any adequate feminism (or marxism or anti-racism) must take account of the simultaneity of social relations that more traditional accounts have tried to separate analytically. Without naturalizing ethnic differences, she attends to embodiedness, whether writing about her own experience of teaching in Canadian universities or about the sexual harassment of a Black woman working in a Canadian factory, analyzed as the product of a pervasive "racist sexism" woven into economic relations.

Chandra Talpede Mohanty (1991a,b), drawing on the study of colonialism and its legacy, seeks a social science that will contribute to the worldwide project of decolonization. She emphasizes multiple levels of work: consciousness raising (of both researcher and others), a reformulation of disciplines that have supported the colonial enterprise, and empirical investigations that reconstruct understandings of women's histories and contexts. Like Bannerji, she envisions a social science that encompasses the daily activities of third world women as well as the ruling relations that construct their oppression, and like Bannerji, she draws on the work of Dorothy Smith, suggesting that Smith's attention to "relations of ruling" may be especially useful in the investigation of colonial and postcolonial social organization.

Mohanty also begins to rework issues of consciousness, identity, and writing, noting that "the very practice of remembering and rewriting leads to the formation of politicized consciousness" (34). Though she links this statement to the legacy of feminist consciousness raising, she also suggests that the texts of third world women challenge the "individualist subject" of much feminist writing. She argues that the feminism of women of color calls for rethinking the idea that "the personal is political," not because starting from experience is wrong, but because of the richness of collective rather than individual stories of agency and resistance. Drawing from Gloria Anzaldúa (1990b) and echoing Sandoval's notion of differential consciousness, she points to the strategic value of a multiple or "mestiza" consciousness, attentive to borders and negotiations through multiple locations.

This kind of methodological innovation is related to philosopher Maria Lugones's (1987) use of the term "'world'-traveling" to refer to the ability to move across social boundaries that seems so central to the experiences of Black and third world women (and so foreign to the over-privileged). Lugones inspired political scientist Christine Sylvester's (1995) discussion of western encounters with African feminisms. However, these provocative discussions of fluid and shifting identities sit somewhat uneasily alongside the analyses of Collins and Bannerji, whose methods emphasize the obduracy of social categories associated with ethnicity and their significance for people's recruitment into social relations.

These writers are rarely included in discussions of "feminist methodology," but I believe they point to the next stages in the project of building more adequate research practices. Their writings, and the roots of these writings in communities of resistance, lend some credence to notions of epistemic privilege—the idea that people in subordinated locations have access to perspectives that others miss. On the other hand, these writings begin to "open up" the histories, experiences, and self-representations of such communities, so that it seems more possible, and urgent, for all knowers to attend to the perspectives of others. These writers challenge scholars to think more carefully about what is at stake in how one gains such knowledge, and how it is used.

Finally, it may be worth noting that the gender-related isolation and stress of doing research have been discussed in the writing of some non-European feminists (Hull, Bell Scott, & Smith 1982, Ramazanoglu 1989). Annecka Marshall (1994) writes poignantly of the pain and isolation she felt as a student and scholar in sexist-racist institutional contexts, giving an account of serious health problems that she tried to ignore, but ultimately had to resolve before continuing her work. I do not mean to suggest that these kinds of problems are suffered only by third world feminists, but to highlight the fact that institutional settings which may have become increasingly comfortable for white feminist academics continue to be painfully alienating for others, and to suggest that these different positionings continue to shape the work produced by feminist scholars.

CONCLUSION: FEMINISM AND SOCIOLOGY

I close, in keeping with the sociology of knowledge approach I have adopted throughout this chapter, with a brief discussion of the connections through which feminist sociologists construct and sustain a discourse on feminist methodology. Strategizing about research practice has been strongly connected to feminist theory and necessarily so: Feminist understandings drive methodological innovation. Still, theory does not translate unproblematically to the questions of empirical investigation, and those working on methodology must shape the insights of theorists to their own needs. Feminist sociologists also value connections to feminists in other disciplines, whose related projects can often provide models for experimentation. Working across disciplines also helps to reveal disciplinary power and thus aids in strategizing about how to use it well and avoid its pitfalls. Feminist scholars are always more or less directly linked to activism, by virtue of their origins, but maintaining such connections requires continuing attention; sustaining connections to policymakers who might use feminist research requires another kind of attention.

Connections to our own disciplines are among the most vexed questions that occupy feminist sociologists. Some argue convincingly for a strategic "disloyalty to the disciplines" (Stacey 1995), while others advocate strategic uses of disciplinary authority and legitimacy (Risman 1993). My approach in this essay relies on (and attempts to contribute to) a sense of distinctiveness in feminist sociological practice, and a commitment to articulating the value of disciplinary traditions. Paradoxically, but not for the first time, sociological approaches have provided tools for unmasking their own coercive power. Though feminists are in struggle with the discipline, it is the struggle of committed participants.

ACKNOWLEDGMENTS

My title is inspired by hooks (1989). The bibliography prepared by Nancy Naples and participants in the Sex and Gender Section's preconference workshop at the 1994 Annual Meeting of the American Sociological Association provided a valuable resource in my literature search. In addition, I am grateful for comments on an earlier draft from Susan Borker, Robert Chibka, Julia Loughlin, Shulamit Reinharz, Dorothy Smith, Barrie Thorne, and Judith Wittner, though I have not done justice to all their suggestions.

Literature Cited

Acker J, Barry K, Esseveld J. 1983. Objectivity and truth: problems in doing feminist research. *Women's Stud. Int. Forum* 6(4):423–35

Allen P. 1973. Free space. In *Radical Feminism*, ed. A Koedt, E Levine, A Rapone, pp. 271–79. New York: Quadrangle

Anderson K, Armitage S, Jack D, Wittner J. 1990. Beginning where we are: feminist methodology in oral history. See Nielsen 1990, pp. 94–112

Anzaldúa G, ed. 1990a. *Making Face, Making Soul, Haciendo Caras: Creative and Critical Perspectives by Feminists of Color.* San Francisco: Aunt Lute Books

Anzaldúa G. 1990b. La conciencia de la mestiza: towards a new consciousness. See Anzaldúa 1990a, pp. 377–89

Baca Zinn M, Cannon LW, Higginbotham E, Dill BT. 1986. The costs of exclusionary practices in women's studies. *Signs* 11(2):290–303

Bannerji H. 1995. *Thinking Through: Essays on Feminism, Marxism, and Anti-Racism.* Toronto: Women's Press

Bauer J. 1993. Ma'ssoum's tale: the personal and political transformations of a young Iranian "feminist" and her ethnographer. *Fem. Stud.* 19(3):519–48

Beoku-Betts J. 1994. When Black is not enough: doing field research among Gullah women. *Natl. Women's Stud. Assoc. J.* 6(3):413–33

Bhavnani KK. 1993. Tracing the contours: feminist research and feminist objectivity. *Women's Stud. Int. Forum* 16(2):95–104

Billson JM. 1991. The progressive verification method: toward a feminist methodology for studying women cross-culturally. *Women's Stud. Int. Forum* 14(3):201–15

Bolles AL. 1993. Doing it for themselves: women's research and action in the Commonwealth Caribbean. In *Researching Women in Latin America and the Caribbean*, ed. E Acosta-Belen, CE Bose, pp. 153–74. Boulder, CO: Westview

Bowles G, Duelli Klein R, eds. 1983. *Theories*

of Women's Studies. London: Routledge & Kegan Paul

Bulkin E, Pratt MB, Smith, B. 1984. *Yours in Struggle: Three Feminist Perspectives on Anti-Semitism and Racism.* Brooklyn, NY: Long Haul

Campbell M, Manicom A, eds. 1995. *Knowledge, Experience, and Ruling Relations: Studies in the Social Organization of Knowledge.* Toronto: Univ. Toronto Press

Cancian F. 1992. Feminist science: methodologies that challenge inequality. *Gender Soc.* 6(4):623–42

Cancian F. 1993. Reply to Risman, Sprague and Howard. *Gender Soc.* 7(4):610–11

Cannon LW, Higginbotham E, Leung MLA. 1988. Race and class bias in qualitative research on women. *Gender Soc.* 2(4):449–62

Clough PT. 1993. On the brink of deconstructing sociology: critical reading of Dorothy Smith's standpoint epistemology. *Sociol. Q.* 34(1):169–82

Cockburn C. 1992. Technological change in a changing Europe: does it mean the same for women as for men? *Women's Stud. Int. Forum* 15(1):85–90

Collins PH. 1990. *Black Feminist Thought: Knowledge, Consciousness, and the Politics of Empowerment.* Boston: Unwin Hyman

Collins PH. 1992. Transforming the inner circle: Dorothy Smith's challenge to sociological theory. *Soc. Theory* 10(1):73–80

Combahee River Collective. 1982. A Black feminist statement. See Hull et al 1982, pp. 13–22

Cook JA, Fonow MM. 1986. Knowledge and women's interests: issues of epistemology and methodology in feminist sociological research. *Sociol. Inq.* 56(1):2–29

Cotterill P. 1992. Interviewing women: issues of friendship, vulnerability, and power. *Women's Stud. Int. Forum* 15(5/6):593–606

DeVault ML. 1990. Talking and listening from women's standpoint: feminist strategies for interviewing and analysis. *Soc. Probl.* 37(1):96–116

DeVault ML. 1995. Ethnicity and expertise: racial-ethnic knowledge in sociological research. *Gender Soc.* 9(5):612–31

Dill BT. 1979. The dialectics of Black womanhood. *Signs* 4(3):543–55

Dixon-Mueller R. 1991. Women in agriculture: counting the labor force in developing countries. See Fonow & Cook 1991, pp. 226–47

Edwards R. 1990. Connecting method and epistemology: a white woman interviewing Black women. *Women's Stud. Int. Forum* 13(5):477–90

Eichler M. 1988. *Nonsexist Research Methods: A Practical Guide.* Boston: Unwin Hyman

Ellis C. 1993. "There are survivors": telling a story of sudden death. *Sociol. Q.* 34(4):711–30

Farran D. 1990. "Seeking Susan": producing statistical information on young people's leisure. See Stanley 1990a, pp. 91–102

Ferree MM, Martin PY, eds. 1995. *Feminist Organizations: Harvest of the New Women's Movement.* Philadelphia: Temple Univ. Press

Fonow MM, Cook JA, eds. 1991. *Beyond Methodology: Feminist Scholarship as Lived Research.* Bloomington: Ind. Univ. Press

Frontiers. 1993. Special issue "Feminist Dilemmas in Fieldwork." *Frontiers* 13(3):1–103

Game A. 1991. *Undoing the Social: Towards a Deconstructive Sociology.* Toronto: Univ. Toronto Press

Gelsthorpe L. 1992. Response to Martyn Hammersley's paper "On feminist methodology." *Sociology* 26(2):213–18

Glazer-Malbin N, Waehrer HY, eds. 1971. *Woman in a Man-Made World.* Chicago: Rand McNally

Gluck SB, Patai D, eds. 1991. *Women's Words: The Feminist Practice of Oral History.* New York/London: Routledge

Gordon DA. 1993. Worlds of consequences: feminist ethnography as social action. *Crit. Anthropol.* 13(4):429–43

Gorelick S. 1989. The changer and the changed: methodological reflections on studying Jewish feminists. See Jaggar & Bordo 1989, pp. 336–58

Gorelick S. 1991. Contradictions of feminist methodology. *Gender Soc.* 5(4):459–77

Greenhalgh S, Jiali Li. 1995. Engendering reproductive policy and practice in peasant China: for a feminist demography of reproduction. *Signs* 20(3):601–41

Haraway D. 1985. A manifesto for cyborgs: science, technology, and socialist feminism in the 1980s. *Social. Rev.* 15(2):65–107

Haraway D. 1988. Situated knowledges: the science question in feminism and the privilege of partial perspective. *Fem. Stud.* 14(3):575–99

Harding S. 1986. *The Science Question in Feminism.* Ithaca, NY: Cornell Univ. Press

Harding S, ed. 1987. *Feminism and Methodology: Social Science Issues.* Bloomington, IN: Ind. Univ. Press

Harding S. 1991. *Whose Science? Whose Knowledge?* Ithaca, NY: Cornell Univ. Press

Harding S. 1992. Rethinking standpoint epistemology: what is "strong objectivity?" *Centen. Rev.* 36(3):437–70

Haug F, ed. 1987. *Female Sexualization: A Collective Work of Memory.* London: Verso

Hill B. 1993. Women, work and the census: a problem for historians of women. *Hist. Workshop J.* 35:78–94

hooks b. 1989. *Talking Back: Thinking Femi-*

nist, Thinking Black. Boston: South End

Hull GT, Bell Scott P, Smith B, eds. 1982. *All the Women Are White, All the Blacks Are Men, But Some of Us Are Brave: Black Women's Studies.* Old Westbury, NY: Feminist Press

Ingraham C. 1994. The heterosexual imaginary: feminist sociology and theories of gender. *Soc. Theory* 12(2):203–19

Inscriptions. 1988. Special issue on "Feminism and the critique of colonial discourse," ed. D Gordon. *Inscriptions* Nos. 3/4

Jackson JJ. 1973. Black women in a racist society. In *Racism and Mental Health,* ed. CV Willie, BM Kramer, BS Brown, pp. 185–268. Pittsburgh: Univ. Pittsburgh Press

Jaggar AM. 1989. Love and knowledge: emotion in feminist epistemology. See Jaggar & Bordo 1989, pp. 145–71

Jaggar AM, Bordo SR, eds. 1989. *Gender/Body/Knowledge: Feminist Reconstructions of Being and Knowing.* New Brunswick, NJ: Rutgers Univ. Press

Kasper A. 1994. A feminist, qualitative methodology: a study of women with breast cancer. *Qual. Sociol.* 17(3):263–81

Keller EF. 1985. *Reflections on Gender and Science.* New Haven: Yale Univ. Press

Kelly L, Burton S, Regan L. 1994. Researching women's lives or studying women's oppression: what constitutes feminist research? See Maynard & Purvis 1994, pp. 27–48

Kondo DK. 1990. *Crafting Selves: Power, Gender, and Discourses of Identity in a Japanese Workplace.* Chicago: Univ. Chicago Press

Kramarae C, Spender D, eds. 1992. *The Knowledge Explosion: Generations of Feminist Scholarship.* New York: Teachers College Press

Krieger S. 1991. *Social Science and the Self: Personal Essays on an Art Form.* New Brunswick, NJ: Rutgers Univ. Press

Ladner JA. 1971. *Tomorrow's Tomorrow: The Black Woman.* Garden City, NY: Doubleday

Lather P. 1991. *Getting Smart: Feminist Research and Pedagogy With/In the Postmodern.* London: Routledge

Lather P. 1993. Fertile obsession: validity after poststructuralism. *Sociol. Q.* 34(4):673–93

Leveque-Lopman L. 1988. *Claiming Reality: Phenomenology and Women's Experience.* Totowa, NJ: Rowan & Littlefield

Linden RR. 1993. *Making Stories, Making Selves: Feminist Reflections on the Holocaust.* Columbus: Ohio State Univ. Press

Lugones M. 1987. Playfulness, "world"-travelling, and loving perception. *Hypatia* 2(2):3–19

Maguire P. 1987. *Doing Participatory Research: A Feminist Approach.* Amherst, MA: Cent. Int. Educ., Univ. Mass.

Mansbridge J. 1995. What is the feminist movement? See Ferree & Martin 1995, pp. 27–34

Marshall A. 1994. Sensuous Sapphires: a study of the social construction of Black female sexuality. See Maynard & Purvis 1994, pp. 106–24

Maynard M, Purvis J, eds. 1994. *Researching Women's Lives from a Feminist Perspective.* London: Taylor & Francis

McDermott P. 1994. *Politics and Scholarship: Feminist Academic Journals and the Production of Knowledge.* Urbana: Univ. Ill. Press

Mies M. 1983. Towards a methodology for feminist research. See Bowles & Duelli Klein 1983, pp. 117–39

Mies M. 1991. Women's research or feminist research? The debate surrounding feminist science and methodology. See Fonow & Cook 1991, pp. 60–84

Millar J. 1992. Cross-national research on women in the European Community: the case of solo women. *Women's Stud. Int. Forum* 15(1):77–84

Millman M, Kanter RM, eds. 1975. *Another Voice: Feminist Perspectives on Social Life and Social Science.* Garden City, NY: Anchor Doubleday

Mohanty CT. 1991a. Cartographies of struggle: third world women and the politics of feminism. See Mohanty et al 1991, pp. 1–47

Mohanty CT. 1991b. Under western eyes: feminist scholarship and colonial discourses. See Mohanty et al 1991, pp. 51–80

Mohanty CT, Russo A, Torres L, eds. 1991. *Third World Women and the Politics of Feminism.* Bloomington: Ind. Univ. Press

Moraga C, Anzaldúa G, eds. 1981. *This Bridge Called My Back: Writings by Radical Women of Color.* Watertown, MA: Persephone. 2nd ed. 1983. New York: Kitchen Table Women of Color Press

Narayan U. 1989. The project of feminist epistemology: perspectives from a nonwestern feminist. See Jaggar & Bordo 1989, pp. 256–69

Nebraska Feminist Collective. 1983. A feminist ethic for social science research. *Women's Stud. Int. Forum* 6(5):535–43

Nebraska Sociological Feminist Collective, ed. 1988. *A Feminist Ethic for Social Science Research.* Lewiston, NY: Edwin Mellen

Nielsen JM, ed. 1990. *Feminist Research Methods: Exemplary Readings in the Social Sciences.* Boulder, CO: Westview

Oakley A. 1981. Interviewing women: a contradiction in terms. In *Doing Feminist Research,* ed. H Roberts, pp. 30–61. London: Routledge & Kegan Paul

Opie A. 1992. Qualitative research, appropriation of the "other" and empowerment. *Fem.*

Rev. 40:52–69

Oppong C. 1982. Family structure and women's reproductive and productive roles: some conceptual and methodological issues. In *Women's Roles and Population Trends in the Third World,* ed. R Anker, M Buvinic, NH Youssef, pp. 133–50. London: Croon Helm

Orr J. 1990. Theory on the market: panic, incorporating. *Soc. Probl.* 37(4):460–84

Park J. 1992. Research partnerships: a discussion paper based on case studies from "The place of alcohol in the lives of New Zealand women" project. *Women's Stud. Int. Forum* 15(5/6):581–91

Personal Narratives Group, ed. 1989. *Interpreting Women's Lives: Feminist Theory and Personal Narratives.* Bloomington: Ind. Univ. Press

Phoenix A. 1994. Practising feminist research: the intersection of gender and "race" in the research process. See Maynard & Purvis 1994, pp. 49–71

Pugh A. 1990. My statistics and feminism—a true story. See Stanley 1990a, pp. 103–12

Ramazanoglu C. 1989. Improving on sociology: the problems of taking a feminist standpoint. *Sociology* 23(3):427–42

Reay D. 1995. The fallacy of easy access. *Women's Stud. Int. Forum* 18(2):205–13

Reinharz S. 1979. *On Becoming a Social Scientist.* San Francisco: Jossey-Bass

Reinharz S. 1983. Experiential analysis: a contribution to feminist research. See Bowles & Duelli Klein 1983, pp. 162–91

Reinharz S. 1985. Feminist distrust: problems of content and context in sociological research. In *The Self in Social Inquiry,* ed. D Berg, K Smith, pp. 153–72. Beverly Hills, CA: Sage

Reinharz S, with Davidman L. 1992. *Feminist Methods in Social Research.* New York: Oxford

Reinharz S. 1993. Neglected voices and excessive demands in feminist research. *Qual. Soc.* 16(1):69–76

Reinharz S, Bombyk M, Wright J. 1983. Methodological issues in feminist research: a bibliography of literature in women's studies, sociology, and psychology. *Women's Stud. Int. For.* 6(4):437–54

Richardson L. 1993. Poetics, dramatics, and transgressive validity: the case of the skipped line. *Sociol. Q.* 34(4):695–710

Riessman CK. 1987. When gender is not enough: women interviewing women. *Gender Soc.* 1(2):172–207

Risman BJ. 1993. Methodological implications of feminist scholarship. *Am. Sociol.* 24(3/4):15–25

Risman BJ, Sprague J, Howard J. 1993. Comment on Francesca M. Cancian's "Feminist Science." *Gender Soc.* 7(4):608–9

Roby P. 1992. Women and the ASA: degendering organizational structures and processes, 1964–1974. *Am. Sociol.* 23(1):18–48

Rofel L. 1993. Where feminism lies: field encounters in China. *Frontiers* 13(3):33–52

Sandoval C. 1991. U.S. Third World feminism: the theory and method of oppositional consciousness in the postmodern world. *Genders* 10(Spring):1–24

Scanlon J. 1993. Challenging the imbalances of power in feminist oral history: developing a take-and-give methodology. *Women's Stud. Int. Forum* 16(6):639–45

Scott JW. 1991. The evidence of experience. *Crit. Inq.* 17(Summer):773–97

Skeggs B. 1994. Situating the production of feminist ethnography. See Maynard & Purvis 1994, pp. 72–92

Smith DE. 1987. *The Everyday World as Problematic: A Feminist Sociology.* Boston: Northeastern Univ. Press

Smith DE. 1990a. *The Conceptual Practices of Power: A Feminist Sociology of Knowledge.* Boston: Northeastern Univ. Press

Smith DE. 1990b. *Texts, Facts, and Femininity: Exploring the Relations of Ruling.* New York: Routledge

Smith DE. 1992. Sociology from women's experience: a reaffirmation. *Soc. Theory* 10(1):88–98

Smith DE. 1993. High noon in textland: a critique of Clough. *Sociol. Q.* 34(1):183–92

Smith MD. 1994. Enhancing the quality of survey data on violence against women: a feminist approach. *Gender Soc.* 8(1):109–27

Spalter-Roth RM, Hartmann HI. 1991. Science and politics and the "dual vision" of feminist policy research: the example of family and medical leave. In *Parental Leave and Child Care: Setting a Research and Policy Agenda,* ed. JS Hyde, MJ Essex, pp. 41–65. Philadelphia: Temple Univ. Press

Spelman EV. 1988. *Inessential Woman: Problems of Exclusion in Feminist Thought.* Boston: Beacon

Sprague J, Zimmerman M. 1993. Overcoming dualisms: a feminist agenda for sociological methodology. In *Theory on Gender/Feminism on Theory,* ed. P England. New York: Aldine

Stacey J. 1988. Can there be a feminist ethnography? *Women's Stud. Int. Forum* 11(1):21–27

Stacey J. 1994. Imagining feminist ethnography: a response to Elizabeth E. Wheatley. *Women's Stud. Int. Forum* 17(4):417–19

Stacey J. 1995. Disloyal to the disciplines: a feminist trajectory in the borderlands. In *Feminisms in the Academy,* ed. DC Stanton, AJ

Stewart, pp. 311–29. Ann Arbor: Univ. Mich. Press

Stanko EA. 1994. Dancing with denial: researching women and questioning men. See Maynard & Purvis 1994, pp. 93–105

Stanley L, ed. 1990a. *Feminist Praxis: Research, Theory and Epistemology in Feminist Sociology.* New York: Routledge

Stanley L. 1990b. "A referral was made": behind the scenes during the creation of a Social Services Department "elderly" statistic. See Stanley 1990a, pp. 113–22

Stanley L, Wise S. 1979. Feminist research, feminist consciousness, and experiences of sexism. *Women's Stud. Int. Q.* 2(3):359–74

Stanley L, Wise S. 1983/93. *Breaking Out: Feminist Consciousness and Feminist Research* and *Breaking Out Again: Feminist Ontology and Epistemology.* New ed. London: Routledge

Strobel M. 1995. Organizational learning in the Chicago Women's Liberation Union. See Ferree & Martin 1995, pp. 145–64

Sylvester C. 1995. African and Western feminisms: world-traveling the tendencies and possibilities. *Signs* 20(4):941–69

Waring M. 1988. *If Women Counted.* San Francisco: Harper & Row

Wheatley EE. 1994. How can we engender ethnography with a feminist imagination? a rejoinder to Judith Stacey. *Women's Stud. Int. Forum* 17(4):403–16

Wheatley EE. 1994. Dances with feminists: truths, dares, and ethnographic stares. *Womens Stud. Int. For.* 17(4):421–23

Windebank J. 1992. Comparing women's employment patterns across the European Community: issues of method and interpretation. *Women's Stud. Int. Forum* 15(1):65–76

Zavella P. 1993. Feminist insider dilemmas: constructing ethnic identity with "Chicana" informants. *Frontiers* 13(3):53–76

Annu. Rev. Sociol. 1996. 22:51–78

GENDER IN THE WELFARE STATE

Ann Orloff

Department of Sociology, University of Wisconsin, Madison, Wisconsin 53706

KEY WORDS: social policy, women, feminization of poverty, states

ABSTRACT

Gender relations—embodied in the sexual division of labor, compulsory hetero-sexuality, gendered forms of citizenship and political participation, ideologies of masculinity and femininity, and the like—profoundly shape the character of welfare states. Likewise, the institutions of social provision—the set of social assistance and social insurance programs and universal citizenship entitlements to which we refer as "the welfare state"—affect gender relations. Until recently, two broad approaches to gender relations and welfare states predominated: one which saw states contributing to the social reproduction of gender hierarchies, and a second which saw states having an ameliorative impact on gender inequal-ity. More recently, two new strands of research have emerged emphasizing the variation in the effects of social policies on gender.

INTRODUCTION

Gender relations, embodied in the sexual division of labor, compulsory hetero-sexuality, discourses and ideologies of citizenship, motherhood, masculinity and femininity, and the like, profoundly shape the character of welfare states. Likewise, the institutions of social provision—the set of social assistance and social insurance programs, universal citizenship entitlements, and public ser-vices to which we refer as "the welfare state"—affect gender relations in a variety of ways. Studies of the welfare state have turned strongly comparative and lately have been concerned with understanding qualitative differences in the origins and trajectories of social policy in different countries, and in con-sequence also with developing typologies identifying the range of forms taken by welfare states: "regime types" or "worlds of welfare capitalism." However, comparative study has so far given little systematic attention to gender. Most

51

0360-0572/96/0815-0051$08.00

feminist work, though concerned with elaborating a gendered analysis of welfare states, has not been systematically comparative. (In short, we see the persistence of sex segregation in studies of the welfare state.[1]) This means that we lack a sense of the range of variation in how gender relations and welfare states mutually influence each other.

Some exciting new work is investigating precisely these issues either by tracing the historical development of state social provision and its gendered effects or by exploring comparative variation in the linkages between specific characteristics of gender relations and particular features of welfare states. In this article, I assess this new comparative and historical work. Thus, I do not focus on contemporary single-country case studies, nor do I attend to comparative studies of welfare states that entirely neglect gender. My goal is to summarize the current state of understanding about the varying effects of welfare states on gender relations and vice versa.

The "welfare state" typically is conceptualized as a state committed to modifying the play of social or market forces in order to achieve greater equality (Ruggie 1984, p. 11). It is often operationalized as the collection of social insurance and assistance programs that offer income protection to those experiencing unemployment, industrial accident, retirement, disability, ill health, death or desertion of a family breadwinner, or extreme poverty—all of which have developed over the past century or so across the western industrialized world. Other analysts, feminists prominent among them, have argued for a broader definition that includes provision of daycare, education, housing, medical services, and other services dedicated to the care of dependent citizens. I define the welfare state, or state social provision, as interventions by the state in civil society to alter social forces, including male dominance, but I do not judge a priori that all interventions are aimed at, or actually produce, greater equality among citizens.

By "feminist," I refer to analyses that take gender relations into account as both causes and effects of various social, political, economic, and cultural processes and institutions. I do not assume, however, that categories of gender—women and men—are internally homogeneous. By "gender relations" I mean the set of mutually constitutive structures and practices which produce gender differentiation, gender inequalities, and gender hierarchy in a given society. I am informed by multidimensional theoretical frameworks of gender relations, such as Connell's (1987) "gender order" comprised of three types of structures: labor,

---

[1]A review of books on the welfare state from 1991 to the present (reviewed in the *American Journal of Sociology* and carried out by Greg Maney, who provided research assistance on this project), revealed that almost all recent "mainstream" scholarship ignores the relationship between gender and the welfare state; further information is available by writing to Ann Orloff.

power, and cathexis, and Scott's (1986) four interrelated elements of gender: symbolic representations, normative interpretations of these symbols, social institutions (including kinship, the labor market, education, and the polity), and subjective gender identity. This approach allows for investigation of variation across states and over time in the intensity, character, and mix of different structural sources of gender differentiation and inequality in, e.g., the division of paid and unpaid labor, political power, and the character of sexual relationships.

GENDER AND THE WELFARE STATE

Over the past two decades, we have amassed a large body of research showing that state policies of all kinds are shaped by gender relations and in turn affect gender relations. Until recently, one of two broad understandings of the relationship between the state and gender has predominated in analyses of social policy. The first sees states contributing in one way or another to the social reproduction of gender hierarchies. In contrast, the second sees states varying in terms of their ameliorative impact on social inequality, including gender inequality.

The Social Reproduction of Gender Hierarchy

One school of thought emphasizes the ways in which state social policies regulate gender relations and contribute to the social reproduction of gender inequality through a variety of mechanisms (see Jenson 1986 for a review). Analysts saw the emergence of modern welfare states as a transition from "private" to "public" patriarchy (e.g. Holter 1984). Key mechanisms for the maintenance of gender hierarchy include: (i) gendered divisions of labor, with men responsible for families' economic support and women responsible for caregiving and domestic labor as well as for producing babies; (ii) the family wage system, in which men's relatively superior wages (and tax advantages) are justified partly in terms of their responsibility for the support of dependent wives and children; women are excluded from the paid labor force (or from favored positions within it) and therefore are economically dependent on men; (iii) traditional marriage (which implies the gender division of labor) and a concomitant double standard of sexual morality. Analysts in the United States and other English-speaking countries tended to see all of these mechanisms operating together—for example, Abromovitz (1988) refers to a "family ethic" enforced on women as analogous to the work ethic enforcing paid labor on men, while Gordon (1988) refers to welfare as reinforcing the family wage system, that is, acting as a backup by giving support to those suffering from market or family "failures," even while contributing to the reproduction of the system of gender relations (see also Lister 1992, Gordon 1990). Scandinavian—but also British—analysts have emphasized women's responsibility for care work, the continuing dependence of the society on women's unpaid care work, and the ways in which welfare states reward care work less well than the paid labor that characterizes men's lives (e.g. Land 1978, Waerness 1984, Ungerson 1990, Hernes 1987, 1988, Sassoon 1987, Finch & Groves 1983). Finally, many have called attention to the ways in which these various mechanisms—even when not associated with women's absolute material deprivation—are coupled with women's exclusion from political power (e.g. Lewis & Åström 1992, Nelson 1984, Hernes 1987, Borchorst & Siim 1987).

The social reproduction analysts highlighted the ways in which welfare states reinforced pre-existing (traditional) gender roles and relations. More recently, there has been a greater focus on the ways in which state practices themselves constitute gender. Thus, some have focused particularly on the construction of gendered citizenship, with its encodings of male "independence" based on wage-earning (rather than the older basis in military service) and female "dependence," and associated gender-differentiated social provision (Gordon & Fraser 1994, Knijn 1994, Saraceno 1994, Cass 1994, Pateman 1988, Lister 1990). Another formulation highlights the state's production of gender differentiation (and inequality) through the process of claiming benefits from the state: men tend to make claims on the welfare state as workers while women make claims as members of families (as wives or mothers) and through the very existence of "masculine" and "feminine" programs—the former protecting against labor market failures and targeting a male clientele, the latter providing help for family-related problems and targeting a female clientele (e.g. Fraser 1989). Similarly, Bryson (1992) describes a "men's welfare state" and a "women's welfare state." In the United States especially, scholars speak of a "two-tier" or "two-track" welfare state in which programs targeted on men and labor market problems tend to be contributory social insurance while those primarily for women and family-related are means-tested social assistance; they emphasize the disadvantages of relying on second-tier programs in terms of benefit generosity, the restrictiveness of eligibility regulations and the extent of concomitant supervision and intrusion (e.g. Fraser 1989, Nelson 1990).

There is clearly some truth in this portrait of the welfare state helping to maintain hierarchical gender relations even as women's material position is sometimes improved. However, this picture is also incomplete—and, to some extent, inaccurate. Crucially, it ignores cross-national and historical variation that is significant for women and for gender relations because almost all studies in this tradition have focused on a single country; if the experiences of a number of countries are mentioned, it is largely to illustrate similarity rather than variation in social policy effects (e.g. Bryson 1992).

Ameliorating Gender Inequalities?

The second understanding of gender relations and the welfare state is based on the common idea that welfare states work to ameliorate social inequalities; feminist versions of this view focus on gender as well as class inequalities, especially in vulnerability to poverty. These analysts generally note that although poverty rates for the population as a whole fell in the post–World War II era, women made up an increasing proportion of poor adults, and households headed by women became an ever-larger proportion of all poor households; these trends are due partly to the improving situation of other demographic groups (e.g. the elderly) but also to some women's deteriorating position in the labor market and the rising rates of solo motherhood (McLanahan, Sorenson and Watson 1989). Income transfer programs sometimes offer buffers against women's poverty (Piven 1985). Although less sophisticated in their understanding of gender relations than the social reproduction analyses, these studies have sometimes noted cross-national variation in policy outcomes (see, e.g. Kamerman 1986, Goldberg & Kremen 1990, Mitchell 1993, Smeeding, Torrey & Rein 1988). For example, studies focusing on the poverty of women and/or women-maintained families consistently find the United States has the highest poverty levels, followed closely by Canada and Australia; Britain looks considerably better than its "daughter" countries, while Germany's poverty rates for solo-mothers are quite a bit higher than is the case in other European countries (Mitchell 1993). Analysts link these variations to a key characteristic of welfare states—the relative generosity of benefit levels and levels of overall social spending (Kamerman 1986, Goldberg & Kremen 1990). The implication of these studies is that disadvantaged groups—including women—have an interest in higher spending.

While the concern of poverty researchers with cross-national variation is important, this view of welfare states and gender is also inadequate—it examines only linear variation in the effects of state policies on women's status. This is particularly problematic if one is concerned with states' impacts on gendered social institutions (e.g. the gendered division of labor, especially women's responsibility for unpaid care work), and on gendered power (e.g. that accruing to men from their status as breadwinners receiving a family wage or public benefits to replace it). For example, in their comparison of seven industrialized countries, Goldberg & Kremen (1990) found that several factors in addition to the level of public benefits—the proportion of families headed by single mothers, the extent of women's labor force participation, and the degree of gender equality in the labor market—affect the level of women's poverty. In Sweden, good labor market conditions and generous benefits minimize single women's poverty; in Japan, despite very unequal labor market conditions and low benefits, feminization of poverty has not emerged as an area of concern because few mothers are single. But while Swedish social policy is recognized in most cross-national studies of poverty for its effectiveness in virtually eliminating poverty among women, analyses concentrating on poverty alone may miss other significant issues, such as the high concentration of women in part-time (albeit well-remunerated) employment and their continuing disproportionate responsibility for housework and care of children and the elderly (Ruggie 1988).

A focus on poverty rates alone can be misleading; when marriage rates are high, one sees relatively low poverty rates for women and low gender poverty gaps, but the extent of women's vulnerability to poverty is occluded. Moreover, quantitative poverty studies typically overlook the ways in which regulation may accompany benefits, as in the case of many benefits for solo parents that are conditioned on cooperation in paternity establishment (Monson 1996). In addition, the ways in which the systemic characteristics of social provision affect gender interests are ignored. For example, in the United States, increased levels of income transfers would not address the political marginalization of the status of "client" in a context where citizenship is linked strongly to the status of "worker" (Nelson 1984); nor would this strategy counter stereotypes of dependency deeply embedded in relations of class, race/ethnicity, and gender (Roberts 1995, Quadagno 1994, Collins 1990). Others have argued that the residual character of American social provision undermines popular support for social spending generally, and in such a context, calls for increased benefits in targeted programs such as Aid to Families with Dependent Children (AFDC) may actually exacerbate the political difficulties of welfare (Weir et al 1988). In other words, access to cash benefits is not always an unmixed blessing.

Toward Understanding Variation

These social reproduction and amelioration approaches to gender and social policy fail to capture the full complexity of policy variation—the first assumes uniformity, while the second attends only to one, linear dimension of variation (generosity of benefits or levels of social spending). Moreover, their analytic focus makes it difficult to identify women's activity in policymaking. More recently, two new strands of research have emerged from theoretically informed comparative and/or historical analyses of gender and social policies, emphasizing the variation in the effects of social policies on gender: Male dominance is not necessarily reproduced; indeed, it is often transformed. Some amelioration is possible, although it is sometimes coupled with greater regulation by the state. Historical analyses of the development of gendered social policy have challenged the assumptions that ungenerous and punitive policies have simply been imposed on women; such analyses uncovered the activities of women reformers in shaping early programs targeted on women and their children. Rather than assuming that all (Western) countries' systems operate similarly, they find that policy may promote qualitatively different types of gender relations. Of particular importance have been studies of countries (e.g. Sweden, France) and groups (e.g. US African-Americans) that do not display the family wage system that prevails in most other countries and among dominant racial groups, but feature instead higher levels of married women's paid work.

MATERNALISM AND THE ORIGINS OF WELFARE STATES

Recent studies of the origins of modern social provision have challenged some key assumptions of both mainstream and earlier feminist scholarship. First, these studies have revealed the significant amount of state activity aimed at the welfare of mothers and children and the activities of women reformers, ignored in the mainstream literature's focus on labor market regulation and class actors. Second, they have challenged some of the assumptions of the social reproduction analysts by highlighting women's participation (even as subordinate actors) in the shaping of policies directed at women and families.

Many women (and some male) reformers were motivated by the ideas and discourses of maternalism. Koven & Michel (1993, p. 4) define maternalism as "ideologies and discourses which exalted women's capacity to mother and applied to society as a whole the values they attached to that role: care, nurturance and morality." The widespread acceptance of ideals of gender differentiation did not deter women from entering the political sphere—indeed, they entered it largely on the basis of "difference," claiming their work as mothers gave them unique capacities for developing state policies that would safeguard mothers and children, leading to "equality in difference." Koven & Michel emphasize the ambiguous meanings and uses of maternalism, noting that it can encompass pronatalists most concerned with population increase, women who accepted the ideal of a family wage for men as the source of support for mothers, and feminists who called for an independent state-supplied income for mothers (Pedersen 1993, Lake 1992). Others (e.g. Ladd-Taylor 1994, p. 5) prefer a more restricted definition that contrasts maternalism to feminism, particularly in terms of their positions on the desirability of the family wage and women's economic dependence (maternalists supported them, feminists opposed them). Finally, Skocpol (1992) distinguishes between "maternalist" and "paternalist" welfare states; both are premised on gender differentiation and the family wage, but institutionalize different types of linkages between states and citizens. In Europe and the Antipodes, elite male political leaders established and administered programs "for the good of" working-class men, often organized in trade unions and labor parties, who gained access to benefits based on their labor-force participation. Yet these men were also understood in terms of their family status—as heads of families and supporters of dependent wives and children. A maternalist welfare state would feature "female-dominated public agencies implementing regulations and benefits for the good of women and their children" (p. 2). Skocpol writes that such a welfare state never came fully to fruition in the United States, although an impressive range of legislation targeted on women in their role as mothers was passed in most states.

Koven & Michel (1993) distinguish between outcomes in "strong" and "weak" states; paradoxically, while women's movements were stronger and their involvement was greater in the so-called weak states—Britain and the United States—than in the strong—Germany and France, policies aimed at protecting women and children were better developed and more generous in the latter. While weak states provided greater political opportunities for women's political activism, they had fewer capacities for enacting and financing generous social policies and women's movements were not yet strong enough to press for better outcomes. Bock & Thane (1991) point to differences between countries that maintained democratic governments in the 1930s and 1940s and those that became fascist dictatorships. All these countries started with policies that could be called maternalist (by the broader definition), although organized women were not equivalently active in their initiation and administration. Fascist governments made significant changes; Bock (1991), Saraceno (1991), and Nash (1991) argue that it was the attention to men, masculinity, and fatherhood rather than pronatalism that distinguished the fascist countries. For example, payment of allowances for children was made to fathers, often as part of the wage packet, rather than to mothers, as was the case in the democracies. (Interestingly, these patterns have continued even after the return to democracy—Wennemo (1994) finds that these countries offer support to children through employment-based schemes, which go disproportionately to men). Germany was internationally unique, Bock (1991) contends, in its antinatalist policies carried out against Jewish people and those considered "defective" by the National Socialist regime—policies that eventually culminated in genocide.

The few explicitly comparative studies of this period offer some clues to which factors were most significant in shaping the character of social policies aimed at the support of motherhood, parenthood, and children—variations that in many cases continue to distinguish the systems of social provision in the contemporary west. Of particular significance are: (i) the balance of power among labor, employers, and the state; (ii) discourses and ideologies of motherhood, especially whether or not mothering was seen as compatible with paid work; and (iii) concerns about population quality and quantity, particularly in the context of international military competition.

Jenson's (1986) comparison of British and French policies for the support of reproduction was influential in questioning the generalizations about women and the state that predominated in the early 1980s. Both French and British elites operated within an international context that raised concerns about population, particularly about declining birthrates and rates of infant mortality perceived to be too high. Yet Jenson showed that differences in the capacities of organized workers and employers, different levels of demand for female labor, and different discourses about motherhood and paid work, produced strikingly different policies. British policy worked to make the support of babies primarily dependent on fathers' wages, while France developed policies that allowed for mothers' paid work, offering both material support and health-related services to working mothers and their children. Klaus (1993) compares maternal and infant health policies in the United States and France, and finds that the relative level of international military competition was important in shaping outcomes. It was fiercer in France than in the United States, providing a greater incentive to political actors for conserving infant and maternal life and promoting population growth; these concerns were reflected in the development of more generous and far-reaching policies. Concerns about population also feature in Hobson's (1993) comparison of New-Deal America and Sweden in the 1930s around the issue of married women's right to engage in paid work. She finds that fears about population decline were utilized by Swedish women reformers to create new protections for women workers, while their American counterparts were marginalized and found no comparable national discourse which could justify such protections.

Pedersen's (1993) study of Britain and France elaborates some of the themes initially put forward by Jenson. She argues that the balance of power among workers, employers, and the state was the most significant factor determining policies vis-á-vis dependent children and women's labor force participation in the ensuing years. But trade unionists and employers (and others) had gender and familial as well as occupational or class interests, and were influenced as well by the discursive connotations of various policies. British and French trade unionists—mainly men—defended a "family wage" which would give them control of the resources flowing to their families; they preferred that their wives be kept out of the labor market (wives did not always disagree, of course). Employers in both countries appreciated cheap female labor. British unions had the capacity to keep most married women out of paid work and to block the use of family allowances to restrain wages, while French employers had the capacity to block measures keeping married women out of the labor market and acceded to state-mandated family allowances, which promoted wage restraint while funneling funds to families with children. Pedersen also attends to the role of feminists and other women's groups, social scientists, intellectuals, political leaders, church officials, and pronatalists in constructing the discourse of family issues and policy. Differences in the strength of feminist and women's groups were reflected in how family allowances were carried into political discourse and consequently how they were perceived politically, contributing in this way to the different outcomes in the two countries. Pedersen notes unintended effects of the patterns institutionalized in the interwar years. France's "parental welfare state" gave less institutionalized support for family wages; in Britain, strong male-dominated unions succeeded in making the family wage central to social provision. Once political forms of women's oppression were lifted, the French system has offered excellent support for two-earner families and ensures children's welfare more effectively than has been the case in Britain, where children must depend almost exclusively upon the wages of their fathers in an economy marked by great inequalities and a society in which women cannot always depend on access to male wages.

American social policy exceptionalism is shown to have a gender dimension in recent studies. Koven & Michel (1993) group the United States and Britain as "weak" states featuring strong women's movements but relatively weaker public protections for women and children. But Sklar (1993) and Skocpol (1992, also Skocpol & Ritter 1991) describe key institutional differences between Britain and the United States that made gender more salient as a political identity to Americans and offered opportunities for the development of autonomous women's organizations even before women had the vote; these included the relatively open structure of religion and higher education, as well as the existence of universal white manhood suffrage. Sklar (1993) provocatively argues that in the United States, gender substituted for class as the organizing principle in welfare politics as organized middle-class women played the role of welfare champions elsewhere undertaken by organized labor and working-class parties.

Skocpol's (1992) analysis is significant for drawing attention to the impact of political structures and processes on gendered identities, capacities for mobilization, and potential for successfully influencing policy. Her work differs from both mainstream and feminist analyses in simultaneously analyzing men's and women's political activities and the differing fates of maternalist and paternalist policies. She examines the ways in which the American polity was particularly receptive to women's organizing, even when women lacked the vote, while at the same time it was unreceptive to demands for paternalist, class-based policies. The work is distinctive in focusing on the activities of married ladies' voluntary organizations in the Midwest and West in addition to investigating elite reformers in the Northeast. These groups were essential to a cross-class alliance among women that gave administrators such as Julia Lathrop of the

United States Children's Bureau (identified as a core woman-dominated state agency; see also Muncy 1991)—at least for a time—the capacity to initiate and maintain their innovative policies. In a related quantitative analysis of state-level mothers' pensions (Skocpol et al 1993), women's voluntary groups are shown to be the most important predictor of the timing of passage of these programs.

Gordon (1994, pp. 7–8) notes a paradox: today, "programs for women are inferior to programs for men. ... Many feminists have understandably assumed that women were slotted into inferior programs because of 'patriarchy' and men's monopoly on state power. But the fact is that ADC [which later became AFDC] was designed by... feminist women." (pp. 7–8). Gordon traces the origins of these developments through, among other things, an examination of different approaches to welfare by networks of white male and female reformers and of African-American reformers and their involvement in the policymaking process from the late nineteenth century through the Social Security Act. (See Skocpol 1993 and Gordon 1993 for a debate about their respective analyses of welfare programs.)

No one disagrees that today, AFDC represents a stigmatized and ungenerous program; however, analysts of early United States social policy disagree about the character of early programs, the forerunners of today's "welfare," about the interests and actions of the elite women who were responsible for their initiation and administration, and about what factors led to the degradation of social provision for poor single women. One group of analysts traces at least some of the problems of AFDC to the vision of those who initiated mothers' pensions. A particularly important component of this vision was their preference for supervision in the programs that were to assist poor women. Gordon (1994) contends that this was tied to the social work and casework background of women elites, reflecting their class and racial interests. Goodwin (1992) and Michel (1993) note their acceptance of a family wage ideology and preference for women's domesticity, which made supervision a necessity. Mink (1994) focuses on their views about the necessity of "Americanizing" the predominantly immigrant clients of mothers' pensions. The flaws in mothers' pensions were not corrected when they were given federal funding and somewhat standardized as ADC under the Social Security Act in 1935; even later reforms of the 1960s and 1970s were only partial remedies. Another group highlights the universalistic character of the maternalists' claims and contrasts this with the ways in which policies came to be implemented and eventually undermined (Skocpol 1992, Orloff 1991, 1993b, Ch. 5). Ladd-Taylor (1994) locates these universalistic aspects of maternalism in women's private lives—their common vulnerability to death in childbirth and to loss of their children. Mothers' pensions and other programs were seen to recognize the socially valuable work of mothering, even if women had no access to a male breadwinner's wage—their service to the state was understood as parallel to men's soldiering or industrial service. Lack of administrative capacities, which meant that on the local level programs were often turned over to those who had initially opposed them, the inability of women's groups to monitor programs after implementation, and inadequate financing all undermined the universalist promise of maternalist policies.

Analyses of maternalism have provided some opening for consideration of the ways in which race, ethnicity, and nationalism have also shaped gendered policies. In the United States, a number of studies have shown that maternalist policies such as mothers' pensions and the Sheppard-Towner maternal health programs were not equally aimed at or accessible to African-Americans and other women of color (Bellingham & Mathis 1994, Goodwin 1992, Gordon 1994, Mink 1994, Boris 1995). Thus, the motherhood (and infant life) to be supported was bounded in racial and ethnic terms; analysts disagree about the extent to which this reflects the interests of maternalist reformers or is simply a reflection of the power of racist forces in American society. Similar considerations obtained in Australian policy, which simultaneously supported white motherhood (largely through state-regulated male wages, but also with maternalist measures), banned non-European immigration under the rubric of the "White Australia" policy, and systematically deprived aboriginal mothers of custody of their children (Lake 1992, Shaver 1990, Burney 1994). A debate in Germany about the character of social provision under National Socialism features disagreement about the interests of dominant-group women. Bock (1991) emphasizes that only some group's reproduction was supported—pronatalism for "Aryans" was accompanied by antinatalism for Jews, Gypsies and "defectives." Yet Bock and Koonz (1987) have disagreed about the extent to which Christian German women benefited from Nazi policies—Bock has argued that because Nazi policies channeled benefits to men, German women were not implicated as beneficiaries of Nazism, while Koonz has argued that German Christian women did benefit from the pronatalist aspects of the Nazi regime.

The New Deal period in American social provision has been less studied from a gendered perspective than have the Progressive Era and the 1920s. Still, few would dispute that the institutionalization of national contributory social insurance targeted on (mostly male) wage-earners, which soon after incorporated their (almost exclusively female) dependent spouses, while support for single mothers remained a largely state-run social assistance program was significant for the emergence of the bifurcated welfare state we have today (Weir, Orloff & Skocpol 1988, Orloff 1993b, Gordon 1994, Chs. 7–10). Quadagno's (1994) study of the War on Poverty and the Nixon Era is one of the few to bring the gendered history of American social policy development close to the present; she is able to show, for example, the ways in which the proposed Family Assistance Plan depended on notions of the desirability of a traditional gender division of labor—although in the end, racial politics and federal institutional structures "trumped" those concerns and left AFDC in place.

COMPARING GENDER IN CONTEMPORARY WELFARE STATES

In comparative work, scholars from—or familiar with the cases of—the Scandinavian countries have been particularly prominent in pointing out that assumptions about the inevitability of the reproduction of patriarchy are too narrowly based on the experiences of countries where the the family wage was (and to some extent still is) the starting premise of social policy, and policies seem unlikely to promote women's interests (e.g. Siim 1988, Hernes 1987, 1988, Borchorst & Siim 1987, Ruggie 1984, Haas 1992, Leira 1992). The centrality of the family wage and women's domesticity to gender-related social policies has been questioned also by analysts of the French case (Jenson 1986) and of the situation of nonwhite women in the United States and elsewhere (e.g. Roberts 1995). In these cases, women's paid work is far more accepted— indeed promoted—than has been the case for women of the dominant racial group in the English-speaking countries and in Central Europe. A number of analysts have therefore tried to explain the difference between the Scandinavian and other cases; the strength and organization of working-class groups looms large as an explanatory factor.

Ruggie's (1984) analysis of Swedish and British policies toward working women revealed that the overall relationship between state and society— determined by the character of governing coalitions—affected women workers' progress: "for the successful achievement of their employment pursuits, women must be incorporated into labor, and labor must be incorporated into the governing coalition" (p. 346). Similarly, Hill & Tigges (1995) compared women's public pension quality across 20 industrialized countries and found that working-class strength is associated with improved income security and adequacy for older women, while women's participation in working-class political and economic organizations increases older women's economic equality with men. In a comparison of policies supporting care work and caretakers in Britain and Denmark, Siim (1990) argued that the extent to which increased social welfare benefits also increased women's political power depended in part on the organization of social reproduction. In Denmark, women's dual roles as worker and mother are supported by social and family policy that gives the state a larger role in organizing and financing care for dependents, which facilitates women's integration into the workforce. In Britain, a "familist" social policy assigns primary responsibility for care work to "the family," assuming this contains a breadwinner husband and a wife who has time to attend to (unpaid) caregiving work; this seriously undercuts women's capacities to enter the paid labor force on an equal footing with men.

Interest in comparatively based explanations has also been stimulated by the persistence of "traditional" gender relations, particularly relatively low rates of women's labor force participation (see, e.g. on Ireland, Jackson 1993; on the Netherlands, Knijn 1994, Bussemaker & van Kersbergen 1994; and on Germany and other German-speaking countries, Schmidt 1993, Ostner 1993). European integration has raised the issue of how gender relations and social policies will be changed by processes of economic integration and by formal institutions such as the European court and the European Union equality directive (e.g. Schunter-Kleemann 1992, Lewis 1993).

Gender and Regime Types

A particularly promising development in comparative scholarship has come with the elaboration of the concept of "social policy regimes," which offers a way to analyze the qualitative variation across national systems. As Shaver (1990) describes them, social policy regimes are institutionalized patterns in welfare state provision establishing systematic relations between the state and social structures of conflict, domination, and accommodation. Such patterns refer to the terms and conditions under which claims may be made on the resources of the state, and reciprocally, the terms and conditions of economic, social, and political obligation to the state. These regimes are to be found in both individual institutions of the welfare state and in common patterns cutting across domains of social provision, such as health or income maintenance. Mainstream analysts of regime types have been concerned with the effects of welfare states on class relations and particularly with whether the state can "push back the frontiers of capitalism" (Esping-Andersen 1990). Feminist analysts using the regime type concept are interested in the gendered effects of state social policy; some are also attempting to define and measure gender interests [e.g. "woman-friendliness," in the felicitous phrase coined by Helga Hernes (1988)].

Much recent feminist work on regime types builds on Esping-Andersen's *Three Worlds of Welfare Capitalism* (1990). While Esping-Andersen's work only incidentally takes account of gender differences among different types of welfare states, his ideal-typical scheme has inspired fruitful research on the variation among regimes as investigators have utilized or reworked his schema to incorporate gender. Esping-Andersen proposes three dimensions that characterize welfare states, including the relationship between the state and the market in providing income and services and the effects of the welfare state on social stratification. Central to the understanding of how welfare states affect class relations are the concepts of social rights and the "decommodification of labor," defined as the degree to which the individual's typical life situation is freed from dependence on the labor market. These rights affect the class balance of power by insulating workers to some extent from market pressures and by contributing to working-class political capacities.

Esping-Andersen has constructed a typology of regimes representing "three worlds of welfare capitalism"—liberal, conservative-corporatist and social-democratic—based on where they fall out on the three dimensions. Liberal regimes promote market provision wherever possible, encourage social dualisms between the majority of citizens who rely mainly on the market and those who rely principally on public provision, and do little to offer citizens alternatives to participating in the market for services and income. The welfare state is well-developed in both social-democratic and conservative-corporatist regimes, bringing almost all citizens under the umbrella of state provision, but in other ways the two types differ. The former are universalistic and egalitarian, while the latter preserve status and class differentials. Only social-democratic regimes promote significant decommodification of labor, for conservative-corporatist regimes condition their relatively generous benefits on strong ties to the labor market. Significant for gender relations is the fact that conservative regimes promote subsidiarity (thereby strengthening women's dependence on the family), while social-democratic regimes have promoted an individual model of entitlement and provide services allowing those responsible for care work—mostly married mothers—to enter the paid labor force. Liberal regimes, he argues, are indifferent to gender relations, leaving service provision to the market. Despite the fact that "there is no single pure case," Esping-Andersen classified the United States, Canada, Australia, and (probably) Great Britain as liberal regimes; the Nordic countries are identified as social-democratic regimes; and Austria, France, Germany, Italy, and the Netherlands are conservative-corporatist regimes.

Many feminist analysts have critiqued Esping-Andersen for the gender-blindness of his scheme: His citizens are implicitly male workers; his dimensions tap into states' impact on class relations and the relationship between states and markets without considering gender differences within classes or the relations between states and families; he leaves invisible women's work on behalf of societal welfare (i.e. unpaid caring/domestic labor); and his framework fails to consider states' effects on gender relations, inequalities, and power (see e.g. Langan & Ostner 1991, O'Connor 1993a, Orloff 1993a, Sainsbury 1994a,b,c,

Bussemaker & van Kersbergen 1994, Borchorst 1994a). Still, Esping-Andersen is not entirely uninterested in questions relevant for gender. The second half of his book considers the effects of welfare regimes on labor markets, with an in-depth analysis of the United States, Germany, and Sweden, and he here must confront patterns of gender within employment (albeit without any systematic understanding of how this is linked to gender relations overall). Swedish women's employment depends on the state both for jobs and for the services that make employment for those with caregiving responsibilities a possibility. German women are largely marginalized by an employment regime that revolves around the needs of predominantly male industrial workers, a relatively underdeveloped service sector, and state policies that prize subsidiarity over the public provision of services. US women's rising employment and the advances women have made into the upper ranks of the labor force are largely market-driven, although state anti-discrimination activity has been important in opening opportunities in the realm of private employment. While some US women have benefited from private employment opportunities and can afford private provision of services, others have suffered from the low wages and benefits of the lower rungs of the service sector.

Analysts have tried to make sense of gendered relations and patterns using the regime-type framework, evaluating whether or not liberal, conservative, and social-democratic regime types have distinctive effects on gender relations. Extending the analysis of regime types to consider the ways in which care work (broadly defined) is organized and supported has been a key area of concern for those interested in states and gender relations. Taylor-Gooby (1991) enriches Esping-Andersen's model by considering regime-type differences in the organization of the unpaid care work and the connected issue of how governments deal with issues of gender equality (principally in access to paid work). Gustafsson (1994) finds that childcare policies in the United States, the Netherlands, and Sweden reflect the regime-type differences specified by Esping-Andersen, that is, that public services are best developed in Sweden, market provision of services is prominent in the United States, and the Netherlands offers little public provision, in effect opting to support mothers' caregiving work rather than offering daycare. In a study of family support in the OECD countries, Wennemo (1994) finds two clusters: the countries of continental Europe—corresponding to Esping-Andersen's conservative regimes, which channel benefits through the wage system and therefore largely to men, and the English-speaking and Scandinavian countries—i.e. the liberal and social-democratic regimes—which offer public family allowances that are paid to mothers.

Sainsbury (1993) considers the effects on women of one aspect of social rights, the bases for making welfare claims, and the programmatic characteristics (i.e. social assistance, social insurance, or universal entitlements) of four different welfare states—the United States, the United Kingdom, the Netherlands, and Sweden [which, although she is not explicit as to her selection criteria, do correspond to Esping-Andersen's three types (allowing for Britain's status as a mixed type)]. She shows that indeed, whether claims are based on labor market status, need, or citizenship is significant for gendered outcomes; women do best in Sweden, a system with strong universal characteristics, and fare worst in the United States and Britain, the countries with claims based principally on labor market participation. Lewis & Åström (1992) claim that Sweden's "woman-friendly" universalism is actually based on the fact that most Swedish women are in the paid labor force, thus successfully laying claim to the status of "worker citizens" as they also press demands based on "difference" [echoing Ruggie's (1984) argument]. Ruggie (1988, p. 174) has recently argued that Swedish politics had important limitations for further progress to the extent that "women's interests go beyond or are different from the interests of 'workers as a whole'." This would imply that the claims bases delineated by Esping-Andersen, Korpi, and others as important for the character of social rights must also be considered in terms of their gender content and that some concerns of women cannot be satisfied even by the generous social-democratic policy approach.

Many analyses of Luxembourg Income Study data have assessed regime-type concepts. For example, McLanahan and her colleagues have used LIS data to examine women's poverty levels, the association of different women's roles with poverty rates, and differences in men's and women's poverty in countries said by Esping-Andersen and others to represent different regime types (McLanahan et al 1995, Caspar et al 1994). These studies find relatively high poverty rates for single mothers and relatively high gender gaps in poverty (i.e. the difference between men's and women's rates) in Germany and Britain, but most notably in the United States, Canada, and Australia. Moreover, the policy strategies of countries that have relatively low poverty rates for women and low gender gaps differ qualitatively and in ways which seem to be related to regime types as defined by Esping-Andersen: Sweden reduces women's poverty by promoting their employment, Italy by reinforcing marriage [so that women's access to men's wages is (they assume) assured], the Netherlands by providing generous social transfers to all citizens. However, it is worth noting that gender roles have a significant influence on outcomes apart from differences in regimes types: "marriage and work reduce the risk of poverty for women in all countries, whereas motherhood increases the chances of being poor. The only mothers who have a better than average chance of staying out of poverty are mothers who combine parenthood and work with marriage" (McLanahan et al 1995, p. 275).

States clearly differ to some extent in their effects on gender relations. However, conclusions based on analyses that contrast countries purporting to represent different regime types are very likely influenced by the country chosen to "stand in" for any given regime cluster, when we have not carefully assessed their differences and similarities across dimensions relevant for gender. Thus, a "most-similar nations" comparative strategy can be very useful. Leira (1992) and Borchorst (1994b) examine the Scandinavian (i.e. social-democratic) states and find that there is significant variation within this group in the level of public child-care provision, with concomitant differences in women's labor force participation; Denmark and Sweden offer greater support for combining motherhood with paid work, particularly for mothers of very young children, than does Norway. Leira argues that this results from differing models of motherhood, a dimension that seems to cross-cut the regimes as classified by Esping-Andersen's dimensions. Similarly, investigations of the policies of countries classified as "liberal" using explicitly gendered dimensions reveal some important differences. Shaver (1993) finds a difference in reproductive policies. In the United Kingdom and Australia, women gain access to abortion through medical entitlement—universal health coverage gives them a social right to abortion understood as a medical procedure. In Canada and the United States, women have legal entitlement to "body rights"—including abortion with little medical or social regulation—but have no social right to help in providing the service. Orloff (1996) finds that different models of motherhood, as institutionalized in policies for the support of single mothers, hold sway in the United States as opposed to the United Kingdom, Australia, and Canada; while the United States is moving to require paid work as the only route for the support of households, whether headed by couples or single mothers, (poor) solo mothers are still offered a period of state-supported full-time caring for their children in the other three. O'Connor (1993b) notes that Australia offers greater support for women's and mothers' paid work than do other "liberal" regimes; she attributes this to greater involvement by the central state in setting terms and conditions of paid work and the influence of state-oriented feminist movements.

GENDERED DIMENSIONS FOR ASSESSING WELFARE STATES

All of the approaches I have reviewed have helped to show the importance of gender relations in the welfare state and the significance of welfare states for the situations of men and women and their relationships. Yet these studies share some analytic weaknesses: an inadequate theorization of the political interests of gender and a failure to specify the dimensions of social provision and other state interventions relevant for gender relations (Orloff 1993a, Borchorst 1994a). The two weaknesses are related; if one wants to argue that welfare states help to promote patriarchy or that welfare state benefits help women, one needs to specify the yardsticks for measuring these effects. One may ask the social reproduction analysts: What will constitute evidence that a given policy works for or against male dominance? One may ask the poverty researchers: Are women's interests only economic? Comparative analyses have generally had a more nuanced view of gender and state policies, but the understandings of gender interests and their measures often remain implicit and, to some extent, idiosyncratic. Finally, one may ask those who have used Esping-Andersen's regime-type scheme whether gender interests are fully correlated with class interests, and whether women's interests are limited to entering paid work. We need an explicit framework for assessing the gendered effects of social policy that is informed by an understanding of gender interests.

Gender Interests

Defining gender interests is necessary to the task of assessing the gendered effects of welfare states, but not simple. A prominent theme in recent feminist scholarship concerns conflicts of interests. For example, in addition to pointing out that men and women may have conflicting interests based on who has family wage–paying jobs or who has access to domestic or sexual services, feminist analysts have noted ways in which women's interests cohere and/or compete with children's interests. Others argue that it is falsely homogenizing to speak of women's interests per se, since the "interests that women (or men) have" (the descriptive sense of the concept) vary by class, race, ethnicity, nationality, sexual orientation, and so on (e.g. Molyneux 1985, Collins 1990). Molyneux (1985) calls attention to gender interests—those based on one's position within structures of gender relations (e.g. the gender division of labor, heterosexuality, or access to political power). This would imply that neither men's nor women's gender interests can be limited to the economic realm (Connell 1987, Jónasdóttir 1994, Fraser 1994). Thus conflicts of interests based both on gender relations and on other types of cleavages among women (and men) are quite likely in heterogeneous societies like our own. Molyneux further distinguished two types of gender interests: practical gender interests, those that if realized would improve women's (or men's) material situation but would not in themselves fundamentally challenge the gender order, and strategic gender interests, which for women are those that if realized would undermine some aspects of gender subordination. Post-structuralist theorists and those influenced by institutionalism argue further for shifting attention away from the question of "how women's interests can be most accurately represented to the processes whereby they are constituted" (Pringle & Watson 1992, p. 63). Here, one needs to understand how the character of different welfare states' policies both shapes and is shaped by the content of women's (and men's) practical and strategic gender interests, and how these change over time and vary within and across countries.

Political power and participation are also of concern in understanding interests. Jonasdottir (1988) contends that everyone has an interest in participating in the construction of choices in the policy areas that which affect them. Thus, being the subject as well as the object of policy is a critical aspect of women's and men's interests (see also Lewis 1992, Orloff 1993a, Lister 1990, O'Connor 1993a, Nelson 1984). Participation takes on a specifically gendered character in that women have been so long formally and informally excluded from the policymaking that shapes the structures of their incentives to work for pay and bear children, and to care for children, their husbands, or the disabled.

Gendered Dimensions for Assessing Welfare States

Feminist analysts note that Esping-Andersen's framework was developed to address issues of class rather than gender power. Therefore, they argue, one cannot fully tap into states' effects on gender relations simply by looking at how women and men fare in different regime types using his (or others') gender-blind dimensions. Rather, specifically gendered dimensions based on an understanding of gendered interests are needed to assess the impact of state policies on gender relations.

Lewis (1992) argues for considering policy regimes in terms of their different levels of commitment to a male breadwinner-female housewife household form, which in ideal-typical form would "find married women excluded from the labour market, firmly subordinated to their husbands for the purposes of social security entitlements and tax, and expected to undertake the work of caring (for children and other dependents) at home without public support" (p. 162). Women's interests, she thereby implies, are least well served by policies supporting this traditional set of arrangements, but they fare somewhat better when policy supports dual-earner households. She contrasts France, Sweden, Britain and Ireland, finding Britain and Ireland strongly committed to the breadwinner form, France less strongly so, and Sweden only weakly so, tending to a dual-breadwinner form. Although these cases are also in different regime clusters in Esping-Andersen's scheme, there is considerable variation in the extent to which states approximate the ideal-type within his clusters (e.g. Germany vs. France within the corporatist type or Norway vs. Sweden within the social-democratic cluster). Lewis shows that her gendered dimension does not correlate neatly with class-related dimensions, but the model seems to conflate a number of potentially separable dimensions, notably women's exclusion from paid work and their subordination within a male-headed family.

Sainsbury (1994c) proposes examining states in terms of their similarity to one of two gendered ideal-types: the breadwinner model (similar to Lewis's conception) and what she calls an individual model, where both men and women are earners and carers, benefits are targeted on individuals, and much caring work is paid and provided publicly. (One may also need to consider whether some elements of the individual model can be provided by nonstate sources.) She draws out specific dimensions of variation that differentiate the two models: the character of familial ideology, entitlement (including its basis, recipient, benefit unit, contribution unit, and mode of taxation), employment and wage policies, and organization of care work.

Shaver's (1990) earlier work on the gendered character of policy regimes argues that such regimes have components concerned with personhood and the rights of the individual, with the social organization of work, and with social bonding in emotional and reproductive relationships. These have close congruence with the terms use by RW Connell (1987) to map the structures of gender relations more generally. Connell identifies three underlying structures—labor, power, and cathexis. Shaver shows that the gender dimensions of policy regimes are shaped by state policies and legal frameworks. This approach then calls for an investigation of the gender basis of legal personhood, particularly with reference to "body rights" such as access to control over reproduction (see also Shaver 1993); how the sexual division of labor is institutionalized in paid employment and how it is affected by related policies such as child care; and how family, reproduction, and sexuality are affected by the institutionalization of dependency or individualization and the privileging of heterosexuality.

Langan & Ostner (1991) develop a gendered extension of Leibfried's (1992) empirically based classificatory scheme, which differentiated among Scandinavian, Bismarckian, Anglo-Saxon, and Latin Rim regimes on the basis of their relative emphasis on the market or citizenship, the extent to which traditional household forms remain, and the extent to which public social provision has been institutionalized and extended to the entire population. They examine each regime type in terms of whether the traditional family or individuals are the basis for social policy and how women are treated as unpaid and paid workers (occupational segregation, pay); however, their assessment criteria are not spelled out.

Orloff (1993a) and O'Connor (1993a) have worked to gender the conceptual apparatus of regime types as developed by Esping-Andersen, Korpi and others. Both argue that the organization of state-market relations and of the power balance among labor, state, and capital are significant for gender, as they affect the character of women's labor force participation and the organization of family support systems (e.g. unpaid care work, services). They also argue for including a stratification dimension, to include both gender differentiation and gender inequality. Gender differentiation exists on the systemic level (e.g. through creating different programs for labor market and family "failures") and on the individual level (e.g. through processes of making claims on the state, where men have typically made claims as individuals and workers, women often as dependents and family members). Access to benefits of similar quality for men and women in a range of different statuses (e.g. solo parent, unemployed worker, married person, retiree) is a key element of women's interests in the welfare state. In contrast, Lewis's scheme seems to give inadequate attention to women's situation when they are not linked to men through marriage. As Hobson notes (1994, p. 175), "to cluster Britain, the Netherlands and Germany into a strong breadwinner model is to ignore the differences in poverty among solo mothers, who are the residuum in the male breadwinner ideology."

O'Connor (1993a) and Orloff (1993a) argue for retaining and augmenting the decommodification dimension. Decommodification "protects individuals, irrespective of gender, from total dependence on the labor market for survival. . . . [a] protection from forced participation, irrespective of age, health conditions, family status, availability of suitable employment, [that] is obviously of major importance to both men and women" (O'Connor 1993a, p. 513). But not all social groups have equal access to the jobs that allow personal independence and access to decommodifying benefits. Both argue that access to paid work and to the services that facilitate employment for caregivers are critical gender dimensions of welfare regime variability, and reflect core gendered interests of women. O'Connor (1993a, p. 511) conceptualizes these dimensions as aspects of the ways in which the state affects "personal autonomy and insulation from personal and/or public dependence," which centrally affects gender relations. Paid work is a principal avenue by which women have sought both to enhance their independence from husbands and fathers in families (thereby undermining the breadwinner-housewife family form) and to claim full status as "independent" citizens; it is also a prerequisite for gaining access to work-related benefits which decommodify labor.

Orloff (1993a) proposes also to consider how benefits contribute to women's capacity to form and maintain an autonomous household, a dimension that indicates "the ability of those who do most of the domestic and caring work—almost all women—to form and maintain autonomous households, that is, to survive and support their children without having to marry to gain access to breadwinners' income." This should enhance women's power vis-á-vis men within marriages and families (see also Hobson 1990). Men typically gain this capacity through their market work, backed up by income maintenance programs. State policies have differed in how (if at all) this capacity is achieved for women; some regimes have promoted women's employment through varying combinations of childcare services, wage subsidies, or improved-access policies, or by reducing levels of and eligibility for public support; this overlaps, then, with the dimension of access to paid work. Other regimes have offered support for solo mothers to stay at home to care for their children; this maintains core features of the gender division of labor—women remain responsible for caretaking—but undermines economic dependence on husbands. Orloff (1996) argues that the capacity to form and maintain a household embodies "the right to a family," implying more than individual independence, and reflects the character of laws regulating sexuality, marriage, and household formation (e.g. laws on divorce, custody, homosexuality).

Political philosopher Fraser (1994) has proposed a set of evaluative standards for social policy based on an analysis of gender equity that recognizes that it is "a complex notion comprising a plurality of distinct normative principles" (p. 595). The principles include prevention of poverty, prevention of exploitable dependency, gender equality in income, leisure and respect, promotion of women's participation on a par with men in all areas of social life, and the reconstruction of "androcentric institutions so as to welcome human beings who can give birth and who often care for relatives and friends, treating them not as exceptions, but as ideal-typical participants" (pp. 599–600). She argues that the only way to satisfy these principles would be to deconstruct gender by "inducing men to become more like what most women are now—that is, people who do primary care work" (p. 611); this would dismantle "the gendered opposition between breadwinning and caregiving." Women's gender interests are expressed in overcoming the gender division of labor and concomitant economic dependency and marginalization as well as in equality in access to valued resources (income, respect, time).

These various frameworks offer researchers a range of ways to take gender into account in evaluating welfare states. In addition to assessing the effects of state social provision on various aspects of gender relations, many of the analysts involved in these efforts to theorize gender and the welfare state have called for attention to the dimension of political participation (Lewis 1992, Orloff 1993a, O'Connor 1993a, Shaver 1990).

CONCLUSION

On the basis of this review, I recommend that future research include a comparative dimension; case studies should be situated in the context of the range of cross-national variation in relations between welfare states and gender relations. Moreover, I would encourage the use of gendered dimensions of variation to give greater specificity to findings and to allow the further development of a body of comparable findings concerning the mutual effects of gender relations and welfare states. These findings may also speak to the question of the extent to which different gendered interests are reflected in state social provision, including the "woman-friendliness" of the state (Hernes 1988).

Out of this juxtaposition of studies coming from several different disciplines, modes of analysis, and theoretical emphases, I am struck by the potential to evaluate comparatively explanations for the variation in states' gendered effects documented over time and across state boundaries. Research has established the causal significance of several factors: the balance of power between organized labor and employers; state capacities; the character of production and labor markets; the character of organized women's groups (and men's groups—usually manifest in organized labor); the character of discourses and ideologies of motherhood, population, femininity and masculinity; demographic characteristics; the extent of international military and economic competition (and the kind of wars for which countries need to prepare). Several case studies have also argued for the importance of race, ethnicity, and nationality (e.g. different population compositions and histories of immigration and settlement) to policy outcomes (see Williams 1995 for a proposed framework for comparison); gender relations differ across races, ethnicities, and nationalities within national contexts and are thus differently affected by social provision and contribute differently to social politics. The relative causal importance of these factors can now be assessed more explicitly, and the specific conjunctures of factors associated with particular outcomes identified. It seems likely as well that the political and programmatic legacies of different manifestations of "maternalist" policy will help in developing explanations for contemporary regime differences.

A focus on states as constitutive of gender relations—without the functionalist baggage of early research—has already been useful, and further refinements promise to be fruitful. For example, one might look at whether state capacities function in the same ways when the state is organized along formally gender-neutral principles as when it is characterized by gender differentiation and explicit masculine authority. Research on the maternalist policies and politics of the first part of the century suggest that when state administrative capacities are extensive, women's autonomous organizations are less likely to emerge, but these capacities are also associated with relatively well-developed programs targeting women as mothers (and their children). However, in the contemporary era, state capacities in particular political contexts (e.g. social-democratic or labor parties in power) are associated with the development of "state feminism" and the promotion of various kinds of equality policies (e.g. Franzway, Court & Connell 1989, Stetson & Mazur 1995). Analysts are also highlighting the effects of discourse on gendered political participation (e.g. social movements, institutional participation) and on policymaking more generally; here, too, specification of how these effects are shaped within particular economic, political, and institutional contexts would be welcome.

Research on gender relations and welfare states is engaged with many of the same issues as those that occupy "mainstream" research (i.e. research not concerned with gender)—but also offers some new perspectives on some vexing issues (e.g. American social policy exceptionalism). Moreover, it is increasingly clear that women are central to labor market developments, that social politics are at least partly gender politics, and that much welfare state restructuring is and has been a response to changes in gender relations. I close with the suggestion that we fully integrate gender into all studies of the welfare state.

ACKNOWLEDGMENTS

I am grateful to Renee Monson for helpful discussions of many of the issues raised in this review, particularly the feminization of poverty and gendered interests. Thanks to Kathrina Zippel for general research assistance on this project, and for providing a summary of the literature on gender and the welfare state in Germany, including many works written in German. Also thanks to the members of the Research Network on Gender, State and Society, subscribers to H-State, H-Women and Socpol-l, and contributors to Social Politics who supplied copies of their work and made suggestions for material to be included.

Literature Cited

Abramovitz M. 1988. *Regulating the Lives of Women: Social Welfare Policy from Colonial Times to the Present.* Boston, MA: South End Press

Bellingham B, Mathis MP. 1994. Race, citizenship, and the bio-politics of the maternalist welfare state: "traditional" midwifery in the American South under the Sheppard-Towner Act, 1921–29. *Soc. Polit.* 1:157–89

Bock G. 1991. Antinatalism, maternity and paternity in National Socialist racism. See Bock & Thane 1991, pp. 233–55

Bock G, Thane P, eds. 1991. *Maternity and Gender Policies: Women and the Rise of the European Welfare States. 1880s–1950s.* New York: Routledge

Borchorst A. 1994a. Welfare state regimes, women's interests, and the EC. See Sainsbury 1994a, pp. 26–44

Borchorst A. 1994b. The Scandinavian welfare states—patriarchal, gender neutral or woman-friendly? *Int. J. Contemp. Sociol.* 31:1–23

Borchorst A, Siim B. 1987. Women and the advanced welfare state—a new kind of patriarchal power? See Sassoon 1987, pp. 128–57

Boris E. 1995. The racialized gendered state: constructions of citizenship in the United States. *Soc. Polit.* 2:160–80

Bryson L. 1992. *Welfare and the State.* London: Macmillan

Burney L. 1994. An Aboriginal way of being Australian. *Aust. Fem. Stud.* 19:17–24

Bussemaker J, van Kersbergen K. 1994. Gender and welfare states: some theoretical reflections. See Sainsbury 1994a, pp. 8–25

Caspar L, McLanahan S, Garfinkel I. 1994. The gender-poverty gap: What we can learn from other countries. *Am. Sociol. Rev.* 59:594–605

Cass B. 1994. Citizenship, work and welfare:

the dilemma for Australian women. *Soc. Polit.* 1:106–24

Collins PH. 1990. *Black Feminist Thought. Knowledge, Consciousness, and the Politics of Empowerment.* New York: Routledge

Connell RW. 1987. *Gender and Power.* Stanford, CA: Stanford Univ. Press

Esping-Andersen G. 1990. *The Three Worlds of Welfare Capitalism.* Princeton, NJ: Princeton Univ. Press

Ferree MM. 1995. Patriarchies and feminisms: the two women's movements of postunification Germany. *Soc. Polit.* 2:10–24

Finch J, Groves D. 1983. *A Labour of Love: Women, Work and Caring.* Boston, MA: Routledge & Kegan Paul

Franzway S, Court D, Connell RW. 1989. *Staking a Claim: Feminism, Bureaucracy, and the State.* Oxford: Polity Press

Fraser N. 1989. Women, welfare and the politics of need. In *Unruly Practices,* pp. 144–60. Minneapolis, MN: Univ. Minn. Press

Fraser N. 1994. After the family wage: gender equity and the welfare state. *Polit. Theor.* 22:591–618

Goldberg G, Kremen E. 1990. *The Feminization of Poverty: Only in America?* New York: Praeger

Goodwin J. 1992. An American experiment in paid motherhood: the implementation of mothers' pensions in early twentieth century Chicago. *Gender Hist.* 4:323–42

Gordon L. 1988. What does welfare regulate? *Soc. Res.* 55:609–30

Gordon L, ed. 1990. *Women, the State and Welfare.* Madison, WI: Univ. Wisc. Press

Gordon L. 1993. Gender, state and society: a debate with Theda Skocpol. *Contention* 2:139–56

Gordon L. 1994. *Pitied But Not Entitled: Single Mothers and the History of Welfare.* New York: Free Press

Gordon L, Fraser N. 1994. "Dependency" demystified: inscriptions of power in a keyword of the welfare state. *Soc. Polit.* 1:14–31

Gustafsson S. 1994. Childcare and types of welfare states. See Sainsbury 1994a, pp. 45–61

Haas L. 1992. *Equal Parenthood and Social Policy: A Study of Parental Leave in Sweden.* Albany: State Univ. New York Press

Hernes H. 1987. *Welfare State and Woman Power.* Oslo, Norway: Norway Univ. Press

Hernes H. 1988. The welfare state citizenship of Scandinavian women. See Jones & Jonasdottir 1988, pp. 187–213

Hill DCD, Tigges L. 1995. Gendering welfare state theory: a cross-national study of women's public pension quality. *Gender Soc.* 9:99–119

Hobson B. 1993. Feminist strategies and gendered discourses in welfare states: married women's right to work in the United States and Sweden. See Koven & Michel 1993, pp. 396–430

Hobson B. 1994. Solo mothers, social policy regimes and the logics of gender. See Sainsbury 1994a, pp. 170–87

Holter H, ed. 1984. *Patriarchy in a Welfare Society.* Oslo: Universitetsforlaget

Jackson PC. 1993. Managing the mothers: the case of Ireland. See Lewis 1993, pp. 72–91

Jenson J. 1986. Gender and reproduction: or, babies and the state. *Stud. Polit. Econ.* 20:9–45

Jónasdóttir AG. 1988. On the concept of interest, women's interests, and the limitations of interest theory. See Jones & Jonasdottir 1988, pp. 33–65

Jónasdóttir AG. 1994. *Why Women Are Oppressed.* Philadelphia, PA: Temple Univ. Press

Jones K, Jónasdóttir A, eds. 1988. *The Political Interests of Gender.* Newbury Park, CA: Sage

Kamerman SB. 1986. Women, children and poverty: public policies and female-headed families in industrialized countries. In *Women and Poverty,* ed. B Gelpi, N Hartsock, C Novak, M Strober, pp. 41–63. Chicago, IL: Univ. Chicago Press

Klaus A. 1993. *Every Child a Lion: The Origins of Maternal and Infant Health Policy in the United States and France, 1890–1920.* Ithaca, NY: Cornell Univ. Press

Knijn T. 1994. Fish without bikes: revision of the Dutch welfare state and its consequences for the (in)dependence of single mothers. *Soc. Polit.* 1:83–105

Koonz C. 1987. *Mothers in the Fatherland: Women, the Family and Nazi Politics.* New York: St. Martin's

Koven S, Michel S, eds. 1993. *Mothers of the New World: Maternalist Politics and the Origins of the Welfare State.* New York: Routledge

Ladd-Taylor M. 1994. *Mother-Work: Women, Child Welfare and the State, 1890–1930.* Urbana, IL: Univ. Ill. Press

Lake M. 1992. Mission impossible: how men gave birth to the Australian nation—nationalism, gender and other seminal acts. *Gender Hist.* 4:305–22

Land H. 1978. Who cares for the family? *J. Soc. Policy* 7:257–84

Langan M, Ostner I. 1991. Gender and welfare: toward a comparative framework. In *Toward a European Welfare State?* ed. G Room, pp. 127–50. Bristol, UK: Sch. Adv. Urban Stud.

Leibfried S. 1992. Towards a European welfare state? Integrating poverty regimes into the European community. In *Social Policy in a*

Changing Europe, ed. S Ferge, JE Kolberg, pp. 245–79. Boulder, CO: Westview

Leira A. 1992. *Welfare States and Working Mothers: The Scandinavian Experience.* New York: Cambridge Univ. Press

Lewis J. 1992. Gender and the development of welfare regimes. *J. Eur. Soc. Policy* 3:159–73

Lewis J, ed. 1993a. *Women and Social Policies in Europe. Work, Family, and the State.* Hants, UK: Edward Elgar

Lewis J. 1993b. Introduction: women, work, family and social policies in Europe. See Lewis 1993a, pp. 1–24

Lewis J, Åström G. 1992. Equality, difference, and state welfare: labor market and family policies in Sweden. *Fem. Stud.* 18:59–86

Lister R. 1990. Women, economic dependency and citizenship. *J. Soc. Policy* 19:445–67

Lister R. 1992. *Women's Economic Dependency and Social Security.* Manchester, UK: Equal Oppor. Comm.

McLanahan S, Casper L, Sørenson A. 1995. Women's roles and women's poverty. In *Gender and Family Change in Industrialized Countries,* ed. K Mason, AM Jensen, pp. 258–78. Oxford, UK: IUSSP/Oxford Univ.

McLanahan S, Sorenson A, Watson D. 1989. Sex differences in poverty, 1950–1980. *Signs* 15:102–22

Michel S. 1993. The limits of maternalism: policies toward American wage-earning mothers during the Progressive era. See Koven & Michel 1993, pp. 277–320

Mink G. 1994. *Wages of Motherhood: Inequality in the Welfare State, 1917–1942.* Ithaca, NY: Cornell Univ. Press

Mitchell D. 1993. Sole parents, work and welfare: evidence from the Luxembourg income study. In *Comparative Perspectives on Sole Parents Policy: Work and Welfare,* ed. S Shaver, pp. 53–89. Univ. NSW Soc. Policy Res. Cent. Rep. Proc. No. 106

Molyneux M. 1985. Mobilization without emancipation? Women's interests, the state and revolution in Nicaragua. *Fem. Stud.* 11:227–54

Monson R. 1996. *State-ing sex and gender in paternity establishment and child support policy.* PhD thesis. Univ. Wis.-Madison

Muncy R. 1991. *Creating a Female Dominion in American Reform, 1890–1935.* New York: Oxford Univ. Press

Nash M. 1991. Pronatalism and motherhood in Franco's Spain. See Bock & Thane 1991, pp. 160–77

Nelson B. 1984. Women's poverty and women's citizenship: some political consequences of economic marginality. *Signs* 10:209–32

Nelson B. 1990. The origins of the two-channel welfare state: workmen's compensation and

mothers' aid. See Gordon 1990, pp. 123–51

O'Connor J. 1993a. Gender, class and citizenship in the comparative analysis of welfare state regimes: theoretical and methodological issues. *Br. J. Sociol.* 44:501–18

O'Connor J. 1993b. Citizenship, class, gender, and labour market participation in Canada and Australia. In *Gender, Citizenship and the Labour Market,* ed. S Shaver, pp. 4–37. Univ. NSW Soc. Policy Res. Cent. Rep. Proc. No. 109

Orloff AS. 1991. Gender in early U.S. social policy. *J. Policy Hist.* 3:249–81

Orloff AS. 1993a. Gender and the social rights of citizenship: the comparative analysis of gender relations and welfare states. *Am. Sociol. Rev.* 58:303–28

Orloff AS. 1993b. *The Politics of Pensions: A Comparative Analysis of Britain, Canada, and the United States, 1880–1940.* Madison, WI: Univ. Wis. Press

Orloff AS. 1996. Gender in the liberal welfare states: Australia, Canada, the United Kingdom and the United States. In *State/Culture,* ed. G Steinmetz. Ithaca: Cornell Univ Press. In press

Ostner I. 1993. Slow motion: women, work and the family in Germany. See Lewis 1993, pp. 92–115

Pateman C. 1988. The patriarchal welfare state. In *Democracy and the State,* ed. A Gutmann, pp. 231–78. Princeton, NJ: Princeton Univ. Press

Pedersen S. 1993. *Family, Dependence, and the Origins of the Welfare State: Britain and France, 1914–1945.* New York: Cambridge Univ. Press

Piven FF. 1985. Women and the state: ideology, power, and the welfare state. In *Gender and the Life Course,* ed. A Rossi, pp. 265–87. New York: Aldine

Pringle R, Watson S. 1992. Women's interests and the post-structuralist state. In *Destabilizing Theory,* ed. M Barret, A Phillips, pp. 53–73. Stanford: Stanford Univ. Press

Quadagno J. 1994. *The Color of Welfare. How Racism Undermined the War on Poverty.* New York: Oxford Univ. Press

Roberts D. 1995. Race, gender, and the value of mothers' work. *Soc. Polit.* 2:195–207

Ruggie M. 1984. *The State and Working Women.* Princeton: Princeton Univ. Press

Ruggie M. 1988. Gender, work, and social progress: some consequences of interest aggregation in Sweden. In *Feminization of the Labour Force,* ed. J Jenson, E Hagen, C Ready, pp. 172–88. New York: Oxford Univ. Press

Sainsbury D. 1993. Dual welfare and sex segregation of access to social benefits: income maintenance policies in the UK, the US, the Netherlands and Sweden. *J. Soc. Policy* 22:69–98

Sainsbury D, ed. 1994a. *Gendering Welfare States.* Thousand Oaks, CA: Sage

Sainsbury D. 1994b. Introduction. See Sainsbury 1994a, pp. 1–8

Sainsbury D. 1994c. Women's and men's social rights: gendering dimensions of welfare states. See Sainsbury 1994a, pp. 150–69

Saraceno C. 1991. Redefining maternity and paternity: gender, pronatalism, and social policies in Fascist Italy. See Bock & Thane 1991, pp. 196–212

Saraceno C. 1994. The ambivalent familism of the Italian welfare state. *Soc. Polit.* 1:60–82

Sassoon AS, ed. 1987. *Women and the State. The Shifting Boundaries of Public and Private.* London, UK: Hutchinson

Schmidt M. 1993. Gendered labor force participation. In *Families of Nations,* ed. FG Castles, pp. 179–237. Aldershot: Dartmouth

Schunter-Kleemann S, ed. 1992. *Mansion Europe—Gender Relations in the Welfare State.* Berlin, Germany: Edition Sigma

Scott J. 1986. Gender: a useful category of historical analysis. *Am. Hist. Rev.* 91:1053–75

Shaver S. 1990. Gender, social policy regimes and the welfare state. Presented at Annu. Meet. Am. Sociol. Assoc., Washington, DC

Shaver S. 1993. Body rights, social rights and the liberal welfare state. *Crit. Soc. Policy* 13(39):66–93

Siim B. 1988. Towards a feminist rethinking of the welfare state. See Jones & Jonasdottir 1988, pp. 160–86

Siim B. 1990. Women and the welfare state: between private and public dependence. a comparative approach to care work in Denmark and Britain. See Ungerson 1990, pp. 80–109

Sklar KK. 1993. The historical foundations of women's power in the creation of the American welfare state, 1830–1930. See Koven & Michel 1993, pp. 43–93

Skocpol T. 1992. *Protecting Soldiers and Mothers.* Cambridge, MA: Harvard Univ. Press

Skocpol T. 1993. Soldiers, workers and mothers: gendered identities in early U.S. social policy. *Contention* 2:157–83

Skocpol T, Abend-Wein M, Howard C, Lehmann SG. 1993. Women's associations and the enactment of mother's pensions in the United States. *Am. Polit. Sci. Rev.* 87:686–701

Skocpol T, Ritter G. 1991. Gender and the origins of modern social policies in Britain and the United States. *Stud. Am. Polit. Dev.* 5:36–93

Stetson D, Mazur M, eds. 1995. *Comparative State Feminism.* Thousand Oaks, CA: Sage

Taylor-Gooby P. 1991. Welfare state regimes and welfare citizenship. *J. Eur. Soc. Policy* 1:93–105

Ungerson C, ed. 1990. *Gender and Caring: Work and Welfare in Britain and Scandinavia.* New York: Harvester Wheatsheaf

Waerness K. 1984. Caregiving as women's work in the welfare state. See Holter 1984, pp. 67–87

Weir M, Orloff AS, Skocpol T, eds. 1988. *The Politics of Social Policy in the United States.* Princeton, NJ: Princeton Univ. Press

Wennemo I. 1994. *Sharing the costs of children: studies on the development of family support in the OECD countries.* Stockholm, Sweden: Swed. Inst. Soc. Res. Diss. Ser., No. 25

Williams F. 1995. Race/ethnicity, gender and class in welfare states: a framework for comparative analysis. *Soc. Polit.* 2:127–59

Annu. Rev. Sociol. 1996. 22:79–102

ADULT CHILD–PARENT RELATIONSHIPS

Diane N. Lye

University of Washington, Department of Sociology, Box 353340, Seattle, Washington 98195-3340

KEY WORDS: intergenerational exchanges, adult child–parent contact, divorce, kinkeeping

---

ABSTRACT

In this essay I review recent studies of adult child–parent relationships, with an emphasis on studies using nationally representative samples. Adult children and their parents have frequent contact and emotionally satisfying relationships, but exchanges of practical and financial assistance are uncommon. Continuing relationships between adult children and their parents depend on women's work as kinkeepers. Parental divorce greatly weakens adult children's relationships with their fathers and also tends to weaken relationships with mothers. Adult child–parent relationships are not stronger in black families than in white families. The most pressing need for future research is the development of new theoretical formulations.

INTRODUCTION

This essay is about the relationships between adult children and their parents: how often adult children and parents are in contact with each other, how they assess the quality of their interactions, what they do for each other, and what they feel they ought to do for each other. I focus on relationships between adult children and parents who do not live together, because coresidence may have different meanings depending on the ages of the parent and child, and on who is head of household. I examine relations between adult children and parents of all ages and health statuses, but I do not review studies of caregiving. Reviews of adult child–parent coresidence and of caregiving and may be found in White (1994) and Mancini (1989).

79

The structure of this essay is as follows. I begin by discussing the theoretical perspectives that have informed research on adult child–parent relations and then describe some of the methodological challenges faced by researchers in this area. In the main part of this essay, I review recent findings concerning patterns of adult child–parent contact, relationship quality, and helping. I pay particular attention to variations in adult child–parent relationships by race and ethnicity, gender, and whether the adult child or parent is divorced. Next I discuss norms concerning adult child–parent relations as well as the connections among various aspects of adult child–parent relations. I conclude with a brief assessment of the strengths and weaknesses of research about adult child–parent relations and offer some suggestions for future research.

THEORETICAL PERSPECTIVES

For the past 40 years research on adult child–parent relations has been dominated by the reaction against structural-functionalist theories of the family. According to theorists such as Parsons (1943) and Burgess & Locke (1945), urbanization and industrialization led to the destruction of traditional extended family ties in favor of nuclear families, and adult children and their elders were left isolated and alienated from each other. While historians challenged the view that families in the past were characterized by close intergenerational ties (see Hareven 1994), family sociologists devoted themselves to dispelling the myth of the isolated nuclear family. A parallel tendency can be seen in research on race and ethnic differences in family relations, where researchers have applied themselves to disproving the claims of the Moynihan report and the myth of the pathological black family.

The myths appears to have been well and truly dispelled (Mancini & Blieszner 1989), but few have attempted to develop alternate theories of intergenerational family relations that yield testable predictions. For the most part researchers have been content to frame their work by reference to the myths of the isolated nuclear family and the pathological black family rather than by proposing new approaches to adult child–parent relations. For example, the convoy model (Antonucci 1990) has been one of the most influential models of helping between adult children and parents. Yet this approach is largely a reaction to structural-functionalism: The central proposition of the convoy model is that adults are not isolated from kin but can call on assistance from a hierarchy of kin (Hogan & Eggebeen 1995). My point is not that the claims of structural-functionalism or the Moynihan report were accurate. Rather we need to move beyond old mythologies and develop new theories that us allow to make sense of the knowledge we have produced about adult child–parent relationships.

Altruism has been suggested as one reason for exchanges of support between adult children and their families: Families members are said to exchange resources (including companionship and affection) because they derive utility both from giving and receiving those resources (Becker 1981). The observation that, over the life course, parents provide more resources to their children than they receive from their children is consistent with the idea that parents act out of altruism. However, the tendency for parents to give more than they receive is also consistent with evolutionary theories of the family that suggest that in low-fertility settings parents act to maximize their investments in their children (Eggebeen & Hogan 1990). Evolutionary theory also predicts that parents would provide most resources to adult children who have or who are more likely to have grandchildren, a hypothesis that is generally confirmed.

The consistent finding that adult child–parent relations are largely characterized by reciprocity has led to renewed interest in exchange theories (Mancini & Blieszner 1989, Hogan et al 1993). These approaches do not require an exact and immediate reciprocation of all support received; rather they posit that parents and children "trade" emotional, practical, and financial support over the life course (Antonucci & Akiyama 1987). The observation that adult children of divorce have weaker relationships with the parent who had not been their custodian might be consistent with exchange theory. Similarly, research suggesting that parents strategically manipulate bequests in order to ensure attention from their children (Bernheim et al 1985) also implies that adult child–parent relations may have an exchange component.

Gender theory has also informed recent research on adult child–parent relations. This perspective focuses on the gendered pattern of family interaction and family work. Specifically, because women perform the gendered work of kinkeeping, they are more involved in kin networks and may control men's access to kin (Furstenberg & Cherlin 1991, Hagestad 1986). Women may be more involved in adult child–parent relationships because they place greater importance on close emotional bonds with family members (Silverstein et al 1995) and are more compassionate and altruistic (Beutel & Marini 1995). In addition, women's greater provision of family services in early and middle adulthood may lead to greater access to support in late adulthood (Spitze & Logan 1989, Rossi & Rossi 1990). In contrast, unmarried men may have only tenuous connection to kin networks (Goldscheider 1990).

METHODOLOGICAL CONSIDERATIONS

In recent years several high-quality survey samples have gathered information about adult child–parent relationships; thus finding adequate data to describe and analyze adult child–parent relations is less of a challenge than in the recent past. There have also been advances in the measurement of adult child–parent relations. Questions are designed to elicit precise information about contact and helping between adult children and parents, usually with reference to a particular time period and type of helping or contact. Few recent studies rely on global measures of helping or contact, and most researchers are careful to distinguish between measures assessing actual assistance and potential assistance. Nevertheless, how to describe and analyze adult child–parent relations continues to be a challenge.

One major concern is the units of analysis. Should the units of analysis be adult children, parents, or adult child–parent dyads? Each approach is likely to yield a different picture of adult child–parent relationships, and not just because adult children and parents may report the same exchanges differently. Studies that assess exchange in any particular dyad will likely find lower levels of exchange than those that assess adult children's or parents' total involvement in exchange. This is because each parent may be involved in exchange with more than one adult child, and each adult child may be involved in exchange with more than one parent. For example, Hogan et al (1993) suggest that one reason for their relatively low estimates of helping between adult children and parents is because they rely on adult children's reports of exchange with one parent, rather than parents' reports of exchange with all their adult children. However, how often adult children and parents are involved in more than one dyad has not been well documented, and the precise implications of assessing adult child–parent relations from these different perspectives are not well understood. Also, in some cases, e.g. gifts to assist with home purchases, it may make more sense to assess transfers between households than between individuals.

In order to examine the impact of adult child and parent characteristics on adult child–parent relations, it is necessary to focus on the relationships between a particular adult child and a particular parent, that is, to use adult child–parent dyads as the unit of analysis. However, in such an analysis it is not appropriate to include all possible dyads because to do so would violate the assumption required by many multivariate statistical techniques that each observation must be independent from all the other observations (Lye et al 1995). Yet the price of statistical correctness is the loss of the information about how, say, one parent's relationship with one child is related to their relationship with another child. One solution to this dilemma may be the application of regression techniques that allow for, and estimate, the correlations between observations (Spitze et al 1994).

A second concern is how to describe adult child–parent relationships. Some researchers have argued that involvement in any exchange of helping or resources is sufficiently uncommon that the best approach is to combine all types of assistance (including emotional support) and to focus on whether respondents are involved in helping at all, and if so whether they are givers or receivers or both (e.g. Hogan et al 1993). In contrast, other researchers stress the conceptual and empirical differences between different types of assistance and the different aspects of adult child–parent relations; they argue that each should be considered separately (e.g. Rossi & Rossi 1990, Spitze & Logan 1990). In addition, although there appear to be widely accepted measures of some aspects of adult child–parent relationships, e.g. contact, there is considerable variation in the measures used to assess other domains of adult child–parent relations, e.g. relationship quality.

With these concerns in mind, I now turn to my review of research describing adult child–parent relations.

CONTACT AND PROXIMITY

Adult child–parent relations in the United States are characterized by frequent visits, telephone calls and letters, and close proximity. For example, data from the 1990 American Association of Retired Persons Intergenerational Linkages Survey (ILS), a nationally representative sample of adults of all ages, show that over half of adult children live within a one hour drive of their parents, 69% of adult children have weekly contact with their mothers, and 20% have daily contact with their mothers (Lawton et al 1994a). Likewise the 1988 National Survey of Families and Households (NSFH) shows that close to 40% of adult children have face-to-face contact with their parents once a week or more (Lye et al 1995). Similar patterns have been found in other national and regional samples (Aldous 1987, Aldous & Klein 1991, Cicirelli 1981, Dietz 1995, Jayakody et al 1993, Leigh 1982, Mancini & Blieszner 1989, Rossi & Rossi 1990, Shanas 1980, Spitze & Logan 1990, 1991a; Streib & Beck 1980, Troll 1971, Umberson 1992).

Variations in sampling strategies and measurement make it difficult to establish trends in adult child–parent contact and proximity. Data from two national surveys show that the fraction of elderly people who saw a child every day declined from one half in 1962 to one third in 1984. Over the same period, the proportion of elderly living within ten minutes of an adult child declined from 47% to 40%, although the fraction of elderly people living within 30 minutes of an adult child remained steady at around two thirds (Crimmins & Ingegneri 1990).

RELATIONSHIP QUALITY

There is no single, widely accepted measure of the quality of adult child–parent relationships. Researchers have examined a wide variety of variables intended to assess the quality of relationships between adult children and their parents, including a single variable assessment of relationship quality (Aquilino 1994, Houser & Berkman 1984, Lye et al 1995), scale measures of relationship quality (Amato & Booth 1991, Booth & Amato 1994, Cooney 1994, Levitt et al 1992, Markides et al 1986), feelings of attachment and closeness (Bengtson & Roberts 1991, Cicirelli 1983, Lawton et al 1994, Spitze & Logan 1991a,b; Rossi & Rossi 1990, White et al 1985), the exchange of emotional support and advice (Umberson 1992), intimacy (Thompson & Walker 1984), strain and parental dissatisfaction with adult children (Umberson 1992), and disagreement (Aldous 1987, Cicirelli 1983). Despite the lack of consensus about how to measure adult child–parent relationship quality, there is broad agreement among researchers concerning the general disposition of adult child–parent relationships as well as the sources of variation in adult child–parent relationship quality.

The overwhelming majority of adult children report close relationships with their parents. Among adult children interviewed in the ILS, 80% had "emotionally close" relationships with their parents (Lawton et al 1994b). Among white adult children interviewed in the NSFH, over one third rated their relationship excellent, and only 10% rated their relationship below the midpoint of the scale (Lye et al 1995). Data from the NSFH also show that emotional help and support are the most common types of support exchanged by adult children and their parents (Eggebeen & Hogan 1990, Hogan & Eggebeen 1995, Cooney & Uhlenberg 1992). Similar findings have been reported in other national and regional samples, including some that assess both parents' and adult children's evaluations of relationship quality (Aldous 1987, Bengtson & Roberts 1991, Booth & Amato 1994, Chatters & Taylor 1993, Jayakody et al 1993, Spitze & Logan 1991a,b, Umberson 1992).

INSTRUMENTAL AND FINANCIAL ASSISTANCE

Based on extensive research conducted over the past 30 years family researchers have concluded that American adults and their parents are engaged in extensive and continuous exchanges of assistance, that most exchange is reciprocal, and that parents do not become net recipients of aid until they become very elderly or frail (for reviews, see Bengtson et al 1990, Mancini & Blieszner 1989, Streib & Beck 1980, Troll 1971).

However, data from the NSFH suggest that earlier studies may have overstated the extent and frequency of exchange between adult children and parents. Among adults of all ages with at least one living parent, 55% provide no support to their parents, and 56% receive no support from their parents. Although around one quarter each report giving and receiving advice and emotional support, only 17% receive money from their parents, and only 4% give money to their parents (Eggebeen & Hogan 1990). Parents also report low levels of exchange with their adult children; the majority were not involved in giving or receiving support (Eggebeen 1992). Among adults aged 55 and over, only around 4% were currently receiving financial assistance from their adult children, and only around 20% were currently receiving practical assistance (Hogan & Eggebeen 1995).

Using NSFH data for adults with at least one living parent and one coresident child under age 16, Hogan et al (1993) classified adult children into four categories: low exchangers, high exchangers, receivers, and advice givers. Over half the adult children were classified as low exchangers, and 72% of the low exchangers were not involved in any exchange. Only 11% of adult children were high exchangers, 19% were receivers, and 17% were advice givers. In a separate analysis of adults aged 45–59, the age group most likely to have both surviving parents and adult children, the most common pattern, reported by one third of the respondents, was not to be involved in exchange with either parents or adult children (Hogan & Eggebeen 1995). These estimates likely overstate the amount of exchange because in addition to assessing exchanges of financial and practical assistance, they include advice and emotional support, which can be viewed as aspects of relationship quality.

Other researchers using recent national probability samples other than the NSFH have also found low levels of adult child–parent exchange. For example, data from the National Survey of Hispanic Elderly, the National Survey of Black Americans, the ILS, and the National Health Interview Survey all show high levels of emotional support and advice giving, but quite limited exchanges of practical assistance (Dietz 1995, Jayakody et al 1993, Lawton et al 1994a, Spitze & Logan 1990).

Although most adults are not involved in on-going, routine exchanges of practical and financial assistance with their parents and adult children, assistance linked to key life course transitions is quite common. Parents make the largest transfers of practical and financial help to their children in early adulthood (Cooney & Uhlenberg 1992, Eggebeen & Hogan 1990, Lawton et al 1994a, Rossi & Rossi 1990). Many parents help launch their children toward independence by providing substantial amounts of assistance with college expenses and home purchases. Data from the High School Class of 1972 show that two thirds of the students who entered college in the fall of 1972 received some financial support from their parents and that on average parents provided 46% of the total college costs (Steelman & Powell 1989). Among adults interviewed in the NSFH who purchased a home since 1980, about 25% received financial help, mostly from parents, and the median amount was $5000 (Bumpass 1990). This type of assistance is of considerable importance since parents' ability and willingness to assist their children affects access to college and the housing market, which are important aspects of social stratification.

DIFFERENTIALS IN ADULT CHILD–PARENT RELATIONSHIPS

Race and Ethnicity

During the 1970s, ethnographic studies of black communities suggested a range of important black-white differences in family relationships (Hayes & Mindel 1973, Martin & Martin 1978, McAdoo 1978, Stack 1974). Blacks were said to be more likely to live in extended families or close to kin, to have stronger kin ties, and to be more likely to exchange financial, practical, and emotional assistance with other kin. These findings have led some researchers to conclude that there are, "long-standing cultural differences in the ways blacks and whites conceive of and carry out their family lives. In particular. . . ties to a network of kin that can extend over more than one household" (Cherlin 1992:109). The implications for adult child–parent relationships are clear: Compared to whites, blacks have been assumed to have more frequent contact with their parents and adult children, higher quality relationships, and to be more involved in exchanges of assistance.

Data from the 1979–1980 National Survey of Black Americans confirm that black adults tend to live close to the majority of their kin and that most have at least weekly contact with members of their extended families (Jayakody et al 1993, Chatters & Taylor 1993). Research on other ethnic minorities is limited. For some groups the frequency of contact with, and proximity to, kin reflects the recency of immigration to the United States; immigrants tend to be further away from their families, which in turn reduces the opportunities for contact (Weeks & Cuellar 1981). However, research on elderly Mexican-Americans suggests that frequent contact is common. Data from the 1988 National Survey of Hispanic Elderly show that around 80% of elderly Hispanics either lived with or lived within a few minutes of an adult child, and among those who did not live with an adult child nearly half had daily face-to-face contact with an adult child (Dietz 1995).

To date few studies have compared adult child–parent relations in different racial and ethnic groups because of the lack of nationally representative data sets with sufficient number of minorities to support comparisons (Markides et al 1990). Studies that include race and ethnic comparisons in adult child–parent contact yield inconsistent results. Some studies have found only small or no race differences in adult child–parent contact (Lawton et al 1994b; Umberson 1992). In contrast, NSFH data show that black adult children visit their parents more often than do whites, and Hispanic adult children visit their parents less often than whites (Lye & Klepinger 1995). In addition, among never-married young adults, blacks were more likely than whites to reside within 25 miles of their mothers, and blacks saw their mothers more frequently than whites (Raley 1995). Also, among young mothers surveyed in the National Longitudinal Survey of Youth (NLSY), blacks lived closer to their mothers than did whites (Hogan et al 1990, Parish et al 1991).

Findings concerning race differences in relationship quality are also inconsistent. In some studies black adult children report closer relationships with their mothers than do whites (Lawton et al 1994b, Umberson 1992), although black mothers report receiving less emotional support from their adult children than do whites (Umberson 1992). Data from the NSFH show that similar proportions of blacks and whites describe their relationships with their parents as excellent, but that Hispanic adult children are less likely than blacks or whites to report an excellent relationship with their parents (Lye & Klepinger 1995). Hispanics also reported lower adult child–parent relationship quality in a small, nonprobability sample (Levitt et al 1992).

Early studies of adult child–parent exchange provided some support for the view that blacks were more likely than whites to be involved in exchange. For example, among adults aged over 65 in a 1974 national sample, blacks were more likely to be involved in giving and receiving assistance (Mutran 1985).

Recent studies of young adults provide mixed support for the hypothesis that blacks are more likely than whites to exchange assistance with family members. Data from the NLSY and the NSFH show that among young mothers, blacks were more likely than whites to receive help with childcare from their mothers and were more likely to receive financial assistance from kin (Benin & Keith 1995, Hogan et al 1990, Parish et al 1991). In contrast, one study of young, never-married adults finds no race differences in giving and that black men are less likely than whites to receive help from their parents (Raley 1995). Data for the High School Class of 1980 show that black adult children are less likely than whites to receive financial help with college expenses, partly because of lower income in black families, but also because more black young adults have only one parent or very young parents (Goldscheider & Goldscheider 1991). Among young adults who do not go to college, blacks are more likely than whites or Hispanics to make financial contributions to their families (Goldscheider & Goldscheider 1991).

Data for adults of all ages do not show higher levels of adult child–parent exchange among minorities; in fact, they show the reverse. Data from two different national samples show that African Americans are less likely to be involved in exchanges of assistance than whites and do not have better access to emergency support networks (Lawton et al 1994a, Eggebeen & Hogan 1990, Hogan et al 1993, Hogan & Eggebeen 1995). For example, in the ILS only 9% of African American parents provided practical help to their adult children, compared with 31% of non-Blacks (Lawton et al 1994a). In addition, Mexican-American adult children are less involved in exchange than are Anglo adult children because they tend to live further away from their parents (Eggebeen & Hogan 1990, Hogan et al 1993).

Gender

In many families one adult occupies the position of "kinkeeper" and assumes responsibility for keeping family members in touch with each other (Hagestad 1986, Milardo 1987, Rosenthal 1985). Because kinkeeping is largely under-taken by women, relationships between mothers and daughter are thought to be emotionally closer and to entail more frequent contact and exchanges of assistance than mixed-gender or male adult child–parent relationships.

Consistent with the view that women serve as kinkeepers, adult child–mother relationships are closer than adult child–father relationships, particularly for daughters (Lawton et al 1994b, Markides et al 1986, Marks 1995, Silverstein et al 1995, White et al 1985). Aging mothers are more likely to choose daughters than sons as confidants (Aldous 1987, Mutran & Reitzes 1984). Mothers receive more emotional support than fathers (Umberson 1992), although mothers are more likely to report disagreements with their adult children (Aldous & Klein 1991), and daughters are more likely than sons to report strain in their relationships with their parents (Umberson 1992).

Mothers and daughters have more frequent contact than fathers and sons or mixed-gender dyads (Lawton et al 1994a, Rossi & Rossi 1990). Adult daughters report more frequent contact with their parents than do adult sons (Aldous 1995, Leigh 1982, Lye et al 1995, Spitze & Logan 1991a,b, Umberson 1992), and adult children report less contact with their fathers than with their mothers (Lawton et al 1994a, Lye et al 1995, Rossi & Rossi 1990). Parents visit and talk on the telephone more with daughters than with sons (Spitze & Logan 1989, Spitze & Miner 1992, Spitze et al 1994). Parents with at least one daughter report more frequent contact than do parents with only sons, and the frequency of contact increases the more daughters the parent has (Spitze & Logan 1990).

Adult daughters are more likely to provide routine help to their parents than are sons (Eggebeen & Hogan 1990, Rossi & Rossi 1990); daughters are more likely to receive help than sons (Eggebeen & Hogan 1990); and mothers are more likely than fathers to provide practical assistance to adult children (Lawton et al 1994a, Parish et al 1991, Rossi & Rossi 1990, Spitze et al 1994). Mothers are also more likely to receive assistance than fathers (Hogan & Eggebeen

1995, Spitze & Logan 1989), although this may reflect greater longevity among women and a greater need for assistance among elderly women. The largest gender difference seems to be in giving as women are no more likely than men to receive unreciprocated assistance (Amato et al 1995, Hogan et al 1993). In addition, parents with at least one daughter are more likely to receive assistance than those with only sons. Apparently, when it comes to providing assistance to elderly parents, gender role norms are so strong they prevent sons from substituting for daughters, but women's involvement in kinkeeping may secure them greater access to support in later life (Rossi & Rossi 1990, Spitze & Logan 1989, 1990).

Parent's Divorce

A large literature has documented the dramatic weakening of relations between fathers and children after divorce (Seltzer 1994), and several authors have predicted that divorced fathers will have weaker relations with their adult children than will continuously married fathers (Goldscheider 1990, Spitze & Miner 1992). Drawing on exchange theory, Smyer & Hofland (1982) argued that divorced fathers may not have "built up enough credit" in their relations with their children to be able to rely on them in later life. In addition, the norms and expectations that define the rights and obligations of family members may be less clear in divorced and remarried families (Cherlin 1978). Predictions concerning relations with divorced mothers, the majority of whom assume responsibility for raising children, are less clear cut. Early research suggested that mothers' relations with their children might be largely unaffected by divorce because of the children's high pre-divorce attachment to their mothers and the tendency for women to have custody of children after divorce (White et al 1986). Other researchers suggested that the decline in resources experienced by divorced mothers might have adverse consequences for the mother–adult child relationship (Brubaker 1990, Umberson 1992). Since the early 1990s several studies have addressed these questions, and there is broad agreement in the findings.

Compared to adult children whose parents are married, adult children with divorced parents report fewer visits, telephone calls, and letters (Amato & Booth 1991, Aquilino 1994, Booth & Amato 1994, Cooney 1994, Lye et al 1995), tend to live further away from their parents than do those with continuously married parents (Lawton et al 1994a), are less likely to be involved in exchanges of practical support, especially with fathers (Amato et al 1995, Furstenberg 1995, Marks 1995, Spitze et al 1994, but see Aquilino 1994), and are less likely to be involved in exchanges of emotional support (Umberson 1992). Similarly, compared to married parents, divorced parents report less contact with their adult children (Crimmins & Ingegneri 1990, Cooney & Uhlenberg 1990, Spitze

& Miner 1992, Umberson 1992, White 1992), tend to live further away from their children (White 1992), are less likely to be involved in exchanges of assistance (White 1992), and report more strain in their relationships with their children (Umberson 1992). Although some studies do not distinguish between parental divorces that occurred before and after the child attained adulthood (e.g. Crimmins & Ingegneri 1990, Lawton et al 1994a; Umberson 1992, White 1992), most attention has been focused on the impact of parents' divorce and remarriage during childhood for subsequent adult child–parent relations.

The effects of parents' divorce during childhood on subsequent adult child–parent contact vary by the gender and custodial status of the parent as well as by whether or not the parents remarried. NSFH data for adult children of all ages show that those who experienced their parents' divorce before age 19 had fewer visits, less contact by telephone and mail, and lower quality relationships than did those raised in intact families. The deficits in visits, contact, and relationship quality were particularly great for noncustodial parents (nearly all of whom were fathers), entailing approximately a 65% reduction in the frequency of visits, but the deficits were also significant for custodial parents (mostly mothers), for whom visits were lower by approximately 35%. Remarriage of the custodial parent was associated with a further deficit in the subsequent frequency of contact and relationship quality with the noncustodial parent, but tended to restore relations with the custodial parent. Further, the reduction in adult child–parent contact associated with living in a single-parent family, or living apart from a biological parent, was greater the longer the duration of that living arrangement (Lye et al 1995). These findings are consistent with those of Amato & Booth (1991) who used data from a national sample of married adults and found that, compared to adult children raised in intact families, adult children whose parents had divorced had lower contact with both mothers and fathers.

Studies of the impact of parents' divorce on adult child–parent relationships that have used samples of young adults also show negative effects of parental divorce on contact and relationship quality with fathers but show no effect of divorce on contact and relationship quality with custodial mothers (Aquilino 1994, Booth & Amato 1994). For example, among young adults interviewed in the NSFH, Aquilino (1994) found that adult children of divorce were no more likely to be in regular contact with their noncustodial fathers than adults who had never lived with their fathers, but that adult children of divorced custodial mothers, adult children of remarried mothers, and adult children of intact marriages all saw their mothers about equally often. Thus studies using samples of young adults suggest that parental divorce does not adversely affect relations with custodial mothers, whereas studies using samples of adults of all age suggest divorce has a lasting adverse effect on relations with custodial mothers.

One explanation for this discrepancy is that the effects of divorce on adult child–mother relationships might be less among younger adults who experienced their parents' divorce in a more recent historical period, when single mothers were subject to less stigma and, perhaps, less hardship. Unfortunately, however, it is not possible to test this hypothesis with cross-sectional survey data because the effects of the historical period of the divorce cannot be distinguished from the effects of the respondent's age. In addition, there are numerous variations in the analytic strategies and measures utilized to assess the impact of parents' divorce on adult child–mother relationships, most notably the measurement of childhood living arrangements, which might also account for the differences in the findings.

The adverse effects of parents' divorce on adult child–father relationship quality and contact may be greater for daughters than for sons, that is, noncustodial fathers may be more likely to maintain contact with sons than with daughters (Amato & Booth 1991, Booth & Amato 1994, Cooney 1994). However, studies using the NSFH do not find this pattern (Aquilino 1994, Lye et al 1995).

In addition to reporting lower-quality relationships and less frequent contact with their parents, adult children of divorce are also less likely than adult children of intact marriages to be involved in exchanges of financial and practical assistance with their parents. Using nationally representative data from the Panel Study of Income Dynamics, Furstenberg et al (1995), found that adult children of divorce were less likely to receive financial or practical help from their parents, and were less likely to provide practical help to their parents. For all three types of transfers the reduction in help was larger for transfers with fathers than for transfers with mothers. Analyses using other data sets generally confirm this pattern (Amato et al 1995, Eggebeen 1992, White 1992).

It appears from the preceding discussion that custody arrangements play a central role in adult child–parent relationships in divorced families. In later life adult children have frequent contact and high-quality relationships with custodial parents and infrequent contact and poor relationships with noncustodial parents. But what happens in the absence of a court-imposed custody arrangement? Cooney (1994) addresses this question by examining adult child–parent contact and affection in a regional sample of 18 to 23 year olds, half of whom had recently experienced their parents' divorce. Cooney finds no effect of parental divorce on contact or affection with mothers, but substantially lower contact and affectionate relations with fathers among the children of divorce. Cooney concludes that the low levels of postdivorce contact between fathers and children cannot be attributed solely to maternal custody.

Divorced fathers' reports of adult child–parent contact also indicate that divorce tends to weaken adult child–parent relations. NSFH data for men aged

50 to 79 reveal that whereas 90% of continuously married fathers had at least weekly contact with one of their children, only 50% of divorced fathers did so. Roughly one third of divorced fathers had effectively lost touch with one child, and one in ten divorced fathers had lost touch with all their children. Finally, divorced fathers were 30 to 45% less likely than married fathers to view their children as potential sources of emergency assistance (Cooney & Uhlenberg 1990).

Many divorced men express concern about loosing touch with their adult children and feel they no longer have a family (Hagestad 1986). However, the tenuous ties between divorced fathers and their adult children cannot be solely attributed to maternal custody, because limited evidence suggests that noncustodial mothers manage to sustain relationships with their children (Aquilino 1994, Cooney 1994, Hagestad 1986). The gender perspective proposed that men's contact with their children is mediated by their wives who serve as kin-keepers, and that when men separate from their wives the link between men and their children is disrupted or severed. It may be that, "men only know how to be fathers indirectly, through the actions of their wives" (Cherlin & Furstenberg 1991:118). Consistent with this hypothesis, the negative impact of parents' divorce on adult child–father relationship quality is greater for noncustodial fathers who do not remarry than for those who do remarry (Amato & Booth 1991, Lawton et al 1994b), perhaps because they have no wife to perform the functions of kinkeeper such as sending holiday and birthday gifts.

Adult Child's Divorce

Several authors have speculated that rising rates of divorce among adult children might tend to depress adult child–parent contact, relationship quality, and exchanges, particularly among adult daughters, due to increased conflict and strain between divorcing children and their parents, increased financial hardship and labor force participation among divorcing daughters, and the constraints on time and energy associated with single parenting (Cicirelli 1984, Hagestad 1986, Milardo 1987, Smyer & Hofland 1982). In contrast, others have argued that the impact of an adult child's divorce is likely to be temporary or very small (Rossi & Rossi 1990), or even positive, as divorcing children seek assistance for their parents (Johnson 1988a,b; Spitze et al 1994).

Studies that compare adult child–parent contact among divorced and married children yield contradictory results. Cicirelli (1984) finds lower contact with parents among divorced adult children than among married adult children, and Umberson (1992) finds that, compared to married adult children, divorced adult children receive less emotional support from their parents and report more strain in their relationships with their parents. In contrast, Spitze et al (1994) find that divorced adult daughters have more frequent contact with their parents than married adult daughters, no differences by marital status in adult sons' contact with parents, and no differences in adult child–parent closeness by child's marital status.

Similar to the findings concerning adult child–parent relations after parents' divorce, gender may be more important than marital status in determining adult children's exchange with their parents. Compared to married adult children, single mothers are more involved in exchange with their parents, and single fathers are less involved (Marks & McLanahan 1993). Divorced daughters receive more help than married daughters, especially if they have custody of grandchildren (Aldous 1987, Spitze et al 1994), but divorced sons receive and provide less help (Spitze et al 1994). Remarried adult children provide more help to their parents than first married adult children, but they are less likely to receive help (Spitze et al 1994). Overall, however, differences in adult child–parent exchange by adult child's marital status are small. Apparently, divorced children and single adult children with children do not pose a special burden for their parents (White & Peterson 1995), perhaps because mothers provide substantial assistance to adult children around the time of the divorce, but quickly become less involved as the initial crisis subsides (Johnson 1988b).

Other Differentials

The conventional picture of adult child–parent relations suggests closer relations when adult children have children (Aldous 1987, 1995). Evolutionary theory predicts that parents will provide more support to adult children who have children (Eggebeen & Hogan 1990). Research on patterns of exchange between adult children and parents supports the second but not the first prediction. Childcare is the most widely provided type of practical assistance (Cooney & Uhlenberg 1992, Eggebeen & Hogan 1990), and exchange is more common in adult child–parent dyads where there are grandchildren (Eggebeen & Hogan 1990). Grandmothers provide more help to their adult children the younger the grandchildren (Lawton et al 1994a). Childcare is also most often provided by women, and the positive effect of the presence of grandchildren on adult children's receipt of help appears largely to reflect help from mothers; help from fathers is unaffected by the presence or age of grandchildren (Rossi & Rossi 1990). National data suggests no effect of the presence of grandchildren on adult child–parent contact or quality (Umberson 1992, Lawton et al 1994b), although regional studies have found both negative (Rossi & Rossi 1990) and positive (Spitze et al 1994) effects of the number of grandchildren on adult child–parent contact.

Parents with more adult children tend to have higher overall contact with their children (Aldous & Klein 1991, Crimmins & Ingegneri 1990), but fewer per-child contacts (Aldous & Klein 1991, Rossi & Rossi 1990) and provide less help for their adult children (Eggebeen & Hogan 1990, Rossi & Rossi 1990). In addition, young adults with more siblings are less likely to receive help with college expenses (Steelman & Powell 1989, 1991). One interpretation of these findings is that parents divide a limited amount of time and resources among their adult children who compete for attention and support (Aldous & Klein 1991). However, contrary to the notion of competition among siblings, Spitze & Logan (1991a) found no effects of the number of siblings on adult child–parent relationship quality or exchanges of assistance and that the more parents visit and help one adult child, the more they visit and help the others. Spitze & Logan suggest that parents follow a norm of equal treatment in their dealings with adult children. Perhaps, too, the effect of number of siblings on adult child–parent relations varies with different types of support.

Widowhood does not appear to affect contact or relationship quality between adult children and the surviving parent (Anderson 1984, Umberson 1992), but widows are less likely to reciprocate practical assistance they receive (Bengtson et al 1990, Eggebeen 1992, Eggebeen & Hogan 1990, Ingersoll-Dayton & Antonucci 1988, Rossi & Rossi 1990; but see Mutran & Reitzes 1984). One study shows that daughters are less close to widowed fathers than to married fathers (Spitze & Logan 1991b), which is consistent with the argument advanced above that men interact with their children through their wives.

Adult children and parents who are in middle class occupations, are more highly educated, and have higher incomes are more likely to be involved in exchanges of emotional and instrumental support than are their working class, less well educated, or lower income counterparts (Hogan et al 1993, Goetting 1990, Kulis 1992, Lawton et al 1994a, Mutran & Reitzes 1984, Rossi & Rossi 1990). Socioeconomic status differentials are particularly marked for parents provision of financial assistance to young adult children for college expenses (Steelman & Powell 1989). These findings suggest that resource availability is a major determinant of adult child–parent exchange.

Contrary to fears that working women would have less time to spend with their aging parents (e.g. Shanas 1980), adult children's weekly work hours are not related to contact with parents, relationship quality, or helping (Matthews & Rosner 1988, Rossi & Rossi 1990, Spitze & Logan 1991b, Stroller 1983). One study found that adult sons and daughters working for pay are more likely to provide assistance to their parents (Lawton et al 1994a).

Finally, contrary to classical sociological theory, urbanism is associated with increased adult child–parent contact and is unrelated to the probability of identifying an adult child or parent as a potential source of emergency assistance (Wilson 1993). However, residence in the largest urban areas is negatively associated with adult child–parent contact (Crimmins & Ingegneri 1990).

NORMS AND EXPECTATIONS

In the contemporary United States, relationships between adult children and parents are framed by two apparently conflicting sets of norms: obligation and independence (Aldous 1995). On the one hand, norms of obligation mandate that adult children and parents should assist and care for each other over the life course. On the other hand, norms of independence mandate that adults should assume responsibility for their own well-being, that nuclear families should maintain themselves independently of wider kin networks, and that outsiders, including kin, should respect the privacy of nuclear families. Relations between adult children and their parents represent a delicate balancing of these two norms.

A number of researchers have suggested that in recent decades norms of obligation have weakened or become subject to considerable uncertainty, while norms of independence have strengthened. Today's young and middle-aged adults are the first generation to have, on average, more living parents than living children, which might increase uncertainty about obligations (Hagestad 1986, Preston 1984, Riley 1984). Increased living standards among the elderly and expanded public programs that transfer resources from the young to the old may have reduced adult children's feelings of obligation toward their parents while, at the same time, promoting greater independence from family support among elderly parents (Rossi & Rossi 1990, Preston 1984). Increased divorce and remarriage, and the consequent increase in complex family structures, may also have increased uncertainty among adult children and parents about their obligations to each other (Cherlin 1978, Riley 1984, Rossi & Rossi 1990). Finally, kin ties in general have become more discretionary, and parents of adult children have not been immune to this trend. Parents and grandparents choose whether and how to have relationships with their children and grandchildren, and they involve themselves in kinship networks on their own terms (Aldous 1987, Cherlin & Furstenberg 1986, Riley 1984, Shanas 1980). To the extent that norms of obligation persist, they are said to emphasize the obligation of the older generation to the younger generation (Rossi & Rossi 1990, Seelbach 1984).

Against this background of sociological speculation that feelings of obligation between adult children and their parents are weakening, data concerning attitudes toward intergenerational obligations are somewhat surprising. Close to three quarters of respondents in the NSFH either agreed or strongly agreed that adult children should provide financial assistance to their parents, and over half agreed that adult children should let their parents live with them. There was less agreement with the items concerning parental obligations: Slightly fewer than half the respondents agreed or strongly agreed that parents should provide financial assistance to their adult children, and only just over one third agreed or strongly agreed that parents should let adult children live with them. The strongest expression of support for parental obligations was that over two thirds agreed or strongly agreed that parents should pay for children's college education (author's own tabulations). Although data from other samples may not be directly comparable because of differences in question wording, researchers using other national and regional samples, as well as vignettes designed to elicit information about family obligations, have consistently found high levels of agreement with attitudes expressing adult children's obligations to their parents, and slightly lower but still high levels of agreement with attitudes expressing parents' obligations to their adult children (Antonucci 1990, Brody et al 1983, 1984, Finley et al 1988, Hanson et al 1983, Lawton et al 1994a, Rossi & Rossi 1990, Sauer et al 1981, Steelman & Powell 1991). In short, available data do not support the view that adult children and parents feel few obligations toward each other or are uncertain about their obligations.

These data should not be interpreted, however, as showing that the majority of adult children and parents feel unconditionally obliged to support each other. Rather, the nature of intergenerational obligations appears to be circumscribed in two important ways. First, there is much greater approval of reciprocal exchanges of support than of nonreciprocal transfers of support, particularly among older adults (Antonucci 1990, Brody et al 1983, Ingersoll-Dayton & Antonucci 1988, Kulis 1992). Second, there is much greater approval of support that does not compromise, or that even facilitates, the continuing independence of the recipient than there is of support that creates dependence in the recipient. Thus, there is greater agreement with attitudes expressing the obligations of adult children and parents to provide each other with companionship and emotional support than with attitudes expressing the obligation of adult children and parents to provide each other with financial and instrumental support (Blieszner & Hamon 1992, Brody et al 1984, Rossi & Rossi 1990, Seelbach 1984). Research reviewed above confirms that in many families exchanges of support are limited in exactly this way: Exchanges of emotional support and companionship are frequent; exchanges of practical assistance are rare. Further, when adult children do assist their parents they often act to maintain their parents' independence, for example, by helping parents secure publicly provided services or paid help and then monitoring the quality of that help, apparently following a "principle of least involvement" (Matthews & Rosner 1988, Seelbach 1984, Kulis 1992).

One of the most consistent findings from research assessing attitudes toward intergenerational obligations is that, compared to younger adults, older adults are less likely to agree that adult children should provide instrumental or financial assistance to their parents and are more likely to favor public programs for the elderly (Blieszner & Hamon 1992, Brody et al 1983, Hanson et al 1983,

Sauer et al 1981). In addition, older adults are more likely to agree that parents should provide assistance to their children (Lawton et al 1994a). For example, a recent study of a range of attitudes toward family obligations, found that older adults were consistently less likely than mid-life adults to endorse attitudes favoring greater provision of assistance to the elderly by their children, but were more likely to agree that the older adults should help their adult children. Unlike some earlier studies, the same study did not find that older adults were more likely to support public programs directed at the elderly (Logan & Spitze 1995). This pattern of findings suggests that self-interest among the elderly is outweighed by a desire to maintain independence and avoid becoming a burden to one's children, and also, perhaps, by a desire to direct resources toward children (Lawton et al 1994a, Logan & Spitze 1995). Taken together, available studies suggest that adult children and parents define their obligations to each other in a manner that is supportive of individual independence and that in this way norms of obligation are reconciled with norms of independence.

LINKAGES AMONG DOMAINS OF ADULT CHILD–PARENT RELATIONS

In the preceding review I have distinguished four different domains of adult child–parent relationships: contact and proximity, relationship quality, exchanges of assistance, and norms and expectations. Clearly these domains are interrelated; for example, some types of helping are not possible without contact. However, the linkages among domains of adult child–parent relationships are not straightforward, and there does not appear to be a single construct that represents all domains of adult child–parent relations (Bengtson & Roberts 1991). In addition, it is not possible to specify the causal direction of associations between different domains of adult child–parent relationships. Nevertheless some generalizations are possible.

According to Rossi & Rossi (1990), accessibility is the foundation of any significant interaction and exchange of help. Adult children and parents who live further apart are less likely to exchange assistance (Hogan et al 1983, Spitze & Logan 1991b), are less likely to be in regular contact (Aldous & Klein 1991, Dewit et al 1988), are less emotionally close (Aldous & Klein 1991), and feel weaker obligations toward each other (Finley et al 1988, Spitze & Logan 1991b). Similarly, regular contact between adult children and their parents is a key correlate of the exchange of assistance (Cicirelli 1983, Eggebeen & Hogan 1990, Hogan et al 1993, Leigh 1982). Adult children who endorse attitudes indicating filial responsibility toward parents have more frequent contact with their parents, higher quality relationships, and are more likely to provide assistance to their parents (Bengtson & Roberts 1991, Cicirelli 1983, Spitze & Logan 1991b).

Finally, adult children and parents who have warmer relationships are more likely to have frequent contact and exchange assistance (Bengtson & Roberts 1991, Lawton et al 1994b; Leigh 1982, Mutran & Reitzes 1984). However, affection between adult children and their parents is not a prerequisite for contact or exchanges of assistance (Aldous 1987, Walker & Thompson 1983).

DISCUSSION

In the contemporary United States, adult children and their parents enjoy frequent contact, are emotionally close to each other, provide each other with emotional support and advice, but do not routinely provide each other with practical or financial assistance. Parents with sufficient resources provide young adult children with financial support to help launch them into independent adulthood. Furthermore, most adults believe this is how relations between adult children and their parents ought to be. Relations between adult children and their parents depend, to a great extent, upon the kinkeeping activities of women and especially on the mother-daughter bond.

Recent changes in the family, and in particular the increase in divorce, appear to have marked consequences for adult–child parent relations. In particular, divorced fathers are less likely to be in contact with their children, are less likely to be emotionally close to their children, and are less likely to be involved in exchanges of assistance with their children. Divorced fathers may also be less likely to help launch their young adult children by helping with college expenses and a home purchase, although this question has not yet been the subject of detailed research.

In view of the findings described above, that most adult children provide little practical or financial assistance to their parents, the loss of support associated with divorce appears to be greater for adult children than for parents. However, many divorced fathers will enter old age with only tenuous connections to their families, and thus without access to the emotional support adult child–parent relationships can offer. The consequences for older divorced men of limited access to adult children is an important topic for future research.

The consequences of divorce for adult child–mother relationships appear to be less severe than the consequences for adult child–father relationships. However, the precise impact of divorce of adult child–mother relationships is not yet fully understood. Specifically, we need to know more about how divorce, and the attendant decline in resources available to mothers, affects transfers of support from mothers to their children, especially in young adulthood. We also know very little about the effects of remarriage on adult child–parent relations. To what extent do adult children form lasting relationships with stepparents, and to what extent do stepparents transfer resources to their adult children?

It appears that African-Americans are less likely than whites to be involved in adult child–parent exchanges of support. African-American kin networks may be more extensive than those of whites; that is, African-Americans may be more likely to exchange support with other kin, and by focusing on solely adult child–parent exchanges, we may understate the level of kin exchange in black families. However, the question of why blacks are less likely than whites to exchange resources with their families is deserving of further study. One possibility is that blacks have fewer resources to exchange. If this is the case, we would expect to see larger race differences for exchanges involving goods and money than for exchanges involving time or emotional support.

Overall, research on adult child–parent relations has yielded impressive results. Recent studies use high-quality data and are methodologically sophisticated. Further, most important findings have been replicated using widely differing samples and methods of analysis. We can be confident that our depiction of adult child–parent relations is broadly accurate. Yet our understanding of the bond between parents and children is primitive. We don't know why ties usually persist in the absence of any exchange of resources, and even sometimes with only occasional contact. We don't know why some ties are irretrievably broken while others endure. We don't know why members of some groups have closer ties to kin than members of other groups, or why certain characteristics seem to predispose some individuals to maintain stronger kin ties. In short, our descriptions are good, but our analyses have barely begun. Clearly the most pressing task for researchers interested in adult child–parent relations is the formulation of theoretical models to organize existing findings and guide new research.

ACKNOWLEDGMENTS

I thank Linda Stephens, Judy Howard, and Dan Klepinger for helpful comments, and Nancy Morrow and Hoa Cung for expert bibliographic assistance.

Literature Cited

Aldous J. 1987. New views on the family life of the elderly and near-elderly. *J. Marriage Fam.* 49:227–34

Aldous J. 1995. New views of grandparents in intergenerational context. *J. Fam. Issues* 16:104–22

Aldous J, Klein DM. 1991. Sentiment and services: models of intergenerational relationships in mid-life. *J. Marriage Fam.* 55:595–608

Amato PR, Booth A. 1991. Consequences of parental divorce and marital unhappiness for adult well-being. *Soc. Forces* 69:895–914

Amato PR, Rezac SJ, Booth AJ. 1995. Helping between adult parents and young adult offspring: the role of parental marital quality, divorce and remarriage. *J. Marriage Fam.* 57:363–74

Anderson TB. 1984. Widowhood as a life transition: its impact on kinship ties. *J. Marriage Fam.* 46:105–14

Antonucci TC. 1990. Social supports and social relationships. See Binstock & George 1990, pp. 205–26

Antonucci TC, Akiyama H. 1987. Social networks in adult life and a preliminary examination of the convoy model. *J. Gerontol.* 42:519–27

Aquilino WS. 1994. Impact of childhood family disruption on young adults' relationships with parents. *J. Marriage Fam.* 56:295–313

Becker GS. 1981. *A Treatise on the Family.* Cambridge: Harvard

Bengtson VL, Roberts REL. 1991. Intergenerational solidarity in aging families: an example of formal theory construction. *J. Marriage Fam.* 53:856–70

Bengtson V, Rosenthal C, Burton L. 1990. Families and aging: diversity and heterogeneity. See Binstock & George 1990, pp. 263–87

Benin M, Keith VM. 1995. The social support of employed African-American and Anglo mothers. *J. Fam. Issues* 16:275–97

Bernheim BD, Shleifer A, Summers LH. 1985. The strategic bequest motive. *J. Polit. Econ.* 93:1045–76

Beutel AM, Marini MM. 1995. Gender and values. *Am. Sociol. Rev.* 60:436–48

Binstock RH, George LK, eds. 1990. *Handbook of Aging and the Social Sciences.* New York: Academic. 3rd ed.

Blieszner RR, Hamon RR. 1992. Filial responsibility: attitudes, motivators, and behaviors. In *Gender, Families and Elder Care*, ed. JW Dwyer, RT Coward, pp. 105–19. Newbury Park, CA: Sage

Booth A, Amato PR. 1994. Parental marital quality, parental divorce and relations with parents. *J. Marriage Fam.* 56:21–34

Brody EM, Johnsen PT, Fulcomer MC. 1984. What should adult children do for elderly parents? Opinions and preferences of three generations of women. *J. Gerontol.* 39:736–46

Brody EM, Johnsen PT, Fulcomer MC, Lang AM. 1983. Women's changing roles and help to elderly parents: attitudes of three generations of women. *J. Gerontol.* 38:597–607

Brubaker TH. 1990. Families in later life: a burgeoning research area. *J. Marriage Fam.* 52:959–81

Bumpass LL. 1990. What's happening to the family? Interactions between demographic and institutional change. *Demography* 27:483–98

Burgess E, Locke H. 1945. *The Family: From Institution to Companionship.* New York: American

Chatters LM, Taylor RJ. 1993. Intergenerational support: the provision of assistance to parents by adult children. In *Aging in Black America*, ed. JS Jackson, LM Chatters, RJ Taylor, pp. 69–83. Newbury Park, CA: Sage

Cherlin AJ. 1978. Remarriage as an incomplete institution. *Am. J. Sociol.* 84:634–50

Cherlin AJ. 1992. *Marriage Divorce Remarriage.* Cambridge: Harvard. 2nd ed.

Cherlin AJ, Furstenberg FF. 1986. *The New American Grandparent.* New York: Basic Books

Cicirelli V. 1983. Adult children's attachment and helping behavior to elderly parents: a path model. *J. Marriage Fam.* 45:815–26

Cicirelli V. 1984. Adult children's helping behavior to elderly parents: the influence of divorce. *J. Fam. Issues* 5:419–40

Cooney TM. 1994. Young adults' relations with parents: the influence of recent parental divorce. *J. Marriage Fam.* 56:45–56

Cooney TM, Uhlenberg P. 1990. The role of divorce in men's relations with their adult children after mid-life. *J. Marriage Fam.* 52:677–88

Cooney TM, Uhlenberg P. 1992. Support from parents over the life course: the adult child's perspective. *Soc. Forces* 71:63–84

Crimmins EM, Ingegneri DG. 1990. Interaction and living arrangements of older parents and their children. *Res. Aging* 12:3–35

Dewit DJ, Wister AV, Burch TK. 1988. Physical distance and social contact between elders and their adult children. *Res. Aging* 10:56–80

Dietz TL. 1995. Patterns of intergenerational assistance within the Mexican-American family: Is the family taking care of the older generation's needs? *J. Fam. Issues* 16:344–56

Eggebeen DJ. 1992. Family structure and intergenerational exchanges. *Res. Aging* 14:427–47

Eggebeen DJ, Hogan DP. 1990. Giving between generations in American families. *Hum. Nat.* 1:211–32

Finley NJ, Roberts MD, Banahan BF. 1988. Motivators and inhibitors of attitudes of filial obligation toward aging parents. *Gerontologist* 28:73–78

Furstenberg FF, Cherlin AJ. 1991. *Divided Families: What Happens to Children When Parents Part.* Cambridge: Harvard

Furstenberg FF, Hoffman SD, Shrestha L. 1995. The effect of divorce on intergenerational transfers: new evidence. *Demography* 32:319–33

Goetting A. 1990. Patterns of support among in-laws in the United States. *J. Fam. Issues* 11:67–90

Goldscheider FK. 1990. The aging of the gender revolution: What do we know and what do we need to know? *Res. Aging* 12:531–45

Goldscheider FK, Goldscheider C. 1991. The intergenerational flow of income: family structure and the status of Black Americans. *J. Marriage Fam.* 53:499–508

Hagestad GO. 1986. The family: women and grandparents as kinkeepers. In *Our Aging Society*, ed. A. Pifer, L. Bronte, pp. 141–60. New York: Norton

Hanson SL, Sauer WJ, Seelbach WC. 1983. Racial and cohort variations in filial responsibility norms. *Gerontologist* 23:626–31

Hareven T. 1994. Aging and generational relations: a historical and life course perspective. *Annu. Rev. Sociol.* 20:437–61

Hayes WC, Mindel CH. 1973. Extended kinship relations in Black and White families. *J. Marriage Fam.* 35:51–57

Hogan DP, Eggebeen DJ. 1995. Sources of emergency help and routine assistance in old age. *Soc. Forces* 73:917–36

Hogan DP, Eggebeen DJ, Clogg CC. 1993. The structure of intergenerational exchanges in American families. *Am. J. Sociol.* 98:1428–58

Hogan DP, Hao L, Parish WL. 1990. Race, kin networks, and assistance to mother headed families. *Soc. Forces* 68:797–812

Houser BB, Berkman SL. 1984. Aging parent/mature child relationships. *J. Marriage Fam.* 46:295–99

Ingersoll-Dayton B, Antonucci TC. 1988. Reciprocal and nonreciprocal sides of intimate relationships. *J. Gerontol.* 43:S65–73

Jayakody R, Chatters LM, Taylor RJ. 1993. Family support to single and married African American mothers: the provision of financial, emotional and child care assistance. *J. Marriage Fam.* 55:261–76

Johnson CL. 1988a. Postdivorce reorganization of relationships between divorcing children and their parents. *J. Marriage Fam.* 50:221–31

Johnson CL. 1988b. Active and latent functions of grandparenting during the divorce process. *Gerontologist* 28:185–91

Kulis SS. 1992. Social class and the locus of reciprocity in relationships with adult children. *J. Fam. Issues* 13:482–504

Lawton L, Silverstein M, Bengtson VL. 1994a. Solidarity between generations in families. In *Intergenerational Linkages: Hidden Connections in American Society*, ed. VL Bengtson, RA Harootyan, pp. 19–42. New York: Springer

Lawton L, Silverstein M, Bengtson VL. 1994b. Affection, social contact and geographic distance between adult children and their parents. *J. Marriage Fam.* 56:57–68

Leigh GK. 1982. Kinship interaction over the family life span. *J. Marriage Fam.* 44:197–208

Levitt MJ, Guacci N, Weber A. 1992. Intergenerational support, relationship quality and well-being: a bicultural analysis. *J. Fam. Issues* 13:465–81

Logan JR, Spitze GD. 1995. Self-interest and altruism in intergenerational relations. *Demography* 32:353–64

Lye DN, Klepinger D. 1995. *Race, Hispanic ethnicity, childhood living arrangements and adult child–parent relations.* Presented at Annu. Meet. Popul. Assoc. Am., San Francisco

Lye DN, Klepinger D, Hyle PD, Nelson A. 1995. Childhood living arrangements and adult children's relations with their parents. *Demography* 32:261–80

Mancini JA, ed. 1989. *Aging Parents and Adult Children.* Lexington, MA: Lexington

Mancini J, Blieszner R. 1989. Aging parents and adult children: research themes in intergenerational relations. *J. Marriage Fam.* 51:275–90

Markides KS, Boldt JS, Ray LA. 1986. Sources of helping and intergenerational solidarity: a three-generations study of Mexican Americans. *J. Gerontol.* 41:506–11

Markides KS, Liang J, Jackson JS. 1990. Race, ethnicity and aging: conceptual and methodological issues. See Binstock & George 1990, pp. 112–29

Marks NF. 1995. Midlife marital status differences in social support relationships with adult children and psychological well-being. *J. Fam. Issues* 16:5–28

Marks NF, McLanahan SS. 1993. Gender, family structure and social support among parents. *J. Marriage Fam.* 55:481–93

Martin JM, Martin EP. 1978. *The Helping Tradition in the Black Family.* Chicago: Univ. Chicago

Matthews SH, Rosner TT. 1988. Shared filial responsibility: the family as the primary caregiver. *J. Marriage Fam.* 50:185–95

McAdoo HP. 1978. Factors related to stability in upwardly mobile Black families. *J. Marriage Fam.* 40:761–76

Milardo RM. 1987. Changes in social networks of women and men following divorce. *J. Fam. Issues* 8:78–96

Mutran E. 1985. Intergenerational family support among blacks and whites: response to culture or to socioeconomic differences. *J. Gerontol.* 40:832–89

Mutran E, Reitzes DC. 1984. Intergenerational support activities and well-being among the elderly. *Am. Sociol. Rev.* 49:117–30

Parish WL, Hao L, Hogan DP. 1991. Family support networks, welfare and work among young mothers. *J. Marriage Fam.* 53:203–15

Parsons T. 1943. The kinship system of the contemporary United States. *Am. Anthropol.* 45:22–38

Preston SH. 1984. Children and the elderly: divergent paths for America's dependents. *Demography* 21:435–57

Raley RK. 1995. Black-white differences in kin contact and exchange among never married adults. *J. Fam. Issues* 16:77–103

Riley MW. 1983. The family in an aging society: a matrix of latent relationships. *J. Fam. Issues* 4:439–54

Rosenthal CJ. 1985. Kinkeeping in the familial division of labor. *J. Marriage Fam.* 47:965–74

Rossi AS, Rossi PH. 1990. *Of Human Bonding: Parent-Child Relations across the Life Course.* New York: Aldine

Sauer WJ, Seelbach WC, Hanson SL. 1981. Rural-urban and cohort differences in filial responsibility norms. *J. Minority Aging* 5:299–305

Seelbach WC. 1984. Filial responsibility and the care of aging family members. In *Independent Aging: Family and Social Systems Perspectives*, ed. WH Quinn, GA Hughston, pp. 92–105. Rockville, MD: Aspen

Seltzer JA. 1994. Consequences of marital dissolution for children. *Annu. Rev. Sociol.* 20:235–66

Shanas E. 1980. Old people and their families: the new pioneers. *J. Marriage Fam.* 42:9–15

Silverstein M, Parrott TM, Bengtson VL. 1995. Factors that predispose middle-aged sons and daughters to provide social support to older parents. *J. Marriage Fam.* 57:465–75

Smyer MA, Hofland BF. 1982. Divorce and family support in later life: emerging concerns. *J. Fam. Issues* 3:61–77

Spitze G, Logan JR. 1989. Gender differences in family support: Is there a payoff? *Gerontologist* 29:108–13

Spitze G, Logan JR. 1990. Sons, daughters and intergenerational social support. *J. Marriage Fam.* 52:420–30

Spitze G, Logan JR. 1991a. Sibling structure and intergenerational relations. *J. Marriage Fam.* 53:871–84

Spitze G, Logan JR. 1991b. Employment and filial relations: Is there a conflict? *Sociol.*

Forum 6:681–97

Spitze G, Logan JR, Deane G, Zerger S. 1994. Adult children's divorce and intergenerational relationships. *J. Marriage Fam.* 56:279–93

Spitze G, Miner S. 1992. Gender differences in adult child contact among Black elderly parents. *Gerontologist* 32:213–18

Stack CB. 1974. *All Our Kin.* New York: Harper & Row

Steelman LC, Powell B. 1989. Acquiring capital for college: the constraints of family configuration. *Am. Sociol. Rev.* 54:844–55

Steelman LC, Powell B. 1991. Sponsoring the next generation: parental willingness to pay for higher education. *Am. J. Sociol.* 96:1505–29

Streib GF, Beck RW. 1980. Older families: a decade review. *J. Marriage Fam.* 42:937–56

Stroller EP. 1983. Parental care giving by adult children. *J. Marriage Fam.* 45:851–58

Thompson L, Walker AJ. 1984. Mothers and daughters: aid patterns and attachment. *J. Marriage Fam.* 46:313–22

Troll LE. 1971. The family of later life: a decade review. *J. Marriage Fam.* 33:263–90

Umberson D. 1992. Relationships between adult children and their parents: psychological consequences for both generations. *J. Marriage Fam.* 54:664–74

Walker AJ, Thompson L. 1983. Intimacy and intergenerational aid and contact among mothers and daughters. *J. Marriage Fam.* 45:841–49

Weeks J, Cuellar J. 1981. The role of family members in the helping networks of older people. *Gerontologist* 21:388–94

White L. 1992. The effect of parental divorce and remarriage on parental support for adult children. *J. Fam. Issues* 13:234–50

White L. 1994. Coresidence and leaving home: young adults and their parents. *Annu. Rev. Sociol.* 20:81–102

White L, Peterson D. 1995. The retreat from marriage: its effect on unmarried children's exchange with parents. *J. Marriage Fam.* 57:428–34

White LK, Brinkerhoff DB, Booth A. 1985. The effect of marital disruption on child's attachment to parents. *J. Fam. Issues* 6:5–23

Wilson TC. 1993. Urbanism and kinship bonds: a test of four generalizations. *Soc. Forces* 71:703–12

Annu. Rev. Sociol. 1996. 22:103–28

MASS MEDIA EFFECTS ON VIOLENT BEHAVIOR

Richard B. Felson

Department of Sociology, State University of New York at Albany, Albany, New York 12222

KEY WORDS: violence, aggression, exposure to television violence, media violence

ABSTRACT

The literature on the effect of exposure to media violence (including exposure to violent pornography) on aggressive behavior is critically reviewed. Evidence and theoretical arguments regarding short-term and long-term effects are discussed. Three points are emphasized: 1. Exposure to violence in laboratory and field experiments is as likely to affect nonaggressive antisocial behavior as it does aggressive behavior. The pattern is consistent with a sponsor effect rather than a modeling effect: an experimenter who shows violent films creates a permissive atmosphere; 2. the message that is learned from the media about when it is legitimate to use violence is not much different from the message learned from other sources, with the exception that illegitimate violence is more likely to be punished in media presentations; 3. the fact that violent criminals tend to be versatile—they commit nonviolent crimes as well—is inconsistent with explanations that emphasize proviolence socialization (from the media or other sources). I conclude that exposure to television violence probably does have a small effect on violent behavior for some viewers, possibly because the media directs viewer's attention to novel forms of violent behavior that they would not otherwise consider.

INTRODUCTION

Watching violence is a popular form of entertainment. A crowd of onlookers enjoys a street fight just as the Romans enjoyed the gladiators. Wrestling is a popular spectator sport not only in the United States, but in many countries in the Middle East. People enjoy combat between animals, e.g, cock fights in Indonesia, bull fights in Spain, and dog fights in rural areas of this country. Violence is frequently depicted in folklore, fairy tales, and other literature. Local news shows provide extensive coverage of violent crimes in order to increase their ratings.

103

0360-0572/96/0815-0103$08.00

Technological advances have dramatically increased the availability of violent entertainment. The introduction of television was critical, particularly in making violent entertainment more available to children. More recently, cable systems, videocassette recorders, and video games have increased exposure. Hand-held cameras and video monitors now permit filming of actual crimes in progress. Economic competition for viewers, particularly young viewers, has placed a premium on media depictions of violence.

Not long after the introduction of television in American households, there occurred a dramatic increase in violent crime (Centerwall 1989). Some scholars and commentators see a causal connection. The most common argument is that children imitate the violence they see on television. The process of imitation is emphasized by social learning theory—a well-established approach in social psychology (Bandura 1983). For both practical and theoretical reasons, then, an interest developed in examining whether exposure to violence in the media affects the incidence of violence.

Violence usually refers to physical aggression. Aggression is usually defined as any behavior involving an intent to harm another person. Some studies of media effects, however, examine behaviors that do not involve an intent to harm. For example, a common procedure is to see whether children will hit a "Bobo" doll after observing an adult model do so or after being exposed to media violence. It seems unlikely that hitting a Bobo doll involves an intent to do harm (Tedeschi et al 1974). Other studies include measures of nonviolent criminal behavior, most of which do not involve an intent to do harm. Of course, it depends on what is meant by intent, a term most researchers do not define. Tedeschi & Felson (1994) define an intent to do harm as a behavior in which the actor expects the target will be harmed and values that harm.[1] Offenders who commit larceny and other nonviolent crimes know that the victim will be harmed, but in most cases they do not value that harm; harm is not their goal.

In the first section of this review, I discuss the empirical evidence regarding whether media violence has a causal effect on the aggressive behavior of viewers. I review the classic studies, the meta-analyses, and some more recent research. In the second section I examine the theoretical processes that might explain short-term effects, should they exist, and discuss relevant evidence. I do the same for long-term effects in the third section.[2]

---

[1] An alternative definition is that intentional harm involves deliberate harm or expected harm. However, teachers sometimes give low grades with the expectation that it will make their students unhappy, but their behavior should not be defined as aggressive, unless they also value that harm. Tedeschi & Felson (1994) substitute the term coercion for aggression and include coercive actions in which the actor values compliance as well as harm.

[2] This chapter borrows from Tedeschi & Felson (1994).

EMPIRICAL EVIDENCE REGARDING MEDIA EFFECTS ON AGGRESSION

The relationship between exposure to media violence and aggression has been examined using laboratory experiments, field experiments, natural experiments, and longitudinal analyses based on correlational data. I review some of the key research in each of these domains.

Laboratory Experiments

Laboratory experiments examine short-term effects of media violence. Most studies show that subjects in laboratory experiments who observe media violence tend to behave more aggressively than do subjects in control groups. A meta-analysis of these studies reveals consistent and substantial media effects (Andison 1977). However, research is inconsistent in showing whether it is necessary to provoke subjects before showing violence to get an effect (Freedman 1984). Thus, it is not clear whether media exposure acts as instigator of aggression in the laboratory or merely as a facilitator.

Researchers have raised questions about the external validity of laboratory experiments in this area (Freedman 1984, Cook et al 1983). They point out that the laboratory situation is very different from situations leading to violence outside the laboratory (e.g. Tedeschi & Felson 1994). For subjects to engage in aggressive behavior in the laboratory, the behavior must be legitimated. Subjects are told, for example, that the delivery of shocks is a teaching method or a part of a game. Subjects are then subjected to an attack by a confederate and given a chance to retaliate. Unlike aggressive behavior outside the laboratory, there is no possibility that this will be punished by third parties or subject them to retaliation from the target. It is unknown to what extent these differences limit the generalizability of experimental studies. Evidence suggests that aggression measures in many laboratory studies do involve an intent to harm (Berkowitz & Donnerstein 1982). Experimental subjects may not be so different from those who engage in violence outside the laboratory, who see their behavior as legitimate and who do not consider its costs.[3]

The demand cues in these studies are probably a more significant problem. Demand cues are instructions or other stimuli that indicate to subjects how the

---

[3] According to Freedman (1984), effects outside the laboratory are likely to be weaker than laboratory effects because violent programs are mixed with other types of programs. Friedrich-Cofer & Huston (1986) dispute this point, arguing that experimental research underestimates media effects. They claim that the stimuli used in experimental research are brief and often less violent than typical television programs and that the presence of experimenters inhibits subjects from engaging in aggressive behavior in laboratory settings.

experimenter expects them to behave.[4] Experimenters who show violent films are likely to communicate a message about their attitudes toward aggression. A violent film may imply to subjects that the experimenter is a permissive adult or someone not particularly offended by violence. Just a few subjects aware of the demand and compliant could account for the mean differences in aggression found between experimental conditions.

The laboratory is a setting that exaggerates the effects of conformity and social influence (see Gottfredson & Hirschi 1993). The extent of compliance in laboratory settings is dramatically demonstrated in Milgram's (1974) well-known research on obedient aggression. Subjects' behavior is easily influenced for at least three reasons: (*a*) The standards for behavior are unclear and the situation is novel (Nemeth 1970); (*b*) subjects are influenced by the prestige of the experimenter and the scientific enterprise; (*c*) subjects want to avoid being perceived as psychologically maladjusted by the psychologist-experimenter (Rosenberg 1969).

Field Experiments

Concerns about external validity have stimulated researchers to employ field experiments. Field experiments retain the advantages of experimental design but avoid the problem of demand cues since subjects do not usually know they are being studied. A number of such studies have been carried out in institutionalized settings (Feshbach & Singer 1971, Leyens et al 1975, Parke et al 1977). In these studies, boys are exposed to either violent or nonviolent programming, and their aggressive behavior is observed in the following days or weeks. Each of the studies has some important methodological limitations (see Freedman 1984). For example, although the boys in each treatment lived together, the studies used statistical procedures that assumed that each boy's behavior was independent. Even if one overlooks the limitations, the results from these studies are inconsistent. In fact, one of the studies found that the boys who watched violent television programs were less aggressive than the boys who viewed nonviolent shows (Feshbach & Singer 1971).

The results of field experiments have been examined in at least three meta-analyses. Hearold's (1986) meta-analysis of a broad range of experimental studies revealed an effect for laboratory experiments but no effect for field experiments. A meta-analysis that included more recent studies, however, did find an effect for field experiments (Paik & Comstock 1994). Finally, Wood et al's meta-analysis (1991) was restricted to field studies of media violence

---

[4]Any cue that indicates which direction the experimenter prefers would be a demand cue. In their strongest form demand cues give away the experimenter's hypothesis to subjects, who then compliantly act to confirm the hypothesis. In their weaker form, demand cues simply guide behavior without creating awareness of the hypothesis.

on unconstrained social interaction.[5] In all of these studies children or adolescents were observed unobtrusively after being exposed to an aggressive or nonaggressive film. In 16 studies subjects engaged in more aggression following exposure to violent films, while in 7 studies subjects in the control group engaged in more aggression. In 5 of the studies there was no difference between control and experimental groups.

Natural Experiments: The Introduction of Television

These studies take advantage of the fact that television was introduced at different times in different locations. They assume that people who are exposed to television will also be exposed to a high dose of television violence. This is probably a reasonable assumption given the extremely high correlation between television viewing and exposure to television violence (Milavsky et al 1982).

Hennigan et al (1982) compared crime rates in American cities that already had television with those that did not. No effect of the presence or absence of television was found on violent crime rates in a comparison of the two kinds of cities. Furthermore, when cities without television obtained it, there was no increase in violent crime. There was an increase in the incidence of larceny, which the authors attributed to relative deprivation suffered by viewers observing affluent people on television.[6]

Joy et al (1986) examined changes in the aggressive behavior of children after television was introduced into an isolated Canadian town in the 1970s. The town was compared to two supposedly comparable towns that already had television. Forty-five children in the three towns were observed on the school playground in first and second grade and then again two years later. The frequency of both verbal and physical aggression increased in all three communities, but the increase was significantly greater in the community in which television was introduced during the study. Some of the results were not consistent with a television effect, however. In the first phase of the study, the children in the community without television were just as aggressive as the children in the communities that already had television. Without television they should have been less aggressive. The children in the community where television was introduced then became more aggressive than the children in the other communities in the second phase, when all three communities had television. At this point, the level of aggressive behavior in the three communities should have been similar. To accept the findings, one must assume that the community without television at the beginning of the study had more

---

[5]Some of the studies were in laboratory settings, but subjects did not know that their aggressive behavior was being observed as part of the study.

[6]The hypothesis that consumerism, promoted by advertising and the depiction of wealth on television, leads to more financially motivated crime has never been tested, to my knowledge.

aggressive children than the other communities for other reasons, but that this effect was counteracted in the first phase by the fact that they were not exposed to television. That assumption implies that there are other differences between the communities and thus casts doubt on the findings of the study.

Centerwall (1989) examined the relationship between homicide rates and the introduction of television in three countries: South Africa, Canada, and the United States. Television was introduced in South Africa in 1975, about 25 years after Canada and the United States. The white homicide rate increased dramatically in the United States and Canada about 15 years after the introduction of television, when the first generation of children who had access to television were entering adulthood. The white homicide rate declined slightly in South Africa during this time period. While Centerwall ruled out some confounding factors (e.g. differences in economic development), causal inference is difficult, given the many differences between the countries involved. In addition, Centerwall could not determine at the time he wrote whether the level of violence had increased 15 years after the introduction of television in South Africa; thus an important piece of evidence was missing.

Centerwall also examined the effect of the introduction of television in the United States. He found that urban areas acquired television before rural areas, and their homicide rates increased earlier. However, social changes in general are likely to occur in urban areas before they occur in rural areas. He also found that households of whites acquired television sets before households of blacks, and their homicide rates increased earlier as well. It is difficult to imagine an alternative explanation of this effect.

Still, the methodological limitations of these studies make it difficult to have confidence in a causal inference about media effects. The substantial differences between the comparison groups increase the risk that the relationship between the introduction of television and increases in aggression is spurious.

Natural Experiments: Publicized Violence

The effects of highly publicized violent events on fluctuations in homicide and suicide rates over time have been examined in a series of studies (see Phillips 1986 for a review). Phillips (1983) found an increase in the number of homicides after highly publicized heavyweight championship fights. Modeling effects were only observed when the losing fighter and the crime victims were similar in race and sex. The loss of prize fights by white fighters was followed by increases in deaths through homicide of white males on days 2 and 8. The loss of prize fights by blacks was followed by an increase in homicide deaths for black males on days 4 and 5. The rise in the homicide rate was not canceled out by a subsequent drop, suggesting that the prize fights affected the incidence and not just the timing of homicides.

Baron & Reiss (1985) attribute these effects to the fact that prize fights tend to occur during the week and homicides are more likely to occur on weekends. They were able to replicate Phillips' findings selecting weeks without prizefights and pretending that they had occurred. In response to this critique, Phillips & Bollen (1985) selected different weeks and showed that the weekend effect could not account for all of the findings. Miller et al (1991) replicated some of Phillips' results, but found that the effect only occurred on Saturdays following highly publicized fights.

Freedman (1984) has criticized Phillips' research on other methodological grounds, and Phillips (1986) has addressed these criticisms. There are still unresolved questions such as why effects tended to occur on different days for different races. In addition, experimental results suggest that watching boxing films does not affect the viewer's aggressive behavior. Geen (1978) found that, when provoked, college students were more aggressive after viewing vengeful aggression but not after viewing a boxing match (see also Hoyt 1970).

Longitudinal Surveys

Survey research demonstrates that the correlation between the amount of exposure to television violence and frequency of aggressive behavior generally varies between .10 and .20 (Freedman 1984, see Paik & Comstock 1994 for slightly higher estimates). There are good reasons to think the relationship is at least partly spurious. For example, children with favorable attitudes toward violence may be more likely to engage in violence and also more likely to find violence entertaining to watch. Also, children who are more closely supervised may be less likely to engage in violence and less likely to watch television. Intelligence, need for excitement, level of fear, and commitment to school are other possible confounding variables. Wiegman et al (1992) found that intelligence was negatively associated with both exposure to violence and aggressive behavior.

Longitudinal data has been used to examine whether viewing television violence produces changes in aggressive behavior. These studies statistically control for aggression at T1 in order to isolate causal effects on aggression at T2. Spuriousness is still possible if some third variable is associated with exposure to media violence and changes in aggressive behavior over time.

The main longitudinal evidence for a causal link between viewing violence and aggressive behavior has been provided by Eron, Huesmann, and their associates (Eron et al 1972, Huesmann & Eron 1986). In the first study, they examined the effect of children's exposure to television violence at age eight on aggressive behavior at age eighteen. A measure of viewing television violence at Time 1 was obtained by asking parents the names of their children's favorite television shows. These shows were coded for the level of violence depicted.

Aggressive behavior at Time 2 was measured by ratings of aggressiveness by peers, self-reports, and the aggression subscale on the MMPI.[7] Effects of television violence were found only for boys and only on the peer nomination measure.

In addition to the inconsistent results, there are some measurement problems in this study (see Surgeon General's Report on Television Violence 1972, Freedman 1984). First, the aggression measure included items referring to antisocial behavior that do not involve aggression. Second, the measure of television exposure is based on parents' beliefs about the favorite programs of their children. Later research found that parental reports of their children's favorite programs are not strongly correlated to children's self-reports of total exposure (Milavsky et al 1982).

Three-year longitudinal studies of primary school children were later carried out in five countries: Australia, Israel, Poland, Finland, and the United States (Huesmann & Eron 1986). Aggression was measured by the same peer nomination measure as the one used in the earlier research. The children were asked to name one or two of their favorite programs and to indicate how often they watched them. Complex and inconsistent results were obtained. In the United States, television violence had a significant effect on the later aggressiveness of females but not males, a reversal of the effect found in their first study (Huesmann & Eron 1986). An effect of the violence of favorite programs on later aggression was found only for boys who rated themselves as similar to violent and nonviolent television characters. A similar conditional effect was found for males in Finland, but there was no effect of viewing television violence on later aggressiveness of females (Lagerspetz & Viemero 1986). In Poland a direct effect of violence in favorite programs was found on later aggressiveness for both males and females (Fraczek 1986). No effect of early viewing of television violence was found on subsequent aggressiveness for either males or females in Australia (Sheehan 1986), or among children living in a Kibbutz in Israel (Bachrach 1986). A television effect was found for city children in Israel when the measure of aggression was a single item asking "who never fights." But the effect did not occur on the same peer nomination measure that had been used in the other cross-national studies.

Negative evidence was obtained in a large-scale, methodologically sophisticated, longitudinal study carried out by Milavsky et al (1982). Their study was based on data collected from 3200 students in elementary and junior high schools in Fort Worth and Minneapolis. Students identified the programs they

---

[7]An important requirement of such studies is that they control for the aggressiveness of the viewer at the earlier time period, when looking at the effect of earlier exposure on later aggression. Eron & Huesmann do so in later reanalyses of their data.

had watched in the last four weeks and indicated how many times they had watched them; these were coded for violent content.[8] The authors refined the peer nomination measure of aggression used by Eron et al to include intentional acts of harm-doing, but not general misbehavior.

There was no evidence that any of the measures of exposure to television violence produced changes in aggressive behavior over time. The authors corrected for measurement error and used a variety of time lags, subsamples, and measures of exposure to television violence and aggressive behavior. In spite of a thorough exploration of the data, they found no evidence that exposure to violence on television affected the aggressive behavior of children. While the coefficients in most of the analyses were positive, they were all close to zero and statistically insignificant. The abundance of positive correlations led some critics to reject Milavsky et al's conclusion of no effect (e.g. Friedrich-Cofer & Huston 1986).

A more recent longitudinal study in the Netherlands also failed to find a media effect (Wiegman et al 1992). The children were surveyed in either the second or fourth grade and then again two years later. Peer nominations were used as a measure of aggressive behavior. The lagged effect of exposure on aggressive behavior was small and statistically insignificant.

It is difficult to reach a conclusion on the long-term effects of viewing television violence from these longitudinal studies. The studies that used better measurement failed to find an effect. In the studies where an effect was found, the relationship was between favorite show violence and subsequent aggression, rather than the amount of exposure to television violence, and Milavsky, et al did not replicate that effect. The findings reported in the cross-national studies were inconsistent and had as many negative findings as positive ones. Therefore one must conclude that longitudinal studies have not demonstrated a relationship between the amount of violence viewed on television and subsequent aggressive behavior.[9]

THEORETICAL EXPLANATIONS OF SITUATIONAL EFFECTS

The experimental results described above show that exposure to media violence can have at least a short-term effect on aggressive behavior. In this section, I

[8] Also included were parental reports of a child's favorite programs, and self-reports of children of their favorite programs. These measures of exposure to television violence were poor indicators of overall exposure.

[9] Valkenburg et al (1992) found that violent programming increased the level of aggressive-heroic fantasies found in a longitudinal analyses among Dutch children. However, nonviolent dramatic programming had the same effect.

consider theoretical reasons for expecting situational effects. I also review some of the evidence regarding these theoretical mechanisms.

Cognitive Priming

According to a cognitive priming approach, the aggressive ideas in violent films can activate other aggressive thoughts in viewers through their association in memory pathways (Berkowitz 1984). When one thought is activated, other thoughts that are strongly connected are also activated. Immediately after a violent film, the viewer is primed to respond aggressively because a network of memories involving aggression is retrieved. Evidence indicates that media violence does elicit thoughts and emotional responses related to aggression (Bushman & Geen 1990).

Huesmann (1982) makes a similar argument. He suggests that children learn problem-solving scripts in part from their observations of others' behavior. These scripts are cognitive expectations about a sequence of behaviors that may be performed in particular situations. Frequent exposure to scenes of violence may lead children to store scripts for aggressive behavior in their memories, and these may be recalled in a later situation if any aspect of the original situation—even a superficial one—is present.

The classic studies of these effects involve the exposure of subjects to the fight scene from a film, *The Champion*, starring Kirk Douglas. In one of these studies subjects were either shocked frequently or infrequently by a confederate, witnessed the fight scene, or viewed a neutral film, and then had an opportunity to shock the confederate, whose name was either Bob or Kirk (Berkowitz & Geen 1966). Subjects gave the confederate the most shocks in the condition when they had been provoked, had viewed the violent film, and the confederate had the same name as the film's star.

Tedeschi & Norman (1985) attribute the results from these studies to demand cues (see also Tedeschi & Felson 1994). They point out that experimenters mention the fact that the confederate's first name is the same as Kirk Douglas' in their instructions, and that they justify to subjects the beating that Kirk Douglas received. A series of studies have shown that it is necessary to provide this justification to get a violent film effect (Geen & Berkowitz 1967, Berkowitz 1965, Berkowitz et al 1962, Berkowitz & Rawlings 1963, Meyer 1972b).

Josephson (1987) examined the combined effects of exposure to a violent film and retrieval cues in a field experiment with second and third grade boys. The boys were exposed to either a violent film—in which a walkie-talkie was used—or a nonviolent film. The boys were also frustrated either before or after the film. Later they were interviewed by someone holding either a walkie-talkie or a microphone. After the interview, the boys played a game of field hockey and their aggressive behavior was recorded. It was predicted that boys who were exposed to both violent television and a walkie-talkie would be most aggressive in the game, since the walkie-talkie would lead them to retrieve scripts associated with the violent film. The hypothesis was confirmed for boys who were, according to teacher ratings, aggressive. Boys who were identified as nonaggressive inhibited their aggression when exposed to the walkie-talkie and the film. Josephson suggested that for these nonaggressive boys, aggression may be strongly associated with negative emotions such as guilt and fear which, when primed, may inhibit aggression. If we accept this post-hoc interpretation, it suggests that media violence may increase or inhibit the violent behavior of viewers depending on their initial predisposition. Such effects are likely to be short-term, and they may have no effect on the overall rate of violence.

Arousal from Pornography

According to Bandura (1973), emotional arousal facilitates and intensifies aggressive behavior. The facilitating effect of emotional arousal occurs only when the individual is already prone to act aggressively. If the individual is predisposed to behave in some other way, then emotional arousal will facilitate that behavior. Arousal energizes any behavior that is dominant in the situation.

Zillmann (1983) explains the facilitative effects of arousal in terms of excitation transfer. He has proposed that arousal from two different sources may combine with one another and be attributable to the same source. When the combined arousal is attributed to anger, the individual is likely to be more aggressive than would have been the case if only the anger-producing cue has been present.

Some research has examined whether the arousal produced by pornography facilitates aggressive behavior. A series of experiments have been carried out in which subjects are exposed to sexual stimuli and then allowed to aggress against another person, who may or may not have provoked them. The prediction is that arousal produced by pornography should increase aggression when a subject has been provoked. The message communicated by pornography and the gender of actor and target should not matter unless they affect the level of arousal.

Experiments that have examined the effects of arousal from pornography have produced mixed results. Some studies have found that erotic films increased the aggressiveness of subjects who had been provoked by the victim, while others have shown that pornography has an inhibitory effect (Zillman 1971, Meyer 1972a, Zillmann et al 1974, Baron & Bell 1973, 1977, Donnerstein et al 1975).

Researchers have developed hypotheses to provide explanations for the conditions under which opposite effects are obtained (Baron 1974, White 1979). Zillmann et al (1981) explained the contradictory findings using an arousal-affect hypothesis. They proposed that arousal has both an excitation component and an affective component. If arousal is accompanied by negative affect, it should add to the arousal produced by anger, and increase the level of aggression. If arousal is accompanied by positive affect, it should subtract from the arousal produced by anger, and decrease the level of aggression. The findings from research on the arousal-affect hypothesis are inconclusive (see Sapolski 1984, Tedeschi & Felson 1994 for reviews).

Even if these results are real, their significance for pornography effects outside the experimental lab seems trivial. They suggest, for example, that a man enjoying a pornographic film is less dangerous when provoked, while a man who dislikes the film, but is still aroused by it, is more likely to retaliate for a provocation. Perhaps the findings have more implications for the effects of arousal from other sources. For example, it is possible that arousal from the car chase in the Rodney King incident contributed to the violent behavior of the police.

It is difficult to manipulate arousal in the laboratory without also affecting the meanings subjects give to those manipulations (Neiss 1988). Experimenters who show pornographic films communicate information about their values and expectations and thus create demand cues. I discuss this issue in the next section.

Sponsor Effects

Demand cues provide a general explanation of short-term media effects in the experimental laboratory. Wood et al (1991) suggest that demand cues may be a type of "sponsor effect" that occurs outside the experimental laboratory as well:

> Viewers are likely to believe that the violent presentation is condoned by the media sponsor, whether it be an experimenter, one's family, the television networks or movie studios, or society in general.... Sponsor effects are not artifacts of laboratory procedures; they also occur in field settings (Wood 1991:373).

Wood et al's (1991) concept of sponsor effects appears to include both social learning and situational conformity. Social learning involves socialization and enduring effects on the viewer. Viewers may be more likely to internalize a media message if they think it is sponsored by someone they respect. A sponsor effect would enhance whatever message is being conveyed.

Field and laboratory experiments seem more likely to produce sponsor effects involving situational conformity. By showing a violent film, sponsors may communicate that they are not very strict or that they have a permissive attitude toward aggressive behavior. Young people, who are normally inhibited in front of adults, may engage in aggressive behavior if they think that they can get away with it. For example, students often misbehave when they encounter less experienced substitute teachers. According to this line of thinking, young people who are exposed to media violence should feel disinhibited and should be more likely to misbehave in a variety of ways, at least while adults are present. When the sponsors of the film are no longer present, the effects should disappear.

Meta-analyses show that exposure to violence is related to nonaggressive forms of antisocial behavior. Hearold (1986) performed a meta-analysis of experiments that included studies of effects of exposure to media violence on antisocial behavior generally. The effects of media violence on antisocial behavior were just as strong as the effects of media violence on violent behavior. A more recent meta-analysis that focused on all types of studies yielded similar results (Paik & Comstock 1994).

A study performed by Friedrich & Stein (1973) provides an example of an experiment showing general effects of exposure to media violence on antisocial behaviors. They found that nursery school children exposed to violent cartoons displayed more aggression during free play than children exposed to neutral films. However, they also found that children exposed to violence had lower tolerance for minor delays, lower task persistence, and displayed less spontaneous obedience in regard to school rules. These behaviors clearly do not involve an intent to harm.

Additional evidence for a sponsor effect comes from a study by Leyens et al (1975). They found that subjects delivered more shock to another person when they anticipated that the experimenter would show them violent films; it was not necessary for them to actually see the films. The investigators attributed this effect to priming, based on the assumption that the mere mention of violent films primes aggressive thoughts. It seems just as likely that sponsor effects were involved: an experimenter who is willing to show a violent film is perceived as more permissive or more tolerant of aggression.

The effects of exposure to television violence on antisocial behavior generally cast doubt on many of the theoretical explanations usually used to explain media effects on violence. Explanations involving cognitive priming or arousal cannot explain why those who view violence should engage in deviant behavior generally. Explanations that stress modeling (to be discussed) cannot explain this pattern of effects either. It is possible, however, that viewers imitate the low self-control behaviors of the characters they observe in television and films, rather than violence specifically. Children model the self-control behavior of adults in experimental situations (Bandura & Walters 1963), but it is not clear whether socialization or short-term situational effects are involved.

Sponsor effects may also explain the results of experimental studies involving exposure to pornography. Paik & Comstock's (1994) meta-analysis shows effects of both pornography and violent pornography on antisocial behavior in general. Experimenters who show pornography, especially violent pornography, may imply that they condone or at least are tolerant of taboo behavior (Reiss 1986). Subjects may be disinhibited in this permissive atmosphere and engage in more antisocial behavior.

In sum, these studies suggest that subjects may assume a more permissive atmosphere when they are shown a violent film, and their inhibitions about misbehavior generally are reduced. It is not yet clear whether their behavior reflects short-term conformity or longer-term socialization. Research is needed to determine whether subjects who view violent films in experiments engage in more aggression and other misbehavior in the absence of sponsors.

Television Viewing as a Routine Activity

According to the routine activity approach, crime should be less frequent when the routine activities of potential offenders and victims reduce their opportunities for contact (e.g. M Felson 1986). Any activity that separates those who are prone to violence from each other, or from potential victims, is likely to decrease the incidence of violence.

Messner uses this approach to argue that watching television can decrease the incidence of violence in society (Messner 1986, Messner & Blau 1987). Since people watch television at home, the opportunities for violence, at least with people outside the family, are probably reduced. When people watch television, they may also interact less often with other family members, so the opportunities for domestic violence may also be reduced. Messner found that cities with high levels of television viewing have lower rates of both violent and nonviolent crime (Messner 1986, Messner & Blau 1987). However, in an aggregate analysis of this type, one cannot determine the specific viewing habits of offenders or victims of criminal violence.[10]

The routine activities of young adult males are particularly important since they are most prone to use violence. Young adult males do not spend as much time as other groups watching television (Dimmick et al 1979). According to the routine activity approach, their level of violence would be lower if they did.

THEORETICAL EXPLANATIONS INVOLVING SOCIALIZATION

It is widely believed that people are more violent because they learn to be violent from their parents, their peers, and the mass media. These socialization effects

[10]Viewing violent television and viewing television are so highly correlated across cites that it does not matter which measure is used in analysis. The notion of catharsis provides an alternative explanation, but it cannot explain the negative relationship between exposure to television violence and the incidence of nonviolent crime.

tend to endure since they involve changes in the individual. The evidence on the versatility of criminal offenders casts doubt on the importance of this socialization process. Considerable evidence suggests that those who commit violent crime tend to commit nonviolent crime and other deviant acts as well. Studies of arrest histories based on both official records and self-reports show a low level of specialization in violent crime. For example, West & Farrington (1977) found that 80% of adults convicted of violence also had convictions for crimes involving dishonesty. Violent acts were also related to noncriminal forms of deviant behavior, such as sexual promiscuity, smoking, heavy drinking, gambling, and having an unstable job history.

The evidence that most offenders are versatile challenges the notion that violent offenders are more violent because of a special proclivity to engage in violence, due to exposure to media violence or any other factor. Individual differences in the propensity to engage in criminal violence reflect for the most part individual differences in antisocial behavior generally. Variations in the socialization of self-control and other inhibitory factors are probably important causal factors (Gottfredson & Hirschi 1990). Theories that emphasize specific socialization to violence are likely to be limited in their utility, since most violent offenders are generalists.

The versatility argument should not be overstated. Some people do specialize in violence, and exposure to media violence may play a role in their socialization. There are a variety of reasons one might expect viewers to learn aggressive behavior from the media. First, media depictions of violence may suggest novel behaviors to viewers that they otherwise might not have considered. Second, vicarious reinforcements and legitimation of violent actions may increase the tendency to model media violence. Third, viewers become desensitized about violence after a heavy diet of it on television. Finally, people may get a false idea of reality from observing a great deal of violence on television and develop unrealistic fears. I now examine each of the processes more closely.

Learning Novel Forms of Behavior

Bandura (1983) has argued that television can shape the forms that aggressive behavior takes. Television can teach skills that may be useful for committing acts of violence, and it can direct the viewer's attention to behaviors that they may not have considered. For example, young people may mimic karate and judo moves, or they may learn effective tactics for committing violent crime. This information may give direction to those who are already motivated to engage in aggression. Such a modeling process could lead to more severe forms of aggression. It could increase the frequency of violence if people who are motivated to harm someone choose a violent method they have observed on television.

There is anecdotal evidence that bizarre violent events have followed soon after their depiction on television, suggesting a form of copycat behavior. In one widely reported case in Boston, six young men set fire to a woman after forcing her to douse herself with fuel. The scene had been depicted on television two nights before. In another instance, four teenagers raped a nine-year-old girl with a beer bottle, enacting a scene similar to one in the made-for-TV movie *Born Innocent.* Such incidents may be coincidental, but they suggest the possibility that unusual and dramatic behaviors on television are imitated by viewers who might never otherwise have imagined engaging in such behaviors.

Modeling can also be used to explain contagion effects observed for highly publicized violence, such as airline hijackings, civil disorders, bombings, and political kidnaping. The tendency for such events to occur in waves suggests that at least some viewers imitate real events that are reported on television. However, the central argument about the relationship of viewing violence on television and viewers' aggressive behavior focuses on fictional events.

Vicarious Reinforcement and Legitimations

Bandura (1983) also suggested that television may inform viewers of the positive and negative consequences of violent behavior. Audiences can be expected to imitate violent behavior that is successful in gaining the model's objectives in fictional or nonfictional programs. When violence is justified or left unpunished on television, the viewer's guilt or concern about consequences is reduced. Thus Paik & Comstock's (1994) meta-analysis found that the magnitude of media effects on antisocial behavior was greater when the violent actor was rewarded or the behavior was legitimated.

It is not at all clear what message is learned from viewing violence on television. In most plots, the protagonist uses violence for legitimate ends while the villain engages in illegitimate violence. The protagonist usually uses violence in self-defense or to mete out an appropriate level of punishment to a dangerous or threatening criminal. Television conveys the message that while some forms of violence are necessary and legitimate, criminal violence is evil.

The consequences of the illegitimate violence portrayed in fictional television and film are more negative than the consequences of illegitimate violence in real life. In real life violent people often evade punishment, while in television, the villain is almost always punished. Thus, one could argue that television violence might reduce the incidence of criminal violence, since crime doesn't pay for TV criminals. Another difference is in the appeal of those who engage in illegitimate violence. In fictional television, those who engage in illegitimate violence tend to lack any attractive qualities that would lead to sympathy or identification. In real life, illegitimate violence may be committed by loved ones or others who are perceived to have desirable qualities.

Other factors may limit the effects of any message about the legitimacy, or the rewards and costs of violence. First, the lessons learned from the media about violence may be similar or redundant to the lessons learned about the use of violence conveyed by other sources. In fact, most viewers probably approve of the violent behavior of the protagonists. The influence of television on viewers who already agree with its message would be weak at best. Second, the audience may not take the message from fictional plots seriously. Modeling is more likely to occur after viewing nonfiction than after viewing fiction (Feshbach 1972, Berkowitz & Alioto 1973).[11] Third, the violent contexts and provocations observed on television are likely to be very different from the contexts and provocations people experience in their own lives. Evidence suggests that viewers take context and intentions into account before they model aggressive behavior (Geen 1978, Hoyt 1970). Straus (Baron & Straus 1987), on the other hand, suggests that people are likely to be influenced by the violence they observe regardless of its context, message, or legitimacy. According to cultural spillover theory, violence in one sphere of life leads to violence in other spheres.

Finally, some young children may miss the more subtle aspects of television messages, focusing on overt acts rather than on the intentions or contexts in which such acts occur. Collins et al (1984) found that kindergarten and second grade children were relatively unaffected by an aggressor's motives in their understanding of a violent program. They focused more on the aggressiveness of the behavior and its ultimate consequences. However, even if young children imitate the violence of models, it is not at all clear that they will continue to exhibit violence as they get older. When they are older, and they pay attention to the intentions and context in violent television, their behavior is more likely to reflect the messages they learn. It is also at these later ages that violent behavior, if it should occur, is likely to be dangerous.

Creating Unrealistic Fear

Bandura (1983) claims that television distorts knowledge about the dangers and threats present in the real world. The notion that television viewing fosters a distrust of others and a misconception of the world as dangerous has been referred to as the "cultivation effect" (Gerbner & Gross 1976). Research shows that heavy television viewers are more distrustful of others and overestimate their chances of being criminally victimized (see Ogles 1987 and Gunter 1994 for reviews).[12] The assumption is that these fears will lead viewers to perceive

---

[11]In Paik & Comstock's (1994) meta-analyses the strongest effects were observed for cartoon programs. However, the subjects in these studies were children, and children may be more easily influenced.

[12]There is some evidence that the relationship is spurious; see Gunter's (1994) review.

threats that do not exist and to respond aggressively. It is just as plausible that such fears would lead viewers to avoid aggressive behavior against others, if they feel it is dangerous, and might lead to victimization. Persons who fear crime may also be less likely to go out at night or go to places where they may be victimized. If viewing television violence increases fear, it might decrease the level of violence.

Desensitization

Frequent viewing of television violence may cause viewers to be less anxious and sensitive about violence. Someone who becomes desensitized to violence may be more likely to engage in violence. This argument assumes that anxiety about violence inhibits its use.

Desensitization has been examined indirectly using measures of arousal. Research shows that subjects who view violent films are less aroused by violence later on (Thomas et al 1977; see Rule & Ferguson 1986 for a review). In addition, heavy viewers of television violence tend to respond less emotionally to violence than do light viewers.

There is no evidence that desensitization produces lower levels of violent behavior.[13] Nor is it clear what effect should occur. Studies of desensitization measure arousal not anxiety, and arousal can facilitate violent behavior, according to the literature cited earlier (e.g. Zillmann 1983). If viewers are exposed to a heavy diet of television violence, one might argue that they will be less aroused by violence and therefore less likely to engage in violence. In addition, if viewers become desensitized to violent behavior on television, they may become indifferent to its message. Desensitization could thereby weaken the effect of a heavy diet of television violence.

Messages from Pornography

The discussion of situational effects of pornography on aggression focused on arousal as a mediating variable. Feminists have argued that pornography has special effects on violence against women because of the message it communicates (Dworkin 1981, MacKinnon 1984). Exposure to pornography supposedly leads to negative attitudes toward women which, in turn, affects the likelihood of rape and other forms of violence against women. It is argued, for example, that pornography leads male viewers to think of women as sex objects or as promiscuous (Linz & Malamuth 1993). Furthermore, some erotica portrays scenes of rape and sadomasochism. In such fictional forms the female victim may express pleasure during and after being raped, suggesting that women enjoy such treatment. Males who view such films may be induced to believe that

---

[13]Emergency room personnel may become desensitized to the consequences of violent behavior, but there is no evidence that they are more violent than other groups of people.

forceful sexual acts are desired by women. In addition, unlike illegitimate violence not associated with sex, violence in pornographic films rarely has negative consequences for the actor (Palys 1986, Smith 1976).

Evidence does not support the hypothesis that exposure to nonviolent pornography leads to violence toward women. Most experimental studies show no difference in aggression toward women between subjects exposed to pornographic films and control groups (for reviews, see Donnerstein 1984, Linz & Malamuth 1993). Research outside the laboratory has not demonstrated that exposure to pornography and violence toward women are even correlated, much less causally related. There is evidence that rapists report less exposure to pornography than controls, not more (see Linz & Malamuth 1993 for a review). Studies of the relationship between exposure to pornography and use of sexual coercion among college students yields mixed results (Demare et al 1993, Boeringer 1994).

Research using aggregate data has also failed to demonstrate a relationship between exposure to pornography and violence against women. Studies of the effect of changes in restrictions on pornography on rape rates show inconsistent results. States in which sex-oriented magazines are popular tend to have high rape rates (Baron & Straus 1987). However, it is questionable whether the state is a meaningful unit of analysis, given the heterogeneity within states. Gentry (1991) found no relationship between rape rates and circulation of sexually oriented magazines across metropolitan areas.

Effects of violent pornography have been reported in laboratory experiments, at least under certain conditions (see Linz & Malamuth 1993 for a review). Some studies show that an effect is obtained only if the sexual assault has positive consequences. In this case, subjects are told that the woman became a willing participant in the coercive sexual activities, and she is shown smiling and on friendly terms with the man afterwards (Donnerstein 1980). However, in a more recent study, exposure to a rape scene with positive consequences did not increase subjects' aggression toward women (Fisher & Grenier 1994).

The effects of exposure to violence with positive consequences have been examined in a field experiment. College students were exposed either to two films that showed women responding positively to men who had attacked them or to two neutral films (Malamuth & Check 1981). Subjects completed a survey that they thought was unrelated to the films several days later. Males who had viewed the violent films showed greater acceptance of violence against women. Note that these films did not involve pornography. Pornographic films in which the victim of sexual aggression is perceived as experiencing a positive outcome are quite rare (Garcia & Milano 1990).

The experimental evidence is mixed concerning whether pornography or violent pornography affects male attitudes toward women, according to Linz's (1989) review of the literature. Evidence that men who have negative attitudes toward women are more likely to engage in violence against women is also inconsistent. Some studies find that men who engage in sexual coercion have different attitudes toward women and rape than do other men, while other studies do not (Kanin 1969, Malamuth 1986, Ageton 1983, Rapapport & Burkhart 1984). It may be that sexually aggressive men are more likely to have antisocial attitudes generally. Thus, convicted rapists are similar to males convicted of other offenses in their attitudes toward women and women's rights (e.g. Howells & Wright 1978) and in their belief in rape myths (Hall et al 1986).

The literature on violence and attitudes toward women is plagued by conceptual and measurement problems. Measures of belief in rape myths are problematic (Tedeschi & Felson 1994). In addition, traditional attitudes about gender roles do not necessarily involve negative attitudes toward women and may be negatively associated with violence toward women and exposure to pornography. Thus, rape rates are twice as high at private colleges and major universities than at religiously affiliated institutions (Koss et al 1987). Males who report greater exposure to pornography have more (not less) liberal attitudes toward gender roles (Reiss 1986). Finally, even if a correlation between certain attitudes regarding women and violence could be established, the causal interpretation would be unclear. For example, it may be that men express certain beliefs to justify coercive behavior already performed (Koss et al 1985).

One limitation on the impact of pornography or any media effect is selective exposure (McGuire 1986). Media effects are likely to be limited to the extent that viewers choose programming that already reflects their values and interests. The argument in regard to media violence is that violence is so pervasive on television that all viewers, including impressionable children, are exposed. In the case of pornography, particularly violent pornography, there is much more selective exposure, since those interested in viewing this material must make a special effort to do so. In addition, the viewers of pornography are usually adults, not children.

Pornography provides fantasies for masturbation. Viewers may select material depicting activities that they already fantasize about. When they substitute commercially produced fantasies for their own fantasies, the content is not necessarily more violent. Palys (1986) found that less than 10% of scenes in pornography videos involved some form of aggression. A study of college students revealed that approximately 39% of men and women reported that they had fantasized about forced sex (Loren & Weeks 1986).

The versatility evidence is also relevant to the literature on pornography and rape. Most rapists do not specialize in rape nor in violent crime (Alder 1984, Kruttschnitt 1989). Therefore, theories that emphasize socialization of rape-supportive attitudes, whether learned from the media or elsewhere, are going to have limited utility for understanding individual differences in the proclivity to rape.

In summary, some experimental research suggests that violent pornography that depicts women enjoying the event can lead male subjects to engage in violence against women in the laboratory. The effect of these films appears to be similar to the effects of violent films without a sexual theme. Demand cues provide an alternative explanation of these results as well (see Reiss 1986). The external validity of these studies is questionable given the rarity of these themes in pornography, and given selective exposure.

SUMMARY AND CONCLUSIONS

The inconsistencies of the findings make it difficult to draw firm conclusions about the effects of exposure to media violence on aggressive behavior. Most scholars who have reviewed research in the area believe that there is an effect (Friedrich-Cofer & Huston 1986, Centerwall 1989). Other scholars have concluded that the causal effects of exposure to television have not been demonstrated (Freedman 1984, McGuire 1989).

Given the pervasiveness of media violence, it would be surprising if it had no effect on viewers. I agree with those scholars who think that exposure to television violence probably does have a small effect on violent behavior (Cook et al 1983). The reason that media effects are not consistently observed is probably because they are weak and affect only a small percentage of viewers. These weak effects may still have practical importance since, in a large population, they would produce some death and injuries. However, it seems unlikely that media violence is a significant factor in high crime rates in this country. Changes in violent crimes mirror changes in crime rates generally. In addition, the people who engage in criminal violence also commit other types of crime. An explanation that attributes violent behavior to socialization that encourages violence cannot easily explain the versatility of most violent criminals.

It seems likely that some people would be more susceptible to media influence than others. Therefore it is puzzling that research has not shown any consistent statistical interactions involving individual difference factors and media exposure. The failure to find individual difference factors that condition the effects of media exposure on aggressive behavior contributes to skepticism about media effects.

It seems reasonable to believe that the media directs viewers' attention to novel forms of violent behavior they might not otherwise consider. The anecdotal evidence is convincing in this area. There appear to be documented cases in which bizarre events on television are followed by similar events in the real world; the similarities seem too great to be coincidental. In addition, hijackings and political violence tend to occur in waves. Many parents have observed their children mimicking behaviors they've observed in films. Whether this process leads to a greater frequency of violence is unclear.

There is some evidence that the effects observed in laboratory experiments, and less consistently in field experiments, are due to sponsor effects. The fact that children who are exposed to violence tend to misbehave generally casts doubt on most of the other theoretical explanations of media effects. The issue has particular significance for laboratory research, where subjects know they are being studied and may be responding to demand cues. Research is needed in which sponsor effects are isolated and controlled. A field experiment in which subjects imitate violent behavior they have observed in the absence of the sponsor, but do not misbehave otherwise, would be convincing. Alternatively, there may need to be further development of the theoretical argument that self-control behavior is modelled.

It is not clear what lesson the media teaches about the legitimacy of violence, or the likelihood of punishment. To some extent that message is redundant with lessons learned from other sources of influence. The message is probably ambiguous and is likely to have different effects on different viewers. Young children may imitate illegitimate violence, if they do not understand the message, but their imitative behavior may have trivial consequences. Out of millions of viewers, there must be some with highly idiosyncratic interpretations of television content who intertwine the fantasy with their own lives, and as a result have an increased probability of engaging in violent behavior.

Literature Cited

Ageton S. 1983. *Sexual Assault Among Adolescents.* Lexington, MA: Lexington

Alder C. 1984. The convicted rapist: a sexual or a violent offender? *Crim. Justice Behav.* 11:157–77

Andison FS. 1977. TV violence and viewer aggression: a cumulation of study results: 1956–1976. *Public Opin. Q.* 41:314–31

Bachrach RS. 1986. The differential effect of

observation of violence on kibbutz and city children in Israel. In *Television and the Aggressive Child: A Cross-National Comparison,* ed. LR Huesmann, LD Eron, pp. 201–38. Hillsdale, NJ: Erlbaum

Bandura A. 1973. *Aggression: A Social Learning Analysis.* Englewood Cliffs, NJ: Prentice-Hall

Bandura A. 1983. Psychological mechanisms of

aggression. In *Aggression: Theoretical and Empirical Reviews,* ed. RG Geen, EI Donnerstein, 1:1–40. New York: Academic

Bandura A, Walters RH. 1963. *Social Learning and Personality Development.* New York: Holt, Rinehart & Winston

Baron JN, Reiss PC. 1985. Same time next year: aggregate analyses of the mass media and violent behvaior. *Am. Sociol. Rev.* 50:347–63

Baron L, Straus MA. 1987. Four theories of rape: a macrosocial analysis. *Soc. Probl.* 34:467–89

Baron RA. 1974. The aggression-inhibiting influence of heightened sexual arousal. *J. Pers. Soc. Psychol.* 30:318–22

Baron RA, Bell PA. 1973. Effects of heightened sexual arousal on physical aggression. *Proc. 81st Annu. Conv. Am. Psychol. Assoc.* 8:171–72

Baron RA, Bell PA. 1977. Sexual arousal and aggression by males: effects of type of erotic stimuli and prior provocation. *J. Pers. Soc. Psychol.* 35:79–87

Berkowitz L. 1965. Some aspects of observed aggression. *J. Pers. Soc. Psychol.* 2:359–69

Berkowitz L. 1984. Some effects of thought on anti- and pro-social influences of media effects. *Psychol. Bull.* 95:410–27

Berkowitz L, Alioto JT. 1973. The meaning of an observed event as a determinant of its aggressive consequences *J. Pers. Soc. Psychol.* 28:206–17

Berkowitz L, Corwin R, Heironimus M. 1962. Film violence and subsequent aggressive tendencies. *Public Opin. Q.* 27:217–29

Berkowitz L, Donnerstein E. 1982. External validity is more than skin deep: some answers to criticism of laboratory experiments. *Am. Psychol.* 37:245–57

Berkowitz L, Geen RG. 1966. Film violence and the cue properties of available targets. *J. Pers. Soc. Psychol.* 3:525–30

Berkowitz L, Rawlings E. 1963. Effects of film violence: an inhibition against subsequent aggression. *J. Abnorm. Soc. Psychol.* 66:405–12

Boeringer S. 1994. Pornography and sexual aggression: associations of violent and nonviolent depictions with rape and rape proclivity. *Deviant Behav.* 15:289–304

Bushman BJ, Geen RG. 1990. Role of cognitive-emotional mediators and individual differences in the effects of media violence on aggression. *J. Pers. Soc. Psychol.* 58:156–63

Centerwall BS. 1989. Exposure to television as a cause of violence. In *Public Communication and Behavior,* ed. G. Comstock, 2:1–58. Orlando: Academic

Collins WA, Berndt TJ, Hess VL. 1984. Observational learning of motives and consequences for television aggression: a developmental study. *Child Dev.* 45:799–802

Cook TD, Kendzierski DA, Thomas SV. 1983. The implicit assumptions of television: an analysis of the 1982 NIMH Report on Television and Behavior. *Public Opin. Q.* 47:161–201

Demare D, Lips HM, Briere J. 1993. Sexually violent pornography, anti-women attitudes, and sexual aggression: a structural equation model. *J. Res. Pers.* 27:285–300

Dimmick JW, McCain TA, Bolton WT. 1979. Media use and the life span. *Am. Behav. Scientist* 23:7–31

Donnerstein E. 1980. Aggressive erotica and violence against women. *J. Pers. Soc. Psychol.* 39:269–77

Donnerstein E. 1984. Pornography: its effect on violence against women. In *Pornography and Sexual Aggression,* ed. NM Malamuth, E Donnerstein, pp. 53–81. New York: Academic

Donnerstein E, Donnerstein M, Evans R. 1975. Erotic stimuli and aggression: facilitation or inhibition. *J. Pers. Soc. Psychol.* 32:237–44

Dworkin A. 1981. *Pornography: Men Possessing Women.* New York: GP Putnam's Sons

Eron LD, Huesmann LR, Lefkowitz MM, Walder LO. 1972. Does television violence cause aggression? *Am. Psychol.* 27:253–63

Felson M. 1986. Routine activities, social controls, rational decisions and criminal outcomes. In *The Reasoning Criminal: Rational Choice Perspectives on Offending,* ed. D Cornish, R Clarke. New York: Springer-Verlag

Feshbach S. 1972. Reality and fantasy in filmed violence. In *Television and Social Behavior,* ed. JP Murray, E Rubinstein, GA Comstock, pp. 318–45. Vol. 2: *Television and Social Learning.* Washington DC: US Govt. Printing Off.

Feshbach S, Singer R. 1971. *Television and Aggression.* San Francisco: Jossey Bass

Fisher WA, Grenier G. 1994. Violent pornography, antiwoman thoughts, and antiwoman acts: in search of reliable effects. *J. Sex Res.* 31:23–38

Fraczek A. 1986. Socio-cultural environment, television viewing, and the development of aggression among children in Poland. In *Television and the Aggressive Child: A Cross-National Comparison,* ed. LR Huesmann, LD Eron, pp. 119–60. Hillsdale, NJ: Erlbaum

Freedman JL. 1984. Effects of television violence on aggressiveness. *Psychol. Bull.* 96:227–46

Friedrich LK, Stein AH. 1973. Aggressive and prosocial television programs and the natural behavior of preschool children. *Monogr. Soc. for Res. in Child Dev., 38 4, Serial No. 151*

Friedrich-Cofer L, Huston AC. 1986. Television violence and aggression: the debate continues. *Psychol. Bull.* 100:364–71

Garcia LT, Milano L. 1990. A content analysis of erotic videos. *J. Law Psychiatry* 14:47–64

Geen RG. 1978. Some effects of observing violence upon the behavior of the observer. In *Progress in Experimental Personality Research,* Vol. 8, ed. B Maher. New York: Academic

Geen RG. 1983. Aggression and television violence. In *Aggression: Theoretical and Empirical Reviews,* ed. RG Geen, EI Donnerstein, 2:103–25. New York: Academic

Geen RG, Berkowitz L. 1967. Some conditions facilitating the occurrence of aggression after the observation of violence. *J. Pers.* 35:666–76

Gentry CS. 1991. Pornography and rape: an empirical analysis. *Deviant Behav.* 12:277–88

Gerbner G, Gross L. 1976. Living with television: the violence profile. *J. Commun.* 26:173–99

Gottfredson M, Hirschi T. 1990. *A General Theory of Crime.* Stanford: Stanford Univ. Press

Gottfredson M, Hirschi T. 1993. A control theory interpretation of psychological research on aggression. In *Aggression and Violence: Social Interactionist Perspectives,* ed. RB Felson, JT Tedeschi, pp. 47–68. Washington, DC: Am. Psychol. Assoc.

Gunter B. 1994. The question of media violence. In *Media Effects: Advances in Theory and Research,* ed. J. Bryant, D. Zillman, pp. 163–212. Hillsdale: Lawrence Erlbaum

Hall ER, Howard JA, Boezio SL. 1986. Tolerance of rape: a sexist or antisocial attitude. *Psychol. Women Q.* 10:101–18

Hearold S. 1986. A synthesis of 1043 effects of television on social behavior. In *Public Communication and Behavior,* ed. G. Comstock, 1:65–133. San Diego, CA: Academic

Hennigan KM, Del Rosario ML, Heath L, Cook TD, Wharton JD, Calder BJ. 1982. The impact of the introduction of television on crime in the United States. *J. Pers. Soc. Psychol.* 42:461–77

Howells K, Wright E. 1978. The sexual attitudes of aggressive sexual offenders. *Br. J. Crimnol.* 18:170–73

Hoyt JL. 1970. Effect of media violence 'justification' on aggression. *J. Broadcast.* 14:455–64

Huesmann LR. 1982. Television violence and aggressive behavior. In *Television and Behavior: Ten Years of Scientific Progress and Implications for the Eighties,* Vol. 2. *Technical Reviews,* ed. D Pearl, L Bouthilet, J Lazar eds, pp. 220–56. Washington, DC: Natl. Inst. Mental Health

Huesmann LR, Eron LD. 1986. The development of aggression in American children as a consequence of television violence viewing. In *Television and the Aggressive Child: A Cross-National Comparison,* ed. LR Huesmann, LD Eron, pp. 45–80. Hillsdale, NJ: Erlbaum

Josephson WL. 1987. Television violence and children's aggression: testing the priming, social script, and disinhibition predictions. *J. Pers. Soc. Psychol.* 53:882–90

Joy LA, Kimball MM, Zaback ML. 1986. Television and children's aggressive behavior. In *The Impact of Television: A Natural Experiment in Three Communities,* ed. TM Williams, pp. 303–60. New York: Academic

Kanin EJ. 1969. Selected dyadic aspect of male sex aggresssion *J. Sex Res.* 5:12–28

Koss MP, Gidycz CA, Wisniewski N. 1987. The scope of rape: incidence and prevalence of sexual aggression and victimization in a national sample of students in higher education. *J. Consult. Clin. Psychol.* 55:162–70

Koss MP, Leonard KE, Beezley DA, Oros CJ. 1985. Non-stranger sexual aggression: a discriminate analysis classification. *Sex Roles* 12:981–92

Kruttschnitt C. 1989. A sociological, offender-based, study of rape. *Sociol. Q.* 30:305–29

Lagerspetz K, Viemero V. 1986. Television and aggressive behavior among Finnish children. In *Television and the Aggressive Child: A Cross-National Comparison,* LR Huesmann, LD Eron, pp. 81–118. Hillsdale, NJ: Erlbaum

Leyens JP, Camino L, Parke RD, Berkowitz L. 1975. Effects of movie violence on aggression in a field setting as a function of group dominance and cohesion. *J. Pers. Soc. Psychol.* 32:346–60

Linz D. 1989. Exposure to sexually explicit materials and attitudes toward rape: a comparison of study results. *J. Sex Res.* 26:50–84

Linz D, Malamuth N. 1993. *Pornography.* Newbury Park: Sage

Loren REA, Weeks G. 1986. Sexual fantasies of undergraduates and their perceptions of the sexual fantasies of the opposite sex. *J. Sex Educ. Ther.* 12:31–36

MacKinnon C. 1984. Not a moral issue. *Yale Law Policy Rev.* 2:321–45

Malamuth NM. 1986. Predictors of naturalistic sexual aggression. *J. Pers. Soc. Psychol.* 50:953–62

Malamuth NM, Check JVP. 1981. The effects of mass media exposure on acceptance of violence against women: a field experiment. *J. Res. Pers.* 15:436–46

McGuire WJ. 1986. The myth of massive media impact: Savagings and salvagings. In *Public Communication and Behavior,* ed. G. Comstock, 1:175–257. Orlando: Academic

Messner SF. 1986. Television violence and violent crime: an aggregate analysis. *Soc. Probl.* 33:218–35

Messner SF, Blau JR. 1987. Routine leisure activities and rates of crime: a macro-level analysis. *Soc. Forces* 65:1035–52

Meyer TP. 1972a. The effects of sexually arousing and violent films on aggressive behavior. *J. Sex Res.* 8:324–31

Meyer TP. 1972b. Effects of viewing justified and unjustified real film violence on aggressive behavior. *J. Pers. Soc. Psychol.* 23:21–29

Milavsky JR, Stipp HH, Kessler RC, Rubens WS. 1982. *Television and Aggression: A Panel Study.* New York: Academic

Milgram S. 1974. *Obedience to Authority: An Experimental View.* New York: Harper & Row

Miller TQ, Heath L, Molcan JR, Dugoni BL. 1991. Imitative violence in the real world: a reanalysis of homicide rates following championship prize fights. *Aggressive Behav.* 17:121–34

Neiss R. 1988. Reconceptualizing arousal: psychobiological states in motor performance. *Psychol. Bull.* 103:345–66

Nemeth C. 1970. Bargaining and reciprocity. *Psychol. Bull.* 74:297–308

Ogles RM. 1987. Cultivation analysis: theory, methodology and current research on television-influenced constructions of social reality. *Mass Comm. Rev.* 14:43–53

Padget VR, Brislin-Slutz J, Neal JA. 1989. Pornography, erotica, and attitudes toward women: the effects of repeated exposure. *J. Sex Res.* 26:479–91

Paik H, Comstock G. 1994. The effects of television violence on antisocial behavior: a meta-analysis. *Comm. Res.* 21:516–45

Palys TS. 1986. Testing the common wisdom: the social content of video pornography. *Can. Psychol.* 27:22–35

Parke RD, Berkowitz L, Leyens JP, West S, Sebastian RJ. 1977. Some effects of violent and nonviolent movies on the behavior of juvenile delinquents. In *Advances in Experimental Social Psychology*, ed. L. Berkowitz, 10:135–72. New York: Academic

Phillips DP. 1983. The impact of mass media violence on U.S. homicides. *Am. Sociol. Rev.* 48:560–68

Phillips DP. 1986. The found experiment: a new technique for assessing the impact of mass media violence on real-world aggressive behavior. In *Public Communication and Behavior*, ed. G Comstock, 1:259–307. San Diego, CA: Academic

Phillips DP, Bollen KA. 1985. Same time last year: selective data dredging for unreliable findings. *Am. Sociol. Rev.* 50:364–71

Rapaport K, Burkhart BR. 1984. Personality and attitudinal characteristics of sexually coercive college males. *J. Abnorm. Psychol.* 93:216–21

Reiss IL. 1986. *Journey into Sexuality: An Exploratory Voyage.* Englewood Cliffs, NJ: Prentice

Rosenberg MJ. 1969. The conditions and consequences of evaluation apprehension. In *Artifacts in Behavioral Research*, ed. R Rosenthal, R Rosnow. New York: Academic

Rule BG, Ferguson TJ. 1986. The effects of media violence on attitudes, emotions, and cognitions. *J. Soc. Issues* 42:29–50

Sapolsky BS. 1984. Arousal, affect, and the aggression-moderating effect of erotica. In *Pornography and Sexual Aggression*, ed. NM Malamuth, E Donnerstein, pp. 83–115. New York: Academic

Sheehan PW. 1986. Television viewing and its relation to aggression among children in Australia. In *Television and the Aggressive Child: A Cross-National Comparison*, ed. LR Huesmann, LD Eron, pp. 161–200. Hillsdale, NJ: Erlbaum

Smith DD. 1976. The social content of pornography. *J. Comm.* 29:16–24

Straus N. 1991. Discipline and divorce: physical punishment of children and violence and other crime in adulthood. *Soc. Probl.* 38:133–54

Surgeon General's Scientific Advisory Committee on Television and Social Behavior. 1972. Television and growing up: the impact of televised violence. *Rep. to the Surgeon General, US Public Health Serv. HEW Publ. No. HSM 72–9090.* Rockville, MD: Natl. Inst. Mental Health, USGPO

Sykes G, Matza D. 1961. Juvenile delinquency and subterranean values. *Am. Sociol. Rev.* 26:712–19

Tedeschi JT, Felson RB. 1994. *Violence, Aggression, and Coercive Actions.* Washington, DC: Am. Psychol. Assoc.

Tedeschi JT, Norman N. 1985. Social mechanisms of displaced aggression. In *Advances in Group Processes: Theory and Research*, ed. EJ Lawler, Vol. 2. Greenwich, Conn.: JAI

Tedeschi JT, Smith RB III, Brown RC Jr. 1974. A reinterpretation of research on aggression. *Psychol. Bull.* 89:540–63

Thomas MH, Horton RW, Lippincott EC, Drabman RS. 1977. Desensitization to portrayals of real-life aggression as a function of exposure to television violence. *J. Pers. Soc. Psychol.* 35:450–58

Valkenburg PM, Vooijs MW, Van der Voort TH. 1992. The influence of television on children's fantasy styles: a secondary analysis. *Imagination, Cognition, Pers.* 12:55–67

West DJ, Farrington DP. 1977. *The Delinquent Way of Life.* London: Heinemann

White LA. 1979. Erotica and aggression: the influence of sexual arousal, positive affect, and negative affect on aggressive behavior. *J. Pers. Soc. Psychol.* 37:591–601

Wiegman O, Kuttschreuter M, Baarda B. 1992. A longitudinal study of the effects of television viewing on aggressive and antisocial behaviors. *Br. J. Soc. Psychol.* 31:147–64

Wood W, Wong FY, Chachere JG. 1991. Effects of media violence on viewers aggression in unconstrained social interaction. *Psychol. Bull.* 109:371–83

Zillman D. 1971. Excitation transfer in communication-mediated aggressive behavior. *J. Exp. Soc. Psychol.* 7:419–34

Zillman D. 1983. Arousal and aggression. In *Aggression: Theoretical and Empirical Reviews,* ed. RG Geen, EI Donnerstein, 1:75–101. New York: Academic

Zillmann D, Bryant J, Comisky PW, Medoff NJ. 1981. Excitation and hedonic valence in the effect of erotica on motivated intermale aggression. *Eur. J. Soc. Psychol.* 11:233–52

Zillmann D, Hoyt JL, Day KD. 1974. Strength and duration of the effect of aggressive, violent, and erotic communications on subsequent aggressive behavior. *Comm. Res.* 1:286–306

Annu. Rev. Sociol. 1996. 22:129–52

FOCUS GROUPS

David L. Morgan

Institute on Aging, School of Urban and Public Affairs, Portland State University, Portland, Oregon 97201

KEY WORDS: qualitative research methods, methodology, focus groups, group interviews

ABSTRACT

Over the past decade, focus groups and group interviews have reemerged as a popular technique for gathering qualitative data, both among sociologists and across a wide range of academic and applied research areas. Focus groups are currently used as both a self-contained method and in combination with surveys and other research methods, most notably individual, in-depth interviews. Comparisons between focus groups and both surveys and individual interviews help to show the specific advantages and disadvantages of group interviews, concentrating on the role of the group in producing interaction and the role of the moderator in guiding this interaction. The advantages of focus groups can be maximized through careful attention to research design issues at both the project and the group level. Important future directions include: the development of standards for reporting focus group research, more methodological research on focus groups, more attention to data analysis issues, and more engagement with the concerns of the research participants.

INTRODUCTION

Although some form of group interviewing has undoubtedly existed for as long as sociologists have been collecting data (e.g. Bogardus 1926), the past decade has produced a remarkable surge of interest in group interviews generally and focus groups in particular. Much of this interest first surfaced in the mid-1980s. In 1987, Robert Merton published remarks that compared his pioneering work on "focused interviews" (Merton & Kendall 1946) with marketers' uses of the focus group, while John Knodel and his collaborators (Knodel et al 1987) published a summary of their focus group research on demographic changes in Thailand. The next year produced two book-length treatments of focus groups

129

0360-0572/96/0815-0129$08.00

by social scientists (Krueger 1988/1994, Morgan 1988). This initial burst of interest was followed by other texts (Stewart & Shamdasani 1990, Vaughn et al 1996), a reissuing of Merton et al's original manual (Merton et al 1956/1990), an edited collection of more advanced material (Morgan 1993a), and at least two special issues of journals (Carey 1995, Knodel 1995).

The current level of interest in focus group interviews is evident from searches of *Sociological Abstracts, Psychological Abstracts,* and the *Social Science Citation Index.* All of these sources show a steady growth in research using focus groups, indicating that well over a hundred empirical articles using focus groups appeared in refereed journals during 1994 alone. These searches also show interesting patterns in the use of focus groups. In particular, a content analysis of the materials from *Sociological Abstracts* revealed that over 60% of the empirical research using focus groups during the past decade combined them with other research methods, although the proportion of studies that rely solely on focus groups has been increasing in recent years. Hence, this review pays attention to uses of focus groups both as a "self-contained" method and in combination with other methods. Before examining the uses of focus groups, however, I examine how focus groups are related to group interviews in general.

FOCUS GROUPS AND GROUP INTERVIEWS

This chapter defines focus groups as a research technique that collects data through group interaction on a topic determined by the researcher. This definition has three essential components. First, it clearly states that focus groups are a research method devoted to data collection. Second, it locates the interaction in a group discussion as the source of the data. Third, it acknowledges the researcher's active role in creating the group discussion for data collection purposes.

While this definition is intentionally quite broad, each of its three elements does exclude some projects that have occasionally been called focus groups. First, focus groups should be distinguished from groups whose primary purpose is something other than research; alternative purposes might be: therapy, decision making, education, organizing, or behavior change (although focus groups that are primarily for data collection may have some of these outcomes as well). Second, it is useful to distinguish focus groups from procedures that utilize multiple participants but do not allow interactive discussions, such as nominal groups and Delphi groups (these techniques are reviewed in Stewart & Shamdasani 1990). Finally, focus groups should be distinguished from methods that collect data from naturally occurring group discussions where no one acts as an interviewer. The distinction here is not whether the group existed prior to the research, but whether the researcher's interests directed the discussion, since focus groups are often conducted with existing groups (Morgan 1989).

Lying behind this effort to define focus groups is the fundamental question of whether focus groups should be distinguished from other types of group interviews. In one camp are those who use an inclusive approach that treats most forms of group interviews as variants on focus groups. In another camp, however, are those who use an exclusive approach that treats focus groups as a narrower technique not to be confused with other types of group interviews. One version of the exclusive approach, which is particularly common in marketing research (Greenbaum 1988, 1993, McQuarrie 1996), is a statement that focus groups must meet some specified set of criteria, typically that they consist of structured discussions among 6 to 10 homogeneous strangers in a formal setting. The problem with this approach is that it fails to demonstrate any advantages of either limiting the definition of focus groups to studies that meet these criteria or excluding group interviews that deviate from them.

In contrast to such unthinking reliance on an exclusive definition of focus groups, Frey & Fontana (1991) have created a typology that locates focus groups as one among several categories of group interviews. The typology includes some that the present definition already distinguishes from focus groups (nominal and Delphi groups and observations of naturally occurring groups), and some (brainstorming groups and field interviews in naturally occurring settings) that the current definition would treat as variations on focus groups. (See Khan & Manderson 1992 for a similar but more anthropologically based typology). One way to assess the usefulness of a typology such as Frey & Fontana's is to ask if it can determine whether a particular group interview is or is not a focus group. According to the dimensions that define their typology, group interviews are something other than focus groups if they: (i) are conducted in informal settings; (ii) use nondirective interviewing; or (iii) use unstructured question formats. Yet applied demographers such as Knodel (1987, 1995) have held focus group interviews throughout the world and have concluded that they can be adapted to a wide variety of settings and culture practices. Similarly, social science texts on focus groups (Krueger 1993, Morgan 1988, Stewart & Shamdasani 1990) describe ways to conduct focus groups with more or less directive interviewing styles and more or less structured question formats, depending on the purposes of the particular project. It would thus, in actual practice, be quite difficult to apply Frey & Fontana's typology to determine whether any given group interview was or was not a focus group.

In the long run, the question of whether sociologists should use a more inclusive or exclusive definition of focus groups will depend on which approach maximizes both the effective application of available techniques and the innovative development of new techniques. For the present, this remains an open question. Consequently, this chapter follows an inclusive approach that treats focus groups as a set of central tendencies, with many useful variations that can be matched to a variety of research purposes.

CURRENT USES FOR FOCUS GROUPS

This review necessarily concentrates on the uses of focus groups by sociologists. Still, it should be obvious that focus groups, like other qualitative methods, are used across a wide variety of different fields. Other disciplines in which focus groups are relatively widespread include communication studies (Albrecht et al 1993, Staley 1990), education (Brotherson & Goldstein 1992, Flores & Alonzo 1995, Lederman 1990), political science (Delli Carpini & Williams 1994, Kullberg 1994), and public health (Basch 1987). Outside of academia, focus groups are well known to be popular in marketing (Goldman & McDonald 1987, Greenbaum 1993), where they have been used for everything from breakfast cereals (Templeton 1987) to political candidates (Diamond & Bates 1992). This acceptance in applied marketing has not, however, carried over to the academic field of marketing (McQuarrie 1990), although there does seem to be a trend toward more methodological research in this field (McDonald 1993, Nelson & Frontczak 1988).

Given the breadth of possible applications of focus groups and group interviews, it is hardly surprising that they have found uses in many of the specialty areas that interest sociologists, including: aging (Knodel 1995, Duncan & Morgan 1994), criminology (Sasson, 1995), medical sociology (Morgan & Spanish 1985, McKinlay 1993), political sociology (Gamson 1992), social movements (Cable 1992), and the sociology of work (Bobo et al 1995). In addition, many applications of focus groups do not fit within the neat, traditional boundaries of sociology's subdisciplines. For example, Shively's (1992) study of how American Indians and Anglos responded to cowboy movies used focus groups within a cultural studies framework; Jarrett's (1993, 1994) work on low-income, African American women combined elements of family sociology, inequality, and race and ethnicity; and Pinderhughes' (1993) investigation of racially motivated violence mixed elements of urban sociology, criminology, and race relations.

Despite this wide-ranging interest in focus groups, they have found more currency within several specific areas of sociological interest. In particular, marketing's legacy of using focus groups to hear from consumers has carried over into their use in the development and evaluation of programs ranging from substance abuse (Lengua et al 1992) to curricular reform (Hendershott & Wright 1993). Program development efforts use focus groups to learn more about the potential targets of these programs in order to reach them more effectively.

This use often occurs under the explicit rubric of "social marketing," which applies tools such as focus groups to socially valued goals, as in Bryant's (1990) program to encourage breast feeding among low-income women. On the program evaluation side, focus groups have become an important tool in qualitative evaluation research, including not only post-program evaluation, but also needs assessment and strategic planning (Krueger 1994).

Two specific research areas where the applied use of focus groups has had a major and continuing link to sociology are family planning and HIV/AIDS. The application of focus groups to research on fertility first emerged in the early 1980s (e.g. Folch-Lyon et al 1981). These studies typically sought a better understanding of knowledge, attitudes, and practices with regard to contraception in the Third World; in particular, advocates of a social marketing approach to contraceptives (Schearer 1981) argued that focus groups could supplement the kind of attitudinal data that surveys produced. Since that time, focus groups have been an important source of data on fertility and family planning preferences around the world, as in the work of Ward et al (1991) in Guatemala, Honduras, and Zaire, or Knodel et al (1987) in Thailand. This established application in the study of sexual behavior also led to the use of focus groups in research on the spread of HIV, both in the Third World (Irwin et al 1991) and the West (Kline et al 1992, Pollak et al 1990).

An important theme that reappears in many of these uses of focus groups is their ability to "give a voice" to marginalized groups. For example, in early HIV/AIDS research (Joseph et al 1984), epidemiologists used focus groups to gain a better understanding of at-risk groups with whom they had little prior experience, such as gay and bisexual men. Focus groups have thus been used in many applied settings where there is a difference in perspective between the researchers and those with whom they need to work. Others have argued, however, that the value of focus groups goes well beyond listening to others, since they can serve as either a basis for empowering "clients" (Magill 1993, Race et al 1994) or as a tool in action and participatory research (Hugentobler et al 1992, Padilla 1993). Similarly, feminist researchers have noted the appeal of focus groups because they allow participants to exercise a fair degree of control over their own interactions (Nichols-Casebolt & Spakes 1995, Montell 1995).

USES IN COMBINATION WITH OTHER METHODS

As noted at the outset of this review, a content analysis of *Sociological Abstracts* revealed that a majority of the published research articles using focus groups combined them with other methods. Further examination of the specific combinations of focus groups with other methods showed that the most frequent pairings were with either in-depth, individual interviews or surveys.

Between these two, the use of focus groups with individual interviews is the more straightforward, since both are qualitative techniques. (This does not, however, imply that the two methods are interchangeable; the following section contains a comparison of individual and group interviews.) Investigators' reasons for combining individual and group interviews typically point to the greater depth of the former and the greater breadth of the latter (Crabtree et al 1993). For example, individual interview studies have used follow-up group interviews to check the conclusions from their analyses and to expand the study populations included in the research (Irwin 1970). This strategy has the advantage of getting reactions from a relatively wide range of participants in a relatively short time. In a complementary fashion, focus group studies have used follow-up interviews with individual participants to explore specific opinions and experiences in more depth, as well as to produce narratives that address the continuity of personal experiences over time (Duncan & Morgan 1994). This strategy has the advantage of first identifying a range of experiences and perspectives, and then drawing from that pool to add more depth where needed. Thus, depending on the varied needs that a qualitative study has for breadth and depth, there is little difficulty in combining individual and group interviews.

While studies that bring together focus groups and surveys are one of the leading ways of combining qualitative and quantitative methods, such designs also raise a complex set of issues, since the two methods produce such different kinds of data. Morgan (1993c) presented a conceptual framework to clarify these issues by distinguishing four ways of combining qualitative and quantitative methods in general and focus groups and surveys in particular. The four ways of combining the methods are based on which method received the primary attention and whether the secondary method served as a preliminary or follow-up study.

Thus, the first combination contains studies in which surveys are the primary method and focus groups serve in a preliminary capacity. Survey researchers typically use this design to develop the content of their questionnaires. Because surveys are inherently limited by the questions they ask, it is increasingly common to use focus groups to provide data on how the respondents themselves talk about the topics of the survey. Although this practice has long been common in marketing research, systematic publications in this area did not appear until social scientists renewed their interest in focus groups (Fuller et al 1993, O'Brien 1993, Zeller 1993b). Still, this is an area that is just beginning to receive attention, and many issues are only now arising, such as the need to find other means of pursuing focus group insights that are not amenable to survey research (Laurie 1992, Laurie & Sullivan 1991). At present, this is easily the most common reason for combining focus groups and surveys.

In the second combination, focus groups are the primary method while surveys provide preliminary inputs that guide their application. Studies following this research design typically use the broad but "thin" data from surveys to assist in selecting samples for focus groups or topics for detailed analysis. With regard to sampling, Morgan & Zhao (1993) and O'Connor et al (1992) both used surveys of medical records to divide a larger population into different "segments" that they then compared using separate sets of focus groups. With regard to analysis, Morgan (1994) and Shively (1992) both illustrated the use of findings from a brief preliminary survey with focus group participants to guide the more detailed interpretive analysis of the data from the group discussions. Compared to the first combination, studies that use surveys as a secondary method to assist focus group research are relatively rare.

The third combination once again uses surveys as the primary method, but the focus groups now act as a follow-up that assists in interpreting the survey results. One increasingly common use for qualitative follow-up methods, including focus groups, is to recontact survey respondents for illustrative material that can be quoted in conjunction with quantitative findings. More interesting from a methodological perspective are efforts to clarify poorly understood results, such as Knodel's (1987) and Wolff et al's (1993) efforts to account for fertility rates and education levels in Thailand, Morgan's (1989) investigations of the ineffectiveness of social support among recent widows, and Harari & Beaty's (1990) deeper probing of surface similarities in the survey responses of black workers and white managers in South Africa under apartheid. Among the four combinations, these designs are the second most frequent, but they have yet to receive any systematic methodological attention.

The final combination of surveys and focus groups uses focus groups as the primary method and surveys as a source of follow-up data. One such application would examine the prevalence of issues or themes from the focus groups. For example, Nichols-Casebolt & Spakes (1995:53) followed up their focus groups by locating secondary data from surveys that showed policy makers "the scope of the problems associated with the issues identified by the participants." Another possibility would be to survey a large number of sites to determine where the results from a more limited focus group study might be most immediately transferable. But studies that employ designs from this fourth combination are easily the rarest of this set. One likely reason that those who conduct focus group studies seldom do smaller follow-up surveys is their desire to avoid any implication that quantitative data are necessary to "verify" the results of the qualitative research. In other words, the issues that accompany combining methods from different "paradigms" (Lincoln & Guba 1985) involve not just technical considerations, but epistemological and political issues as well (Bryman 1988). Still, the current popularity of work from the first combination, where focus groups aid in developing surveys, demonstrates the potential value of combining focus groups with quantitative methods. It thus seems likely that research using various combinations with surveys will continue to be not only one of the major uses of focus groups but also one of the most practical ways of bringing together qualitative and quantitative methods.

HOW FOCUS GROUPS COMPARE TO OTHER SOCIOLOGICAL METHODS

Despite the increasingly widespread use of focus groups as a method within sociology and the other social sciences, virtually all this work has occurred in the past ten years. This "newcomer" status has encouraged comparisons between focus groups and the various traditional methods in each of these areas, but researchers have offered two very different reasons for comparing methods. One reason for comparing focus groups to more familiar methods has been to determine whether the two methods produce equivalent data. According to this view, focus groups are most useful when they reproduce the results of the standard methods in a particular field. A different reason for comparing focus groups to existing methods has been to locate the unique contributions that each can make to a field of studies. According to this view, focus groups are most useful when they produce new results that would not be possible with the standard methods in a particular field. There is an obvious paradox here, as focus groups cannot produce results that are simultaneously the same as and different from results of familiar techniques. Unfortunately, the failure to recognize these divergent goals has limited the cumulative knowledge from studies that compare focus groups to other methods. Nonetheless, these comparisons are useful for summarizing the strengths and weaknesses of focus groups.

COMPARISONS TO SURVEYS

In one of the earliest reports of a major social science application of focus groups, Folch-Lyon et al (1981) also included a detailed comparison to a survey on the same topic. This study investigated attitudes toward contraception in Mexico using two independent research teams. One team conducted 44 focus groups with some 300 participants, while the other did household surveys with over 2000 respondents. Overall, the authors had little difficulty in matching the investigation of their substantive topics across the two methods; their results showed an overwhelming convergence. As Stycos (1981) pointed out, however, most of Folch-Lyon et al's judgments about the convergence between the two methods were based on subjective assessments of the correspondence of the findings; fortunately, more recent efforts have used more systematic comparisons.

Ward et al (1991) compared survey and focus group results from three studies on family planning in Guatemala, Honduras, and Zaire. For each of their three studies, they matched topic areas where methods contained similar questions, and they judged results from the two methods to be similar when "they would lead to the same conclusions" (p. 272). Based on explicit comparisons across a total of 60 variables, they found that the results from the two methods were: (i) highly similar for 30% of the variables; (ii) similar, but focus groups provided more information for 42% of the variables; (iii) similar, but surveys provided more information for 17% ; and (iv) dissimilar for 12% of the variables. The biggest difference found between the methods was the ability of the focus groups to produce more in-depth information on the topic at hand.

In another systematic comparison of survey and focus group results, Saint-Germain et al (1993) reported on two studies of the barriers to breast cancer screening services for older Hispanic women in the southwestern United States. To assess the comparability of the results, the authors rank-ordered a list of barriers according to how often survey respondents had experienced each, and then they compared this to a rank-order of how often each barrier was mentioned in the focus groups. Saint-Germain et al's conclusions (1993:363) matched those of Ward et al: "The findings of the focus group interviews, in most cases, confirmed the findings of the previous population surveys. In many cases, the focus group interviews went beyond the information obtained in the survey, amplifying our understanding of the various facets of barriers to breast cancer screening and specifying more exactly how some of the barriers work in practice."

Although each of these studies emphasized the convergence of the results from focus groups and surveys, a consistent set of differences did occur in all three studies. First, the survey interview setting limited what respondents said about sensitive topics, in comparison to what they revealed in focus groups. Second, the differences in response options meant that surveys were better able to elicit yes/no answers about specific behaviors and experiences, even though the forced-choice format of the survey items limited what respondents could say on general attitude areas, in comparison to the more open-ended discussions in the focus groups. Finally, Ward et al explicitly noted that all of these comparisons used only the variables that occurred in both studies, thus downplaying the fact that the surveys typically covered many more topics than did the focus groups. There was thus a key tradeoff between the depth that focus groups provided and the breadth that surveys offered.

COMPARISONS TO INDIVIDUAL INTERVIEWS

Fern's (1982) work on the relative productivity of individual interviews and focus groups was one of the very few methodological studies that involved a head-to-head comparison between the two methods. Using an "idea generation" task, Fern compared focus groups to an equivalent number of aggregated responses from individual interviews (i.e. "nominal groups"). He determined that each focus group participant produced only 60% to 70% as many ideas as they would have in an individual interview; he also had raters judge the quality of ideas from the two methods, and again an advantage appeared for individual interviews. These results clearly argue against the notion that focus groups have a "synergy" that makes them more productive than an equivalent number of individual interviews. Instead, the real issue may well be the relative efficiency of the two methods for any given project. For example, Fern's results suggest that two eight-person focus groups would produce as many ideas as 10 individual interviews. As Crabtree et al (1993) have pointed out, however, a number of logistical factors, such as location of the interviews, the mobility of the participants, the flexibility of their schedules, would determine which study would actually be easier to accomplish.

The major issue in studies of individual and group interviews has not, however, been the number of ideas they generate, but the comparability of the results they produce. Wight (1994) reported one of the rare studies on this issue. The study involved both group and individual interviews with the same adolescent males concerning their sexual experiences, and systematic variation in which of the two types of interviews was done first. Wight concluded that the greatest number of discrepancies occurred between reports of boys who participated in individual interviews first and then in focus groups, while boys who started in group interviews gave similar accounts in subsequent individual interviews. Kitzinger (1994a,b) reported that the conclusions about the results from her study on HIV issues validated those of Wight's, although she also found that the difference between individual and group interviews was limited to heterosexual males. Kitzinger thus argued against a generalized effect of groups on conformity, and she called for more attention to how such processes are affected by the group's composition, the topic, the relationship of the interviewer to the group, and the general context of the interview.

Kitzinger (1994b:173) also reached the more general conclusion that, "Differences between interview and group data cannot be classified in terms of validity versus invalidity or honesty versus dishonesty. ...The group data documenting macho or sexual harassing behaviour is no more 'invalid' than that showing the research participants' relatively acceptable behaviour in interview settings." It thus seems a safe conclusion that, if one searches, one is bound to find differences in how some interviewees talk about some topics in individual versus group interviews. For those cases where we are interested only in a specific social context, this interest will determine which form of data is more valid. In general, however, the existence of differences between what is said in individual and group interviews is as much a statement about our culture as our methods, and this is clearly a research topic of interest in its own right.

STRENGTHS AND WEAKNESSES OF FOCUS GROUPS

One benefit of comparing focus groups to other methods is a more sophisticated understanding of the strengths and weaknesses of focus groups. For example, rather than just listing exploratory research as a strength of focus groups, it is now necessary to note that individual, nominal interviews can be a more effective technique for idea generation (Fern 1982) and that surveys can be more effective for determining the prevalence of any given attitude or experience (Ward et al 1992). Comparisons to other methods have thus led to the conclusion that the real strength of focus groups is not simply in exploring what people have to say, but in providing insights into the sources of complex behaviors and motivations (Morgan & Krueger 1993).

Morgan & Krueger also argued that the advantages of focus groups for investigating complex behaviors and motivations were a direct outcome of the interaction in focus groups, what has been termed "the group effect" (Carey 1994, Carey & Smith 1994). An emphasis on the specific kinds of interactions that occur in focus groups is also an improvement over vague assertions that "synergy" is one of their strengths. What makes the discussion in focus groups more than the sum of separate individual interviews is the fact that the participants both query each other and explain themselves to each other. As Morgan & Krueger (1993) have also emphasized, such interaction offers valuable data on the extent of consensus and diversity among the participants. This ability to observe the extent and nature of interviewees' agreement and disagreement is a unique strength of focus groups. A further strength comes from the researcher's ability to ask the participants themselves for comparisons among their experiences and views, rather than aggregating individual data in order to speculate about whether or why the interviewees differ.

The weaknesses of focus groups, like their strengths, are linked to the process of producing focused interactions, raising issues about both the role of the moderator in generating the data and the impact of the group itself on the data. With regard to the role of the moderator, Agar & MacDonald (1995) used discourse analysis to compare the conversations between interviewers and interviewees in a single focus group and a set of individual interviews. They concluded that the dynamics of the individual interviews put more burden on the informants to explain themselves to the interviewer, while the moderator's efforts to guide the group discussion had the ironic consequence of disrupting the interaction that was the point of the group. Saferstein (1995) also used discourse analysis to make a similar point about moderator control in a comparison of focus groups and naturally occurring talk at a job site. In particular, he noted that it is the moderator, rather than the ongoing work of the group, that determines the agenda and form of the discussion. Both of these articles directly questioned the assertion that focus groups mimic a conversation among the participants, and each independently suggested that a meeting would be a better analogy, due to the control exercised by the moderator.

Although the issues that Agar & MacDonald (1995) and Saferstein (1995) raised are of most concern with more directive styles of moderating, there is no denying that the behavior of the moderator has consequences for the nature of the group interviews. But the issue of interviewer effects is hardly limited to focus groups, as is shown in work from both survey research (Fowler & Mangione 1990) and individual interviewing (Mischler 1986). All of these issues point to the importance of understanding the range of variation that is possible across different styles of moderating, a range discussed in the following section.

In terms of weaknesses that are due to the impact of the group on the discussion itself, Sussman et al (1991) used a design from small group research and administered questionnaires before and after focus groups to find out if the discussions changed the participants' attitudes. They found the predicted "polarization" effect—attitudes became more extreme after the group discussion. The magnitude of this effect was small, however, as it accounted for only 4% of the variance in attitude change; this may be significant in an analysis of variance, but it is not likely to skew the results of most focus group research. Nonetheless, the point is well taken that we know little about how group members affect each other, and research designs from the social psychological study of small groups can offer useful tools for investigating this issue.

A final weakness due to the impact of the group on its participants concerns the range of topics that can be researched effectively in groups. Because group interaction requires mutual self-disclosure, it is undeniable that some topics will be unacceptable for discussion among some categories of research participants. At present, however, assertions about this weakness of focus groups are based more on intuition than data, since there are no empirical investigations of the range of topics or participants that either can or cannot be studied with group interviews. In particular, claims that focus groups are inappropriate for "sensitive topics" seem to ignore the widespread use of group interviewing to study sexual behavior in all forms. Further, the growing use of focus groups with cultural minorities and marginalized groups suggests that experience is the best predictor of where focus groups will and will not work. Fortunately, several of the researchers who have worked with sensitive topics and minority groups have written about their use of focus groups in these settings (Jarrett 1993, 1994, Hoppe et al 1995, Hughes & DuMont 1993, Kitzinger 1994a,b, Zeller 1993a), and only time will tell how widely these techniques apply to other topics and populations.

RESEARCH DESIGNS FOR SOCIOLOGICAL APPLICATIONS OF FOCUS GROUPS

As the previous sections demonstrate, sociologists and other social scientists have used focus groups in many ways for many purposes. Yet, if there are many ways of doing focus groups, then how does a practicing researcher make choices between doing focus groups one way versus another? And how does an outside reviewer determine whether a focus group project was done in a proper and effective fashion? The emerging consensus is that these issues can be resolved through an emphasis on research design in focus groups.

An emphasis on research design has advantages both for the field of focus groups as a whole and for individual investigators. For the field of focus groups, Morgan (1992a) has argued that an emphasis on research design would generate explicit principles that would replace the "rules of thumb" that have guided past practice. Thus, rather than simply asserting that focus groups should consist of structured discussions among 6 to 10 homogeneous strangers in a formal setting, an emphasis on research design would systematically investigate the implications of conducting more structured versus less structured discussions, of using smaller versus larger groups, etc. For the individual investigator, such research design principles would provide a means for linking the purposes of the research and the specific procedures that best achieve these purposes. For example, in his research on the political consciousness of ordinary citizens, Gamson (1992) first noted that his procedures departed from the prevailing rules of thumb when he used loosely moderated groups of four to six familiar acquaintances who met at one of the participants' homes; he then justified each of these design decisions by stating why it would produce data better suited to his purposes.

In considering the set of issues involved in designing focus group research, it is useful to distinguish between decisions that apply to the research project as a whole (i.e. project-level design issues), and those that apply to the conduct of a particular group (i.e. group-level design issues). While decisions at the project level specify the kinds of data that the focus groups should produce, group-level design decisions largely determine how to conduct the groups in order to produce such data. In particular, many of the group-level decisions are related to issues of group dynamics that help to ensure a productive discussion.

PROJECT-LEVEL DESIGN ISSUES

Standardization

As a project-level design issue, standardization addresses the extent to which the identical questions and procedures are used in every group. At one extreme would be an emphasis on "emergence" that lets the questions and procedures shift from group to group in order to take advantage of what has been learned in previous groups. At the other extreme, a project could begin by determining a fixed set of questions and procedures that would apply throughout. Of course, standardization is actually a matter of degree, and even standardized designs allow minor variations that accommodate the unique aspects of each group, in order to avoid what Merton et al (1990) called the fallacy of adhering to fixed questions.

Although nothing like a census of focus group designs among sociologists exists, it is quite clear that the majority of these research projects have used a fixed research design that relied on a consistent set of predetermined questions and procedures. This tendency toward standardized research designs has not gone unexamined. Orosz (1994) has argued that this aspect of focus groups is inconsistent with many of the key tenets of qualitative research, while Brotherson & Goldstein (1992) made the case for pursuing standardization within an emergent research design. According to the present argument for making decisions according to research design principles, whether to standardize the questions and procedures in a focus group project should not be based on past tradition, within either the more standardized practices of focus group researchers or the less standardized approach favored by practitioners of other qualitative methods. Instead, it should be based on a conscious assessment of the advantages and disadvantages of standardization with regard to the goals of a particular project.

The great advantage of standardization, and its most common justification, is the high level of comparability that it produces across groups. This comparability is particularly valuable when the goal of the research is to compare the responses of different categories of participants (see the discussion of segmentation in the next section). As Knodel (1993) pointed out, standardization has the particular advantage of facilitating the analysis of focus groups by allowing for direct comparisons of the discussions from group to group. The obvious disadvantage of standardization is that one must live with whatever questions and procedures were chosen prior to entering the field, which would be inimical to many truly exploratory applications of focus groups.

Morgan (1993c) has described two types of designs that combine the advantages of more standardized and more emergent designs (see Morgan 1992b for a partial application of these procedures). The first such design breaks the project into phases that move from less standardized to more standardized groups. This has the advantage of allowing the early groups in the project to take a more exploratory approach, which then serves as the basis for developing a later set of standardized questions and procedures grounded in the data themselves. The second compromise design organizes the questions in each group according to a "funnel" pattern that begins with a fixed set of core questions and then proceeds to a variable set of specific issues. This has the advantage of maintaining comparability across groups for the first part of each discussion but allowing the later section of each group to vary according to the emergent needs of the research.

Sampling

Focus group research reveals its historical association with marketing research by using the term "segmentation" to capture sampling strategies that consciously vary the composition of groups. This use of segmentation to create groups that consist of particular categories of participants is a longstanding practice, as illustrated by Folch-Lyon et al's (1981) study on family planning, where they composed groups that were as homogeneous as possible by sex, age, marital status, contraceptive use, socioeconomic status, and geographical location. The most obvious kinds of segmentation capture something about the research topic itself. For example, if gender differences were of interest, then one might conduct separate groups of men and women, or an evaluation study might segment the groups into more frequent and less frequent users of the program in question.

Segmentation offers two basic advantages. First, it builds a comparative dimension into the entire research project, including the data analysis. For example, Folch-Lyon et al (1981) analyzed their data according to the categories described above and found the most wide-ranging differences between groups of men and women, with some additional differences between groups in rural and urban areas. Second, segmentation facilitates discussions by making the participants more similar to each other. For example, even if the behavior of men and women does not differ greatly on a given topic, discussion still may flow more smoothly in groups that are homogeneous rather than mixed with regard to sex. The same logic applies to dividing groups according to the age, race, or social class of the participants, although the value of segmenting to facilitate a free-flowing discussion obviously depends on the research topic.

The obvious disadvantage of segmentation is that it can greatly multiply the number of groups. As Knodel (1993) pointed out, it is seldom wise to run just one group per segment, since what one learns about that segment is confounded with the group dynamics of that unique set of participants. As Knodel also noted, however, using multiple segmentation criteria can produce acceptable designs that have only one group "per cell" in the overall design, as long as there are multiple groups in each separate segment (e.g. there may be several groups of women, several rural groups, and several groups of older participants, but only one group of older, rural women). Even so, using multiple segmentation criteria can easily lead to projects that involve large numbers of focus groups, like the 44 groups conducted by Folch-Lyon et al (1981).

Number of Groups

The most common rule of thumb is that most projects consist of four to six focus groups. The typical justification for this range is that the data become "saturated" and little new information emerges after the first few groups, so moderators can predict what participants will say even before they say it (Zeller 1993b). Morgan (1992a) has suggested that diversity in either the participants or the range of topics to be covered will increase the number of groups necessary to achieve saturation. For example, Kitzinger wished to hear about views on AIDS from a wide range of different populations and thus conducted 52 groups, while Gamson (1992) wanted each of his groups to give their opinions on four different political issues and thus conducted 37 groups in order to produce enough discussion on each topic.

As the previous section noted, using multiple segments will increase the number of groups needed, which is a special case of diversity in the study population. Projects that use a lower level of standardization will also typically need more groups, since this produces more variation in the topics that are raised group to group. The connection between the number of groups and issues of standardization and segmentation raises the question of how different aspects of research design for focus groups intersect—a topic addressed at the end of this section.

GROUP-LEVEL DESIGN ISSUES

Level of Moderator Involvement

The presence of a moderator is one of the most striking features of focus groups. Groups in which the moderator exercises a higher degree of control are termed "more structured," and Morgan (1992a) has called attention to two senses in which a group can be more structured. First, it can be more structured with regard to asking questions, so that the moderator controls what topics are discussed (e.g. directing attention away from what are deemed less important issues). Second, it can be more structured with regard to managing group dynamics, so that the moderator controls the way that the participants interact (e.g. trying to get everyone to participate equally in the discussion). Both of these aspects of moderator involvement can be elements of the research design.

With regard to the moderator's involvement in asking questions, a less structured discussion means that the group can pursue its own interests, while a more structured approach means that the moderator imposes the researcher's interests, as embodied in the questions that guide the discussion. A key factor that makes groups more or less structured is simply the number of questions. Thus, if the average focus group lasts 90 minutes, and the moderator has the responsibility for covering a great many questions during that time, then the moderator will be heavily involved in controlling the group's discussion. Unfortunately, there is currently little consensus about what constitutes a more structured or less structured approach to questioning. For example, Lederman (1990:123) characterized a guide that contained five broad questions as "quite structured," while Byers & Wilcox (1991:65) termed a guide with 17 specific questions "relatively unstructured."

One possible cause for this confusion is the failure to distinguish between structure that controls questioning and structure that controls group dynamics. In managing group dynamics, a less structured approach allows participants to talk as much or as little as they please, while a more structured approach means that the moderator will encourage those who might otherwise say little and limit those who might otherwise dominate the discussion. Although most marketing approaches to focus groups (e.g. Greenbaum 1993) have typically advocated a more structured control of group dynamics, many social science approaches have explicitly favored a less directive style of interviewing (e.g. Krueger 1994, Merton et al 1990). Morgan's (1988) instructions for how to conduct "self-managed" groups, in which the moderator does not even sit at the same table as the participants, probably represent the extreme in social science advocacy of less structured approaches to group dynamics.

In general, marketing researchers, more than social science researchers, prefer research designs with high levels of moderator involvement that impose more structure with regard to both asking questions and managing group dynamics. Morgan (1988) has suggested that this reflects a difference between the marketing goal of answering questions from an audience of paying customers and the social science goal of generating new knowledge for an audience of peer reviewers. To the extent that this broad generalization does hold, it is a nice illustration of the general principle that research designs should follow from research goals. This conclusion—that approaches to moderating should be linked to research goals—is strongly supported by one of the few instances of systematic research that evaluates differences in moderator style (McDonald 1993). Further, it implies that arguments about whether moderators should use a more or less structured approach are meaningless unless one specifies the goals of the research.

Group Size

The number of participants who are invited to a focus group is one element of the research design that is clearly under the researcher's control. Morgan (1992a) reviewed the bases for determining group size, concluding that smaller groups were more appropriate with emotionally charged topics that generated high levels of participant involvement, while larger groups worked better with more neutral topics that generated lower levels of involvement. On the one hand, a smaller group gives each participant more time to discuss her or his views and experiences on topics in which they all are highly involved. On the other hand, a larger group contains a wider range of potential responses on topics where each participant has a low level of involvement. In addition, small groups make it easier for moderators to manage the active discussions that often accompany high levels of involvement and emotional topics, whereas large groups are easier to manage when each participant has a lower level of involvement in the topic.

This last point once again raises an issue that involves the intersection of two different design principles: group size and moderator involvement. Although it is generally the case that design dimensions cannot be considered in isolation from each other, current knowledge about how design issues impinge on each other is limited to a few obvious considerations. In addition to the linkage between group size and moderator involvement, earlier portions of this section noted connections between standardization and sample segmentation, and between the number of groups and both standardization and segmentation. There is thus an increasing but still limited stock of knowledge about how design issues go together. This limitation is understandable, given that most of the explicit investigations of research design in focus groups have come from social scientists and consequently reflect only a decade or so of activity.

DATA QUALITY CONCERNS

The basic goal in specifying research designs for focus groups is to ensure that the research procedures deliver the desired data. Despite the best research designs, however, things can still go wrong due to poor planning or the inappropriate implementation of otherwise optimal designs. Krueger (1993) and Morgan (1995) have both noted that data quality depends on a number of factors, including whether the researcher locates enough participants, selects appropriate samples, chooses relevant questions, has a qualified moderator(s), and uses an effective analysis strategy.

Standards for reporting on research procedures are one practical step to improve the quality of focus group research. At present, the reporting of focus group procedures is a haphazard affair at best. Based on the studies reviewed for this chapter, the following is one effort to develop such standards. First, to learn the overarching context for the research, readers should know whether a standardized set of questions and procedures applied throughout the project. Then, most basically, readers should know the number of groups conducted and the size range of these groups. There should also be information on the group composition, including relevant background data on the participants. In particular, when groups are divided into different sample segments, there should be information on the basis for this sampling strategy and the number of groups per segment. Regardless of whether the study used segmentation, it is important to report the sources for locating participants and other information about recruitment procedures. In terms of the interview itself, thorough summaries of the question content are needed; surprisingly, many current publications say very little about the questions that were asked. Similarly, most current reports say little about moderating, and useful information would include concrete descriptions of the degree of structure that the moderator(s) imposed, how many moderators were used, and what their training and qualifications were. Finally, ethical issues need to be discussed, and, although the field as a whole has been slow to address ethical concerns in focus group research, there now is at least one discussion of this topic (Smith 1995).

This kind of information would aid not only reviewers in judging the quality of the research design and procedures but also other researchers in adapting these practices into future work. For both of these purposes, it would be highly desirable for research reports to go beyond merely presenting factual information to including justifications for the more crucial design decisions. This process of making public the basis for our decisions about why to do focus groups one way and not another is a vital step in the growth of our field.

FUTURE DIRECTIONS FOR FOCUS GROUPS

The steady increase in the use of focus groups over the past decade clearly demonstrates that sociologists and other social scientists have found them to be a useful and practical method for gathering qualitative data. The leading role that sociologists have played in this field has been most evident in methodological research on focus groups, which has given sociologists a major influence on both their current uses and future directions. In terms of future directions, a group of social science researchers participated in focus groups, funded in part by the American Sociological Association, that led to a statement on "Future Directions for Focus Groups" (Morgan 1993b). Not surprisingly, several of the specific topics considered there have been echoed here, such as the need to set standards for focus groups and the need to further define the strengths and weaknesses of the method.

The major theme raised in the focus group discussions on future direction was the need to do more research on focus groups as a method, and several of the studies reviewed here provide concrete examples of how to accomplish this. For example, both Agar & MacDonald (1995) and Saferstein (1995) demonstrate the value of discourse analysis for investigating interactions between moderators and participants. Sociologists who have experimented with discourse analysis (e.g. Gamson 1992) have concluded that the time and expense spent in producing such data have little value for substantive analyses of what was said in groups. Yet, methodological analyses of how things are said in focus groups may well be a more profitable use of these tools. Another potentially useful technique from another field is Sussman et al's (1991) application of procedures from small group research. As Morgan & Krueger (1993) note, however, it is important not to confuse the standard decision-making paradigm in small groups research with the data gathering goals of focus groups. One particularly promising aspect of the Sussman et al procedures is the post-group questionnaire, and other focus group researchers (Pies 1993, Swenson et al 1992) have used this technique to investigate not only the impact that the discussion had on the participants, but also their feelings about the discussion, including the extent to which they were able to share their true opinions on the topics they discussed. One final promising technique for methodological research on focus groups is McDonald's (1993) use of an archive of focus group transcripts to investigate how differences in project goals were linked to differences in moderator style. Unfortunately, qualitative researchers have been slower in archiving their work than their quantitative counterparts; still, the opportunity to compare the qualitative procedures of multiple investigators across multiple topics would be an exciting opportunity that should not be limited to focus groups.

Data analysis is another topic for future work on focus groups. To date, most discussions of how to analyze focus groups have occurred within broader discussions of the method (e.g. Knodel 1993), and only one article is specifically dedicated to analysis of issues (Bertrand et al 1992). Although it is true that many of the analytic issues in focus groups are the same as in other qualitative methods, it is also true that focus groups raise some unique issues, such as the ongoing debate about the circumstances under which the unit of analysis should be the groups, the participants, or the participants' utterances (Carey & Smith 1994, Gamson 1992, Morgan 1995). In addition, focus groups offer some special opportunities for the application of computer technologies in the analysis of qualitative data (Javidi et al 1991).

Beyond such strictly methodological concerns, there are also promising new uses for focus groups. The most notable of these involves researchers who are more actively engaged with the participants and their concerns. In an earlier section, this was summarized as an increasing interest in focus groups among those who pursue goals such as empowerment or approaches such as action and participatory research. Underlying many of these efforts is a desire to break down the division between using groups as a means for gathering data and as a means for educating, mobilizing, or intervening with participants. This matches a widespread concern in the social sciences about the artificiality of the division between researchers and those who are researched. This issue is especially relevant for focus groups, since they have been widely touted (e.g. Morgan & Krueger 1993) as a means for helping to bridge the gap between those in authority and the people they control.

One question about focus groups that has remained unasked, however, is why they have reemerged with such popularity at this particular time. One segment of our future work on focus groups should thus go beyond practical concerns with the method itself to ask about their place within the history of sociology— especially since this is the discipline that is self-consciously charged with the study of humans in groups. Part of the present popularity of focus groups may indeed be due to their unique advantages for addressing such contemporary issues as empowerment and diversity. Whether this is true or not, it is clear that focus groups are both being shaped by the directions that our discipline is taking and playing a role in shaping those directions.

Literature Cited

Agar M, MacDonald J. 1995. Focus groups and ethnography. *Hum. Organ.* 54:78–86

Albrecht TL, Johnson GM, Walther JB. 1993. Understanding communication processes in focus groups. See Morgan 1993a, pp. 51–64

Basch CE. 1987. Focus group interview: an underutilized research technique for improv-

ing theory and practice in health education. *Health Educ. Q.* 14:411–48

Bertrand JE, Brown JE, Ward VM. 1992. Techniques for analyzing focus group data. *Eval. Rev.* 16:198–209

Bobo L, Zubrinsky CL, Johnson JH, Oliver ML. 1995. Work orientation, job discrimination,

150   MORGAN

and ethnicity: a focus group perspective. *Res. Sociol. Work* 5:45–55

Bogardus ES. 1926. The group interview. *J. Appl. Sociol.* 10:372–82

Brotherson MJ, Goldstein BL. 1992. Quality design of focus groups in early childhood special education research. *J. Early Interv.* 16:334–42

Bryant CA. 1990. The use of focus groups in program development. *Natl. Assoc. Pract. Anthropol. Bull.* 39:1–4

Bryman A. 1988. *Quality and Quantity in Social Research.* London: Unwin Hyman

Byers PY, Wilcox JR. 1991. Focus groups: a qualitative opportunity for researchers. *J. Bus. Comm.* 28:63–78

Cable ES. 1992. Women's social movement involvement: the role of structural availability in recruitment and participation processes. *Sociol. Q.* 33:35–50

Carey MA. 1994. The group effect in focus groups: planning, implementing and interpreting focus group research. In *Critical Issues in Qualitative Research Methods,* ed. J Morse, pp. 225–41. Thousand Oaks, CA: Sage

Carey, MA. 1995. Issues and applications of focus groups. *Qual. Health Res.* 5:413–530 (Special issue)

Carey MA, Smith M. 1994. Capturing the group effect in focus groups: a special concern in analysis. *Qual. Health Res.* 4:123–27

Crabtree BF, Yanoshik MK, Miller WL, O'Connor PJ. 1993. Selecting individual or group interviews. See Morgan 1993a, pp. 137–49

Delli Carpini MX, Williams B. 1994. The method is the message: focus groups as a method of social, psychological, and political inquiry. *Res. Micropolit.* 4:57–85

Diamond E, Bates S. 1992. *The Spot: The Rise of Political Advertising on Television.* Cambridge, MA: MIT Press. 3rd ed.

Duncan MT, Morgan DL. 1994. Sharing the caring: family caregivers' views of their relationships with nursing home staff. *The Gerontologist* 34:235–44

Fern EF. 1982. The use of focus groups for idea generation: the effects of group size, acquintanceship, and moderator on response quantity and quality. *J. Mark. Res.* 19:1–13

Flores JG, Alonso CG. 1995. Using focus groups in educational research. *Eval. Rev.* 19:84–101

Folch-Lyon E, de la Macorra L, Schearer SB. 1981. Focus group and survey research on family planning in Mexico. *Stud. Fam. Plan.* 12:409–32

Fowler FJ, Mangione TW. 1990. *Standardized Survey Interviewing.* Thousand Oaks, CA: Sage

Frey JH, Fontana A. 1991. The group interview in social research. *Soc. Sci. J.* 28:175–87. See also Morgan 1993a, pp. 20–34

Fuller TD, Edwards JN, Vorakitphokatorn S, Sermsri S. 1993. Using focus groups to adapt survey instruments to new populations: experience from a developing country. See Morgan 1993a, pp. 89–104

Gamson WA. 1992. *Talking Politics.* Cambridge, UK: Cambridge Univ. Press

Goldman AE, McDonald SS. 1987. *The Group Depth Interview: Principles and Practice.* Englewood Cliffs, NJ: Prentice Hall

Greenbaum TL. 1988/1993. *The Practical Handbook and Guide to Focus Group Research.* Lexington, MA: Lexington. Rev. ed.

Harari O, Beaty D. 1990. On the folly of relying solely on a questionnaire methodology in cross-cultural research. *J. Manage. Issues* 2:267–81

Hendershott A, Wright S. 1993. Student focus groups and curricular review. *Teach. Sociol.* 21:154–59

Hoppe MJ, Wells EA, Morrison DM, Gillmore MR, Wilsdon A. 1995. Using focus groups to discuss sensitive topics with children. *Eval. Rev.* 19:102–14

Hugentobler MK, Israel BA, Schurman SJ. 1992. An action research approach to workplace health: integrating methods. *Health Educ. Q.* 19:55–76

Hughes D, DuMont K. 1993. Using focus groups to facilitate culturally anchored research. *Am. J. Community Psychol.* 21:775–806

Irwin J. 1970. *The Felon.* Englewood Cliffs, NJ: Prentice Hall

Irwin K, Bertrand J, Mibandumba N, Mbuyi K, Muremeri C, et al. 1991. Knowledge, attitudes and beliefs about HIV infection and AIDS among healthy factory workers and their wives, Kinshasa, Zaire. *Soc. Sci. Med.* 32:917–30

Jarrett RL. 1993. Focus group interviewing with low-income, minority populations: a research experience. See Morgan 1993a, pp. 184–201

Jarrett RL. 1994. Living poor: family life among single parent, African-American women. *Soc. Probl.* 41:30–49

Javidi M, Long LW, Vasu ML, Ivy DK. 1991. Enhancing focus group validity with computer-assisted technology in social science research. *Soc. Sci. Comput. Rev.* 9:231–45

Joseph JG, Emmons CA, Kessler RC, Wortman CB, O'Brien K, et al. 1984. Coping with the threat of AIDS: an approach to psychosocial assessment. *Am. Psychol.* 39:1297–302

Khan ME, Manderson L. 1992. Focus groups in tropical diseases research. *Health Policy Plan.* 7:56–66

Kitzinger J. 1994a. The methodology of focus groups: the importance of interaction between research participants. *Sociol. Health Illn.* 16:103–21

Kitzinger J. 1994b. Focus groups: method or madness. In *Challenge and Innovation: Methodological Advances in Social Research on HIV/AIDS*, ed. M Boulton, pp. 159–75. New York: Taylor & Francis

Kline A, Kline E, Oken E. 1992. Minority women and sexual choice in the age of AIDS. *Soc. Sci. Med.* 34:447–57

Knodel J. 1993. The design and analysis of focus group studies: a practical approach. See Morgan 1993a, pp. 35–50

Knodel J. 1995. Focus group research on the living arrangements of elderly in Asia. *J. Cross-Cult. Gerontol.* 10:1–162 (Special issue)

Knodel J, Chamratrithirong A, Debavalya N. 1987. *Thailand's Reproductive Revolution: Rapid Fertility Decline in a Third-World Setting.* Madison, WI: Univ. Wisc. Press

Krueger RA. 1993. Quality control in focus group research. See Morgan 1993a, pp. 65–85

Krueger RA. 1988/1994. *Focus Groups: A Practical Guide for Applied Research.* Thousand Oaks, CA: Sage. 2nd ed.

Kullberg JS. 1994. The ideological roots of elite political conflict in post-Soviet Russia. *Eur. Asia Stud.* 46:929–53

Laurie H. 1992. Multiple methods in the study of household resource allocation. In *Mixing Methods: Qualitative and Quantitative Research*, ed. J Brannen, pp. 145–68. Brookfield, VT: Avebury

Laurie H, Sullivan O. 1991. Combining qualitative and quantitative data in the longitudinal study of household allocations. *Sociol. Rev.* 39:113–30

Lederman LC. 1990. Assessing educational effectiveness: the focus group interview as a technique for data collection. *Commun. Educ.* 39:117–27

Lengua LJ, Roosa MW, Schupak-Neuberg E, Michaels ML, Berg CN, Weschler LF. 1992. Using focus groups to guide the development of a parenting program for difficult-to-reach, high-risk families. *Fam. Relat.* 41:163–68

Lincoln YS, Guba EG. 1985. *Naturalistic Inquiry.* Thousand Oaks, CA: Sage

Magill RS. 1993. Focus groups, program evaluation, and the poor. *J. Sociol. Soc. Welfare* 20:103–14

McDonald WJ. 1993. Focus group research dynamics and reporting: an examination of research objectives and moderator influences. *J. Acad. Mark. Sci.* 21:161–68

McKinlay JB. 1993. The promotion of health through planned sociopolitical change: challenges for research and policy. *Soc. Sci. Med.* 36:109–17

McQuarrie EF. 1990. Review of: Morgan, *Focus Groups as Qualitative Research*, and McCracken, *The Long Interview. J. Mark. Res.* 13:114–17

McQuarrie EF. 1996. *The Market Research Toolbox.* Thousand Oaks, CA: Sage

Merton RK. 1987. The focused interview and focus groups: continuities and discontinuities. *Public Opin. Q.* 51:550–66

Merton RK, Fiske M, Kendall PL. 1956/1990. *The Focused Interview.* New York: Free Press. 2nd ed.

Merton RK, Kendall PL. 1946. The focused interview. *Am. J. Sociol.* 51:541–57

Mischler EG. 1986. *Research Interviewing: Context and Narrative.* Cambridge, MA: Harvard Univ. Press

Montell FB. 1995. *Focus group interviews: a new feminist method.* Presented at Annu. Meet. Am. Sociol. Assoc., Washington, DC

Morgan DL. 1988. *Focus Groups as Qualitative Research.* Thousand Oaks, CA: Sage

Morgan DL. 1989. Adjusting to widowhood: do social networks really make it easier? *Gerontologist* 29:101–7

Morgan DL. 1992a. Designing focus group research. In *Tools for Primary Care Research*, ed. M Stewart, et al, pp. 177–93. Thousand Oaks, CA: Sage

Morgan DL. 1992b. Doctor caregiver relationships: an exploration using focus groups. In *Doing Qualitative Research in Primary Care: Multiple Strategies*, ed. B Crabtree, W Miller, pp. 205–30. Thousand Oaks, CA: Sage

Morgan DL. 1993a. *Successful Focus Groups: Advancing the State of the Art.* Thousand Oaks, CA: Sage

Morgan DL. 1993b. Future directions for focus groups. See Morgan 1993a, pp. 225–44

Morgan DL. 1993c. *Focus groups and surveys.* Presented at Annu. Meet. Am. Sociol. Assoc., Pittsburg, PA

Morgan DL. 1994. *Seeking diagnosis for a family member with Alzheimer's disease.* Presented at Annu. Meet. Am. Sociol. Assoc., Los Angeles, CA

Morgan DL. 1995. Why things (sometimes) go wrong in focus groups. *Qual. Health Res.* 5:516–22

Morgan DL, Krueger RA. 1993. When to use focus groups and why. See Morgan 1993a, pp. 3–19

Morgan DL, Spanish MT. 1985. Social interaction and the cognitive organisation of health-relevant behavior. *Sociol. Health Illness* 7:401–22

Morgan DL, Zhao PZ. 1993. The doctor-caregiver relationship: managing the care of family members with Alzheimer's disease. *Qual. Health Res.* 3:133–64

Nelson JE, Frontczak NT. 1988. How acquaintanceship and analyst can influence focus group results. *J. Advert.* 17:41–48

Nichols-Casebolt A, Spakes P. 1995. Policy research and the voices of women. *Soc. Work Res.* 19:49–55

O'Brien KJ. 1993. Improving survey questionnaires through focus groups. See Morgan 1993a, pp. 105–17

O'Connor PJ, Crabtree BF, Abourizk NN. 1992. Longitudinal study of a diabetes education and care intervention. *J. Am. Board Fam. Practice* 5:381–87

Orosz JF. 1994. *The use of focus groups in health care service delivery: understanding and improving the health care experience.* Presented at Qual. Health Res. Conf., Hershey, PA

Padilla R. 1993. Using dialogical methods in group interviews. See Morgan 1993a, pp. 153–66

Pies C. 1993. *Controversies in context: ethics, values, and policies concerning NORPLANT.* PhD thesis. Univ. Calif., Berkeley

Pinderhughes H. 1993. The anatomy of racially motivated violence in New York City: a case study of youth in southern Brooklyn. *Soc. Probl.* 40:478–92

Pollak M, Paicheler G, Pierret J. 1992. AIDS: a problem for sociological research. *Curr. Sociol./La Sociol. Contemp.* 40:1–134

Race KE, Hotch DF, Packer T. 1994. Rehabilitation program evaluation: use of focus groups to empower clients. *Eval. Rev.* 18:730–40

Saferstein B. 1995. *Focusing opinions: conversation, authority, and the (re)construction of knowledge.* Presented at Annu. Meet. Am. Sociol. Assoc., Washington, DC

Saint-Germain MA, Bassford TL, Montano G. 1993. Surveys and focus groups in health research with older Hispanic women. *Qual. Health Res.* 3:341–67

Sasson T. 1995. *Crime Talk: How Citizens Construct a Social Problem.* Hawthorne, NY: Aldine

Schearer SB. 1981. The value of focus group research for social action programs. *Stud. Fam. Plan.* 12:407–8

Shively JE. 1992. Cowboys and Indians: perceptions of Western films among American Indians and Anglos. *Am. Sociol. Rev.* 57:725–34

Smith MW. 1995. Ethics in focus groups: a few concerns. *Qual. Health Res.* 5:478–86

Staley CS. 1990. Focus group research: the communication practitioner as marketing specialist. In *Applied Communication Theory and Research,* ed. D O'Hair, G Kreps, pp. 185–201. Hillsdale, NJ: Erlbaum

Stewart DW, Shamdasani PN. 1990. *Focus Groups: Theory and Practice.* Thousand Oaks, CA: Sage

Stycos JM. 1981. A critique of focus group and survey research: the machismo case. *Stud. Fam. Plan.* 12:450–56

Sussman S, Burton D, Dent CW, Stacy AW, Flay BR. 1991. Use of focus groups in developing an adolescent tobacco use cessation program: collective norm effects. *J. Appl. Soc. Psychol.* 21:1772–82

Swenson JD, Griswold WF, Kleiber PB. 1992. Focus groups: method of inquiry/intervention. *Small Groups Res.* 23:459–74

Templeton JF. 1987. *Focus Groups: A Guide for Marketing and Advertising Professionals.* Chicago: Probus

Vaughn S, Shumm JS, Sinagub S. 1996. *Focus Group Interviews in Education and Psychology.* Thousand Oaks. CA: Sage

Ward VM, Bertrand JT, Brown LF. 1991. The comparability of focus group and survey results. *Eval. Rev.* 15:266–83

Wight D. 1994. Boys' thoughts and talk about sex in a working class locality of Glasgow. *Sociol. Rev.* 42:702–37

Wolff B, Knodel J, Sittitrai W. 1993. Focus groups and surveys as complementary research methods: a case example. See Morgan 1993a, pp. 118–36

Zeller RA. 1993a. Focus group research on sensitive topics: setting the agenda without setting the agenda. See Morgan 1993a, pp. 167–83

Zeller RA. 1993b. Combining qualitative and quantitative techniques to develop culturally sensitive measures. In *Methodological Issues in AIDS Behavioral Research,* ed. D Ostrow, R Kessler, pp. 95–116. New York: Plenum

Annu. Rev. Sociol. 1996. 22:153–85

GENDER INEQUALITY AND HIGHER EDUCATION

Jerry A. Jacobs

Department of Sociology, University of Pennsylvania, Philadelphia, Pennsylvania
19104

KEY WORDS: women's education, educational history, women's colleges, college majors, fields
of study

ABSTRACT

This paper reviews a diverse literature on gender and higher education. Gender
inequality is more pronounced in some aspects of the educational systems than
in others. The analysis distinguishes 1) access to higher education; 2) college
experiences; and 3) postcollegiate outcomes. Women fare relatively well in the
area of access, less well in terms of the college experience, and are particularly
disadvantaged with respect to the outcomes of schooling. Explanations of gender
inequality in higher education should distinguish between these different aspects
of education and should explain those contexts in which women have attained
parity as well as those in which they continue to lag behind men.

INTRODUCTION

In this essay I draw on a disparate literature to discuss several key questions regarding the relationship between gender inequality and higher education. What
aspects of education exhibit the most pronounced gender disparities? How does
the education of women interface with gender inequality in the workplace and
in the family? Has the expansion of education for women stimulated changes
in other arenas, or has the educational system merely reflected developments
in the rest of society?

I found research pertinent to these questions in diverse fields outside of
sociology, including economics, history, social psychology, career counseling,
and educational policy. One recent review of the literature on the effects of
college on students included a bibliography running 150 pages (Pascarella &

153

0360-0572/96/0815-0153$08.00

Terenzini 1991). Rather than review every study that considers the question of sex differences, I focus on those issues that are central to the question of gender inequality. I examine areas that have been vigorously debated—such as the effects of single-sex colleges on women's achievements. I also highlight topics that call for more careful scrutiny—such as why women's achievements in higher education in the United States surpass those in many other industrial countries.

Educational theory and research remain focused on social class disparities. Classic studies of inequality in education typically have focused on disparities by social class among men (Blau & Duncan 1967, Bourdieu & Passeron 1977, Collins 1979, Karabel & Halsey 1977). When gender inequality is discussed, it receives relatively limited attention. For example, Aronowitz & Giroux (1993) devote less than 2 of 256 pages to gender issues. Gender often is mentioned as a variation on the central theme of social class inequalities (Davies 1995). Scholars who do focus on gender issues often treat all aspects of education as working to the disadvantage of women (Sadker & Sadker 1993, Sandler 1986, Byrne 1978). In contrast, I suggest that education is often a relatively advantaged sphere of social life for women, and that gender inequality is more pronounced in some aspects of the educational system than others. My analysis focuses on three processes: 1. access to higher education; 2. college experiences; and 3. postcollegiate outcomes. Women fare relatively well in the area of access, less so in terms of the college experience, and are particularly disadvantaged with respect to the outcomes of schooling. Explanations of gender inequality in higher education should distinguish between these different aspects of education and should explain those contexts in which women have attained parity as well as those in which they continue to trail men.

Many important issues are not covered in this essay: women's athletics, gender equity in standardized testing, part-time and adult study, and the community college experience. The focus on gender differentials also means that relatively little attention has been devoted to variation among women—by class, race, and ethnicity. It is my hope that the focus on gender issues provides insights that help to situate future research on particular groups of women.

ACCESS

Women's Access to College in the United States

In this section I review findings on the enrollment and degree completion of women compared to men, drawing on contemporary and historical data on the United States, as well as international comparisons. I then turn to explanations offered for these patterns, with theories organized under four broad rubrics:

critical or reproductionist, status attainment, comparative historical, and economic.

One of the striking features of education in the United States is the prominence of women among college students. In 1992, women represented 53.1% of enrolled college students. Of women who graduated from high school in 1992, 65.4% enrolled in college the following fall, compared with 59.7% of men. Women's share of degrees climbed steadily during the 1970s and 1980s (Karen 1991), during a period when the fraction of college-age young adults enrolled in school increased slowly but steadily (US Department of Education 1995). By 1982, women surpassed men in the number of bachelor's degrees earned. Women have garnered more bachelor's degrees than their male counterparts ever since. By 1992, 54.2% of bachelor's degree recipients were women. Women earned 58.9% of two-year degrees, 51.5% of master's and professional degrees, and 37.3% of PhD degrees (National Center for Educational Statistics 1994).

In recent years, women's advantage in college enrollment has been similar to that observed for earned degrees, which suggests that women and men complete their degrees at similar rates. Progression to graduate and professional degrees is now at parity by gender. This represents a marked change from earlier periods in this century, when women's completion rates trailed men's (Goldin 1995). Only among PhD recipients does women's representation continue to lag.

Are women equally represented at top-tier institutions? Hearn (1990) and Persell et al (1992) report, based on an analysis of data on 1980 high school seniors, that women were disadvantaged in access to elite schools. While women have made progress since 1980 (Karen 1991), they remain slightly overrepresented in schools with higher acceptance rates, lower faculty/student ratios, lower standardized test scores, and lower fees (Jacobs 1996). The small remaining sex gap at top-tier schools is due to two factors: 1. the relative scarcity of women in schools with large engineering programs and 2. the tendency of women to enroll in school part-time (lower-status institutions are more likely to accept part-time students). Selected reports on admissions as well as enrollment from leading institutions indicate that women are well represented among recent entering classes, except in schools that prominently feature engineering programs (Monthly Forum on Women in Higher Education 1995).

Adult or continuing education represents a substantial fraction of tertiary schooling in the United States (Kasworm 1990). Over one third (35.8%) of college students enrolled in the fall of 1991 were over age 24, including 17.1% of full-time students and 63.9% of part-time students. Women represent 61.8% of these older students, including 57.0% of those enrolled full-time and 63.7% of those enrolled part-time.

The parity women have achieved in college completion is a recent phenomenon, but the 1950s and 1960s represented a historically depressed level. Women represented 41.3% of college graduates in 1940, slipping to 23.9% in 1950, and remaining at a historically low 35.0% in 1960 (US Bureau of the Census 1975). Goldin (1995) estimates, based on retrospective reports from the 1940 Census, that women's college enrollment rates exceeded 90% of men's from the late 1890s until the mid 1920s, although the inclusion of "normal schools," which were often less academically rigorous than other institutions, arguably inflates Goldin's figures (see also Graham 1978).

For the entire twentieth century in the United States, women have comprised a large proportion of students in primary and secondary schools. Women's rate of enrollment among 5–19 year olds has exceeded 90% of men's rate since as early as 1850, and 98% since 1890. Women have represented the majority of high school graduates since at least 1870—in 1920 over 60% of high school graduates were women (US Bureau of the Census 1975: pp. 369–70, 379). Analysis of individual-level data from the 1910 Census indicates that women's enrollments in elementary and high schools were comparable to their male counterparts for most immigrant groups (Jacobs & Greene 1994), although attendance data strongly favor males for certain ethnic groups, such as the Italians (US Immigration Commission 1911, Olneck & Lazerson 1974). The median years of schooling completed by women exceeded those by men for most of this century (Folger & Nam 1967), until the GI Bill after World War II enabled men to surpass women.

International Comparisons

Women in the United States surpassed their counterparts in other countries in access to schooling at both the secondary and tertiary levels for more than a century (Klemm 1901, US Commissioner of Education 1900). Today, the United States enrolls more college students per capita than virtually any other country, and women's share of college enrollments in the United States exceeds that in most other countries (see Stromquist 1989, Kelly 1989, Kelly & Slaughter 1991, King & Hill 1993, and Finn et al 1979 for informative reviews of women and education in developing countries). Data for selected countries are presented in Table 1. In most of the advanced industrial countries of Europe, women's share of enrollments is quite high. But even here, substantial variation persists, with women's share ranging from 40% of college students in Switzerland and 41% in Germany to 55% in France and 61% in Portugal (see also Byrne 1978). Women also fared well in terms of schooling in the socialist countries of Eastern Europe (Kelly 1991, Finn et al 1979), and socialist regimes in developing countries, in their initial years in power, typically emphasized schooling for girls (Carnoy & Samoff 1990). The postsocialist experience warrants close scrutiny, as women's status is eroding in many spheres in these countries (Biaecki &

Heyns 1993, Heyns & Biaecki 1992, Einhorn 1993).

Women's share of enrollment in Latin American colleges and universities is often quite high—Brazil, 53%; Argentina, 47%; Chile, 42%. Asian countries follow: In both China and India one third of college students are women. African countries include many with the lowest share of female enrollments in the world. Within each of these regions, there is substantial variation in women's share of enrollment.

Gender disparities are highest at the tertiary level, as young men typically pursue college before the women in their cohort do. Gender disparities in expenditures are greater than those in enrollments, because college education is more expensive than elementary or secondary schooling.

In terms of adult education, the United States ranked third among eight countries studied—behind Norway and Finland, but just ahead of Sweden and Switzerland—in the proportion of college-level adult students (OECD 1995). However, these figures include those in on-the-job training, in which the United States trails other countries (Lynch 1994). The standing of the United States on continuing education alone might well have been higher.

In some countries, including the United States, education has been relatively favorable to women, compared to other spheres of social life. Why do women get so much education? And why is there more access in the United States than elsewhere?

Explaining Access: Critical Approaches

Theorists who have focused most directly on the issue of gender inequality have approached the subject from a critical, feminist, or neomarxist perspective (Holland & Eisenhart 1990, Stromquist 1989, Connell et al 1982). Critical scholars seek to explain how the educational system reproduces gender inequality in society despite its provoking resistance to such inequality on the part of women students. Holland & Eisenhart argue that a culture of romance leads young women away from a focus on their studies and careers. Based on in-depth interviews and observations with students spanning several years at two southern colleges, they conclude that the college experience is tangential to intellectual and career development among young women. Their ethnographic research is the latest in a series of detailed investigations of undergraduate culture dating back to the 1930s (Hulbert & Schuster 1993, Angrist & Almquist 1975, Komarovsky 1971 (1953), 1985, Waller 1937).

Some basic flaws in the reproductionist approach make it unlikely that this perspective will be useful for elucidating gender issues. In my view, the central theoretical problem with the reproductionist model is that schools do not simply mirror the demands of the economy. Educational systems are surely influenced by vocational exigencies, but schools can easily expand in advance of employ-

Table 1 Comparative data on enrollment, and student and faculty sex composition[1]

Country	Tertiary Enrollment (Per 100,000 Population)	University Faculty Percent Female	University Students Percent Female
North & Central America			
Canada	7197	21(%)	55(%)
Cuba	1836	47	58
El Salvador	1512	26	31
Haiti	107	26	29
Jamaica	950	29	63
Mexico	1478	–	45
Nicaragua	814	31	50
Panama	2377	–	58
United States	5687	31	53
South America			
Argentina	3293	35	47
Brazil	1075	38	53
Chile	2144	–	42
Columbia	1554	25	50
Ecuador	1958	–	39
Paraguay	769	–	46
Peru	3465	16	34
Uruguay	2180	30	53
Venezuela	2847	–	47
Europe			
Austria	2847	24	45
Belgium	2772	21	45
Czech Republic	1128	34	56
Denmark	2917	–	51
France	3414	28	55
Germany	3051	20	41
Greece	1928	29	53
Italy	2795	–	50
Netherlands	3280	21	43
Norway	3883	21	50
Poland	1521	38	52
Portugal	1935	31	61
Russian Federation	1900	–	50
Spain	3335	31	52
Switzerland	2147	12	40

(*continued*)

Table 1 *(continued)*

Country	Tertiary Enrollment (Per 100,000 Population)	University Faculty Percent Female	University Students Percent Female
Middle East			
Algeria[a]	1163	20	31
Egypt	1697	29	38
Iran	1061	18	31
Iraq[a]	1240	25	38
Israel	2790	32	51
Jordan	2497	12	42
Kuwait	1135	22	68
Saudi Arabia	1064	25	42
Syria	1695	20	38
Turkey	1569	33	37
Asia & Pacific			
Afghanistan	147	22	42
Bangladesh	382	12	20
China[a]	191	12	20
Hong Kong	1534	23	40
India	556	19	32
Indonesia[a]	1032	8	14
Japan	2338	12	29
Korea (South)	4208	22	30
Malaysia	679	24	46
Pakistan	266	17	24
Philippines[a]	2596	53	54
Thailand	2060	51	53
Vietnam	153	22	24
Australia	3178	31	53
New Zealand	4332	26	52
Sub-Sarahan Africa			
Ivory Coast	204	–	19
Kenya	187	–	28
Liberia	–	20	24
Morocco	158	19	37
Nigeria	320	10	27
Senegal	266	15	22
S. Africa	1231	29	48
Tanzania	21	6	15
Zimbabwe	582	16	26

[1] Source: UNESCO, 1995. Figures pertain to most recent year, typically early 1990s. No data are earlier than 1980.

[a] Figures pertain to all tertiary education, not just universities and equivalent institutions.

ment needs or lag behind the economy. Many European countries developed extensive educational systems well in advance of industrialization (Graff 1979, 1987); some produced far more college graduates than their economies could absorb (Barbagli 1982). Moreover, the mechanisms that explain the correspondence that does occur must be specified.

There are also fundamental problems with extending the logic of class reproduction to the case of gender inequality. The analogy between class and gender fails because these two forms of inequality bear a fundamentally different relationship to the educational system. Differential access to higher education is a principal support for racial and social class inequality. In other words, the disadvantaged social position of (*a*) those holding less prestigious positions in society, (*b*) racial and ethnic minorities, and (*c*) the unemployed stems in large part from the fact that they do not have the educational credentials—especially college degrees—of the more socioeconomically successful groups. However, as we have seen, in the United States women have attained access to higher education more or less on par with their male counterparts (although among middle-aged and older women the gender disparity in education attained during the 1950s remains). Gender inequality in earnings persists despite rough equality in access to education, whereas class inequality is based on sharp differences in access to education.

My objection to the resistance approach is that it sometimes infers resistance among students where none exists, while it ignores organized feminist activism in higher education. In the search for student resistance, Holland & Eisenhart, along with others (Lees 1986, Griffin 1985, McRobbie 1982), drew on Willis's (1977) influential study of working class boys in a British secondary school. Holland & Eisenhart found only relatively subtle and individualistic resistance to the culture of romance, compared with somewhat more strident and collective disobedience on the part of Willis's subjects. Yet Holland & Eisenhart look for resistance in the wrong place. Feminist activism is responsible for much of the expansion in opportunities for women, from the founding of elite women's schools (Woody 1929, Solomon 1985, Rosenberg 1982) to the ongoing organizing activity of the American Association of University Women (AAUW) (Levine 1995), to Betty Friedan's (1963) influential critique of the narrow options available to college-educated women, to the passage of equal educational opportunity legislation for women (Stromquist 1993). Women's access to higher education did not emerge because of the dictates of the captains of industry, but because women successfully demanded a place. This does not mean that interviews with a small group of women students during a conservative period in history will reflect clear-cut resistance to patriarchy.

Explaining Access: Status Attainment

Status attainment is an alternative framework for explaining gender inequality. For attainment researchers, gender is an ascriptive characteristic like race. Early attainment studies included gender as a predictor of years of schooling completed (Alexander & Eckland 1974, Marini & Greenberger 1978). More recent studies have not devoted a great deal of attention to gender, although there are some some notable exceptions (Alexander et al 1987a, 1987b, Hearn 1992), because gender tends not to be a significant predictor of educational attainment. Anderson & Hearn (1992) review the literature on educational status attainment (see also Karen 1991).

Some research that explores family composition effects has investigated the possibility that particular combinations of brothers and sisters might reduce parental investments in daughters' schooling (Powell & Steelman 1989, 1990, Butcher & Case 1994). However, given the relatively high levels of educational attainment of women in recent years, there is little reason to expect that parents continue to favor sons over daughters in terms of the decision to pursue college (Hauser & Kuo 1995; see also Behrman et al 1986). The number and spacing of siblings undoubtedly influence the enrollment of children, but at present in the United States these constraints probably do not inhibit parental investments in daughters more than in sons.

The lack of sex differences is viewed as evidence for the triumph of achievement over ascription, but the problem is accounting for universalism that exists in some contexts but not others. In attainment terminology, how does relatively universalistic access in the United States coexist with sharp ascriptive differences in educational process and outcomes? Status attainment researchers are well positioned to determine whether gender per se or other factors are responsible for whatever sex gaps may be observed, but as yet they have not offered a theory of when gender can be expected to matter and when its effects are attenuated. Moreover, international variation has not been explored. To the best of my knowledge, no attainment studies have attempted to explain why young women trail young men in college graduation in some countries more than others.

In principle, proponents of the attainment framework should be able to address gender inequality just as easily as they have addressed race and socioeconomic inequality. At its broadest, the attainment framework is designed to explain later outcomes from earlier inputs. Its individualistic bias can easily be modified by the incorporation of context-level variables. Development of the framework has been stymied by the absence of gender inequality in educational attainment and in the preferred measure of career outcomes, socioeconomic status (England 1979, Jacobs & Powell 1987). This combination has led attainment researchers to focus little attention on gender inequality in the college experience and has led researchers interested in gender to explore different indicators of gender inequality.

Mickelson (1989) has attempted to explain women's high levels of educational attainment. The puzzle, as she poses it, is why women persist in schooling despite the limited financial returns they face. She considers four possible explanations for this paradox: female reference groups, unrealistic expectations, improved access to high status husbands, and sex-role socialization. While there may be some truth to each of these suggestions, none explains why the attainment of women relative to men is so much higher in the United States than in many other industrial countries, and moreso in developed countries than in less developed ones. Neither can these suggestions account for the rise over time in the level of women's education relative to men's.

Explaining Access: Comparative Historical Approaches

Another sociological approach explores comparative and historical variation in education experiences (Meyer & Hannan 1979, Meyer et al 1979, Rubinson 1986). Again, this approach should be ideally suited for elucidating gender inequality. Yet practitioners of this approach remain focused on class and race issues and have yet to devote sustained attention to the connection between schooling and gender inequality. Only a few studies explore gender patterns of schooling, and not all of these have focused on explaining the extent of gender disparities. For example, Walters (1986) finds that expanding employment opportunities contributed to the growth of higher education for women between 1952 and 1980. But the remaining puzzle is why the gender gap in education has narrowed more than that observed in labor force participation.

Ramirez & Boli (1987) explore international trends in enrollment through 1975 (see also Ramirez 1980, Ramirez & Weiss 1979). They suggest that there has been diffusion across countries of a model of the relationship between states and individuals that is predicated on the compulsory education of all citizens, and which inevitably results in the incorporation of females into the educational system. They suggest that the demands of citizenship predict an increasing female share of higher education, although applying the notion of citizenship to explain enrollments in higher education seems like a bit of a stretch. More such studies with a longer time frame and more countries would be informative. [See Behrman & Rosenzweig (1994) for cautions regarding the comparability of educational data across countries.]

Clark (1992) reports that the more multinational investment in a developing country, the less higher education is provided for girls. He argues that this is due to the influence of multinational corporations on local political systems as well as on gender role ideology and job opportunities for women. Clark's research is part of a growing interest in the effect of the world system on women's status and employment opportunities (Ward 1990).

Comparative studies of international enrollment trends conducted by economists focus on the influence of national income levels, urbanization, and fertility. Schultz (1987) shows that the enrollment of girls climbed faster than that of boys in the poorest countries during the period 1961–1980. Specifically, he finds that the elasticity of enrollment with respect to national income is higher for girls than for boys. His findings are consistent with those of Tan & Mingat's research in Asia (1992), who show that gender disparities in elementary and secondary enrollments taper off as countries approach universal enrollment. However, it does not necessarily follow that the same pattern will characterize higher education, since universal enrollment remains unlikely at the college and university level.

A number of informative studies of US women's educational history have been conducted, although most of the focus is on elite schools for women (Solomon 1985, Horowitz 1993, Schwager 1987, Cott 1993, Woody 1929; see also Delamont 1989). Yet a comprehensive comparative historical account of women's access to higher education that highlights the relatively favorable position of US women remains to be done. Some factors that might well contribute to the distinctive position of women in higher education in the United States are 1. the decentralized structure of higher education (Jencks & Reisman 1968), with over 3000 public and private institutions, which allowed for the creation of specialized colleges for women; 2. the existence of the social space for the independent political mobilization of women, which enabled them to create some of the first schools for women; and 3. the ideology of individual opportunity, which women successfully exploited to justify their pursuit of higher education.

Culture and politics feature prominently in comparative historical research, while they are frequently relegated to a minor role in other treatments of education. To what extent do cultural factors impede schooling for girls? The case of women's education in Muslim societies may be instructive in this regard. In some traditional Muslim societies, the requirement that boys and girls attend separate schools may reduce access for girls. The education of girls can suffer when there are not enough schools for girls or when the distance to these schools creates parental concerns about safety, propriety, and the loss of daughter's time for household chores. But this effect is most pronounced in poor countries: oil-related wealth has produced marked improvements in the education of girls. In Kuwait, for example, elementary and secondary education is universal for both sexes, and women attend college in larger numbers than do men (El-Sanabary 1993).

The Muslim preference for same-sex teachers reduces the job opportunities available to women, who otherwise generally garner the lion's share of elementary teaching positions. On the other hand, the expectation of same-sex doctors creates an opportunity for women physicians in some Muslim countries that exceeds women's share of medical positions in many western countries.

The rapid rise of women's education in the oil-producing countries may be interpreted by some as evidence that traditional constraints on women can be overcome by modernization. Put in economic terms, culture acts as a drag on rational allocation of resources, but this lag is overcome more or less easily as incomes rise. Traditional cultures are assumed to be static, acting only as a lag on the forces of modernization and universalism (Ogburn 1922).

But cultures can be dynamic as well as static. Cultural change often occurs with the formation of a nation state. Ramirez & Weiss (1979) stress the importance of political centralization in educational diffusion for women at the elementary and secondary levels in developing countries. Their approach follows Meyer et al's (1979) emphasis on educational expansion as a key step in nation building.

Education serves many gods: It can be used to pursue salvation, vocation, civilization, participation, and recreation (Kelly 1983, cited in Coats 1994). The relative importance of these goals is a matter of history, politics, and culture. The connection between culture and education for women, both positive and negative, needs more thorough exploration.

Wars tend to create employment openings for women, but also educational opportunities as well. The case of women's higher education in Germany during the Third Reich is a case in point. Pauwels (1984) shows that women's enrollment in universities declined markedly from 1933–1939 both in absolute numbers and relative to men, as the Nazis stressed women's familial roles, sought to boost women's fertility, and questioned the intellectual capabilities of women. Ironically, the growing enlistment of young men in the military created a vacuum in college for women to fill, and the war years saw a sharp increase in women's enrollments, both in absolute and relative terms. Barbagli (1982) presents similar evidence for Italy during both the First and Second World Wars (see also De Grazia 1992). In both Germany and Italy these gains were rather quickly eroded in the postwar period (UNESCO 1967). In the United States, women's share of college degrees soared during the Second World War, but women's college enrollment actually declined in absolute terms relative to prewar levels (US Bureau of the Census 1975: 385–386). Women's enrollment in particular fields, such as medicine, did sharply increase during the war, only to tumble abruptly to prewar levels at the conclusion of hostilities (Walsh 1977).

Explaining Access: Economic Models

While the comparative literature on education remains sparse, there is an extensive literature on the returns to schooling and individual-level determinants of education in particular countries (King & Hill 1993, Stromquist 1989, Moore 1987). Parental economic resources are central determinants of attainment, but this effect is often greater for girls than for boys (Stromquist 1989). The same holds for parental education. Distance from school is often more important for girls than boys, especially in countries with single sex schools and a cultural emphasis on propriety. Boys often have more opportunity to make money that draws them into the labor market and out of school, but girls often have more obligations to help with housekeeping and childcare activities. Some studies in moderate income countries find that many girls who are not attending school are engaged in neither income-generating activities nor household chores (Stromquist 1989; see Durbin & Kent (1989) for similar evidence on the United States). My discussion of the economic approach to education centers on whether this perspective captures how children and their families decide to pursue or terminate schooling. In particular, does this literature help us to understand the share of schooling conferred on young women?

Several prominent economists have offered distinctive approaches to understanding women's educational investments. Becker (1975) writes that parents would be rational to invest less in their daughters' schooling than in their sons, even if the percentage change in earnings with an additional year of schooling were identical for both sexes, because their daughters could be expected to work full time for fewer years than do sons. The expected lifetime payoff of a son's education would thus exceed that of a daughter's. This is the private (sometimes referred to as internal) return in terms of earnings to education. This prediction was consistent with the lower investments in young women's college education when Becker formulated this approach during the 1960s, and it is consistent with the lower level of college enrollment for women in many countries today. But this approach does not account for the parity in college enrollments women have achieved in recent years in the United States and in a number of other developed countries.

Becker and others also seem to ignore the fact that men have a larger base level of earnings than do women, so the same percentage return is worth more for sons than daughters. I suspect parents would rather get a 10% return on a $20,000 earnings base (for a son) as opposed to a 10% return on a $15,000 base (for a daughter).

Schultz (1993a,b) maintains that Becker's approach is flawed because it ignores the increased social productivity of women who do not work. He posits that the increased productivity of women in nonmarket work is identical to that in market work. He also emphasizes that the social returns to schooling—those reaped by society at large rather than the family itself—for women are high, and consequently he urges more investment in their education (see discussion of outcomes of schooling below). This recommendation is consistent with Benavot's (1989) findings that educating girls gives a larger boost to economic development than does educating boys. But Schultz is left with the problem of explaining why parents underinvest in their daughters' schooling.

A third approach to calculating the payoff from women's schooling is offered by Goldin (1992, 1995), who holds that husbands' earnings should be included in the calculation of the costs and benefits of a college education (see also Becker 1975, Behrman et al 1986, Boulier & Rosenzweig 1984). Educational homogamy in marriages is extensively documented (Mare 1991, Lichter 1990). It is evident in second marriages as well as in first marriages (Jacobs & Furstenberg 1986) and characterizes interethnic and interracial marriages as well as endogamous ones (Jacobs & Labov 1995).

Goldin (1995) suggests that during the 1950s women were drawn into college by the financial value of the "Mrs." degree. College attendance increased the chances of marrying a college-educated husband with high earnings potential: 64% of women aged 30–39 in 1960 with 16 or more years of schooling married college-educated husbands, compared with only 11% for women with a high school degree. Indeed, Goldin estimates that 57% of women graduates married before or during their year of college graduation. Goldin concludes that the private rate of return to college approximately doubles if husband's earnings are added to what a college-educated woman could bring home herself.

However, Goldin applies this logic only to the cohort attending college during the 1950s. Ironically, this was the cohort of daughters with the lowest share of college attendance compared to their brothers. If this logic motivated college attendance, the gap between young women and men should have narrowed, rather than widened. The gender gap in enrollment did not narrow until the 1960s, when the career dimension rather than marital dimension of women's college decisions began to rise.

Moreover, if husbands' incomes were included in the financial calculus for the first generation of women college graduates, the total returns to college would be negative, since nearly one third of this group never married (Goldin 1995, Solomon 1985, Rosenberg 1982) and thus lost the prospect of a husband's earnings. The positive effect of college on women's marriage prospects was not taken for granted by the first generation of women attending college. Indeed, there was widespread concern over the low marriage rates of college-educated women (Solomon 1985, Cookingham 1984). If one applies Goldin's family income calculus consistently, one would have to conclude that the decision to enroll in college was a poor investment for the first generation of women college graduates.

By the 1920s, however, the marriages rates of college-educated women markedly improved, and the marriage-market dimension of college became evident (Horowitz 1993, Frankfort 1977). Smock & Youssef (1977) describe a similar transformation in attitudes regarding educated wives in Egypt, while Hooper (1984) reports that male Chinese college students voice reluctance to seek a college-educated bride (cited in Tilak 1993). This transformation of women's education from marriage-inhibiting to marriage-promoting deserves further attention. In a number of countries, however, men remain ambivalent about, if not actively hostile to, educated wives.

Finally, there is a problem in including husband's earnings for international comparisons. If educational homogamy is the rule, this logic would predict that college is typically a good deal for women, since it helps them secure an affluent husband. The task of explaining the high historical level of women's college enrollments in the United States must do so in a way that differentiates the United States from other countries with much lower shares of college attendance by women.

Manski (1993) points out that economists assume adolescents and their families are able to make exceedingly complicated calculations regarding the costs and benefits of college. The approaches of Becker, Schultz & Goldin make it clear that estimating the economic payoff to college for women is probably even more complicated than the standard economic formulation. Nor do these approaches exhaust the range of economic considerations: Education after all may be viewed as consumption and not strictly as an investment (Schultz 1987).

In summary, parents and children surely take the financial consequences of schooling into account when making educational decisions. However, there are many relevant considerations, and many ways to be rational. Consequently, in my view, economic calculations contribute to but are not sufficient to explain variation across countries and over time in the share of schooling obtained by women.

PROCESS

If college provided an undifferentiated education conferred equally on young men and women, then the issue of access would settle the question of gender inequality. But in fact women and men experience college differently and face markedly different outcomes. Of the many respects in which the college experience differs by gender, I consider five: fields of study, women's studies, faculty, harassment, and women's colleges.

Fields of Study

Women and men pursue different fields of study in college. In the United States, 30% of women would have to change fields of study in order for women to be distributed in the same manner as men (Jacobs, 1995a). The sex typing of fields of study is a worldwide phenomenon (Moore 1987), yet it varies between countries. For example, 51.6% of engineering students are women in Kuwait, compared with 3.3% in Switzerland and Japan (UNESCO 1995). One of the most striking contrasts is within the divided Germany: in the former East Germany, 32.4% of engineering graduates were women, compared with only 7.5% in West Germany. In Poland, 62.7% of mathematics and computer science degrees went to women, compared with 35.9% in the United States and 21.0% in Egypt. Kelly (1989) suggests that segregation of fields of study increases as women's representation in higher education increases, but she does not marshall specific evidence in support of this hypothesis.

In the United States during the early 1960s, women were concentrated in an extremely limited range of fields. Education drew almost half of women undergraduates, and over 70% of women graduates were concentrated in just six fields: education, English, fine arts, nursing, history, and home economics. Now business is the leading field of study for women. In 1990, women garnered 51% of life science bachelor's degrees, 47% of mathematics degrees, 47% of business degrees, but only 14% of engineering degrees. Segregation across majors declined substantially from the mid-1960s through the mid-1980s but has reached a plateau during the last 10 years (Jacobs 1995a).

Women have not always been segregated into separate fields from men. Founders of the most prominent women's colleges tried hard to maintain curricula that matched or exceeded men's in scope (Solomon 1985, Horowitz 1993). During the early years of land-grant schools, no separate curriculum for women existed (Thorne 1985). A peculiarly feminine curriculum began to emerge with the development of home economics. This development reflected an enduring emphasis on female domesticity but also was promoted in part by women academics, who were excluded from other fields and sought to create a field of expertise and set of job opportunities for which they would be uniquely suited (Solomon 1985, Rosenberg 1982, Clifford 1989). At the same time, this development contributed to the emergence of a distinctively feminine college experience for young women that served to limit the career prospects of most graduates.

Studies of choice of majors have addressed many issues. Social psychologists have searched for personality congruence between students and their majors (Betz & Fitgerald 1988, Betz et al 1990, Wolfle & Betz 1981). Vocational counseling research has explored the vocational maturity of students and their career realism (Holland 1985, Walsh & Osipow 1994).

The sex typing of fields can be attributed to precollege socialization (Wilson & Boldizar 1990), since students enter college roughly as segregated as they leave. However, about half of students change subjects during college. Therefore, college plays an essential role in maintaining level of segregation (Jacobs 1995, 1989). Many studies have attempted to document the effect of college on students. For example, Hearn & Olzak (1981) suggest that high status majors are competitive, and both men and women leave such fields. Their results also show that women fared poorly in high status fields with close occupational linkages. Yet most research on college effects is typically ahistorical. The net change in the sex segregation of students during college has varied over the last three decades. During the late 1960s and 1970s, the college experience resulted in students being less segregated as seniors than they were as freshmen; during the 1980s there was little or no net change during the college years (Jacobs 1995a, 1989). This finding suggests that change during the college years may reflect social changes in society at large in addition to the experiences unique to the college environment.

Economists have sought to explain the sex typing of fields as due to the desire for women to maximize their lifetime earnings. Polachek (1978) has suggested that female-dominated fields lead to jobs with high rewards early in life and a low earnings trajectory. By entering these majors, women position themselves to earn the most during the period when they are most likely to be working. This hypothesis has not been supported by the evidence. Women's fields pay less initially and exhibit slower earnings growth than do male fields, so that earnings maximization cannot be the explanation of such choices (England 1984, England et al 1988).

Decisions regarding majors in part reflect options in the labor market, but it should be noted that there has been more change in college than in the labor market. Sex segregation in college majors declined by 40% between 1960 and 1990, while sex segregation in the labor market declined by approximately 20% (Jacobs 1995a, Reskin 1993).

Much attention has been devoted to why women are underrepresented in science and engineering (Brush 1991, Yarrison-Rice 1995). The research has focused on sex differences in preparation (Ethington & Wolfle 1988), career orientation (Ware & Lee 1988), parental influences (Maple & Stage 1991) and attrition (Strenta et al 1994, Seymour 1992, Frehill 1996). This line of research has identified many of the steps needed to plug the leaky pipeline that results in relatively few women pursuing careers in mathematics and science. Most of these studies focus on such individual issues as psychological obstacles or lack of social support, or examine specific programs designed to improve women's achievement. However, some studies connect the issues of math and science to broader patterns in education and society. Green (1989) notes that the scarcity of women in scientific fields needs to be understood in the context of low overall enrollments in science. As we have seen, the sex gap in science and mathematics enrollment varies substantially across countries.

Women's Studies

Another important change in the curriculum has been the creation of women's studies (Musil 1992, Chamberlain 1988, Guy-Sheftall 1995, Stimpson 1986). Since the first women's studies program was founded in the 1969–1970 academic year, over 600 schools have established programs. The number of women's studies programs listed by *Women Studies Quarterly* continues to rise, from 449 in 1984, to 502 in 1989, to 606 in 1994. Wood (1981) showed that larger, more selective schools offering graduate degrees were the first to institute this organizational innovation. Women's studies now exists in many countries, although the extent of its institutionalization varies widely (Kelly 1989).

The National Center for Educational Statistics reports that only 189 bachelor's degree recipients majored in women's studies in 1990 (187 women and 2 men), although undoubtedly there were many more students who included women's studies as a second major or a minor area of concentration within a traditional field of study, such as history or literature. Colleges and universities now offer upwards of 20,000 women's studies courses. (Guy-Sheftall 1995).

Women's studies has had an important impact on the intellectual development of the humanities and the social sciences, most notably in the fields of literature, history, sociology, and anthropology (Farnham 1987, Langland & Gove 1983). Evaluations of the disciplinary impact of women's studies will necessarily be ongoing, as women's studies and the relevant fields evolve. A number of innovative programs have attempted to promote the mainstreaming of gender issues in courses outside women's studies programs (National Council for Research on Women 1991, Fiol-Matta & Chamberlain 1994). It would be valuable to know the extent to which gender issues have been incorporated in courses outside women's studies.

More research assessing the impact of women's studies on students is in order. Luebke & Reilly (1995) show that women's studies majors report that their major significantly enhanced their feminist consciousness and personal self confidence, but unfortunately the study samples students chosen on the recommendation of women's studies program directors. This study is not likely to be any more representative than that of Patai & Koertge (1994), which is largely based on interviews with faculty disillusioned with women's studies. Some studies have examined the impact of women's studies courses, although these assessments tend to be short term (Pascarella & Terenzini 1991:316, Stake & Rose 1994). It would be interesting and valuable to know what fraction of undergraduates take one or more women's studies courses and what if any lasting impact these courses have on students. Such information would provide sound basis for a discussion of curriculum reform and might displace the shrill charges and countercharges often made regarding feminism, multiculturalism, and the decline of the established canon.

Faculty

Men represent the great majority of college and university faculty worldwide (see Table 1). The figures cited in Table 1 include women at marginal institutions and in marginal positions, and thus they surely overstate women's attainments. In the United States, 31.8% of faculty were women in 1991. Women's representation declines with the prestige of the institution: 37.9% in public two-year schools, 28.9% in the public comprehensive schools, and 19.5% in private research universities. The number of women also declines with faculty rank. Women represent 47.9% of lecturers and instructors, 39.7% of assistant professors, and 17.2% of professors (National Center for Educational Statistics 1994). The US record actually looks quite favorable by comparison with the professoriat in Britain and France, which were 2.3% and 8.7% female, respectively, during the early 1980s (Clark 1987). Graham (1978) notes that women's representation on the faculty of US colleges and universities actually declined between 1930 and 1970, before beginning a sustained advance during the 1970s and 1980s.

There are many reasons that women's entrance into faculty positions is so low. Until recently women were a small proportion of PhD recipients; women are concentrated in a limited number of fields; women entered academia in large numbers during a period of retrenchment, and pursued fields that were facing sharp declines in enrollments (Slaughter 1993). Nonetheless, women's progress remains far slower than would be expected. Viewed optimistically, if a sizable fraction of women who are currently assistant professors are granted tenure, then the sex composition of the faculty will change dramatically during the next decade or two. Parity is unlikely for quite a long time because of the number of fields in which women PhDs remain severely underrepresented (Ransom 1990).

Much research has examined the position of women faculty members (Chamberlain 1988). Studies have examined gender inequality with respect to hiring patterns (Tolbert & Oberfield 1991, Konrad & Pfeffer 1991, Bowen & Schuster 1986, Bach & Perrucci 1984), promotion rates (Hurlbert & Rosenfeld 1992, Long et al 1993, Long & Fox 1995), publication rates (Ward & Grant 1995), mobility between institutions (Rosenfeld 1987), job satisfaction (Tack & Patitu 1992), turnover (Tolbert et al 1995), salaries (Bellas 1994, Tolbert 1986, Fox 1981, Bowen & Schuster 1986, Astin & Snyder 1982, Langton & Pfeffer

1994), and the sense of personal and professional marginalization (Aisenberg & Harrington 1988).

The notion of cumulative disadvantage seems to be a reasonable summary of the underrepresentation of women in faculty positions. In other words, women have been disadvantaged to some extent in every stage of the academic career process. This would account for women's underrepresentation in the higher echelons of university administration (Touchon et al 1993, Chamberlain 1988, Sandler 1986, Sagaria 1988, Sturnick et al 1991), in higher ranks and in higher status institutions. Graham (1978) suggests that the extreme exclusion of women from Ivy League institutions undermined the position of all women faculty, because, with the emergence of the research university as the pinnacle of the higher education system, these schools came to set the pattern for higher education as a whole.

A number of researchers see the position of women faculty as evidence of a chilly climate for women throughout higher education (Sandler 1986). But the effects of faculty composition on students continue to be debated. Tidball (1986, 1980) finds that the proportion of female faculty is strongly associated with the number of women high achievers, even in coeducational schools. This finding is probably less vulnerable to the lack of institutional controls than are Tidball's other findings (see below) and is a result that bears further scrutiny with longitudinal data. Rothstein (1995) finds that women students with female advisors are more likely to continue their education after college. Evidence on student satisfaction with same sex advisors (Erkut & Mokros 1984) and faculty (Ehrenberg et al 1995) is mixed. These issues require more detailed investigation of particular environments on particular groups of women, such as math and science majors. Sadker & Sadker (1993) make the case for gender bias in the classroom, but this evidence is principally based on research in high schools.

There are ironies in the history of women faculty as role models. The first generation of women faculty was expected to forego marriage. As Horowitz (1993) notes, by the 1920s women college students, most of whom planned marriage and not career, did not entirely identify with their female faculty mentors, who had sacrificed so much for the sake of women's education. The faculty were often perplexed and disappointed at the students who followed them (Clifford 1989). Same-sex role models can of course be beneficial, but it is important to understand the context of the student-faculty relationships in order to develop firm generalizations in this area.

Harassment

Sexual harassment as a legal concept is quite new, dating back to MacKinnon's (1979) treatise on the subject. Since that time, a substantial body of research has been conducted on the issue (Borgida & Fiske 1995, Tinsley & Stockdale 1993, Gruber 1992, 1989, Paludi 1990). The incidence of harassment varies with the status of the perpetrator, the type of behavior, and the length of exposure (Rubin & Borgers 1990). Peer harassment exceeds faculty-student harassment, and verbal harassment is much more common than demands of sexual favors or physical assault, but estimates of the latter are disturbingly high.

Roiphe (1993) sheds much heat but little light on this subject. Criticisms of the estimates of sexual assault launched by Gilbert (1993) were rebutted in detail by Koss & Cook (1993). One of Gilbert's main points is that sexual assault figures from college surveys surpass those found in federal crime reports. However, it is possible that the figures included in crime reports are too low. Indeed, federal statistics on sexual assault are being revised upwards, reflecting an adjustment in survey procedures to more closely follow those used by Koss and others (Sniffen 1995).

Faculty harassment can be especially consequential for graduate students, who have more exposure to faculty and who depend more on a limited set of advisors for their career prospects (Schneider 1987). Williams et al (1992) show that the incidence of faculty/student harassment declined after a sexual harassment policy and grievance procedure was established. More research on which policies work best is in order (Paludi & Barickman 1991).

Harassment may be viewed as part of a hostile climate for women on campuses (Sandler 1986), although little research to date has made such connections. The potential connections between harassment and the choice of major, the extent of career commitment, and other long-term consequences remain to be explored.

The topic of harassment is one aspect of a larger question of whether the college environment is equitable to women (American Association of University Women 1992). This larger set of issues includes classroom interactions (Wilkinson & Marrett 1985), informal counseling of students by faculty (Pascarella & Terenzini 1991:478–80), and the broader social scene (Holland & Eisenhart 1990), including sororities and fraternities (Sanday 1990).

Coeducation and Women's Colleges

One way to assess the effect of college environments on female students is to compare all-female schools to coeducational ones. If the former are more supportive environments for women, the difference in outcomes between the two can be viewed as an estimate of the sum of all of the deleterious effect of college environment on women in coeducational schools. The research on women's colleges has great theoretical importance even though only about 1.3% of women receive degrees from such colleges today (author's calculation, based on school-level Earned Degrees Conferred data, National Center for

Educational Statistics), and less than 3% of female high school seniors even consider attending such schools (Horowitz 1993).

In a series of papers, Tidball and her colleagues document the disproportionate number of graduates of women's colleges among prominent women (as listed in *Who's Who*) (1980), women medical school students (1985), and women scientists (1986). The initial *Who's Who* research pertained mostly to students who had graduated before 1960 (Tidball & Kistiakowsky 1976), but the medical school and natural science PhD data include information on the 1970s as well. Rice & Hemmings (1988) find a decline in the advantage of women's colleges in producing achievers during the 1960s and 1970s, but because they do not control for the declining share of graduates attending such institutions, their results are suspect.

The problem with this line of research is that controls for institutional characteristics, such as selectivity, are not included, nor are controls for the attributes of incoming students available for analysis (Crosby 1994). Tidball shows that her results are not solely due to the effects of the elite seven sister colleges, but she does not control for potential selectivity of other women's schools. Tidball's results may be due in part to student self-selection in terms of socioeconomic status and desire to pursue careers, and not solely due to the college experience per se.

Crosby et al (1994) reanalyzed Tidball's data on entrants into medical school and found that the positive effect of single-sex schools disappeared after selectivity was taken into account. Stoecker & Pascarella (1991) find no effect of female schools on four student outcomes measured nine years after students' freshman year. Unfortunately, the high sample attrition in the data they employ (reported in Astin 1982 and not in their article) introduces uncertainty into Stoecker & Pascarella's conclusions. Riordan's (1992) findings are consistent with Tidball's in a study of the High School Class of 1972 in results for both 1979 and 1986. Bressler & Wendell (1980) and Solnick (1995) find more movement of women into male-dominated fields of study in single-sex than in coeducational schools during the period 1967–1971. Smith (1990) finds students in women's colleges report greater satisfaction with all aspects of the college experience except social life. Further research in this area is needed that includes individual and institutional controls and that follows students for a long period of time after college.

Single-sex schools are just one instance of a broader question of how gender inequality varies across schools. Organizational sociologists have treated schools as "loosely coupled systems" (Ingersoll 1993, 1994) but have not focused on the organizational correlates of gender inequality in the educational context. In other words, Acker's (1990) approach to gendered organizations has yet to take hold in the context of higher education. This area promises much, since surely substantial variation exists among the several thousand colleges and universities in the United States, as well as between countries in the organization of higher education. Two exceptions are Studer-Ellis's (1995) examination of the determinants of the founding of women's colleges and Wood's (1981) analysis of the diffusion of women's studies programs (see also Pascarella & Terenzini for a review of studies on college effects).

OUTCOMES

Much of the discussion of gender inequality in the labor market has been written in response to the writings of the human capital school of economics, which holds that gender inequality stems from inadequate investments on the part of women (Jacobs 1995b). As we have seen, this is no longer the case in the United States. England (1993) has noted that working women have surpassed men in median years of schooling completed for much of the century; only during the period since the GI Bill have men surged past women. By 1990, working women once again had caught up with men in average educational attainment (author's estimate, based on the March 1993 *Current Population Survey*).

Gender differences in earnings persist despite the parity in education attained by women. Table 2 displays annual earnings by sex by years of schooling completed. Women earn less than men even with the same level of education. Indeed, the sex gap in earnings hardly varies by educational level.

The economic benefits of college have increased since the mid-1970s (Freeman 1994). The gender gap in earnings has narrowed at all educational levels, due in part to the decline in men's earnings (Bernhardt et al 1995). Yet the gender gap in earnings among college graduates remains similar to that at other educational levels.

A significant portion of the gender gap in earnings can be attributed to gender differences in majors (Gerhart 1990, Eide 1994, Fuller & Schoenerger 1991, Angle & Wissman 1981, Daymont & Andrisani 1984, Wilson & Smith-Lovin

Table 2   Median annual income of year-round full-time workers, by years of school completed and sex, 1990

	Women	Men	Women/Men
Less than 9 years	$12,251	$17,394	.70
1–3 years high school	$14,429	$20,902	.69
4 years high school	$18,319	$26,653	.69
1–3 years college	$22,227	$31,734	.70
4 years college	$28,017	$39,238	.71
5 or more years college	$33,750	$49,304	.68

U.S. Bureau of the Census, "Money income of families and persons in the united states" current population reports, series p-60, no. 174, 1991.

1983). Majors play a larger role in early-career earnings, although they may influence later career earnings indirectly through occupational tracking.

Formal schooling does not exhaust the range of possible sources of skill differences between men and women. The gender gap in wages may be due in part to gender differences in skills acquired in on-the-job training (Lynch 1994, Jacobs 1985b) and informal experience. Space does not permit an in-depth exploration of all the sources of gender inequality in the labor market. The point here is that the gender gap in earnings in the United States does not stem from the fact that women spend too few years in formal schooling. Some feminists have found reason for despair in these figures. Gender inequality can persist despite high levels of education for women. However, there are important additional effects of schooling on gender inequality besides earnings that bear mention.

Studies find that higher education results in more support for egalitarian gender role attitudes on the part of women (Pascarella & Terenzini 1991:293–97), particularly if the students took courses related to women's roles in society (Pascarella & Terenzini 1991:316). Klein (1984) finds education increases women's support for feminism. Freeman (1975) suggests that education raised women's expectations and created a sense of relative deprivation, leading them to support feminism.

Woody (1929) suggests that highly educated women leaders were indispensable to the success of the suffrage movement. Campbell (1979) found that highly educated women with small families, and especially those employed as professionals, were disproportionately represented among suffragists, based on analysis of a sample of 879 prominent women in 1914. On the other hand, Kelly (1991) reviewing the international evidence is more skeptical that additional education for women leads to greater political power.

As noted above, economists distinguish between the private returns to schooling—such as higher wages and higher household income—and the social or public returns, which may involve improvements to health, welfare, and society. Two principal nonmonetary effects of schooling for women that have been extensively researched are improved health of their infants and lower fertility. In developing countries, women with more education marry later, are more likely to use contraceptives, desire smaller families, have their first child later (but breastfeed for fewer months), and have a lower total fertility rate than do less educated women (Schultz 1993a,b). Much of the research described by Schultz compares girls with primary education to those with no education in developing countries, but the depressing effect of education on fertility is a consistent finding in affluent countries as well (Sweet & Rindfuss 1983, Martin 1995).

The 1994 United Nations International Conference on Population and De-velopment (1995) held in Cairo stressed the importance of empowering women in order to promote sustainable economic development and population control. Women's education is a central element in this agenda. Education may thus have significant implications for women's status with respect to gender relations throughout society, but these effects are historically contingent and depend on the character as well as the extent of women's education.

CONCLUSION

I have suggested that access, process, and outcomes are distinct aspects of higher education that need to be examined separately. The trends in these areas often do not coincide with one another, and consequently separate explanations of these facets of higher education are needed. For example, women remain a minority of faculty and are disadvantaged in terms of rank and institutional prestige. Yet as students in the United States, women represent a majority of students at nearly all levels of higher education and are not distinctly disadvantaged in terms of institutional position. Clearly, treating women's standing among the faculty and in the student body as one phenomenon will not do, since the extent of women's progress differs between these two statuses.

I remain surprised at how much mainstream research in the sociology of education ignores women, and how much of the rest considers gender interactions rather than gender inequality. In other words, gender often becomes a matter of variations on the main theme of socioeconomic or racial inequality. My first recommendation for further research, then, is that gender deserves the attention of sociologists of education. Gender presents many interesting puzzles, when gender inequality is evident as well as when it is not. We need a theory of when gender is likely to be consequential and when it is likely to be unimportant. We also need a theory of what economic, social, cultural, and political trends can be expected to affect the role of gender in the educational sphere.

Second, I believe that educational decision-making processes need more attention. Studies relying on widely available panel data sets tend to promote an input-output view of education. While this may make reasonable sense for studying certain outcomes, such as test scores, it tends to downplay individuals' views of their own motives. Moreover, this data framework abstracts away from socially embedded processes.

Third, aspects of the college experience need to be incorporated into a general account of educational inequality. As we have seen, gender inequality in the United States is now less a matter of inequality in access, and more a matter of gender differentiation in educational experiences and outcomes. Process and outcomes need to be linked to access in a general analysis of the educational system. There are many studies in the area of educational process, but these have not been synthesized into a general account of gender disparities.

Fourth, the relationship between gender and institutional development needs further attention. Educational research focuses heavily on individuals and tends to deemphasize the role of the institutional setting. More research that highlights the institutional context pertaining to gender inequality would be welcome.

Fifth, international comparisons also warrant further research. Accounting for women's share of access across countries would seem to be the logical first step. Assessing the role of gender in the educational process across countries would appear to pose more fundamental conceptual and measurement challenges, but it should also be addressed. The study of outcomes is complicated by international variation in linkages between school and work, but this analysis is needed.

In my view, the principal challenge facing research on gender in education is to go beyond documenting specific gender effects to developing a more theoretically motivated account of the status of women in the educational system. This perspective would have to account for the relative status of women in each aspect of the educational system as well as for variation across time and space. The challenge is to situate gender inequality economically, historically, culturally, and politically. The substantial research in various fields on women in education should set the stage for the next generation of researchers to tackle some of the fundamental issues regarding gender and the educational system. In particular, the relationship between gender inequality in education and that in the rest of society is a fundamental question for future theory and research.

ACKNOWLEDGMENTS

The author wishes to thank Kevin Dougherty, James Hearn, Barbara Heyns, David Karen, Demie Kurz, Brian Powell, Rachel Rosenfeld, and Susan Sturm for their constructive comments and suggestions, and Keren Polsky for her efficient research assistance.

Literature Cited

Acker J. 1990. Hierarchies, jobs, bodies: a theory of gendered organizations. *Gender Soc.* 4:139–58
Aisenberg N, Harrington M. 1988. *Women of Academe: Outsiders in the Sacred Grove.*

Amherst, MA: Univ. Mass. Press
Alexander KL, Eckland BE. 1974. Sex differences in the educational attainment process. *Am. Sociol. Rev.* 39:668–82
Alexander KL, Holupka S, Pallas AM. 1987a.

Social background and academic determinants of two-year versus four-year college attendance: evidence from two cohorts a decade apart. *Am. J. Educ.* 96:56–80

Alexander KL, Pallas AM, Holupka S. 1987b. Consistency and Change in Educational Stratification: Recent Trends Regarding Social Class Background and College Access. *Res. Soc. Strat. Mobility* 6:161–85

American Association of University Women. 1992. *How Schools Shortchange Girls.* Washington, DC: AAUW & Natl. Educ. Assoc.

Anderson MS, Hearn JC. 1992. Equity issues in higher education outcomes. In *The Economics of American Higher Education,* ed. WE Becker, DR Lewis, pp. 301–34. Boston: Kluwer Acad.

Angle J, Wissman DA. 1981. Gender, college major, and earnings. *Sociol. Educ.* 54:25–33

Angrist SS, Almquist EM. 1975. *Careers and Contingencies: How College Women Juggle with Gender.* New York: Dunelen

Aronowitz S, Giroux HA. 1993. *Education Still Under Siege.* Westport, CT: Gergin & Garvey. 2nd ed.

Astin AW. 1982. *Minorities in American Higher Education.* San Francisco: Jossey Bass

Astin H, Snyder MB. 1982. Affirmative action 1972–1982—a decade of response. *Change* July-Aug, pp. 26–31; 59

Bach RL, Perrucci CC. 1984. Organizational influences on the sex composition of college and university faculty: a research note. *Sociol. Educ.* 57:193–98

Barbagli M. 1982. *Educating for Unemployment: Politics, Labor Markets, and the School System—Italy, 1859–1973.* New York: Columbia Univ. Press

Becker G. 1975. *Human Capital.* Chicago: Univ. Chicago Press, for the Natl. Bur. Econ. Res. 2nd ed.

Behrman JR, Pollak RA, Taubman P. 1986. Do parents favor boys? *Int. Econ. Rev.* 27(1):33–54

Behrman JR, Rosenzweig MR. 1994. Caveat emptor: cross-country data on education and the labor force. *J. Dev. Econ.* 44(1):147–71

Bellas ML. 1994. Comparable worth in academia: the effects on faculty salaries of the sex composition and labor market conditions of academic disciplines. *Am. Sociol. Rev.* 59:807–21

Benavot A. 1989. Education, gender, and economic development: a cross-national study. *Sociol. Educ.* 62:14–32

Bernhardt A, Morris M, Handcock MS. 1995. Women's gains or men's losses: a closer look at the shrinking gender gap in earnings. *Am. J. Sociol.* 101(2):302–28

Betz NE, Fitzgerald LF. 1988. *The Career Psy-chology of Women.* Orlando, FL: Academic

Betz NE, Heesacker RS, Shuttleworth C. 1990. Moderators of the congruence and realism of major and occupational plans in college students: a replication and extension. *J. Counsel. Psychol.* 37(3):269–76

Biaecki I, Heyns B. 1993. Educational attainment, the status of women, and the private school movement. In *Democratic Reform and the Position of Women in Transitional Economies,* ed. VM Moghadam, pp. 111–34. Oxford: Clarendon

Blau P, Duncan OD. 1967. *The American Occupational Structure.* New York: John Wiley

Borgida E, Fiske ST. 1995. Gender stereotyping, sexual harassment, and the law. Special issue. *J. Soc. Issues* 51(1):1–193

Boulier BL, Rosenzweig MR. 1984. Schooling, search and spouse selection: testing the economic theory of marriage and household behavior. *J. Polit. Econ.* 92:712–32

Bourdieu P, Passeron J. 1977. *Reproduction: In Education, Culture and Society.* Beverly Hills: Sage

Bowen HR, Schuster JH. 1986. *American Professors: A National Resource Imperiled.* New York: Oxford Univ. Press

Bressler M, Wendell P. 1980. The sex composition of selective colleges and gender differences in career aspirations. *J. Higher Educ..* 51:650–63

Brush SG. 1991. Women in science and engineering. *Am. Scientist* 79:404–19

Butcher KF, Case A. 1994. The effect of sibling sex composition on women's education and earnings. *Q. J. Econ.* 109(3):531–63

Byrne EM. 1978. *Women and Education.* London: Tavistock

Campbell BK. 1979. *The Liberated Woman of 1914.* Ann Arbor, MI: UMI Res. Press

Carnoy M, Samoff J. 1990. *Education and Social Transition in the Third World.* Princeton, NJ: Princeton Univ. Press

Chamberlain MK. 1988. *Women in Academe: Progress and Prospects.* New York: Russell Sage Foun.

Clark BR, ed. 1987. *The Academic Profession: National Disciplinary and Institutional Settings.* Berkeley: Univ. Calif. Press

Clark R. 1992. Multinational corporate investment and women's participation in higher education in noncore nations. *Sociol. Educ.* 65:37–47

Clifford GJ, ed. 1989. *Lone Voyagers: Academic Women in Coeducational Universities, 1870–1937.* New York: Feminist Press at City Univ. NY

Coats M. 1994. *Women's Education.* Bristol, PA: Soc. Res. into Higher Educ., Open Univ. Press

Collins R. 1979. *The Credential Society.* New York: Academic

Connell RW, Ashenden DJ, Kessler S, Dowsett GW, et al. 1982. *Making the Difference: Schools, Families and Social Division.* Boston: Allen & Unwin

Cookingham ME. 1984. Bluestockings, spinsters and pedagogues: women college graduates, 1865–1910. *Popul. Stud.* 38:349–64

Cott NF, ed. 1993. *History of Women in the United States.* Vol. 12. *Education.* New Providence, CT: Saur

Crosby F, Allen B, Culbertson T, Wally C, Morith J, et al. 1994. Taking selectivity into account, how much does gender composition matter? A re-analysis of M. E. Tidball's research. *Natl. Women's Stud. Assoc. J.* 6(1):107–18

Davies S. 1995. Leaps of faith: shifting currents in critical sociological education. *Am. J. Sociol.* 100(6):1448–78

Daymont TN, Andrisani PJ. 1984. Job preferences, college major, and the gender gap in earnings. *J. Hum. Resourc.* 19:408–34

Delamont S. 1989. *Knowledgeable Women. Structuralism and the Reproduction of Elites.* London: Routledge

de Grazia V. 1992. *How Fascism Ruled Women: Italy, 1922–1945.* Berkeley: Univ. Calif. Press

Durbin N, Kent L. 1989. Postsecondary education of white women, in 1900. *Sociol. Educ.* 62:1–13

Ehrenberg RG, Goldhaber DD, Brewer DJ. 1995. Do teachers' race, gender and ethnicity matter? Evidence from NELS. *Indust. Labor Relat. Rev.* 48(3):547–61

Eide E. 1994. College major and changes in the gender wage gap. *Contemp. Econ. Policy* 12(2):55–64

Einhorn B. 1993. *Cinderella Goes to Market: Citizenship, Gender and Women's Movements in East Central Europe.* London: Verso

El-Sanabary N. 1993. Middle East and North Africa. In *Women's Education in Developing Countries: Barriers, Benefits and Policies,* ed. EM King, MA Hill, pp. 136–74. Baltimore, MD: Johns Hopkins Univ. Press

England P. 1979. Women and occupational prestige: a case of vacuous sex equality. *Signs* 5:252–65

England P. 1984. Wage appreciation and depreciation: a test of neoclassical economic explanations of occupational sex segregation. *Soc. Forces* 62:726–49

England P. 1993. *Comparable Worth: Theories and Evidence.* New York: Aldine de Gruyter

England P, Farkas G, Kilbourne B, Dou T. 1988. Explaining occupational sex segregation and wages: findings from a fixed effects model.

Am. Sociol. Rev. 53(4):544–88

Erkut S, Mokros JR. 1984. Professors and models and mentors for college students. *Am. Educ. Res. J.* 21(2):399–417

Ethington CA, Wolfe LM. 1988. Women's selection of quantitative undergraduate fields of study: direct and indirect influences. *Am. Educ. Res. J.* 25:157–75

Farnham C, ed. 1987. *The Impact of Feminist Research in the Academy.* Bloomington, IN: Indiana Univ. Press

Fiol-Matta L, Chamberlain MK, eds. 1994. *Women of Color and the Multicultural Curriculum: Transforming the College Classroom.* New York: Feminist Press

Finn JD, Dulberg L, Reis J. 1979. Sex differences in educational attainment: a cross-national perspective. *Harvard Educ. Rev.* 49(4):477–503

Folger JK, Nam CB. 1967. *Education of the American Population.* Washington, DC: US Bur. Census

Fox MF. 1981. Sex, salary and achievement: reward-dualism in academia. *Sociol. Educ.* 54:71–84

Frehill L. 1996. *We just can't keep them: the myth of women's attrition from engineering.* Paper pres. Eastern Sociol. Soc. Meet., Boston, March

Freeman J. 1975. *The Politics of Women's Liberation.* New York: Longman

Fuller B. 1983. Youth job structure and school enrollment, 1890–1920. *Sociol. Educ.* 56:145–56

Fuller R, Schoenberger R. 1991. The gender salary gap: Do academic achievement, internship experience, and college major make a difference? *Soc. Sci. Q.* 72(4):715–26

Frankfort R. 1977. *Collegiate Women: Domesticity and Career in Turn-of-the-Century America.* New York: New York Univ. Press

Friedan B. 1963. *The Feminine Mystique.* New York: Dell

Freeman R, ed. 1994. *Working Under Different Rules.* New York: Russell Sage Found.

Gerhart B. 1990. Gender differences in current and starting salaries: the role of performance, college major and job title. *Indust. Labor Relat. Rev.* 43(4):418–33

Gilbert N. 1993. Examining the facts: advocacy research overstates the incidence of date and acquaintance rape. In *Current Controversies on Family Violence,* ed. RJ Gelles, DR Loseke, pp. 120–32. Newbury Park, CA: Sage

Goldin C. 1992. *The meaning of college in the lives of American women: the past one-hundred years. Work. Pap. No. 4099.* Cambridge, MA: Natl. Bur. Econ. Res.

Goldin C. 1995. Career and family: College

women look to the past. Unpubl. Ms. Dep. Econ., Harvard Univ., Cambridge, MA

Graff HJ. 1979. *The Literacy Myth.* New York: Academic

Graff HJ. 1987. *The Legacies of Literacy.* Bloomington, IN: Ind. Univ. Press

Graham PA. 1978. Expansion and exclusion: a history of women in American higher education. *Signs* 3(4):759–73

Green KC. 1989. A profile of undergraduates in the sciences. *Am. Scientist.* 77:475(6)

Greene M, Jacobs JA. 1992. Urbanism and education in 1910: evidence from the 1910 public use sample. *Am. J. Educ.* 101:29–59

Griffin C. 1985. *Typical Girls? Young Women from Schools to the Job Market.* London: Routledge & Kegan Paul

Gruber J. 1989. How women handle sexual harassment: a literature review. *Sociol. Soc. Res.* 74:3–9

Gruber J. 1992. A typology of personal and environmental sexual harassment: research and policy implications for the 1990s. *Sex Roles* 26:447–64

Guy-Sheftall B, Heath S. 1995. *Women's Studies: A Retrospective.* New York: Ford Found.

Hauser RM, Kuo HD. 1995. Does the gender composition of sibships affect educational attainment? Unpubl. ms. Cent. Demography & Ecol., Univ. Wisc., Madison, WI

Hearn JC. 1990. Pathways to attendance at the elite colleges. In *The High-Status Track: Studies of Elite Schools and Stratification,* ed. PW Kingston, LS Lewis, pp. 121–46. Albany, NY: SUNY Press

Hearn JC. 1992. Emerging variations in postsecondary attendance patterns: an investigation of part-time, delayed and nondegree enrollment. *Res. Higher Educ.* 33(6):657–87

Hearn JC, Olzak S. 1981. The role of college major departments in the reproduction of sexual inequality. *Sociol. Educ.* 53:195–205

Heyns B, Bialecki I. 1992. Educational inequality in Poland. In *Persistent Inequality: Changing Educational Stratification in Thirteen Countries,* ed. Y Shavit, H-P Blossfeld, pp. 303–35. Boulder, CO: Westview

Holland D, Eisenhart M. 1990. *Educated in Romance.* Chicago: Univ. Chicago Press

Holland JL. 1985. *Making Vocational Choices: A Theory of Careers.* Englewood Cliffs, NJ: Prentice Hall. 2nd ed.

Hooper B. 1984. China's modernization: Are young women going to lose out? *Modern China* 10:317–43

Horowitz HL. 1993. *Alma Mater: Design and Experience in the Women's Colleges from Their Nineteenth-Century Beginnings to the 1930s.* Amherst, MA: Univ. Mass. Press. 2nd ed.

Hulbert KD, Schuster DT, eds. 1993. *Women's Lives Through Time: Educated American Women of the Twentieth Century.* San Francisco: Jossey-Bass

Hurlbert JS, Rosenfeld RA. 1992. Getting a good job: rank and institutional prestige in academic psychologists' careers. *Sociol. Educ.* 65(3):188–207

Ingersoll R. 1993. Loosely coupled organizations revisited. *Res. Sociol. Organ.* 11:81–112

Ingersoll R. 1994. Organizational control in secondary schools. *Harvard Educ. Rev.* 64:150–72

Jacobs JA. 1989. *Revolving Doors: Sex Segregation and Women's Careers.* Stanford, CA: Stanford Univ. Press

Jacobs JA. 1995a. Gender and academic specialties: trends among college degree recipients during the 1980s. *Sociol. Educ.* 68(2):81–98

Jacobs JA, ed. 1995b. Introduction. In *Gender Inequality at Work,* ed. JA Jacobs, pp. 1–22. Thousand Oaks, CA: Sage

Jacobs JA. 1996. Gender and access to higher education. Unpubl. ms. Dep. Sociol., Univ. Penn.

Jacobs JA, Furstenberg FF. 1986. Changing places: conjugal succession and the marital mobility of women. *Soc. Forces* 64(3):714–32

Jacobs JA, Greene ME. 1994. Race and ethnicity, social class and schooling in 1910. In *After Ellis Island: Newcomers and Natives in the 1910 Census,* ed. SC Watkins, pp. 209–56. New York: Russell Sage Found.

Jacobs JA, Labov T. 1995. Sex differences in intermarriage: exchange theory reconsidered. Unpubl. ms. Dep. Sociol., Univ. Penn.

Jacobs JA, Powell B. 1987. On comparing the social standing of men and women. Unpubl. ms. Dep. Sociol., Univ. Penn.

Jencks C, Riesman D. 1968. *The Academic Revolution.* Chicago: Univ. Chicago Press

Karabel J, Halsey AH. 1977. *Power and Ideology in Education.* New York: Oxford Univ. Press

Karen D. 1991. The politics of class, race and gender: access to higher education in the United States, 1960–1986. *Am. J. Educ.* 99:208–37

Kasworm CE. 1990. Adult undergraduates in higher education: a review of past research perspectives. *Rev. Educ. Res.* 60(3):345–72

Kelly GP. 1989. *International Handbook of Women's Education.* New York: Greenwood

Kelly GP, Slaughter S, eds. 1991. *Women's Higher Education in Comparative Perspective.* Dordecht, The Netherlands: Kluwer Acad.

Kelly T. 1983. The historical evolution of adult education in Great Britain. In *Educational Opportunities for Adults,* , ed. M Tight, Vol. II. London: Croom Helm

King EM, Hill MA. 1993. *Women's Education in Developing Countries: Barriers, Benefits and Policies.* Baltimore, MD: Johns Hopkins Univ. Press

Klein E. 1984. *Gender Politics.* Cambridge: Harvard Univ. Press

Klemm LR. 1901. Translator's Introduction. In *Higher Education of Women in Europe,* ed. Helene Lange. New York: Appleton

Komarovsky M. 1971 (1953). *Women in the Modern World: Their Education and Their Dilemmas.* Dubuque, Iowa: Brown Reprints

Komarovsky M. 1985. *Women in College: Shaping New Feminine Identities.* New York: Basic

Konrad AM, Pfeffer J. 1991. Understanding the hiring of women and minorities in educational institutions. *Sociol. Educ.* 64:141–57

Koss MP, Cook SL. 1993. Facing the facts: date and acquaintance rape are significant problems for women. In *Current Controversies on Family Violence,* ed. RJ Gelles, DR Loseke, pp. 104–19. Newbury Park, CA: Sage

Langland E, Gove W, eds. 1983. *A Feminist Perspective in the Academy: The Difference it Makes.* Chicago: Univ. Chicago Press

Langton N, Pfeffer J. 1994. Paying the professor: sources of salary variation in academic labor markets. *Am. Sociol. Rev.* 59:236–56

Lees S. 1986. *Losing Out: Sexuality and Adolescent Girls.* London: Hutchinson

Levine S. 1995. *Degrees of Equality: The American Association of University Women and the Challenge of Twentieth-Century Feminism.* Philadelphia, PA: Temple Univ. Press

Lichter DT. 1990. Delayed marriage, marital homogamy, and the male selection process among white women. *Soc. Sci. Q.* 71:802–11

Long JS, Allison PD, McGinnis R. 1993. Rank advancement in academic careers: sex differences and the effects of productivity. *Am. Sociol. Rev.* 58:703–22

Long JS, Fox MF. 1995. Scientific careers: universalism and particularism. *Annu. Rev. Sociol.* 21:45–71

Luebke BF, Reilly ME. 1995. *Women's Studies Graduates: The First Generation.* New York: Teachers Coll. Press

Lynch L, ed. 1994. *Training and the Private Sector: International Comparisons.* Chicago: Univ. Chicago Press.

Manski CF. 1993. Adolescent econometricians: How do youth infer the returns to schooling? In *Studies of Supply and Demand in Higher Education,* ed. C Clotfelter, M Rothschild, pp. 43–57. Chicago: Univ. Chicago Press

Maple SA, Stage FK. 1991. Influences on the choice of math/science major by gender and ethnicity. *Am. Educ. Res. J.* 28(1):37–60

Mare RD. 1991. Five decades of educational assortative mating. *Am. Sociol. Rev.* 56:15–32

Marini MM, Greenberger E. 1978. Sex differences in educational aspirations and expectations. *Am. Educ. Res. J.* 15:67–79

Martin TC. 1995. Women's education and fertility: results from 26 demographic and health surveys. *Stud. Family Planning* 26(4):187–202

McRobbie A. 1982. The politics of feminist research: between talk, text and action. *Feminist Rev.* 12:46–57

Meyer J, Hannan M, eds. 1979. *National Development and the World System.* Chicago: Univ. Chicago Press

Meyer JW, Tyack D, Nagel J, Gordon A, et al. 1979. Public education as nation-building in America: enrollments and bureaucratization in the American states, 1870–1930. *Am. J. Sociol.* 85:591–613

Mickelson RA. 1989. Why does Jane read and write so well? The anomaly of women's achievement. *Sociol. Educ.* 62:47–63

Monthly Forum on Women in Higher Education. 1995. Enrollment ratios of first-year women students at the nation's highest ranked colleges and universities. *Monthly For. Women Higher Educ.* 1(1):6–8

Moore KM. 1987. Women's access and opportunity in higher education. *Compar. Educ.* 23:23–34

Musil C. 1992. *The Courage to Question: Women's Studies and Student Learning.* Washington, DC: Assoc. Am. Coll. & Natl. Women's Stud. Assoc.

National Center for Educational Statistics. 1994. *Digest of Educational Statistics.* Washington, DC: US Govt. Printing Off.

National Council for Research on Women. 1991. *Mainstreaming Minority Women's Studies.* Washington, DC: Natl. Council for Res. Women

OECD. 1995. *Education at a Glance: OECD Indicators.* Paris: OECD

Ogburn W. 1922. *Social Change.* New York: Viking

Olneck MR, Lazerson M. 1974. The school achievement of immigrant children, 1900–1930. *Hist. Educ. Q.* 14:453–82

Paludi M, ed. 1990. *Ivory Power: Sexual Harassment on Campus.* Albany, NY: SUNY Press

Paludi MA, Barickman RB. 1991. *Academic and Workplace Sexual Harassment: A Resource Manual.* Albany: State Univ. NY

Press
Pascarella ET, Terenzini PT. 1991. *How College Affects Students*. San Francisco: Jossey-Bass
Patai D, Koertge N. 1994. *Professing Feminism: Cautionary Tales from the Strange World of Women's Studies*. New York: Basic Books
Pauwels JR. 1984. *Women, Nazis, and Universities: Female University Students in the Third Reich, 1933–1945*. Westport, CT: Greenwood
Persell CH, Catsambis S, Cookson PW. 1992. Differential asset conversion: class and gendered pathways to selective colleges. *Sociol. Educ.* 65:208–25
Polachek S. 1978. Sex differences in college major. *Indust. Labor Relat. Rev.* 31(4):498–508
Powell B, Steelman LC. 1989. The liability of having brothers: paying for college and the sex composition of the family. *Sociol. Educ.* 62:134–47
Powell B, Steelman LC. 1990. Beyond sibship size: sibling density, sex composition and educational outcomes. *Soc. Forces* 69:181–206
Ramirez FO, Boli J. 1987. Global patterns of educational institutionalization. In *Institutional Structure: Constituting the State, Society and the Individual*, ed. GM Thomas, JW Meyer, FO Ramirez, J Boli, pp. 150–72. Beverly Hills, CA: Sage
Ramirez F, Weiss J. 1979. The political incorporation of women. In *National Development and the World System*, ed. J Meyer, M Hannan, pp. 238–49. Chicago: Univ. Chicago Press
Ransom MR. 1990. Gender segregation by field in higher education. *Res. Higher Educ.* 31(5):477–94
Reskin B. 1993. Sex segregation in the workplace. *Annu. Rev. Sociol.* 19:241–70
Rice JK, Hemmings A. 1988. Women's colleges and women achievers: an update. *Signs* 13(3):546–59
Riordan C. 1992. Single- and mixed-gender colleges for women: education and occupational outcomes. *Rev. Higher Educ.* 15:327–46
Roiphe K. 1993. *The Morning After: Sex, Fear and Feminism on Campus*. Boston, MA: Little Brown
Rosenberg R. 1982. *Beyond Separate Spheres: Intellectual Roots of Modern Feminism*. New Haven: Yale Univ. Press
Rosenfeld RA. 1987. Patterns and effect of geographic mobility for academic women and men. *J. Higher Educ.* 58(5):493–515
Rothstein DS. 1995. Do female faculty influence female students' educational and labor market attainments? *Indust. Labor Relat. Rev.* 48(3):515–30
Rubin LJ, Borgers SB. 1990. Sexual harassment in universities during the 1980's. *Sex Roles* 23:397–411

Rubinson R. 1986. Class formation, politics and institutions: schooling in the United States. *Am. J. Sociol.* 92:519–48
Sadker M, DM. 1993. *Failing at Fairness: How America's Schools Cheat Girls*. New York: Scribner
Sagaria MA. 1988. Administrative mobility and gender: patterns and processes in higher education. *J. Higher Educ.* 59:305–26
Sanday P. 1990. *Fraternity Gang Rape: Sex, Brotherhood and Privilege on Campus*. New York: New York Univ. Press
Sandler BR. 1986. *Campus Climate Revisited: Chilly for Women Faculty, Administrators, and Graduate Students*. Washington, DC: Assoc. Am. Coll.
Schneider BE. 1987. Graduate women, sexual harassment, and university policy. *J. Higher Educ.* 58(1):46–65
Schultz TP. 1993a. Returns to women's education. In *Women's Education in Developing Countries: Barriers, Benefits and Policies*, ed. EM King, MA Hill, pp. 51–99. Baltimore: Johns Hopkins Univ. Press
Schultz TP. 1993b. Investments in the schooling and health of women and men. *J. Hum. Resourc.* 28:694–734
Schultz TP. 1987. School expenditures and enrollments, 1960–1990. In *Population Growth and Economic Development*, ed. DG Johnson, R Lee. Madison: Univ. Wisc. Press
Schwager S. 1987. Educating women in America. *Signs* 12(2):333–72
Seymour E. 1992. Undergraduate problems with teaching and advising in SME majors—explaining gender differences in attrition rates. *J. Coll. Sci. Teaching* 22:284–92
Slaughter S. 1993. Retrenchment in the 1980s: the politics of prestige and gender. *J. Higher Educ.* 64(3):250–82
Smith DG. 1990. Women's colleges and coed colleges: Is there a difference for women? *J. Higher Educ.* 61:181–97
Smock AC, Youssef NH. 1977. Egypt: from seclusion to limited participation. In *Women: Roles and Status in Eight Countries*, ed. JZ Giele, AC Smock, pp. 33–79. New York: Wiley
Sniffen MJ. 1995. US doubles estimates of rapes, attempted rapes to 310,000. *Philadelphia Inquirer*, August 17, p. A-25
Solnick S. 1995. Changes in women's majors from entrance to graduation at women's and coeducational colleges. *Indust. Labor Relat. Rev.* 48(3):505–14
Solomon BM. 1985. *In the Company of Educated Women: A History of Women and Higher Education in America*. New Haven: Yale Univ. Press
Stake JE, Rose S. 1994. The long-term impact of

women's studies on students' personal lives and political activism. *Psychol. Women Q.* 18(3):403–12

Stimpson CR, Cobb NK. 1986. *Women's Studies in the United States.* New York: Ford Foundation

Stoecker JL, Pascarella ET. 1991. Women's colleges and women's career attainments revisited. *J. Higher Educ.* 62:394–406

Strenta AC, Elliott R, Adair R, Matier, Scott J, et al. 1994. Choosing and leaving science in highly selective institutions. *Res. Higher Educ.* 35(5):513–47

Stromquist NP. 1989. Determinants of educational participation and achievement of women in the third world: a review of the evidence and a theoretical critique. *Rev. Educ. Res.* 59:143–83

Stromquist NP. 1993. Sex equity legislation in education: the state as promoter of women's rights. *Rev. Educ. Res.* 63(4):379–407

Studer-Ellis EM. 1995. Springboards to mortarboards: women's college foundings in Massachusetts, New York and Pennsylvania. *Soc. Forces* 73(3):1051–70

Sturnick JA, Milley JE, Tisinger CA. 1991. *Women at the Helm: Pathfinding Presidents at State Colleges and Universities.* Washington, DC: Am. Assoc. State Coll. and Univ.

Sweet JA, Rindfuss RR. 1983. Those ubiquitous fertility trends: United States, 1945–1979. *Soc. Biol.* 30:127–39

Tack MW, Patitu CI. 1992. *Faculty Job Satisfaction: Women and Minorities in Peril.* Washington, DC: Geo. Wash. Univ., Clearinghouse on Higher Educ., for Assoc. for Study of Higher Educ.

Tan J, Mingat A. 1992. *Education in Asia: A Comparative Study of Cost and Financing.* Washington, DC: World Bank

Thorne AC. 1985. *Visible and Invisible Women in Land-Grant Colleges, 1890–1940.* Logan, Utah: Utah State Univ. Press

Tidball ME. 1980. Women's colleges and women achievers revisited. *Signs* 5(3):504–17

Tidball ME. 1985. Baccalaureate origins of entrants into American medical schools. *J. Higher Educ.* 56:385–402

Tidball ME. 1986. Baccalaureate origins of recent natural science doctorates. *J. Higher Educ.* 57(6):606–20

Tidball ME, Kistiakowsky V. 1976. Baccalaureate origins of American scientists and scholars. *Science* 193:646–52

Tilak JBG. 1993. East Asia. In *Women's Education in Developing Countries,* ed. EM King, MA Hill, pp. 247–85. Baltimore, MD: Johns Hopkins Univ. Press

Tinsley HEA, Stockdale MS. 1993. Special issue on sexual harassment in the workplace. *J. Vocat. Behav.* 42(1):1–153

Tolbert PS. 1986. Organizations and inequality: sources of earnings differences between male and female faculty. *Sociol. Educ.* 59:227–35

Tolbert PS, Simmons T, Andrews A, Rhee J, et al. 1995. The effects of gender composition in academic departments on faculty turnover. *Indust. Labor Relat. Rev.* 4893:562–79

Tolbert PS, Oberfield AA. 1991. Sources of organizational demography: faculty sex ratios in colleges and universities. *Sociol. Educ.* 64:305–15

Touchon JG, Shavlik D, Davis L, eds. 1993. *Women in Presidencies.* Washington, DC: Am. Council Educ.

Tyack D, Hansot E. 1990. *Learning Together: A History of Coeducation in American Schools.* New York: Russell Sage Found.

UNESCO. 1967. *Access to Higher Education in Europe.* Vienna: UNESCO

United Nations. 1987. *Fertility Behaviour in the Context of Development: Evidence from the World Fertility Survey.* New York: United Nations

United Nations International Conference on Population and Development. 1995. *Population and Development.* New York: United Nations

US Bureau of the Census. 1975. *Historical Statistics of the United States: Colonial Times to 1970.* Washington, DC: US Govt. Printing Off.

US Commissioner of Education. 1900. *Report of the Commissioner of Education for the Year 1898–1899.* Washington, DC: USGPO

US Department of Education. 1995. *The Condition of Education.* Washington, DC: USGPO

US Immigration Commission. 1911. *Reports of the Immigration Commission.* Washington, DC: USGPO

Waller W. 1937. The rating and dating complex. *Am. Sociol. Rev.* 2:727–34

Walsh HB, Osipow SH. 1994. *Career Counseling for Women.* Hillsdale, NJ: Erlbaum

Walsh MR. 1977. *Doctors Wanted: No Women Need Apply: Sexual Barriers in the Medical Profession, 1835–1975.* New Haven, CT: Yale Univ. Press

Walters PB. 1986. Sex and institutional differences in labor market effects on the expansion of higher education, 1952–1980. *Sociol. Educ.* 59:199–211

Ward K, ed. 1990. *Women Workers and Global Restructuring.* Ithaca, NY: ILR Press

Ward K, Grant L. 1995. Gender and academic publishing. In *Higher Education: Handbook of Theory and Research,* ed. A Bayer, J Smart. New York: Agathon

Ware NC, Lee VE. 1988. Sex differences in

choice of college science majors. *Am. Educ. Res. J.* 25(4):593–614

Wilkinson LC, Marrett CB. 1985. *Gender Influences in Classroom Interaction.* Orlando, FL: Academic

Williams EA, Lam JA, Shively M. 1992. The impact of a university policy on the sexual harassment of female students. *J. Higher Educ.* 63(1):50–64

Willis PE. 1977. *Learning to Labour.* Aldershot, UK: Gower

Wilson KL, Boldizar JP. 1990. Gender segregation in higher education: effects of aspirations, mathematics achievement, and income. *Sociol. Educ.* 63:62–74

Wilson K, Smith-Lovin L. 1983. Scaling the prestige, authority and income potential of college curricula. *Soc. Sci. Res.* 12:159–86

Wolfle LK, Betz NE. 1981. Traditionality of choice and sex-role identification as moderators of the congruence of occupational choice in college women. *J. Vocat. Behav.* 18:43–55

Wood DJ. 1981. Academic women's studies programs: a case of organizational innovation. *J. Higher Educ.* 52(2):155–72

Woody T. 1929. *A History of Women's Education in the United States.* New York: Science

Yarrison-Rice JM. 1995. On the problem of making science attractive for women and minorities: an annotated bibliography. *Am. J. Physics* 63(3):203–11

Annu. Rev. Sociol. 1996. 22:187–212

LAW AND INEQUALITY: Race, Gender... and, of Course, Class

Carroll Seron

School of Public Affairs, Baruch College, Department of Sociology, Graduate Center, City University of New York, New York, NY 10010

Frank Munger

Faculty of Law, State University of New York, Buffalo, New York 14260

KEY WORDS: sociology of law, class theory, legal institutions

---

ABSTRACT

This chapter discusses the concept of class in an important subfield, the sociology of law. Class, a pivotal institution of society, was central to the earliest studies of legal institutions and of law and inequality in particular. More recently, class has played a less important role. This chapter argues for the continuing importance of class and provides examples of its potential use in contemporary sociolegal research. The first part reviews early work that employed class and instrumental models of the state. Grounded, anti-formal models of law provided a contrasting view. Following wider trends in the discipline, sociology of law turned from structural models to theories of law as an ideology, and most recently, as reviewed in the second part, to law as an element of consciousness and experience. While acknowledging the value of contemporary research that documents a deeply textured, paradoxical, and nuanced analysis of the role of law in society, the third part argues for theorizing the link between experience and context, including the role of social class, and presents a research agenda for a sociology of law, where the relationship between law and class is considered both as institution and experience.

"The plain fact is that in a new stage of capitalism, class divides as ruthlessly as it did in the age of the Robber Barons."

Richard Sennett,[1] 1942

[1] As quoted in "Back to Class Warfare," The New York Times, December 27, 1994.

0360-0572/96/0815-0187$08.00

INTRODUCTION

In this essay we review the ways in which class has been conceptualized and used to explain the role of legal institutions in society. Though always controversial in American social science, class is nonetheless central in thought and theorizing about society, including its legal institutions. In the past two decades, theories of class and social structure have been endlessly critiqued, and the importance of class as a research concept reduced to the point of near extinction. Class is only now beginning to be reconsidered—as one more anchor of personal identity like gender, race, and ethnicity. The contemporary turn from structural theory toward interpretive studies of experience emphasizes nuanced descriptions of actors' orientations to law in a particular context, but it has offered little to explain the interaction between individual agency and continuing patterns of political or economic hierarchy.

Understanding the structural foundations of class continues to be important in the postmodern world. Class describes an individual's position with respect to the central economic and cultural institutions of society and, in turn, relates that position to the social resources available to the individual. Just as new ways have been found to bring the state back in or to create a new institutionalism that acknowledges the importance of complex continuing patterns in social life—but purged of deterministic claims—so class must be reconceptualized. Indeed, our review of sociolegal research shows that class has continued to be an important, if largely implicit, concept not only making possible a clearer understanding of the distributive effects of economies but also providing a key to understanding power in contemporary society.

We show here that class, as a marker for the distributive effects of law, has been of great importance in sociolegal studies. In the 1970s, structural theories began to decline in importance. In the sociology of law, the importance of class was diminished still further by the weight of arguments of neo-Marxists and others that law is an ideological force, not a straightforward reflection of resource inequality or a simple instrument of domination.

The interpretive and postmodern turn in sociology is reflected in contemporary sociolegal research on legal culture and legal consciousness, and on narrative and discourse about law. The critique and decline of grand theory did not undercut interest in the concrete distributive consequences of law, the bread and butter of the field, but the shift did sever these studies conceptually from their roots in general theories of society. The second part of this chapter describes the shift as well as the conceptual limits of this paradigm: Agency alone will not provide an understanding of the group-life of a society or its institutions or the ways in which class continues to form an important bridge between those contingencies that comprise elements of an actor's own understanding of action and those of which the actor is unaware.

Finally, the third part of the chapter presents a research agenda for a sociology of law where the tension between structure and agency, class and law, frames the undertaking. Using recent studies as examples, we show why the institutions of class continue to explain dimensions of inequality and hierarchy and how incorporating a nuanced, agency-sensitive concept of class will contribute to the development of sociology of law and to class theory.

THEORY AND THE PROBLEM OF LAW AND INEQUALITY

The sociology of law has always drawn on theories prevailing in the discipline. Early sociology of law was shaped by mainstream theories, including conflict, structural-functional, and grounded theories of society (Dahrendrof 1959, Parsons 1964, Glaser & Strauss 1967). Conflict and structural-functional theories have been particularly influential in the sociology of law. Both were derived from nineteenth century social theory of industrial society in which class structure was understood as fundamental, as a source of both order and conflict. The purpose of the state was to make the differentiation of social roles at the heart of class structure work smoothly (structural-functional theory) or to contain the inevitable conflict that resulted from inequality created by class structure (conflict theory). Marxist conflict theory also viewed the state as an instrument of the ruling class or some combination of dominant classes (Marx & Engels 1950). In all of these theories of the class-state, the law legitimates state authority, enabling the state to carry out its purposes (see Evans 1963). Almost all early sociology of law accepted this fundamental ordering of class, law, and the state. Weber's theory of legal formalism and the role of the legal profession in maintaining the authority of law has also been influential. It is not surprising, therefore, given the lineage of the theories dominating the early sociology of law, that economic class was universally and uncontroversially the measure employed in research on law and inequality.

A second perspective in the sociology of law was employed in studying inequality, but without connection to grand theory. Sociology of law shares with the discipline at large a body of research that begins with an anti-instrumental and anti-formal model of the relationship between law and inequality. Growing out of symbolic interactionism and inductive, grounded theory of society, law and inequality are explained as social processes marked by situation and context (Goffman 1956, 1961, Berger & Luckmann 1966).

Research within the sociology of law thus grew from widely shared theoretical perspectives within the discipline, and the contradictory premises of these perspectives, structural on one hand and antistructural on the other, contained the seeds of tensions that have driven debates within the field about the role of structure and class. Sociology of law has also been deeply influenced by intellectual traditions specific to legal scholarship, particularly liberal legalism. In contrast to conflict, structural-functional, and grounded theories, liberal legalism is not a theory, but rather a "description of ideal practices on which law as we know it is said to depend" (Munger 1993:99). In this model of a sociology of law, social science helps policymakers achieve the law's ideals of fairness and equality. The influence of liberal legalism explains, in part, the tendency of American sociology of law to focus on description of legal problems rather than on theory development.[2]

Law and Inequality From the Top Down

Law and society scholars, finding the egalitarian pretensions of both liberal legalism and state theories of law an easy target, produced a vast literature exploring the inevitable gap between an ideal of equal justice on the books and the biases introduced by social organization into the law in action (Abel 1980). Class was often an important element of the explanation of the "gap," but it was rarely developed theoretically.

Numerous studies examined access to justice for persons of limited means. Research projects at the American Bar Foundation and elsewhere documented the legal problems of the poor. The poor, it was shown, made only limited use of lawyers and law, and a resources theory (Mayhew & Reiss 1969) was developed to explain the failure to act in terms of lack of knowledge, lack of material resources, or passivity in the face of oppression (Levine & Preston 1970, Curran 1977, Carlin, Howard & Messinger 1966, Mayhew 1968).

Abel (1973) reviewed this literature and reframed its agenda in more general terms as a theory of the structure of dispute processing. While dispute processing theory and research has been criticized for failing to examine underlying social conflict (including class conflict) as well as the interplay and contestation that "socially constructs" all of social life (Kidder 1980–1981, Berger & Luckmann 1966), Abel's model provided a more precise conceptualization of the effects of structural inequalities on legal and prelegal conflict resolution than did any prior work (see also Felstiner, Abel & Sarat 1980–1981, Miller & Sarat 1980–1981).

Studies examined the stratification of the legal profession, especially in large cities (Smigel 1964, Carlin 1962, Handler 1967). Smigel's seminal study of the Wall Street lawyer, for example, documented the ways in which class and status intersected to create a closed world of elite, WASP law practice dominated and controlled by men. Class background and the privileges of status, as measured by such indices as membership in the Social Register, were of no significance for women, as Epstein's (1983) work made abundantly clear: Daughters of

---

[2] As a number of scholars have reported, in projects growing out of this model sociologists often played a second-class role to legal academics (see Simon and Lynch 1989, Skolnick 1965).

the elite were systematically denied entry to the Wall Street firms of their brothers. Epstein's work demonstrates how gender alters the effects of class on the stratification of legal practice. If gender was one key to exclusion from the professional elite, so was service to clients at the lowest extreme of the class structure, and several studies examined the careers and commitment of lawyers for the poor (Handler et al 1978, Katz 1982).

Research showed the dependence of lawyers on the class structure of society. A market-dependence theory of the legal profession, linking professional organization and individual lawyer behavior to economic dependence on a capitalist market, profoundly influenced empirical research on both stratification and the role of the profession in society (Abel 1989). A more sophisticated theory of market dependence, combining literatures on the lawyer-client relationship, network analysis, and theories of mobility showed that lawyers in Chicago were stratified into two hemispheres of law practice defined by networks of professionals embodying distinct differences in clients, organization of practice, career lines, and values (Heinz & Laumann 1982).

A large body of research on the role of courts and adjudication (see Galanter 1986 for an extensive review), documented the gap between the promises of fairness and equality and the practices of the legal process. Research examined the stratified functions and effects of courts (Wanner 1974, 1975), their relationship to external social organization, and the construction of roles within the courts (Boyum & Mather 1986, Baum et al 1981–1982, Kagan et al 1977, 1978, Galanter 1986). Tracking social movements for reform of adjudication led to interest in the redistributive effects of judicial rationalization (Heydebrand & Seron 1990), mediation, and alternative dispute resolution [described at length by Menkel-Meadow (1984) and Galanter (1986) and extensively critiqued by Abel (1982)].

At the focal point of the literature on law and inequality is an article by Galanter, perhaps the most frequently cited in all of the earlier law and society research literature, which attempts to summarize the vast array of findings up to the mid-1970s (1975). The article presents a process model of the cumulative effects of disadvantage between those Galanter calls one-shot players in law and those he terms repeat players. The disadvantages stem from differences in knowledge, experience, material resources, and the social context of typical pairings between one-shotters and repeat players. In addition, the differences in knowledge, resources, and organizational capacity are exacerbated by the institutional biases of legal process itself—unequal access to lawyers and ability to command their best efforts, the complexities of litigation that favor the knowledgeable and the rich, and the advantages of being able to "play for rules" in legislatures and before courts. In all but explicit terms, the article presents a comprehensive summary of the sociology of law research showing that the system of justice is thoroughly embedded in the class structure, and indeed the title of the article carries the message—"Why the Haves' Come Out Ahead." While Galanter presents a clear and powerful description, he does so, much as does the field itself, without developing a strong conceptual or theoretical scheme: In an article laced with evidence of inequality and hierarchy, the term Haves', like social class itself, is neither defined nor theorized.[3]

Law and Inequality From the Ground Up

There is a second, anti-instrumental and anti-formal tradition of research and theory development in the sociology of law. In contrast to structural models of law and society, grounded theory gives much greater weight to agents' roles in constructing frames of reference.[4] For example, Blumberg (1967), Sudnow (1965), and Macaulay (1963) assume that the relationship between inequality and law can be understood primarily from the interactions among actors in the settings studied. Blumberg & Sudnow describe the construction of typifications through interaction between the regular participants in criminal court proceedings—the judge, prosecutor, and defense counsel. "Normal" crimes receive well-understood, routine treatment, based on typification of the defendant and the crime situation. Mutual commitments are made between court regulars about the expeditious disposition of cases that leave defendants, usually poor, out of the negotiation.

Macaulay's study of noncontractual relations in business has been highly influential in shaping this microsociology of law. Macaulay observed that sales transactions between businesses led to the establishment of continuing relations between sales personnel and the creation of sales practices based on mutual commitment established through long-term dealings (Macaulay 1963). The law, though technically applicable, was largely irrelevant to such practices when continuing relations developed between actors. The continuing-relations hypothesis, quite similar to observations on conflict resolution by anthropologists, makes understanding the effects of inequality considerably more complex,

---

[3] The lone effort to develop a general theory of law and inequality (Black 1976) also fails to do more than offer a set of unexplained categories. Black predicts a patterning of legal relationships according to the relative position of parties in the social order. For example, he predicts that the greater the social distance between two individuals, the more law will govern the relationship and the greater the likelihood of third-party intervention to resolve a dispute. Black's insistence that theory consider only observable behavior, not meaning or understanding from the actor's viewpoint, has been highly controversial. By providing a target for such criticism, Black helped to coalesce interest in the ideological analysis of the role of law and in interpretive theory.

[4] An anthropology of law also played an important intellectual role in the development of socio-legal studies. Indeed, much of the work on dispute processing borrows heavily from anthropology (Nader 1969, Collier 1973, Moore 1978, Mather & Yngvesson 1980–1981, Merry 1982).

as Macaulay himself noted. Among his purchasing agents, continuing relations developed among relative equals, but not between large and small or among the very large businesses. Commenting on the generalizability of Macaulay's study, Yngvesson argued that continuing relations need not involve equals nor be based on trust, and they may involve coercion to prevent recourse to the law (1985, see also Macaulay 1966).

Reflecting on the implications of the line of research inspired by his study, Macaulay has suggested that continuing relations in the form of social networks, private associations, organizations, and informal groups break down formal structure and instrumental legal processes, rendering the state-society boundary meaningless. Sociology of law thus constructed from the ground up supports many of the impulses that led to rejection of class-structural theory of the state, including the claim that agency is more important than the invisible hand of class. Anticipating this turn in sociology of law, Macaulay has remained firmly committed to the importance of the role of social life in explaining the relationship between law and inequality (1984).

Legal Ideologies and Social Class

The failed social reforms and revolutions of the 1960s and 1970s fueled disillusionment with structural theories of law, in particular theories of class-instrumentalism. Empirical studies of contemporary and historical legal conflict by Marxist scholars pointed to a more ambiguous role for class in determining the long-run benefits and burdens imposed by law. A study of the court dispositions of participants in riots by African-Americans in Detroit in 1968 (Balbus 1973) showed that even in response to a serious episode of class and racial strife the courts followed conflicting imperatives. The findings of the study cast serious doubt on the ability of any one perspective, in particular class theory, to explain the behavior of courts even in the middle of a serious episode of class conflict. Similarly, studies by Hay (1975) and Thompson (1964, 1975) of the enforcement of repressive eighteenth century English criminal laws showed that law aided class rule by being violent but also by seeming, and to a degree by being, just. Thompson concluded that the law displayed a "relative autonomy" from class control:

> It is true that the law did mediate existent class relations to the advantage of the rulers. . . On the other hand, the law mediated these class relations through legal forms, which imposed again and again, inhibitions upon the actions of the rulers (1975:264).

The sociology of law was deeply influenced by the European Marxists and neo-Marxists on the subject of legal ideology (Gramsci 1992, Hunt 1981, 1985). The concept of ideology provided a means of avoiding simplistic claims about mechanical class rule and false consciousness. The new challenge was to examine the politics of law—the playing out of class conflicts in contests about the meaning of law in a process that was class-biased but historically contingent. Instrumentalism, state-centered law, structural models of society, and ahistorical social science all came into question as ideology became the vehicle for explaining the relationship between law and social class.[5] Reviewing the literature on the study of law as ideology, Hunt cautioned "ideology is and will remain a difficult, slippery, and ambiguous concept" (1985:31), though it endures as a powerful lens for explaining the role and power of the legal form in social relations.

Some who have contributed to the growing body of research on legal ideology have assumed, as did most Marxist scholars, that legal ideology is a terrain of struggle, conflict, and indeterminacy, but also that ideology is related to "broader social forces rooted in economic, political, and other practices and to institutions" (Hunt 1985:32), i.e. the reproduced patterns of social life that we have called structure. For example, Larson (1977) examined the historically contingent ways in which lawyers and other professionals secured a powerful class position by using ideological claims—merit, science, and service—coupled with political closure and control over access through university-based education and licensure by the state. Abel and his collaborators (1982) describe the rise of the politics and ideology of informalism in law and the reasons for its seemingly contradictory effect—extending the legitimacy and power of the state to new disputes and new parties. Both studies document the historically contingent impulses embedded in legal institutions with a view toward explaining their role in legitimating a structurally unequal, class-based society.

Studies like those of Larson and Abel that located legal ideology in an institutional structure have avoided a simplistic base-superstructure reading of Marx by emphasizing the complex and often contradictory functions of law in society, including the ways in which law constrains both the dominated and the dominating and the contingencies that mediate the law's effects. Some scholars have criticized the lingering instrumentalism and structuralism in such sociological studies of ideology (Harding 1986, Trubek 1984). Indeed, some scholars of legal ideology begin from altogether different premises.

As we show in the next section, a growing body of research focuses on interpretation, holding "that the meanings of cultural and social forms are

---

[5]Feminist scholarship made a particularly important contribution by expanding the horizons of investigations, raising critical questions about method, and questioning whether there is even a distinction between theory and method (Menkel-Meadow & Diamond 1991). Within the sociology of law, feminist scholars have examined the entry of women into male bastions such as law practice (Epstein 1981, Menkel-Meadow 1989), courts (Cook 1978), and alternative dispute resolution (Menkle-Meadow 1984).

constituted in their use" (Greenhouse 1988:687, emphasis added). The relationship between law and inequality is to be understood as the social and
cultural processes by which things (genders, races, individuals, nations, and so
on) come to be recognized as differentiable... from the eye of the beholder"
(1988:688). Because this perspective also holds that there are no intrinsically
or historically prior differences, the interpretivist task is to study only how some
symbols of difference become "legitimate 'givens' of public life" while others
do not (Sarat & Felstiner 1988, 1995).

Grounded sociological theory of law and inequality (described earlier) privileges agency by emphasizing the sociological task of explaining the ways in
which agents act and construct social meanings in the process. Interpretive theory in the sociology of law takes this one step further by being anti-institutional
as well. Social difference—race, class, gender, or sexual preference—is explained entirely through the words, meanings, and language used by actors in the
process of going about their business as citizens, employees, legal professionals,
plaintiffs, or defendants. Interpretive explanations of difference are theoretically severed from any analysis of ongoing patterns of society outside the framework by which meaning is created for the actors being considered. There is no
place for a classical sociological concept of structure in such an analysis, and in
particular there is no room for analysis of relational inequalities such as class.

NARRATING THE STORIES OF LEGAL EXPERIENCE

An emerging sociology of law employs interpretive methods to examine narratives and texts in order to understand legal ideology, legal consciousness, and
law in everyday life. A constitutive theory of law attempts to understand the
ways in which law forms identity and experience and is, in turn, constituted
by the everyday interactions that give law meaning. Constitutive theory shares
with Michel Foucault's (1977) description of cultural history a belief that culture
determines the micro-distribution of power, thus decentering—but also largely
determining—the allocation of power in society. As we noted in the first part
of the chapter, some studies of legal ideology acknowledge the importance of
the institutional dimension of action. Others, including those based upon constitutive theory, pursue the origins of meaning but not the dimension of social
interaction that we term structure (Geertz 1983, Sarat & Felstiner 1995).

Narratives of legal consciousness are among the most common forms of
interpretive scholarship employed on behalf of the constitutive perspective.
Narratives have been used to demonstrate that power is contingent and specifically that power may not be determined by categories such as race, gender,
or class. For example, the narratives of a welfare mother (White 1993), an
African-American law professor (Williams 1991), a female defendant (Ewick

& Silbey 1992), and parents of children with disabilities (Engel 1993) have been used to show that the expected hierarchies of wealth, race, or professional status can be subverted.[6]

In a recent review of this literature, Ewick & Silbey attempt to explain the contingent relationship between reproduction of the social order and narratives of legal consciousness (1995). They argue that there are limits to the power of narrative to subvert the existing social order because "[a]ll stories are produced and communicated interactively with a social context" (p. 211). While "narratives are likely to bear the marks of existing social inequities, disparities of power and ideological effects," yet, the "assumption that 'society' is an ongoing production that is created daily anew, rather than a fixed and external entity" is a reminder of the "dual capacity of reproduction and invention" (p. 222). Although they attempt to come to grips with the stability of "existing social inequities" and other patterns of social order that condition the timing, content, and interpretation of narratives, Ewick & Silbey's formulation of "reproduction and invention" offers no means of explaining such patterns other than the narratives themselves. Similarly, those who present narratives of the legal consciousness of the poor assume that such narratives, by themselves, provide a full understanding of law and poverty (see, e.g. Sarat 1991, Ewick & Silbey 1992, White 1991). Such studies collapse the distinction between idea and action. Put differently, by taking poverty to be what the poor say about poverty, such studies of narratives, methodologically and conceptually, abandon analysis of the social patterns or institutional practices and histories of poverty and law.[7]

Interpretive sociology of law is well illustrated by Felstiner & Sarat's observational study of lawyer-client interactions during divorce counseling (1995). Lawyer-client exchanges are interpreted to show how power "unfolds," "shifts," "permeates," and "moves" between lawyer and client in the process of defining, negotiating, and settling a divorce. For the lawyer, "interaction takes place in a familiar space and a space of privilege" symbolized by, for example,

---

[6]Although there are passing references to the working class, welfare poor, or the occupational status of the individuals' whose consciousness is described, these typifications are not carefully identified apart from the holism of oppressed consciousness, and there is often little or no systematic evidence of relevant group characteristics (Merry 1990, White 1990, Sarat 1990, Ewick & Silbey 1992, Alfieri 1992). Equally common are interpretive accounts that imply that social differences or power are completely dependent on contingencies that occur during social interaction (Abrams 1993, Sarat & Felstiner 1995).

[7]Critical race scholars claim that (auto)biography, legal cases, personal experience, and historical chronicles are powerful forms of "storytelling in the law" (Lawrence 1992:2278), which permit the reader to live in the writer's world as she thinks about identity, law, and action (Williams 1991, Bumiller 1988, Engel 1991, Ewick & Silbey 1992, Sanger 1993). For example, White (1991) writes about an African-American welfare mother who speaks up at a welfare hearing, contrary to her attorney's advice, a story that shows the possibility of autonomous action in spite of the repressive power of the context and the woman's own attorney.

the office, law books, language, or rituals. But the lawyer's power over the client is "malleable." Sarat & Felstiner acknowledge that "structure" circumscribes and shapes "a limited reservoir of possibility defined by history and habit" (1995:23), but the outcome of the circumscription of possibility is rarely predictable or routine. From the interpretive perspective, inequality in power unfolds "in its use."

We are left to speculate: Are gender, race, class, or power so completely malleable? Is there no power in such differences to create inequality that shapes, or compels, or moves individual action or group interaction whether conscious or not? Does the power of class, gender, or race—difference—exist only as experience "in the eye of the beholder?" Is there no institutional and social history of the power of class, race, or gender beyond individual experience? As White has recently suggested:

> While the Foucaltian lens reveals the fluidity of power, it does not show how power can be congealed in social institutions in ways that sustain domination. It may be true that everyday interactions create and maintain social institutions, but this insight does not enable us to map those interactions against the institutional matrices they create. Nor does this insight show us how institutions constrain the circulation of power, channeling it to flow toward some social groups and away from others (1992:1505).

BRINGING CLASS BACK IN: AN AGENDA FOR THE SOCIOLOGY OF LAW

Our review of sociolegal research has shown that analysis of class has declined in importance and that the recent interpretive research on law and inequality has abandoned the institutional and social organizational perspectives of earlier research. The theoretical framework for class analysis employed throughout much of the twentieth century has been challenged by the emergence of a global economy, indeed a global society, in which local movements for human rights can be linked across continents by e-mail and fax, by changes in the organization of work, and by the rise of new cultural themes of consumerism and personal identity. The turn toward an interpretive sociology of law offers a nuanced and microsocial understanding of the asymmetry, paradoxes, and contradictory relations of once familiar experiences across a range of social institutions.

Nonetheless, interpretive research on law and inequality often inadequately addresses how individual lives are interwoven to become part of larger patterns, or why such patterns evolve and persist over time (Sewell 1992). Contemporary society—including the role of law in attorneys' offices, in public agencies, and in everyday life—does not emerge on a tabula rasa and cannot be explained exclusively by examining the interpretations of individuals outside of time and place. The limitation of an interpretive sociology, in particular the analysis of narratives, is in large part a limitation of method. While narratives may capture variation, improvisation, or resistance, by definition they cannot account for the institutional contexts of action, including the institution of class.

In this concluding part we focus our attention on the continuing importance of relative differences in institutional power and resources for the sociology of law. Economic class remains one important element of inequality. Economic class position, associated with employment (and unemployment), income, and ownership of economic resources, is a nearly universal part of social experience.[8] Because class is necessarily relational, everyone experiences inequality, difference, and almost universally, subordination in a fundamentally important aspect of social life.[9] Notwithstanding the continuing importance of economic class, in the late twentieth century, a group's position is defined only partly by its economic class endowments. Other sources of capital—cultural and symbolic—also create hierarchies, power, and subordination as well as opportunities for change.

The class theory of Pierre Bourdieu, to offer one promising example, examines the variation, improvisation, and even indeterminacy of agency without losing sight of group trajectories or the tendency toward reproduction of patterns in social relations (Bourdieu 1985, 1987, Bourdieu & Wacquant 1992). Groups are positioned by patterns in the distribution of endowments of capital. Bourdieu broadens the concept of capital to include the positioning power not only of economic relationships but also of cultural, social, and symbolic capital. Bourdieu's theory of agency considers the effects of a great range of resources while linking those resources to the societal processes that create or maintain them. The habitus, the interpretive context for action generated by a group's experience in society, is a system of "lasting, transposable dispositions which, integrating past experiences, functions at every moment as a matrix of perceptions, appreciations, and actions and makes possible the achievement of infinitely diversified tasks" (1977:82–83). Bourdieu's concept of class is flexible and empirical, providing a means of understanding both the positioning

---

[8] As Rosemary Crompton remarks in the course of an exhaustive assessment of research on class, "although 'work' may possibly have declined as a significant source of social identity, work is still the most significant determinant of the material well-being of the majority of the population" (1993:18). Our point is somewhat broader, namely that work is not only an important source of material resources but also a relational position that places individuals in a hierarchy of authority as well as hierarchies of symbolic and material power.

[9] Class is a system of relational inequalities created by the economy. Class is a relational inequality because, unlike height or talent, it exists through a social process which requires that some individuals acquire more benefits, including authority, status, and income, than others.

power of historical conjunctions of capital endowments for particular groups and the contingency of individual action.

While a theory of class such as Bourdieu's is complex and open ended, it offers a means of making more precise distinctions and observations about contemporary social relations. One consequence of failing to conceptualize class in more theoretical terms is to rely on even more problematic categorical descriptions by using holistic labels such as "working class American," "middle class family," "underclass African-American," or simply "poor," which are found in contemporary ethnographic studies of law and inequality. A theoretically informed concept of class, such as that employed by Bourdieu, will suggest specific institutional processes, generating inequality through endowments of capital and the formation of a habitus. Further, more precise concepts will make possible both comparison and extension of findings across studies. Herein lies the challenge—to build our understanding of the sources and continuity of social hierarchy while respecting the complexities of power and agency.

Class and Law in Everyday Life

Studies in the sociology of law reviewed in the first part of this chapter include research on everyday encounters with legal institutions, documenting the ways in which law may (or may not) be mobilized by individuals of different class, race, or gender. The early studies of legal mobilization have been criticized because they seemed to provide only static portraits of individuals, a characteristic that has weakened categorical approaches to inequality. But the authors of many earlier studies were well aware of the dynamic and interpretive dimensions of action, conflict, and the assertion of rights that have become the focus of attention in more recent qualitative research. Findings of such studies offer guidance for contemporary sociolegal research attempting to link class and law in everyday life.

For example, research by Levine & Preston (1970) attributed a low rate of legal problem-solving among their low-income respondents to a lack of knowledge about rights and to lack of the legal competence often associated with higher income. Yet they considered that "subjects were probably experiencing powerlessness and a feeling of resignation in the face of circumstances about which they thought little could be done" (109) (compare Carlin et al 1966, Felstiner 1980–1981). Mayhew & Reiss termed this perspective the personal resources theory, and they argued that it represented one aspect of their broader theoretical proposition that the role of law in everyday life is a product of the ongoing organization of social life and its institutional structure (1969).

The recent turn to research on legal consciousness can expand our understanding of the social organizational perspective. Studies of legal consciousness directly examine what was merely inferred from very thin data in the early studies—passivity or activism, legal competence, powerlessness, resignation, and the like. Studies of legal consciousness also have a direct bearing on institutional structure. The meaning of such concepts as employment, authority, market, and property are the foundation for the institutions that shape "legal contacts" (to employ Mayhew & Reiss' phrase) linking class to rights and justice (Sennett & Cobb 1972, Willie 1985, Hochschild 1981), to legal conflict (Crowe 1978, Baumgartner 1988), or to beliefs about entitlements (Newman 1988, Munger 1991).

While research on legal consciousness could fill a gap in our understanding of the relationship between meaning and structure, such studies often overlook any process that informants themselves do not describe. In some research the social organizational understanding of action, and specifically class organization, has been lost altogether. Few studies of legal consciousness examine the social organization of work, or more generally the class structure, as a source of the ideological matrix comprising legal consciousness.

For example, most recent community-based studies of legal conflict and dispute resolution pay only limited attention to class, for there is no systematic tapping of class experience as such unless class is mentioned by the subjects (Greenhouse et al 1994). Such studies have focused on inductive discovery of the groups—social networks, neighborhoods, and families—whose interpretations shape disputes and legal conflicts. While some scholars pursuing these studies have suggested that the silence of their informants concerning class may itself have significance (see Greenhouse et al 1994:185), there is no way to determine which aspects of the legal experience or consciousness described by means of the research are attributable to the effects of social class.

A more robust research agenda must attend to the social organizational elements deemed important for the formation of consciousness. As the focus and site of research in the sociology of law has shifted from formal legal institutions to the routines and events of everyday life that are only occasionally touched, if ever, by formal legal institutions, a broad invitation exists to explore beyond the outer edges of the narrative. Beyond the limits of narrative lie the patterns that connect the individual to jobs as well as to organizations, neighborhoods, families, associations, communities (with public authorities), and networks that enable or limit action, whether they are fully understood by their members or not. In these ongoing connections, class is the local embodiment of larger patterns shaped by property holding, market institutions, cultural preferences, and political organization, patterns that may be reconstructed locally, but as variations on themes that play more widely in society.

Class Hierarchy, the Economy, and the Legal Profession

Sociolegal research on lawyers has encompassed research on professional careers and on the social role of lawyers. In both lines of study scholars have examined the effects of class hierarchy, mapping the effects of social stratification on lawyers' careers and examining the effects of clients' wealth and power on lawyers' services. While the studies have been attentive to the effects of social hierarchies on professional stratification and differentiation, the research seldom considers lawyers in relation to class as an institution—namely the role of lawyers in the creation, maintenance, or changes in class organization. Further, both lines of inquiry began with studies of the external factors explaining the behavior of lawyers; more recently they have begun to take greater account of the ways lawyers themselves understand their careers and social roles. This shift from deductive to inductive research has enriched our understanding of the organization of professional work but has exacerbated the tendency of researchers to ignore the relationship between the profession and other institutions in society.

Studies of the career patterns of attorneys have closely paralleled the development of research on social stratification. The earliest work on lawyers' careers relied on conventional mobility models (Ladinsky 1963, Carlin 1962). Later research turned to network models to explain career patterns (Heinz & Laumann 1982, Nelson et al 1987, Seron 1996).

Two recent studies of lawyers' careers draw on contemporary theory of class formation to examine how the organization of lawyers' work helps construct class differences. Hagan et al (1988) employ a relational definition of class, i.e. focusing on domination within the work place, while Hagan & Kay (1995) apply Bourdieu's analysis of noneconomic class endowments to describe the careers of women lawyers entering the professional workplace. The work of Hagan & Kay suggests a means of extending the internal network model of professional stratification (Heinz & Laumann 1982, Nelson 1987) by examining the positioning of lawyers in a general class system. Contemporary theories of class formation (Bourdieu 1977, 1985) and agency (Sewell 1992) may help guide examination of the sources and significance of the social endowments possessed by lawyers and the development of their orientations as agents within a habitus created by class.

A second illustration of the potential contribution of the concept of class to research on professional careers is a recent study by Seron of New York City lawyers (1993, 1996). Reflecting a more grounded, inductive research tradition, Seron showed how lawyers are able to pursue a variety of adaptive strategies for reorganizing their work in response to changing economic pressures. Within a system of stratification among law practices created by market opportunities and lawyers' career endowments, lawyers demonstrate the possibilities for "regulated improvisation" (Bourdieu 1977:77) by a group for which the habitus of professional role is well defined. Seron's perspective could be extended. For example, contemporary research on the relationship between economic restructuring and reorganization within large law firms (Galanter & Paley 1991) would be greatly enriched by considering how lawyers form ideas about reorganizing large law firms and adapt to altered endowments of economic class capital and other forms of social capital implicated in market changes.

A large sociology of law literature considers the social role of the legal profession. Early research on the part played by the profession in promoting justice and ameliorating social inequality (Handler et al 1978, Capelletti et al 1975) found an easy target in the structural-functional theory which specified that the profession stabilized and legitimated the social order (Parsons 1964). Alternative theories suggested that a self-interested monopoly of professional knowledge (Freidson 1986, Abbott 1988) or control of market position (Larson 1977, Abel 1989) motivated professional organizations and individual lawyer's behavior.

The relationship between lawyers and the evolution of major institutions of the society, including the class system, should be a prime area for continuing development of theory and research. A great deal of empirical evidence has been amassed to show the uneven distribution of lawyer's services, reflecting the market power of clients and professional self-interest. Yet this literature initially failed to consider the institutional questions raised by such findings— why social inequality persists and why it persists in particular forms (Currie 1971). Later research on the organization and the social role of lawyers partially addressed such questions by drawing on market dependency theory, which described the contribution of market pressure to the formation of professional organizations and the creation of a professional monopoly. But market dependency theory, by itself, does not account for the nature of economic hierarchy, or the complex relationship between class, the work of lawyers, and the production of professional culture (Nelson et al 1992). Thus, in spite of decades of research showing that lawyers are influenced by client wealth and power, few broad theoretical attempts have been made to understand the role lawyers play in maintaining or transforming fundamental social institutions (Munger 1994).

Weber maintained that lawyers' commitment to law, irrespective of lawyers' class origins or class loyalties, is an important prop for legitimate authority in a plural society (1954), while, in contrast, Marx argued that the professions served the interests of those who held ultimate power—the capitalist class (1950). Heinz & Laumann's study of stratification among lawyers in Chicago raised questions about whether any significant core values are shared by all lawyers

(1982). Their finding that lawyers are separated into two distinct hemispheres representing organizations and individuals, and subdivided further by types of practice within each hemisphere, suggests rather that lawyers' values vary considerably as a function of client influence (and by the class of the client). The turn to grounded research on lawyers' work has also suggested that lawyers create culture, as well as reflect culture, when they serve their clients (Gordon 1982, Sarat & Felstiner 1995). For example, Dezalay & Garth conclude from their research on lawyers in international business transactions that lawyers are important carriers of legal and economic culture in the internationalization of trade and business relations (1995).

As grounded research continues to explore the interplay between professional work and the creation of social organization, economic change, or the control of conflict, class theory offers a means of looking beyond the situated lawyer to the normatively constructed habitus of professional life and to the institutional pressures and limitations imposed by the economic organization of society (see Simon 1988, Alfieri 1992, Bezdek 1992, Seron 1993, 1996). Contemporary qualitative research on the work of the profession should examine the conditions under which lawyers contribute to the reproduction or change in fundamental patterns in society such as markets and classes (Harrington 1985, Halliday 1987, Shamir 1993).

Class Structure and the Administration of the Law

By linking the internal practices of public and private organizations directly to the class structure of society, the theories of Marx & Weber posed a powerful hypothesis about the scope of social control.[10] Yet empirical research has increasingly demonstrated the importance of institutional, organizational, and professional practices as ends in themselves (Heimer forthcoming; Reichman 1989, Hawkins 1989, Heydebrand & Seron 1990). "Law from the bottom up" refers to the analysis of the practices of those who are the first-in-line (at the bottom of the authority ladder) to apply legal authority. Their practices do not merely alter the terms upon which law will be applied; they are the law (Cohen 1985, Massell 1968, Edelman et al 1993, Macaulay 1963). The research has undermined to a considerable extent the Weberian master-narrative of organizational order (cf Suchman & Edelman forthcoming; Lempert 1991).

Such findings have made understanding the relationship of legal institutions to class structure both more difficult and more direct. To the extent that lower

---

[10]Instrumental and structural Marxism argued that in the last analysis law reflected class domination. Weber argued that law was upheld by an autonomous legal profession, but he also argued that legal authority existed in constant tension with the social hierarchies of class and status that distorted such authority. Much sociolegal research supports the existence of direct effects of class on legal institutions, and we have reviewed these in first part of this chapter.

levels of officials, judges, police, prosecutors, and social workers are not controlled by higher level authorities, the structural theories of the state and class seem to lose their relevance. To the same extent, however, organizations may be permeated much more directly by class organization or culture and other influences on bureaucrats and functionaries, whose jobs are defined through a mixture of situational constraints and grass roots accommodations (Cohen 1985, Handler 1990). While innovation and change may come from the bottom, more often the effect is to permit routinization of decision-making according to locally generated norms about what constitutes a "normal" case or a "last resort" case. These typifications are subject to class, race, and gender biases (Sudnow 1965, Emerson 1981, Daly 1994).

Studies of social control suggest not only that class is a factor in the treatment of individuals but also that social control is organized quite differently to deal with different social classes. Through policing and welfare, the poor and especially the underclass experience a special kind of "government of the poor" (Simon 1993, Cohen 1985, Sampson & Laub 1993). In addition to a long line of studies showing that white collar crimes are treated relatively leniently (Sutherland 1955, Hagan et al 1980, Shapiro 1987), Cohen argues that the "soft" technologies for social control—self-help, therapeutic guidance, education— are reserved for those who have greater social and economic capital (1985). Simon suggests that the disparity in class treatment is increasing because growing income differences, increasing numbers of permanently unemployed, and the Africanization and ghettoization of poverty in political discourse are contributing to a shift in emphasis from rehabilitation and reform of the poor to surveillance and control (Simon 1993, Feeley & Simon 1992).

"Loose coupling" (Hagan 1979) between and within the agencies of social control that is apparent from studies of crime control raises still broader questions about the relationship between class, state, and society. Loose coupling between state agencies as well as extensive interpenetration of state and society often renders the state's attempts to regulate ineffective because power is shared among state agencies, private institutions, associations, and networks (Moore 1978, see especially Macaulay 1986). This state is not the class-state described by Marx, Weber, or Durkheim but is rather a more complex institution; it is dependent on the power of class but, absent special conditions, far less instrumental in its capacity. What implications do these findings have for the relationship between class structure and the role of the state's regulatory efforts over time?

Four research strategies are suggested by current work on the relationship between class, law, and the state. The first is to study the formation of the habitus of routine decision-making by the bureaucrats responsible for disposing of most of the state's business. Though the existing studies are revealing, they often do not approach their analysis of case decisions from the perspective of a wider set of cultural and institutional influences beyond the office setting.

Second, the state may be studied as a collection of concrete critical decisions and ongoing relatively stable processes. Calavita's study of the Immigration and Naturalization Service's handling of the bracero farmworker program shows that the theory that state bureaucrats are dependent on the resources of those with continuing access to the means of producing wealth must be supplemented with knowledge of the particular state managers involved in a particular decision (1992). The intersection of biography and the momentum of agency history exposes both the lasting dependencies between state and economy and their contingency.

Third, the state-class connection may be usefully considered in light of a nonfunctional systems theory articulated by Block (1987) to take account of surprising, counterintuitive patterns, e.g. the strong response by law enforcement agencies to the savings and loan crisis (Calavita & Pontell 1994). Politics always creates an important contingency in law enforcement, especially in the United States (see Savelsberg 1994).

Finally, as sociology of law becomes more international and more global in its subject matter, the endowments of class, the links between societies, and the institutional response to change take on new complexities. Hierarchy, domination, and resistance are altered by the pressures of a global economy, the interactions between cultures, or simply by the power of modern communications that makes it possible to bypass the courts and even the nation state to assert claims for rights. The juxtaposition of the use of local, national, and international legal institutions reminds us that the relations of domination and exploitation take on new forms in a global society, forms that are often constituted in ways unfamiliar to western sociologists (Upham 1987, Winn 1994).

Class Mediation of Law and Social Change

Classic social theory placed law in an instrumental role. Law could both create and respond to social change; indeed, state capacity to respond to or manage the consequences of industrialization was a core concern of the theories of Marx, Durkheim, and Weber. The poignant ineffectiveness and contingency of legislation and litigation during America's civil rights era in the 1960s had an impact (Scheingold 1974, see Gordon 1984), but skepticism about the instrumental effectiveness of law is an older theme in American sociology of law, reflecting, among other sources, the influence of legal realism (Arnold 1935). Authors such as Handler (1978) and Rosenberg (1991), who amass evidence of the failure of social movements for legal rights, base their skepticism on theories about the direct effects of class and inequality on the state, and they challenge the liberal legal ideal of an effective, neutral, and responsive state. Handler and Rosenberg show that an imbalance in class resources combined with the inertia and bureaucracy of the state will nearly always defeat redistributive change (for an important critique of this view see Simon 1992).

An important locus of the relationship between law and change lies outside formal legal process. Sumner's claim that folkways always prevail over stateways was clearly wrong. Law directly influences ordinary life. The ways that it influences ordinary life are many—by contributing to the creation of social norms, by producing knowledge that becomes a foundation for action, and by direct enforcement of change. The effects of law vary, but they are not always marginal or inevitably invisible. Based on what we know about class differences in knowledge, moral decisions, values, styles of conflict resolution, and their interaction with gender and race, there is surely a class component to the social change that law can create. Now we have come full circle, because to understand such effects we must understand the context in which action is contemplated and undertaken in everyday life.

Michael McCann's study of the role of legal rights in the pay equity movement (1994) takes seriously the challenges of studying legal change and legal consciousness at the grass roots. He applies a discourse theory of legal mobilization in which "law is understood to consist of a complex repertoire of discursive strategies and symbolic frameworks that structure ongoing social intercourse and meaning-making activities among citizens" (1994:282). Further, he argues that rights are "inherently indeterminate, pluralistic, and contingent in actual social practice (ibid)." While he also acknowledges the importance of institutional attributes such as social class and organizational or political context, his findings, like those in many recent studies that follow the turn to discourse and narrative, do not systematically locate the individuals interviewed in relevant group contexts—in the continuing patterns of association and experience that were either similar across all workplaces or unique to particular settings. Thus, McCann's study brings us back to the concerns with which we began this essay, namely, appreciating the connection between the larger institutional patterns of a class society and the role of law.

CONCLUSION

Research without a structural concept of class impoverishes our understanding of law and inequality. Underlying the reluctance of many to examine class is a generation-long skepticism about the concept of structure. The structure-agency problem goes to the core of sociological theory and method, and to what it means to conduct empirical research with conceptual rigor. A review of the literature in the sociology of law revealed swings between analyses that emphasized structure or agency. Just as earlier theory in the sociology of law tended toward a more instrumental view of social action, so contemporary theory tends to focus on the indeterminacy of action. While interpretive work presents an important critique of structural theory, structure and class have not gone away.[11] Class continues to describe an important aspect of social life, namely the powerful link between the lives of individuals and the economic organization of society that is beyond the control and often beyond the knowledge or full understanding of those individuals.

Our review of ways that more careful attention to the role of class might enrich the sociology of law leads to several suggestions for incorporating the concept of class into sociolegal research:

• The *experience* of class is a starting point. Biography—the experiences of individual and group through time—is fundamental.

• The relationship of class structure to the activities of members of a class is complex.

The direct effects of class structure are modified by the experience of race and gender, the roles occupied by individuals in complex organizations, and by the emergent and creative possibilities of social action.

• Research on class requires a comparative perspective.

Ultimately sociology studies the social group. Narrative and case-study methodology treat the subject as representative of a larger group. Identification of the similarities and differences between sites and subjects should be made explicit, and class is one of the important dimensions on which narrative and case studies can be compared.

• The concept of class evolves through empirical research.

Class theory suggests possible connections between the experience of the situated individual and the group-habitus and the larger patterns of social life, but our understanding of class rests on discovery of the precise role of class and habitus through empirical research.

• The element of time is essential.

[11]Attempts to grapple with the structure-agency problem are in evidence across a variety of subfields, including the sociology of professions (Abbott 1988), comparative sociology (Orren & Skowronek 1994, Orren & Skowronek forthcoming; Somers & Gibson 1994), criminology (Savelsberg 1994), and organizations (Powell & DiMaggio 1991). The pivotal question is: "How [can] sociological theories which do accept the sui generis collective character of social arrangements. . . retain a conception of individual freedom and voluntarism?" (Alexander 1982).

Both as situated experience and as a larger pattern in social life, class is best understood through biography and through community history. Class, so understood, is one important element in the accretion of particular routines, knowledge, and relationships that constitute the trajectory of a group through time. Out of these grow change and, equally, the tendency to reproduce the patterns of social life.

The turn to narrative studies in sociolegal research reflects awareness of the importance of context and agency. But in taking this turn, contemporary studies of law and society have sidestepped the capacity to explain the sources and significance of difference and inequality in terms that individuals themselves cannot employ. While biographies are individually experienced and understood, they are also shaped by history not only of the individual's making (Calavita & Seron 1992). As C. Wright Mills (1959) concluded, the promise of the sociological imagination lies in explaining the link between the meanings of the private lives of individuals and "the larger historical scene."

ACKNOWLEDGMENTS

We would like to acknowledge the contributions of colleagues who read earlier versions of this essay. In particular we would like to thank Kitty Calavita, Marcus Dubber, Cynthia Fuchs Epstein, John Hagan, Bonnie Oglensky, Renate Reiman, Jack Schlegel, Susan Silbey, and Rob Soute. We have tried to follow their good advice, but our success or failure in doing so remains our responsibility alone. We would like to thank Kevin Zanner & Jason Yots for their assistance with our research.

Literature Cited

Abbott A. 1988. *The System of Professions: An Essay on the Division of Expert Labor.* Chicago: Univ. Chicago Press

Abel RL. 1989. *American Lawyers.* New York: Oxford Univ. Press

Abel RL, ed. 1982. *The Politics of Informal Justice.* Vols. 1, 2. New York: Academic

Abel RL. 1980. Redirecting social studies of law. *Law Soc. Rev.* 14:(3)805–29

Abel RL. 1973. A comparative theory of dispute institutions in society. *Law Soc. Rev.* 8(2):217–347

Abrams K. 1993. Unity, narrative and law. In *Studies in Law, Politics and Society,* ed. A

Sarat, SS Sibley, 13:3–35. Greenwich, CT: JAI

Alexander J. 1982. Positivism, presuppositions, and current controversies. In *Theoretical Logic in Sociology,* Berkeley/Los Angeles: Univ. Calif. Press

Alfieri AV. 1992. Disabled clients, disabling lawyers. *Hastings Law J.* 43:769–851

Arnold TW. 1935. *The Symbols of Government.* New Haven, CT: Yale Univ. Press

Balbus I. 1973. *The Dialectics of Legal Repression: Black Rebels Before the American Criminal Courts.* New York: Russell Sage

Baum L, Goldman S, Sarat A. 1981/1982. Research note: the evolution of litigation in the federal courts of appeal, 1895–1975. *Law Soc. Rev.* 16(2):291–309

Baumgartner MP. 1988. *The Moral Order of a Suburb.* New York: Oxford Univ. Press

Berger P, Luckmann T. 1966. *The Social Construction of Reality: A Treatise in the Sociology of Knowledge.* Garden City, NY: Doubleday

Bezdek B. 1992. Silence in the court: participation and subordination of poor tenants' voices in the legal process. *Hofstra Law Rev.* 20:533–608

Black D. 1976. *The Behavior of Law.* New York: Academic

Block F. 1987. *Revising State Theory: Essays on Politics and Postindustrialism.* Philadelphia: Temple Univ. Press

Blumberg A. 1967. *Criminal Justice.* Chicago: Quadrangle

Bourdieu P. 1985. The social space and the genesis of groups. *Theory Soc.* 14:723–75

Bourdieu P. 1977. *Outline of a Theory of Practice.* Cambridge, MA: Cambridge Univ. Press

Bourdieu P, Wacquant LJD. 1992. *An Invitation to Reflexive Sociology.* Chicago: Univ. Chicago Press

Boyum K, Mather L. 1986. *Empirical Theories About Courts.* New York: Longman

Bumiller K. 1988. *The Civil Rights Society: the Social Construction of Victims.* Baltimore: Johns Hopkins Press

Calavita K. 1992. *Inside the State: the Bracero Program, Immigration, and the I.N.S.* New York: Routledge

Calavita K, Pontell H. 1994. The state and white-collar crime: saving the savings and loans. *Law Soc. Rev.* 28:297–324

Calavita K, Seron C. 1992. Postmodernism and protest: recovering the sociological imagination. *Law Soc. Rev.* 26(4):756–71

Capelletti M, Gordley J, Johnson E. 1975. *Toward Equal Justice: a Comparative Study of Legal Aid in Modern Societies.* Milan: Guiffre/Dobbs Ferry, NY: Oceana

Cohen S. 1985. *Visions of Social Control: Crime, Punishment and Classification.* Cambridge, UK: Polity

Collier J. 1973. *Law and Social Change in Zinacantan.* Stanford: Stanford Univ. Press

Cook BB. 1978. Women judges: the end of tokenism. In *Women in the Courts,* ed. W Hepperle, L Crites, pp. 84–105. Williamsburg, VA: Natl. Cent. State Courts

Crompton R. 1993. *Class and Stratification: An Introduction to Current Debates.* Cambridge, UK: Polity Press

Crowe PW. 1978. Complainant reactions to the Massachusetts commission against discrimination. *Law Soc. Rev.* 12(2):217–35

Curran BA. 1977. *The Legal Needs of the Public: the Final Report of a National Survey.* Chicago: The Foundation

Currie E. 1971. Sociology of law: the unasked questions. *Yale Law J.* 81:134–47

Dahrendorf R. 1959. *Class and Class Conflict in Industrial Society.* Stanford: Stanford Univ. Press

Daly K. 1994. *Gender, Crime and Punishment.* New Haven, CT: Yale Univ. Press

Dezalay Y, Garth B. 1995. Merchants of law as moral entrepreneurs: constructing international justice from the competition for transnational business dispute. *Law Soc. Rev.* 29(1):27–64

Edelman LB, Erlanger HS, Lande J. 1993. Internal dispute resolution: the transformation of civil rights in the workplace. *Law Soc. Rev.* 27(3):497–534

Emerson R. 1981. On last resorts. *J. Sociol.* 87:1–22

Engel D. 1993. Law in the domains of everyday life: the construction of community and difference. In *Law in Everyday Life,* ed. A Sarat, T Kearns, pp. 123–70. Ann Arbor: Univ. Mich. Press

Engel D. 1991. Law, culture, and children with disabilities: educational rights and the construction of difference. *Duke Law J.* 1991:166–205

Epstein CF. 1981. *Women in the Law.* New York: Basic Books

Evans W, ed. 1962. *Law and Sociology: Exploratory Essays.* Glencoe, IL: Free

Ewick P, Silbey S. 1995. Subversive stories and hegemonic tales: toward a sociology narrative. *Law Soc. Rev.* 29(2):197–226

Ewick P, Silbey S. 1992. Conformity, contestation and resistance: an account of legal consciousness. *New Engl. Law Rev.* 26:731–49

Feeley M, Simon J. 1992. The new prophecy: notes on the emerging strategy of corrections and its applications. *Criminology* 30:449–74

Felstiner WLF, Abel R, Sarat A. 1980/1981. The emergence and transformation of disputes: naming, blaming, claiming. *Law Soc. Rev.* 15(3–4):631–54

Foucault M. 1977. *Discipline and Punish: The Birth of the Prison.* New York: Pantheon

Freidson E. 1986. *Professional Powers: a Study of the Institutionalization of Formal Knowledge.* Chicago: Univ. Chicago Press

Galanter M. 1986. Adjudication, litigation, and related phenomena. In *Law and the Social Sciences,* ed. L Lipson, S Wheeler, pp. 151–258. New York: Russell Sage

Galanter M. 1975. Why the "Haves" come out ahead: speculations on the limits of legal change. *Law Soc. Rev.* 9(1):95–160

Galanter M, Paley T. 1991. *Tournament of*

Lawyers: The Transformation of the Big Law Firms. Chicago: Univ. Chicago Press

Geertz C. 1983. *Social Knowledge: Further Essays in Interpretive Anthropology*. New York: Basic

Glaser BG, Strauss A. 1967. *The Discovery of Grounded Theory: Strategies for Qualitative Research*. Chicago: Aldine

Goffman E. 1961. *Encounters*. Indianapolis: Bobbs-Merrill

Goffman E. 1956. *The Presentation of Self in Everyday Life*. Garden City, NY: Doubleday

Gordon R. 1984. Legal thought and legal practice in the age of American enterprise. In *Profession and Professional Ideologies in America*, ed. G Geison, pp. 70–110. Chapel Hill: Univ. N Carolina

Gordon R. 1982. New developments in legal theory. In *The Politics of Law: A Progressive Critique*, ed. D Kairys, pp. 281–93. New York: Pantheon

Gramsci A. 1992. *Prison Notebooks*. New York: Columbia Univ. Press

Greenhouse CJ. 1988. Courting difference: issues of interpretation and comparison in the study of legal idealism. *Law Soc. Rev.* 22(4):687–707

Greenhouse CJ, Engel DM, Yngvesson B. 1994. *Law and Community in Three American Towns*. Ithaca: Cornell Univ. Press

Hagan J. 1979. Ceremonial justice: crime and punishment in a loosely coupled system. *Soc. Forces* 58(2):506–27

Hagan J, Huxter M, Parker P. 1988. Class structure and legal practice: inequality and mobility among Toronto lawyers. *Law Soc. Rev.* 22(1):9–55

Hagan J, Nagel I, Albonetti C. 1980. The differential sentencing of white-collar offenders in ten federal district courts. *Am. Sociol. Rev.* 45:802–20

Halliday T. 1987. *Beyond Monopoly: Lawyers, State Crisis and Professional Empowerment*. Chicago: Univ. Chicago Press

Handler J. 1967. *The Lawyer and His Community: The Practicing Bar in a Middle-Sized City*. Madison: Univ. Wis. Press

Handler JF. 1990. *Law and the Search for Community*. Philadelphia: Univ. Penn. Press

Handler JF. 1978. *Social Movements and the Legal System: A Theory of Law Reform and Social Change*. New York: Academic

Handler JF, Hollingsworth EJ, Erlanger H. 1978. *Lawyers and the Pursuit of Legal Rights*. New York: Academic

Harding S. 1986. *The Science Question in Feminism*. Ithaca: Cornell Univ. Press

Harrington C. 1985. *Shadow Justice: the Ideology and Institutionalization of Alternatives to Court*. Westport, CT: Greenwood

Hawkins K. 1989. "FATCATS" and prosecution in a regulatory agency: a footnote on the social construction of risk. *J. Law Policy* 11(3):370–91

Hay D, et al, eds. 1975. *Albion's Fatal Tree: Crime and Society in Eighteenth-Century England*. New York: Pantheon

Heimer C. 1996. Explaining variation in the impact of law: organizations, institutions, and professions. In *Fifteen Studies in Law, Politics, and Society*, ed. A Sarat, S Sibley. In press

Heinz JP, Laumann EO. 1982. *Chicago Lawyers: The Social Structure of the Bar*. New York: Russell Sage

Hochschild J. 1981. *What's Fair?: American Beliefs about Distributive Justice*. Cambridge: Harvard Univ. Press

Hunt A. 1985. The ideology of law: advances and problems in recent application of the concept of ideology to the analysis of law. *Law Soc. Rev.* 19(1):11–37

Hunt A. 1981. Dichotomy and contradiction in the sociology of law. *Br. J. Law Soc.* 8(1):47–78

Heydebrand W, Seron C. 1990. *Rationalizing Justice: the Political Economy of Federal District Courts*. Albany: SUNY Press

Kagan R, Cartwright B, Friedman L, Wheeler S. 1978. The evolution of state supreme courts. *Mich. Law Rev.* 76:961–1001

Kagan R, Cartwright B, Friedman L, Wheeler S. 1977. The business of state supreme courts, 1870–1980. *Stanford Law Rev.* 30:121–56

Katz J. 1982. *Poor Peoples Lawyers in Transition*. New Brunswick, NJ: Rutgers Univ. Press

Kidder R. 1980/1981. The end of the road: problems in the analysis of disputes. *Law Soc. Rev.* 15(3–4):717–25

Ladinsky J. 1963. *Career Development Among Lawyers: a Study of Social Factors in the Allocation of Professional Labor*. Ann Arbor: Univ. Microfilms

Larson MS. 1977. *The Rise of Professionalism: A Sociological Analysis*. Berkeley: Univ. Calif. Press

Lawrence CR. 1992. The word and the river: pedagogy as scholarship as struggle. *South. Calif. Law Rev.* 65:2231–98

Lempert R. 1991. Dependency on the welfare state: beyond the due process vision. *Contemp. Sociol.* 20(1):84–86

Levine FJ, Preston E. 1970. Community resource orientation among low income groups. *Wis. Law Rev.* 1970:80–113

Macaulay S. 1986. Private government. In *Law and Social Science*, ed. L Lipson, S Wheeler, pp. 445–518. New York: Russell Sage Found.

Macaulay S. 1984. Law and the social sciences: Is there any there there? *J. Law Policy* 6(2):149–87

Macaulay S. 1966. *Law and the Balance of Power: the Automobile Manufacturers and their Dealers.* New York: Russell Sage Found.

Macaulay S. 1963. Non-contractual relations in business: a preliminary study. *Am. Sociol. Rev.* 28:55–69

Marx K, Engels F. 1950. *Basic Writings on Politics and Philosophy,* ed. L Furer. Garden City, NY: Doubleday

Massell G. 1968. Law as an instrument of revolutionary change in a traditional milieu: the case of Soviet Central Asia. *Law Soc. Rev.* 2(2):179–228

Mather L, Yngvesson B. 1980/1981. Language, audience, and the transformation of disputes. *Law Soc. Rev.* 15(3–4):775–821

Mayhew L. 1968. *Law and Equal Opportunity: A Study of the Massachusetts Commission Against Discrimination.* Cambridge: Harvard Univ. Press

Mayhew L, Reiss AJ. 1969. The social organization of legal contacts. *Am. Sociol. Rev.* 34(3):309–18

McCann M. 1994. *Rights at Work: Pay Equity Reform and the Politics of Legal Mobilization.* Chicago: Univ. Chicago Press

Menkel-Meadow C. 1989. Feminization of the legal profession: the comparative sociology of women lawyers. In *Lawyers in Society: Comparative Theories,* ed. RL Abel, PSC Lewis, pp. 196–256. Berkeley: Univ. Calif. Press

Menkel-Meadow C. 1984. Toward another view of legal negotiation: the structures of problem-solving. *UCLA Law Rev.* 31:754–842

Menkel-Meadow C, Diamond S. 1991. The content, method, and epistemology of gender in sociological studies. *Law Soc. Rev.* 25(2):221–38

Merry SE. 1990. *Getting Justice and Getting Even: Legal Consciousness Among Working Class Americans.* Chicago: Univ. Chicago Press

Merry SE. 1982. The social organization of mediation in nonindustrial societies: implications for informal community justice in America. See Abel 1982, 2:17–46

Miller R, Sarat A. 1980/1981. Grievances, claims and disputes: assessing the adversary cultures. *Law Soc. Rev.* 15(3–4):525–66

Mills CW. 1959. *The Sociological Imagination.* New York: Oxford Univ. Press

Moore SF. 1978. *Law as Process: An Anthropological Approach.* London: Routledge & Kegan Paul

Munger F. 1994. Miners and lawyers: law practice and class conflict in Appalachia, 1872–1920. In *Lawyers in a Postmodern World,* ed. M Cain, CB Harrington, pp. 185–228. New York: New York Univ. Press

Munger F. 1993. Sociology of law for a postliberal society. *Loyola Law Rev.* 27:89–125

Munger F. 1991. Legal resources of striking miners: notes for a study of class conflict and law. *Soc. Sci. Hist.* 15(1):1–33

Nader L. 1969. *Law in Culture and Society.* New York: Academic

Nelson R. 1987. *Bureaucracy, Professionalism, and Commitment: Authority Relationships in Large Law Firms.* Chicago: Am. Bar Found.

Nelson R, Trubek D, Solomon RL. 1992. *Lawyers' Ideals/Lawyers' Practices: Transformations in the American Legal Practice.* Ithaca: Cornell Univ. Press

Newman K. 1988. *Falling From Grace: the Experience of Downward Mobility in the American Middle Class.* New York: Free

Orren K, Skowronek S. 1994. Beyond the iconography of order: notes for a new institutionalism. In *The Dynamics of American Politics: Approaches and Interpretations,* ed. LC Dodd, C Jilson, pp. 311–30. Boulder: Univ. Colo. Press

Orren K, Skowronek S. 1996. Forthcoming. Institutions and intercurrents: theory building in the fullness of time. In *Nomos: Political Order,* ed. R Hardin, I Shapiro. Vol. 37. In press

Parsons T. 1964. *Essays in Sociological Theory.* New York: Free

Powell W, DiMaggio P. 1991. *The New Institutionalism in Organizational Analysis.* Chicago: Univ. Chicago Press

Reichman N. 1989. Breaking confidences: organizational influences on insider trading. *Sociol. Q.* 30(2):185–204

Rosenberg GN. 1991. *The Hollow Hope: Can Courts Bring About Social Change?* Chicago: Univ. Chicago Press

Sampson R, Laub J. 1993. Structural variations in juvenile court case processing: inequality, the underclass and social control. *Law Soc. Rev.* 27(2):285–311

Sanger C. 1993. *Law as litany: teenage abortion hearings.* Presented at Annu. Meet. Law Soc. Assoc., Chicago

Sarat A. 1990. ". . . the law is all over:" power, resistance and the legal consequences of the welfare poor. *Yale J. Law Hum.* 2:343–79

Sarat A, Felstiner WLF. 1995. *Divorce Lawyers and Their Clients: Power and Meaning in the Legal Process.* New York: Oxford Univ. Press

Sarat A, Felstiner WLF. 1988. Law and social relations: vocabularies of motive in lawyer/client interaction. *Law Soc. Rev.*

22(4):737–69

Savelsberg JJ. 1994. Knowledge, domination and criminal punishment. *Am. J. Sociol.* 99(4):911–43

Scheingold SA. 1974. *The Politics of Rights: Lawyers, Public Policy and Political Change.* New Haven, CT: Yale Univ. Press

Sennett R, Cobb J. 1972. *The Hidden Injuries of Class.* New York: Vintage

Seron C. 1996. *The Business of Practicing Law: the Worklives of Solo and Small Firm Attorneys.* Philadelphia: Temple Univ. Press

Seron C. 1993. New strategies for getting clients: urban and suburban lawyers' views. *Law Soc. Rev.* 27(2):399–420

Sewell WH. 1992. A theory of structure: duality, agency and transformation. *Am. J. Sociol.* 98(1):1–29

Shamir R. 1993. Professionalism and monopoly of expertise: lawyers and administrative law, 1933–37. *Law Soc. Rev.* 27(2):361–97

Shapiro S. 1987. *Wayward Capitalists: Target of the Securities and Exchange Commission.* New Haven, CT: Yale Univ. Press

Simon J. 1993. *Poor Discipline: Parole and the Social Control of the Underclass, 1890–1990.* Chicago: Univ. Chicago Press

Simon J. 1992. "The long walk home" to politics. *Law Soc. Rev.* 26(4):923–41

Simon R, Lynch J. 1989. The sociology of law: Where we have been and where we might be going. *Law Soc. Rev.* 23(5):825–47

Simon W. 1988. Ethical discretion in lawyering. *Harvard Law Rev.* 101:1083–145

Skolnick J. 1965. The sociology of law in America: overview and trends. *Soc. Probl.* 12(4):4–39

Smigel E. 1964. *The Wall Street Lawyer, A Professional Organization Man?* New York: Free Press

Somers MR, Gibson G. 1994. Reclaiming the epistemological "other": narrative and the constitution of identity. In *Social Theory and the Politics of Identity,* ed. C Calhoun, pp. 37–99. Cambridge, MD: Blackwell

Suchman D, Edelman LB. 1995. Legal rational myths: lessons for the new institutionalism from the law and society tradition. *Law Soc. Issues* Nov.

Sudnow D. 1965. Normal crimes: sociological features of the penal code in a public defender office. *Soc. Probl.* 12(3):255–76

Sutherland EH. 1955. *Principles of Criminology.* Philadelphia: Lippencott

Thompson EP. 1975. *Whigs and Hunters: The Origins of the Black Act.* New York: Pantheon

Thompson EP. 1964. *The Making of the English Working Class.* New York: Vintage Books

Trubek DM. 1984. Where the action is: critical legal studies and empiricism. *Stanford Law Rev.* 36:575–622

Upham FK. 1987. *Law and Social Change in Postwar Japan.* Cambridge: Harvard Univ. Press

Wanner C. 1975. The public ordering of private relations, part two: winning civil court cases. *Law Soc. Rev.* 9(2):293–306

Wanner C. 1974. The public ordering of private relations, part one: initiating civil cases in urban trial courts. *Law Soc. Rev.* 8(3):421–40

Weber M. 1954. *Max Weber on Law in Economy and Society,* ed. E Shils, M Rheinstein. Cambridge: Harvard Univ. Press

White L. 1993. No exit: rethinking welfare dependency: from a different ground. *Georgetown Law J.* 81:1961–2002

White L. 1992. Seeking "…the faces of otherness…": a response to professors Sarat, Felstiner, and Cahn. *Cornell Law Rev.* 77:1499–511

White L. 1991. Subordination, rhetorical survival skills, and Sunday shoes: notes on the hearing of Mrs. G. In *At the Boundaries of Law,* ed. MA Fineman, NS Thomadsen, pp. 40–58. New York: Routledge

Williams PJ. 1991. *The Alchemy of Race and Rights.* Cambridge: Harvard Univ. Press

Willie CU. 1985. *Black and White Families: a Study in Complementarity.* Bayside, NY: General Hall

Winn JK. 1994. Rational practices and the marginalization of law: informal financial practices of small businesses in Taiwan. *Law Soc. Rev.* 28(2):193–232

Yngvesson B. 1985. Re-examining continuing relations and the law. *Wis. Law Rev.* 1985(3):623–46

Annu. Rev. Sociol. 1996. 22:213–38
Copyright © 1996 by Annual Reviews Inc. All rights reserved

COMPUTER NETWORKS AS SOCIAL NETWORKS: Collaborative Work, Telework, and Virtual Community

Barry Wellman, Janet Salaff, Dimitrina Dimitrova, Laura Garton, Milena Gulia, Caroline Haythornthwaite

Centre for Urban and Community Studies, University of Toronto, Toronto, Canada M5S 2G8

KEY WORDS: computer supported cooperative work, virtual community, telework, electronic mail, social networks, internet communication

ABSTRACT

When computer networks link people as well as machines, they become social networks. Such computer-supported social networks (CSSNs) are becoming important bases of virtual communities, computer-supported cooperative work, and telework. Computer-mediated communication such as electronic mail and computerized conferencing is usually text-based and asynchronous. It has limited social presence, and on-line communications are often more uninhibited, creative, and blunt than in-person communication. Nevertheless, CSSNs sustain strong, intermediate, and weak ties that provide information and social support in both specialized and broadly based relationships. CSSNs foster virtual communities that are usually partial and narrowly focused, although some do become encompassing and broadly based. CSSNs accomplish a wide variety of cooperative work, connecting workers within and between organizations who are often physically dispersed. CSSNs also link teleworkers from their homes or remote work centers to main organizational offices. Although many relationships function off-line as well as on-line, CSSNs have developed their own norms and structures. The nature of the medium both constrains and facilitates social control. CSSNs have strong societal implications, fostering situations that combine global connectivity, the fragmentation of solidarities, the de-emphasis of local organizations (in the neighborhood and workplace), and the increased importance of home bases.

213

0360-0572/96/0815-0213$08.00

COMPUTER-SUPPORTED SOCIAL NETWORKS

When computer networks link people as well as machines, they become social networks, which we call computer-supported social networks (CSSNs). Three forms of CSSNs are rapidly developing, each with its own desires and research agendas. Members of virtual community want to link globally with kindred souls for companionship, information, and social support from their homes and workstations. White-collar workers want computer-supported cooperative work (CSCW), unencumbered by spatial distance, while organizations see benefits in coordinating complex work structures and reducing managerial costs and travel time. Some workers want to telework from their homes, combining employment with domestic chores and Arcadian retreats; management foresees reduced building and real estate costs, and higher productivity.

We examine here the extent to which people work and find community on CSSNs. Is it possible to sustain productive or supportive relationships on-line with network members who may never meet in-person? What will the composition and structure of CSSNs be like, with their weaker constraints of distance and time, their easy connectivity, and limited social presence? What are the implications of such changes for the societies within which they are proliferating?

These questions have captured the public's imagination. Pundits argue about whether we will have computer-supported utopias—"the most transforming technological event since the capture of fire" (Barlow 1995:40)—or dystopias—"this razzle-dazzle... disconnects us from each other" (Hightower, quoted in Fox 1995:12). The popular media is filled with accounts of life in cyberspace (e.g. Cybergal 1995), much like earlier travellers' tales of journeys into exotic unexplored lands. Public discourse is (a) Manichean, seeing CSSNs as either thoroughly good or evil, (b) breathlessly present-oriented, writing as if CSSNs had been invented yesterday and not in the 1970s, (c) parochial, assuming that life on-line has no connection to life off-line, and (d) unscholarly, ignoring research into CSSNs as well as a century's research into the nature of community, work, and social organization.

The Nets Spread

CSSNs began in the 1960s when the US Defense Department's Advanced Projects Research Agency developed ARPANET to link large university computers and some of their users (Cerf 1993). The Electronic Information Exchange System, modeled after a government emergency communications network, started supporting computerized conferences of scientific researchers (including social network analysts) in the mid-1970s (Freeman 1986, Hiltz & Turoff 1993). Other systems were also proposed and partially implemented in this period.

Since the mid-1980s personal computers have become increasingly connected (through modems, local networks, etc) to central communication hosts. These hosts have become linked with each other through the worldwide "Internet" and the "World Wide Web" (encompassing information access as well as communications). Together with other interconnecting computer networks, the overall network has become known simply as "The Net," a "network of networks" (Craven & Wellman 1973) that weaves host computers (using high-capacity communication lines), each of which is at the center of its own local network. While the Net originally only encompassed nonprofit (principally university) computers, commercial users were allowed on in the early 1990s. Between October 1994 and January 1995, the number of Internet hosts grew by 26% (Treese 1995).

Other computer networks have grown concomitantly, while the cost of access has decreased. Those principally for leisure use range from community bulletin board systems (Marx & Virnoche 1995) to global, for-profit networks such as America OnLine that have developed commercial activity and the structured provision of information (e.g. airline guides, movie reviews). In late 1995, America OnLine had an estimated 4.5 million subscribers worldwide, CompuServe had 4 million, while Prodigy had 1.5 million (Lewis 1996). The development of World Wide Web services may displace such commercial systems. Local low-cost Internet service providers are proliferating, and Windows95 comes ready to connect to the Internet.

Competitive pressures have led these commercial systems to link with the Internet, making the Net even more widely interconnected. The Net has been growing, perhaps doubling its users annually. Its rapid growth and structure as a network of networks makes it difficult to count the number of users, for one must count both the computer systems directly connected to the Net and the users on each system. For example, estimates of recent Internet use in mid-1995 ranged between 27 million and 10 million adults (*Insight New Media* 1995, Lewis 1995). Besides exchanging private e-mail messages, internet members participated (as of January 27, 1996) in 24,237 collective discussion groups (Southwick 1996). There is much scope for growth: In 1994 only 17% of the 2.2 million Canadian computer users logged onto the Net (Frank 1995). Moreover, users vary between those who rarely log on to those who are continuously connected. Given such uncertainties and the tendency of enthusiasts and marketers to forecast high levels of network membership, many estimates of the number of users are unreliable.

There is little published information about the demographic composition of Net users, although this should change as it develops as a commercial marketing milieu. There is general agreement that users are largely politically conservative white men, often single, English-speaking, residing in North America, and professionals, managers, or students (*Newsweek* 1995; Treese 1995). One survey of Web users in Spring 1995 found that women comprised less than one fifth of their sample, although the proportion of women users had doubled in the past six months (Pitkow & Kehoe 1995). Two thirds of this sample had at least a university education, an "average" household income of US $59,600, and three quarters lived in North America. By contrast, Algeria had 16 registered internet users in July 1995 and Bulgaria had 639 (Danowitz et al 1995). Trends suggest an increasing participation of women, non-English speakers, and people of lower socioeconomic status (Gupta et al 1995, Kraut et al 1995, On-line Research Group 1995). Nevertheless, French President Jacques Chirac (1995) has warned that if English continues to dominate the information highway, "our future generations will be economically and culturally marginalized. ... To defend the influence of the French language is to defend the right to think, to communicate, to feel emotions and to pray in a different way."

Possibly more people participate in private organizational networks than on the Net, either using CSCW from offices or teleworking from homes. They use proprietary systems such as Lotus Notes or Internet tools adapted for use on private "intranets." In 1991 there were 8.9 million participants in Fortune 2000 companies (Electronic Mail Association 1992). In late 1995, there probably were still more users of private networks than of the Net, but there were no available estimates. There is also no published demographic information about private network participants, but presumably they are even more homogeneous than those on the Net. To protect organizational security, private networks often are not connected to the Net. However, pressure from professional employees to have access to colleagues and information elsewhere is leading many organizations to connect to the Net (Pickering & King 1995).

Types of Systems

Almost all CSSNs support a variety of text-based interactions with messages entered on keyboards and transmitted in lowest-common denominator ASCII code. Basic electronic mail (e-mail) is asynchronous communication from one person to another or from one person to a distribution list. When e-mail messages are forwarded, they concatenate into loosely bounded intergroup networks through which information diffuses rapidly. E-mail is bidirectional, so that recipients of messages can reply with equal ease. By contrast to these single-sender arrangements, "groupware" (Johnson-Lenz & Johnson-Lenz 1978) supports computerized conferencing that enables all members of a bounded social network to read all messages. Many private networks support computerized conferencing as does the Net through "list servers" (such as the Progressive Sociology Network) and leisure-time "Usenet newsgroups."

The on-line storage of most messages allows computer-mediated communication (CMC) to be asynchronous so that participants can be in different places and on different schedules. This gives people potentially more control over when they read and respond to messages. Moreover, the rapid transmission of large files between individuals and among groups increases the velocity of communication, supports collaborative work, and sustains strong and weak ties (Feldman 1987, Finholt & Sproull 1990, Eveland & Bikson 1988, Sproull & Kiesler 1991). On-line storage and digital transmission also help intruders to read files and messages, although computerization does provide cryptographic means of protecting privacy (Weisband & Reinig 1995).

Far fewer people participate in synchronous "real-time" CSSNs, although improved technology should lead to their growth. The "chat lines" of commercial services and the Internet Relay Chat (IRC) system operate in real time, providing multithreaded conversations like cocktail parties (Bechar-Israeli 1995, Danet et al 1996). As widespread Internet access and microcomputer multitasking develop, it is likely that many currently asynchronous users will see messages when they arrive, creating the potential for more widespread synchronic social exchanges. Multi-User Dungeons (MUDs) and kindred systems are a special play form of real-time computerized conferencing. Those who enter MUDs don pseudonymous personas and role play in quests, masquerades, and other forms of intense on-line communal interaction (Danet et al 1995, 1996, Reid 1996, Smith 1996).

Current trends supplement text with graphics, animation, video, and sound, increasing social presence. However, this increases cost and requires good hardware and communication lines. Desktop and group videoconferencing is currently limited to research groups and large-screen corporate meeting rooms (Ishii 1992, Mantei et al 1991, Buxton 1992, Moore 1997). Other experimental systems include video walls (in which large-screen videos link widely separated lounges to promote informal coffee-machine conversation), video hallways (Fish et al 1993, Dourish & Bly 1992) that allow participants to check the availability of others at a glance, and agents or avatars that move, speak and search on-line (Maes 1995, Riecken 1994, Stephenson 1992). Hence we focus in this chapter on the most widely used, text-based, forms of CSSNs such as e-mail and computerized conferences. We look only at interpersonal communication. We do not cover impersonal broadcast e-mail (such as electronic newsletters), distance education, passively accessible sites (such as file transfer [FTP] and Web sites), and the exchange of data on-line (as in manufacturing processes or airline reservation systems).

Research into CSSNs has involved several disciplines—principally computer science, communication science, business administration, and psychology.

There are annual CSCW conferences with published proceedings. Despite the inherently sociological nature of the matter, sociology is underrepresented, and gatekeepers are mostly members of other disciplines (Dillon 1995). Although mutually germane, studies of virtual community, CSCW, and telework generally have not informed each other.

COMMUNICATION ON-LINE

Early research developed from "human-computer" analysis of single-person interfaces with computer systems to analyzing how small group communication is mediated by computer systems. Many of these studies examined how the limited "social presence" of CMC (as compared to in-person contact) affects interactions and group decision-making. What are the effects of losing verbal nuances (e.g. voice tone, volume), nonverbal cues (e.g. gaze, body language) physical context (e.g. meeting sites, seating arrangements) and observable information about social characteristics (e.g. age, gender, race)? Research in this approach links the technical characteristics of CMC to task group outcomes such as increased participation, more egalitarian participation, more ideas offered, and less centralized leadership (Hiltz et al 1986, Kiesler et al 1984, Rice 1987, Adrianson & Hjelmquist 1991, Weisband et al 1995). Limited social presence may also encourage people to communicate more freely and creatively than they do in person, at times "flaming" others by using extreme, aggressive language (Kiesler et al, 1984).

Although groups supported by CMC often produce higher quality ideas, reaching agreement can be a lengthy and more complex process as the greater number of ideas and the lack of status cues hinder group coordination (Hiltz et al 1986, Kiesler & Sproull 1992, Valacich et al 1993). However, status cues are not completely absent, as social information is conveyed through language use, e-mail address, and signatures such as "VP-Research" (Walther 1992). As messages are often visibly copied to others, they also indicate social network connections. Some participants prefer in-person contact to CMC for ambiguous, socially sensitive, and intellectually difficult interactions (Culnan & Markus 1987, Daft & Lengel 1986, Rice 1987, Fish et al 1993, Jones 1995). However, CMC is also used to maintain social distance, document contentious issues, or when the message involves fear, dislike, awkwardness, or intimidation (Markus 1994a, Walther 1996).

Much CMC research has been individualistic and technologically deterministic, assuming a single person rationally choosing among media (Lea 1991). To go beyond this, some CMC analysts now consider how social relationships, organizational structures, and local norms affect the use of communication media (Finholt & Sproull 1990, Orlikowsi et al 1995, Huber 1990, Markus 1990,

1994b, Sproull & Kiesler 1991, Lea et al 1995, Orlikowski et al 1996b, Zack & McKenney 1995). For example, people do not "choose" to use e-mail in many organizations: It is a condition of employment (Fulk & Boyd 1991). Even when e-mail use is voluntary, a critical mass of users affects the extent to which people use it (Markus 1990). Thus the laboratory basis of most CMC research sets limits for understanding CSSNs in natural settings. Sociological research needs to take into account the social characteristics of participants (e.g. gender, SES), their positional resources (CEO or mail-room clerk, broker or densely knit star), the interplay between ongoing on-line and off-line relationships, and their ongoing social relationships.

SUPPORT ON-LINE

Information

Much of the communication on CSSNs involves the exchange of information. For example, in two weeks of March 1994 the 2295 newsgroups in the top 16 Usenet newsgroup hierarchies received 817,638 messages (Kling 1996b). On-line digital libraries are growing, along with search tools (Kling & Lamb 1996), although locating the right information is difficult in large organizations and communities. The nature of the medium supports a focus on information exchanges, as people can easily post a question or comment and receive information in return. Broadcasting queries through CSSNs increases the chances of finding information quickly and alters the distribution patterns of information. It gives those working in small or distant sites better access to experienced, skilled people (Constant et al 1996).

However, as anyone can contribute information to most newsgroups and distribution lists, the Net can be a repository of misleading information and bad advice, as some health care professionals have charged (Foderaro 1995). Such worries discount the fact that people have always given each other advice about their bodies, psyches, families, or computers (e.g. Wellman 1995, Kadushin 1987). The Net has just made the process more accessible and more visible to others, including experts whose claims to monopolies on advice are threatened (Abbott 1988).

The flow of information through CSSNs itself generates access to new information. On-line information flows spill over unexpectedly through message forwarding, providing access to more people and new social circles, thus increasing the probability of finding those who can solve problems (Kraut & Attewell 1993). People often bump into new information or new sources of information unintentionally through "leaky. . . quasi social networds" (Brent 1994:on-line). Information obtained serendipitously helps solve problems before they occur and helps keep people aware of organizational news. Weak on-line ties are bridges between diverse sources of information. In one large organization, those with more diverse ties obtained better on-line advice (Constant et al 1996).

Social Support

If CSSNs were solely a means of information exchange, then they would mostly contain narrow, specialized relationships. However, information is only one of many social resources exchanged on-line. Despite the limited social presence of CMC, people find social support, companionship, and a sense of belonging through the normal course of CSSNs of work and community, even when they are composed of persons they hardly know (Rice & Love 1987, McCormick & McCormick 1992, Haythornthwaite et al 1995, Walther 1996, Wellman & Gulia 1996). Although providing such types of support often does not require major investments of time, money, or energy, CSSN members have also mobilized goods, services, and long-term emotional support to help each other (e.g. Lewis 1994). Thus while most of the elderly users of the "SeniorNet" virtual community joined to gain access to information, their most popular on-line activity has been companionable chatting (Furlong 1989, see also Hiltz et al 1986, Walther 1994, Rheingold 1993, Meyer 1989, Kraut et al 1995). An informal support group sprang up inadvertently when the "Young Scientists' Network" aimed primarily at providing physicists with job hunting tips and news stories. Similarly, the "Systers" mailing list, originally designed for female computer scientists to exchange information, has become a forum for companionship and social support (Sproull & Faraj 1995). The members of a computer science laboratory frequently exchange emotional support by e-mail. Because much of their time is spent on-line, and many of their difficulties happen at their terminals, it is natural for them to discuss problems on-line (Haythornthwaite et al 1995).

Some CSSNs are explicitly set up to be support groups that provide emotional aid, group membership, and information about medical treatment and other matters (Foderaro 1995, King 1994). One therapist who provides one-to-one counseling through a bulletin board reports that, while she has less social presence and cues than through in-person sessions, the greater anonymity of CMC allows her clients to reveal themselves more (Cullen 1995). For example, Peter and Trudy Johnson-Lenz (1990, 1994) have organized on-line groups for 20 years, working to build self-awareness, mutually supportive activities, social change, and a sense of collective well-being. Their software tools, such as passing around sacred "talking sticks," rearrange communication structures, vary exchange settings, mark group rhythms, and encourage lurkers to express themselves.

RELATIONSHIPS ON-LINE

Specialized and Multiplex Ties

CSSNs contain both specialized and multiplex relationships. The structure of the Net encourages specialized relationships because it supports a market approach to finding social resources in virtual communities. With more ease than in almost all real life situations, people can shop for resources from the safety and comfort of their homes or offices, and with reduced search and travel time. The Usenet alone houses more than 3500 newsgroups (Kling 1996b) to which anyone may subscribe, with diverse foci including politics (e.g. feminism), technical problems (e.g. SPSS), therapeutics (e.g. alcoholism), socializing (e.g. singles), and recreation (e.g. BMWs, sexual fantasies). Net members can browse through specialized channels on synchronous chat lines before deciding to join a discussion (Danet et al 1996). Relationships in these virtual communities are often narrowly defined.

The narrow focus of newsgroups, distribution lists, and chat lines allows people to take risks in specialized relationships that may only exist in a single partial on-line community. Some CSSNs even allow people to be anonymous or use nicknames when they want to speak freely or try on different personas (Hiltz & Turoff 1993). However, the inclusion of e-mail addresses in most message headers provides the basis for more multiplex relationships to develop. In the absence of social and physical cues, people are able to get to know each other on the Net on the basis of their communication and decide later to broaden the relationship or move it off-line (Rheingold 1993). Thus more than half of the recovering addicts on electronic support groups also contact each other by phone or in-person (King 1994). Soon after an especially intense computerized conference, many "of the participants altered their business and vacation travel plans to include a face-to-face meeting with one another" (Hiltz & Turoff 1993:114).

Strong Ties

Can the medium support the message if the limited social presence of computer-mediated communication works against the maintenance of socially close, strong ties on CSSNs? Many on-line ties do meet most of the criteria for strong ties. They facilitate frequent, reciprocal, companionable, and often supportive contact, and the placelessness of CSSN interactions facilitates long-term contact without the loss of relationships that often accompanies residential mobility. Virtual communities are quite voluntary, while CSSN participation varies between voluntary and mandatory in CSCW and telework (Hiltz & Turoff 1993, Johnson-Lenz & Johnson-Lenz 1994, Rheingold 1993). Certainly many accounts report great involvement in on-line relationships. Community members came to regard each other as their closest friends even though they seldom or never met in-person (Hiltz & Turoff 1993). Net members tend to base their feelings of closeness on shared interests rather than on shared social characteristics such as gender and SES. That the siren call of CSSNs sometimes lures net members away from "real-life" argues for the potential strength of on-line relationships and networks.

Many computer-mediated communication ties are moderately strong "intimate secondary relationships" that are frequent and supportive but only operate in one specialized domain (Wireman 1984). Over time, some of these relationships become more personal and intimate. Perhaps the limited social presence and asynchronicity of CMC only slows the development of intimacy, with on-line interactions eventually developing to be as sociable and intimate as in-person ones (Walther 1995).

In part, concerns about whether on-line ties can be strong ties are wrongly specified. Although CSSNs do transcend time and space, not all ties are either totally on-line or off-line. Much on-line contact is between people who see each other in person and live locally. At work, computer scientists intermingle in-person and e-mail communication. At some offices, employees chat privately by e-mail while they work silently side-by-side (Garton 1995, Labaton 1995). In such situations, conversations started on one medium continue on others. As with the telephone and the fax (Wellman & Tindall 1993), the lower social presence of CMC may be sufficient to maintain strong ties between persons who know each other well. For example, kinship networks use the Net to arrange weddings and out-of-town visits (Hiltz & Turoff 1993), while an American woman gave up her job and flew to Britain to marry a Net friend whom she had never met in person (Toronto News Radio 680, Sept. 3, 1995).

Weak Ties

There are low logistical and social costs to participating in CSSNs. People can participate within the comfort and safety of their own homes or offices, at any time, and at their own convenience. Limited social cues on-line encourage contact between weak ties. Very often, the only social characteristic that people learn about each other on-line is a Net address, which provides very little information. The egalitarian nature of the Net encourages responses to requests. It also generates a culture of its own, as when humorous stories sweep CSSNs, possibly fostering a revival of folk humor.

On the face of it, CSSNs should not support much reciprocity. Many on-line ties are between persons who have never met face to face, who are weakly tied, socially and physically distant, and not bound into densely knit work or community structures. Computerized conferences allow free-rider "lurkers" to read others' messages invisibly without contributing (Kollack & Smith 1996a).

Nevertheless, there is evidence of reciprocal supportiveness on CSSNs, even between people with weak ties (Hiltz et al 1986, Walther 1994). Providing reciprocal support and information on-line is a means of increasing self-esteem, demonstrating technical expertise, earning respect and status, and responding to norms of mutual aid (e.g. Constant et al 1994, 1996, Kraut & Attewell 1993, Kollock & Smith 1996b). In some organizations, employees are encouraged to help each other or to direct those in need to others who could help. Computerized conferences and public archives reinforce this supportiveness by making it visible to all co-workers and managers (Constant et al 1995, Kraut & Attewell 1993, Kollock & Smith 1996b). Such processes also arise in densely knit virtual communities and are common among frequent contributors to computerized conferences. People having a strong attachment to an organization or electronic group will be more likely to participate and provide assistance to others. For example, computer hackers involved in illegal activities are reluctant to change their pseudonyms because the status they gain through on-line demonstrations of technical expertise accrues to that pseudonym (Meyer 1989).

Some commentators have warned about the consequences of making connections on CSSNs teeming with strangers whose biographies, social positions, and social networks are unknown (Stoll 1995). Nevertheless CSSN members tend to trust strangers, much as people gave rides to hitchhikers in the flowerchild days of the 1960s. This willingness to engage with strangers on-line contrasts with in-person situations where bystanders are often reluctant to intervene and help strangers (Latané & Darley 1976). Yet bystanders are more apt to intervene when they are the only ones around and they can withdraw easily in case of trouble. Analogously, on-line requests for aid are read by people alone at their screens. Even if the request is to a newsgroup and not by personal e-mail, as far as the recipient of the request knows, s/he is the only one who could provide aid. At the same time, on-line intervention will be observed by entire groups and will be positively rewarded by them. It is this visibility that may foster the kindness of strangers. Just as physical proximity provides the opportunity for observing face-to-face interaction, CSSNs provide social exemplars to large numbers of passive observers as well as to active participants. Individual acts can aggregate to sustain a large community because each act is seen by the entire group and perpetuates a norm of mutual aid (Rheingold 1993, Barlow 1995, Lewis 1994).

Stressful Ties

Most research into antisocial behavior on-line has studied uninhibited remarks, hostile flaming, nonconforming behavior, and group polarization (Hiltz et al 1978, Kiesler et al 1985, Siegal et al 1986, Sproull & Kiesler 1991, Lea et al 1992, Walther et al 1994). The limited social presence of computer-mediated communication encourages the misinterpretation of remarks, and the asyn-chronous nature of most conversations hinders the immediate repair of dam-ages, stressing and even disrupting relationships. There are numerous anecdotes about antisocial behavior on-line. Hackers disseminate viruses, entrepreneurs "spam" (flood) the Net with unwanted advertisements, stalkers harass partic-ipants on-line, and scoundrels take on misleading roles such as men posing on-line as women to seduce others electronically (Cybergal 1995, Slouka 1995).

SOCIAL NETWORKS ON-LINE

In what kinds of social networks are on-line relationships embedded? Because they operate somewhat differently, we separately discuss virtual community and computer-supported work groups. For both community and work, we consider the composition of computer-supported social networks—the nature of the participants in them, and the structure of CSSNs—the network pattern of relationships and hierachies of power.

Size and Composition

VIRTUAL COMMUNITY   Although contemporary people in the western world may know 1000 others, they actively maintain only about 20 community ties (Kochen 1989). Easy access to distribution lists and computerized confer-ences should enable participants to maintain more ties, including more strong ties. Communication also comes unsolicited through distribution lists, news-groups, and forwarded messages from friends. These provide indirect contact between previously disconnected people, allowing them to establish direct con-tact. Newsgroups and distribution lists also provide permeable, shifting sets of members, with more intense relationships continued by private e-mail. The resulting relaxation of constraints on the size and proximity of one's personal community can increase the diversity of people encountered (Lea & Spears 1995). Thus the Net facilitates forming new connections between people and virtual communities.

The relative lack of social presence on-line fosters relationships with Net members who have more diverse social characteristics than are normally en-countered in person. It also gives participants more control over the timing and content of their self-disclosures (Walther 1995). This allows relationships to de-velop on the basis of shared interests rather than to be stunted at the onset by dif-ferences in social status (Coate 1994, Hiltz & Turoff 1993, Jones 1995, Kollock & Smith 1996a). This is a technologically supported continuation of a long-term shift to communities organized by shared interests rather than by shared neighborhoods or kinship groups (Fischer 1975, Wellman 1979, 1994). When their shared interests are important to them, those involved in the same virtual community may have more in common than those who live in the same building or block (Rheingold 1993). Indeed, people have strong commitments to their on-line groups when they perceive them to be long-lasting (Walther 1994). There is a danger, though, that virtual communities may develop homogeneous interests (Lea & Spears 1992). Furthermore, the similarity of social characteristics of most current Net participants also fosters cultural homogeneity.

This emphasis on shared interests rather than social characteristics can be empowering for members of lower-status and disenfranchised social categories (Mele 1996). Yet although social characteristics have become less apparent on CSSNs, they still affect interactions. Women often receive special attention from males (Shade 1994, Herring 1993, O'Brien 1996). In part, this is a function of the high ratio of men to women on-line. "Reveal your gender on the Net and you're toast" claims one (fictional) female participant (Coupland 1995:334).

COOPERATIVE WORK   The evidence is mixed about whether CSSNs reduce the use of other communication media, add to the total amount of communication, or boost the use of other communication media (Garton & Wellman 1995). One study found that work groups using CMC have a higher level of communication than those that do not (Bikson & Eveland 1990), while another found that heavy CMC use reduces face-to-face and telephone communication (Finholt et al 1990).

People can greatly extend the number and diversity of their social contacts when they become members of computerized conferences or broadcast information to other CSSN members. In one large, physically dispersed organization, four fifths of the e-mail messages were from electronic groups and not individuals. More than half of these messages were from unknown people, different buildings, or people external to their department or chain of command (Finholt & Sproull 1990, Kiesler & Sproull 1988). In another study, an on-line work team formed more subcommittees than did an off-line team and was better able to involve its members in its activities (Bikson & Eveland 1990). Where the organizational climate fosters open communication, the lack of status cues fosters connections across hierarchical or other forms of status barriers (Sproull & Kiesler 1991, Eveland & Bikson 1988).

Structure

VIRTUAL COMMUNITY   The architecture of the Net may nourish two contradictory trends for the structure of virtual communities. First, the Net fosters membership in multiple, partial communities. People often belong to several computerized conferences, and they can easily send out messages to separate personal distribution lists for different kinds of conversations. Moreover, they can vary in their involvements in different communities, participating actively in some and occasionally in others. Second, the ease of responding to entire groups and forwarding messages to others foster the folding in of on-line networks into broader communities (Marx & Virnoche 1995). Moreover, MUDs and similar role-playing environments resemble village-like structures if they capture their members' attention.

The proliferation of CSSNs may produce a trend counter to the contemporary privatization of community. People in the western world are spending less time in public places waiting for friends to wander by, and where they can to introduce them to other friends (Wellman 1992, Economist 1995). Community has moved indoors to private homes from its former semi-public, accessible milieus such as cafés, parks, and pubs. This dispersion and privatization means that people must actively contact community members to remain in touch instead of visiting a café and waiting for acquaintances to drop by. By contrast, computerized conferences support connections with large numbers of people, providing possibilities for reversing the trend to less public contact. Because all members of newsgroups and discussion groups can read all messages—just as in a café conversation—groups of people can talk to each other casually and get to know the friends of their friends. "The keyboard is my café," William Mitchell enthuses (1995:7). Moreover, each participant's personal community of ties connects specialized, partial communities, providing cross-cutting links between otherwise disconnected groups.

WORK GROUPS   There has not been much research into how widespread use of CSSNs affect broad organizational structures of management and control. Research has focused more narrowly on CSSNs themselves. For example, organizational CSSNs are maintained by system administrators who may support management goals by monitoring on-line activities and devising procedures that affect social outcomes. Some administrators promote the "appropriate" use of the CSSN and admonish those who use it for recreational or noncompany purposes (Chiu 1995, Orilowski et al 1995). Managers fear that CSSNs will threaten control by accelerating the flow of (mis)information, including rumors, complaints, jokes, and subversive communications (Finholt & Sproull 1990). For example, management closed an employee "Gripenet" when group discussions challenged long-standing corporate practices (Emmett 1982). Even when organizations support informal electronic groups, managers often view them with distrust (Perin 1991). When women in a large corporation established a computerized conference to discuss careers, management monitored the messages because they feared it would lead to demands for unionization and affirmative action (Zuboff 1988).

Nevertheless, CSSNs support a variety of agendas, not only those sanctioned by the organization. For example, striking Israeli university professors used both private and group messages to coordinate their nationwide strike (Pliskin & Romm 1994). Less confrontationally, managers and staff use discussion groups to cross status and power boundaries by exchanging information about shared leisure interests. In one decentralized corporation, more than half of those surveyed use e-mail at least occasionally to keep in touch, take work breaks, and take part in games and other entertaining activities (Steinfield 1985). Such groups are larger, more dispersed, and more spontaneous than the distribution lists which the organization requires employees to be on, and their exchanges emphasize fun rather than displays of competence (Finholt & Sproull 1990). Such informal messaging may reduce work stress (Steinfield 1985), integrate new or peripheral employees (Eveland & Bikson 1988, Rice & Steinfield 1994, Steinfield 1985), and increase organizational commitment (Huff et al 1989, Kaye 1992, Sproull & Kiesler 1991).

Much "groupware" has been written to support the social networks of densely knit and tightly bounded work groups in which people work closely with a focused set of colleagues. For example, video conferencing systems enable spatially dispersed coworkers to confer instantly (Moore 1997), while co-writing systems support joint authorship (Sharples 1993). Yet both the Internet and within-organization intranets are also well-suited to support work relationships in sparsely knit, loosely bounded organizations whose members switch frequently and routinely among the people with whom they are dealing throughout the day, as they move between projects or need different resources (Fulk & DeSanctis 1995, Kling & Jewett 1994, Koppel et al 1988, Weick 1976, Wellman 1996). In such organizations, work outcomes depend more on the ability of people and groups to bridge cognitive distances than on having people and other resources located in the same place (Mowshowitz 1994). This relatively autonomous mode of work is often found among professionals, scholars, or academics who have to make multiple, often unexpected, contacts with colleagues within and outside their own organizations (Abbott 1988, Burt 1992, Hinds & Kiesler 1995, Star 1993, Walsh & Bayama 1996).

From an organizational perspective, dispersed work teams require social as well as technical support (Wellman et al 1994, Garton 1995). Studies of collaboration among scientific communities suggest that an initial period of physical proximity is necessary to build trust and to come to consensus on the focus of proposed projects (Carley & Wendt 1991). Such collaborations may need different forms of CMC support at different points in a project. For example, work groups tightly focused on a single project need different types of CSCW support than do individuals switching among multiple tasks and relationships (Mantei & Wellman 1995).

Shifting boundaries characterize networked virtual organizations, not only within the organizations but between them. Interorganizational CSSNs can help an organization in negotiations between buyers and sellers and in coordinating joint projects. They also help managers and professionals maintain a large network of potentially useful contacts, stockpiling network capital for the time when they need to obtain information externally. These interorganizational networks also help employees to maintain a sense of connection with former colleagues and can provide support during job changes and other stressful events. CSSNs blur organizational boundaries, supporting "invisible colleges" of dispersed professionals. (Constant et al 1994, 1996, Hesse et al 1993, Hiltz & Turoff 1993, Kling 1996, Meyer 1989, Carley 1990, Kaufer & Carley 1993, Huff et al 1989, Kaye 1992, Rice & Steinfield 1994, Walsh & Bayama 1996). They can knit scientific researchers into "highly cohesive and highly cooperative research groups, ... geographically dispersed yet coordinated" (Carley & Wendt 1991:407). However, there is less use of CSSNs in disciplines such as chemistry where practitioners want to protect unwanted commercial use of their knowledge (Walsh & Bayama 1996).

TELEWORK ON-LINE

Implementation

To date, most developments in organizational CSCW have been to improve connections between existing workplaces. However, CSSNs provide opportunities for developing relatively new forms of work organization. Thus, telework (aka "telecommuting") is a special case of CSCW in which CMCs link organizations to employees working principally either at home or at remote work centers (Fritz et al 1994). Most writing about telework has been programmatic, forecasting, or descriptive, assuming that the technology of telework will determine its social organization (e.g. Hesse & Grantham 1991, Helms & Marom 1992, Grey et al 1993). Yet teleworking's growth has been driven by new market conditions that are promoting organizational restructuring, reducing employees, eliminating offices, and giving more flexibility to remaining employees (Salaff & Dimitrova 1995a,b). Although teleworkers now comprise a tiny fraction of the work force (DiMartino & Wirth 1990), their growing number includes many salespeople, managers, professionals, and support personnel. Entire offices of data entry clerks and telephone services have moved to home or other remote offices (Kugelmass 1995).

Research is moving from technological determinism to studying the interplay between telework and work organization. Several analysts have shown managerial inertia and organizational lethargy to be barriers to telework. Many employees favor telework to gain more work autonomy or to accommodate family, but many managers feel their power threatened (Kraut 1988, 1989, Olson 1988, Huws et al 1990, Grantham & Paul 1994, Tippin 1994). Although there have been concerns that the careers of teleworking managers and professionals would suffer because of less visibility in organizations, this has not yet been the case (Tolbert & Simons 1994). Despite the proliferation of telework and great public interest in the subject, there has not been much systematic research into what teleworkers actually do, their connections with their main offices, their links with coworkers (peers, subordinates, and supervisors), and the implications of their physical isolation for their careers within organizations or for labor solidarity.

Communication

Teleworkers do not communicate more frequently on-line with coworkers or supervisors than do similarly occupied nonteleworkers (Kinsman 1987), although teleworkers do have less postal and in-person contact (see also Olszewski & Mokhtarian 1994). However, teleworking leads to more structured and formalized communication with supervisors and, to a lesser extent, with coworkers. This may be due as much to physical separation from the organizational office as to the use of CMC (Olson 1988, Heilmann 1988, Huws et al 1990, Olson & Primps 1984).

There has been contradictory evidence about how teleworking affects informal communication among coworkers. One study notes that personal conversations among teleworking programmers have decreased and their informal relationships have deteriorated (Heilmann 1988). Another study finds that the restructuring of work accompanying the shift to telework among pink-collar workers curtails informal communication (Soares 1992). By contrast, university employees, both white- and pink-collar, who work at home have more informal contact with other employees (McClintock 1981). At the same time, teleworkers can increase autonomy by being slow to respond to on-line messages (Wellman et al 1994). The nature of informal communications by teleworkers appears to depend on the employees' social status, their previous relationships, and the support of the organization. For example, British Telecom reports (1994) that pink-collar teleworkers complain less about isolation than about the slowness of help in fixing computers and the lack of news about main office events (see also Shirley 1988).

Telework may only be a continuation of existing task independence and work flows already driven by messages and forms on computer screens (Dimitrova et al 1994). This may explain why some studies find that professional teleworkers maintain work-related networks, but pink-collar clerical workers become more isolated (Durrenberger et al 1996). New work force hierarchies that emerge from teleworking segregate those who lack informal contacts, while those that have them benefit richly (Steinle 1988). In this way, CSSNs may further bifurcate the work force.

Work Organization

Most research on the impact of telework addresses workplace issues such as the control and autonomy of teleworkers, flexibility of work schedules, job redesign, remote supervision, and productivity. Although much post-Fordist hype suggests that teleworking will liberate workers (e.g. Toffler 1980), research supports the neo-Fordist conclusion that managers retain high-level control of planning and resources but decentralize the execution of decisions and tasks. Companies that implement teleworking to cut costs often tighten control. This strategy is most effective with abundant pink-collar labor, typically women with children. The more severe the employees' personal constraints (e.g. child-care, disabilities) and the less the demand for their skills, the more likely they are to experience tighter control (Olson 1987). Thus management has increasing control of clerks who become teleworkers, while professionals have gained more autonomy (Olson & Primps 1984, Simons 1994, Soares 1992).

Thus the divergent impact of telework on control and job design follows the logic of the dual nature of labor markets, with company strategy determining the outcome (Steinle 1988, Huws et al 1990). Where a company seeks to retain scarce skills by reducing personal constraints, teleworking provides more discretion over work arrangements. Professionals often obtain greater autonomy, flexibility, skills, and job involvement, but they may have more uncertainties about their careers and incomes (Olson 1987, Simons 1994, Bailyn 1989).

Telework, Domestic Work, and Gender

Telework is part of changing relationships between the realms of work and nonwork: a high proportion of women working, more part-time and flextime work, and the bifurcation of workers into the information-skilled and -deskilled (Hodson & Parker 1988, Olson 1988, Steinle 1988). Women and men often experience telework differently, although the evidence is somewhat contradictory.

Telework reinforces the gendered division of household labor because women teleworkers do more family care and household work. Women are more likely to report high stress over the conflict of work and family demands, and the lack of leisure time (Olson & Primps 1984, Christensen 1988). Women say they are satisfied with teleworking, possibly because blending work and family space may ease role strain between family and work, and it may improve family relations (Falconer 1993, Higgins et al 1992, Duxbury 1995). Thus, female teleworking clerks are more family oriented than are their office counterparts (French 1988, DuBrin 1991).

Yet fusing domestic and work settings can be disruptive and can embed women more deeply in the household (Ahrentzen 1990, Calabrese 1994, Heck et al 1995). Women doing paid work at home spend a similar amount of time on domestic work regardless of their job status, number and ages of their children, part-time or full-time employment, or the structure of their household (Ahrentzen 1990). Although teleworking women may benefit from flexibility in their "double load," managers and researchers alike claim that doing paid work at home is not a good way to provide early childcare (Christensen 1988). Teleworkers are almost as likely to use paid childcare, and indeed most have higher childcare expenses than do office workers (Falconer 1993). Yet mothers with older children are better able to work while their children are in school, to greet them after school, and to be available in emergencies.

Fathers who telework report better relationships with their children than do comparable nonteleworkers. They have more leisure time and less stress than before they began teleworking, and they play more with their children (Olson & Primps 1984). Yet gender dynamics are different. Men see teleworking as a privilege because they want more autonomy, and they get more interaction with their families as a bonus. Women see teleworking as a compromise because family responsibilities limit their employment opportunities, and they want flexible scheduling (Olson 1987, Gerson & Kraut 1988).

GLOBAL NETWORKS AND LITTLE BOXES

Despite their limited social presence, CSSNs successfully maintain strong, supportive ties with work and community as well as increase the number and diversity of weak ties. They are especially suited to maintaining intermediate-strength ties between people who cannot see each other frequently. On-line relationships are based more on shared interests and less on shared social characteristics. Although many relationships function off-line as well as on-line, CSSNs are developing norms and structures of their own. The are not just pale imitations of "real life." The Net is the Net.

Organizational boundaries are becoming more permeable just as community boundaries already have. The combination of high involvement in CSSNs, powerful search engines, and the linking of organizational networks to the Net enables many workers to connect with relevant others elsewhere, wherever they are and whomever they work for. If organizations grow toward their information and communication sources (Stinchcombe 1990), CSSNs should affect changes in organizational structures.

Social networks are simultaneously becoming more global and more local as worldwide connectivity and domestic matters intersect. Global connectivity de-emphasizes the importance of locality for work and community; on-line relationships may be more stimulating than suburban neighborhoods and alienated offices. Even more than before, on the information highway each person is at the center of a unique personal community and work group.

The domestic environment around the workstation is becoming a vital home base for neo–Silas Marners sitting in front of their screens day and night. Nests are becoming well feathered. Telework exaggerates both trends. Although it provides long-distance connections for workers, it also moves them home, providing a basis for the revival of neighborhood life. Just as before the Industrial Revolution, home and workplace are being integrated, although gender roles have not been renegotiated.

The privatization of relationships affects community, organizational, and coworker solidarity. Virtual communities are accelerating the ways in which people operate at the centers of partial, personal communities, switching rapidly and frequently between groups of ties. Whether working at home or at an office workstation, many workers have an enhanced ability to move between relationships. At the same time, their more individualistic behavior means the weakening of the solidarity that comes from working in large groups.

Such phenomena give sociologists wonderful opportunities. A Bellcore vice president says that when "scientists talk about the evolution of the information infrastructure, . . . [we don't] talk about. . . the technology. We talk about ethics, law, policy and sociology. . . . It is a social invention" (Lucky 1995:205). Yet there has been little sociological study of computer-supported social networks. Research in this area engages with important intellectual questions and social issues at all scales, from dyadic to world system. It offers stimulating collaborations with other disciplines, industry, labor, and government. It provides opportunities to develop social systems and not just study them after the fact. As our computer science colleague William Buxton tells us, "the computer science is easy; the sociology is hard."

ACKNOWLEDGMENTS

More than 100 scholars responded to our on-line requests for germane work. We regret that we are unable to cite them all or to include relevant references to mainstream sociology. We thank Aaron Dantowitz, Paul Gregory, and Emmanuel Koku for help in gathering information, Beverly Wellman for editorial advice, and Ronald Baecker, William Buxton, and Marilyn Mantei for introducing us to computer science. Our work has been supported by the Social Science and Humanities Research Council of Canada, Bell Canada, the Centre for Information Technology Innovation, and the Information Technology Research Centre's Telepresence project.

Literature Cited

Abbott A. 1988. *The System of Professions: An Essay on the Division of Expert Labor.* Chicago: Univ. Chicago Press

Adrianson L, Hjelmquist E. 1991. Group processes in face-to-face and computer-mediated communication. *Behav. Info Tech.* 10(4):281–96

Ahrentzen SB. 1990. Managing conflicts by managing boundaries: how professional homeworkers cope with multiple roles at home. *Environ. Behav.* 22(6):723–52

Bailyn L. 1989. Toward the perfect workplace. *Commun. ACM* 32(4):460–71

Barlow JP. 1995. Is there a there in cyberspace? *Utne Reader:*50–56

Bechar-Israeli H. 1995. From <Bonehead> to <cLonehEad>: nicknames, play and identity on Internet Relay Chat. *J. Computer-Mediated Commun.* 1(2):on-line URL:http-//www.usc.edu/dept/annenberg/vol1/ issue2

Bikson T, Eveland JD. 1990. The interplay of work group structures and computer support. See Galegher et al 1990, pp. 245–90

Brent DA. 1994. Information technology and the breakdown of "places" of knowledge. *EJournal* 4(4):Online

British Telecommunications. 1994. Teleworking: BT's Inverness. London: Br. Telecommun. 16 pp.

Burt R. 1992. *Structural Holes.* Chicago: Univ. Chicago Press

Buxton W. 1992. *Telepresence: integrating shared task and person spaces.* Pres. Graphics Interface '92 Conference, Vancouver

Calabrese A. 1994. Home-based telework and the politics of private women and public man. In *Women and Technology,* ed. UE Gattiker, pp. 161–99. Berlin: Walter de Gruyter

Carley K. 1990. Structural constraints on communication: the diffusion of the homomorphic signal analysis technique through scientific fields. *J. Math. Soc.* 15(3–4):207–46

Carley K, Wendt K. 1991. Electronic mail and scientific communication. *Knowledge* 12(4):406–40

Cerf V. 1993. How the Internet came to be. In *The Online User's Encyclopedia,* ed. Bernard Aboba, pp. 527–35. Boston: Addison-Wesley

Chirac J. 1995. Speech to La Francophonie summit. (Transl. and reported by John Stackhouse), *Toronto Globe and Mail,* Dec. 4,

1995, pp. A1, A10

Chiu Y. 1995. E-mail gives rise to the E-wail: a blizzard of personal chat raises worries about office productivity. *Washington Post* (August 18): D1, D8

Christensen K, ed. 1988. *The New Era of Home Based Work.* Boulder, CO: Westview. 213 pp.

Coate J. 1994. *Cyberspace innkeeping: building online community.* On-line paper: tex@sfgate.com

Constant D, Kiesler SB, Sproull LS. 1994. What's mine is ours, or is it? A study of attitudes about information sharing. *Info. Sys. Res.* 5(4):400–21

Constant D, Sproull LS, Kiesler SB. 1996. The kindness of strangers: the usefulness of electronic weak ties for technical advice. *Organ. Sci.* 7(2): In press

Coupland, Douglas. 1995. *Microserfs.* New York: HarperCollins

Craven P, Wellman BS. 1973. The network city. *Soc. Inquiry* 43:57–88

Cullen DL. 1995. Psychotherapy in cyberspace. *Clinician* 26(2):1, 6–7

Culnan MJ, Markus ML. 1987. Information technologies. In *Handbook of Organizational Communication,* ed. FM Jablin, LL Putnam, KH Roberts, LW Porter, pp. 420–43. Newbury Park, CA: Sage

Cybergal. 1995. The year of living dangerously. *Toronto Life-Fashion* 1995:104–9

Daft R, Lengel R. 1986. Organizational information requirements, media richness and structural design. *Manage. Sci.* 32:554–71

Danet B, Rudenberg L, Rosenbaum-Tamari Y. 1996. Hmmm...Where's all that smoke coming from? Writing, play and performance on Internet Relay Chat. In *Network and Netplay,* ed. S Rafaeli, F Sudweeks, M McLaughlin. Cambridge, MA: MIT Press. In press

Danet B, Wachenhauser T, Bechar-Israeli C, Cividalli A, Rosenblum-Tamari Y. 1995. Curtain time 20:00 GMT: Experiments in virtual theater on internet relay chat. *J. Computer-Mediated Commun.* 1(2):online URL http-//www.usc.edu/dept/annenberg/vol1/issue2

Danowitz AK, Nassef Y, Goodman SE. 1995. Cyberspace across the Sahara: computing in North Africa. *Commun. ACM* 38(12):23–28

Dillon T. 1995. Mapping the discourse of HCI researchers with citation analysis. *Sigchi Bull.* 27(4):56–62

Di Martino V, Wirth L. 1990. Telework: a new way of working and living. *Int. Labour Rev.* 129(5):529–54

Dimitrova D, Garton L, Salaff J, Wellman B. 1994. *Strategic connectivity: communications and control.* Pres. Sunbelt Soc. Networks Conf., New Orleans

Dourish P, Bly S. 1992. Portholes: supporting awareness in a distributed work group. In *Proc. CHI '92*, ed. P Bauersfeld, J Bennett, G Lynch, pp. 541–47. NY: ACM Press

DuBrin AJ. 1991. Comparison of the job satisfaction and productivity of telecommuters versus in-house employees. *Psychol. Rep.* 68:1223–34

Dürrenberger G, Jaegerand C, Bieri L, Dahinden U. 1996. Telework and vocational contact. *Technol. Stud.* In press

Duxbury L, Higgins C. 1995. *Summary Report of Telework.* Pilot Product Number 750008XPE, Statistics Canada. 57 pp.

The Economist. 1995. Mais où sont les cafés d'antan. *The Economist* June 10, p. 50

Electronic Mail Association. 1992. *Electronic Mail Market Research Results.* Arlington, VA.

Emmett R. 1982. VNET or GRIPENET. *Datamation* 4:48–58

Eveland JD, Bikson TK. 1988. Work group structures and computer support. *ACM Trans Office Info. Sys.* 6:354–79

Falconer KF. 1993. *Space, gender, and work in the context of technological change: telecommuting women.* PhD thesis. Univ. Kentucky, Lexington. 202 pp.

Feld S. 1982. Social structural determinants of similarity among associates. *Am. Sociol. Rev.* 47:797–801

Feldman MS. 1987. Electronic mail and weak ties in organizations. *Office Tech. People* 3:83–101

Finholt T, Sproull L. 1990. Electronic groups at work. *Organ. Sci.* 1(1):41–64

Finholt T, Sproull L, Kiesler S. 1990. Communication and performance in ad hoc task groups. See Galegher et al 1990, pp. 291–325

Fischer C. 1975. Toward a subcultural theory of urbanism. *Am. J. Sociol.* 80:1319–41

Fish R, Kraut R, Root R, Rice R. 1993. Video as a technology for informal communication. *Commun. ACM* 36(1):48–61

Foderaro L. 1995. Seekers of self-help finding it on line. *New York Times,* March 23

Fox R. 1995. Newstrack. *Commun. ACM* 38(8):11–12

Frank J. 1995. Preparing for the information highway: information technology in Canadian households. *Can. Soc. Trends* Autumn:2–7

Freeman L. 1986. The impact of computer based communication on the social structure of an emerging scientific speciality. *Soc. Networks* 6:201–21

French KJF. 1988. *Job satisfactions and family satisfactions of in home workers compared with out of home workers.* PhD thesis. Univ. Calif., Berkeley

Fritz ME, Higa K, Narasimhan S. 1994. Telework: exploring the borderless office. In *Proc. 27th Ann. Hawaii Int. Conf. on Sys. Sci.,* ed. JF Nunamaker, RH Sprague Jr., IV:149–58. Washington, DC: IEEE Press. 971 pp.

Fulk J, Boyd B. 1991. Emerging theories of communication in organizations. *J. Manage.* 17(2):407–46

Fulk J, DeSanctis G. 1995. Electronic communication and changing organizational forms. *Organ. Sci.* 6(4):337–349

Fulk J, Steinfield CW. 1990. *Organizations and Communication Technology.* Newbury Park, CA: Sage

Furlong MS. 1989. An electronic community for older adults: the SeniorNet network. *J. Commun.* 39(3):145–153

Galegher J, Kraut R, Egido C. ed. 1990. *Intellectual Teamwork.* Hillsdale, NJ: Erlbaum

Garton L. 1995. *An Empirical Analysis of Desktop Videoconferencing and Other Media in a Spatially Distributed Work Group.* Laval, Que: Ctr. for Inform. Technol. Innovation

Garton L, Wellman B. 1995. Social impacts of electronic mail in organizations: a review of the research literature. *Commun. Yearbk.* 18:434–53

Gerson J, Kraut R. 1988. Clerical work at home or in the office? See Christensen 1988, pp. 49–64

Grantham CE, Paul ED. 1994. *The greening of organizational change: a case study.* Work. Pap. Inst. Study of Distributed Work. Oakland, CA. 26 pp.

Grey M, Hodson N, Gordon G. 1993. *Teleworking Explained.* Toronto: Wiley. 289 pp.

Gupta S, Pitkow J, Recker M. 1995. *Consumer Survey of WWW Users.* Website: http://www.wmich.edu/sgupta/hermes.html

Haythornthwaite C, Wellman B, Mantei M. 1995. Work relationships and media use. *Group Decisions & Negotiations* 4(3):193–211

Heck R, Owen A, Rowe B. eds. 1995. *Home-Based Employment and Family Life.* Westport, CT: Auburn House

Heilmann W. 1988. The organizational development of teleprogramming. See Korte et al 1988, pp. 39–61

Helms R, Marom R. 1992. *Telecommuting: A Corporate Primer: IBM Tech. Rep. No. TR-74.098.* Toronto: IBM

Herring SC. 1993. Gender and democracy in

computer-mediated communication. *Elect. J. Commun.* 3(2):On-line/unpaginated. (Available through Comserve at vm.its.rpi.edu)

Hesse BW, Grantham CE. 1991. *Electronically distributed work communities.* Work. Pap. Ctr. for Res. on Tech., Am. Inst. for Res. 33 pp.

Hesse BW, Sproull LS, Kiesler SB, Walsh JP. 1993. Returns to science computer networks in oceanography. *Commun. ACM.* 36(8):90–101

Higgins C, Duxbury L, Lee C. 1992. *Balancing work and family: a study of Canadian private sector employees.* Work. Pap. Sch. Bus. Admin, Univ. Western Ontario. 107 pp.

Hiltz SR, Johnson K, Agle G. 1978. *Replicating Bales Problem Solving Experiments on a Computerized Conference.* Computerized Conferencing and Communications Ctr. New Jersey Inst. Technol.

Hiltz SR, Johnson K, Turoff M. 1986. Experiments in group decision making: communication process and outcome in face-to-face versus computerized conferences. *Hum. Commun. Res.* 13(2):225–52

Hiltz SR, Turoff M. 1993. *The Network Nation.* Cambridge, MA: MIT Press

Hinds P, Kiesler S. 1995. Communication across boundaries: work, structure, and use of communication technologies in a large organization. *Organ. Sci.* 6(4):373–393

Hodson R, Parker R. 1988. Work in high-technology settings: a review of the empirical literature. *Res. Soc. Work* 4:1–29

Huber GP. 1990. A theory of the effects of advanced information technologies on organizational design, intelligence, and decision making. See Fulk & Steinfield 1990, pp. 237–74

Huff C, Sproull LS, Kiesler SB. 1989. Computer communication and organizational commitment: tracing the relationship in a city government. *J. Appl. Soc. Psych.* 19:1371–91

Huws U. 1988. Remote possibilities: some difficulties in the analysis and quantification of telework in the UK. See Korte et al 1988, pp. 61–76

Huws U, Korte WB, Robinson S. 1990. *Telework: Towards the Elusive Office.* Chichester, England: Wiley. 273 pp.

Insight New Media. 1995. *Internet facts: anti-hype for the information age.* Work. Pap. December

Ishii H. 1992. ClearBoard: A seamless medium for shared drawing and conversation with eye contact. In *Proc. ACM Conf. on Human Factors in Comp. Sys. CHI '92*, 525–32. NY: ACM Press. 714 pp.

Johnson-Lenz P, Johnson-Lenz T. 1978. On facilitating networks for social change. *Connections* 1:5–11

Johnson-Lenz P, Johnson-Lenz T. 1990. Islands of safety for unlocking human potential. *Awakening Technol.* 3:1–6

Johnson-Lenz P, Johnson-Lenz T. 1994. Groupware for a small planet. In *Groupware in the 21st Century*, ed. P Lloyd, pp. 269–85. Westport, CT: Praeser

Jones SG. 1995. Understanding community in the information age. In *CyberSociety: Computer-Mediated Communciation and Community*, ed. SG Jones, pp. 10–35. Thousand Oaks, CA: Sage

Kadushin C, Lerer N, Tumelty S, Reichler J. 1987. *"With a little help from my friends": Who helps whom with computers?* Work. Pap. Ctr. Soc. Res., City Univ. of New York. 54 pp.

Kaufer D, Carley K. 1993. *Communication at a Distance: The Influence of Print on Sociocultural Organization and Change.* Hillsdale, NJ: Erlbaum. 474 pp.

Kaye AR. 1992. Computer conferencing and mass distance education. In *Empowering Networks*, ed. M Waggoner, Englewood Cliffs, NJ: Educational Technology

Kiesler SB, Siegal J, McGuire TW. 1984. Social psychological aspects of computer-mediated communication. *Am. Psychol.* 39 (10):1123–34

Kiesler SB, Sproull LS. 1988. *Technological and Social Change in Organizational Communication Environments.* Pittsburg: Carnegie Mellon Univ. Press

Kiesler SB, Sproull LS. 1992. Group decision making and communication technology. *Org. Behav. Hum. Decision Proc.* 52:96–123

Kiesler SB, Sproull LS, Eccles JS. 1985. Pool halls, chips, and war games: women in the culture of computing. *Psychol. Women Q.* 9:451–62

King S. 1994. Analysis of electronic support groups for recovering addicts. *Interpersonal Comp. Tech.* 2(3):47–56

Kinsman F. 1987. *The Telecommuters.* Chichester, UK: Wiley. 234 pp.

Kling R. 1996. Synergies and competition between life in cyberspace and face-to-face communities. *Soc. Sci. Comp. Rev.* 14(1):50–54

Kling R. 1996a. *Computerization and Controversy.* San Diego: Academic Press. 2nd ed. In press

Kling R. 1996b. Social relationships in electronic forums: Hangouts, salons, workplaces and communities. See Kling 1996a

Kling R, Jewett T. 1994. The social design of worklife with computers and networks: an open natural systems perspective. *Adv. Computers* 39:239–293

Kling R, Lamb R. 1996. Analyzing visions of electronic publishing and digital libraries. In *Scholarly Publishing: The Electronic Frontier,* eds. GB Newby, R Peek. Cambridge MA: MIT Press. In press.

Kochen M. 1989. *The Small World.* Norwood, NJ: Ablex

Kollock P, Smith MA. 1996a. *Communities in Cyberspace.* Berkeley: Univ. Calif. Press

Kollock P, Smith MA. 1996b. Managing the virtual commons: cooperation and conflict in computer communities. In *Computer-Mediated Communication,* ed. S Herring. Amsterdam: John Benjamins. In press

Koppel R, Appelbaum E, Albin P. 1988. Implications of workplace information technology: control, organization of work and the occupational structure. *Res. Soc. Work* 4:125–152

Korte WB, Robinson S, Steinle WJ. 1988. *Telework: Present Situation and Future Development of a New Form of Work Organization.* Bonn: Elsevier Science

Kraut RE. 1988. Homework: What is it and who does it? See Christensen 1988, pp. 30–48

Kraut RE. 1989. Telecommuting: the trade-offs of home work. *J. Commun.* 39(3):19–47

Kraut RE, Attewell P. 1993. *Electronic mail and organizational knowledge.* Work. Pap. Carnegie Mellon Univ.

Kraut RE, Scherlis W, Mukhopadhyay T, Manning J, Kiesler S. 1995. HomeNet: A field trial of residential internet services. HomeNet 1(2):1–8

Kugelmass J. 1995. *Telecommuting: A Manager's Guide to Flexible Work Arrangements.* New York: Lexington. 226 pp.

Labaton, S. 1995. Clinton papers' index in Foster office vanished after suicide, aide says. *New York Times,* August 2

Latané B, Darley J. 1976. *Help in a Crisis: Bystander Response to an Emergency.* Morristown, NJ: General Learning

Lea M. 1991. Rationalist assumptions in cross-media comparisons of computer-mediated communication. *Behav. Info. Tech.* 10(2):153–172

Lea M, Spears R. 1992. Paralanguage and social perception in computer-mediated communication. *J. Org. Comp.* 2(3–4):321–41

Lea M, Spears R. 1995. Love at first byte? Building personal relationships over computer networks. In *Understudied Relationships,* ed. JT Wood, S Duck, pp. 197–233. Thousand Oaks, CA: Sage

Lea M, O'Shea T, Fung P. 1995. Constructing the networked organization. *Organ. Sci.* 6(4):462–78

Lea M, O'Shea T, Fung P, Spears R. 1992. 'Flaming' in computer-mediated communication. In *Contexts of Computer-Mediated Communication,* ed. M Lea, pp. 89–112. New York: Harvester Wheatsheaf

Lewis PH. 1994. Strangers, not their computers, build a network in time of grief. *New York Times,* 8 March: A1, D2

Lewis P. 1995. Report of high internet use is challenged. *New York Times* (December 13).

Lewis P. 1996. Prodigy said to be in role of a silent son. *New York Times* (January 16).

Lucky R. 1995. What technology alone cannot do. *Sci. Am.* 273(3):204–5

Maes P. 1995. Artificial life meets entertainment: lifelike autonomous agents. *Commun. ACM* 38(11):108–114

Mantei MM, Baecker R, Sellen A, Buxton W, Milligan T, Wellman BS. 1991. Experiences in the use of a media space. In *CHI '91 Conf. Proc.,* ed. SP Roberson, GM Olson, JS Olson, pp. 203–208. Reading, MA: Addison-Wesley. 511 pp.

Mantei MM, Wellman BS. 1995. *From groupware to netware.* Work. Pap. Ctr Urban & Commun. Stud., Univ. Toronto

Markus ML. 1990. Toward a "critical mass" theory of interactive media. See Fulk & Steinfield 1990, pp. 194–218

Markus ML. 1994a. Finding a happy medium: explaining the negative impacts of electronic communication on social life at work. *ACM Trans. Info. Sys.* 12(2):119–149

Markus ML. 1994b. Electronic mail as the medium of managerial choice. *Organ. Sci.* 5:502–27

Marx G, Virnoche M. 1995. *Only connect':* E.M. Forster in an age of computerization: a case study of the establishment of a community network. Pres. Am. Sociol. Assoc., Washington, DC

McClintock CC. 1981. *Working Alone Together: Managing Telecommuting.* Pres. at Natl. Telecommun. Conf., Houston

McCormick N, McCormick J. 1992. Computer friends and foes: content of undergraduates' electronic mail. *Computers in Hum. Behav.* 8:379–405

McKinney E. 1995. New data on the size of the internet and the matrix. Online URL: http://www.tic.com, October.

Mele C. 1996. Access to cyberspace and the empowerment of disadvantaged communities. See Kollock & Smith 1996

Meyer GR. 1989. *The Social Organization of the Computer Underground.* Master's thesis. N. Ill. Univ.

Mitchell W. 1995. *City of Bits: Space, Time and the Infobahn.* Cambridge, MA: MIT Press

Moore G. 1997. Sharing faces, places and spaces: the Ontario Telepresence Project. In *Video-Mediated Communication,* ed. K Finn, A Sellen, S Wilbur. Mahwah, NJ: Lawrence

Erlbaum. Forthcoming

Mowshowitz A. 1994. Virtual organization: a vision of management in the information age. *Info. Soc.* 10:267–88

Newsweek. 1995. Cyberspace tilts right. Jan. 27:30

O'Brien J. 1996. Gender on (the) line: an erasable institution? See Kollock & Smith 1996

Olson MH. 1987. Telework: Practical experience and future prospects. In *Technology and the Transformation of White-Collar Work,* ed. R Kraut, pp. 135–55. Hillsdale, NJ: Erlbaum

Olson MH. 1988. Organizational barriers to telework. See Korte et al 1988, pp. 77–100

Olson MH, Primps SB. 1984. Working at home with computers: work and nonwork issues. *J. Soc. Iss.* 40(3):97–112

Olszewski P, Mokhtarian P. 1994. Telecommuting frequency and impacts for state of California employees. *Tech. Forecasting Soc. Change* 45:275–86

Online Research Group. 1995. *Defining the Internet Opportunity 1994–1995.* Sebastopol, CA: O'Reilly

Orlikowski WJ, Yates J, Okamura K, Fujimoto M. 1995. Shaping electronic communication: the metastructuring of technology in the context of use. *Organ. Sci.* 6(4):423–44

Perin P. 1991. Les usages privés du téléphone. *Commun. & Stratégies* (2):157–62

Pickering JM, King JL. 1995. Hardwiring weak ties: interorganizational computer-mediated communication, occupational communities, and organizational change. *Organ. Sci.* 6(4):479–86

Pitkow J, Kehoe C. 1995. *Third WWW User Survey: Executive Summary.* Online. Internet: WWW http://www.cc.gatech.edu/gvu/usersurveys/survey/or/1995, Graphic, Visualizaton and Usability Center, Georgia Inst. Technol.

Pliskin N, Romm CT. 1994. *Empowerment effects of electronic grcup Communication: a case study.* Work. Pap. Dep. Manage., Faculty Commerce, Univ. Wollongong

Reid E. 1996. Hierarchy and power: social control in cyberspace. See Kollock & Smith 1996

Rheingold H. 1993. *The Virtual Community.* Reading, MA: Addison-Wesley. 325 pp.

Rice R. 1987. Computer-mediated communication and organizational innovation. *J. Commun.* 37(4):65–95

Rice R, Love G. 1987. Electronic emotion: socioemotional content in a computer-mediated communication network. *Commun. Res.* 14(1):85–108

Rice R, Steinfeld C. 1994. Experiences with new forms of organizational communication via electronic mail and voice messaging. In

Telematics and Work, ed. JE Andriessen, R Roe, pp. 109–137. E. Sussex, UK: Lea

Riecken D. ed. 1994. Intelligent agents. *Commun. ACM* 37(7):18–146

Salaff J, Dimitrova D. 1995a. *Teleworking: a review of studies of this international business application of telecommunications.* Work. Pap. Toronto, Ctr for Urban Community Stud., Univ. Toronto

Salaff J, Dimitrova D. 1995b. *Teleworking: a review of studies of this international business application of telecommunications.* Pres. Conf. Global Business in Transition: Prospects for the 21st Century, Hong Kong

Shade LR. 1994. Is sisterhood virtual?: Women on the electronic frontier. Trans. Royal Society Canada VI 5:131–42

Sharples M, ed. 1993. *Computer Supported Collaborative Writing.* London: Springer-Verlag

Shirley S. 1988. Telework in the UK. See Korte et al 1988, pp. 23–33

Siegel J, Dubrovsky V, Kiesler S, McGuire TW. 1986. Group processes in computer-mediated communication. *Org. Behav. Hum. Decision Proc.* 37:157–87

Simons T. 1994. *Expanding the boundaries of employment: professional work at home.* PhD thesis. Cornell Univ. 215 pp.

Slouka M. 1995. *War of the Worlds: Cyberspace and the High-Tech Assault on Reality.* New York: Basic Books. 185 pp.

Smith AD. 1996. Problems of conflict management in virtual communities. See Kollock & Smith 1996

Soares AS. 1992. Telework and communication in data processing centres in Brazil. In *Technology-Mediated Communication,* ed. UE Gattiker, pp. 117–145. Berlin: Walter de Gruyter

Southwick S. 1996. Liszt: *Searchable Directory of E-Mail Discussion Groups.* http://www.liszt.com. BlueMarble Inform. Serv.

Sproull LS, Faraj S. 1995. Atheism, sex and databases. In *Public Access to the Internet,* ed. B. Kahin, J Keller, 62–81. Cambridge, MA: MIT Press

Sproull LS, Kiesler SB. 1991. *Connections: New Ways of Working in the Networked Organization.* Boston, MA: MIT Press. 205 pp.

Star SL. 1993. Cooperation without consensus in scientific problemsolving: dynamics of closure in open systems. In *CSCW: Cooperation or Conflict?,* ed. S Easterbrook, pp. 93–106. Berlin: Springer-Verlag

Steinfield C. 1985. Dimensions of electronic mail use in an organizational setting. *Org. Behav. Hum. Dec. Proc.* 37:157–87

Steinle WJ. 1988. Telework. See Korte et al

1988, pp. 7–19

Stephenson N. 1992. *Snow Crash.* New York: Bantam

Stinchcombe AL. 1990. *Information and Organizations.* Berkeley: Univ. Calif. Press. 391 pp.

Stoll C. 1995. *Silicon Snake Oil: Second Thoughts on the Information Highway.* New York: Doubleday. 247 pp.

Tippin D. 1994. *Control processes in distant work situations: the case of satellite offices.* Presented at Can. Sociol. & Anthro. Assoc., Calgary

Toffler A. 1980. *The Third Wave.* New York: Morrow

Tolbert PS, Simons T. 1994. *The impact of working at home on career outcomes of professional employees.* Work. Pap. 94-04: School of Industrial and Labor Relations, Ctr. for Adv. Human Resource Studies, Cornell Univ. 21 pp.

Treese W. 1995. *The Internet Index Number 6.* On-line: treese@openmarket.com

Valacich JS, Paranka D, George JF, Nunamker JF Jr. 1993. Communication concurrency and the new media. *Commun. Res.* 20:249–76

Walsh JP, Bayama T. 1996. Computer networks and scientific work. *Soc. Stud. Sci.* 26(4): In press

Walther JB. 1992. Interpersonal effects incomputer-mediated interaction: a relational perspective. *Commun. Res.* 19(1):52–90

Walther JB. 1994. Anticipated ongoing interaction versus channel effects on relational communication in computer-mediated interaction. *Hum. Commun. Res.* 20(4):473–501

Walther JB. 1995. Relational aspects of computer-mediated communication. *Organ. Sci.* 6(2):186–203

Walther JB. 1996. Computer-mediated communication: impersonal, interpersonal and hyperpersonal interaction. *Commun. Res.* 23(1):3–43

Walther JB, Anderson JF, Park DW. 1994. Interpersonal effects in computer-mediated interaction: a meta-analysis of social and anti-social communication. *Commun. Res.* 21(4):460–87

Weick K. 1976. Educational organizations as loosely coupled systems. *Admin. Sci. Q.* 21:1–19

Weisband S, Reinig B. 1995. Managing user perceptions of email privacy. *Commun. ACM* 38(12):40–47

Weisband SP, Schneider SK, Connolly T. 1995. Computer-mediated communication and social information: status salience and status difference. *Acad. Manage. J.* 38(4):1124–1151

Wellman BS. 1979. The community question. *Am. J. Sociol.* 84:1201–31

Wellman BS. 1992. Men in networks: private communities, domestic friendships. In *Men's Friendships,* ed. P Nardi, 74–114. Newbury Park, CA: Sage

Wellman BS. 1994. I was a teenage network analyst: the route from the Bronx to the information highway. *Connections* 17(2):28–45

Wellman BS. 1995. Lay referral networks: using conventional medicine and alternative therapies for low back pain. *Soc. Health Care* 12:213–23

Wellman BS. 1996. An electronic group is virtually a social network. In *Research Milestones on the Information Highway,* ed. S Kiesler. Hillsdale, NJ: Lawrence Erlbaum. In press

Wellman BS, Gulia M. 1996. Net surfers don't ride alone: virtual communities as communities. In *Communities in Cyberspace,* ed. P Kollock, M Smith. Berkeley: Univ. Calif. Press

Wellman BS, Salaff J, Dimitrova D, Garton L. 1994. *The virtual reality of virtual organizations.* Pres. at Am. Sociol. Assoc., Los Angeles

Wellman BS, Tindall D. 1993. Reach out and touch some bodies: how social networks connect telephone networks. *Progress Commun. Sci.* 12:63–93

Wireman P. 1984. *Urban Neighborhoods, Networks and Families.* Lexington, MA: Lexington Books

Zack MH, McKenney JL. 1995. Social context and interaction in ongoing computer-supported management groups. *Organ. Sci.* 6(4):394–422

Zuboff S. 1988. *In the Age of the Smart Machine.* New York: Basic

Annu. Rev. Sociol. 1996. 22:239–70

COMPARATIVE MEDICAL SYSTEMS

David Mechanic

Institute for Health, Health Care Policy, and Aging Research, Rutgers University, 30 College Avenue, New Brunswick, New Jersey 08903

David A. Rochefort

Department of Political Science, Northeastern University, Boston, Massachusetts 02115

KEY WORDS: comparative health systems, convergence hypothesis, demography, health policy, health services, medical care, medical profession, mental health care, public health

ABSTRACT

National health systems throughout the world face a number of pressures in common related to demography, epidemiology, developments in science and technology, medical demand, and rising public expectations. These pressures are producing convergence in the objectives and activities of these systems in several key areas, including cost-containment, health promotion, expansion of access, primary health care, patient choice, and the linkage between health and social services. At the same time, it is also necessary to recognize the role of political and governmental processes, as well as clinical and professional variables, in shaping different societal responses to health care challenges.

INTRODUCTION

Since Mechanic's 1975 *Annual Review* paper (Mechanic 1975a), there has been an increasing growth in publication on health care delivery and medical organization in countries throughout the world. In the United States, this interest in recent years reflects the unresolved US health care debate and the search abroad for potential reform ideas that could be adapted to the American context. The broad reach of mass communications, the reduction of trade barriers in Western Europe and North America, and the rapid diffusion of technology have

239

0360-0572/96/0815-0239$08.00

also furthered the "global village" phenomenon. Finally, more than ever before, scholars from many disciplines recognize the theoretical and practical insights that may be gained by examining the relationship between cultural, social, political, and economic forces and the organization and output of national health care systems. Even those specializing in the health care system processes of a single nation can see the simple truth of Kipling's suggestion that they don't know England "who only England know."

Despite this contagious interest in comparative health systems analysis, the field as a whole is poorly developed in theoretical sophistication and the rigor of much of the empirical research. van Atteveld et al (1987) reviewed 144 studies on comparative and international health care research published in leading journals between 1970 and 1985. They found that most studies were descriptive and dominated by a quantitative economic approach with little interdisciplinary input. Even those studies with analytic objectives lacked clear analytic models. Many studies were comparative in name only, making no comparisons across different systems.

In 1975, Mechanic stated a hypothesis of convergence in which health systems were seen to be responding both to the developing dynamics of science and technology, on the one hand, and to a variety of exogenous factors associated with resource levels, patterns of morbidity, demography, and mass culture, on the other. The 20 years since the presentation of this hypothesis have confirmed its general utility, while highlighting needed clarifications and refinements. Accordingly, this review is organized around primary elements of the convergence approach. Beyond this, it also considers the distinctive impact of the state on national and international health sector trends; it notes how clinical and social aspects of illness can work to shape health system responses and their effectiveness; and it records the shifting position of the medical profession amidst powerful eddies of change. Taken together, these perspectives yield an encompassing overview of comparative health care developments.

As an introduction to this discussion, we begin with alternative conceptual methods for classifying national health systems.

CLASSIFYING NATIONAL HEALTH CARE SYSTEMS

Various classifications of health systems have been developed whose purposes are largely descriptive. Even from the point of view of system description, however, there is as yet no accepted taxonomy "which provides detailed qualitative information on the eligibility, benefits, reimbursement, financing, and delivery system characteristics, as well as quantitative measures of the availability and use of specific health services based on standard definitions" (Schieber et al 1991, p. 25). These limitations notwithstanding, a few words about past typological work is in order because it has served to organize much of the comparative health care field.

One of the very earliest comparative typologies was suggested by Terris (1978). He identified three basic systems of medical care: public assistance systems that serve the majority of a nation's population via government facilities supported by general tax revenues; health insurance systems that rely on public and private third-party mechanisms to cover the population for fee-for-service medicine; and national health service systems that cover the entire population by means of salaried health care providers working in public facilities.

Offering a more extensive set of categories with greater conceptual elaboration was another influential early schema by Field (1980). Field proposed five types of systems: anomic, pluralistic, insurance/social security, national health service, and socialized. These are defined according to the status of health care as a national social good. Field asserted that the five forms represented a progression, with systems not yet at the point of socialized medicine moving predictably in that direction. (For one application of Field's typology, see Leichter & Rodgers 1984; for an attempt to blend Terris's and Field's approaches, see Ertler et al 1987).

Numerous other health system typologies have been conceived that tend to place primary emphasis on either political or economic definitional criteria. Of the former are those from Babson (1972), Maxwell (1974), Leichter (1979), Anderson (1972, 1989), Graig (1993), and Kirkman-Liff (1994). The latter can be found in the work of Evans (1981), Hurst (1991), Organization for Economic Co-operation and Development (1992), Hsiao (1992), and Saltman & Von Otter (1989, 1992). Roemer (1991, 1993) combined political and economic dimensions in a sixteen-celled matrix depicting the extent of health-market intervention against the economic level of a country. Elling (1989, 1994) also fused politics and economics in a neo-Marxist framework that ties health care provision to a nation's position in the "capitalist world-system" and the strength of its workers movements.

Many theoretical and empirical problems undermine the value of these classifying approaches. Categories are not always distinct, nor do they typically encompass all health systems. Scholars have sometimes neglected their own schemas when choosing which nations to compare, although theoretically informed sample selection is a main purpose of system classification (van Atteveld et al 1987). A typology, however, used too rigidly for structuring analysis can assume answers to questions that are properly the object of study. Elling (1989, 1994), for example, becomes circular in recommending his class-based typology as a tool for research investigating the role of class struggle in health care change.

Rather than continue the search for a single all-purpose framework, future typology development needs to be matched more closely to particular study purposes, for example, public policy change versus theoretical analysis (van Atteveld et al 1987). The issues facing different components of health systems—e.g. acute care, long-term care, and mental health—are also distinct enough to warrant varied typologies. Last, insufficient attention has been paid to system groupings incorporating a significant cultural dimension.

THE CONVERGENCE HYPOTHESIS REVISITED

The concept of health systems moving toward convergence in response to certain scientific, technological, economic, and epidemiological imperatives has commonly been misunderstood or misrepresented. As originally noted, "The hypothesis of convergence does not imply that medical systems, which develop out of the particular historical and cultural background of a nation and its dominant ethos, will not continue to have distinct social and cultural characteristics reflecting the ideological orientations and socio-cultural context of a country" (Mechanic 1975a, p. 62). Nor does the concept negate the importance of competition among health occupations for defining and controlling the division of labor. Finally, there is no implication, as some critics have argued (Elling 1994), that the convergence hypothesis indicates "automatic" change outside the unique history and political dynamics of any society.

To state the matter as plainly as possible, then, many social, historical, and situational factors affect the particularities of any medical system, and no exact form of organization is inevitable (Leichter 1979, Immergut 1992, Rosenberg 1987, Starr 1982, Stevens 1989). At any point, there are alternative pathways a nation can follow. Cultural processes, local politics, and even individual personalities may be sufficiently dominant to overcome probabilistic trends. What the convergence hypothesis does imply, however, is a certain macro process in which a narrowing of system options takes place, compared with those theoretically possible, due to forces that generally lie beyond the control of particular national actors or institutions and to which more and more societies are being exposed.

The convergence hypothesis has received strong empirical corroboration in the recent comparative health services literature. For example, a study of health policy in nations associated with the Organization for Economic Co-operation and Development (OECD 1994) concluded that "The most remarkable feature of health care system reform among the seventeen countries is the degree of emerging convergence. Whether intentionally or not, the reforms follow in the general direction of those pioneered in other countries" (p. 45). Similarly, Anderson (1989) found in his research on a group of six industrialized democratic nations: "The most astonishing observation may be that, regardless of country, scientific medicine seems to have created similar types of health services, facilities, and personnel" (p. 6). In addition, Kirkman-Liff (1994) traced how common strategies of health system reform are, in turn, resulting in convergence in the issues confronting health care managers.

We turn now to a more detailed analysis of both the sources and consequences of this convergence phenomenon.

FACTORS AFFECTING CONVERGENCE

Among the most important factors affecting health system convergence are the dynamic character of medical knowledge and technology and the forces that sustain it; the effect of medical demand on national economies; changing demography and, particularly, the aging of populations; changing disease patterns; and increasingly rapid mass communication coupled with rising public expectations. No nation, of course, starts anew; all must build on preexisting social institutions and professional organization in reacting to the currents of change. Yet many of the most profound challenges that have already arrived, and those that loom ahead, are strikingly similar internationally and define common societal predicaments.

Medical Knowledge and Technology

Biomedical knowledge and technological development has become an enormous world industry, reflecting the high value national populations put on medical intervention (Mechanic 1975b). In recent decades, extraordinary advances have occurred in genetics, body imaging, microsurgery, transplantation, and in the technical ability to sustain life. The latest developments in genetics, immunology, and molecular biology suggest an enormous range of new possibilities (Galjaard 1994). And varied innovative procedures are on the horizon, including such interventions as skin replacement, new uses for lasers, blood substitutes, new vaccines, disc transplantation, and cancer susceptibility testing (Health Care Technology Institute 1994).

The momentum in biomedical science and technology is sustained by a variety of significant interests (Waitzkin 1983) that depend on continued research and development support, including medical industries, universities, health science centers, and consultant firms, as well as scientists, physicians, and other professionals whose livelihood and professional success depend on their expertise in manipulating new technologies. Medical industries and drug companies aggressively market technologies on a worldwide basis, encouraging rapid adoption often before efficacy or cost effectiveness has been demonstrated. Physicians and other professionals often have strong incentives for acquiring or using these technologies because they increase the range of reimbursable services, because technical procedures pay better than cognitive services (Hsiao et al 1988), and because such technology when purchased can be amortized quickly, leading to significant additional income. New technical procedures are also welcomed by professionals because they add novelty to routine practice, because they provide new opportunities to acquire and demonstrate expertise, and because they often bring prestige. In the United States, and in much of Europe, these patterns also receive support from populations that value technology and believe in its potential. Both professionals and the public at large have strong faith in solving problems through applied knowledge and technology, and they welcome medical innovation for its therapeutic possibilities.

Effect of National Economies on Health Services Development

As medicine demonstrates its capacities for intervention, all nations face increased demand for the provision of medical services. As national economies in western developed countries have grown, nations have responded to population demands not only by spending more, but also by spending a larger proportion of gross national product (GNP) for health services. Nowhere is such expenditure as large as in the United States, where they now exceed a trillion dollars a year and approach 15% of GNP (Levit et al 1994). From 1980–1992 in the United States, the average annual growth rate in per capita health expenditures was 9.3% (Schieber et al 1994), much larger than the expansion of the economy as a whole, and this has created enormous pressures for cost-containment. Similar growth has occurred throughout Europe, with average annual health expenditure increases of 7.5% for OECD countries during the period 1980–1992. For these same countries in 1992, health expenditures averaged 8.1% of gross domestic product (GDP) (Schieber et al 1994).

The poorer countries of Eastern Europe, countries comprising the former Soviet Union, most countries in Asia and Africa, and such struggling nations as Cuba have been less able to sustain health care programs in the face of faltering economies. In Cuba, for example, loss of subsidy from the Soviet Union, a US boycott, and a failing economy have seriously damaged what many saw as a model public health system (Stein & Susser 1972, Susser 1993). In much of the developing world, economic recession, AIDS, war, and other large-scale disasters have significantly disrupted public health development (Desjarlais et al 1995).

Economic crisis and the social dissolution of the Soviet Union and the Eastern bloc have led to great ferment in the national health systems of these countries. The former socialist countries of Europe, including Hungary, Poland, the Czech and Slovak Republics, Albania, Bulgaria, Romania, Slovenia, and the various non-European republics of the former Soviet Union previously supported centralized funding, universal access to care, and networks of poly-clinics and hospitals (Ensor 1993). With economic collapse these systems have not been sustainable and the trend has been away from universal entitlement supported by centralized funding based on taxes. As these countries attempt to develop market economies, their medical structures have moved toward plu-ralistic approaches depending on payroll contributions and new market-like arrangements. Similar market-like approaches have been introduced in Asia, resulting in extensive cost escalation (Hsiao 1994). These trends vary and depend in part on the degree to which nations endorse market ideologies as a solution to their health care problems. In the Czech Republic, for exam-ple, decentralization and privatization have taken place rapidly, while in the Slovak Republic a preference for centralization persists (Potek 1993). Some have linked the push toward competitive markets in health care to misplaced confidence in American economic concepts and to the role played by Amer-ican economists in international organizations and in advising many of these countries (Glaser 1993). An inevitable result in many of these countries will be to widen disparities in access to health care services.

Even in the most resource-rich Western countries, technical medical pos-sibilities and public expectations put extraordinary pressures on government budgets and/or sickness funds. In the United States, government pays more than two fifths of health care expenditures directly, even in the absence of uni-versal coverage, and substantial amounts indirectly through tax exemptions and other subsidies (Deleuw & Greenberg 1994).

Changing Demography

Since 1950, the countries of North America, Western Europe, and Oceania have continued to experience population aging, a trend accompanied by increases in the wealth and education of the population (Uhlenberg 1992). The elderly population has also been growing in the developing countries, but within a much shorter time span and without comparable economic improvements (Preston 1975). Longevity advances in these countries can be attributed primarily to improved nutrition, the application of public health knowledge, and to particular medical interventions such as immunization, antibiotic treatment, and improved prenatal and child care.

Both the magnitude and type of health care demands depend on the compo-sition of populations and the needs of inhabitants at varying ages. As people live longer they have more chronic disease and disabilities. Aging is associated with greater need across the entire spectrum of health services, but especially for long-term care of both institutional and noninstitutional forms (Kirkman-Liff 1994). As Table 1 illustrates, the elderly now constitute from one seventh to almost one fifth of the populations of developed countries, with expected

Table 1 Comparative demographics and vital statistics of selected developed and developing nations

Country	Population structure[1]- % < 15 years	Population structure[1]- % > 65 years	Fertility rate[1] (births per 1,000 population)	Infant mortality rate[2]- (deaths per 1,000 live births)	Life expectancy at birth[2], males (years)	Life expectancy at birth[2], females (years)	Life expectancy at age 70[3], males (years)	Life expectancy at age 70[3], females (years)
Australia	22	12	14	7.1	74.4	80.4	12.1	15.26
Austria	18	15	11	7.4	72.6	79.2	11.71	14.24
Belgium	18	15	12	8.4	72.8	79.5	10.91	14.41
Canada	21	12	14	6.8	73.8	80.4	11.79	15.44
Denmark	17	16	12	7.3	72.2	77.7	11.1	14.21
Finland	19	14	12	5.8	71.4	79.3	10.74	13.82
France	20	15	13	7.3	73.0	81.1	12.29	15.80
Germany	16	15	11	6.7	72.9	79.3	10.67	13.78
Italy	16	15	11	8.3	73.6	80.3	11.57	14.69
Netherlands	18	13	13	6.5	74.1	80.2	11.28	15.12
Sweden	18	18	14	6.1	74.9	80.5	12.02	15.24
U.K	19	16	13	7.4	73.2	78.8	10.90	14.09
U.S	22	13	15	8.9	72.0	78.9	12.10	15.20
China	28	6	18	52[1]	68.0[3]	79.9[3]	N/A	N/A
India	36	4	28	78[1]	55.4[3]	55.67[3]	9.68	11.01

[1] *World Almanac* (1995), various country entries. Most data are for 1994, with the exception of Germany, whose population distribution predates 1990.

[2] Schieber, Poullier, and Greenwald (1994, Exhibit 5, p. 108), Most data are for 1990; some are for the late 1980s.

[3] *United Nations Demographic Yearbook* (1992, Table 25, pp. 710–39), various country entries. Most data are for 1990, with the exception of Germany, whose data are for 1985–87.

remaining life at age 70 in the range of 10 to 15 years. Birth rates and infant mortality rates are low.

Populations are growing slowly, if at all, in the developed countries (Hugman 1994). This is significant because of increasing dependency ratios between nonworking and working segments of society. Such trends are only somewhat mitigated by the increased participation of women in the workforce. It is a sign of the times that new ways to increase the productivity and reduce the dependency of the old, or to reduce existing public financial commitment to them, are not only being seriously debated but also implemented (Uhlenberg 1992, Pierson 1994).

Already by 1980, most of the world's large global regions were experiencing sharply rising old-age dependency ratios (Roemer 1991). From 1950 to 1980, the percentage of elderly in comparison to the working-age population between 15 and 64 years increased from 12.5% to 16.7% in North America, and from 13.2% to 20.1% in Europe. Though a slower trend, a similar pattern occurred in Latin America (from 6.0% to 7.6%) and East Asia (from 5.9% to 8.5%). As dramatic reductions in fertility take place in many underdeveloped areas where birth rates have been high (Mosley et al 1990), these societies will eventually confront rapidly greying populations with the health and welfare burdens this implies (Hauser 1986, Häfner et al 1986).

As one extreme example, The People's Republic of China is aggressively pursuing a one-child family policy that could ultimately lead to a disruptive social transition. Compulsory sterilization, contraception, and other methods have enabled China to reach family planning targets originally set for the year 2010 (Kristof 1993a,b). The current trend is for Chinese women to have on average 1.73 children, the lowest rate in Chinese history. Putting aside international controversy over the coerciveness of adopted population control measures, significant health and economic advances could be realized in Chinese society from this policy. However, strong economic growth will be needed if "baby bust" generations are to accommodate the future support needs of current adult cohorts. As Table 1 illustrates, China has already attained life expectancies comparable to developed nations.

Changing Patterns of Disease

It is commonly hypothesized that the nations of the world are moving through a health transition involving three fundamental transformations (Frenk 1993, Wilkinson 1994). The first transformation consists of the decline in importance of the infectious diseases, as well as the growing prevalence of chronic degenerative conditions, injuries, and behavioral disorders that result in profound disabilities and dependency. As illustrated in Figure 1, the disease profile of developing nations is projected to move steadily closer to that found in developed nations in the coming decades (Mosley et al 1990).

Although the balance between infectious and chronic illness is surely shifting globally, it is premature to discount the importance of new infections such as AIDS or the resurgence of older diseases like tuberculosis and malaria. Increasing resistance to antibiotics and other drugs also poses renewed threats from formerly devastating conditions. Yet, however unevenly it occurs across and within different societies, the disease burden will increasingly result from pathologies and disabilities that evolve over long periods of time and that are persistent. Those instances of chronic disease that are not averted by effective primary prevention will require continuing medical management with drugs and other palliative measures.

A second characteristic of the health transition is the changing age prevalence of illness, as public health measures and treatment of acute infections make childhood safer. With infant mortality and early infant death sharply reduced, the preponderance of mortality will occur among the older cohorts, and increasingly among those over 80 years of age.

Third, changes in disease patterns are altering conceptions of illness and what patients expect. Illness less often threatens life itself, but more often endangers the ability of persons to perform their usual activities and achieve a desired quality of life. While the health sector can provide useful assistance with many of these problems, it is also under mounting pressure as a result of the medicalization of a variety of personal and social conditions ranging from infertility to personal maladjustments.

Mass Communication and Rising Public Expectations

The accessibility of mass communication, particularly television and films, throughout the world, and increasing educational levels of populations make it inevitable that reference groups will extend beyond the local situation and even beyond national boundaries. People are increasingly aware of what is possible in health care, and the media heighten expectations and demands by focusing on advances in medical knowledge and technology. Patients seem increasingly

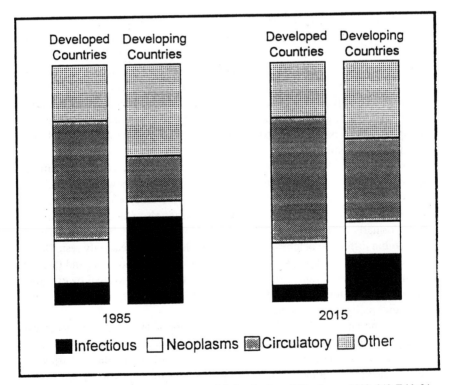

Figure 1   A shifting disease profile. (Source: Mosley, Jamison, & Henderson, 1990: 343, Table 2.)

less prone to be convinced by those in authority that little more can be done for them, and they insist on the same opportunities that are known to be available in other localities. Rising wants inevitably result in multitier health systems unless government prohibits them. But governments themselves, facing growing "cultures" of wants and rights, are struggling to maintain legitimacy, and most are not in a position to resist strong pressures from their middle and upper classes.

Although much could be said for pluralism and market competition, they lead to major dilemmas, particularly for middle-income countries and much of the developing world. In these countries, three systems of care are typical: a private system for the wealthy, who either acquire private insurance or purchase services directly; a government-funded social security insurance system that covers important government employees and other high-priority occupational groups; and a resource-strained public sector for the vast majority of the population. Usually, the private and social security sectors, while serving a small proportion of the population, account for the greatest proportion of expenditures. Thus, one finds in the developing world situations where some populations lack potable water and even the most rudimentary public health services, while others partake of the highest levels of medical technology.

POLITICS, THE STATE, AND HEALTH SYSTEM DEVELOPMENT

Politics and government deserve special consideration as variables influencing the organization of national medical care systems. This much is suggested by the many health system typologies that use some form of government intervention as a defining dimension. Such typologies alone, however, do not guide us on how and why different public sector roles come to be established. While societies face common health system pressures, these are filtered through collective decision-making processes to produce the reimbursement, regulatory, and other health policy decisions that shape a particular service delivery structure (Walt 1994). The collapse of national health reform legislation in the United States in late 1994 underscores that a range of political response to contemporary health care challenges is possible in different societies.

These observations are consistent with an upsurge of interest in the role of the state within comparative social analysis (Evans et al 1985). According to this perspective, the state is capable of autonomous policy choices, which, in turn, may have far-reaching impacts not only on the allocation of resources, but also on a society's political dynamics (Skocpol & Amenta 1986). Whether such autonomy actually is exercised depends on the polity's degree of independence from organized private interests and dominant economic classes. But numerous forces in the contemporary world seem to be pushing in this direction, including the expansion of state capacities and increasing involvement of states in "transnational structures and international flows of communication" (Skocpol 1985, p. 9).

Several studies have used comparative historical analysis to examine the impact of health politics and policymaking on the evolution of national health care systems. Through this approach, researchers seek "to weigh the social determinants of policy and, in particular, to distinguish culturally specific from other determinants of policy outcomes" (Marmor et al 1983, p. 46). A principal theme of recent writing is the impact of political institutions on policy design. For example, Immergut (1992) studied the development of national health insurance legislation in Sweden, France, and Switzerland. She concluded that different health policy outcomes resulted from different "rules of the game" in these societies, which determined group influence and the framing of debates. Wilsford (1991) cited some of the same factors in his comparison of the role of organized medicine in health policymaking in France and the United States. He connected the relative decline of physicians' political power in France to the "tactical advantages" enjoyed by a stronger French state, including a stronger executive, a weaker legislature and judiciary, a more powerful bureaucracy, and ideologically fragmented interests.

In her study of national health insurance proposals in Canada and the United States during the 1940s, Maioni (1995) argued that critical policymaking differences reflected divergent political party configurations in the two countries. As Canada was pulled toward the left by a social-democratic third party, so was the United States pulled away from the left by a potent conservative congressional coalition of southern Democrats and Republicans. Adopting a "culturalist interpretation of institutional change," Jacobs (1993) stressed the influence of public opinion on both the "broad policy goals and administrative details" of health policy formulation in Britain in the 1940s and the United States in the 1960s. Yet Jacobs, too, notes that public opinion and political institutions interact; state actors have their own "strategic calculations" that condition their reactions to public views.

States may also influence health system processes in societies other than their own by exporting, in effect, components of a specific organizational model. The fall of socialist regimes in Eastern Europe has presented new opportunities of this kind, eagerly pursued by certain Western powers. Thus, in January, 1994, the US Agency for International Development announced the awarding of a $44 million contract to Abt Associates, Inc., a Cambridge, Massachusetts, social policy consulting firm, to help institute market-based health care reforms in the former Soviet Republics, including, possibly, an employment-based private insurance system (Stein 1994, Borghesani 1994). States also act through various international organizations, such as those belonging to the United Nations system (Walt 1994). One of these, the World Bank, is a major lender of conditionally based development aid. Dominated by Anglo-American interests, the World Bank has been expanding its health sector program, with a published agenda of stimulating market-oriented finance and delivery systems.

A focus on health politics and state policymaking can help to explain both the process of health system convergence and circumstances when divergence occurs. Increasingly confronted by similar kinds of health system problems, societies are also exposed to the same policy currents about effective health system management. But the processing of these ideas in particular cultural and political contexts is subject to variation. As Skocpol (1985) points out, not only do states differ in their capacity for autonomy, but states have differing capacities in different policy sectors. Seeking to combine political and convergence explanations of health sector evolution, Wilsford (1991) maintains that "there is a universal logic in health care that drives policies toward the same goals across countries and across cultures. This holds in spite of the fact that over the short term there is clearly broad variation across countries and cultures in the timing of policy, in the nature of policy instruments, and in the distribution of health care responsibilities" (p. 5). This seems a reasonable conclusion, and one buttressed by the increasing transcendence of cost-containment activities across public/private sectors, which we examine in the next section, among other major convergence tendencies. Yet even in the long-term, it is difficult to predict the stubbornness of exceptionalist trends in a nation like the United States, which repeatedly has stood on the verge of universalizing health insurance coverage, then faltered, and whose per capita medical costs are so high relative to other countries.

The concept of a "laggard" state was addressed in early theoretical formulations of welfare state development (see, e.g., Wilensky & Lebeaux 1965) and is not inconsistent with a general hypothesis of systemic convergence. That said, neither describing nor accounting for such deviation is easy, especially when the analytic lens is intended to capture a moving picture rather than a snapshot. Consider again the Canada/United States comparison. During the recent US health care debate, many single-payer advocates emphasized an extreme contrast in the two nations' health policy philosophies and operations. Today these differences, while still real and important, seem at least somewhat less marked, as financial problems force coverage cutbacks in some Canadian provinces and managed care legislation (Farnsworth 1996, Rathwell 1994). Similarly, as to the origins of Canadian/US health policy differences, there is little scholarly consensus on how distinct social values in the two nations truly are, much less the relationship between these values and governmental choices (see, e.g., Lipset 1990, Baer et al 1990, Ogmundson & Fisher 1994).

TYPES OF CONVERGENCE

In a world of more than 150 countries representing widely contrasting levels of economic and social development, cross-national patterns can easily be obscured. Moreover, health systems vary so much in cultural and organizational aspects that it is difficult to make empirical comparisons with the assurance that terms are even remotely comparable. Criteria for reporting national statistics vary substantially, and small changes in definition can have large analytic implications (Klein 1991). One can impose a standard definition of units, but the units themselves function differently in varying systems and have different implications. A few examples from English-speaking industrialized countries that share a common cultural heritage will make these difficulties clear.

Doctors vary a great deal in training and function. Thus, in theory, one might select for comparison doctors who have comparable training and perform similar functions in contrasting systems. One might argue, for example, that general practitioners (GPs), family physicians, general internists, and pediatricians in the United States are comparable to British general practitioners. There might be more controversy about including general obstetricians, although British GPs, unlike most American GPs, do obstetrics. But British GPs work only outside the hospital and thus function quite differently from American doctors, who retain continuing responsibility for both inpatient and outpatient care.

One conclusion is that it is futile to compare practitioners since medical systems are organized around structures and functions, and it is more appropriate to describe how each major function is carried out within systems. One function, for example, is primary care, which provides patients with a point of first contact, takes continuing responsibility for routine care, and makes referrals to other levels when needed. Even this comparison is too simple, however, because some primary practitioners are gatekeepers to care, as in the National Health Service (NHS) of the United Kingdom and in many health maintenance organizations (HMOs) in the United States, while in other systems patients have open access and go where they wish. But reasonable subclassifications are possible. A significant comparative difficulty arises because the same function may be performed by personnel who vary greatly in training; for example, primary care practitioners have as little as a few weeks or as much as ten years of educational preparation. Even the comparative financial data that are so glibly cited encompass major differences in how countries do their national accounts, as well as how budgets are divided between health, social welfare, social services, and the like. All of this suggests the need for great caution in cross-national comparisons.

Nonetheless, at least six fundamental types of convergence affect nations that vary greatly in government, culture, stage of economic development, and population characteristics. These forms of convergence reflect both the nature of medical knowledge and technology and the various exogenous factors already discussed, and also the international nature of medical care. Medicine is a world culture with well-developed routes of communication. Even before the computer and fax machine, medical knowledge diffused quickly. Now, new developments are known throughout the world almost as they occur. Thus, nations learn from one another, and often adopt each other's priorities, adjusting them to their own national needs and circumstances (OECD 1994).

We discuss six major areas of convergence: (i) Nations are concerned with cost control and efforts to improve efficiency and effectiveness of health services. (ii) As a consequence of the foregoing, and of the realization that health status is substantially a product of circumstances outside the medical care system, many nations are developing initiatives to promote health and improve health-related behaviors. (iii) Most nations are concerned about inequalities in health outcomes, as well as access to medical care, and seek to develop initiatives to reduce them. (iv) All nations are struggling with the effects of technology and specialization, and many are seeking to develop or strengthen their primary health care systems. (v) There is growing interest throughout the world with patient satisfaction and increased efforts to enhance patient participation, choice, and voice in the organization of health services. (vi) With aging populations and growing prevalence of chronic disease, nations are giving attention to the linkage between health and social services and seeking to reduce fragmentation so evident in this area. Each of these points requires elaboration.

Controlling Costs and Increasing Efficiency and Effectiveness

Because of factors already reviewed, nations throughout the world are struggling with ways to control expenditures and particularly the pressures on public budgets. Frequently, this is accomplished by increasing insurance premiums and patient cost-sharing, reducing the range of procedures covered under national insurance programs, and controlling reimbursement of professionals, hospitals, and other institutions through global budgets, prospective payment methods, (including diagnostically related groups), and fixed fee schedules. Efforts are also being made to control the introduction and diffusion of new technologies by certificate of need and other regulatory devices that specify the establishment of new facilities. Countries with centralized budgetary and regulatory authority control new technologies by budgetary allocations, by manpower policies that control the numbers and distribution of specialists, and by restricting new medical practices in overdoctored areas.

In the United States and Europe, there has been increased focus on the idea of competition as a way of promoting efficiency in the delivery of health services. The work of Alain Enthoven has had important influence in the translation of competitive ideas to varying contexts (Enthoven 1985, OECD 1992). Enthoven (Enthoven 1980, Enthoven & Kronick 1989) advocated a system of managed competition for the United States, where individual purchasers of health insurance would have incentives to select carefully and economically among competing health care plans. This is to be achieved by subsidizing insurance only to a standard level, with the consumer at risk for any additional cost. He also recommended that employer-provided insurance be taxed to reduce the existing incentive for overinsurance because of the federal tax subsidy. The logic of managed competition is that consumers at financial risk would be motivated to make more efficient choices, leading to a boost in enrollment in health maintenance organizations, which function more efficiently than fee-for-service practice (Luft 1987). Competition, Enthoven maintained, must be managed to ensure that health plans compete on efficiency and quality rather than by risk selection.

The European countries already have in place either national health insurance systems or national health services, and thus the concept of a competitive marketplace seems irrelevant. Many of these countries, however, are seeking ways to introduce greater cost consciousness and efficiency among providers and greater choice and responsiveness for clients. Enthoven, for example, suggested that purchasers of care and providers of care within the British NHS be separated to create an internal market where purchasers could take their contracts elsewhere should providers be too expensive or unresponsive (Enthoven 1985). The internal market in theory would result in more competition among providers and more efficient provision of services. This concept of a quasi-market (Le Grand & Bartlett 1993) in which competition is induced within the framework of public systems is being applied in a variety of sectors, including education, and is being adopted in various ways by different European countries. Consider, once more, the case of the United Kingdom.

The British have the only nationalized health service in Western Europe. Basically, the Department of Health distributes its budget to health districts, responsible for population areas of approximately 500,000, which then assess needs and purchase the necessary services for their populations from hospitals and community providers. Most pre-existing NHS institutions have become self-governing trusts and must gain their revenue by contracting with health districts (Ham 1994, Klein 1995, Butler 1992, Ranade 1993). Part of the budget is also allocated to GP fundholders, who purchase a specified range of services for patients within the budget allocated (Glennester et al 1994). At the margins, this gives GPs some leverage to affect the responsiveness of hospital consultants and community services. In a sense, GP fund holders, who now serve approximately one half of the population, function as mini-HMOs, although the GPs are not at personal financial risk (Mechanic 1995c). Fund-holding is now being expanded to more GPs, and experiments are in place examining fundholding for a much broader array of services (NHS Executive 1994). Budgets are still allocated to GPs based on historical cost experience. But development of the scheme will require the use of a risk-adjusted capitation, that is, a fixed payment per patient adjusted for age, sex, and illness risk (Glennester et al 1994).

Adaptations of the American HMO and British fundholding practice are being introduced in experiments in other countries, such as Sweden, where public ambulatory clinics are given budgets to manage that include the purchase of inpatient care (Glennester & Matasaganis 1994). In these quasi-markets, however, providers and purchasers are at very little or no financial risk, and it is not clear that they have significant incentives to much alter traditional behaviors. Equally uncertain is whether the benefits of trying to introduce quasi-markets can compensate for the large increase in transaction costs associated with the addition of many more managers, as well as the burdens of negotiating detailed contracts. In Enthoven's concept, the English health district was large enough to be an efficient purchaser, something comparable to the purchasing cooperatives advocated for the United States (Starr 1993). GP fundholding, in contrast, fragments purchasing among many small entities, making it difficult to develop a coherent purchasing strategy. A major argument in favor of such small entities is that they are close to patients and know their needs, and increasingly GP fundholders are coming together in larger cooperative ventures to increase their influence in the marketplace. Whether quasi-markets are simply a diversion reflecting marketplace ideologies presently dominant in many European countries or something more lasting is impossible to say at present.

Initiatives to Promote Health

Improvements in health status are only marginally affected by medical care systems; most such advances come instead from improved environmental conditions and public health, better nutrition, and increased living standards (McKeown 1965, Frank & Mustard 1994). Major inequalities in health status and longevity by socioeconomic status have persisted and have even worsened in some countries, reflecting the wide range of health influences associated with social class differences and income inequalities (Pappas et al 1993, Feinstein 1993). Most forms of mortality are preventable or can be delayed, but they depend greatly on social and environmental conditions and on health behavior

(Bunker 1994). Important risk factors include smoking, diet, exercise, substance abuse, risk-taking, and violence (Mechanic 1994).

Accompanying the concern with escalating health care costs has come a new emphasis on individual responsibility, improved lifestyles, and prevention of illness. Having little flexibility over macro policy relating to inequalities such as the redistribution of income, health policymakers have concentrated on changing individual behaviors. Legislative initiatives have been taken to control smoking and alcohol use through taxes and regulation and to reduce accidents through regulation of transportation and workplace conditions, but most effort is at the individual level to reduce smoking and drug use, change diet, promote safe sexual behavior, and the like.

The issue of prevention was first explicitly raised by the Lalonde report issued by the Canadian Government in 1974 (Lalonde 1974), soon followed by the Forward Plan for Health issued by the Public Health Service of the United States (US Department of Health, Education, and Welfare 1975). Subsequently, many other countries also developed elaborate goals to promote health of the population by centering on changes in individual behavior (US Department of Health, Education, and Welfare 1979; Secretaries of State for Health 1992; World Health Organization 1978). The most developed agenda of this kind, however, is found in the Year 2000 objectives of the US Department of Health and Human Services (1991). A major deficiency of all these efforts is poor specification of the causal processes underlying targeted risks and uncertain technologies for altering behaviors (Mechanic 1989, 1994). Thus, the objectives often function more as symbolic aspirations than as practical strategies. Still, the potential benefits of successfully altering behaviors are very substantial, guaranteeing that attention to these matters will continue. In some areas, such as prevention of HIV infection, prevention strategies offer the only pragmatic option for controlling the spread of disease.

Despite the common belief that prevention is a significant way to control cost, prevention is often not cost effective (Russell 1986, 1993). The utility of preventive efforts hinges on many factors, including the size of the target population, the resource requirements and impact of the intervention, the proportion of persons in the population who would have developed the condition without intervention, and the needed frequency of repeating the intervention. A number of national governments are now sponsoring clinical epidemiological studies and decision analyses to provide better assessments of the cost-benefit outcomes of preventive screening at different intervals (Eddy 1994, Russell 1994).

Reducing Inequalities

Countries throughout the world have enacted policies meant to reduce inequalities in access to health care. Almost all developed Western countries now have universal insurance systems (OECD 1994), but even in these instances many factors other than insurance coverage affect the accessibility of services, such as the geographic location of specialized facilities, the distribution of doctors and other health personnel, the effectiveness of health delivery systems, the size of patient queues, etc. In the United States, some 35–40 million people have been uninsured in recent years, and many more are underinsured, resulting in differential access to services and differences in morbidity and mortality across social groups (Weissman & Epstein 1994). Considerable concern exists worldwide to achieve a better fit between medical need and the manner in which resources are allocated.

The argument in many countries extends to the appropriateness of allocating services to reduce inequalities in health status as well as in access to care. And since outcomes are substantially related to factors exogenous to the medical care system (Adler et al 1993), it is clearly implied that disproportionate resources would be allocated to the most disadvantaged groups. Compensatory initiatives of this kind have been controversial.

Current approaches to reducing health care inequalities depend on the financing and organization of care within particular national systems. The US Medicaid program, for example, is a federal-state program for certain low-income persons and people with disabilities that features a range of services exceeding what is commonly available in private insurance, including transportation assistance and case-management (Schlesinger & Mechanic 1993). In universal public services, financed and often run by government health agencies, attempts to address inequalities focus on centralized budgeting decisions that determine funds allocation among geographic areas and competing types of service (e.g. public health, primary care, acute inpatient services, and long-term care).

In all countries, patterns of allocation arise from prior historical patterns, and dominant medical professionals and other interests resist major alterations (Walt & Gilson 1994). The flow of funds often is tied to the infrastructure of existing facilities and personnel distribution. Major reallocations are painful and contentious. In the United Kingdom, for example, efforts have been made over several years to reallocate the national health budget among geographic areas in closer relation to population size, age distribution, and illness burden (Ranade 1993, Mechanic 1995c). Traditionally, because of population concentrations and medical care and medical education patterns, resources have been concentrated in London and some other large cities. Equalization of funding across regions required substantial reductions, for example, in London beds and the merger or closure of well-known hospitals and medical schools. This has been an acrimonious process. Within geographic areas, enormous differences remain in allocation of resources across and within health districts, reflecting the difficulties of reversing long-standing patterns in the use of resources (Clinical Standards Advisory Group 1993, Frankel & West 1993). Everywhere in the world, very large resource variations among practice areas can be readily documented (Wennberg & Gittelsohn 1982), and these patterns are difficult to explain on the basis of any objective medical criteria (Wennberg 1985).

Thus, a major challenge for all modern systems is to reduce variations in care that cannot be justified on medical grounds. This problem is being approached through outcomes research, the development of practice guidelines for treating common and expensive medical conditions, and the use of medical peer review and medical audits. Although scientific work is international in scope and widely shared among nations, countries are sufficiently different in medical professional cultures and in patients' expectations so that nations go through their own exercise of establishing such guidelines. The form these processes take depends on the power of the medical profession and the countervailing strength of external managers.

Primary Health Care

The World Health Organization's (1978) "Health for All" initiative puts great stress on the development of primary care. Primary care is the point of first contact and continuing responsibility for management of common acute and chronic illnesses, simple patient-oriented preventive measures, and case-management with referral when necessary. In many systems of care, the primary practitioner is a gatekeeper who controls access to specialists and inpatient care. Relative to specialty care and inpatient services, primary care is a low-technology service and relatively inexpensive. In primary care systems in some underdeveloped countries, the cost of prescribed drugs constitutes the single largest category of expenditure (US Department of Health and Human Services 1980).

As noted earlier in this paper, primary care is a set of interrelated functions that can be performed in alternative ways with varying types of personnel or teams. How primary care is organized in any situation depends on how it is embedded in the structure of health services and whether it is part of an organized health services system. In the United States, for example, the primary care physician in traditional practice is just another practitioner, and patients may refer themselves to specialists at will. In health maintenance organizations, in contrast, primary care physicians function as a central component of a system and the main point for triage to more specialized services. Currently, many countries are attempting to bolster the gatekeeping aspects of primary care practitioners as one initiative to control health care costs.

Conceiving primary care as a set of functions rather than as a particular type of personnel allows many alternative approaches, depending on culture and patient expectations, available resources, and existing personnel (Lewis et al

1976). Even in the United States, nurse practitioners and physician assistants are used as primary care personnel in some settings, and much research has been done demonstrating that they function as well or even better than physicians in certain circumstances (Ford 1992). Other countries lacking sufficient doctors and nurses may use trained ancillaries to perform primary care functions, and in underdeveloped countries such persons may have very limited preparation. A substantial amount of primary medical care, however, takes little technical skill and depends essentially on how well the primary care provider relates to patients. Often, workers with little training do this very well. They learn simple preventive modalities such as immunization, treat common problems like infections and diarrhea, distribute birth control devices, and carry out simple health education. The differences in training between nurse practitioners/physician assistants and well-trained doctors probably only matter at the margins, and thus such personnel serve resource-poor countries well.

Patient Choice and Voice

With the erosion of social authority generally, and the loss of authority of physicians specifically, people expect and are demanding more alternatives in their health care and more involvement in setting priorities. These developments are most apparent in the United States but are also gaining momentum in Europe and elsewhere, even in nations that have had highly paternalistic health service systems.

In the United States, patients' aversion to having their choices limited has restricted the growth of prepaid group practice, a form of medical organization capable of providing adequate care at lower cost than traditional care (Luft 1987). Instead, the type of HMO growing most rapidly is the Independent Practice Association, a prepaid program that offers patients a wide choice of doctors. Insurance companies responding to consumer preferences have also developed "point of service" plans, which allow patients virtually unlimited choice of physicians within a preferred provider arrangement, but with some financial penalty for going out-of-plan.

At the treatment level in the United States, providers are giving more attention to informed consent, presenting patients with treatment options, living wills, and many other devices that increase patient influence. Organized practices increasingly have developed complaints mechanisms and monitor patient satisfaction. In competing for patients, health programs try to structure special health promotion and educational efforts that attract healthy patients who are interested in such services. Despite cost controls and managed care, medical care is increasingly a buyer's market attentive to patient choice and voice.

Until recently, the NHS of the United Kingdom was a relatively paternalistic system with little patient choice except in the selection of one's GP. Patients had difficulty changing doctors, and GPs were not inclined to take on patients who wished to make such shifts. The generation that lived through World War II was especially appreciative of the universal coverage and easy access to doctors which came with the NHS and, in general, was not looking to be critical of personal medical arrangements. This situation has changed appreciably with younger cohorts, different historical circumstances, and the effects of mass communication. Clearly, many patients today wish and even insist on more choice (Klein 1995).

In recent years, the NHS has made changes that would have been inconceivable just a few decades ago. Now, for example, there are patient councils at the district level advising on priorities. There is also a charter of patients' rights (Prime Minister and the Chancellor of the Duchy of Lancaster 1994). Recent reforms allow patients to change GPs more easily (Ranade 1993), and some health districts are conducting surveys to learn about public priorities for resource allocation. As in the United States, strong advocacy organizations have developed arguing the case for the needs of varying client groups and disease categories, and such interests often use the media effectively to focus attention on health service deficiencies. While some of the changes described have come more from a desire within government to increase responsiveness among providers than from the insistence of patients, it is also evident that patients are increasingly less docile and more demanding.

Linkage Between Health and Social Services

The national populations of Western Europe have higher proportions of elderly than does the United States, some substantially so (OECD 1994, Saltman 1992), and they share with us the need to develop service patterns appropriate to long-term care responsibilities. With the growing prevalence of chronic disease and disability, sociomedical services of a longitudinal kind must be developed with socially supportive arrangements that allow the disabled and frail population to continue to function and maintain themselves in their homes and communities. Moreover, concepts of patients' rights and of the least restrictive types of care have diffused throughout nations, and in many countries there has been significant deinstitutionalization of the mentally ill, persons with developmental disorders, and the physically handicapped (Scull 1984). The disability rights movement, so evident in the United States, is growing in many other countries as well.

Providing appropriate long-term care requires a mix of traditional medical and social services, organized and administered by different bureaucracies in varying nations (Mechanic 1995a). The professionals associated with these bu-reaucracies have their own priorities and reward structures that hamper effective coordination. Most countries have had only mixed success developing mecha-nisms to reduce fragmentation and confusion among the varying agencies that provide services to elderly people and the disabled. In the United States, the federal government has sponsored a demonstration and evaluation of social health maintenance organizations, structures designed to broaden the defini-tion of relevant services and to allow effective tradeoffs among varying types of services (Harrington & Newcomer 1990, 1991). In many countries, case-management models are used to orchestrate care among varying participating agencies (Marshall et al 1995).

It is difficult to divorce long-term care problems from other changes in mod-ern societies that shift responsibility from the family and neighborhood to formal services systems (Doty 1986). Much of the responsibility for long-term care continues to reside with family caretakers, and governments are cautious about allowing shifts of responsibility to the public purse. Yet, there is a point in all systems when patients are so disabled, incontinent, and confused that mainte-nance in the household, even if possible, excessively burdens other household members. With smaller families, and more women in the workforce, the family is less able to cope with long-term care needs without formal services. Even in countries with extremely strong family systems and a high sense of responsi-bility for elders, newly emerging conditions pose unprecedented challenges for the health services in replacing traditional family care or in supporting families so that they can continue caregiving responsibilities.

In response to aging populations and community care values, more health care expenditures are being devoted to providing care in the home and other community settings (Doty 1986). In addition, advancements have made it possible to do highly sophisticated surgery and other medical procedures on an outpatient or one-day basis and to bring sophisticated medical technologies into the home. The latter has served to moderate the growth of long-term beds in nursing homes, but with greater reliance on home-based care.

COMPARATIVE LESSONS OF THE MENTAL HEALTH SECTOR

The mental health sector illustrates many of our critical points about health system convergence, for example the use of new drug treatments (Reid et al 1993), the influence of demographic change on levels and types of illness (Kramer 1983), the drive for cost-containment through management controls (Goldman & Feldman 1993), and heightened attention to the linkage between health and social services (Rochefort 1993). However, key differences also distinguish mental health care from general medical care that provide valuable insights for comparative health system analysis. Although international mental health care trends have not attracted nearly the scholarly interest given the general health sector, one finds a growing body of research in this area.

Rochefort's (1992) comparison of the United States and Canada described shared mental health sector deficiencies, despite contrasting national health care structures. He identified five problem areas: discriminatory fee-for-service restrictions; two-tiered care between public and private sectors; resource shortages; inequitable funding for community-based programs; and poorly coordinated care. In a study of the components of effective community mental health care, Huxley (1990) reported that the United States and United Kingdom face similar issues in service provision, such as case finding through primary care and integrating specialist and nonspecialist mental health services. Hollingsworth (1992) studied services for the chronically mentally ill in the United States, Germany, and the United Kingdom and concluded: "There seems to be no systematic association between the type of medical care system a nation has and its success in establishing a widespread community-based system of care for the chronically mentally ill. In all three countries, conditions for care of the chronically mentally ill are poor" (p. 921).

More broad-based comparative investigation has also pointed to the commonality of mental health care challenges and attempted responses in different nations. A recent special edition of the *International Journal of Social Psychiatry* usefully employed the concept of "continuing care" to delineate the diverse and intensive service requirements generated by the most severely and chronically mentally ill in modern society (Ramon & Mangen 1994). Apart from a degree of variation in policymaking activity and program implementation, the general rule across numerous health systems was limited organizational innovation, inadequate and maldistributed funding, poor services integration, and, consequently, vast unmet population needs (Mangen 1994, Mechanic 1995a).

What the mental health sector portrays is a distinctive form of convergence that is a part of, yet also separate from, larger health system dynamics. This situation results from the interaction of many factors. Foremost among these are the intricate clinical demands of a disease that can be at once psychologically and socially disabling, the limited acceptance of responsibility for mental health care problems within either the health or welfare sectors, and the absence of public support for a patient group lacking in popular appeal and political influence. Noting this pattern, Mangen (1994) writes: "There can be few fields of social policy other than mental health where national differences in politics and welfare state traditions are of comparatively minor relevance" (pp. 235–36).

THE WANING OF PROFESSIONAL DOMINANCE

Although the social status of doctors may vary from one country to another depending on the priority given to varying components of the economy, doctors have come to dominate the medical division of labor throughout the world during the twentieth century, due in large part to the concentration of medicine in hospitals (Freidson 1970a,b, Starr 1982, Stevens 1989). While nurses and other health workers far outnumber doctors, the medical profession has successfully legitimized its authority to define and control how sickness is to be managed. Increasingly, however, the changing nature of medical services and the universal concern with health care costs are eroding doctors' authority. As medical care moves away from the hospital, the modern doctor's workplace, other occupations have a more credible claim that their services are distinct from medicine and not properly under its jurisdiction (Abbott 1988).

It is necessary to distinguish the cultural authority of medicine from the power, authority, and autonomy of its individual practitioners (Mechanic 1991). Ironically, as medicine's cultural dominance and share of societal resources have grown, individual practitioners have had to protect their domains on many sides from competitors and regulators (McKinlay & Stoeckle 1990). Moreover, medicine itself is more politically fragmented, with competition among specialties, types of medical functions, and organizational alignments. Doctors are increasingly challenged not only by other health occupations, but also by professionals from their own ranks who represent the perspectives of particular specialized concerns or of management. Medical authority may continue in a larger sense, but doctors on the front line are becoming more constrained in what they do and how they do it.

While in some countries budget limits are established by centralized governmental decisions, in others privatized regulatory organizations have developed to achieve the same objectives. In the United States, for example, employers and government often contract with utilization management companies which take on financial risk in curtailng physicians' use of expensive medical resources (England & Vaccaro 1991, Mechanic et al 1995). Whatever the direct or indirect methods used in varying national contexts, the ultimate aim is the same, to ration the delivery of care.

Rationing of Care

Medical care has always been rationed by the ability to purchase services, by the geographic availability of facilities and personnel, and by decisions at every level of care to give either more or less services (Mechanic 1977). As governments throughout the world have assumed responsibility for health care by either mandating or providing services for the population, and as care has become more expensive, obvious measures are being taken to control aggregate expenditures. An impressive variety of devices to do this have been introduced in various countries (Glaser 1987, 1990), but all approaches fall within three general categories: cost-sharing, implicit rationing, and explicit rationing.

The theory underlying cost-sharing is that when patients pay a larger proportion of their bills, they are more prudent purchasers, differentiating between needed and efficacious services and more trivial ones. The evidence is persuasive that cost-sharing reduces the use of services over which patients have some control (particularly ambulatory services), but it does so in an unselective way (Newhouse and the Insurance Experiment Group 1993). Thus, cost-sharing functions as a barrier to care rather than as a judicious way of sifting between different types of services. It has the further disadvantage of differential effects on those with more and less resources, producing inequities in care.

The most common form of rationing in national health services and in such organizations as health maintenance organizations is to require serving a defined population within a fixed budget that is typically established by prospective payment or by capitation (a fixed payment for each patient regardless of the number of services used) (Mechanic 1979, 1986). Such budgets require health organizations to ration care through distributing resources among different types of services, establishing waiting lists, and making decisions as to which patients should get priority. The great advantage of such implicit rationing is its flexibility, but it is associated with decisions that reflect the social and personal preferences of practitioners as well as the needs of patients (Mechanic 1992, 1995b).

Explicit rationing involves centralized decisions about how available resources are to be allocated. At its most simple level, it includes decisions under health insurance as to which services are covered and not covered, which practitioners qualify for reimbursement, and eligible service settings. At more complex levels, it includes decisions about the availability and locations of technologies and facilities, decisions about the relative size of budgets to be given to varying types of services, and specific decisions about what illnesses will be treated and with what technologies. Oregon's rationing plan—which orders illnesses and medical procedures on a hierarchy and only funds those above a cutting point established by the available budget—represents perhaps the most dramatic example of explicit rationing (US Congress 1992).

The case for explicit rationing is that it allows for decisions based on community preferences and assessment of the best available scientific information, rather than on the individualistic inclinations of practitioners. Moreover, explicit rationing is seen as more equitable than implicit rationing, less susceptible to personal privilege and prejudices (Churchill 1987, Sheldon & Maynard

1993). The weaknesses of such rationing include its distance from the ambiguities and complexities of clinical medicine, its inflexibility to deal with unanticipated contingencies, and its rigidity in the face of everchanging medical knowledge and technology. Nor is it clear that heterogeneous societies can make allocation decisions explicit without engendering high levels of political conflict (Mechanic 1992, 1995b).There is some indication that systems that have moved toward very explicit forms of rationing revert to greater discretion as they confront pressures from groups whose needs have been excluded by particular decisions (Redmayne et al 1993).

Most health systems, in fact, use all three forms of rationing strategies, and the critical issue focuses on the appropriate mix more than on any single approach. All Western medical systems are struggling to develop rational approaches for dealing with the large variabilities in medical practice across even small geographic areas. Current techniques include developing sophisticated outcomes research, practice guidelines, and varying types of peer review and clinical audits. The appropriateness of various rationing criteria is increasingly being discussed, particularly the question of whether rationing is justified on the basis of age (Callahan 1987, 1994). Many implicit systems already use age as a rationing criterion (Aaron & Schwartz 1984, Halper 1989), but efforts to make such considerations explicit result in acrimonious debate (Mechanic 1995b). The inevitability of more stringent rationing of care as nations face increasingly severe cost pressures represents the single greatest, and perhaps most divisive, challenge in future health care.

CONCLUSIONS

While a great deal is known about health care systems, we are far from developing an appropriate analytic framework that makes sense of all the extraordinary structural and procedural variations among individual nations. No particular set of economic, organizational, political, or cultural factors suffices. Compounding the difficulties is the fact that scientific medicine is a world culture with rapid communications, and countries readily borrow ideas from one another, adapting them to their particular settings. Moreover, the history of each medical system, to the extent that we have adequate social and political histories, makes clear that no particular form is inevitable but that it depends importantly on the actors and circumstances prevalent at any particular time. Who would have expected the NHS of the United Kingdom, given its history, to have substantially introduced a market orientation to its bureaucratized health service, or even more so, many of the nations of Eastern Europe? What could have predicted that American medicine, while espousing an ideology of free choice and professional autonomy, would have developed perhaps the most intrusive system of micro management over medical decision-making (utilization management) seen in the world today? Who would have believed that the doctor in nationalized systems like the NHS could be an object of envy by American doctors for the freedom they have in clinical decisions? But that too is changing.

We are left with the conclusion that while there are many internal variations among medical care systems reflecting national history, culture, and politics, a productive way of understanding major current and future health care developments is to focus on the exogenous factors that increasingly put common burdens on systems throughout the world. The strength of these factors is not identical from one country to another, and they occur at varying rates and interact in different ways. Nonetheless, they provide an excellent window through which to monitor and evaluate the evolution of medical care in its principal outlines.

ACKNOWLEDGMENTS

Special thanks are given to Lisa Smolski, a student in Northeastern University's Master of Public Administration program, for her help in organizing the reference list and compiling data for Table 1 and for her insightful reactions to an early draft of this paper.

Literature Cited

Aaron HJ, Schwartz WB. 1984. *The Painful Prescription: Rationing Hospital Care*. Washington, DC: Brookings Inst.
Abbott AD. 1988. *The System of Professions: An Essay on the Division of Expert Labor*. Chicago: Univ. Chicago Press
Adler NE, Boyce T, Chesney MA, Folkman S, Syme L. 1993. Socioeconomic inequalities in health: no easy solution. *JAMA* 269(24):3140–45
Anderson OW. 1972. *Health Care: Can There be Equity? The United States, Sweden and England*. New York: Wiley & Sons
Anderson OW. 1989. *The Health Services Continuum in Democratic States*. Ann Arbor, MI: Health Admin. Press
Babson JH. 1972. *Health Care Delivery Systems: A Multinational Survey*. Bath, Engl: Pitman
Baer D, Grabb E, Johnston WA. 1990. The values of Canadians and Americans: a critical analysis and reassessment. *Soc. Forces* 68(3):693–713
Borghesani J. 1994. Abt lands $44M Russian contract. *Boston Bus. J.* Jan. 28:1
Bunker JP, Frazier HS, Mosteller F. 1994. Improving health: measuring effects of medical care. *Milbank Q.* 72(2):225–58
Butler JR. 1992. *Patients, Policies, and Politics: Before and After Working for Patients*. Buckingham/Philadelphia: Open Univ. Press
Callahan D. 1987. *Setting Limits: Medical Goals in an Aging Society*. New York: Simon & Schuster
Callahan D. 1994. Setting limits: a response. *Gerontologist* 34(3):393–98
Churchill LR. 1987. *Rationing Health Care in America: Perceptions and Principles of Justice*. Notre Dame, IN: Univ. Notre Dame Press
Clinical Standards Advisory Group. 1993. *Access to and Availability of Specialist Services*. London: HMSO

Deleuw N, Greenberg G. 1994. United States. In *The Reform of Health Care Systems: A Review of Seventeen OECD Countries, Health Policy Stud.* 5:317–36. Paris: OECD

Desjarlais R, Eisenberg L, Good B, Kleinman A. 1995. *World Mental Health: Problems and Priorities in Low-Income Countries.* New York: Oxford Univ. Press

Doty P. 1986. Family care of the elderly: the role of public policy. *Milbank Q.* 64:34–75

Eddy D. 1994. Rationing resources while improving quality: how to get more for less. *JAMA* 272:817–24

Elling RH. 1989. The comparison of health systems in world-system perspective. *Res. Soc. Health Care* 8:207–26

Elling RH. 1994. Theory and method for the cross-national study of health systems. *Int. J. Health Serv.* 24(2):285–309

England MJ, Vaccaro VA. 1991. New systems to manage mental health care. *Health Aff.* 10(4):129–37

Ensor T. 1993. Health system reform in former socialist countries of Europe. *Int. J. Health Plan. Manage.* 8(3):169–87

Enthoven AC. 1980. *Health Plan: The Only Practical Solution to the Soaring Cost of Medical Care.* Reading, MA: Addison-Wesley

Enthoven AC. 1985. *Reflections on the Management of the National Health Service.* London: Nuffield Provincial Hospitals Trust

Enthoven AC, Kronick R. 1989. A consumer-choice health plan for the 1990s. *N. Engl. J. Med.* 320(1):29–37, 320(2):94–101

Ertler W, Schmidl H, Treytl JM, Wintersberger H. 1987. The social dimensions of health and health care: an international comparison. *Res. Soc. Health Care* 5:1–62

Evans PB, Rueschemeyer D, Skocpol T. 1985. *Bringing the State Back In.* Cambridge: Cambridge Univ. Press

Evans RG. 1981. Incomplete vertical integration: the distinctive structure of the health-care industry. In *Health, Economics, and Health Economics,* ed. J van der Gaag, M Perlman, pp. 329–54. Amsterdam: North Holland

Farnsworth, CH. 1996. Will Ontario Wrap Doctors in Red Tape? *New York Times,* Jan. 15, p. A6

Feinstein JS. 1993. The relationship between socioeconomic status and health: a review of the literature. *Milbank Q.* 71(2):279–322

Field MG. 1980. The health system and the polity: a contemporary American dialectic. *Soc. Sci. Med.* 14:397–413

Ford L. 1992. Advanced nursing practice: future of the nurse practitioner. In *Charting Nursing's Future: Agenda for the 1990s,* ed. LH Aiken, CM Fagin, pp. 287–99. Philadelphia: Lippencott

Frank JW, Mustard JF. 1994. The determinants of health from a historical perspective. *Daedalus* 123(4):1–19

Frankel S, West R. 1993. *Rationing and Rationality in the National Health Service: The Persistence of Waiting Lists.* Houndsmills: Macmillan

Freidson E. 1970a. *Profession of Medicine: A Study of the Sociology of Applied Knowledge.* New York: Dodd, Mead

Freidson E. 1970b. *Professional Dominance: The Social Structure of Medical Care.* New York: Atherton

Frenk J. 1993. The public/private mix and human resources for health. *Health Policy Plan.* 8:315–26

Galjaard H. 1994. Genetic technology in health care: a global view. *Int. J. Technol. Assessment Health Care* 10:527–45

Glaser WA. 1987. *Paying the Hospital: The Organization, Dynamics, and Effects of Differing Financial Arrangements.* San Francisco: Jossey-Bass

Glaser WA. 1990. Designing fee schedules by formulae, politics, and negotiations. *Am. J. Public Health* 80(7):804–9

Glaser WA. 1993. The competition vogue and its outcomes. *Lancet* 341(8848):805–12

Glennerster H, Matasaganis M. 1994. The English and Swedish health care reforms. *Int. J. Health Serv.* 24(2):231–51

Glennerster H, Matasaganis M, Owens P, Hancock S. 1994. *Implementing GP Fundholding: Wild Card or Winning Hand?* Buckingham/Philadelphia: Open Univ. Press

Goldman W, Feldman S, eds. 1993. *Managed Mental Health Care. New Directions for Mental Health Services, Managed Mental Health Care.* San Francisco: Jossey-Bass

Graig LA. 1993. *Health of Nations: An International Perspective on U.S. Health Care Reform.* Washington, DC: Congressional Q.

Häfner H, Moschel G, Sartorius N, eds. 1986. *Mental Health of the Elderly.* Berlin: Springer-Verlag

Halper T. 1989. *The Misfortunes of Others: End-Stage Renal Disease in the United Kingdom.* Cambridge/New York: Cambridge Univ. Press

Ham C. 1994. Reforming health services: learning from the UK experience. *Soc. Policy Admin.* 28(4):293–98

Harrington C, Newcomer RJ. 1990. Social health maintenance organizations. *Generations* 14:49–54

Harrington C, Newcomer RJ. 1991. Social health maintenance organizations' service use and costs, 1985–89. *Health Care Financ.*

Rev. 12(3):37–52

Hauser PM. 1986. Aging and increasing longevity of world population. See Häfner et al 1986, pp. 9–14

Health Care Technology Institute. 1994. *Reference Guide for the Health Care Technology Industry.* Alexandria, VA: Health Care Technol. Inst.

Hollingsworth EJ. 1992. The mentally ill: falling through the cracks. *J. Health Polit. Policy Law* 17:899–928

Hsiao W. 1992. Comparing health systems: What nations can learn from one another. *J. Health Polit. Policy Law* 17:613–36

Hsiao W. 1994. Marketization: the illusory magic pill. *Health Econ.* 3:351–57

Hsiao WC, Braun P, Dunn D, Becker ER, DeNicola M, Ketcham TR. 1988. Results and policy implications of the resource-based relative-value study. *N. Engl. J. Med.* 319(13):881–88

Hugman R. 1994. *Ageing and the Care of Older People in Europe.* New York: St. Martin's

Hurst JW. 1991. Reforming health care in seven European countries. *Health Aff.* 10(3):7–21

Huxley P. 1990. *Effective Community Mental Health Services.* Aldershot, Engl: Avebury

Immergut EM. 1992. *Health Politics: Interests and Institutions in Western Europe.* Cambridge/New York: Cambridge Univ. Press

Jacobs LR. 1993. *The Health of Nations: Public Opinion and the Making of American and British Health Policy.* Ithaca: Cornell Univ. Press

Kirkman-Liff BL. 1994. Management without frontiers: health system convergence leads to health care management convergence. *Front. Health Serv. Manage.* 11:3–48

Klein R. 1991. Risks and benefits of comparative studies: notes from another shore. *Milbank Q.* 69(2):275–91

Klein R. 1995. *The New Politics of the National Health Service.* London/New York: Longman. 3rd ed.

Kramer M. 1983. The continuing challenge: the rising prevalence of mental disorders, associated chronic diseases, and disabling conditions. *Am. J. Soc. Psychiatry* 3:13–24

Kristof ND. 1993a. China's crackdown on births: a stunning, and harsh, success. *New York Times,* April 25, p. 1

Kristof ND. 1993b. Peasants of China discover new way to weed out girls. *New York Times,* Aug. 21, p. A1

Lalonde M. 1974. *A New Perspective on the Health of Canadians: A Working Document.* Ottawa: Gov. Canada

Le Grand J, Bartlett W, eds. 1993. *Quasi-Markets and Social Policy.* Houndsmills: Macmillan

Leichter HM. 1979. *A Comparative Approach to Policy Analysis: Health Care Policy in Four Nations.* Cambridge/New York: Cambridge Univ. Press

Leichter HM, Rodgers HR. 1984. *American Public Policy in a Comparative Context.* New York: McGraw-Hill

Levit KL, Sensenig Al, Gowen CA, Lazenby HC, McDonnell PA, et al. 1994. National health expenditures, 1993. *Health Care Financ. Rev.* 16:247–94

Lewis CE, Fein R, Mechanic D. 1976. *A Right to Health: The Problem of Access to Primary Medical Care.* New York: Wiley Intersci.

Lipset SM. 1990. *Continental Divide: The Values and Institutions of the United States and Canada.* New York: Routledge

Luft HS. 1987. *Health Maintenance Organizations: Dimensions of Performance.* New Brunswick, NJ: Transaction Books

Maioni A. 1995. Nothing succeeds like the right kind of failure: postwar national health insurance initiatives in Canada and the United States. *J. Health Polit. Policy Law* 20:5–30

Mangen SP. 1994. Continuing care: an emerging issue in European mental health policy. *Int. J. Soc. Psychiatry* 40:235–45

Marmor TR, Bridges A, Hoffman WL. 1983. Comparative politics and health policies: notes on benefits, costs, limits. In *Political Analysis and American Medical Care,* ed. TR Marmor, pp. 45–57. Cambridge: Cambridge Univ. Press

Marshall M, Lockwood A, Gath D. 1995. Social services case management for long-term mental disorders: a randomized controlled trial. *Lancet* 345:409–12

Maxwell R. 1974. *Health Care, The Growing Dilemma: Needs Versus Resources in Western Europe, the U.S., and the U.S.S.R.* New York: McKinsey

McKeown T. 1965. *Medicine in Modern Society: Medical Planning Based on Evaluation of Medical Achievement.* London: Allen & Unwin

McKinlay JB, Stoeckle JD. 1990. Corporatization and the social transformation of doctoring. In *The Corporate Transformation of Health Care: Issues and Directions,* ed. JW Salmon, 1:133–49. Amityville, NY: Baywood

Mechanic D. 1975a. The comparative study of health care delivery systems. *Annu. Rev. Sociol.* 1:43–65

Mechanic D. 1975b. Ideology, medical technology, and health care organization in modern nations. *Am. J. Public Health* 65(3):241–47

Mechanic D. 1977. The growth of medical technology and bureaucracy: implications for medical care. *Milbank Q.* 55:61–78

Mechanic D. 1979. *Future Issues in Health Care: Social Policy and the Rationing of Medical Services.* New York: Free Press

Mechanic D. 1986. *From Advocacy to Allocation: The Evolving American Health Care System.* New York: Free Press

Mechanic D. 1989. Socioeconomic status and health: an examination of underlying processes. In *Pathways to Health: The Role of Social Factors,* ed. JP Bunker, D Gomby, B Kehrer, pp. 9–26. Menlo Park, CA: Kaiser Family Found.

Mechanic D. 1991. Sources of countervailing power in medicine. *J. Health Polit. Policy Law* 16(3):485–98

Mechanic D. 1992. Professional judgment and the rationing of medical care. *Univ. Penn. Law Rev.* 140:1713–54

Mechanic D. 1994. *Inescapable Decisions: The Imperatives of Health Reform.* New Brunswick, NJ: Transaction

Mechanic D. 1995a. Challenges in the provision of mental health services: some cautionary lessons from U.S. experience. *J. Public Health Med.* 17:132–39

Mechanic D. 1995b. Dilemmas in rationing health care services: the case for implicit rationing. *Br. Med. J.* 310:1655–59

Mechanic D. 1995c. The Americanization of the British National Health Service. *Health Aff.* 14:51–67

Mechanic D, Schlesinger M, McAlpine D. 1995. Management of mental health and substance abuse services: state of the art and early results. *Milbank Q.* 73(1):19–55

Mosley WH, Jamison DT, Henderson DA. 1990. The health sector in developing countries: problems for the 1990s and beyond. *Annu. Rev. Public Health* 11:335–58

National Health Service Executive. 1994. *Developing National Health Service Purchasing and GP Fundholding.* Quarry House, Leeds: Dept. Health. 20 Oct., EL(94)79

Newhouse JP, Insurance Experiment Group. 1993. *Free For All? Lessons from the Rand Health Insurance Experiment.* Cambridge: Harvard Univ. Press

Ogmundson R, Fisher L. 1994. Beyond Lipset and his critics: an initial reformulation. *Can. Rev. Sociol. Anthropol.* 31 (2):196–99

Organisation for Economic Co-operation and Development. 1992. *The Reform of Health Care: A Comparative Analysis of Seven OECD Countires, Health Policy Stud.* No. 2. Paris: OECD

Organisation for Economic Co-operation and Development. 1994. *The Reform of Health Care Systems: A Review of Seventeen OECD Countries, Health Policy Stud.* No. 5. Paris: OECD

Pappas G, Queen S, Hadden W, Fisher G. 1993. The increasing disparity in mortality between socioeconomic groups in the United States, 1960 and 1986. *N. Engl. J. Med.* 329(2):103–9

Pierson P. 1994. *Dismantling the Welfare State?: Reagan, Thatcher, and the Politics of Retrenchment.* Cambridge/New York: Cambridge Univ. Press

Potek M. 1993. Current social policy developments in the Czech and Slovak Republics. *J. Eur. Soc. Policy* 3:209–26

Preston SH. 1975. The changing relation between mortality and level of economic development. *Popul. Stud.* 29:231–48

Prime Minister and the Chancellor of the Duchy of Lancaster. 1994. *The Citizen's Charter: Second Report.* London: HMSO, CM. 2540

Ramon S, Mangen SP, eds. 1994. The continued care client: a European perspective. *Int. J. Soc. Psychiatry* 40 Special Issue

Ranade W. 1993. *A Future for the National Health Service? Health Care in the 1990s.* London/New York: Longman

Rathwell T. 1994. Health care in Canada: a system in turmoil. *Health Policy* 24:5–17

Redmayne R, Klein R, Day P. 1993. *Sharing Our Resources: Purchasing and Priority Setting in the NHS.* Natl. Assoc. Health Authorities and Trusts, No. 11

Reid WH, Pham VA, Rago W. 1993. Clozapine use by state programs: public mental health systems respond to a new medication. *Hosp. Community Psychiatry* 44:739–43

Rochefort DA. 1992. More lessons, of a different kind. *Hosp. Community Psychiatry* 43:1083–90

Rochefort DA. 1993. *From Poorhouses to Homelessness: Policy Analysis and Mental Health Care.* Westport, CT: Greenwood

Roemer MI. 1991. *National Health Systems of the World,* Vols. 1, 2. New York: Oxford Univ. Press

Roemer MI. 1993. National health systems throughout the world. *Annu. Rev. Public Health* 14:335–53

Rosenberg CE. 1987. *The Care of Strangers: The Rise of America's Hospital System.* New York: Basic Books

Russell LB. 1986. *Is Prevention Better than Cure?* Washington, DC: The Brookings Inst.

Russell LB. 1993. The role of prevention in health reform. *N. Engl. J. Med.* 329(5):352–54

Russell LB. 1994. *Educated Guesses: Making Policy About Medical Screening Tests.* Berkeley: Univ. Calif. Press

Saltman RB. 1992. Recent health policy initiatives in Nordic countries. *Health Care Financ. Rev.* 13(4):157–66

Saltman RB, Von Otter C. 1989. Public competition versus mixed markets: an analytic comparison. *Health Policy* 11:43–55

Saltman RB, Von Otter C. 1992. *Planned Markets and Public Competition: Strategic Reform in Northern European Health Systems.* Buckingham/Philadelphia: Open Univ. Press

Schieber GJ, Poullier J-P, Greenwald LM. 1991. Health care systems in twenty-four countries. *Health Aff.* 10:22–38

Schieber GJ, Poullier J-P, Greenwald LM. 1994. Health system performance in OECD countries, 1980–1992. *Health Aff.* 13(4):100–12

Schlesinger M, Mechanic D. 1993. Challenges for managed competition from chronic illness. *Health Aff.* 12:123–37 (Suppl.)

Scull A. 1984. *Decarceration: Community Treatment and the Deviant–A Radical View.* New Brunswick, NJ: Rutgers Univ. Press. 2nd ed.

Secretaries of State for Health. 1992. *The Health of the Nation: A Strategy for Health for England.* London: HMSO, Cmnd. 1986

Sheldon TA, Maynard A. 1993. Is rationing inevitable? In *Rationing in Action,* pp. 3–14. London: BMJ

Skocpol T. 1985. Bringing the state back in: strategies of analysis in current research. See Evans et al 1985, pp. 3–43

Skocpol T, Amenta E. 1986. States and social policies. *Annu. Rev. Sociol.* 12:131–57

Starr P. 1982. *The Social Transformation of American Medicine: The Rise of a Sovereign Profession and the Making of a Vast Industry.* New York: Basic Books

Starr P. 1993. Design of health insurance purchasing cooperatives. *Health Aff.* 12:58–64 (Suppl.)

Stein C. 1994. Abt wins $44M pact in Russia. *Boston Globe,* Jan. 28, p. 59

Stein Z, Susser M. 1972. The Cuban health system: a trial of a comprehensive service in a poor country. *Int. J. Health Serv.* 2:551–66

Stevens R. 1989. *In Sickness and in Wealth: American Hospitals in the Twentieth Century.* New York: Basic Books

Susser M. 1993. Health as a human right: an epidemiologist's perspective on the public health. *Am. J. Public Health* 83:418–26

Terris M. 1978. The three world systems of medical care: trends and prospects. *Am. J. Public Health* 68(11):1125–31

Uhlenberg P. 1992. Population aging and social policy. *Annu. Rev. Sociol.* 18:449–74

United Nations Demographic Yearbook. 1992. *United Nations Demographic Yearbook.* New York: Dept. Econ. Soc. Aff., Stat. Off., UN

US Congress, Office of Technology Assessment. 1992. *Evaluation of the Oregon Medicaid Proposal. OTA H-531.* Washington, DC: US Gov. Print. Off.

US Dep. Health, Education, and Welfare. 1975. *Forward Plan for Health FY 1977–1981.* DHEW Publ. No. (05) 76–50024, 97–121. Washington, DC: USGPO

US Dep. Health, Education, and Welfare. 1979. *Healthy People: The Surgeon General's Report on Health Promotion and Disease Prevention.* DHEW (PHS) Publ. No. 79–55071. Washington, DC: USGPO

US Dep. Health and Human Services. 1980. *Rural Health in the People's Republic of China.* NIH Publ. No. 81–2124. Washington, DC: USGPO

US Dep. Health and Human Services. 1991. *Healthy People: National Health Promotion and Disease Prevention Objectives.* DHHS Publ. No. (PHS) 91–50212. Washington, DC: USGPO

van Atteveld L, Broeders C, Lapré R. 1987. International comparative research in health care: a study of the literature. *Health Policy* 8:105–36

Waitzkin H. 1983. *The Second Sickness: Contradictions of Capitalist Health Care.* New York: Free Press

Walt G. 1994. *Health Policy: An Introduction to Process and Power.* London: Zed Books

Walt G, Gilson L. 1994. Reforming the health sector in developing countries: the central role of policy analysis. *Health Policy Plan.* 9:353–70

Weissman J, Epstein A. 1994. *Falling Through the Safety Net: Insurance Status and Access to Health Care.* Baltimore: Johns Hopkins Univ. Press

Wennberg J. 1985. On patient need, equity, supplier-induced demand, and the need to assess the outcome of common medical practices. *Med. Care* 23:512–20

Wennberg J, Gittelsohn A. 1982. Variations in medical care among small areas. *Sci. Am.* 246(4):120–34

Wilensky HL, Lebeaux CN. 1965. *Industrial Society and Social Welfare.* New York: Free Press

Wilkinson RG. 1994. The epidemiological transition: from material scarcity to social disadvantage? *Daedalus* 123(4):61–77

Wilsford D. 1991. *Doctors and the State: The Politics of Health Care in France and the United States.* Durham, NC: Duke Univ. Press

World Almanac. 1995. Mahwah, NJ: Funk & Wagnalls

World Health Organization. 1978. *ALMA-ATA. Primary Health Care.* Geneva: WHO

Annu. Rev. Sociol. 1996. 22:271–98

WHAT DO INTERLOCKS DO? An Analysis, Critique, and Assessment of Research on Interlocking Directorates

Mark S. Mizruchi

Department of Sociology, University of Michigan, Ann Arbor, Michigan 48109-1382

KEY WORDS: boards of directors, corporations, interorganizational relations, social networks,
corporate interlocks

ABSTRACT

Research on interlocking directorates has gained increasing prominence within the field of organizations, but it has come under increasing criticism as well. This chapter presents an in-depth examination of the study of interlocking directorates. I focus initially on both the determinants and the consequences of interlocking directorates, reviewing alternative accounts of both phenomena. Special attention is paid to the processual formulations implied by various interlock analyses. I then address the two primary criticisms of interlock research and evaluate the tenability of these criticisms. I conclude with a discussion of future directions for interlock research.

INTRODUCTION

An interlocking directorate occurs when a person affiliated with one organization sits on the board of directors of another organization. The causes and consequences of this seemingly minor, even innocuous event, have been the source of extensive debate since the Pujo Committee identified interlocks as a problem in the early twentieth century. Relatively simple to identify in publicly available information from highly reliable sources, interlocks have become the primary indicator of interfirm network ties. Research using interlocks flourished in the 1970s and 1980s, and with the explosion of research on interorganizational relations, it has become even more prominent in the 1990s. But despite its virtues, research on interlocks has always attracted its critics. Perhaps it

271

0360-0572/96/0815-0271$08.00

is unsurprising that as the prominence of interlock research has increased, the frequency of criticisms against it have also increased.

Given the swirl of controversy surrounding interlock research, it is time for a detailed assessment of its contributions. In this paper I describe and evaluate the primary strands of work within interlock research. I deal with both the claims of interlock researchers and the criticisms leveled against the approach. I argue that, although they are not the answer to all questions about interorganizational relations, interlocks remain a powerful indicator of network ties between firms. When properly applied, I suggest, they continue to yield significant insights into the behavior of firms.

HOW AND WHY DO INTERLOCKS FORM?

All publicly traded corporations in the United States are required to have a board of directors of at least three persons. In most small, family-controlled firms, the board is likely to consist of the firm's president, some relatives and/or managers, and perhaps the firm's attorney and a few trusted friends. Large corporations tend to have boards with ten or more members; the size of boards has increased steadily since the 1950s. The typical board of a large firm consists of a range of inside and outside directors. Inside directors are those whose primary affiliation is with the firm and who usually include the firm's CEO and other top officers. Retired officers and (in some cases of long-standing family interest) stockholding family members are also included in this group. Outside directors are individuals whose primary affiliations are with organizations other than the focal firm. Most outside directors of large firms are officers of other large firms, especially financial institutions. They include bankers, insurance company executives, investment bankers, attorneys, accountants, and officers of firms in a variety of nonfinancial sectors. Many boards of the larger firms include so-called public directors, who represent groups such as civil rights organizations. Representatives of large external stockholders, including those involved in recent acquisitions of the firm, are also frequently represented on boards.

Interlocks are created by both inside and outside directors. A firm's inside directors, especially its leading officers, often sit on the boards of other firms. A study of 456 Fortune 500 manufacturing firms in 1981 (Mizruchi et al 1993) revealed that more than 70% of the firms had at least one officer who sat on the board of a financial institution. This does not include cases in which a firm's officers sit on the boards of other nonfinancial corporations. But most interlocks are created by a firm's outside directors. Any board member who is primarily affiliated with another firm automatically creates an interlock between the two organizations. The sum of the affiliations of a firm's outside directors constitute the majority of its interlocks, which comprise about three fourths of all ties with financial institutions among the 456 firms in the above-mentioned study.

This automatic creation of an interlock is important to recognize because it means that interlocks need not be the result of conscious decisions by a firm's management to link the firms in question. It is therefore worthwhile to consider both explicit and inadvertent reasons for the formation of interlocks. Several have been stipulated, including collusion, cooptation and monitoring, legitimacy, career advancement, and social cohesion.

Collusion

Congressional investigations of interlocks dating back to the turn of the century have been concerned primarily with the effect of interlocks on the workings of the market. Prior to 1914, there were no prohibitions on who could interlock with whom. At the turn of the century, it was common for several firms within industries to share directors. The National Bank of Commerce, for example, shared directors with virtually every other major New York bank. Critics of big business argued that interlocks between competitors provided a means of restricting competition. Section 8 of the Clayton Act of 1914 expressly prohibited interlocks between firms deemed to be competing in the same markets. The number of interlocks among leading US firms dropped sharply after this point (Mizruchi 1982).

It is legitimate to ask whether interlocks between competitors actually facilitate collusion. The electrical price-fixing scandals of the early 1960s occurred long after interlocks within the industry were prohibited, and the Clayton Act prohibition on competitor ties did not deter numerous other price-fixing conspiracies that have been uncovered (Baker & Faulkner 1993). This raises the questions of whether interlocks between competitors were motivated by attempts to collude, whether they were effective in facilitating such collusion, or whether they were ultimately irrelevant.

Evidence on this issue has been difficult to identify. There are virtually no systematic data on firms' motives for interlocking. Instead, researchers have examined correlates and consequences of horizontal (within-industry) interlocks. Studies of US firms by Pennings (1980) and Burt (1983) examined the association between industry concentration and horizontal ties. Pennings found a positive association between the two, while Burt found an inverted U-shaped function, in which intraindustry interlocks were highest in industries with intermediate levels of concentration. This finding is consistent with the suggestion that, up to a point, concentration facilitates intraindustry ties but that the most highly concentrated industries, because of their small numbers of producers, have little need for interlocking in order to set prices. As for whether such ties improve firm performance, Pennings (1980:147–158) found virtually no association between a firm's interlocks with competitors and its profitability. Burt too found little association between within-industry interlocking and industry profitability once concentration was controlled. Carrington (1981), however, in a study of Canadian firms, found positive associations among concentration, interlocking, and profitability.

The fact that within-industry interlocks continue to occur suggests that some interlocks may have been established with the aim of restricting competition. There is little evidence that such interlocks are effective in this venture, however, or more importantly, whether interlocks are necessary to reduce competition. Perhaps for this reason, research on the anticompetitive effects of interlocks has virtually disappeared.

Cooptation and Monitoring

A less sinister interpretation of interlocking is that it reflects attempts by organizations to coopt sources of environmental uncertainty. This idea has spawned considerable research and continues to influence organizational theory. In his classic study of the Tennessee Valley Authority (1949), Selznick defined cooptation as the absorption of potentially disruptive elements into an organization's decision-making structure. Drawing on Selznick, Thompson & McEwen (1959) presented a hypothetical example of cooptation, in which a corporation invites onto its board of directors a representative of a bank to which the firm is heavily indebted. This example later became the subject of several studies. Works by Dooley (1969), Pfeffer (1972), Allen (1974), Bunting (1976), Pfeffer & Salancik (1978), Pennings (1980), Burt (1983), Ornstein (1984), Ziegler (1984), Galaskiewicz et al (1985), Palmer et al (1986), Mizruchi & Stearns (1988), Lang & Lockhart (1990), and Sheard (1993) all examined the extent to which interfirm dependence contributed to the existence of interlocks. Although the findings have been mixed, on balance they support the view that interlocks are associated with interfirm resource dependence.

These studies had at least two problems, however. First, because the authors lacked data on direct business transactions between firms, they were forced to measure resource dependence at the industry level and then either restrict themselves to industry-level conclusions (as in Burt's work) or infer back to the firm level from the industry-level data. In studies of financial dependence, for example, researchers hypothesized that firms with high levels of debt would have higher numbers of bankers on their boards. Because of the absence of lending data, these researchers were unable to determine whether the bankers on the boards represented the firms' lenders.

A second problem with these studies was that they were able to account for only a subset of a firm's existing interlocks. This problem was highlighted by a series of studies (Koenig et al 1979, Ornstein 1980, Palmer 1983) that showed that the majority of interlocks broken accidentally (through the death or retirement of the person creating the interlock) among US and Canadian firms were not reconstituted within four years after the break. This suggested that, at best, resource dependence accounted for a minority of actual interlocks.

Does cooptation work? Do firms that have coopted sources of environmental uncertainty report higher levels of performance than do firms that have not coopted? Studies of the relation between interlocking and profitability have yielded a wide range of findings. Pennings (1980), Carrington (1981), and Burt (1983) found generally positive but slight associations between interlocking and profitability, although only Carrington's findings (based on Canadian data) were unequivocal. Meeusen & Cuyvers (1985), in a comparative analysis of the Netherlands and Belgium, found positive associations between financial interlocking and profitability in both countries, but negative associations between profitability and several types of "holding" interlocks (involving ownership) in Belgium. In a study of 266 US firms over a ten-year period, Baysinger & Butler (1985) found a positive association between a firm's proportion of outside directors and its profitability compared to its industry average. Fligstein & Brantley (1992), however, found a negative association between interlocks and profitability among a sample of large US firms.

The ambiguous nature of these findings may be a reflection of uncertainty over the causal order of the interlock-profitability association. Several studies have found that unprofitable firms are more likely to interlock (Dooley 1969, Allen 1974, Richardson 1987, Mizruchi & Stearns 1988, Lang & Lockhart 1990, Boeker & Goodstein 1991). Bunting (1976) found a curvilinear relation between the two: Up to a point, profitability increased with increasing interlocking; as interlocks continued to increase, however, profitability began to decline. Several authors have suggested, and interviews with bankers have confirmed (Richardson 1987), that bankers often join a board when a firm is in financial difficulty. Thus it is precisely when profits are lowest that interlocking may occur.

This finding points to an alternative interpretation of the basis for interlocking: an attempt to monitor (Aldrich 1979:296, Stiglitz 1985, Eisenhardt 1989). From the formation of US Steel and International Harvester at the turn of the century, in which every board member of both firms was personally approved by JP Morgan, firms have employed board seats as devices to monitor other firms. Large stockholders, bankers, and customers frequently expect to achieve board representation. This phenomenon has led some theorists to suggest that interlocks are instruments of corporate control. Researchers have identified links between stock ownership and board representation (Mizruchi 1982: Ch. 2; Berkowitz et al 1979, Burt 1983, Caswell 1984), and the finding that the appointments of bankers to a firm's board tend to follow periods of declining performance (Richardson 1987, Mizruchi & Stearns 1988) is consistent with a monitoring perspective. Empirically, however, it is often impossible to distinguish monitoring, or influence-driven, interlocks from cooptation ones. In both cases, the interlock follows resource dependence flows. In fact, several researchers have suggested that cooptation and influence occur simultaneously in any resource dependence–based interlock (Pfeffer 1972:222, Allen 1974: p. 401, Pfeffer & Salancik 1978: pp. 164–65, Pennings 1980: pp. 23–24, Mizruchi & Stearns 1988: p. 195). Since, in the resource dependence model, control of resources is said to confer power on an organization, then the existence of a dependent firm will provide an opportunity for the exercise of power over that firm. One form of this exercise may involve the monitoring function that board representation entails.

On the other hand, both Pennings and Meeusen & Cuyvers suggest that outside directors prefer to join the boards of well-performing firms. This certainly makes sense from the perspective of the individual involved in the interlock, a point I address below. It is significant to note, however, that both an organization's preference to monitor poorly performing firms and an individual's preference to sit on the boards of well-performing firms could exist concurrently. If so, it would explain the inverted U-shaped function identified by Bunting. What remains unresolved here is the causal direction of the interlocking-profitability association. Both of these examples suggest that profitability (or lack of profitability) drives interlocking. Yet components of the resource dependence model suggest that interlocking promotes profitability. Exactly what interlocks do, and how they affect firm behavior, is an issue that we address at length below.

Legitimacy

Boards of directors perform an important function regarding the reputation of a firm (Selznick 1957, Parsons 1960). When investors decide whether to invest in a company, they consider the firm's strength and the quality of its management. By appointing individuals with ties to other important organizations, the firm signals to potential investors that it is a legitimate enterprise worthy of support. The quest for legitimacy is thus a further source of interlocking. In this formulation, firms are seeking not so much an alliance with another firm as the prestige that an association with such a firm may convey.

Legitimacy may also be a prerequisite for the securing of resources discussed in the previous section. A bank may be more willing to lend money to a firm if it believes that the firm is directed by reputable individuals (DiMaggio & Powell 1983). The probability of the bank lending money to the firm may thus increase if the firm already has bankers on its board.

Although the concept of legitimacy has always played a prominent role in organizational theory (Scott 1992), the legitimacy model has received little attention from interlock researchers. The model is difficult to test, and its predictions are closely related to those of the resource dependence model. Cooptation itself in part involves an attempt to gain the legitimacy that may be necessary for the acquisition of resources. The existing literature on board appointments certainly implies, however, that the quest for legitimacy underlies the formation of many interlocks.

Career Advancement

Interlocks occur between organizations, but they are created by individuals. A tie is often instituted at the behest of both organizations. Certainly the firm whose board an outside director joins is making an organizational-level decision to invite the person. But the outside director's decision to join may be the decision either of the firm or of the individual, or a combination of both.

Two studies (Stokman et al 1988, Zajac 1988) have proposed theories of interlock formation that treat interlocks in terms of the individuals who create them rather than from the perspective of interfirm relations. According to Zajac, individuals join boards for financial remuneration, prestige, and contacts that may prove useful in securing subsequent employment opportunities. The existence of interlocks is viewed as an inadvertent consequence of decisions made for reasons having little to do with the desire to link organizations. For a 20-year period among a sample of large Dutch firms, Stokman et al show that the vast majority of new director appointments were drawn from a relatively small number of persons with high levels of experience and expertise. They suggest, in line with Zajac's point, that these directors were chosen for their individual characteristics rather than for the organizations they represent. Useem, in his study of the inner circle (1984), develops a similar theme, suggesting that individuals who sit on multiple boards benefit from what he calls "business scan." As one executive told Useem (1984:47–48):

> You're damn right it's helpful to be on several boards. It extends the range of your network and acquaintances, and your experience. That's why you go on a board, to get something as well as give. . . . It just broadens your experience, the memory bank that you have to test things against.

From the perspective of the host organization, outside directors are chosen as individuals for a number of reasons (Mace 1971). First, firms want board members who will add prestige to their organization (see the discussion of legitimacy above). Among the largest firms, the majority of corporation-based outside directors are CEOs of their respective firms. Second, firms want board members who are capable of providing input and advice, often on issues specific to already-identified corporate strategies. Third, firms want board members who are "good citizens," individuals known by reputation to be both conscientious and noncontroversial. Those most likely to meet the third criterion are people known to the CEO and other firm leaders, including those who are friends of the CEO. Outside directors, therefore, are often selected from within a relatively small circle of eligible individuals. As one director with representative views told Mace (1971:99):

> Here in Baltimore there is a relatively small group of leading businessmen who dominate all the principal company boards in the area. They are all fine men, they are public-spirited men, they have high standards and are widely admired. Individually and collectively their names are a credit to the boards they are on. They are friends of friends, and new board vacancies are filled from their ranks and their rosters.

These findings suggest that interlocks provide benefits to both the inviting firm and the invited outside director that are independent of specific relations between the connected organizations but are a function instead of the individuals involved. But this view is in no way incompatible with either of the interorganizational models described above. On the one hand, as in the cases described by Mace, it is likely that the interlocks created by these individuals are largely independent of relations between the firms themselves. On the other hand, specific individuals are often experts because of their organizational affiliations.[1] Therefore, the fact that an individual is a banker matters, even if the specific bank from which the individual is drawn does not. Even here, one must ask why a particular banker is chosen. This could be a result of a prior or ongoing business relation between the inviting firm and the bank, a friendship relation between leaders of the firms, or the lack of availability of alternative directors. All three of these cases involve factors related to social structural conditions: a business transaction between the firms; a social tie between the firm leaders; and a limited availability of suitable candidates as a result of already established obligations involving other firms. The career advancement models, therefore, are as much complements as alternatives to the interorganizational models described above.

---

[1]Directors who are heavily interlocked are more likely to be chosen for new board positions (Davis 1993). In fact, the severance of an organizational affiliation may render a given outside director less desirable. In an example cited by Useem (1984:39), an outside director of an insurance company was not renominated to the board after the retail firm of which he had been president was acquired by another firm. As a director of the insurance company told Useem, "The president suddenly was without a job; he devoted his time to working with the local art museum, but he didn't keep up with the business community because he hadn't any base.... His being on the board does not add anything."

Social Cohesion

An alternative to both the interorganizational and career advancement models is the view that interlocks represent social ties among members of the upper class. An early (and oft-quoted) statement of this position was presented by Mills (1956:123):

> "Interlocking Directorate" is no mere phrase: it points to a solid feature of the facts of business life, and to a sociological anchor of the community of interest, the unification of outlooks and policy, that prevails among the propertied class.

The model of interlocks as representing social ties is implied in Mace's findings as well. As one director told Mace (1971:99):

> Here in New York it's a systems club. They are all members of the Brook Club, the Links Club, or the Union League Club. Everybody is washing everybody else's hands.

Following Mills, several theorists, including Domhoff (1967), Zeitlin (1974), and Useem (1984), viewed interlocks as elements of capitalist class integration. Zeitlin (1976:900) proposed this position as an explicit alternative to the interorganizational model:

> Neither "financiers" extracting interest at the expense of industrial profits nor "bankers" controlling corporations, but finance capitalists on the boards of the largest banks and corporations preside over banks' investments as creditors and shareholders organizing production, sales, and financing, and appropriating the profits of their integrated activities (emphasis in the original).

The early analyses of interlock networks operated broadly within this framework (Levine 1972, Bearden et al 1975, Mariolis 1975, Sonquist & Koenig 1975, Mintz & Schwartz 1981, Mizruchi 1982, Scott & Griff 1984, Stokman et al 1985), although the extent to which these studies viewed interlocks as organizational- or class-level phenomena was often unclear. The issue of whether interlocks were primarily organizational or class phenomena was at the root of the first broken ties studies. For Koenig et al (1979), Ornstein (1980), and Palmer (1983), the frequency with which accidentally broken interlocks between firms were reconstituted was an indicator of the extent to which such interlocks represented significant links between the firms in question. The fact that the majority of broken ties were not reconstituted with the same firm suggested to these authors that interlocks were not primarily organizational phenomena. They inferred from this that the majority of interlocks reflected intraclass social ties rather than interorganizational resource dependence or control ties.

This interpretation, although plausible, was difficult to sustain because of its true-by-default character. Stearns & Mizruchi (1986) argued that even resource dependence–based interlocks will not necessarily be replaced with a tie to the same firm (see also Pfeffer 1987). Some links will involve what they term functional, as opposed to direct, reconstitutions, in which a broken tie is filled by a tie to a different firm in the same industry as the previous tie. Even when functional reconstitutions were taken into account, Stearns & Mizruchi found that more than half of the broken ties they examined were not reconstituted. Still, their analysis suggested that the incidence of organization-based interlocks was higher than had been found in the earlier broken ties studies. Subsequent studies in this area moved from computing the frequency of broken-tie reconstitutions toward attempting to predict the conditions under which reconstitutions occur (Ornstein 1984, Palmer et al 1986). This contributed to the recognition that interlocks reflected both interorganizational and intraclass ties. A synthesis of the organizational and class models (Mizruchi 1989, 1992: Ch. 4) suggested that even ties developed for organizational purposes could have the consequence of facilitating interfirm political unity.

SO WHAT?: CONSEQUENCES OF INTERLOCKING

Whatever the disputes over the causes of interlocks, they pale compared to what I call the "So what?" question. If interlocks are to be worth studying, it is essential that they be shown to have consequences for the behavior of firms. Most of the analyses of the determinants of interlocks have implied various consequences. As collusive mechanisms, interlocks are assumed to facilitate communication among competitors. As mechanisms of cooptation, interlocks are assumed to pacify the resource provider's management. As monitoring mechanisms, interlocks are assumed to provide the monitoring firm with information on the receiving firm's operations as well as potential influence on its operations. And as reflections of social cohesion, interlocks are assumed to facilitate the political unity necessary for effective political action.

One difficulty in addressing this issue is the problem of how interlocks have been employed by various researchers. Some have treated interlocks as significant phenomena sui generis. The presence of an interlock is expected to actually affect a firm's behavior, even if all other conditions are identical. Others, however, have treated interlocks as representative of a more general social relation between firms. For these researchers, it is not the existence of the interlock per se that is crucial but the presence of a more basic tie between firms that the interlock is likely to reflect. As we shall see, researchers have not always been explicit about the meanings they have assigned to interlocks.

Interlocks and Corporate Control

The most explicit early studies to assume behavioral consequences of interlocks were those dealing with corporate control. After the publication of Berle &

Means's classic work, *The Modern Corporation and Private Property* ([1932] 1968), managerialism became the dominant model of corporate control. In this view, which held sway among US social scientists well into the 1970s, as corporations became increasingly large and stockholdings became increasingly dispersed around the turn of the twentieth century, control of the firm passed by default to the managers who ran the firm's daily operations. This separation of ownership from control was believed to have had a series of consequences for corporate behavior (less emphasis on profit maximization) and for the society as a whole (the dissolution of the capitalist class; see Mizruchi 1982:17–21 for a discussion of this issue). Dating back to the Congressional investigations of the early 1900s, interlocks had been viewed by some observers as a means by which control of corporations could be traced. The assumption was that a firm that had extensive representation of banks and other corporations on its board was subject to control by those institutions. In the 1970s, sociologists rekindled their interest in this topic.

Among the first sociological analyses to use interlocks to trace control was a work by Mariolis (1975). Examining the Fortune 800 from 1969, Mariolis employed network methods to examine the centrality of various types of firms, based on the assumption that highly central firms would be the most powerful. In a test of the hypothesis that the control of corporations in the United States was centered in banks, Mariolis found that major commercial banks were disproportionately represented among the most central corporations. Banks tended to have the highest numbers of interlocks with other firms and to be interlocked with other highly interlocked firms, the latter feature forming the basis of their high centrality.

Mariolis's study raised questions about the extent to which interlocks function as mechanisms of control. He acknowledged that banks might be able to control a firm, through such mechanisms as stock ownership (US bank trust departments frequently invest pension funds in nonfinancial corporations) and control of loan capital, even in the absence of board representation. It is also true (1975:426) that even the presence of two or three representatives on the board of a firm does not guarantee a bank control of that firm. Nor is it clear what difference such control would have for the firm's behavior. As with many pioneering studies, this one raised more questions than it answered.

Whether board representation is effective at all depends on the role of boards of directors. Although it is not well known, Berle & Means had actually defined management as the board ([1932] 1968:196), implying that directors, rather than officers, were the dominant force in management-controlled firms. By the 1950s, however, managerialists began to suggest that boards were mere tools of top management. Certainly there is a considerable amount of evidence that boards of large nonfinancial corporations are largely passive and typically accede to the wishes of the CEO (Mace 1971, Herman 1981, Lorsch & MacIver 1989). On the other hand, simply because officers make most of the day-to-day decisions does not ensure that they, rather than the board, control the firm (Mizruchi 1983). A board that has been passive for many years while a firm performed well may find itself pressed into service when performance drops. It is not uncommon for boards to oust CEOs during periods of crisis (James & Soref 1981, Mizruchi 1983). In that sense, a firm with strategically placed representatives on the boards of a range of companies might in fact exercise considerable power in the corporate world, even if these board memberships do not ensure control over particular firms.

Building on this conception of interlock centrality as an indicator of general influence, Mintz & Schwartz (1985) developed a model of bank hegemony, in which banks exercise power not by controlling firms but by defining, through their routine actions, limits on the discretion of corporate managers. Mintz & Schwartz flesh out their model in their first five chapters, using theoretical argument and illustrations from the business press. They then turn to a detailed analysis of interlock patterns among US firms during the 1960s.

Some interlocks, Mintz & Schwartz suggest, fulfill one or more of the roles attributed to them by the theories cited above, primarily control or cooptation. But most interlocks, in their view, reflect not dyadic ties between firms but "instruments of discretion within a system defined by structural constraints" (1985:128). Interlocks may be driven by firms' information needs, as well as by personal ties between firm managers. As suggested above, they may also be driven by the directors' specific qualifications or experiences. Importantly, an interlock may simultaneously reflect two or more of these characteristics. A firm's need for information about a particular industry may lead to the appointment of a friend of the CEO from that industry who is also personally ambitious and views the outside directorship as a valuable career opportunity. "The most compelling interpretation of the overall network created by the collection of individual reasons for and responses to director recruitment is a general communication system" (1985:141).

The primary feature of the interlock network, in addition to the centrality of banks, is the predominance of representatives of nonfinancial corporations on the boards of banks. In Mintz & Schwartz's view, this reflects the desire of major players in the corporate world to participate in decisions about capital allocation (1985:151). Banks, meanwhile, by appointing directors from a wide range of industries gain valuable information about industry conditions and investment opportunities. Mintz & Schwartz suggest, then, that bank centrality results from the corporate officials' desire for influence over the allocation of capital. The range of corporate officials on bank boards participates collectively, according to Mintz & Schwartz, in broad decisions about economy-wide capital allocation. Consistent with, although not explicit in, their model is the view that banks fulfill the function of mediating interfirm disputes so that business can approach the state as a unified political actor. The authors do not examine business political activity, however.

Because the Mariolis and Mintz & Schwartz studies were based primarily on cross-sectional data, which therefore provided no basis for comparison, it was impossible to determine the extent to which the networks they identified demonstrated a unified business community. To provide such a comparison, Mizruchi (1982) conducted a historical analysis of interlock networks at seven different points from 1904 through 1974. Claiming that the managerialist argument implied a declining level of cohesion in the US business community, Mizruchi showed that the density of the network of interlocks among 167 large firms declined sharply between 1912 and 1935 but stabilized and actually increased slightly thereafter. He concluded that business unity was a continuing phenomenon into the 1970s. As with the other studies, however, Mizruchi presented no evidence of the behavioral consequences of these networks. The comparative studies of interlock networks in 12 countries, compiled by Stokman et al (1985), likewise paid little attention to behavioral consequences of interlocks.[2]

Interlocks as Indicators of Network Embeddedness

By the early 1980s, interlock researchers had become increasingly aware of the need to study the behavioral consequences of interlocks. This realization coincided with the publication of Granovetter's (1985) important statement on network embeddedness. Granovetter argued that economic behavior, as with human behavior in general, is socially embedded; that is, economic actors are affected by their relations with other actors. It is these relations, more than abstract notions of norms or self-interest, that have the primary impact on economic behavior, he argued. This suggested that a range of firm behaviors—strategies, structures, and performance—could be affected by the firm's relations with other firms. Interlocking directorates, as the most widely employed measure of interfirm networks, provide a logical site from which to test the embeddedness model.[3]

---

[2]The study by Meeusen & Cuyvers in this volume was an exception.

[3]Gerlach (1992) has conducted an exhaustive study of Japanese keiretsu, business groups tied together by a system of interlocks and other formal relations. Uzzi (1996) has recently completed a study that employs detailed interfirm transaction data from the apparel industry to test the embeddedness model. Gulati (1995) has examined the determinants of a range of interfirm alliances, including joint ventures, R&D agreements, and technology exchanges.

In recent years, the emphasis on interlocks has moved increasingly toward their value as a communication mechanism rather than as a mechanism of control. This is reflected not only in the work of Mintz & Schwartz but also in that of Useem (1984). It is also implied by Granovetter's embeddedness model. Much of the research that attempts to identify the behavioral consequences of interlocks has thus treated interlocks as a communication mechanism rather than as a means of control. Nevertheless, evidence that the behavior of firms is systematically affected by social structures has only recently begun to appear.

One reason for the earlier paucity of behavioral evidence on interlocks was that it was unclear exactly what consequences interlocks were supposed to predict. Those who examined interlocks in terms of either collusion or cooptation implied that interlocks improved firm performance, including profits. As we saw earlier, the evidence for this association has been mixed at best. Those who examined interlocks within the corporate control tradition predicted either of two sets of outcomes. Interlocks were viewed as altering the behavior of firms, as, for example, forcing firms to transact business with some firms rather than others even if the latter provided more favorable terms. Or interlocks were viewed as indicative of business political cohesion, which was expected to increase corporate political power. For some theorists, the behavioral consequences of interlocks were unspecified.

Except for the few attempts to predict profits from interlocks, only two studies prior to the mid-1980s systematically examined the effect of interlocking on corporate behavior. These were Koenig's (1979) dissertation on corporate contributions to Richard Nixon's presidential reelection campaign, and Ratcliff's (1980) study of elite networks and lending behavior among St. Louis banks. In a study of Fortune 800 companies, Koenig found that firms that were centrally located in the interlock network were, ceteris paribus, more likely to contribute to Nixon's campaign. Ratcliff found, in a study of the lending activities of all 78 banks based in the St. Louis metropolitan area in 1975, that a given bank's number of interlocks with 350 St. Louis-based firms was positively associated with lending to corporations and negatively associated with mortgage lending.

Explicit or implicit in many of the interlock studies of the 1970s and early 1980s was the view that interlock networks among large corporations were indicative of the cohesion within the capitalist class, which helped solidify business into an effective, and dominant, political actor. Mizruchi's (1982) study of the evolution of the US interlock network during the twentieth century, referred to earlier, was an example of this work. After finding that interlocked directors were more likely to be active in various policy planning organizations (1979), Useem (1984) conducted interviews with interlocked directors in the

United States and Britain. Useem found a high level of political consciousness among these directors in both countries, suggesting that they formed a leading edge of the capitalist class, which he termed the "inner circle." Although Useem's study was a major advance, there remained a need for a systematic demonstration of the effect of interlocks on corporate political behavior.

By the mid-1980s, the newly available data on the campaign contributions of corporate political action committees (PACs) among US firms became a rich source of data on corporate political behavior. Just as the meaning of interlocks has been the subject of considerable debate, so has the meaning of PAC contributions. But most observers agree that corporate PACs take their contributions very seriously and that the contributions stand as legitimate indicators of a firm's political preferences (see Mizruchi 1992: Ch. 5, Clawson et al 1992 for detailed discussions and references on this issue). PAC data became a means to examine whether interlocks actually affected the political behavior of firms.

In one early formulation, Mizruchi & Koenig (1986) assumed that firms with similar PAC contribution patterns could be viewed as politically cohesive. If interlocking directorates contributed to political cohesion, they reasoned, then interlocked firms should have more similar contribution patterns than would noninterlocked firms. Unfortunately, although the other results of this pilot study were promising, the interlocking component yielded null and possibly even negative results. There was a small, negative association between the degree of interlocking between industries and the similarity of campaign contributions between them.

In a more systematic study, reported first in a series of articles (Mizruchi 1989, 1990, for example) and then fleshed out in detail in a subsequent book (1992), Mizruchi moved from the interindustry to the interfirm level of analysis, dealt with a more extensive data set, and incorporated a wider range of variables. In these works, Mizruchi found a consistent positive association between interlocking and similarity of contribution patterns. Interestingly, it was not so much direct interlock ties between firms but rather their indirect ties through financial institutions (situations in which two firms were interlocked with the same banks and insurance companies) that were associated with similar contribution patterns. Because firms with indirect ties have several common sources of information, this suggested the value of interlocks for what Useem (1984) called a firm's "business scan," its awareness of its environment. Mizruchi (1992: Ch. 7) also showed that, controlling for several other factors, interlocked firms were more likely than noninterlocked firms to express the same positions on political issues in Congressional hearings. These findings were the first to demonstrate a systematic link between interlocking and corporate political unity.

At the same time, organizational researchers were uncovering several findings that showed that interlocks were associated with a wide range of corporate strategies. Many of these did not deal explicitly with interlocks but were concerned instead with the composition of firms' boards, especially the number and/or proportion of outside directors. Because outside directors are a primary source of ties to other firms, however, studies showing the effects of board composition on firm behavior are highly relevant to the interlock literature. In one of the earliest such board composition studies, Cochran et al (1985) found that firms with high proportions of outside directors were more likely than those with high proportions of inside directors to provide top managers with "golden parachute" packages (lucrative severance agreements). Subsequent studies of golden parachutes by Singh & Harianto (1989) and Wade et al (1990) revealed similar findings. The authors of the first two studies had hypothesized that firms with insider-dominated boards would be more likely to provide golden parachutes because of the CEO's greater influence over insider-dominated boards. Wade et al developed a possible explanation for this paradoxical result, noting that the key issue may be the extent to which the outside directors were appointed during the particular CEO's reign. If so, they suggested, then even an outsider-dominated board would not be independent of the CEO. Unfortunately, the authors measured only the outsiders appointed after the appointment of the current CEO and ignored those appointed prior to the appointment of the current CEO. They did find, however, that CEOs with high numbers of outside board seats were more likely to receive golden parachute agreements, suggesting that integration into the interfirm social network (as described by Useem, Zajac, and Stokman et al) was associated with more favorable outcomes at the individual level. A study by Davis (1994) further confirmed this interpretation. As in the previous studies, Davis found a positive association between prevalence of outside directors and adoption of golden parachute plans. But a stronger predictor of golden parachute adoption in Davis's model was whether a firm was interlocked with a previous adopter.[4]

In a related study, Kosnik (1987) found that firms with high numbers of outside directors were less likely to repurchase their own stock at an above-market price (a takeover-prevention tactic known as "greenmail") than were firms with fewer outside directors. According to Kosnik, this finding suggested that firms with more outside directors were more effective. Kosnik (1990) replicated this in a subsequent study with an additional set of predictors. In a study of hospital boards, Goodstein & Boeker (1991) found that increases in the proportion of outside directors were associated with expansions of hospital

[4]Westphal & Zajac (1995) found that CEO compensation tends to be higher when CEOs are demographically similar to board members.

services. Davis (1991) found that firms were more likely to adopt "poison pill" takeover defenses (changes in bylaws explicitly preventing the firm from being acquired) when they were centrally located in interlock networks and were interlocked with firms that had already adopted poison pills. Palmer et al (1993) found, in a study of large US firms in the 1960s, that firms interlocked through non-officer ties with firms that had already adopted the multidivisional form were more likely to adopt the MDF during that decade than were firms without such ties.[5] D'Aveni & Kesner (1993) found that takeover attempts in which the top managers of both the bidder and target firms shared elite connections (including multiple directorships) were less likely to involve resistance than were takeover attempts without such characteristics. And Stearns & Mizruchi (1993a,b, Mizruchi & Stearns 1994) found a positive association between bank representation on a nonfinancial firm's board and the amount of external financing the firm employed.

On some issues, the association between interlocking and corporate strategies is less clear. In a study of campaign contributions during the 1982 election cycle by 443 large US corporations, Burris (1987) found no association between a firm's interlocks with 100 large US corporations and its tendency to contribute to incumbents, Republicans, or conservatives. Clawson & Neustadtl (1989), on the other hand, found, in a study of 243 US firms, that firms with high numbers of interlocks with a group of 250 large firms were more likely to contribute to incumbents and less likely to contribute to conservatives during the 1980 election cycle.

In studies of mergers and takeovers the findings have been similarly ambiguous. In a study of all takeover bids of Fortune 500 firms during the 1980s, Davis & Stout (1992) found no association between the presence of a banker on a firm's board and the likelihood of the firm being a target of a takeover bid. Fligstein & Brantley (1992) similarly found no association between bank interlocks and merger activity among 100 large US firms during the 1970s. On the other hand, in a study of large US firms during the 1960s, Palmer et al (1995) found that firms with interlocks with commercial and investment banks were more likely to be acquired in a friendly than a predatory fashion. Haunschild (1993), in a study of 327 firms in four US industries, found that firms whose officers sat on the boards of other firms that had recently engaged in acquisitions were more likely to engage in subsequent acquisitions themselves. And in a study of 120 large US firms between 1979 and 1987, Fligstein & Markowitz (1993) found that firms with bank officers on their boards were more likely

---

[5]Palmer et al also found, paradoxically, that firms with officer ties to prior MDF-adopters were less likely than firms without such ties to adopt the MDF. (See Palmer 1993:122–23 for an interpretation of this finding.)

to be targets of takeovers than were firms without bank officers. Fligstein & Markowitz suggest from this finding that bankers are often appointed to boards to encourage the sale of firms experiencing financial difficulties.

The Process of Embeddedness: An Example

It is clear from the studies cited above that a substantial and rapidly growing literature suggests that interlocks are associated with a wide range of corporate behavior. This evidence is not without some controversy; at least a few studies show no interlock effects. But a much larger number do reveal such effects. And all of the studies cited above could be used to support the argument that the behavior of firms is socially embedded.

As critics have pointed out (Hirsch 1982, Stinchcombe 1990, Davis & Powell 1992, Pettigrew 1992), however, very little is known about the processes through which interlocks might affect corporate behavior. The studies cited above rely on publicly available archival data, in which authors theoretically deduce causal hypotheses about the effects of interlocks or board structures in general and then examine these hypotheses with various regression techniques. Still, most of these researchers have worked hard to specify the processes implied by their models.

Any number of these works could be cited to illustrate this point. The work by Davis (1991) on adoption of poison pill takeover defenses provides a good example. Davis develops agency theory hypotheses to predict the likelihood of adoption. Because agency theory and network hypotheses are often similar (Mizruchi & Stearns 1994), Davis develops interorganizational hypotheses that he believes distinguish network formulations from agency theory ones. In addition to examining the proportion of outside directors (a variable predicted by agency theorists to influence board behavior; see Kosnik 1987), Davis predicts positive effects on poison pill adoption for two explicitly network variables: a firm's centrality in the interlock network and the extent to which a firm is interlocked with other firms that have already adopted. Both variables are strong predictors of poison pill adoption, providing powerful support to the network model.

The logic of Davis's argument is instructive. Network centrality, as reflected in interlock ties, is a form of social capital that provides access to information that flows through the network (1991:592). Heavily interlocked directors constitute a vanguard of the corporate elite, integrated into the community and often in the forefront of innovations. Poison pills were an innovation designed to limit takeovers that core members of the corporate elite viewed as dangerous. Thus, firms centrally located in the interlock network would be among the first to employ this innovation. A second component of the embeddedness argument is the process by which innovations spread. According to Davis (1991:593–94), direct contact with an innovator helps clarify the value of the innovation. Thus, firms interlocked with current adopters will be more likely to adopt themselves.

Significant for our purposes is the role of interlocks in these hypotheses. Davis is not claiming that interlocks are the only means by which the corporate elite is integrated or by which information spreads among firms. He argues only that they are a mechanism through which information may pass. Would the diffusion of the poison pill have occurred as rapidly, or in the same way, in the absence of interlock ties? One way to answer this is to consider the variables that were controlled in Davis's model: proportion of inside directors; several variables related to stock ownership, including concentration of ownership and holdings by board members and institutions; number of prior adopters within the firm's industry; incorporation in either New York or Delaware (to control for legal idiosyncrasies); and several market and performance variables. Perhaps, had the data been available, Davis could have examined friendship patterns or geographic proximity among top corporate managers. Both variables would probably have been correlated with interlock ties, without the advantage of capturing the importance of corporate affiliation. Do the interlock patterns actually reflect a deeper set of social relations among members of the corporate elite? Perhaps they do, but no one has proposed an indicator that surpasses interlocks as a measure of social relations among firms. Davis's article provides convincing evidence not only that networks matter, but that interlock networks matter, and that they influence the behavior of firms.

INTERLOCKS AND LONGITUDINAL ANALYSES: CAUSE, CONSEQUENCE, OR BOTH?

Most studies of the consequences of interlocking have been cross-sectional in nature. Although for some of these, the proposed causal ordering is compelling and the reverse implausible, there are other studies in which it is less clear.

Consider our earlier discussion of the link between interlocks and profits, for example, with a few exceptions (Carrington 1981, Meeusen & Cuyvers 1985, Baysinger & Butler 1985), researchers have generally failed to find a positive effect of interlocks on firm profitability. A repeated finding, however, is a negative effect of profitability on interlocking. Low profits seem to invite interlocks, but interlocks do not appear typically to improve profits. Most studies of the interlock-profit link have been cross-sectional, however, and researchers have failed to consider the possibility that outsiders prefer to join the boards of well-performing firms (Meeusen & Cuyvers 1985, Stokman et al 1988, Zajac 1988). There have, nevertheless, been some longitudinal studies. Mizruchi & Stearns (1988), in a longitudinal study of the creation of interlocks by 22 large US manufacturing firms, found that firms whose profits declined in a given year were more likely than those whose profits did not decline to appoint representatives of financial institutions to their boards. Lang & Lockhart (1990) reported similar findings in a longitudinal study of the airline industry. Using a cross-lagged panel model on 204 leading Canadian firms, Richardson (1987) examined, simultaneously, the effect of profits in 1963 on interlocks in 1968 and the effect of interlocks in 1963 on profits in 1968.[6] He found virtually no effect of interlocks on subsequent profitability. Consistent with the literature, however, he found that the effect of profits on interlocking was negative, in line with other studies that showed bankers tending to sit on the boards of unprofitable firms.[7]

Although Richardson's findings appear to solidify the earlier findings on the link between interlocks and profitability, in other areas even longitudinal data may not be sufficient to resolve interpretive disputes. In a study of 22 large US manufacturing firms between 1955 and 1983, Stearns & Mizruchi (1993a,b, Mizruchi & Stearns 1994) have examined the determinants of firms' use of external financing. One of their hypotheses, drawn from the embeddedness model, is that firms with representatives of financial institutions on their boards will be more likely than firms without such representatives to employ high levels of external financing. The findings support this hypothesis (Mizruchi & Stearns 1994).

This formulation contains a causal ordering problem, however. Although the presence of a banker on a firm's board may indeed have an independent effect on the firm's decision-making, the presence of the banker in the first place may be a consequence of the firm's strategy. One advantage of time-series data is that they should allow the analyst to avoid this problem: It must only be ensured that the presence of the banker on the board precedes the firm's borrowing, using a lagged dependent variable.

Unfortunately, it is not that simple. A firm's decision to borrow could have preceded both the borrowing and the appointment of the board member. For example, a firm may have decided in 1959 to embark on a long-term expansion

---

[6] The interlocks examined by Richardson were those directional ties (created by officers of one of the firms) accidentally broken in 1963 that had been reconstituted by 1968.

[7] Although their paper was not framed within the interlock literature, Baysinger & Butler (1985) also used a cross-lagged panel model to examine the relation between "board independence" (the proportion of outside directors) and performance. They found a positive association between a firm's proportion of outside board members in 1970 and its performance relative to its industry in 1980, but no significant association between performance in 1970 and the proportion of outsiders in 1980. As noted above, this is one of the few studies that showed a positive association between outside directors and profits. The ten-year time gap between the two panels in the study raises questions about the nature of the effects, however.

that would require large amounts of external financing. As part of this strategy, the firm in 1960 or 1961 appoints one or more bankers to its board. Then in 1961 or 1962 the firm's borrowing increases sharply. Did the interlock influence the borrowing, or did the borrowing influence the interlock? Or did the decision to borrow influence the interlock, which then influenced the specific character of the decision to borrow?

Notice that even if interlocking were a consequence of an initial decision to borrow, it is still viewed as significant by the firm's management. Notice also that to the extent that an interlock improves a firm's access to financing, it plays an important role even if it is part of a larger strategy. Still, it is undeniable that in the absence of detailed information about the firm's decision-making policies, the reasons for the interlock, and the process by which the interlock affects subsequent decision-making, the causal ordering will be difficult to untangle. In the Mizruchi & Stearns study, this was less of a problem because at a given point, financial representatives had been members of the board in question for an average of more than 12 years. This means that in the vast majority of cases, it is unlikely that a particular decision to borrow was part of a single strategy that involved the board appointment as well. But the larger issue raised by this study remains: What is the causal ordering between interlocking and corporate strategies? To what extent are interlocks the consequences rather than the causes of such strategies? After all, interlocking itself can be viewed as a strategy (Pfeffer & Salancik 1978). The factors that predict decisions to expand or restructure could affect decisions to interlock as well.

TWO CRITICISMS OF INTERLOCK RESEARCH

The basic criticisms of interlock research fall into two categories. The first type generally accepts the legitimacy of the use of quantitative indicators to predict corporate behavior but argues that interlocking directorates fail to account for these behaviors. The second type questions the use of quantitative indicators altogether and suggests that interlock analyses fail to capture not only the richness and complexity but even the general outlines of board dynamics and interfirm relations.

The first criticism, that interlocking directorates fail to predict corporate behavior, has been presented most forcefully in a recent article by Fligstein & Brantley (1992). Drawing on 100 large US industrial corporations between 1969 and 1979, Fligstein & Brantley hypothesize that interlocks with banks should be positively associated with corporate performance and debt/equity ratios. Fligstein & Brantley's findings revealed a negative association between bank interlocks and most measures of profitability. Although this finding ran counter to the authors' hypothesis, it is consistent with that of several studies cited above and is thus not surprising. Bank interlocking did not predict strategic variables such as mergers or product strategies (related versus unrelated). Because the authors had presented no hypotheses for the effect of interlocking on these variables, the null findings prove little about the relevance of interlocks as a variable.

It is difficult to quarrel with the authors' statement that "We should abandon our concentration on boards of directors as a source of network data... *unless their possible relevance can be specified theoretically*" (1992:304, emphasis added). It would be a mistake, however, to assume from this study that interlocks "just do not predict much that is interesting in the strategic choices of firms" (1992:304). This fails to accord with the results of the numerous studies cited above, such as the works by Kosnik on greenmail; Cochran et al, Singh & Harianto, and Wade et al on golden parachutes; Davis on poison pill adoptions; Palmer et al and Haunschild on mergers; Goodstein & Boeker on hospital strategies; and Stearns & Mizruchi on corporate financing—not to mention the studies showing positive impacts of interlocking on profitability and those showing effects of interlocking on corporate political strategies, a topic that Fligstein & Brantley concede (1992:282) is beyond their scope. This conclusion is also contradicted by a study by Fligstein himself (Fligstein & Markowitz 1993) that showed that the presence of bank interlocks was associated with the likelihood of a firm engaging in merger activity during the 1980s.

Interlocks may not be useful in predicting every significant form of corporate activity, nor have they always proven to be as powerful as predictors as early adherents of their study prophesied back in the 1970s. But it is incorrect to claim that interlocks "just do not predict much that is interesting in the strategic choices of firms" (1992:304). The evidence that they do predict such choices is overwhelming.

The second criticism of interlock research, that interlock analyses fail to capture the richness and complexity of board dynamics and interfirm relations, has been made by several analysts. Among the most powerful statements have been those by Hirsch (1982), Stinchcombe (1990), Davis & Powell (1992), and Pettigrew (1992).

Although business researchers such as Mace (1971) and Lorsch & MacIver (1989) have conducted extensive interviews with corporate directors, Hirsch (1982) and Useem (1984) are, to my knowledge, the only sociologists who have systematically interviewed board members. Pettigrew & McNulty (1995) have begun systematic interviews with directors in large British firms. All three of these latter studies have addressed the topic of interlocks, but Hirsch in particular was sharply critical of interlock analysis. Hirsch asked board members about both the role of interlocks and the positions of bankers on boards. He found in almost every case that directors considered their own power to be extremely limited, that interlocks were of limited significance for the organizations involved, and that bankers were viewed as wielding no particular influence as outside directors. Even actions as potentially benign as business transactions with a firm's interlock partners were assiduously avoided, according to Hirsch, because directors feared being cited by the Securities and Exchange Commission for conflicts of interest.

Hirsch's study raises several interesting questions. First, his finding of virtual unanimity on every issue raises the prospect that board members were conveying generalized norms about appropriate board behavior rather than more probing insights into the details of their activities. Second, even if Hirsch's respondents were entirely sincere, informant reports of their own power are notoriously unreliable. JP Morgan denied before the Pujo Committee that he held a disproportionate share of power within the American business world. David Rockefeller denied to Bill Moyers that he was any more powerful than the average American. It is possible to concede the difficulty of defining power in an objective manner yet still suggest that subjective reports are equally invalid. Third, results from a recent study (Mizruchi et al 1993) reveal that it may be incorrect to accept at face value board members' claims that they rarely do business with the firms with which they are interlocked. Among Fortune 500 US manufacturing firms in 1980 (the approximate period of Hirsch's interviews), nearly half (48.6%) of the cases in which representatives of a financial institution sat on the board of a manufacturing firm were accompanied by a business transaction between the firms. Hirsch is correct that there are numerous reasons that outside directors are appointed to boards and that these reasons often have little to do with specific relations between the organizations involved. But as we have seen, interlocks may have consequences for organizational behavior regardless of whether they were established for primarily organizational purposes.

Stinchcombe's (1990) primary criticism involves concern about what interlock ties actually represent. Because so little is known about the actual operation of interlocks, he suggests that we study "what flows across the links, who decides on those flows in the light of what interests, and what collective or corporate action flows from the organization of links, in order to make sense of intercorporate relations" (1990:381).[8]

This point is made more forcefully by Pettigrew (1992), whose critique is as much a commentary on quantitative research in general as on interlock research in particular. Criticisms of quantitative work for failing to capture the

---

[8]This critique by Stinchcombe was presented in a review of Mizruchi & Schwartz (1987). See Mizruchi & Schwartz (1991) for a reply to Stinchcombe's review.

complexity of human behavior have been around for decades, and it is not surprising that interlock research would be subjected to them. Pettigrew understates the extent to which interlock studies have addressed the "So what?" question, in part because he draws a distinction between board composition studies, which include several of those cited above, and interlock research: Despite their differing orientations and rhetoric, the two bodies of literature touch on many of the same issues. He also understates the findings on the consequences of ties even within explicit interlock analyses. But Pettigrew goes beyond mere restatement of these time-worn criticisms. In proposing detailed study of the selection and behavior of directors and top managers, Pettigrew suggests an emphasis on several levels of analysis, including the internal firm, interfirm, and societal levels, and a focus on the historical contexts that frame organizational decision-making (see Pettigrew 1990 for an illustration of how to conduct such an analysis and Pettigrew & McNulty 1995 for an example).

In making this argument, Pettigrew is treading on much the same ground as contemporary historical sociologists (Abbott 1992, Griffin 1993, for example) who are advocating the abandonment of a focus on variables for a refocus on historical narratives. Sociologists and organizational researchers have operated for several decades primarily within a mode of analysis that assumes that social behavior can be captured in terms of codifications (variables) that capture patterns of activities. Interlocks, one such codification, can be used to "explain" a firm's participation in mergers or the extent to which firms contribute to the same political candidates. Critics of variable analyses acknowledge that there are implicit narratives behind variable-based accounts (Abbott 1992:54–58). In fact, when one examines the development of variable-based hypotheses in academic journals, one sees descriptions of the social processes that the variables are designed to represent. Claims that these variables tend to be "decontextualized" in much sociological research may be true, but estimation approaches are increasingly available to capture the changing social context. Employing time-dependent covariates, it is possible to identify the changing nature of "effects," or processes, over time (Isaac & Griffin 1989). And an increasing number of approaches are available to handle statistically the fact that observations in social groups are often not independent (Krackhardt 1988, Mizruchi 1992: Ch. 5).

What Abbott and others are calling for is not only more attention to narrative, a detailed description of the processes that variables are presumed to capture, but also to systematic means of coding patterns in the narratives to permit generalization. Interlock research is ready for this kind of analysis. In fact, it ultimately will require it. The problem up to this point has been access to data on the operation of corporate boards. A small but growing number of scholars in both the United Kingdom and the United States have conducted interviews with board members. It will be necessary for researchers in a variety of national settings to gain similar access to a wide range of organizations if we are to build a systematic process model of interlocks. In the meantime, researchers working within traditional paradigms will continue to assemble evidence that interlocks predict important organizational phenomena. One can ask for more, but one cannot fail to be impressed with what has been achieved.

ACKNOWLEDGMENTS

This research was supported by two grants from the National Science Foundation (a Presidential Young Investigator Award, SES-9196148, and research grant SBR-9320930) as well as grants from the Dean's Office of the Horace H. Rackham School of Graduate Studies, the Office of the Vice President for Research, and the Dean's Office of the College of Literature, Science, and the Arts, all at the University of Michigan. I would like to thank Don Palmer and Barry Staw for their detailed comments on an earlier draft of this chapter.

Literature Cited

Abbott A. 1992. What do cases do? Some notes on activity in sociological analysis. In *What Is A Case?*, ed. CC Ragin, HS Becker, pp. 53–82. New York: Cambridge Univ. Press

Aldrich HE. 1979. *Organizations and Environments.* Englewood Cliffs, NJ: Prentice-Hall

Allen MP. 1974. The structure of interorganizational elite cooptation: interlocking corporate directorates. *Am. Sociol. Rev.* 39:393–406

Baker WE, Faulkner RR. 1993. The social organization of conspiracy: illegal networks in the heavy electrical equipment industry. *Am. Sociol. Rev.* 58:837–60

Baysinger BD, Butler HD. 1985. Corporate governance and the board of directors: performance effects of changes in board composition. *J. Law Econ. Org.* 1:101–24

Bearden J, Atwood W, Freitag P, Hendricks C, Mintz B, Schwartz M. 1975. *The nature and extent of bank centrality in corporate networks.* Pres. at Annu. Meet. Am. Sociol. Assoc. San Francisco

Berkowitz SD, Carrington P, Kotowitz Y, Waverman L. 1979. The determination of enterprise groupings through combined ownership and directorship ties. *Soc. Netw.* 1:391–413

Berle AA, Means GC. [1932] 1968. *The Modern Corporation and Private Property.* New York: Harcourt, Brace, & World

Boeker W, Goodstein J. 1991. Organizational performance and adaptation: effects of environment and performance on changes in board composition. *Acad. Man. J.* 34:805–26

Bunting D. 1976. Corporate interlocking. Part III. Interlocks and return on investment. *Directors & Boards 1* (fall):4–11

Burris V. 1987. The political partisanship of American business: a study of corporate political action committees. *Am. Sociol. Rev.* 52:732–44

Burt RS. 1983. *Corporate Profits and Cooptation.* New York: Academic

Carrington PJ. 1981. *Horizontal co-optation through corporate interlocks.* PhD thesis. Dept. Sociol., Univ. Toronto

Caswell JA. 1984. An institutional perspective on corporate control and the network of interlocking directorates. *J. Econ. Iss.* 18:619–26

Clawson D, Neustadtl A. 1989. Interlocks PACs, and corporate conservatism. *Am. J. Sociol.* 94:749–73

Clawson D, Neustadtl A, Scott D. 1992. *Money Talks: Corporate PACs and Political Influence.* New York: Basic

Cochran PL, Wood RA, Jones TB. 1985. The composition of boards of directors and incidence of golden parachutes. *Acad. Man. J.* 28:664–71

D'Aveni RA, Kesner IF. 1993. Top managerial prestige, power, and tender offer response: a study of elite social networks and target firm cooperation during takeovers. *Org. Sci.* 4:123–51

Davis GF. 1991. Agents without principles? The spread of the poison pill through the intercorporate network. *Admin. Sci. Q.* 36:583–613

Davis GF. 1993. Who gets ahead in the market for corporate directors: the political economy of multiple board memberships. *Acad. Man. Best Papers Proc.*:202–206

Davis GF. 1994. The interlock network as a self-reproducing social structure. Unpublished manuscript, Kellogg Grad. Sch. Man., Northwestern Univ.

Davis GF, Powell WW. 1992. Organization-environment relations. In *Handbook of Industrial and Organizational Psychology*, ed. M Dunnette, pp. 315–75. Palo Alto: Consulting Psychol. 2nd ed.

Davis GF, Stout SK. 1992. Organization theory and the market for corporate control: a dynamic analysis of the characteristics of large takeover targets, 1980–1990. *Admin. Sci. Q.* 37:605–33

DiMaggio PJ, Powell WW. 1983. The iron cage revisited: institutional isomorphism and collective rationality in organizational fields. *Am. Sociol. Rev.* 48:147–60

Domhoff GW. 1967. *Who Rules America?* Englewood Cliffs, NJ: Prentice-Hall

Dooley PC. 1969. The interlocking directorate. *Am. Econ. Rev.* 59:314–23

Eisenhardt KM. 1989. Agency theory: an assessment and review. *Acad. Man. Rev.* 14:57–74

Fligstein N, Brantley P. 1992. Bank control, owner control, or organizational dynamics: Who controls the large modern corporation? *Am. J. Sociol.* 98:280–307

Fligstein N, Markowitz L. 1993. Financial reorganization of American corporations in the 1980s. In *Sociology and the Public Agenda,* ed. WJ Wilson, pp. 185–206. Newbury Park, CA: Sage

Galaskiewicz J, Wasserman S, Rauschenbach B, Bielefeld W, Mullaney P. 1985. The influence of corporate power, social status, and market position on corporate interlocks in a regional market. *Soc. Forc.* 64:403–31

Gerlach ML. 1992. *Alliance Capitalism: The Social Organization of Japanese Business.* Berkeley: Univ. Calif. Press

Goodstein J, Boeker W. 1991. Turbulence at the top: a new perspective on governance structure changes and strategic change. *Acad. Man. J.* 34:306–30

Granovetter M. 1985. Economic action and social structure: the problem of embeddedness. *Am. J. Sociol.* 91:481–510

Griffin LJ. 1993. Narrative, event-structure analysis, and causal interpretation in historical sociology. *Am. J. Sociol.* 98:1094–133

Gulati R. 1995. Social structure and alliance formation patterns: a longitudinal analysis. *Admin. Sci. Q.* 40:619–52

Haunschild PR. 1993. Interorganizational imitation: the impact of interlocks on corporate acquisition activity. *Admin. Sci. Q.* 38:564–92

Herman ES. 1981. *Corporate Control, Corporate Power.* New York: Cambridge Univ. Press

Hirsch PM. 1982. *Network data versus personal accounts: the normative culture of interlocking directorates.* Pres. Annu. Meet. Am. Sociol. Assoc., San Francisco

Isaac LW, Griffin LJ. 1989. Ahistoricism in time-series analysis of historical process: critique, redirection, and illustrations from U.S. labor history. *Am. Sociol. Rev.* 54:873–90

James DR, Soref M. 1981. Profit constraints on managerial autonomy: managerial theory and the unmaking of the corporation president. *Am. Sociol. Rev.* 46:1–18

Koenig T. 1979. *Interlocking directorates among the largest American corporations and their significance for corporate political activity.* PhD thesis. Dept. Sociol., Univ. Calif., Santa Barbara

Koenig T, Gogel R, Sonquist J. 1979. Models of the significance of interlocking corporate directorates. *Am. J. Econ. & Sociol.* 38:173–86

Kosnik RD. 1987. Greenmail: a study of board performance in corporate governance. *Admin. Sci. Q.* 32:163–85

Kosnik RD. 1990. Effects of board demography and directors' incentives on corporate greenmail decisions. *Acad. Man. J.* 33:129–50

Krackhardt D. 1988. Predicting with networks: nonparametric multiple regression analysis of dyadic data. *Soc. Netw.* 10:359–81

Lang JR, Lockhart DE. 1990. Increased environmental uncertainty and changes in board linkage patterns. *Acad. Man. J.* 33:106–28

Levine JH. 1972. The sphere of influence. *Am. Sociol. Rev.* 37:14–27

Lorsch JW, MacIver E. 1989. *Pawns and Potentates: The Reality of America's Corporate Boards.* Boston: Harvard Bus. Sch.

Mace ML. 1971. *Directors: Myth and Reality.* Boston: Harvard Bus. Sch.

Mariolis P. 1975. Interlocking directorates and control of corporations: the theory of bank control. *Soc. Sci. Q.* 56:425–39

Meeusen W, Cuyvers L. 1985. The interaction between interlocking directorships and the economic behaviour of companies. In *Networks of Corporate Power,* ed. FN Stokman, R Ziegler, J Scott, pp. 45–72. Cambridge, England: Polity

Mills CW. 1956. *The Power Elite.* New York: Oxford Univ. Press

Mintz B, Schwartz M. 1981. Interlocking directorates and interest group formation. *Am. Sociol. Rev.* 46:851–69

Mintz B, Schwartz M. 1985. *The Power Structure of American Business.* Chicago: Univ. Chicago Press

Mizruchi MS. 1982. *The American Corporate Network: 1904–1974.* Beverly Hills: Sage

Mizruchi MS. 1983. Who controls whom? An examination of the relation between management and boards of directors in large American corporations. *Acad. Man. Rev.* 8:426–35

Mizruchi MS. 1989. Similarity of political behavior among large American corporations. *Am. J. Sociol.* 95:401–24

Mizruchi MS. 1990. Determinants of political opposition among large American corporations. *Soc. Forc.* 68:1065–88

Mizruchi MS. 1992. *The Structure of Corporate Political Action.* Cambridge: Harvard Univ. Press

Mizruchi MS, Koenig T. 1986. Economic sources of corporate political consensus: an examination of interindustry relations. *Am. Sociol. Rev.* 51:482–91

Mizruchi MS, Potts BB, Allison DW. 1993. *Interlocking directorates and business transactions: new evidence on an old question.* Pres. Annu. Meet. Am. Soc. Assoc., Miami Beach

Mizruchi MS, Schwartz M. 1987. *Intercorporate Relations: The Structural Analysis of Business.* New York: Cambridge Univ. Press

Mizruchi MS, Schwartz M. 1991. Comment on review of *Intercorporate Relations. Cont. Sociol.* 20:168–69

Mizruchi MS, Stearns LB. 1988. A longitudinal study of the formation of interlocking directorates. *Admin. Sci. Q.* 33:194–210

Mizruchi MS, Stearns LB. 1994. A longitudinal study of borrowing by large American corporations. *Admin. Sci. Q.* 39:118–40

Ornstein MD. 1980. Assessing the meaning of corporate interlocks: Canadian evidence. *Soc. Sci. Res.* 9:287–306

Ornstein MD. 1984. Interlocking directorates in Canada: intercorporate or class alliance? *Admin. Sci. Q.* 29:210–31

Palmer D. 1983. Broken ties: interlocking directorates and intercorporate coordination. *Admin. Sci. Q.* 28:40–55

Palmer D, Barber BM, Zhou X, Soysal Y. 1995. The friendly and predatory acquisition of large U.S. corporations in the 1960s: the other contested terrain. *Am. Sociol. Rev.* 60:469–99

Palmer D, Friedland R, Singh JV. 1986. The ties that bind: organizational and class bases of stability in a corporate interlock network. *Am. Sociol. Rev.* 51:781–96

Palmer DA, Jennings PD, Zhou X. 1993. Late adoption of the multidivisional form by large U.S. corporations: institutional, political, and economic accounts. *Admin. Sci. Q.* 38:100–31

Parsons T. 1960. *Structure and Process in Modern Societies.* Glencoe, IL: Free

Pennings JM. 1980. *Interlocking Directorates.* San Francisco: Jossey-Bass

Pettigrew AM. 1990. Longitudinal field research on change: theory and practice. *Org. Sci.* 1:267–92

Pettigrew AM. 1992. On studying managerial elites. *Strat. Man. J.* 13:163–82

Pettigrew AM, McNulty T. 1995. *Power and influence in and around the boardroom.* Paper pres. Annu. Meet. Acad. Manage., Vancouver

Pfeffer J. 1972. Size and composition of corporate boards of directors: the organization and its environment. *Admin. Sci. Q.* 17:218–28

Pfeffer J. 1987. A resource dependence perspective on intercorporate relations. In *Intercorporate Relations: The Structural Analysis of Business,* ed. MS Mizruchi, M Schwartz, pp. 25–55. New York: Cambridge Univ. Press

Pfeffer J, Salancik GR. 1978. *The External Control of Organizations: A Resource Dependence Perspective.* New York: Harper & Row

Ratcliff RE. 1980. Banks and corporate lending: an analysis of the impact of the internal structure of the capitalist class on the lending behavior of banks. *Am. Sociol. Rev.* 45:553–70

Richardson RJ. 1987. Directorship interlocks and corporate profitability. *Admin. Sci. Q.* 32:367–86

Scott JP, Griff C. 1984. *Directors of Industry.* Cambridge, England: Polity

Scott WR. 1992. *Organizations: Rational, Natural, and Open Systems.* Englewood Cliffs, NJ: Prentice-Hall. 3rd ed.

Selznick P. 1949. *TVA and the Grass Roots.* New York: Harper & Row

Selznick P. 1957. *Leadership in Administration.* New York: Harper & Row

Sheard P. 1993. *An analysis of the supply of executives by banks to boards of large Japanese firms.* Pres. Inst. Asian Res. Conf. on Netw. Action & Org. in Japan, Univ. Br. Columbia

Singh H, Harianto F. 1989. Management-board relationships, takeover risk, and the adoption of golden parachutes. *Acad. Manage. J.* 32:7–24

Sonquist JA, Koenig T. 1975. Interlocking directorates in the top U.S. corporations: a graph theory approach. *Insurg. Sociol.* 5:196–229

Stearns LB, Mizruchi MS. 1986. Broken-tie reconstitution and the functions of interorganizational interlocks: a reexamination. *Admin. Sci. Q.* 31:522–38

Stearns LB, Mizruchi MS. 1993a. Corporate financing: economic and social aspects. In *Explorations in Economic Sociology,* ed. R Swedberg, pp. 279–307. New York: Russell Sage Found.

Stearns LB, Mizruchi MS. 1993b. Board composition and corporate financing: the impact of financial institution representation on borrowing. *Acad. Manage. J.* 36:603–18

Stiglitz JE. 1985. Credit markets and the control of capital. *J. Mon. Cred. Bank.* 17:133–52

Stinchcombe AL. 1990. Weak structural data. *Cont. Sociol.* 19:380–82

Stokman FN, Van der Knoop J, Wasseur FW. 1988. Interlocks in the Netherlands: stability and careers in the period 1960–1980. *Soc. Netw.* 10:183–208

Stokman FN, Ziegler R, Scott J. 1985. *Networks of Corporate Power.* Cambridge, England: Polity

Thompson JD, McEwen WJ. 1959. Organizational goals and environment: goal-setting as an interaction process. *Am. Sociol. Rev.* 23:23–31

Useem M. 1979. The social organization of the American business elite and participation of corporation directors in the governance of American institutions. *Am. Sociol. Rev.* 44:553–72

Useem M. 1984. *The Inner Circle.* New York: Oxford Univ. Press

Uzzi BD. 1996. The sources and consequences of embeddedness for the economic performance of organizations: the network effect. *Am. Sociol. Rev.* In press

Wade J, O'Reilly CA III, Chandratat I. 1990. Golden parachutes: CEOs and the exercise of social influence. *Admin. Sci. Q.* 587–603

Westphal JD, Zajac EJ. 1995. Who shall govern? CEO/board power, demographic similarity, and new director selection. *Admin. Sci. Q.* 40:60–83

Zajac EJ. 1988. Interlocking directorates as an interorganizational strategy. *Acad. Manage. J.* 31:428–38

Zeitlin M. 1974. Corporate ownership and control: the large corporation and the capitalist class. *Am. J. Sociol.* 79:1073–119

Zeitlin M. 1976. On class theory of the large corporation: response to Allen. *Am. J. Sociol.* 81:894–904

Ziegler R. 1984. Das netz der personen- und kapitalverflechtungen deutscher und osterreichischer virtschaftsunternehmen. *Kolner Zeitschrift fur Soziologie und Sozial-Psychologie* 36:585–614

Annu. Rev. Sociol. 1996. 22:299–322

THE DIVISION OF HOUSEHOLD LABOR

Beth Anne Shelton

Department of Sociology and Anthropology, University of Texas at Arlington, Arlington, Texas 76019

Daphne John

Department of Sociology, Oberlin College, Oberlin, Ohio 44074

KEY WORDS: housework, gender, time use, measurement

ABSTRACT

In this chapter we review research on the division of household labor and its consequences. The review summarizes research focused on issues of measurement, including research on methods of gathering data on housework time and time use in general and discussions of various ways to operationalize the division of household labor. Some attention is paid to historical and theoretical work on housework and women's responsibility for it in particular, followed by a more detailed discussion of current empirical approaches to explaining the division of household labor as well as criticisms of these approaches. Finally, we review research that examines the consequences of the division of household labor, focusing on those studies that examine its impact on labor force participation and wages, marital and family satisfaction, psychological well-being, and perceptions of fairness.

INTRODUCTION

The most notable characteristic of the current division of household labor is that, whether employed or not, women continue to do the majority of housework (Brines 1993, Marini & Shelton 1993, Robinson 1988). Current estimates are that men do between 20% (Robinson 1988) and 35% (Presser 1994) of the housework. In spite of disagreement over the significance of change in the division of household labor, the nature of the recent shifts is clear. Women still do the majority of housework, but they are doing less and their spouses more than in the past. In this paper, we review the central issues and questions that arise in research on the division of household labor. In brief, these issues pertain to how housework can and should be measured, what factors, either historical or contemporary, can help us understand the current division of household labor and variation in it, and finally, the consequences of the unequal division of household labor.

MEASUREMENT

Household labor is defined in a variety of ways and even when defined in a consistent way, the precise method of measurement varies from study to study. Housework is rarely defined explicitly in a study except for an indication of whether childcare is included in its definition. Nevertheless, a fairly consistent conceptualization has emerged in the literature. Housework most often refers to unpaid work done to maintain family members and/or a home. As such, emotion work and other "invisible" types of work are typically excluded from analysis, although some studies mention the importance of this invisible labor. In most studies, the definition of housework must be inferred from the way it is measured.

Types of Instruments

TIME DIARIES   One method used to gather information about housework time is the time diary (Harvey 1993). In a time diary, the respondent (and sometimes the spouse/partner) is asked to complete a diary accounting for his/her time for a 24-hour period. Examples of studies of this type are the well-known surveys of time use carried out by the Survey Research Center at the University of Michigan in 1965–1966, 1975–1976, and 1981, and by the Survey Research Center at the University of Maryland in 1985.

Time diaries differ in a variety of ways including whether respondents complete the diary during the day for which data are being collected or whether they complete a diary retrospectively. Retrospective diaries completed one day later are, compared to ongoing diaries, of almost equal value (Robinson 1985), and accurate data about weekends can be obtained up to seven days later (Kalton 1985). Retrospective diaries are less expensive to use since only one visit by an interviewer is required.

Time diaries are problematic to the extent that the diary day is not representative of the general pattern of activities during a day. This potential problem is handled in most studies by ensuring that different days of the week are represented (Robinson 1977, Sanik 1981, Walker & Woods 1976) and, in some cases, that data are collected in different seasons of the year (Hill 1985). In spite of these efforts, it is difficult to obtain data for times around major holidays (Lyberg 1989).

The reliability and validity of time diaries have been assessed by comparing respondents' and spouses' accounts of when an activity occurred (Juster 1985), as well as by comparing activities recorded in time diaries with those occurring when respondents reported their activity at the signal of a beeper set to go off randomly (Robinson 1985). These studies report correlations between estimates obtained by different methods of between .68 and .81.

Although Harvey (1993) reports that the time diary method is relatively robust with respect to minor variations in format, others find that questionnaire format has an effect on responses (Geurts & De Ree 1993). Another limitation of time diaries, and other methods of gathering data about time use, is the difficulty in dealing with tasks performed simultaneously (Nichols 1980, Warner 1986).

DIRECT QUESTIONS   Direct questions about household labor time range from questions that have respondents estimate their usual time spent on a list of household activities (National Survey of Families & Households 1987) to those that have respondents indicate how much time they usually spend on "housework" (Panel Study of Income Dynamics 1976, Quality of Employment Survey 1977). There are few studies that compare time-diary to direct-question data, but those that do find that direct questions typically produce higher time estimates than time diary questions (Juster & Stafford 1991, Niemi 1993), especially for activities that occur frequently (Marini & Shelton 1993). For activities that occur infrequently, direct questions produce lower estimates, possibly because a longer period of recall is required (Hill 1985). Marini & Shelton (1993) compare data from the NSFH and from the Michigan Survey of Time Use (STU) and find that, in general, the NSFH estimates, based on direct questions, result in higher time estimates, but slightly lower estimates of task segregation. In general, the quality of both direct-question and time-diary measures is improved by the use of narrowly defined tasks.

OTHER MEASURES   Some researchers focus on who performs specific tasks rather than how much time is spent on those tasks (Berk & Berk 1978). In a similar method, Blair & Lichter (1991) assess the amount of task segregation by calculating an index of segregation based on the Index of Dissimilarity. This measure assesses gender differences in how women and men allocate their housework time among tasks. Rather than using an estimate of time expenditures, some studies use measures that indicate only the proportion of housework done by the husband or wife (Warner 1986). Proportional measures usually have respondents indicate whether the wife always, wife usually, both wife and husband, husband usually or husband always does a particular household task (Blood & Wolfe 1960, Huber & Spitze 1983, Stafford et al 1977, Ferree 1991), but some researchers calculate proportional measures from time estimates (Ishii-Kuntz & Coltrane 1992a,b, Peters & Haldeman 1987). Finally, some researchers have respondents indicate who is responsible for household tasks, rather than only who performs the tasks (Geerken & Gove 1983), thus allowing some assessment of management responsibility.

In addition to differences in how housework is measured, who provides the information about housework time varies as well. Some studies have one member of a household provide estimates of all household members' housework time, while others have each member of the household, or each adult member, provide an estimate of their time expenditures. Respondents typically overestimate their own housework time and underestimate the time spent by other household members (Marini & Shelton 1993), leading some researchers to use averages of respondent and spouse estimates of time when possible (Marini & Shelton 1993).

The variety of ways housework is measured both complicates any assessment of the literature and indicates the need for development of reliable measures of housework. Up to this point, most researchers are left to use whatever measures of housework are available and then must contend with the problems this poses when comparing their results to other studies.

HISTORICAL TREATMENTS

Historical discussions of household labor range from detailed documentation of changes in how housework is defined and how it has been affected by technological innovations (Bose et al 1984, Cowan 1983, Strasser 1982) to analyses of the impact of industrialization on the distribution of housework.

Technological developments and the mass production of household goods led to the increased availability and use of what are often called laborsaving devices (Bose 1979, Bose et al 1984, Day 1992, Jackson 1992, Strasser 1982). Some argue that such technology homogenized household labor by standardizing what was expected in terms of household labor across social class, although some maintain these standards by hiring outside help (Cowan 1983, Glenn 1992, Jackson 1992, Schor 1991, Strasser 1982). Other research suggests that as women were drawn into the paid labor force, their time available for housework decreased, but technological innovations allowed them to maintain their housework standards even though they were employed (Bose 1979, Bose et al 1984, Day 1992). Still others emphasize how innovations in household technologies served to reallocate women's time to household labor in the form of new tasks that needed to be done (e.g. tub and toilet cleaning) or into upholding higher household standards (e.g. more complicated meals, cleaner carpets) (Cowan 1983, Jackson 1992, McGaw 1982, Schor 1991). In fact, it did both; new household technologies increased women's workload in some areas but reduced the time required to complete other tasks (e.g. sew a garment). Although it is not clear that new household technologies allowed women to enter the paid labor force, they were compatible with their labor force participation.

Industrialization, more generally, has been linked to the separation of paid and unpaid work and the development of the role of "housewife" (Ahlander & Bahr 1995, Bourke 1994, Lopata 1993, Valadez & Clignet 1984) as well as to women's dependence on men through their reliance on their husbands' wages (Jackson 1992, Lamphere 1989, Lopata 1993). Bourke (1994) suggests that increased wages in England in the late nineteenth century encouraged many women to remain in the household instead of entering the paid labor force, thus reinforcing the role of housewife.

EXPLANATIONS FOR THE DIVISION OF HOUSEHOLD LABOR

Marxist/Socialist Feminism

In their analyses of household labor and women's responsibility for it, socialist feminists argue that patriarchy is causally related to the division of labor, with men benefiting, directly and indirectly, from the control of women's labor (Folbre & Hartmann 1989, Hartmann 1979, 1981, Sokoloff 1980). In addition, Delphy (1977) argues that women's relations to men in the household determine not only the nature of their participation in the labor market, but their class position as well (see also Jackson 1992).

Others see capitalism rather than patriarchy as directly related to the division of household labor and to women's position in the family more generally, although these Marxist feminist approaches differ in the way they conceptualize the links between patriarchy and capitalism (Walby 1986, Jaggar 1988). Marxist feminists argue that the requirements of capitalism determine women's oppression (Shelton & Agger 1993, Smith 1983, Vogel 1983), although there is significant disagreement over whether household labor produces surplus value (James & Dalla Costa 1973, Kain 1993, Seccombe 1974).

For the most part, marxist and socialist feminist approaches to understanding the division of household labor have not led to empirical tests of their usefulness, but there are several exceptions. Hardesty & Bokemeier (1989) and Calasanti & Bailey (1991) try to test aspects of the socialist feminist approach to understanding the division of household labor, while Meissner et al (1975) use what they call a *dependent labor model* to account for the fact that women's employment results in a cumulation of demands on them rather than in change in their husbands' housework time. All of these studies characterize the division of household labor as at least partly reflecting structural factors, but the method of testing the influence of these factors is not consistent.

Relative Resource, Time Availability, and Ideology

The empirical research on the division of household labor is dominated by quantitative studies that use one or more of three explanations commonly referred to as the relative resources, time constraints, and ideology/sex role explanations (Godwin 1991, Ross 1987, Shelton 1992).

The relative resources explanation builds on the work of Blood & Wolfe (1960) and conceptualizes the division of housework as reflecting the resources men and women bring to relationships. According to this explanation, the individual with the most resources (education, earnings, occupational prestige) uses those resources to negotiate his/her way out of housework (Brines 1993). This approach assumes that housework is viewed negatively by both women and men and that they are therefore motivated to reduce their share of it.

Evaluations of this explanation yield fairly consistent results, although it is operationalized in a variety of ways. In studies of the impact of earnings on the division of household labor, most researchers find that the smaller the gap between husbands' and wives' earnings the more equal the division of household labor (Blair & Lichter 1991, Brayfield 1992, Kamo 1988, 1991, 1994, Presser 1994, Ross 1987, Shelton & John 1993a) although some argue that this effect, while statistically significant, is small (Goldscheider & Waite 1991). Those studies that assess the effect of earnings on men's and women's housework time separately typically find that earnings have a greater effect on women's housework time than on men's. Brines (1994) interprets this difference in the effect of earnings on women's and men's housework time as support for a gender display interpretation (see page 312). Thus, men who are economically dependent on their wives compensate by "adopting gender-traditional behaviors elsewhere" (Brines 1994: p. 664) (e.g. housework).

Educational attainment also is used as a measure of power or resources. The majority of studies that incorporate education into their analyses use absolute measures of women's and men's educational levels (Berardo et al 1987, Bergen 1991, Brayfield 1992, Calasanti & Bailey 1991, Hardesty & Bokemeier 1989, Kamo 1988, 1991, 1994, Ross 1987, Spitze 1986), although several other studies use relative measures of education (Coverman 1985, Ishii-Kuntz & Coltrane 1992b, Deutsch et al 1993), sometimes in combination with absolute measures (Blair & Lichter 1991, Presser 1994). Most researchers find that men's educational level is positively associated with their participation in housework

(Berardo et al 1987, Bergen 1991, Brayfield 1992, Brines 1993, Haddad 1994, Hardesty & Bokemeier 1989, Kamo 1988, Presser 1994, South & Spitze 1994) and negatively associated with their spouse's or partner's household labor time (Kamo 1991, Shelton & John 1993a). These results are inconsistent with the predictions of the relative resource approach and are sometimes interpreted as indicating the relationship between education and ideology (Coverman 1985, Farkas 1976, Presser 1994) or subculture (Huber & Spitze 1983). Several studies find no association between men's education and housework time (Kamo 1991, McAllister 1990) or that the effect disappears once gender ideology measures are included (Kamo 1994).

The findings on the effect of women's education on the division of household labor generally indicate that women's educational level is negatively associated with their household labor time (Berardo et al 1987, Bergen 1991, Brines 1993, Shelton & John 1993a, South & Spitze 1994) and with the level of task segregation (Blair & Lichter 1991). Although these findings are consistent with the relative resources explanation, they also are consistent with the argument that better educated women hold more egalitarian sex role attitudes and thus do less housework, while better educated men do more (Huber & Spitze 1983).

Occupational prestige, another measure of resources, is less consistently associated with housework time than are earnings or education level in the few models that include it. As predicted by the relative resource model, some researchers report that men's occupational status is negatively associated with their housework time (McAllister 1990), but more find that it is either positively associated with their housework time (Berk & Berk 1978, Deutsch et al 1993) or not associated with it (Aytac 1990, Coverman 1985). Aytac (1990) finds that men whose wives are decision-makers on the job are more likely to share household labor than are men whose wives do not have such authority on the job. Presser (1994) reports that both women and men in professional couples spend less time on housework than women and men in other types of couples.

Most studies find no association between women's occupational status and their household labor time (Calasanti & Bailey 1991, McAllister 1990). Hardesty & Bokemeier (1989) operationalize occupations as male or female dominated and find no association between occupation and housework time for women, but Brayfield's (1992) study reveals that a woman's workplace authority relative to her husband is negatively associated with her housework time for women in higher supervisory positions, but not for women with lower supervisory positions. Studies of the effect of social class on the division of household labor typically find little or no effect of social class (Gregson & Lowe 1993, Wright et al 1992), further suggesting that household labor and standards have been homogenized.

Thus, the most support for the relative resources explanation derives from the association between earnings and housework time, although the gender difference in the association cannot be accounted for in the relative resource model. In addition, the association between earnings and housework time may also reflect households' attempts to distribute housework efficiently (Becker 1981, 1985).

According to the ideology explanation, women and men with more egalitarian attitudes will have a more equal division of household labor than those with more traditional attitudes. Specifically, men with more traditional sex role attitudes are expected to spend less time on housework than those with less traditional attitudes (Huber & Spitze 1983), while the reverse is expected for women (Brayfield 1992). The findings of most studies are consistent with these expectations, although the strength of the association between attitudes and housework time usually is weak.

Most studies find that the more egalitarian men's gender role attitudes, the more equal the division of household labor, but they typically use proportional measures of men's share of housework (Blair & Lichter 1991, Kamo 1988, 1994, Presser 1994, Ross 1987). The results are not completely consistent, however. Brayfield (1992) reports that men's attitudes about whether housework should be shared when both husband and wife are employed full-time are not associated with their share of housework, but she uses only one item to assess attitudes, compared to others who use multiple indicators of attitudes (Blair & Lichter 1991, Kamo 1988, Presser 1994, Ross 1987). To the extent that there is an association between men's gender role attitudes and their proportional share of housework, it is most likely due to its effect on their wives' housework time (Kamo 1991, Shelton & John 1993a, Presser 1994).

Fewer studies find an association between women's gender role attitudes and the division of household labor, but those that do find that women with more egalitarian attitudes spend less time on housework (Brayfield 1992, Presser 1994) and experience less task segregation (see also Atkinson & Huston 1984, Gunter & Gunter 1990). However, a number of other researchers find no effect of women's gender role attitudes on their housework time (Ross 1987, Shelton & John 1993a).

Although gender role attitudes are measured in a variety of ways, most studies indicate that men's attitudes are more strongly associated with the division of household labor than are women's, but that attitudes do not account for very much of the variation in the division of household labor. Those studies that find no association between attitudes and the division of household labor typically have weak measures of attitudes (Shelton & John 1993a) or housework (Ross 1987). Researchers with time estimates of housework and multiple indicators of gender role attitudes usually report an association between them.

The time availability (Hiller 1984), demand/response capability (Coverman 1985), and the situational view (England & Farkas 1986) refer to an explanation that characterizes the division of household labor as the result of women's and men's other time commitments. This explanation suggests that men and women participate in housework and childcare to the extent that there are demands on them to do so and they have available time. The most commonly used indicators of time constraints are employment and/or hours worked, presence or number of children in the household, and work schedule.

Most studies indicate that women's paid work hours are negatively associated with their housework time (Acock & Demo 1994, Almeida et al 1993, Bergen 1991, Brayfield 1992, Brines 1993, Demo & Acock 1993, Fox & Nickols 1983, Kamo 1991, Rexroat & Shehan 1987), with the level of task segregation (Blair & Lichter 1991), with contributions to male-typed tasks (Atkinson & Huston 1984) or female-typed tasks (Brayfield 1992). Nevertheless, no matter what women's paid work time, they continue to do the majority of housework (Kamo 1991, Newell 1993, Rexroat & Shehan 1987, Shelton & John 1993a).

Results of studies of the relationship between women's employment and their husband's housework time are less consistent. Nickols & Metzen (1982), in a longitudinal study, report that men increase their housework time when their wives increase their time spent in paid work. Several other studies also report that women's work hours are positively associated with men's housework time (Blair & Lichter 1991, Brines 1993), but more often with men's proportional share of housework (Barnett & Baruch 1987, Ishii-Kuntz & Coltrane 1992a, Kamo 1988, Rexroat & Shehan 1987, Ross 1987). Atkinson & Huston (1984) find that when women spend more time than their husbands in paid labor, husbands do more female-typed tasks, but Brayfield (1992) finds no association between relative work hours and men's housework time. Other studies find weak, indirect, or nonsignificant associations between women's employment and men's housework time (Kamo 1991, Levant et al 1987, Shelton 1990).

A number of studies find a negative association between men's paid work hours and employment status and their participation in housework (Coltrane & Ishii-Kuntz 1992, Coverman 1985, Hardesty & Bokemeier 1989, Ishii-Kuntz & Coltrane 1992b, Kamo 1988, 1991, McAllister 1990, South & Spitze 1994), although Brines (1993) suggests that the effect may not be linear. Blair & Lichter (1991) find that men's work hours are positively associated with the extent of household task segregation. Few studies consider the relationship between men's work hours and their wives' housework time (but see Kamo 1991 and Rexroat & Shehan 1987).

Taken together, the studies usually indicate that women's paid work time is negatively associated with their housework time, resulting in a more equal

division of household labor, even in the absence of any increase in men's housework time (some studies use only proportional measures but find that the division of household labor is more equal when wives are employed (Maret &
Finlay 1984, Newell 1993, Shamir 1986, Spitze 1986). It is less clear whether
men's housework time varies by their wives' employment status or paid work
time, but if there is some increase it is smaller than the decrease in women's
housework time. Men's paid work is consistently and negatively associated
with their housework time.

Using work schedule to indicate time constraints and the ability to respond to
demands, Presser (1994) reports that men who work different hours than their
wives spend more time on housework than those who work the same hours (see
also Blair & Lichter 1991, Brayfield 1995, Kingston & Nock 1985, Wharton
1994). Pleck & Staines (1985) find that both women's and men's housework
time is positively associated with working different hours than a spouse. However, Barnett & Baruch (1987) find no association between flexibility of wife's
work schedule and husband's participation in household labor.

Similarly, some studies focus on comparisons of dual-earner and single-
earner households. Generally, these studies find that women in dual-earner
households still are responsible for the majority of household labor (Berardo
et al 1987, Bergmann 1986), and that the division is often sex-typed by task
(Coltrane 1990, Mederer 1993), although women in dual-earner households
typically have less responsibility for such tasks than do women in single-earner
households (Maret & Finlay 1984).

The effect of children on women's and men's housework time is similar to the
effect of women's employment in that children have a larger effect on women's
housework time than on men's (Gershuny & Robinson 1988, Shelton 1992).
The more children there are in a household, especially the more preschool children, the more time women, and to a lesser extent men, spend on housework
(Berardo et al 1987, Bergen 1991, Brines 1993, McAllister 1990, Presser 1994,
Shelton & John 1993a,b, South & Spitze 1994), although a few studies, often
with regional or non-US samples, find no association between number of children and women's housework time (Calasanti & Bailey 1991, Douthitt 1989,
Hiller & Philliber 1986).

Although time constraints typically account for the largest amount of variation in the division of household labor, a major problem with this explanation
is that it fails to account for differences in effects for women and men. For
example, although work schedule affects both women's and men's housework
time, the effect is different for women than for men, and this difference is unexplained by the time constraints model. The same holds true for the demands of
children. Although children affect both women's and men's housework time,

the effect is larger for women than for men. Even if women's fewer hours of paid labor fully accounted for their greater housework time, this approach fails to address why women would spend less time in paid labor. These problems as well as inconsistencies in the evaluations of both the relative resource and time constraints perspectives in particular, suggest that some other dynamic is related to how housework is divided.

Other Factors Affecting the Division of Household Labor

MARITAL STATUS   Some of the research on household labor has focused on the relationship between marital status and housework time. Married women spend significantly more time on housework than do cohabiting women (Denmark et al 1985), even after a number of factors (like number of children and paid work hours) have been taken into consideration (Shelton & John 1993a, South & Spitze 1994). While some research suggests that cohabiting men spend more time on housework than do married men (Denmark et al 1985, Kotkin 1983), most studies report no difference in men's household labor time by marital status (Shelton & John 1993a, South & Spitze 1994). Married couples have a more traditional division of household labor than do cohabiting couples (Stafford et al 1977) as well as a more segregated distribution of tasks (Blair & Lichter 1991).

Other researchers find that remarried men spend more time on housework than do men in first marriages, at least for those with biological children in the home (Ishii-Kuntz & Coltrane 1992b). Demo & Acock (1993) note that divorced and first-married mothers spend more hours per week on housework than do remarried or single women. McAllister (1990) finds that single men and women spend less time on housework than their married counterparts, although single women spend more time on housework than single men. South & Spitze (1994) report that married men and single men living with their parents spend less time on housework than do other men and that divorced and widowed men spend more time on female-typed tasks than married men.

Kurdek (1993) and Blumstein & Schwartz (1983) have examined the division of household labor among gay male and lesbian couples. Both studies suggest that although the division of household labor is unequal among both lesbian and gay male couples, more of these couples have an equal division of household labor than is the case for heterosexual couples. Patterson (1995), in a study of lesbian parents, finds that partners report an equal sharing of household tasks, although biological mothers spend more time on childcare than their partners. These studies suggest that the division of household labor reflects gender to some extent but that there are also relational dynamics at work. That is, both gender and marital status are related to housework time.

RACE AND ETHNICITY   Race and ethnicity are often used as independent variables in research on household labor, although few studies focus on racial or ethnic differences in the division of household labor, and those that do yield mixed results. Some studies, for example, conclude that African-American families are more egalitarian in their division of household labor than are white families because African-American men do a larger proportion of household labor than white men do (Ross 1987) or spend more time on housework than white men (Beckett & Smith 1981, Shelton & John 1993b). However, other researchers argue that the division of labor in the African-American family is similar to that of white families: gendered and unequal (Broman 1988, 1991, Cronkite 1977, Hossain & Roopnarine 1993, Wilson et al 1990). In an examination of attitudes about the division of labor, Cronkite (1977) finds that African-American women and men are more likely to think that women should be responsible for housework than are white women and men. Brines (1993) reports that African-American women spend less time on housework than white women (see also Beckett & Smith 1981, Maret & Finlay 1984), but Shelton & John (1993a) find no race effect for women. Wives' employment status appears to be unrelated to African-American men's housework time (Orbuch & Custer 1995). Paid work may have different meanings for African-Americans than for whites, given the long history of high labor force participation by African-American women and the economic marginalization of African-American men.

Even less is known about the division of household labor in Hispanic households. Golding (1990) finds that the division of labor in Mexican-American families is more traditional than in Anglo families but argues that education is the determining factor. Ybarra (1982) argues that it is women's employment that determines the division of household labor in Chicano families, with dual-earner families exhibiting a more egalitarian division of labor than traditional male provider families. Mirande's (1979) conclusions are similar to those from most studies on African-American families in that he suggests that Mexican-American households may appear to be more egalitarian in the division of household labor than other households, but that they are far from dividing labor equally.

Comparative studies provide insight into the variation of household labor across cultures. Several studies indicate that Japanese men spend less time on household labor than do men of other countries, including the United States (Juster & Stafford 1991, Kamo 1994). Sanchez (1994a) notes that South Korean husbands are more likely to regularly share in household labor than US, Taiwanese, Javanese, Sudanese, Indonesian, or Philippine husbands. Lapidus (1988) finds that Soviet women devote a larger percentage of their time to household labor than do Soviet men (see also Juster & Stafford 1991).

CONTRIBUTIONS OF OTHERS   There are an increasing number of studies that focus on the household labor time of children and the contributions children make to family labor. Most researchers agree that although many children do some household labor, their participation is typically occasional and their time investment small (Bird & Ratcliff 1990, Cogle & Tasker 1982, Demo & Acock 1993), although some researchers suggest that children's contributions are significant (Blair 1992a, Peters & Haldeman 1987). It is clear, however, that children's household labor varies by family type, parents' sex-role ideology, mothers' employment status, and age and sex of the child. In addition, Spitze & Ward (1995) find that African-American adult children living at home do more housework than do white adult children living at home.

Many studies conclude that children's household labor is sex-typed in the same way that adult tasks are patterned (Blair 1992a,b; Burns & Homel 1989; Cogle & Tasker 1982; White & Brinkerhoff 1981), although Hilton & Haldeman (1991) found that children's household labor is less sex segregated than that of adults. A number of studies also suggest that girls are more likely to participate in household labor and/or spend more time on housework than boys (Blair 1992b, Bloch 1987, McHale et al 1990), especially among adolescents (White & Brinkerhoff 1981), adult children (Spitze & Ward 1995) or when sibling groups are of mixed sexes (Brody & Steelman 1985). Berk & Berk (1978) find that in households where there are female children between the ages of 16 and 20, children's proportion of household labor is higher than in households with younger children (see also Bird & Ratcliff 1990), but that having boys between 16 and 20 is not associated with any increase in children's housework time.

Several studies examine children's housework by family type, although the classification of household types varies among the studies, thus making comparisons difficult. For example, Demo & Acock (1993) evaluate the variation in children's housework time among a variety of household types and find that children in households of divorced people spend more time on housework than do children in other types of families, with children living in first-marriage households doing the least housework. Other studies suggest that children in single-parent households do less housework than children in two-parent households (Hilton & Haldeman 1991, Peters & Haldeman 1987, Weisner et al 1994). Grief (1985) finds that children share more of the housework in single father families with only female children than in single father families with only male children.

A number of studies find an association between mother's employment status and children's household labor participation. Some researchers find that women's paid work hours are positively associated with children's proportional share of housework in dual-earner households (Blair 1992a) or with daughters' time spent on housework (Blair 1992b), perhaps partially accounting for the weak association between women's employment and husbands' household labor time. Benin & Edwards (1990) find that boys in dual-earner families with mothers who are employed full-time spend less time on housework than do boys in single-earner families, although the opposite is true for girls.

Housework and the Social Construction of Gender

Recently, scholars who study the division of household labor have begun to evaluate its symbolic content to understand why women remain responsible for the majority of housework (Brines 1994, Ferree 1990; see Pestello & Voydanoff 1991 for a similar discussion of the social production of family). This approach identifies gender as something that is created and recreated in interaction with others (Fenstermaker Berk 1985, Potuchek 1992, West & Zimmerman 1987) and as such, this approach provides a way to understand the overriding importance of gender in determining household labor time by conceptualizing housework as a resource through which women and men display (Brines 1994) or produce gender.

Scholars who regard gender as a social construction (Fenstermaker et al 1991, Lorber 1986) argue that housework produces both household goods and services and gender. Thus, what appears to be an irrational arrangement (if only household goods are produced) becomes rational because gender is one of the products of the division of labor. Women's time spent on housework and men's general avoidance of it produce, and sometimes transform, gender (Coltrane 1989, Connell 1985, DeVault 1991, Hochschild 1989, West & Fenstermaker 1993). Hochschild's (1989) study reveals how women and men may view their housework as an expression of their gender, while DeVault (1991) illustrates women's attempts to think of housework as nurturance and love rather than work. Thus, a social constructionist approach not only offers a framework within which the division of household labor can be understood, it also challenges some of the basic assumptions of other approaches to understanding the division of household labor. For example, Brines (1993, 1994) argues that a gender display model is supported by her analysis. Such a model can account for the nonlinear association between economic dependence and men's and women's housework time, as well as for the gender differences in the effects of economic dependence on housework time. Recent work on the social production of race, ethnicity, and/or social class offers insights into how they may also be "produced" interactionally (Hurtado 1989, West & Fenstermaker 1995) and, one could argue, through housework.

Perceptions of Housework

Those studies that address the issue of perceptions of fairness can be classified as focusing on ideological or materialist explanations (Lennon & Rosenfield

1994). Thompson (1991) argues that ideological factors determine perceptions of fairness. She argues that women will perceive the division of household labor as unfair only if they want their husbands to perform more housework, if they compare their husband's housework time to someone who spends more time on housework, and if they do not see any justification for the unequal division of housework. If women want their husbands to spend some minimal amount of time on housework and have no expectation that their housework time will be equal, they will not necessarily view an unequal division of household labor as unfair (Benin & Agostinelli 1988, Thompson 1991). Moreover, if women compare their housework time to other women's, rather than to their husband's time, they may view an unequal division of household labor as fair (Major 1994, Thompson 1991). Finally, if women see acceptable reasons for the unequal division of household labor, they will not view it as unfair (Thompson 1991), although the justifications viewed as acceptable may vary by gender (LaRossa & LaRossa 1981, McKee 1982).

Lennon & Rosenfield (1994) contend that exchange theory can best explain perceptions of fairness; the more power and resources a person has the more likely he or she is to view an unequal division of household labor as unfair. They find only partial support for their hypothesis. They find that women who would fall into poverty should they have to rely on only their own earnings are less likely to view the division of household labor as unfair, although they find no association between contribution to household earnings and perceptions of fairness (see also John et al 1995 and Major 1987 about comparison referents).

In research evaluating the association between the division of household labor and perceptions of fairness, findings are inconsistent. Blair & Johnson (1992) report that men's time spent on female-typed household tasks is the strongest predictor of women's perceptions of fairness (see also Acock & Demo 1994, Benin & Agostinelli 1988), while Lennon & Rosenfield (1994) find that it is men's proportional share of female-typed tasks. In similar research, Sanchez (1994b) and John et al (1995) find that men's housework time is significantly associated with women's and men's perceptions of fairness. Other differences emerge when comparing what division of household labor men and women are most likely to view as fair. Benin & Agostinelli (1988) argue that women want a division of household labor that favors them, and they want their husbands to spend time on traditionally female chores. Men, on the other hand, favor an equitable division of household labor but want to keep their housework hours few. In contrast, John et al (1995) report that both women and men are less likely to view the division of household labor as unfair as the men's proportional share of female-typed tasks increases.

Thompson's (1991) argument that ideological factors affect perceptions of fairness may partially account for the inconsistent findings with respect to the relationship between the division of household labor and perceptions of fairness. In addition, further examination of the exchange approach to understanding perceptions of fairness is necessary, especially analyses evaluating various ways to measure resources.

CONSEQUENCES OF THE DIVISION OF HOUSEHOLD LABOR

Rather than focusing on explaining the division of household labor, a number of studies examine how women's and/or men's housework time affects their labor force participation, earnings, and marital/family satisfaction. This research evaluates the consequences of the division of household labor, sometimes to provide support for their argument that it needs to be changed.

Labor Force Participation and Wages

The research on the relationship between household labor time and labor force participation is complicated by questions about the possible reciprocal nature of the relationship, although Kalleberg & Rosenfeld (1990) report that for women in the United States paid labor time affects housework time, but that women's housework time has no effect on paid work time. The association between women's housework time and their paid labor time may partially account for women's lower average earnings, but some studies show that time spent on housework has a direct, negative effect on women's earnings (Coverman 1983, Hersch 1985, 1991, Hersch & Stratton 1994, McAllister 1990, Shelton & Firestone 1988), although only a few find that men's housework time negatively affects their earnings (Coverman 1983, McAllister 1990). Hersch (1991) argues that the lack of any association between men's housework time and their earnings may be because the negative effect of housework time on earnings occurs at a higher level of housework than men perform or that the types of household tasks women and men perform are different and interfere with work differently.

Neoclassical economists like Becker (1985) argue that the relationship between household labor time and earnings reflects differences in effort (Hersch 1991) as well as differences in human capital investments. That is, women's time spent on housework reduces the energy they have to expend at paid work, and they invest less in human capital because they expect to spend less time in paid work (see England & McCreary 1987 for a discussion). Bielby & Bielby (1988) argue, in contrast, that women expend more effort on their jobs in spite of their greater responsibility for household labor.

Marital/Family Satisfaction and Psychological Well-Being

A number of researchers have examined the effect of household labor on marital or family satisfaction and psychological well-being (Hawkins et al 1994, Lye & Biblarz 1993, Pina & Bengston 1993, Yogev & Brett 1985). Generally, these studies have found that women's marital satisfaction is higher when they feel their husbands do their "fair share" of housework, but few find any consistent relationship between the division of household labor and marital satisfaction (Blair 1993, Perry-Jenkins & Folk 1994, Robinson & Spitze 1992, Yogev & Brett 1985). Pina & Bengston (1993) find that the effect of the division of household labor on various measures of marital satisfaction is mediated by perceptions of how fairly housework is divided, with not all women viewing an unequal division of household labor as unfair. Similarly, Erickson (1993) finds that men's participation in "emotion work" is positively associated with marital well-being and that housework is not associated with marital well-being when emotion work is included in the model (see also Broman 1993, Ward 1993).

Some research suggests that men's marital happiness is affected by their housework time, but not by their perceptions of fairness (perhaps because so few men view the division of household labor as unfair to themselves), but the effects are modest (Robinson & Spitze 1992). Robinson & Spitze (1992) find that men report higher marital happiness when they spend less time on housework, but that men's proportional share of housework is not significant (see also Orbuch & Custer 1993). In contrast, Yogev & Brett (1985) report that men's marital satisfaction is highest for men when they do what they consider to be their "fair share." Broman (1988) finds that African-American men's family satisfaction is affected by their housework time, with men who report that they do most of the housework also reporting lower family satisfaction than men who do a smaller share of housework.

Several studies examine the relationship between housework and conflict. Lye & Biblarz (1993) find that women's household labor time is positively associated with both women's and men's reports of disagreements, while Perry-Jenkins & Folk (1994) find that among dual-earner couples, women's proportional share of female-typed tasks is positively associated with their reports of marital conflict only among working class couples, and with men's reports of conflict among working class couples or couples where the husband is middle class and the wife is working class. Blair (1993) finds no association between women's time spent on female-typed household tasks and reports of marital conflict, but a significant and positive association for men. Each of the studies of marital conflict uses the 1988 NSFH, so the inconsistent results should not reflect differences in data sets. In this case, researchers have quite different models, especially with respect to their measures of housework time. Perry-Jenkins & Folk (1994) use proportional measures of female-typed tasks, while Blair (1993) uses an absolute measure of female-typed tasks and Lye & Biblarz (1993) use an absolute measure of total housework.

A number of studies find that women's time spent on housework and an unequal division of household labor are positively associated with women's depression (Glass & Fujimoto 1994, Golding 1990, Kurdek 1993, Ross et al 1983, Shamir 1986), although some argue that the effect is indirect through housework's impact on household strain (Golding 1990). Bird & Fremont (1991) find that household labor is negatively associated with both women's and men's health and conclude that the greater time women spend on housework is a significant contributor to their higher rates of morbidity (see also Shehan 1984). Several studies that examine full-time housewives find that women who are dissatisfied with housework (e.g. find it boring, isolating) are more likely to be depressed than women who are not dissatisfied (Kibria et al 1990, Krause 1983). However, Bird & Ross (1993) find that housework is viewed as offering more autonomy than paid work, but that it is associated with a lower sense of control over one's life than is paid work [although Shehan (1984) finds that housewives are no more likely than employed women to be depressed].

Rosenfield (1992) finds that husbands who share household labor report feeling more "demoralized," "sad," "anxious" and "helpless/hopeless" than men with a more traditional division of labor (see also Glass & Fujimoto 1994), although a number of other studies find no association between men's housework roles and psychological well-being (Golding 1990, Orbuch & Custer 1995, Ross et al 1983, Shamir 1986). Kurdek (1993) argues that household labor is negatively associated with depression for women in same-sex relationships but positively associated with married women's depression because of housework's symbolic character. Women in same-sex relationships may feel that their participation in housework is by choice, while married women may feel obligated to do housework, a difference that may account for differences in its association with psychological well-being. Using similar logic, Szinovacz (1992) suggests that men's adjustment to retirement may be associated with housework if their participation in housework is viewed as evidence that they are good husbands, or if it provides a source of activity for those men who are unable to participate in other activities (i.e. due to disability, etc). She also finds that housework is positively associated with women's adjustment to retirement, arguing that with the onset of retirement, women's "double burden" is removed, allowing women to "enjoy" housework (see also Kibria et al 1990).

CONCLUSIONS

The burgeoning body of research on the division of household labor is cumulative in some respects, but not as much as it should be. We know that relative resources, time constraints, and ideology affect the division of household labor, but not always as expected. Most notably, gender remains a more important determinant of housework time than any other factor. The argument that gender as well as household utilities are produced by housework not only challenges the logic behind the relative resources and time constraints perspectives, it has the potential to move the research on housework in a direction that may allow us to understand it better. Especially since most women (and men) do not view the division of household labor as unfair, we should begin to address more systematically what varied purposes housework may serve. If we take the insights offered by social constructionists and reevaluate our approach to studying household labor, and avoid using it to formulate just another variable to add to existing models, we may yet achieve better understanding of why the division of household labor is slow to change.

ACKNOWLEDGMENTS

We would like to thank Rimma Ashkinadze, Carrie Conaway, Nena Davis, Sarah Holzman, Julie Jackson, Diane Jones, and Molly Moloney for research assistance. Ben Agger and Paula England gave useful comments. Partial support for this research was provided by Oberlin College.

Literature Cited

Acock A, Demo DH. 1994. *Family Diversity and Well Being.* Thousand Oaks, CA: Sage

Ahlander NR, Bahr KS. 1995. Beyond drudgery, power, and equity: toward an expanded discourse on the moral dimension of housework in families. *J. Marriage Fam.* 57:54–68

Almeida DM, Maggs JL, Galambos NL. 1993. Wives' employment hours and spousal participation in family work. *J. Fam. Psychol.* 7:233–44

Atkinson J, Huston TL. 1984. Sex role orientation and division of labor early in marriage. *J. Pers. Soc. Psychol.* 46:330–45

Aytac I. 1990. Sharing household tasks in the United States and Sweden: a reassessment of Kohn's theory. *Sociol. Spectr.* 10:357–71

Barnett RC, Baruch GK. 1987. Determinants of fathers' participation in family work. *J. Marriage Fam.* 49:29–40

Becker GS. 1985. Human capital, effort, and the sexual division of labor. *J. Labor Econ.* 3:S33–S58

Beckett JO, Smith AD. 1981. Work and family roles: egalitarian marriage in black and white families. *Soc. Serv. Rev.* 55(2):314–26

Benin MH, Agostinelli J. 1988. Husbands' and wives' satisfaction with the division of household labor. *J. Marriage Fam.* 50:349–61

Benin MH, Edwards DA. 1990. Adolescents' chores: the difference between dual- and single-earner families. *J. Marriage Fam.* 52:361–73

318   SHELTON & JOHN

3

Berardo DH, Shehan CL, Leslie GR. 1987. A residue of tradition: jobs, careers, and spouses' time in housework. *J. Marriage Fam.* 49:381–90

Bergen E. 1991. The economic context of labor allocation. *J. Fam. Issues* 12:140–57

Bergmann BR. 1986. *The Economic Emergence of Women.* New York: Basic Books

Berk RA, Berk SF. 1978. A simultaneous equation model for the division of household labor. *Soc. Methods Res.* 6:431–68

Bielby DD, Bielby WT. 1988. She works hard for the money: household responsibilities and the allocation of work effort. *Am. J. Sociol.* 93:1031–59

Bird CE, Fremont AM. 1991. Gender, time use, and health. *J. Health Soc. Behav.* 32:114–29

Bird GW, Ratcliff BB. 1990. Children's participation in family tasks: determinants of mothers' and fathers' reports. *Hum. Relat.* 43:865–84

Bird CE, Ross CE. 1993. Houseworkers and paid workers: qualities of the work and effects on personal control. *J. Marriage Fam.* 55:913–25

Blair SL. 1992a. Children's participation in household labor: socialization versus the need for household labor. *J. Youth Adolesc.* 21(2):241–58

Blair SL. 1992b. The sex-typing of children's household labor: parental influence on daughters' and sons' housework. *Youth Soc.* 24:178–203

Blair SL. 1993. Employment, family, and perceptions of marital quality among husbands and wives. *J. Fam. Issues* 14:189–212

Blair SL, Johnson MP. 1992. Wives' perceptions of fairness of the division of household labor: the intersection of housework and ideology. *J. Marriage Fam.* 54:570–81

Blair SL, Lichter DT. 1991. Measuring the division of household labor: gender segregation of housework among American couples. *J. Fam. Issues* 12:91–113

Bloch MN. 1987. The development of sex differences in young children's activities at home: the effect of the social context. *Sex Roles* 16:279–301

Blood RO, Wolfe DM. 1960. *Husbands and Wives.* Glencoe, IL: Free Press

Blumstein P, Schwartz P. 1983. *American Couples: Money, Work, Sex.* New York: Morrow

Bose C. 1979. Technology and changes in the division of labor in the American home. *Women's Stud. Int. Q.* 2:295–304

Bose CE, Bereano PL, Malloy M. 1984. Household technology and the social construction of housework. *Technol. Cult.* 25(1):53–82

Bourke J. 1994. Housewifery in working class England 1860–1914. *Past Present* 143:167–97

Brayfield A. 1992. Employment resources and housework in Canada. *J. Marriage Fam.* 54:19–30

Brayfield A. 1995. Juggling jobs and kids: the impact of employment schedules on fathers' caring for children. *J. Marriage Fam.* 57:321–32

Brines J. 1993. The exchange value of housework. *Ration. Soc.* 5:302–40

Brines J. 1994. Economic dependency, gender, and the division of labor at home. *Am. J. Sociol.* 100:652–88

Brody CJ, Steelman LC. 1985. Sibling structure and parental sex-typing of children's household tasks. *J. Marriage Fam.* 47:265–73

Broman CL. 1988. Household work and family life satisfaction of blacks. *J. Marriage Fam.* 50:743–48

Broman CL. 1991. Gender, work-family roles, and psychological well-being of Blacks. *J. Marriage Fam.* 53:504–20

Broman CL. 1993. Race differences in marital well-being. *J. Marriage Fam.* 55:724–32

Burns A, Homel R. 1989. Gender division of tasks by parents and their children. *Psychol. Women Q.* 13:113–25

Calasanti TM, Bailey CA. 1991. Gender inequality and the division of household labor in the United States and Sweden: a Socialist-Feminist approach. *Soc. Probl.* 38:34–52

Cogle FL, Tasker GE. 1982. Children and housework. *Fam. Relat.* 31:395–99

Coltrane S. 1989. Household labor and the routine production of gender. *Soc. Probl.* 36:473–90

Coltrane S. 1990. Birth timing and the division of labor in dual-earner families: exploratory findings and suggestions for future research. *J. Fam. Issues* 11:157–81

Coltrane S, Ishii-Kuntz M. 1992. Men's housework: a lifecourse perspective. *J. Marriage Fam.* 54:43–57

Connell RW. 1985. Theorizing gender. *Sociology* 19(2):260–75

Coverman S. 1983. Gender, domestic labor, and wage inequality. *Am. Sociol. Rev.* 48:623–37

Coverman S. 1985. Explaining husbands' participation in domestic labor. *Sociol. Q.* 26:81–97

Cowan RS. 1983. *More Work For Mother: The Ironies of Household Technology from the Open Hearth to the Microwave.* New York: Basic Books

Cronkite RC. 1977. The determinants of spouses' normative preferences for family roles. *J. Marriage Fam.* 39:575–85

Day T. 1992. Capital-labor substitutions in the home. *Technol. Cult.* 33:302–27

Delphy C. 1977. *The Main Enemy.* London: Women's Res. Resourc. Cent.

Demo DH, Acock AC. 1993. Family diversity and the division of domestic labor: how much have things really changed? *Fam. Relat.* 42(3):323–31

Denmark FL, Shaw JS, Ciali SD. 1985. The relationship among sex roles, living arrangements, and the division of household responsibilities. *Sex Roles* 12:617–25

Deutsch FM, Lussier JB, Servis LJ. 1993. Husbands at home: predictors of paternal participation in childcare and housework. *J. Pers. Soc. Psychol.* 65:1154–66

DeVault ML. 1991. *Feeding the Family: The Social Organization of Caring as Gendered Work.* Chicago: Univ. Chicago Press

Douthitt RA. 1989. The division of labor within the home: Have gender roles changed? *Sex Roles* 20:693–704

England P, ed. 1993. *Theory on Gender/Feminism on Theory.* New York: Aldine de Gruyter

England P, Farkas G. 1986. *Households, Employment and Gender: A Social, Economic and Demographic View.* New York: Aldine de Gruyter

England P, McCreary L. 1987. Integrating sociology and economics to study gender and work. *Women Work* 2:143–71

Erickson RJ. 1993. Reconceptualizing family work: the effect of emotion work on perceptions of marital quality. *J. Marriage Fam.* 55:888–900

Farkas G. 1976. Education, wage rates, and the division of labor between husband and wife. *J. Marriage Fam.* 38:473–83

Fenstermaker S, West C, Zimmerman DH. 1991. Gender inequality: new conceptual terrain. In *Gender, Family, and Economy,* ed. RL Blumberg, pp. 289–397. Newbury Park, CA: Sage

Fenstermaker Berk S. 1985. *The Gender Factory: The Apportionment of Work in American Households.* New York: Plenum

Ferree MM. 1990. Beyond separate spheres: Feminism and family research. *J. Marriage Fam.* 52:866–84

Ferree MM. 1991. The gender division of labor in two-earner marriages. *J. Fam. Issues* 12:158–80

Folbre N, Hartmann HI. 1989. The persistence of patriarchal capitalism. *Rethinking Marx.* 2(4):90–96

Fox KD, Nickols SY. 1983. The time crunch: wife's employment and family work. *J. Fam. Issues* 4:61–82

Geerken M, Gove WR. 1983. *At Home and At Work: The Family's Allocation of Labor.* Beverly Hills, CA: Sage

Gershuny J, Robinson JP. 1988. Historical changes in the household division of labor. *Demography* 25:537–52

Geurts J, De Ree J. 1993. Influence of research design on time use estimates. *Soc. Indicators Res.* 30:245–84

Glass J, Fujimoto T. 1994. Housework, paid work, and depression among husbands and wives. *J. Health Soc. Behav.* 35:179–91

Glenn EN. 1992. From servitude to social work: historical continuities in the racial division of paid reproductive labor. *Signs* 18:1–43

Godwin DD. 1991. Spouses' time allocation to household work: a review and critique. *Lifestyles: Fam. Econ. Issues* 12:253–94

Golding JM. 1990. Division of household labor, strain, and depressive symptoms among Mexican Americans and non-Hispanic Whites. *Psychol. Women Q.* 14:103–17

Goldscheider FK, Waite LJ. 1991. *New Families, No Families? The Transformation of the American Home.* Berkeley/Los Angeles/Oxford: Univ. Calif.

Gregson N, Lowe M. 1993. Renegotiating the domestic division of labour? A study of dual career households in north east and south east England. *Sociol. Rev.* 41:475–505

Greif GL. 1985. Children and housework in the single father family. *Fam. Relat.* 34:353–57

Gunter BG, Gunter NC. 1990. Domestic divisions of labor among working couples: Does androgyny make a difference? *Psychol. Women Q.* 14:355–70

Haddad T. 1994. Men's contribution to family work: a re-examination of "time availability." *Int. J. Soc. Fam.* 24:87–111

Hardesty C, Bokemeier J. 1989. Finding time and making do: distribution of household labor in nonmetropolitan marriages. *J. Marriage Fam.* 51:253–67

Hartmann HI. 1979. The unhappy marriage of marxism and feminism: towards a more progressive union. *Cap. Class* 8:1–33

Harvey AS. 1993. Guidelines for time use data collection. *Soc. Indic. Res.* 30:197–228

Hawkins AJ, Roberts TA, Christiansen SL, Marshall CM. 1994. An evaluation of a program to help dual-earner couples share the second shift. *Fam. Relat.* 43:213–20

Hersch J. 1985. Effect of housework on earnings of husbands and wives: evidence from full-time piece rate workers. *Soc. Sci. Q.* 66:210–17

Hersch J. 1991. The impact of nonmarket work on market wages. *Proc. Am. Econ. Assoc.* 44:157–60

Hersch J, Stratton LS. 1994. Housework, wages, and the division of housework time for employed spouses. *Am. Econ. Rev.* 84:120–25

Hill SM. 1985. Patterns of time use. See Juster & Stafford 1985, pp. 133–76

Hiller DV. 1984. Power dependence and division of family work. *Sex Roles* 10:1003–19

Hiller DV, Philliber WW. 1986. The division of labor in contemporary marriage: expectations, perceptions, and performance. *Soc. Probl.* 33:191–201

Hilton JM, Haldeman VA. 1991. Gender differences in the performance of household tasks by adults and children in single-parent and two-parent, two-earner families. *J. Fam. Issues* 12:114–30

Hochschild A. 1989. *The Second Shift: Working Parents and the Revolution at Home.* New York: Viking

Hossain Z, Roopnarine JL. 1993. Division of household labor and child care in dual-earner African-American families with infants. *Sex Roles* 29:571–83

Huber J, Spitze G. 1983. *Sex Stratification: Children, Housework, and Jobs.* New York: Academic

Hurtado A. 1989. Relating to privilege: seduction and rejection in the subordination of white women and women of color. *Signs* 14:833–955

Ishii-Kuntz M, Coltrane S. 1992a. Predicting the sharing of household labor: Are parenting and household labor distinct? *Soc. Perspect.* 35:629–47

Ishii-Kuntz M, Coltrane S. 1992b. Remarriage, step parenting and household labor. *J. Fam. Issues.* 13(2):215–33

Jackson S. 1992. Towards a historical sociology of housework: a materialist feminist analysis. *Women's Stud. Int. Forum* 15:153–72

Jaggar A. 1988. *Feminist Politics and Human Nature.* Totowa, NJ: Rowman & Littlefield

James S, Dalla Costa M. 1973. *The Power of Women and the Subversion of the Community.* Bristol: Falling Water Press

John D, Shelton BA, Luschen K. 1995. Race, ethnicity, gender and perceptions of fairness. *J. Fam. Issues* 16,3:357–79

Juster FT. 1985. The validity and quality of time use estimates obtained from recall diaries. See Juster & Stafford 1985, pp. 63–92

Juster FT, Stafford FP, eds. 1985. *Time, Goods, and Well-Being.* Ann Arbor, MI: Survey Res. Cent., Univ. Mich.

Juster FT, Stafford FP. 1991. The allocation of time: Empirical findings, behavioral models, and problems of measurement. *J. Econ. Lit.* 29:471–522

Kain PJ. 1993. Marx, housework and alienation. *Hypatia* 8(1):121–44

Kalleberg AL, Rosenfeld RA. 1990. Work in the family and in the labor market: a cross-national, reciprocal analysis. *J. Marriage Fam.* 52:331–46

Kalton G. 1985. Sample design issues in time

diary studies. See Juster & Stafford 1985, pp. 93–112

Kamo Y. 1988. Determinants of household division of labor: resources, power, and ideology. *J. Fam. Issues* 9:177–200

Kamo Y. 1991. A nonlinear effect of the number of children on the division of household labor. *Soc. Perspect.* 34:205–18

Kamo Y. 1994. Division of household work in the United States and Japan. *J. Fam. Issues* 15:348–78

Kibria N, Barnett RC, Baruch GK, Marshall NL, Pleck JH. 1990. Homemaking-role quality and the psychological well-being and distress of employed women. *Sex Roles* 22:327–47

Kingston PW, Nock SL. 1985. Consequences of the family work day. *J. Marriage Fam.* 47:619–30

Kotkin G. 1983. Sex roles among married and unmarried couples. *Sex Roles* 9:975–85

Krause N. 1983. Conflicting sex-role expectations, housework dissatisfaction, and depressive symptoms among full-time housewives. *Sex Roles* 9:1115–25

Kurdek LA. 1993. The allocation of household labor in gay, lesbian, and heterosexual married couples. *J. Soc. Issues* 49:127–34

Lamphere L. 1989. Historical and regional variability in Navajo women's roles. *J. Anthropol. Res.* 45:431–56

Lapidus GW. 1988. The interaction of women's work and family roles in the U.S.S.R. *Women Work* 3:87–121

LaRossa R, LaRossa M. 1981. *Transition to Parenthood: How Infants Change Families.* Beverly Hills, CA: Sage

Lennon MC, Rosenfield S. 1994. Relative fairness and the division of housework: the importance of options. *Am. J. Sociol.* 100:506–31

Levant RF, Slattery SC, Loiselle JE. 1987. Father's involvement in housework and child care with school-aged daughters. *Fam. Relat.* 36:152–57

Lopata HZ. 1993. The interweave of public and private: Women's challenge to American society. *J. Marriage Fam.* 55:176–90

Lorber J. 1986. Dismantling Noah's ark. *Sex Roles* 14:567–80

Lyberg I. 1989. Sampling, nonresponse, and measurement issues in the 1984–85 Swedish time budget survey. *Proc. 5th Annu. Res. Conf.* Washington, DC: Bur. Census, US Dep. Commer.

Lye DN, Biblarz TJ. 1993. The effects of attitudes toward family life and gender roles on marital satisfaction. *J. Fam. Issues* 14:157–88

Major B. 1987. Gender, justice, and the psychology of entitlement. In *Review of Personality and Social Psychology,* ed. P Shaver, C Hendricks, 7:124–48. Newbury Park, CA: Sage

Major B. 1994. From social inequality to personal entitlement: the role of social comparison, legitimacy appraisals, and group membership. In *Advances in Experimental Social Psychology,* ed. M Zanna, pp. 293–355. New York: Academic

Maret E, Finlay B. 1984. The distribution of household labor among women in dual-earner families. *J. Marriage Fam.* 46:357–64

Marini MM, Shelton BA. 1993. Measuring household work: recent experience in the United States. *Soc. Sci. Res.* 22:361–82

McAllister I. 1990. Gender and the division of labor: employment and earnings variation in Australia. *Work Occup.* 17:79–99

McGaw J. 1982. Women and the history of American technology: review essay. *Signs* 7:798–828

McHale S, Bartko WT, Crouter AC, Perry-Jenkins M. 1990. Children's housework and psychological functions: the mediating effects of parents' sex-role behaviors and attitudes. *Child Dev.* 61(5):1413–26

McKee L. 1982. Division of labor in two-earner homes: task accomplishment versus household management as critical variables in perceptions about family work. *J. Marriage Fam.* 55:133–45

Mederer HJ. 1993. Division of labor in two-earner homes: task accomplishment versus household management as critical variables in perceptions about family work. *J. Marriage Fam.* 55:133–45

Meissner M, Humphries EW, Meis SM, Scheu WJ. 1975. No exit for wives: sexual division of labor and the cumulation of household demands. *Can. Rev. Sociol. Anthropol.* 12:424–39

Mirande A. 1979. A reinterpretation of male dominance in the Chicano family. *Fam. Coord.* 28:473–80

Newell S. 1993. The Superwoman syndrome: gender difference in attitudes towards equal opportunities at work and towards domestic responsibilities at home. *Work Empl. Soc.* 7:275–89

Nichols SY. 1980. Stand-by care: a measurement problem. In *The Household as Producer: A Look Beyond the Market,* ed. IC Hefferan, pp. 212–14. Washington, DC: Am. Home Econ. Assoc.

Nickols SY, Metzen EJ. 1982. Impact of wife's employment upon husband's housework. *J. Fam. Issues* 3:199–216

Niemi I. 1993. Systematic error in behavioural measurement: comparing results from interview and time budget studies. *Soc. Indic. Res.* 30:229–44

Orbuch TL, Custer L. 1995. The social context of married women's work and its impact on black husbands and white husbands. *J. Marriage Fam.* 57:333–45

Patterson CJ. 1995. Families and the lesbian baby boom: parents' division of labor and childrens' adjustments. *Dev. Psychol.* 31:115–63

Perry-Jenkins M, Folk K. 1994. Class, couples, and conflict: effects of the division of labor on assessments of marriage in dual-earner families. *J. Marriage Rev.* 56:165–80

Pestello FG, Voydanoff P. 1991. In search of mesostructure in the family: an interactionist approach to the division of labor. *Symbol. Interact.* 14:105–28

Peters JM, Haldeman VA. 1987. Time used for household work: a study of school-age children from single-parent, two parent and one-earner and two-earner families. *J. Fam. Issues* 8:212–25

Piña DL, Bengston VL. 1993. The division of household labor and wives' happiness: ideology, employment, and perceptions of support. *J. Marriage Fam.* 55:901–12

Pleck JH, Staines GL. 1985. Work schedules and family life in two-earner couples. *J. Fam. Issues* 6:61–82

Potuchek JL. 1992. Employed wives' orientations to breadwinning: a gender theory analysis. *J. Marriage Fam.* 54:548–58

Presser HB. 1994. Employment schedules among dual-earner spouses and the division of household labor by gender. *Am. Sociol. Rev.* 59:348–64

Rexroat C, Shehan C. 1987. The family life cycle and spouses' time in housework. *J. Marriage Fam.* 49:737–50

Robinson J, Spitze G. 1992. Whistle while you work? The effect of household task performance on women's and men's well-being. *Soc. Sci. Q.* 73:844–61

Robinson JP. 1977. *How Americans Use Time: A Social-Psychological Analysis of Everyday Behavior.* New York: Praeger

Robinson JP. 1985. See Juster & Stafford 1985, pp. 33–62

Robinson JP. 1988. Who's doing the housework? *Am. Demogr.* 10:24–63

Rosenfield S. 1992. The costs of sharing: wives' employment and husbands' mental health. *J. Health Soc. Behav.* 33:213–25

Ross CE. 1987. The division of labor at home. *Soc. Forces* 65:816–33

Ross CE, Mirowski J, Huber J. 1983. Dividing work, sharing work and in-between: marriage patterns and depression. *Am. Sociol. Rev.* 48:809–23

Sanchez L. 1994a. Material resources, family structure resources, and husbands' housework participation: a cross-sectional comparison. *J. Fam. Issues* 15:379–402

Sanchez L. 1994b. Gender, labor allocations, and the psychology of entitlement within the home. *Soc. Forces* 73(2):533–53

Sanik MM. 1981. Division of household work: a decade comparison—1967–1977. *Home Econ. Res. J.* 10:175–80

Schor JB. 1991. *The Overworked American: The Unexpected Decline of Leisure.* New York: Basic Books

Seccombe W. 1974. The housewife and her labour under capitalism. *New Left Rev.* 83:3–24

Shamir B. 1986. Unemployment and household division of labor. *J. Marriage Fam.* 48:195–206

Shehan CL. 1984. Wives' work and psychological well-being: an extension of Gove's social role theory of depression. *Fam. Relat.*37:333–37

Shelton BA. 1990. The distribution of household tasks: does wife's employment status make a difference? *J. Fam. Issues* 11:115–35

Shelton BA. 1992. *Women, Men, and Time: Gender Differences in Paid Work, Housework, and Leisure.* Westport, CT: Greenwood

Shelton BA, Agger B. 1993. Shotgun wedding, unhappy marriage, no-fault divorce? Rethinking the feminism-marxism relationship. See England 1993, pp. 25–42

Shelton BA, Firestone J. 1988. An examination of household labor time as a factor in composition and treatment effects on the male-female wage gap. *Sociol. Focus* 21:265–78

Shelton BA, John D. 1993a. Does marital status make a difference? *J. Fam. Issues* 14:401–20

Shelton BA, John D. 1993b. Ethnicity, race and difference: A comparison of white, black and hispanic men's household labor time. In *Men, Work and Family,* ed. JC Hood, 1:131–50. Newbury Park, CA: Sage. 294 pp.

Smith J. 1983. Feminism and analytic method: the case of unwaged domestic labor. *Curr. Perspect. Soc. Theory* 4:205–23

Sokoloff NJ. 1980. *Between Money and Love: The Dialectics of Women's Home and Market Work.* New York: Praeger

South SJ, Spitze G. 1994. Housework in marital and nonmarital households. *Am. Sociol. Rev.* 59:327–47

Spitze G. 1986. The division of task responsibility in U.S. households: longitudinal adjustments to change. *Soc. Forces* 64:689–701

Spitze G, Ward R. 1995. Household labor in intergenerational households. *J. Marriage Fam.* 57:355–61

Stafford R, Backman E, Dibona P. 1977. The division of labor among cohabiting and married

couples. *J. Marriage Fam.* 50:595–618

Strasser S. 1982. *Never Done: A History of American Housework.* New York: Pantheon

Szinovacz M. 1992. Is housework good for retirees? *Fam. Relat.*41:230–38

Thompson L. 1991. Family work: women's sense of fairness. *J. Fam. Issues* 12:181–96

Valadez JJ, Clignet R. 1984. Household work as an ordeal: culture of standards versus standardization of culture. *Am. J. Sociol.* 89:812–35

Vogel L. 1983. *Marxism and the Oppression of Women: Toward a Unitary Theory.* New Brunswick, NJ: Rutgers Univ. Press

Walby S. 1986. *Patriarchy at Work.* Minneapolis, MN: Univ. Minn.

Walker KE, Woods ME. 1976. *Time Use: A Measure of Household Production of Family Goods and Services.* Washington, DC: Am. Home Econ. Assoc.

Ward RA. 1993. Marital happiness and household equity in later life. *J. Marriage Fam.* 55:427–38

Warner RL. 1986. Alternative strategies for measuring household division of labor: a comparison. *J. Fam. Issues* 7:179–95

Weisner TS, Garnier H, Loucky J. 1994. Domestic tasks, gender egalitarian values and children's gender typing in conventional and non-conventional families. *Sex Roles* 30:23–54

West C, Fenstermaker S. 1993. Power, inequality and the accomplishment of gender: an ethnomethodological view. See England 1993, pp. 151–74

West C, Fenstermaker S. 1995. Doing difference. *Gender Soc.* 9:8–17

West C, Zimmerman DH. 1987. Doing gender. *Gender Soc.* 1:125–51

Wharton CS. 1994. Finding time for the "Second Shift": the impact of flexible work schedules on women's double days. *Gender Soc.* 8:189–205

White LK, Brinkerhoff DB. 1981. The sexual division of labor: evidence from childhood. *Soc. Forces* 60:170–81

Wilson MN, Tolson TFJ, Hinton ID, Kiernan M. 1990. Flexibility and sharing of childcare duties in black families. *Sex Roles* 22(7/8):409–25

Wright EO, Shire K, Hwang SL, Dolan M, Baxter J. 1992. The non-effects of class on the gender division of labor in the home. *Gender Soc.* 6:252–82

Ybarra L. 1982. When wives work: the impact on the Chicano family. *J. Marriage Fam.* 44:169–78

Yogev S, Brett J. 1985. Perceptions of the division of housework and child care and marital satisfaction. *J. Marriage Fam.* 47:609–18

Annu. Rev. Sociol. 1996. 22:323-49

CULTURAL AND SOCIAL-STRUCTURAL EXPLANATIONS OF CROSS-NATIONAL PSYCHOLOGICAL DIFFERENCES[1]

Carmi Schooler

Laboratory of Socio-Environmental Studies, National Institute of Mental Health, National Institutes of Health, Federal Building, Room B1A14, 7550 Wisconsin Avenue, Bethesda, Maryland 20892

KEY WORDS: culture, social structure, attitudes, psychological functioning

ABSTRACT

This chapter examines cross-national differences in individual values, attitudes, and behaviors. The central question raised is how social-structural and cultural factors account for the differences found. After discussing a series of theoretical issues raised by this question, the chapter reviews the findings of four quantitative sociological research programs on modern cross-national differences. The program on individual modernity led by Alex Inkeles established that social-structural conditions associated with industrialization are linked to an increase in individuals' being open to new experience, rejecting traditional authority, and taking a rational, ambitious, orderly approach to both work and human problems. The cross-national research on the Kohn-Schooler hypothesis that self-directed work increases intellectual functioning and self-directed orientations confirmed the generality of that hypothesis and established that the social status and social class differences in these psychological characteristics found within different countries are largely the result of social-structurally determined differences in the opportunity for occupational self-direction. Eric Wright's cross-national research

---

program on class structure and class consciousness provides evidence that in a range of countries social classes directly affect political attitudes, while acting as tangible barriers to mobility and personal relationships. The research deriving from John Meyer's theories on institutionalization highlights the importance of institutions and socially constructed views of reality for the development and maintenance of cross-national differences and similarities in cultural values and their behavioral embodiment. All four of the programs provide evidence of the continuing importance of historically determined cultural differences. All are also congruent with the hypothesis that speed of change generally decreases as we go from psychological to social-structural to cultural levels of phenomena—a possibility whose confirmation would provide a valuable tool for understanding how culture and social structure affect cross-national differences in values and behavior.

INTRODUCTION

This chapter examines cross-national differences in individual values, attitudes and behavior. The central issue raised is how social-structural and cultural factors can account for the differences found. Perhaps the clearest statement of this question was made over two decades ago in a paper by William Caudill (1973).

> [M]odern social structure and traditional culture may be in some conflict, but underneath this, people are, psychologically speaking, much as they have always been. Middle-class managerial personnel in England and France may have more in common than either group has with working-class machine operators in their own country. At the same time, however, I do not think that anyone would say that such Englishmen and Frenchmen are indistinguishable in their approach to work, politics, family life, or sexual activity. They are different in those historically derived and culturally patterned ways of thinking, feeling and behaving that are passed on, often unknowingly, from one generation to the next and are shared in considerable part by all members of a society... (E)ach of these dimensions—position in modern social structure, and continuity of historical culture—exerts a relatively independent influence on human behavior, ... both dimensions need to be considered simultaneously in the investigation of the psychological characteristics of a people....
> There is a... tendency... to blur the distinction between social and cultural dimensions.... [M]y contribution is to stress the relative separateness of these two dimensions of human life.... I think of modern social structure as producing similarities in behavior when one country is compared to another, but equally I think of historically derived cultures as producing differences in behavior in different countries. Empirically the question boils down to the amount of variance accounted for by each of these independent variables in samples of human behavior. (pp. 240–41)

Embedded in Caudill's statement are a series of substantive and theoretical assumptions whose airing raises questions that have to be faced in almost any consideration of the origins of cross-national differences in individual psychology and behavior. At a psychological level, Caudill's statement that "people are, psychologically speaking, much as they have always been (p. 241)" assumes that people are and have been essentially the same no matter where or when they lived or what the nature of their biological make-up. The assumption that at some basic level identical laws of psychological functioning operate among the populations being compared is necessary for any attempt to examine the psychological mechanisms through which culture and/or social structure have their effects. This does not mean that exposure to different social-structural and cultural conditions does not affect individuals' psychological functioning. It is just such effects that are the subject of this paper. Rather, social-structural and cultural explanations of cross-national differences assume that given the same personal histories, individuals in the compared populations would be expected to react similarly to the same stimuli.

Actually, in Caudill's own studies (Caudill & Schooler 1973) of how differences in the parental behavior of Japanese and American mothers lead to the reproduction of cultural differences in behavior patterns, he himself did not blindly accept the assumption of the basic psychological equivalence of all groups of people. He added a Japanese-American group to his original sample to empirically rule out the possibility that the differences he found between Japanese in Japan and Caucasian Americans were not a function of innate psychobiological differences between the two populations [For a full review of Caudill's research, as well as of relevant later research on this issue, see Schooler (1996), which concludes that biological factors are not at the root of the cross-cultural differences Caudill found]. Obviously, it is not always feasible to find a way to rule out the possibility of biological contributions to cross-national differences; nor can the possibility of such biological effects be excluded on a priori grounds. Nevertheless, a growing body of research suggests that there are some fairly universal patterns in the most basic levels of human reactivity (e.g. Baddeley et al 1995, Berry et al 1992, Chomsky & Lightfoot 1990, Ekman 1992, Jackendoff 1994). In the absence of evidence to the contrary, it is probably most parsimonious to assume that the basic learning processes through which individuals are affected by their cultural backgrounds and social-structural positions are essentially the same in the populations being compared.

The question of the universality of the basic psychological processes involved in determining the effects of both culture and social structure is ultimately an empirical one. Theoretically more complex, yet even more relevant to the present chapter, are the definitions and ontological relationships of culture and social structure. In his thinking, Caudill juxtaposes historical culture with modern social structure, but according to most usages of these terms, culture can be modern and social structure is a necessary characteristic not only of present societies, but of those in all historical periods. These difficulties could be avoided by using House's (1981) distinction between culture and social structure. According to House, culture represents what members of a social system collectively believe and social structure represents what members of a social system collectively do. Carrying House's view to its logical extreme, however, would make the question underlying this paper essentially meaningless or at best reduce it to the quite different questions of how beliefs affect behavior and vice versa. Another possible solution is Kohn's (1989) who avoids the issue of the relationship between social structure and culture by limiting himself to cross-national analyses "mainly because 'nation' has a relatively unambiguous meaning (p. 93)." Kohn himself, however, recognizes that such a course "comes at a price: When one finds cross-national differences, it may not be clear whether the crucial 'context' that accounts for the differences is nation or culture..." (p. 94).

SOME FORMAL DEFINITIONS AND THEORETICAL CONSIDERATIONS

If we are to effectively examine the question of the relative importance of social structure and culture in explaining cross-national differences, we are going to have to face forthrightly the problem of formally defining the two concepts in ways that leave the question meaningful, yet are concordant with the common sociological usage of the terms. The definitions that I use are part of a formal conceptualization of human social systems (for a full exposition see Schooler 1994) I developed and extended from my recollection of Merton's late 1950s formulation (Merton 1950–1957)[2], which in turn derived, in part, from earlier conceptualizations of Linton (1936, 1945). Definitions relevant for the present purposes are:

STATUS: A position in a social system occupied by designated actors (i.e. individuals or social organizations) that consists of a set of roles that define the incumbents' expected patterns of interrelationships with incumbents of related statuses.

ROLE: The pattern of expected interrelationships of one status vis-a-vis another.

---

[2]The best published presentation of this conceptualization is in Merton 1957a: see also Merton 1957b. My recall of Merton's views was substantially aided by reading the course notes of Merton's 1957 lectures that my wife, Nina Schooler, carefully took and preserved.

SOCIAL STRUCTURE: The patterned interrelationships among a set of individual and organizational statuses, as defined by the nature of their interacting roles.

CULTURE: An historically determined set of denotative (what is), normative (what should be), and stylistic (how done) beliefs, shared by a group of individuals who have undergone a common historical experience and participate in an interrelated set of social structures.[3]

SOCIETY OR SOCIOCULTURAL SYSTEM: A set of persons and social positions that possesses both a culture and a social structure.

The definition of culture entails subordinate social structures. Furthermore, as is often claimed by anthropologists, culture can be seen as superordinate to social structure in that cultural beliefs shape and integrate the expectations that pattern the relationships among a social structure's constituent statuses and roles. These definitions presuppose that culture and social structure, although causally and ontologically related, represent different levels of reality. The concept of levels of reality implies that phenomena are arranged hierarchically with respect to levels of integration, differentiation, and organizational complexity, and that higher levels are more than simple quantitative accretions. Rather, levels represent qualitative changes in the complexity of integration so that each new level has its own properties and principles. Nevertheless, subordinate and superordinate levels of phenomena can affect each other. (For fuller discussions of this view see Aronson 1984, Schneirla 1951, 1972, Schooler 1991, 1994.) Thus, just as the characteristics of the superordinate cultural level may affect the characteristics of the subordinate social-structural level, the characteristics of the component social-structural level can affect the superordinate cultural level. More generally, causal paths can go both from and to biological, psychological, social-structural and cultural levels of phenomena.

Given the intricacy inherent in such a pattern of possible causal pathways, what instruments can we use to cut the Gordian knot of causal interconnections among cultural, social-structural, and psychological strands of phenomena?

---

[3]The term "historically determined" is included in the definition of culture, but not in the definition of social structure as a matter of emphasis. A social structure is clearly affected by what happened in its past, particularly its relatively recent past. Thus, just as is culture, social structure is influenced by past history (as is everything else if we believe in causality). The distinction, as we shall see, is that a society's culture is slow to change. It tends to remain affected by occurrences in the relatively distant past, including such specific happenstances as which side holding which ideology won what battle, or which unusual person with what abilities and beliefs appeared when. A society's social structure, on the other hand, is not only affected by its historically determined culture, but also by relatively immediate exigencies such as its socioeconomic processes of production and distribution.

Some of the methodologies available to scientists studying more microlevel phenomena are impractical for cross-national sociological and social-psychological comparisons (for a fuller discussion of how the levels of phenomena with which a science deals can affect its canons of proof, see Schooler 1994). For example, we generally cannot randomly assign countries to different experimental conditions and then measure the effects of these conditions. In some circumstances, however, we can develop theoretical or empirical justifications that sufficiently constrain the number and pattern of causal connections among the relevant phenomena so that we can then generate structural equation models to test the possibility of reciprocal effects among the different levels of phenomena. Many of the cross-national comparisons we describe of the causal relationships between social-structurally determined occupational conditions and psychological functioning are based on such analyses.

Unfortunately, we frequently have neither the necessary data nor the theory to identify and test structural equation models that would permit us to tease out the causal connections among the cultural, social-structural, and psychological phenomena in question. Although we can seldom develop fully appropriate statistical models, the dimension of time can, nonetheless, provide a useful instrument for identifying the different ways that cultural, social-structural, and psychological levels of phenomena are causally interconnected. The suggestive possibility that, among these levels, superordinate levels seem likely to affect subordinate levels more quickly than the other way around is raised by a pattern of findings from the cross-national research program on the psychological effects of occupational conditions, originated by Kohn & Schooler (1983) in the Laboratory of Socio-environmental Studies (LSES). The existence of a temporal distinction in the relative speed of the effects of social structure and personality on each other is suggested by the evidence from this research program that, although the effects of social-structurally determined occupational conditions on psychological functioning are generally contemporaneous, the effect of psychological functioning on occupational conditions is generally lagged. These findings imply that, although there is a reciprocal effect between the two, psychological functioning is more quickly affected by occupational conditions than the reverse.

A series of theoretical considerations support the possibility of a temporal ordering in how rapidly psychological, social-structural, and cultural levels of phenomena affect each other (for a full discussion see Schooler 1994). Underlying these considerations is the postulate of stability in the absence of some force for change. This postulate holds that at each of these levels of phenomena, things will stay the same unless something happens to change them. It is not that everything that exists is functional, but rather that everything that exists has not been dysfunctional long enough or severely enough to stop being able to exist. From this perspective the hypothesis about the different speeds at which things change can be reframed in terms of how long an element in a particular system can be dysfunctional before it ceases to exist, possibly by leading to the destruction of the system (e.g. organism, social structure, socio-cultural system) of which it is a part. Thus, perhaps because there is likely to be less redundancy in subordinate than superordinate levels, the lower the level of phenomena the shorter the period it is able to tolerate dysfunctional elements. If more complex levels tend to have a greater degree of redundancy, a greater number of dysfunctional elements would be necessary to disrupt the system. Hence, even if all dysfunctional elements have the same probability of occur-ring and develop at the same rate, the more redundant complex systems would take longer to disintegrate. Dysfunctional elements in the thought processes of a person are likely to threaten the existence of the thinker of the thoughts more quickly than dysfunctional elements in a social structure are likely to lead to the end of the social structure. In a similar manner, cultural level phenom-ena may be more resistant to change than social-structural phenomena, since, as we have noted, sociocultural system level phenomena are superordinate to social-structural level phenomena.

If the postulates about the relative rate of change in psychological, social-structural, and cultural level phenomena are correct, not only would the pro-cesses of firmly embodying something in a culture take longer than the processes involved in psychological change, but once something is included in the cultural corpus it would tend to stay. The ensuing cultural conservatism often has the result that ideologies and customs formed under an earlier set of conditions con-tinue to affect people's behaviors in later, but quite different conditions. Such a cultural time lag may continue unless or until the dysfunctional repercussions of the resulting behavior lead to either modification of the relevant cultural elements or extinction of the relevant statuses and roles. Evidence suggests, for example, the persistence over generations of lagged effects on an ethnic group's culture of historical conditions restricting the individual's autonomy. Americans from ethnic groups with a more recent history of serfdom exhibit the non-selfdirected orientation and lack of intellectual flexibility characteristic of American men working under conditions limiting the individuals' opportunity for self-direction (Schooler 1976).

If we accept that a society's history affects its social structure through its lagged effect on that society's culturally normative role expectations, the ques-tion remains, what besides historically determined culture affects a society's social structure. At least part of the answer stems from the above-mentioned postulate of stability in the absence of some force for change. To the extent that a society's historically derived cultural norms need to have been supplemented or modified to account for its continued existence, nonhistorical elements have to have been incorporated into an existing society's norms and role expectations. Thus, at a social-structural level, the continued existence of a society implies that its roles and statuses were so structured and modified that its modes of production, distribution, and status reproduction were functional enough for it to continue. The research projects reviewed in this chapter have been chosen because their hypotheses compare the effects on individual functioning of recent modifications of a country's social structure, which accommodate changes in its modes of production and distribution, with the effects of longer standing traditional cultural patterns.

REVIEWS OF RESEARCH PROGRAMS

Not least because this is the *Annual Review of Sociology*, and because research done by sociologists is most likely to be framed in ways permitting the comparison of social structure and culture, we focus on studies carried out by card-carrying sociologists.[4] Furthermore, although within sociology there are obviously many germane qualitative and historical studies that examine questions about culture and social structure, given the unmanageable number of potentially relevant studies, our focus is on quantitative sociological research programs on modern cross-national differences. In order to have space to fully describe the studies we discuss, our focus is further limited to research programs that generally compare more than two countries. Since any pair of countries is likely to differ on a wide variety of dimensions that may plausibly explain any differences found between the two, the more countries a research program compares, the more likely are the national characteristics it examines to be truly relevant to explaining the differences in question. (For an excellent general overview of cross-cultural and cross-national social psychology that is not limited by discipline or by number of countries compared and not

[4]Researchers in other disciplines, such as comparative political science and comparative law, also tend to compare the effects of a country's social structure with the effects of longer standing traditional cultural patterns. Anthropologists, on the other hand, who incline to see social structure as secondary to culture, often overlook the psychological effects of social-structural differentiations within nations or ethnic groups. The same tendency to overlook social structure seems even more true of cross-cultural psychologists, whose empirical focus is on the effects of culture on the individual. For example, there is no entry for social structure in the appendix of Triandis' (1994) integrated overview of cross-cultural social psychology. Nor do Markus & Kitayama (1991) consider social structure in their heavily cited paper on the implications for cognition, emotion, and motivation of reported cross-cultural differences in the construal of the self (1991). For a discussion of the mutual relevance of basic psychological research on cognition, on the one hand, and research on social structure and culture, on the other, see Schooler 1989.

specifically concerned with the relative effects of social structure and culture, see Miller-Loessi 1995.)

Alex Inkeles and the Project on the Sociocultural Aspects of Development

The pioneer quantitative, sociological, cross-national study examining the relationship between culture, social structure, and individual attitudes and functioning was the Project on the Sociocultural Aspects of Development. Led by Alex Inkeles, its goal was to test his hypothesis "that the standardized institutional environments of modern society induce standard patterns of response, despite the countervailing randomizing effects of persisting traditional patterns of culture" (Inkeles 1960, p. 1). It did so by examining the degree to which individuals "incorporate as personal attributes qualities which are analogous to or derive from the organizational properties of the institutions and roles in which... [they] are regularly and deeply involved" (Inkeles 1983, p. 8). Tying this question specifically to modern experience, Inkeles and his collaborators selected the factory as an embodiment of many aspects of such experience. From an analysis of factory characteristics they derived a set of qualities which they assumed would be learned and incorporated as personal attributes by men who experienced extended factory employment after growing up in a pre-modern rural village. This set of qualities, which they called individual modernity, consisted of: openness to new experience; independence from traditional authority; belief in science and medicine for solving human problems; educational and occupational ambition; punctuality and orderliness; and interest in civic affairs (Inkeles 1969).

The research was conducted in six industrializing nations—Argentina, Bangladesh, Chile, India, Israel, and Nigeria; almost 6000 men served as survey respondents. Analyses of the data indicated that the various hypothesized aspects of modernity do, in fact, co-occur in a syndrome of individual modernity. Furthermore, the findings demonstrated robust cross-national empirical relationships between the various psychological aspects of individual modernity and work in industrial settings as well as exposure to such other concomitants of modernization as urbanization, education, and mass media. In each of the countries studied, exposure to social-structural conditions associated with industrialization was generally shown to be empirically correlated with the psychological characteristics predicted by the Project's theory.

Using a variety of analytic techniques, Inkeles (1978) directly compared the relative impact of nationality on his measure of psychological modernity with that of the variables influenced by social structure: years of education, years of factory work, exposure to mass media, and possession of consumer goods.

Each type of analysis indicated that nationality had an independent effect. For example, a regression analysis that also included age and rural origin, indicated that nationality (Beta = .22) was a less powerful predictor of modernity than education (Beta = .34), but a more powerful one than years of factory work (Beta = .13). After examining a number of alternative possibilities, he concluded that the national differences he found "are real and they exemplify the impact on individual modernity of the general character of the social milieu in which each individual lived. Those who lived in more modern societies, with more opportunity for contact with modern institutions and objects, and more interaction with decidedly modern men should have become more modern as a result. In other words we have observed true 'contextual' effects" (p. 66).

Despite the strength of its empirical findings, the Project has been criticized for a variety of ideological reasons. For example, from the neo-Marxist perspective, Wallerstein has characterized it as an apologia for the capitalistic, imperialistic status quo (Wallerstein 1974). Somewhat similarly, from the postmodernist perspective, Luke (1991) sees the modernity thesis as a "de-historicized, desocialized and de-culturalized-social theory" (p. 284) that the power elite uses as a legitimating ideology to socially control the masses.

Besides these ideologically based complaints, methodological and theoretical questions have been raised about the modernity concept. Principal among these is the degree of its conceptual differentiation and empirical independence from socioeconomic status (Form 1979). This concern is actually an instance of the more general problem of the conceptual and empirical ambiguity in how the social-structural conditions and psychological characteristics Inkeles and his colleagues associate with modernity relate to each other and to other views and aspects of social structure. Hence, although Inkeles and his associates (Inkeles 1983, Inkeles & Smith 1974) described several mechanisms through which such changes may take place (i.e. reward and punishment, modeling, exemplification and generalization), they never empirically isolate the aspects of the modernization experience that have these effects.

Cross-National Tests of the Kohn-Schooler Hypothesis

The attempt to specify exactly which aspects of experience determined by social structure affect the individual's psychological functioning was a prime aim of the Kohn and Schooler research program on the psychological effects of occupational conditions. Melvin Kohn and I originally conceived the study at the LSES in the early 1960s as a way of explaining social class differences in parental values. Its general purpose was to test the hypothesis that social status differences in people's orientations toward themselves and their environments, in the values they hold for themselves and their children, and even in the ways they think are a function of the nature and conditions of their work.

We wanted to delineate the exact linkages between individuals' conditions of work and psychological characteristics. Instead of comparing specific jobs, we conceived of a job in terms of a series of dimensions, among which were: closeness of supervision, routinization, substantive complexity (seen as indicative of occupational self-direction), ownership, bureaucratization, position in the hierarchy, and time pressure.

The original sample of 3101 men interviewed in 1964 was representative of all men in the United States employed in civilian occupations. In a 1974 follow-up, a representative subsample of these men were re-interviewed, and their wives and children were interviewed for the first time. Analyzing the men's longitudinal data with the then-newly-developed technique of structural equation modeling (Jöreskog 1973), we found that jobs that facilitate occupational self-direction increase intellectual functioning and promote a self-directed orientation to self and to society (Kohn & Schooler 1983). Further findings demonstrated that opportunities for exercising occupational self-direction—especially for doing substantively complex work—are to a large extent determined by a job's location in the social structure of society. Other results indicated that oppressive working conditions produce a sense of distress. In all of these findings there is the consistent implication that the principal process by which occupations affect personality is a generalization from the lessons of the job to life off-the-job. Interviews with the male respondents' wives revealed a similar pattern of psychological effects of occupational conditions among employed women (Miller et al 1979).

From the very beginning we realized that cross-national replication represented one of the best ways to test the generalizability of our hypotheses. In fact, the first cross-national replication (Pearlin & Kohn 1966) was actually carried out in Turin before the planning for the original 1964 US survey was completed. Consequently, its indices, particularly for occupational self-direction are only approximate. Still, the Turin study was the first to provide evidence that the relationship between social stratification and fathers' valuation of self-direction for children is substantially attributable to occupational self-direction. The study even provided evidence that the relationship between men's social stratification position and their wives' values is in part attributable to men's job conditions.

Two other early cross-national studies, one in Taiwan (Olsen 1971), the other in Peru (Scurrah & Montalvo 1975), did not clearly confirm the LSES findings, but it is unclear whether these failures reflect methodological imperfections, particularly in the measurement of occupational self-direction (see Ch. 12 in Kohn & Schooler 1983). More consistent early cross-national support for the Kohn & Schooler hypotheses were found in Canada by Grabb (1981) and Ireland by Hynes (1979); the latter study used indices of occupational self-direction close to those we used.

The cross-national replications that were methodologically closest to the Kohn & Schooler US studies were carried out in Japan and Poland in direct collaboration with the LSES investigators. The major purpose in our undertaking collaborations with investigators from these particular two countries was to ascertain whether social-structural position has similar psychological effects in a Western and a non-Western and in a capitalist and a non-capitalist society. Finding similarities among these three countries in the psychological effects of being in an advantageous social-structural position and in the importance of occupational self-direction in explaining these differences, would provide considerable evidence that our findings have cross-national generality.

The Polish survey, directed by Kazimierz Slomczynski, was conducted in 1978 under the auspices of the Polish Academy of Sciences and with the collaboration of Melvin Kohn (the most complete English description is in Kohn & Slomczynski 1990). The probability sample of 1557 men was representative of men living in urban areas and employed full-time in civilian occupations. The study was designed to be an exact replication of the main parts of the LSES study. Questions about occupational self-direction and psychological functioning were adopted from the Kohn-Schooler interview schedule. Overall, the Polish replication provided very strong confirmation of the LSES hypotheses. The findings "demonstrate that occupational self-direction plays the pivotal role in explaining both the effects of social structure on personality and the effects of personality on achieved position in the social structure. Position in the class structure and in the stratification order affect men's values, intellectual flexibility and self-directedness of orientation primarily because they affect occupational self-direction; occupational self-direction, in turn, affects these facets of psychological functioning. These facets of psychological functioning affect men's positions in the social structure mainly because they affect occupational self-direction, which then affects class placement and status achievement" (p. 170).

Initial analyses of a replication carried out in Poland in 1992 and a companion study carried out in the Ukraine in 1993 (Kohn et al 1995) indicate that radical social change does not change the pattern of relationships between social structure and personality found under stable social conditions. Instead, radical social change affects the relationship of social structure and personality by transforming social structures. Even in the process of transformation, social structures come quickly to exhibit the patterns of psychological effects characteristic of the types of society they are becoming. By late 1992 Poland exhibited the capitalist pattern and early in 1993 the Ukraine was not far behind (Kohn et al 1995). These trends provide striking evidence that the psychological functioning of the individual is quite sensitive to social-structural change.

The Japanese replication was carried out by researchers at Tokyo and Osaka Universities under the direction of Atsushi Naoi with my collaboration. The interview consisted primarily of questions translated from the original Kohn-Schooler US survey. The 629 respondents were drawn from a random probability sample of employed males, 26–65 years old, living in the Kanto area. The results indicated that advantageous social-structural positions are related to parental valuation of self-direction, to intellectual flexibility, and to self-directedness of orientation for Japan very much as they are for the United States and Poland. Occupational self-direction has the same psychological effects and plays precisely the same role in explaining the relationships of social-structural position and personality for Japan as it does for the United States and Poland (A Naoi & Schooler 1985, Schooler & A Naoi 1988). These findings hold true even when traditionality of job settings and economic centrality of industry are statistically controlled. As was the case in the United States, a similar pattern of psychological effects of occupational self-direction was found among the employed wives of the sampled men (M Naoi & Schooler 1990).

Since one of the most consistent themes in accounts of Japanese culture is the deemphasis of individualism and the importance placed on psychological interdependence (A Naoi & Schooler 1985), finding that occupational self-direction has the same effects in Japan as in the more individualistically oriented United States represents a very real increase in the generalizability of our hypotheses about the effects of occupational conditions. The fact that, even in a culture where self-directedness for women is particularly disvalued, occupational self-direction increases the self-directedness of Japanese women's orientations and values is especially compelling.

Japan also provides an example of how cultural inertia may slow down social-structural and consequently psychological change. The evidence is strong that in Japanese culture self-directedness is valued even less for women than for men (Lebra 1984, Schooler & Smith 1978). It is quite plausible that this difference fosters the social-structural differences we find when we compare job roles of Japanese men and their wives (M Naoi & Schooler 1990). The wives' jobs are significantly lower in every component of occupational self-direction than are the men's. Thus, Japanese cultural norms increase the likelihood that women will work in generally subservient, nonself-directed, low-prestige positions. As we have seen, occupying such positions reduces the self-directedness of their orientations. This would increase the likelihood that they will remain amenable to the cultural norms disvaluing women's autonomy (which, of course, played a part in their original discriminatory occupational placement) and decrease their motivation to organize in defense of women's rights.

Although both the Polish and the Japanese replications confirmed the cross-national generalizability of the Kohn and Schooler hypotheses, both studies provided intriguing evidence of how a nation's culture can also affect the ways conditions of work psychologically affect the individual. When we examine Japan we find that most of the cross-national differences relate to the nature and pervasiveness of the psychological effects of organizational position. The pattern of the findings provides support for those who emphasize the general psychological importance of the group to the individual in Japan and the specific importance to the Japanese worker of the organization for which he or she works (A Naoi & Schooler 1985) as well as for those who stress the social importance of hierarchical position (Nakane 1970). In Japan, ownership and position in the work hierarchy increase self-confidence and decrease self-deprecation. These job characteristics have no such effects in the United States (Kohn & Schooler 1983) and may actually have had the opposite effects in socialist Poland (Kohn et al 1990). In Japan, ownership and high hierarchical position at work lead to greater authoritarian conservatism. High hierarchical level at work also leads to more conformity of ideas and less emphasis on personal responsibility in standards of morality. The greater authoritarian conservatism of Japanese in favorable organizational positions may reflect culturally embedded attitudes. The scale measuring authoritarian conservatism in Japan is actually marked by a higher degree of obeisance and respect for authority than its counterpart in the United States. Because of the "strong tendency for consequential human relations to have a vertical structure" (Caudill 1973, p. 249), in accord with Japanese cultural values (Nakane 1970), Japanese in authority may tend to believe that such obeisance is appropriate and that moral principles can be bent to their needs and to believe that others share these beliefs.

Several of the cross-national discrepancies between the Polish and the US findings also center around cultural differences in attitudes toward authority (Kohn et al 1990). Thus, in the United States, the substantive complexity of work is generally the most important aspect of occupational self-direction for explaining the impact of social structure. In then-communist Poland, closeness of supervision was relatively more important. Closeness of supervision had its primary psychological impact in Poland through its effect on authoritarian conservatism, its correlation with authoritarian conservatism being notably higher there than in the United States. Kohn & Slomczynki see this higher correlation "as reflecting the greater saliency of authority in Polish than in American society.... It was in the self-interest of both the state bureaucracy and the church to support those elements of traditional Polish culture that encourage people to obey all forms of authority" (1990, p. 207).

Another cross-national difference that Kohn & Slomczynski see as reflecting the greater cultural acceptance of traditional modes of authority in Poland than the United States is the relative roles of fathers and mothers in the intergenerational transmission of values. In the United States, fathers play at least as important a role as do mothers; in Poland mothers play the predominant role. Kohn & Slomczynski do not attribute this cross-national discrepancy to differing economic and political systems in the two countries. Rather they "think it is a historically rooted cultural contrast: Polish fathers play a more traditional role than do US fathers in the division of labor within the family and in the socialization of children. . . . The traditional Polish pattern where mothers have primary responsibility for child rearing and fathers' roles in the socialization of children focus on control and punishment, still obtains in many families" (Kohn & Slomczynski 1990, p. 208).

Perhaps the most striking cross-national differences that Kohn & Slomczynski (1990) found centered on the relationships among social structure, occupational self-direction, and distress. In then-communist Poland, manual workers had the strongest sense of well-being, and managers were the most distressed. In the United States, managers displayed a strong sense of well-being, and manual workers were the most distressed. In Japan, managers were also least distressed, but it was the nonmanual, not the manual, workers who were particularly distressed. In both the United States and Japan, the relationship between social class and distress, although significant, was relatively modest (Kohn et al 1990).

The experience of occupational self-direction, which is strongly related to a favorable social-structural position in all three countries, significantly reduces distress in the United States and Japan, but did not do so in Poland. Even in the United States and Japan, other social-structural characteristics are more important determinants of distress than is occupational self-direction, and these other characteristics' effects on distress may be at odds with those of occupational self-direction. In the United States, job protections ameliorate distress. Nonetheless, because they lacked opportunities for occupational self-direction, manual workers, the group who enjoyed the greatest job protections, were the most distressed. Were it not for their job protections, these workers would have been even more distressed. In Japan, higher education and the job conditions of working under time pressure and being held responsible for things outside one's control, all of which are related to a favorable socioeconomic position, each increase distress. In both Japan and the United States, the countervailing effects of conditions that increase distress may help explain both the particular patterns of class differences and why the overall relationship of class to distress is modest.

For Poland, although there were few interview questions about occupational conditions other than occupational self-direction, several available pieces of information provide plausible explanations of why manual workers were relatively less distressed and managers relatively more distressed than in the United States and Japan. In 1978, Polish manual workers may have had a sense of well-being because they held a relatively advantageous position in the national economy compared both to the other classes and to their own position in earlier times. This was true in terms of job security and job benefits. In addition, the value placed on their class by Communist ideology led to their having preferential access to housing, health care, and higher education for their children.

A clue to the high level of distress of Polish managers is provided by the finding that one segment of this class was particularly distressed—those who were not members of the Communist Party. Being a non-Party manager in the Polish system of centralized planning may have entailed greater risks than experienced by managers who were Party members, and greater than those experienced by managers in less centralized capitalist countries. Whether or not these historical characteristics of the Polish class structure explain the pattern of relationships between class and distress that Kohn & Slomczynski found in 1978 Poland it is nevertheless the case that by 1992 Poland showed the same relationships between class and distress as found in capitalist societies (Kohn et al 1995). In postcommunist Poland managers have a strong sense of well-being, and manual workers are the most distressed of all classes. Moreover, occupational self-direction now plays a decisive role in explaining the relationship between class and distress, although it had little or no role in doing so in communist Poland.

Unquestionably, the various cross-national studies testing the Kohn & Schooler hypotheses about the psychological importance of occupational self-direction have come up with a variety of findings that indicate that the particular historically determined cultural and political conditions of the different countries examined have direct effects on their inhabitants' psychological functioning. These studies have even provided a variety of examples in which a country's culture and immediate history affect the ways in which occupational conditions have their psychological effects. Nevertheless, the overall pattern of the findings provides firm evidence for the cross-national generalizabilty of the Kohn & Schooler hypothesis that self-directed conditions of work increase intellectual functioning and promote a self-directed orientation to self and to society. Equally supported (Kohn et al 1990) is the corollary hypothesis that, in each of the countries studied, differences in these psychological characteristics related to either the individual's position in the social stratification system (the hierarchical order of society as indexed by education, occupational status, and job income) or social class membership (groups defined in terms of their relationship to ownership and control of the means of production and control over the labor power of others) are to a large extent a direct function of social status and social class differences in the degree to which individuals' jobs permit such self-direction.

Eric Wright and the Comparative Project on Class Structure and Class Consciousness

A concern for empirically legitimating the Marxist belief in the overwhelming importance of social class as a determinant of individual values, attitudes, and behavior appears to be the guiding motivation for the Comparative Project on Class Structure and Class Consciousness initiated in 1977 by Erik Olin Wright. Wright does not personally believe that "quantitative research... should be treated as some kind of privileged basis for developing and reconstructing theoretical arguments" (1989, p. 3). Nevertheless, he has developed, coordinated, and helped secure funding for the extraordinarily extensive and intensive Comparative Project whose "central objective... has been to create a systematic, cross-national data set on class structure and class consciousness which incorporates as rigorously as possible a variety of measures of Marxist and non-Marxist approaches to class" (1989, p. 5). In the early stages of the project, Wright defined classes by ownership and control of the means of production and control over the labor power of others. He then shifted to a definition of class based on the concept of class exploitation—the relationship in which class "X benefits by virtue of appropriating at least part of the social surplus produced by (class) Y" (1989, p. 7). Wright bases his class distinctions on "three principal types of exploitation: capitalist exploitation, based on unequal control over the means of production; bureaucratic or organization exploitation, based on unequal control of organization assets; and skill or credential exploitation, based on unequal control of scarce skills" (1989, p. 8). Categorizing the levels of each of these forms of exploitation, he ends up with a matrix of 12 classes including such traditional marxist classes as the bourgeois and proletarian, but also including new ones like semi-credentialed workers and expert nonmanagers.

Although representative sample survey data for the project seem to have been collected in 11 countries, the presently published cross-national comparisons deal with 2 to 7 countries. The initial cross-national analyses compared the class structures of the United States and Sweden (Wright 1985, 1989). It found that although the class distributions in the two countries were not dramatically different, the working class was larger in Sweden and the supervisory class larger in the United States. Wright interprets these findings in terms of the differences in the social control of production resulting from dissimilarities in labor movement roles and strategies in the two countries.

Examining individual values and behavior, Wright uses the comparison of the United States and Sweden to examine the relationship between class structure and the class consciousness of the individual (Wright 1985). Using a Likert scale measuring pro-capitalist vs pro-working class sentiment, he finds that the patterning of class consciousness is essentially the same in the two countries. No matter whether one is examining "capitalist exploitation," "organizational exploitation," or "skill exploitation," greater levels of exploitation monotonically increase pro-capitalist ideological orientation. Cross-national differences, however, are striking. In Sweden workers are much more anticapitalist than in the United States, and the lines of ideological demarcation between class locations are quite different. In "the United States nearly 40 percent of the labor force is ideologically part of the 'bourgeois coalition' whereas in Sweden this figure is less than 10 percent" (Wright 1989, p. 12). Wright sees these results as indicating that class consciousness is shaped, on the one hand, directly by class location, which determines a set of interests and experiences faced by the individual, and on the other, by the ways that the political strategies of relevant organizations affect how people interpret their experiences and act on their interests.

Later Comparative Project papers seek to demonstrate the tangible reality of the social classes that Wright delineates by demonstrating the relative impermeability of class boundaries to friendships (Wright & Cho 1992) and to intergenerational mobility (Western & Wright 1994). These investigations involve four countries—the United States, Canada, Norway, and Sweden. The patterns of friendship formation across class boundaries proved relatively invariant across the four countries. In each, boundaries based on property ownership were the least permeable, followed by boundaries based on expertise, and then those based on authority. Wright & Cho (1992) point out that, although the prediction of Marxist theory that the property boundary should be least permeable is supported, the expertise boundary is less permeable and the authority boundary more permeable than would be predicted by Wright's theories of class exploitation and common interest. Wright & Cho also note that they had assumed that cross-national differences in the permeability of class boundaries to friendship formation would be important for understanding the cross-national variations in the process by which structurally defined classes become collectively organized as political forces. They see their assumption as undermined by their finding that permeability of class boundaries is largely invariant across countries that differ substantially in patterns of organized class formation.

Western & Wright's (1994) analysis of class boundaries in intergenerational mobility found that in North America class boundaries are broadly consistent with Wright's conceptualization of class. The property boundary is the least permeable, followed by the expertise and then the authority boundary. In the United States and Canada, material resources linked to capitalist property relations are a more significant barrier to mobility than are cultural resources linked to experience. In Sweden and Norway the property and expertise boundaries do not differ significantly in their permeability, primarily because the property boundary is more permeable than in "more purely capitalistic" North America (Western & Wright 1994, p. 624). Since in North America the property boundary is also less permeable for friendships and marriages, the pattern of results suggests that in highly capitalist societies being an employer with even a small business creates barriers to a spectrum of social movements across the property boundary. Another finding that supports Wright's conceptualization of class is the existence of interaction terms suggesting that class structures are "wholes" not simply reducible to the sums of the three underlying dimensions of exploitation.

The most recently published paper from the Comparative Project uses data from seven countries (the United States, Canada, United Kingdom, Australia, Sweden, Norway, and Japan) to examine cross-national differences in the gender gap in workplace authority (Wright et al 1995). The findings indicate that although there is evidence of a gender gap in authority in each of the countries, it is smaller in the English-speaking countries, especially the United States and Canada, large in the Scandinavian countries, and huge in Japan. These cross-national differences are not a function of differences in a range of attributes of firms, jobs, or individuals, nor of self selection, nor of "glass ceiling" processes which limit women's movement up the organizational hierarchy.

In explaining their results, Wright, Baxter and Birkelund hypothesize that if, as in the United States, there are many managerial positions and a relatively strong women's movement oriented to individualistic goals, barriers to authority will be most likely to be breached. If, as in Scandinavia, there are a moderate number of authority positions and the women's movement is oriented toward state welfare policies that reduce the dependency of workers on the market, the workplace gender authority gap will be relatively large. If, as in Japan, there are relatively few managerial positions and the women's movement is weak, the gender gap will be particularly large. They conclude "(b)oth political and economic factors thus seem to be important in explaining the variability in gender inequality in workplace authority, whereas cultural differences more specifically linked to gender ideology seem less significant" (Wright et al 1955, p. 434).

The downgrading of the behavioral and psychological importance of cultural factors in explaining cross-national differences is a general characteristic of the Comparative Project, which generally seeks to explain such differences in terms of present day class structure or in the recent political strategies of class-based organizations. This downplaying of the role assigned to cultural factors becomes particularly evident when we compare the reasons we have seen given for essentially the same phenomena—the particularly subservient occupational positions of Japanese women—by Comparative Project and LSES studies.

A Cross-National Examination of John Meyer's Views on Institutionalization

Although in comparison to Wright's Comparative Project, the LSES program on the psychological effects of occupational conditions may emphasize the importance of cultural factors, it has been cited as a prime example of an approach that underestimates the importance of such factors. In their empirically ground-breaking cross-national study, Frank, Meyer & Miyahara (Frank et al 1995) directly link the prominence of professional psychology to the cultural legitimation and institutionalization of individualism. They contrast their findings with "many classic analyses [that] see western and now worldwide individualism as resulting from the rise of modern social complexity ([e.g.] Foucault 1979, Kohn & Schooler 1983)" (Frank et al 1995, p. 360). They note that "although a range of theories can lead to our core proposition, some important ones do not: These include realist models of modern systems in which individualism derives from social differentiation and economic development and is not an independent property of culture and polity" (p. 362).[5]

Inspired by John Myers' seminal views on institutionalism (Meyer 1977, Meyer & Rowan 1977), Frank, Meyer & Miyahara's paper suggests a variety of ways that culturally institutionalized individualism may lead to a high prevalence of professionalized psychology. For one, elites in individualist countries may be prone to see the improvement of individual performance putatively resulting from the scientific analyses of the individual as a resource for meeting the challenges they face. For another, institutional legitimation of individualism may also increase people's inclination to see their private concerns as intrinsically important and worthy of scientific investigation.

[5]Contrary to Frank, Meyers & Miyahara (1995), the LSES occupation study papers never imply that the value a sociocultural system places on self-direction or individualism can be completely explained by the direct psychological effects of such possible sequelae of modern economic development as structural individualism or environmental complexity. In fact, a number of my papers specifically examine how sociological and cultural processes such as institutionalization affect the acceptance of such values (Schooler 1990a,b, 1994).

Using structural equation modeling, the core hypothesis is tested against the obvious alternative that any form of economic development or modernization generates a greater prominence of psychology. The dependent variable is a latent variable measuring the prevalence of psychology through six indicators (e.g. number of psychologists per million people, number of university level psychology departments per thousand people). The latent variable measuring the degree to which the status of individuals is especially central in national societies is based on four indicators (e.g. a 10-point scale of formal democratic institutions, years since female suffrage). The economic development latent variable is based on GNP and energy consumption per capita. Although plausible arguments can be made against the appropriateness of various of these indicators, the overall properties of the measurement models are highly satisfactory, and in several instances the models were recalculated leaving out potentially problematic indicators, with no change in results. These results, based on a cross-national analysis of 89 countries, indicate that the standardized effect of cultural individualism on the prominence of professionalized psychology (.77) is over three times as great as the effect of economic development. Other analyses indicate that cultural individualism increases the prominence of psychology more than it does that of the social or physical sciences. These results remain essentially the same even with the inclusion of such control variables as English language, population size, state centralization, GNP growth rate, income inequality, and scientific activity.

In concluding, Frank et al state, "[W]e approach the relationship between political-cultural individualism and the prevalence of psychology from an institutionalist perspective, which treats the construction and rationalization of social elements, such as the individual, as a rather direct consequence of the operation of modern liberal society seen as a cultural model. . . [T]he results reflect negatively on those arguments that would view psychology as simply reflecting the structural individualism produced by modern economic development" (p. 373).

Frank et al firmly establish the importance of institutional processes for explaining cross-national differences in values and behavior by providing substantial empirical evidence of how institutional factors affect the societal impact of individualistic values in different countries. In fact, the approach to institutional theory and research in which Meyers has been a central figure clues us to the part institutionalization may play in why cultural level phenomena apparently change at a slower pace than do individual and social level phenomena. According to Jepperson (1991), whose views represent this approach, an institution is a social order or pattern from which departures "are counteracted by repetitively activated, socially constructed controls—that is, by some set of rewards and sanctions. . . [R]outine reproductive procedures support and sustain the pattern, furthering its reproduction— unless collective action blocks, or environmental shock disrupts, the reproductive process. . . . All institutions are frameworks of programs or rules establishing identities and activity scripts for such identities" (pp. 145–46). Thus, in terms of the definitions presented at the beginning of this paper, institutions are social structures that tend to be maintained because the pattern of the role relationships among their statuses are so structured that departures from expectations bring about sanctions enforcing conformity to role expectations.

Further light on the psychological mechanisms through which an institution's culture may be transmitted, kept continuous and resistant to change, is afforded by a series of experiments by Zucker (1991). Their results suggest that, even in the absence of sanctions, the transmission of institutional behaviors is not problematic because the actor doing the transmitting simply communicates them as objective fact, and the actor receiving them treats them as an accurate rendition of objective fact. Knowledge of " the history of transmission provides a basis for assuming that the meaning of the act is part of the common-sense world. As continuity increases, the acts are increasingly objectified and made exterior to the particular situation. . . . Acts high on institutionalization will be resistant to attempts to change them through personal influence because they are seen as external facts, imposed on the setting and at the same time defining it" (p. 88).

All in all, institutional theory and research has demonstrated that some social structures (i.e. institutions) are so patterned that they react to threats to their continued existence by selectively punishing role performances that do not meet their norms and rewarding those that do. At the same time these social structures provide psychological mechanisms for aiding their continuance that do not depend on the possibility of sanctions. In terms of the direct concerns of the present paper, institutionalization provides us with at least part of the reason for the greater inertia of social and cultural as compared to individual level phenomena. Once some set of cultural norms and concomitant behaviors are institutionalized, they are likely to be maintained. The longer they are maintained, the more likely they are to be seen as legitimate and objectively real. It is also possible that actual role performances and relatively specific role expectations (e.g. parenting practices of working mothers) change more readily than more general culturally legitimated role norms (e.g. culturally normative role expectations for mothers), thus contributing to the slower change of cultural than social-structural level phenonena.

Although cross-national differences in the institutionalization of values such as individualism are demonstrably related to cross-national differences in the manifestation of such values, at present institutional theory and research do not come close to providing a basic explanation of such differences in institutionalization. What remains vague are the socioeconomic conditions under which particular institutions begin, change, and end within a given country. Even less clear are the conditions under which an institution developed in one country is accepted as legitimate in another. For example, if we consider the individualist institutions that Frank et al describe, what is left unanswered from an historical perspective is why such institutions were so strongly entrenched in Northwestern Europe. In modern times, even taking into account the direct hand that US occupation officials took in writing the Japanese constitution, it would seem simplistically wrong to explain the complex state of individualist norms and institutions in present-day Japan as merely the direct result of spread from "the Anglo-protestant core countries—the hegemonic source, it seems, of much of the special celebration of the individual in the modern system" (Frank et al 1995, p. 373). (For a discussion of possible causal interconnections in both England and Japan among historical/cultural, social-structural/institutional, economic/production factors and levels of individualism, see Schooler 1990. For a recent innovative sociological examination of historical institutional supports for individulism in Japanese culture, see Ikegami 1995).

CONCLUSIONS, LIMITATIONS, AND IMPLICATIONS

At this point we have discussed four extensive research programs that have used the techniques of quantitative empirical sociology to compare the effects of social structure and culture on present-day values and behavior across a range of countries. The cross-national research on individual modernity led by Alex Inkeles established that social-structural conditions associated with industrialization are almost invariably linked to an increase in the openness of individuals to new experience, rejection of traditional authority, and a rational, ambitious, orderly approach to both work and human problems. The cross-national research on the Kohn and Schooler hypothesis—that self-directed work increases intellectual functioning and promotes self-directed orientations and values—did more than confirm its cross-national generality. These studies also uncovered a variety of national differences reflecting historically determined dissimilarities in cultural values. This research also established that the social status and social class differences in these psychological characteristics found within different countries are largely the result of social-structurally determined status and class differences in the opportunity for occupational self-direction. Wright's cross-national research program provided evidence that in a variety of countries, despite historically determined national differences, social classes, at least as he defines them, directly affect political attitudes, while acting as tangible barriers to mobility and personal relationships. The research deriving from Meyer's theories highlights the importance of institutions and socially constructed views of reality in the development and maintenance of cross-national differences and similarities in cultural values and their behavioral embodiment. As we have seen, institutional theory and research also provide further clues as to why the speed of change seems to decrease as we go from psychological to social-structural to cultural levels of phenomena.

As noted in the introduction, confirming such a temporal tendency would provide a valuable tool for elucidating the causal connections among the different levels of phenomena determining the contribution of culture and social structure to cross-national differences in values and behavior. The need for such help becomes apparent when we compare the outcomes of the four empirically rigorous sociologically based cross-national research programs we have just examined. One points to the general importance of industrialization; the second to the psychological consequences of social-structurally determined conditions of the immediate work environment; the third to the continued relevance of social class based on unequal control over the means of production, organizational assets, or scarce skills; the fourth to the importance of the institutionalization of values. In addition, all four, to varying degrees, provide evidence of the continuing importance of historically determined cultural differences.

Trying to trace the causal connections among cultural, social-structural, and individual level phenomena would be even more complicated if the scope of studies considered were not limited to quantitative sociological research programs on modern cross-national differences that compare more than two countries. Obviously, a variety of potentially relevant studies do not meet these criteria. For example, Lincoln & Kalleberg (1990) find in their quantitative two-nation comparison of the sources of worker commitment in the United States and Japan that while the role of culture is not trivial, "the dedication and commitment of Japanese workers derive from Japan's leading edge status as an adopter and implementer of a new highly successful technology of organization and control" (p. 28). For another example, although his research is not quantitative, Vogel (1991) has tried to determine the commonalities underlying the recent rapid economic growth of Taiwan, Hong Kong, Singapore, and Korea. He concluded that US aid, the destruction of the old order, a sense of political and economic urgency, an eager, plentiful, and skilled labor force, and familiarity with the Japanese model are the common characteristics underlying this unusually rapid development.

The task of sorting out the effects of culture and social structure would become even more daunting if we were also to take into consideration, as we should, the excellent relevant historical research of sociologists such as Goldstone (1987, 1991), let alone relevant historical research in other disciplines. Indeed, although most cross-national research done by psychologists tends to overlook social-structural variables, papers similar to this could well be written reviewing comparative empirical studies of culture and social structure in the fields of political science and anthropology (e.g. the theoretically and methodologically sophisticated cross-cultural studies of interpersonal violence by C Ember and M Ember 1993).

Despite the daunting challenge of what remains undone, elucidating the parts that culture and social structure play in cross-national differences remains a problem worth pursuing. An appropriate theoretical framework exists, as do statistical modeling procedures appropriate for many of the relevant types of data and necessary analyses. Although it should obviously be tested empirically whenever possible, the supposition of a tendency to greater resistance to change as we go from individual to social-structural to cultural level phenomena should also prove useful. Even though we will never achieve an all-encompassing, fully satisfactory understanding of how nations' cultures, social structures, and the psychology of their citizens are causally related, we can learn something. Both what we learn and the theoretical and methodological refinements made while we learn not only have practical import, they are also close to the core issues of sociology.

Any *Annual Review* chapter, as well as any article cited in an *Annual Review* chapter, may be purchased from the Annual Reviews Preprints and Reprints service. 1-800-347-8007; 415-259-5017; email: arpr@class.org

---

Literature Cited

Aronson LR. 1984. Levels of integration and organization: a reevaluation of the evolutionary scale. In *Behavioral Evolution and Integrative Levels,* ed. G Greenberg, E Tobach, pp. 57–81. Hillsdale, NJ: Erlbaum

Baddeley A, Gardner JM, Grantham-McGregor S. 1995. Cross-cultural cognition: developing tests for developing countries. *Appl. Cogn. Psychol.* 9:173–95

Berry JW, Poortinga YH, Segall MH, Dasen PR. 1992. *Cross-Cultural Psychology: Research and Applications.* New York: Cambridge Univ. Press

Caudill WA. 1973. The influence of social structure and culture on human behavior in modern Japan. *J. Nerv. Ment. Dis.* 157:240–57

Caudill WA, Schooler C. 1973. Child behavior and child rearing in Japan and the United States: an interim report. *J. Nerv. Ment. Dis.*

157:323–38

Chomsky N, Lightfoot D. 1990. Language and innateness. In *Mind and Cognition: A Reader,* ed. WG Lycan, pp. 627–59. Oxford, Engl: Blackwell

Ekman P. 1992. Are there basic emotions? *Psychol. Rev.* 99:550–53

Ember CR, Ember M. 1993. Issues in cross-cultural studies of interpersonal violence. *Violence Vict.* 8:217–33

Form WH. 1979. Comparative industrial sociology and the convergence hypothesis. *Annu. Rev. Sociol.* 5:1–25

Foucault M. 1979. *Discipline and Punish: The Birth of the Prison.* Harmondsworth, Engl: Penguin

Frank DJ, Meyer JW, Miyahara D. 1995. The individualist polity and the prevalence of professionalized psychology: a cross-national study. *Am. Sociol. Rev.* 60:360–77

Goldstone JA. 1987. Cultural orthodoxy, risk and innovation: the divergence of East and West in the early modern world. *Sociol. Theory* 5:119–35

Goldstone JA. 1991. *Rebellion in the Early Modern World.* Berkeley: Univ. Calif. Press

Grabb EG. 1981. The ranking of self-actualization values: the effects of class, stratification, and occupational experiences. *Sociol. Q.* 22:373–83

House JS. 1981. Social structure and personality. In *Social Psychology: Sociological Perspectives,* ed. M Rosenberg, RH Turner, pp. 525–61. New York: Basic Books

Hynes E. 1979. *Explaining class differences in socialization values and behavior: an Irish study.* PhD thesis. South. Ill. Univ., Carbondale

Ikegami E. 1995. *The Taming of the Samurai.* Cambridge, MA: Harvard Univ. Press

Inkeles A. 1960. Industrial man: the relation of status to experience, perception, and value. *Am. J. Sociol.* 66:1–31

Inkeles A. 1969. Making men modern: on the causes and consequences of individual change in six developing countries. *Am. J. Sociol.* 75:208–25

Inkeles A. 1983. *Exploring Individual Modernity.* New York: Columbia Univ. Press

Inkeles A, Smith DH. 1974. *Becoming Modern: Individual Changes in Six Developing Countries.* Cambridge, MA: Harvard Univ. Press

Jackendoff R. 1994. *Patterns in the Mind: Language and Human Nature.* New York: Basic Books

Jepperson RL. 1991. Institutions, institutional effects, and institutionalism. In *The New Institutionalism in Organizational Analysis,* ed. WW Powell, PJ DiMaggio, pp. 143–63. Chicago: Univ. Chicago Press

Jöreskog KG. 1973. A general method for estimating a linear structural equation system. In *Structural Equation Models in the Social Sciences,* ed. AS Goldberger, OD Duncan, pp. 85–112. New York: Seminar

Kohn ML. 1989. Cross-national research as an analytic strategy. In *Cross-National Research in Sociology,* ed. ML Kohn, pp. 77–102. Newbury Park, CA: Sage

Kohn ML, Naoi A, Schoenbach C, Schooler C, Slomczynski KM. 1990. Position in the class structure and psychological functioning: a comparative analysis of the United States, Japan and Poland. *Am. J. Sociol.* 95:964–1008

Kohn ML, Schooler C. 1983. Job conditions and personality: a longitudinal assessment of their reciprocal effects. In *Work and Personality: An Inquiry into the Impact of So-cial Stratification,* pp. 125–53. Norwood, NJ: Ablex

Kohn ML, Slomczynski KM. 1990. *Social Structure and Self-direction: A Comparative Analysis of the United States and Poland.* Oxford: Blackwell

Kohn ML, Slomczynski KM, Janicka K, Khmelko V, Mach BW, et al. 1995. Class, work and personality under conditions of radical social change: a comparative analysis of Poland and Ukraine. Presented at Annu. Meet. Am. Sociol. Assoc., 90th, Washington, DC

Lebra TS. 1984. *Japanese Women: Constraint and Fulfillment.* Honolulu: Univ. Hawaii Press

Lincoln JR, Kalleberg A. 1990. *Culture, Control and Commitment: A Study of Work Organization and Work Attitudes in the U.S. and Japan.* Cambridge: Cambridge Univ. Press

Linton R. 1936. *The Study of Man.* New York: Appleton-Century

Linton R. 1945. *The Cultural Background of Personality.* New York: Appleton-Century

Luke TW. 1991. The discourse of development: a genealogy of "developing nations" and the discipline of modernity. *Curr. Perspect. Soc. Theory* 11:71–293

Markus R, Kitayama S. 1991. Culture and self: implications for cognition, emotion and motivation. *Psychol. Rev.* 98:224–53

Merton RK. 1957a. *Social Theory and Social Structure.* New York: Free Press

Merton RK. 1957b. The role set: problems in sociological theory. *Br. J. Sociol.* 8:106–20

Meyer JW. 1977. The effects of education as an institution. *Am. J. Sociol.* 83:53–77

Meyer JW, Rowan B. 1977. Institutionalized organizations: formal structure as myth and ceremony. *Am. J. Sociol.* 83:340–63

Miller J, Schooler C, Kohn ML, Miller KA. 1979. Women and work: the psychological effects of occupational conditions. *Am. J. Sociol.* 85:66–94

Miller-Loessi K. 1995. Comparative social psychology: cross-cultural and cross-national. In *Sociological Perspectives on Social Psychology,* ed. KA Cook, GA Fine, JS House, pp. 397–420. Boston: Allyn & Bacon

Nakane C. 1970. *Japanese Society.* Berkeley: Univ. Calif. Press

Naoi A, Schooler C. 1985. Occupational conditions and psychological functioning in Japan. *Am. J. Sociol.* 90:729–52

Naoi M, Schooler C. 1990. Psychological consequences of occupational conditions among Japanese wives. *Soc. Psychol. Q.* 58:100–16

Olsen SM. 1971. *Family, occupation, and values in a Chinese urban community.* PhD thesis. Cornell Univ., Ithaca, NY

Pearlin LI, Kohn ML. 1966. Social class, occupation, and parental values: a cross-national study. *Am. Sociol. Rev.* 31:466–79

Schneirla TC. 1951. The "levels" concepts in the study of social organization in animals. In *Social Psychology of the Crossroads,* ed. J Rohrer, M Sherif, pp. 83–120. New York: Harper

Schneirla TC. 1972. *Selected Writings.* San Francisco: Freeman

Schooler C. 1976. Serfdom's legacy: an ethnic continuum. *Am. J. Sociol.* 81:1265–86

Schooler C. 1989. Social structural effects and experimental situations: mutual lessons of cognitive and social science. In *Social Structure and Aging: Psychological Processes,* ed. KW Schaie, C. Schooler, pp. 129–47. Hillsdale, NJ: Erlbaum

Schooler C. 1990a. The individual in Japanese history: parallels to and divergences from the European experience. *Sociol. Forum* 5:569–94

Schooler C. 1990b. Individualism and the historical and social-structural determinants of people's concern over self-directedness and efficacy. In *Self Directedness and Efficacy: Causes and Effects Throughout the Life Course,* ed. J Rodin, C Schooler, KW Schaie, pp. 19–49

Schooler C. 1991. Interdisciplinary lessons: the two social psychologies from the perspective of a psychologist practicing sociology. In *The Future of Social Psychology: Defining the Relationships Between Sociology and Psychology,* ed. CW Stephan, WG Stephan, TF Pettigrew, pp. 71–81. New York: Springer-Verlag

Schooler C. 1994. A working conceptualization of social structure: Mertonian roots and psychological and sociocultural relationships. *Soc. Psychol. Q.* 57:262–73

Schooler C. 1996. William Caudill and the reproduction of culture: infant child, and mother's behavior in Japan and the US. In *Japanese Child Development: Classic Stud-*

ies, Retrospects and Prospects, ed. D Shwalb, B Shwalb. New York: Guilford. In press

Schooler C, Naoi A. 1988. The psychological effects of traditional and of economically peripheral job settings in Japan. *Am. J. Sociol.* 94:335–55

Schooler C, Smith KC. 1978. . . . and a Japanese wife: social antecedents of women's role values in Japan. *Sex Roles* 4:23–41

Scurrah MJ, Montalvo A. 1975. *Clase social y valores sociales en Peru.* Lima, Peru: Escuela Admin. Negocios Para Graduados

Triandis HC. 1994. *Culture and Social Behavior.* New York: McGraw-Hill

Vogel E. 1991. *The Four Little Dragons: The Spread of Industrialization in East Asia.* Cambridge: Harvard Univ. Press

Wallerstein I. 1974. The rise and future demise of the world capitalist system: concepts for comparative analysis. *Comp. Stud. Soc. Hist.* 16:287–415

Western M, Wright EO. 1994. The permeability of class boundaries to intergenerational mobility among men in the United States, Canada, Norway and Sweden. *Am. Sociol. Rev.* 59:606–29

Wright EO. 1985. *Classes.* London: New Left Books

Wright EO. 1989. The comparative project on class structure and class consciousness: an overview. *Acta Sociol.* 32:3–22

Wright EO, Baxter J, Birkelund GE. 1995. The gender gap in workplace authority: a cross-national study. *Am. Sociol. Rev.* 57:85–102

Wright EO, Cho D. 1992. The relative permeability of class boundaries to cross-class friendships: a comparative study of the United States, Canada, Sweden and Norway. *Am. Sociol. Rev.* 57:85–102

Zucker LG. 1991. The role of institutionalization in cultural persistence. In *The New Institutionalism in Organizational Analysis,* ed. WW Powell, PJ DiMaggio, pp. 83–107. Chicago, Il: Univ. Chicago Press

Annu. Rev. Sociol. 1996. 22:351–

AN INTRODUCTION TO CATEGORICAL DATA ANALAYSIS

Douglas Sloane

Department of Sociology, Catholic University, Washington, DC 20064

S. Philip Morgan

Department of Sociology, University of Pennsylvania, 3718 Locust Walk, Philadelphia, Pennsylvania 19104-6299

KEY WORDS: methods, statistics, log-linear models, logit models

ABSTRACT

Log-linear methods provide a powerful framework and the statistical apparatus for rigorously analyzing categorical data. These methods were introduced and developed by Leo Goodman and others in the early 1970s. In the late 1970s and the early 1980s, Goodman, Alan Agresti, Clifford Clogg, Otis Dudley Duncan, and others showed how these models could help us to estimate associations between discrete variables, including ordered and unordered polytomies. The last decade has witnessed a set of diverse extensions of these techniques. This paper reviews the basic log-linear strategy and illustrates key concepts. Citations are given to other articles on these topics, many of which are nontechnical and contain substantive sociological applications.

INTRODUCTION

Until the late 1960s, sociologists typically analyzed contingency tables, or two-way tables formed by cross-classifying categorical variables, by calculating chi-square values testing the hypothesis of independence. If independence did not hold, departures from it were typically described in terms of differences in percentages or proportions, or by some global measure of association. Where tables consisted of more than a pair of variables, elaboration procedures

351

0360-0572/96/0815-0351$08.00

(Lazarsfeld 1955, Rosenberg 1969) were often followed, which involved computing chi-squares for two-way tables (like A × B), and then again for multiple subtables formed from them (i.e. A × B, within categories of C). Analysts were typically concerned with determining whether independence held after the subtables were formed but not before (indicating a spurious association), whether it held in some subtables but not others (indicating a partial or conditional association), or whether departures from independence appeared more pronounced in some subtables than others (indicating an interaction). Where departures from independence were exhibited in various subtables, they were frequently described by differences in the percentage differences, or differences in some summary measure of association calculated for the different subtables.[1]

The analysis of cross-classified data changed quite dramatically in the 1970s, with the publication of a series of papers on log-linear models by Goodman (see, for example, 1970, 1971a,b, 1972, 1973a,b), many of which were collected in 1978 into his book *Analyzing Qualitative/Categorical Data*. Other books appeared around that time, many borrowing from and building on Goodman's work; these include important books by Bishop, Fienberg & Holland (1975), Haberman (1974, 1978/1979), and Fienberg (1980). These works, and particularly the work of Goodman, introduced researchers to a wide variety of models, other than the model of independence, that could be fitted to cross-classified data; and provided them with formal and rigorous methods for selecting, from among those models, a model or models that should be preferred over others for describing what's "going on" in a table or, more importantly, in the population that gave rise to the tabulated data.

Two shortcomings appeared in many of the early works on log-linear models. One was that the discussions were impenetrable to substantial numbers of working sociologists, or social scientists generally, who lacked the mathematical sophistication to grasp them. The other was that, at least as they were described by Goodman, the models appeared initially to be most useful for analyzing dichotomous variables, but far less so for analyzing polytomous ones. As Duncan has noted (in his forward to Goodman 1984), all but one of the empirical examples in Goodman's 1978 book pertained to dichotomous variables, and while Goodman was careful to establish their generalizability, many readers may have failed to recognize this. Even those that didn't might have nonetheless considered such models less useful for large tables, or tables with a number of polytomous variables; one of the frequent criticisms of log-linear models was that they seemed to produce, in larger tables, "too many results."

---

[1] Researchers would also sometimes treat discrete variables as if they were continuous and employ regression procedures, a practice that was beset by a number of problems (see Hagenâars 1990).

The second of these problems—the perception that these models might have limited utility in analyzing polytomous variables and larger tables that included them—was addressed, in large measure, by a series of articles and books published in the late 1970s and early 1980s that dealt more specifically with the treatment of ordered and unordered polytomies. Important books on analyzing data involving ordered polytomies were produced by Goodman (1984) and Agresti (1984), and additional articles of note on the same topic were published by Duncan (1979), Duncan & McRae (1979), and Clogg (1982a,b). [For more recent treatments, see also Hout (1984a,b, 1988), Agresti (1989, 1990) and Clogg & Shihadeh (1994).] The Goodman book also contained a formal treatment of how to deal with unordered polytomies via partitioning and collapsing (see in particular Chapter 7 and Appendix A), as did articles by Duncan (1975) and Allison (1980).

The first of these problems (i.e. the fact that many social scientists have not grasped these techniques well enough to feel comfortable using them) has been resolved only partly. Davis's (1974) exegesis of Goodman's early work was helpful in pitching these techniques to a broader audience, as was the Sage publication by Knoke & Burke (1980), and the review essay published by Swafford (1980). An especially lucid nontechnical account of log-linear models is also found in Appendix A of Duncan & Duncan (1978), and a helpful account of how the parameters of log-linear models can be interpreted is provided by Alba (1987; also see Liao 1994). Clogg & Eliason (1987) provide a useful discussion of solutions to some of the common problems in log-linear analysis.

It is also helpful that more and more empirical investigations use these techniques[2], and the lucid accounts of how investigators have proceeded will undoubtedly stimulate others to use them. Social mobility has clearly provided one of the most fertile substantive terrains for innovative log-linear modeling. In earlier volumes of the *Annual Review of Sociology*, Kurz & Muller (1987:419) argue that social mobility research has profited from the "conceptual precision and methodological sophistication" provided by log-linear techniques, and Ganzeboom, Treiman & Ultee (1991) mark the "third generation of social mobility research" (e.g. from the early 1970s to the present) by the introduction and development of log-linear techniques. Mobility research has shown how substantively important claims can be incorporated into statistical models that can then be assessed by comparison to observed data [see for

---

[2]In the journal *Demography*, Teachman, Paasch & Carver (1993) document a dramatic increase in the use of log-linear, logistic, and hazard-rate models in the 1980s. These techniques were rarely used in *Demography* in the 1960–1975 period. Although we have not carried out a systematic study, our impression is that the same trends are observed in many sociological journals.

examples Hauser (1978), Duncan (1979), Hout (1982, 1983, 1984a,b), Sobel (1983), Sobel, Hout, & Duncan 1985, Wong (1990, 1992), Xie (1992), and Yamaguchi (1983, 1987)].[3]

Moreover, a growing number of software programs allow these models to be fitted with far greater ease than was true fifteen years ago. Increased computational ease will likely encourage more users.[4] Still, many who might use these techniques do not, in spite of the fact that the arguments for their use are compelling. We can only guess that there remain a number of people who simply have not figured out that, essentially, these are simple models that can be employed by those with very modest mathematical means, like ourselves.[5]

This review offers a nontechnical introduction to log-linear modeling, at least as it is applied to the common task of disentangling associations in tables that involve a clearly defined dependent variable, and one or more factors whose effects on that dependent variable are of interest. In the course of describing these techniques, we point to related and reasonably nontechnical sources that provide additional details on their use. While our discussion does not cover the most recent innovations in this type of modeling, involving latent structures, log-multiplicative models, and the like, we expect that a simple account of these more basic models will help those who wish to pursue the more technical treatments or more recent developments.

The data employed in our discussion are from the 1974, 1984, and 1994 General Social Surveys, and they provide information on the effects of race and marital status on general happiness. Our interest in these associations was generated, in part, by a question raised by James Davis in a recent article entitled "What's Wrong with Sociology?" According to Davis (1994, p. 194), sociology would benefit from sustained attention to simple causal modeling aimed at accounting for important and interesting correlations, such as: "Married people are distinctly happier than the nonmarried. And white people are distinctly happier than black people. But exactly why—and why is the marital status correlation declining?" We doubt that the little information we offer on these issues will go very far toward curing what Davis thinks is ailing sociology.[6]

---

[3]The "square" (e.g. rows = columns) structure of the mobility table is common to many sociological problems, making the innovative uses of social mobility models highly informative and broadly applicable. For instance, square contingency tables are produced by cross-classifying (i) responses to the same question at two points in time, (ii) two different items with like response categories, or (iii) responses to the same question asked of paired respondents.

[4]Widely used statistical packages such as SAS, SPSS, and BMDP have log-linear and logistic routines. Programs such as GLIM allow a huge array of models to be fitted. In comparison, prior to 1980, a number of special purpose programs were used to fit subsets of log-linear models.

[5]This claim is less credible for some recent extensions of the basic log-linear approach.

[6]Davis argues that the quality of individual sociological research articles is high, but that the

It does, however, illustrate how these types of models can help us to address questions of this sort.

Basic Strategy and Key Concepts

The basic strategy involved in this approach to modeling can be largely understood by reference to a few key concepts. We fit models to the observed frequencies in the cross-tabulation of categoric variables. The models can be represented by a set of expected frequencies that may or may not resemble the observed frequencies. Models vary in terms of the marginals (or observed frequency totals) they fit and can be described in terms of constraints they place on the associations or interactions that are present in the data. We compare models that are hierarchical to one another and chose from among them a preferred model: a model that is preferred over the others on the grounds of parsimony—we want the simplest model possible—and fit—we do not chose models that bears no resemblance to, or do not fit, the observed data. Our choice of a preferred model is typically based on a formal comparison of goodness-of-fit statistics associated with models that are related hierarchically. The goodness-of-fit statistic most often employed is the likelihood-ratio chi-square statistic (L^2), which has the advantage of being exactly partitionable.[7]

Of course, if the above procedure were followed blindly, then the model selection process could be assigned to a computer algorithm. The algorithm could choose a preferred model for any given set of data (weighing fit and parsimony and using a stringent significance level, analogous to step-wise regression procedures). Instead, fit and parsimony are considered with the substantive plausibility of a given model. Ultimately, our preferred model should distinguish the pattern (or structure) in the table from the noise (or sampling variability) and have a substantively defensible interpretation. The pattern of association among variables can be described by a set of odds, and by one or more odds ratios derived from them.[8] This strategy, and the meaning of most of these

research is "incoherent," e.g. not integrated and thus not cumulative. He believes that a sustained focus on producing simple causal models around issues like variation in happiness by marital status and race could produce a cumulative, coherent science.

[7] Knoke & Burke (1980:40–42) suggest that L^2 works best with modest sized samples (i.e. less than 1500 or 2000), but that an R^2 analogue (or pseudo-R^2) may be more useful for much larger samples. Raftery's (1986) BIC statistic, however, which allows comparisons of models and adjusts for sample size, seems to be more widely endorsed and used. Quite recently, Raftery (1995) has made a very strong case, one endorsed by Hauser (1995), that BIC should become the preferred statistic for assessing the tradeoff between fit and parsimony in sociological research, regardless of sample size.

[8] Odds ratios have several desirable properties that traditional measures of association [such as the proportional reduction in error measures (gamma and lambda, for instance) and percentage differences] do not. They are invariant with respect to the interchange of rows and columns, and

Table 1   Observed frequencies in the collapsed version of the Race by General Happiness table, expected frequencies under the independence model fitted to them, and odds and odds ratios derived from the observed and expected frequencies

Race	Observed and expected frequencies-general happiness			Odds on VH:NVH	Odds ratio
	Very happy (VH)	Not very happy (NVH)	Total		
Black	64	321	385	0.20	
	(111.6)	(273.4)	(385.0)	(0.41)	
White	764	1707	2471	0.45	2.3
	(716.4)	(1754.6)	(2471.0)	(0.41)	(1.0)
Total	828	2028	2856		
	(828.0)	(2028.0)	(2856.0)		

(Data are from the 1994 General Social Survey. Unenclosed numbers are observed frequencies and the totals, and odds and odds ratios, derived from them. Numbers in parentheses are expected frequencies under the independence model, and the totals, and odds and odds ratios, derived from them.)
L^2 (Independence—{R}{H}) = 36.29 with 1 df, $P < .001$.

concepts, can be gleaned from an analysis of the simplest cross-tabulation, a 2×2 table, like the one in Table 1.

The 2×2 Table

Table 1 shows the observed frequencies in the 2×2 table formed by cross-classifying race (black or white) by whether respondents reported that they were generally very happy, or not very happy, in the 1994 General Social Survey.[9] These are the four numbers—64, 321, 764, and 1707—which correspond to the numbers of blacks (in the first row) and whites (in the second) who claimed to be very happy and not very happy, respectively. It also shows the row and column marginals, or the total numbers of blacks (385) and whites (2471), and

unaffected by the unevenness of the distributions of the marginals in a table (see Fienberg 1980, Reynolds 1984, or for a nontechnical discussion, Morgan & Teachman 1988).

[9]To simplify, the small number (121, or 4.1%) of respondents whose race was reported as something other than black or white was deleted from the table. The general happiness question on the survey read "All things considered, how would you say things are these days—would you say that you are very happy, pretty happy, or not too happy?" In forming Table 1, we also collapsed (or added together) the "pretty happy" and "not too happy" categories of respondents. Although ignoring 4% of the data might be justified on the basis of our specific interest in the black/white difference on this dimension, the collapsing of the response categories is unjustifiable (as we show below), except for didactic purposes.

of very happy (828) and not very happy (2028) respondents, as well as the grand total of respondents (2856), which is the sum of the row or column marginals or totals.

We can describe the distributions of the race and happiness variables in our sample by calculating marginal odds from the observed marginals and frequencies. The marginal (or overall) odds on being very happy as opposed to not very happy are 828/2028 = 0.41, which implies that for every 100 respondents who were not very happy, there were 41 who were very happy. The overall odds on being black (vs white) are 385/2471 = 0.15, which implies that there were 15 blacks for every 100 whites. These marginal odds (O) provide, like the more familiar proportions (P) that can be derived directly from them, information on the distributions of the two variables in the table, but nothing about their association.[10] The latter requires the calculation of conditional odds and, in the case of our 2 × 2 table, a single odds ratio from them.

We derive conditional odds using the observed frequencies in the table, rather than the marginals or totals. The conditional odds on being very happy for blacks (or under the condition that respondents were black) equals 64/321 = 0.20, while the corresponding odds for whites equals 764/1707 = 0.45. The odds ratio obtained from dividing the latter by the former—i.e. 0.45/0.20 = 2.3—indicates that a fairly sizable association or relationship between race and happiness exists in our sample, inasmuch as the odds on being very happy are more than twice as great for whites as for blacks.[11]

To determine whether this sample difference is simply noise—variation that results from sampling fluctuations, or chance—or whether it reflects a real pattern of association in the population from which we drew our sample, we begin by fitting the model of independence to the table. The expected frequencies associated with the independence model (given in parentheses in the table) fit, or preserve, the row (or race) and column (or happiness) marginals of the table.[12] Notationally, following Goodman (1978), we can symbolize this as

---

[10]Proportions can be derived from the odds by the equation P = O/(1 + O), or odds can be derived from proportions by the equation O = P/(1 − P).

[11]We might have chosen to calculate the conditional odds on being not very happy, which were 321/64 = 5.0 for blacks and 1707/764 = 2.2 for whites, and the odds ratio which reflects how much higher those odds were for blacks than whites, which was by a factor of 5.0/2.2 = 2.3 (i.e. the same as we obtained above). Had we calculated ratios to indicate how much less likely blacks were than whites to be very happy, or how much less likely whites were than blacks to be not very happy, we'd have ended up with the reciprocal of 2.3, or 1/2.3 = 0.43. Each of these ratios, of course, implies the others. The reader should recognize that in this and the other tables we examine in this paper, the odds and odds ratios we calculate are not the only set that might have been calculated.

[12]Note that the sums of the expected frequencies in the rows and columns of the 2 × 2 table equal the sums of the observed frequencies in those rows and columns.

model {R}{H},[13] a model that fits the one-way race and happiness marginals. In fitting only these two one-way marginals, the independence model constrains the association in the data to be nil, or hypothesizes that, in the population from which we drew our sample, race and happiness are independent. We can see this constraint by taking the expected frequencies under the model and calculating from them, as we did from the observed frequencies, the conditional odds on being happy for blacks (111.6/273.4 = 0.41) and whites (716.4/1754.6 = 0.41). The fact that they are equal, or that the odds ratio that can be calculated to compare them equals 1.0, is consistent with the hypothesis of independence, or no association.

The question of whether the independence model is suitable to describe the association in our sample, or in the population from which it was drawn, is answered by calculating a likelihood-ratio chi-square (L^2) statistic, which formally compares the expected frequencies under that model with the observed frequencies in the table. In the case of the 2 × 2 table in Table 1, we obtain $L^2 = 36.29$ which, with one degree of freedom, is highly improbable. We therefore reject the independence model and, in the case of the 2 × 2 table, choose as preferred the only model that is hierarchically related to, and more complex than, the independence model, namely, the trivial (or saturated) model that fits the two-way {RH} marginal and allows an association between race and happiness. Fitting this marginal implies fitting the observed frequencies in the joint categories of race and happiness exactly, and in as much as the trivial model has expected frequencies that equal the observed, it has a $L^2 = 0.00$, with no degrees of freedom, and clearly improves significantly upon the independence model. The choice of the trivial model as preferred implies that (in the population from which we drew our sample) race and happiness are associated, and our best estimate of that association is given by the odds ratio of 2.3 (calculated as above). In that population, in other words, we estimate that whites are more than twice as likely as blacks to be very happy, as opposed to not very happy.

---

[13] All of the models described in this paper fit, at a minimum, the one-way marginals of the variables cross-classified in the tables. The models vary in terms of what associations they allow between those variables, and how those associations are specified or constrained. We specify the nature of the associations in our models using a slightly modified version of Goodman's original marginal notation, and we attempt throughout to describe the associations by odds and odds ratios that we derive from the expected frequencies that underlie the various models we consider. In much of the literature we refer to, models are denoted not by marginals fitted but rather by multiplicative or additive equations (see Knoke & Burke 1980, and Agresti 1990, for examples), which indicate how the odds or log-odds (in the additive case) are affected by which of the combinations of categories a respondent is in. Our approach is more ponderous, we suspect, but hopefully somewhat easier to understand.

Table 2 Observed frequencies in the expanded version of the Race by General Happiness Table, expected frequencies under various models fitted to them, and odds and odds ratios derived from the observed and expected frequencies

| Race | Observed and expected frequencies-general happiness | | | Total | Odds on VH:PH | Odds ratio | Odds on PH:NTH | Odds ratio |
	Very happy (VH)	Pretty happy (PH)	Not too happy (NTH)					
Black	64	233	88	385	0.27		2.64	
	(111.6)	(226.7)	(46.6)		(0.49)		(4.86)	
	[64.0]	[266.2]	[54.8]		[0.24]		[4.86]	
	{62.1}	{236.8}	{86.1}		{0.26}		{2.75}	
White	764	1449	258	2471	0.53	2.0	5.62	2.1
	(716.4)	(1455.3)	(299.4)		(0.49)	(1.0)	(4.86)	(1.0)
	[764.0]	[1415.7]	[291.2]		[0.54]	[2.3]	[4.86]	[1.0]
	{765.9}	{1445.2}	{259.9}		{0.53}	{2.0}	{5.56}	{2.0}
Total	828	1682	346	2856				

(Data are from the 1994 General Social Survey. Unenclosed numbers are observed frequencies and the totals, and odds and odds ratios, derived from them. Numbers in parentheses, square brackets, and curly brackets are expected frequencies and odds and odds ratios, derived from them under the independence model, a partial association model, and a linear model, respectively.)

L^2 (Independence—{R}{H}) = 62.35 with 2 df, P < .001.
L^2 (Partial association = {RH$_1$}) = 26.06 with 1 df, P < .001.
L^2(Linear = {RH$_L$}) = 0.19 with 1 df, P=.662.

The 2 × 3 Table

The happiness variable in the above example was not really dichotomous; we made it so by collapsing two response categories (pretty happy and not too happy) into the single not very happy category. A consideration of the fuller 2 × 3 table, presented as Table 2, provides examples of additional models that can be applied to cross-classified data with ordered or unordered polytomies. As noted in the paper's introduction, a substantial amount of work was published on this topic in the late 1970s and 1980s (see previous references, especially Duncan & McRae 1978 and Clogg 1982b; also see Ishii-Kuntz 1994). The following example illustrates a particularly desirable property of the likelihood ratio chi-square, which is the fact that it can be exactly partitioned (Goodman 1971b, Allison 1980; for the most basic introduction to partitioning, see Reynolds 1984:22–30).

When one of the variables in a two-way table is polytomous, the analysis is more complicated because there is no longer a single odds ratio that describes the association in the observed data, but rather multiple ratios. In the case of the 2 × 3 table, two odds ratios are required. The number of odds ratios equals the number of degrees of freedom (for the cell frequencies) that remain after the table's marginals (row and column totals) are fixed or fitted. In Table 2 we derive these odds ratios by first calculating, within categories of race, the odds on being very happy as opposed to pretty happy, and the odds on being pretty happy as opposed to not too happy, and then taking the ratios of those odds for whites vs blacks. In so doing, we find that whites are more likely than blacks to be very happy vs pretty happy, and more likely to be pretty happy vs not too happy, by factors of 2.0 and 2.1, respectively. Since the polytomous dependent variable is treated as a set of unordered categories, this model is a very simple multinomial logit model (Liao 1994:48–59).

As in the 2×2 table, the independence model fitted to the 2×3 table fits only the one-way marginals {R}{H}, constrains the association in the table to be nil, and the two odds ratios that describe that association to equal 1.0. As could have been anticipated from our previous result, we reject that model, given the $L^2 = 62.35$, with 2 df and P < .001 associated with it, which informs us that the departure of the expected frequencies under the model (given in parentheses in Table 2) from the observed frequencies are too large to have occurred by chance, or as a result of sampling fluctuations. In the 2×3 table, however, unlike the simpler table, we need not resort to the trivial model and the observed odds and odds ratios to describe the associations present, because there are various models that are hierarchically related to both the independence and trivial models. These models constrain the association in various ways.

Three such models are ones we can term partial association models; models that imply an association in part of the table but independence in another part. We can designate these models {RH$_1$}, {RH$_2$}, and {RH$_3$}, where the first model implies that race is associated with whether respondents report being very happy (as opposed to pretty happy or not too happy), the second implies race is associated with whether respondents report being pretty happy (as opposed to very happy or not too happy), and the third model implies that race is associated with the odds on being not too happy (as opposed to very happy or pretty happy). All of these models have a single degree of freedom (one less than the model of independence, and one more than the trivial model) and would require a single odds ratio to describe the departure from independence in the table.

In Table 2 we show (in square brackets) the expected frequencies under the first of these models, which yields odds on being very happy vs pretty happy that are $0.54/0.24 = 2.3$ times higher for whites than blacks, but odds on being pretty happy as opposed to not too happy that are the same (i.e. $266.2/54.8 = 1415.7/291.2 = 4.86$) for both groups. The failure of this model to fit the data—the model {RH$_1$} has $L^2 = 26.06$, with 1 df, and P < .001—implies that independence does not hold between race and the pretty happy and not too happy response categories, or that the odds ratio required to describe the race effect on the odds on being pretty happy vs not too happy is something other than 1.0.

Moreover, recognizing that the difference between the independence model {R}{H} and the partial association model {RH$_1$} is that the latter model allows an association between race and reporting being very happy (vs pretty happy or not too happy) that the former model does not, the difference in the values of L^2 for the two models represents a formal test of the hypothesis of independence between race and reporting being very happy. That is, in our 2 × 3 table the L^2 for {R}{H} minus the L^2 for {RH$_1$} = 62.35 − 26.06 = 36.29, which was the value of L^2 that resulted from fitting the model of independence to the 2 × 2 table (in Table 1) that collapsed over the pretty happy and not too happy response categories and contrasted them with the very happy category.

The foregoing indicates that the likelihood ratio chi-square can be exactly partitioned (see Goodman 1971b, Allison 1980). As a practical matter, this allows us to compare the fit of different models to one another and learn, in so doing, whether models that impose simplifying constraints on associations are appropriate for describing the pattern in the population from which our observed sample data arose. The {RH$_1$} model for the 2 × 3 table is one which asserts that differences across race categories in the observed odds on being very happy (vs pretty happy or not too happy) represent a real pattern in the underlying population, but that differences between race categories in the odds on being pretty happy vs not too happy represent noise, or differences resulting from sampling fluctuations or error. Again, the fact that it improved significantly upon the independence model {R}{H} implies that the former association was not due to chance; and the fact that it didn't fit—or that it is improved upon significantly by the trivial model {RH} which, in this table too, would have expected frequencies that equal the observed and an L^2 = 0.0 with 0 df— implies that race differences in the odds on being pretty happy as opposed to not too happy were too large to be assumed to be due to chance as well. We were, in other words, not justified in collapsing those latter two categories, at least not from a statistical standpoint.

It turns out that neither of the other partial association models (not shown in Table 2) fit the data acceptably either (L^2 {RH$_2$} = 61.86 with 1 df, P < .001, and L^2 {RH$_3$} = 21.28 with 1 df, P < .001). Race is not independent of whether respondents report being very happy vs pretty happy, or pretty happy vs not too happy, or very happy vs not too happy, which is to say that we could not simplify our discussion of this association by employing a model that represents it as a partial association, and we could not justify collapsing over, and ignoring the race differences between, any pair of response categories.

There are, however, different association models that place equality or other relational constraints on the odds ratio values. These constraints reflect the ordinal properties of the dependent variable and are sometimes referred to as ordinal log-linear models (see Ishii-Kuntz 1994).[14] One such model is the linear model, which we can denote {RH$_L$}, to indicate that it places a linear constraint on the way that the ordered happiness categories are involved in the race by happiness association. The expected frequencies under this model are given in curly brackets in Table 2. As we can see by making, as before, a few simple calculations from those expected frequencies, the odds ratios describing the departure from independence, under the linear model, are constrained to be equal. That is, the single ratio of 0.53/0.26 = 5.56/2.75 = 2.0 informs us that whites are more likely than blacks to be very happy as opposed to pretty happy, and pretty happy as opposed to not too happy, in both cases by a factor of 2.0. This model simplifies our description of the association in a way that is clearly consonant with the observed data. We can see this by comparing, informally, the observed frequencies in the table with those expected under this model, or by calculating the L^2 associated with {RH$_L$}, which equals 0.19 with 1 df, and has P = .662. Here too the fact that this model improves significantly upon the independence model implies that a linear pattern of association exists in the population from which the sample was drawn. The fact that it fits the data acceptably (or is not improved upon significantly by the trivial model) implies that the slight departure from linearity we observe in our sample, where we found two different but nearly equal odds ratios of 2.0 and 2.1, is readily attributable to sampling fluctuations.

Larger Two-Way Tables

The utility of models that place simplifying constraints on the associations between variables becomes more apparent when we consider larger two-way tables, like the 5 × 3 cross-tabulation shown in Table 3. Again using data from the 1994 General Social Survey, we cross-classify the three-category happiness variable by marital status, which has five categories. In order to describe fully the association present, it would take eight distinct (or nonredundant) odds ratios, corresponding to the eight degrees of freedom that remain for the cell frequencies when the marginals of the table are fitted. In this table, we can calculate the odds on very happy vs pretty happy and pretty happy vs not too happy, as before, and then take ratios of these odds by comparing married, widowed,

---

[14]In much of the literature, models that impose linear constraints on the row or column variables in two-way tables are referred to as row effects or column effects models (see Agresti 1990, chapter 8). When fitted to a two-way table in which one variable is ordered, and the other is dichotomous, row and column effects models are special cases of the uniform association model, which we describe in the next section (see also Clogg & Shihadeh 1994).

divorced, and separated respondents with never married respondents, in turn. In so doing we find that, in the observed data, married folks have higher odds on being very happy vs pretty happy than do never married respondents, by a factor of 2.3, while widowed respondents have the same odds, and divorced and separated respondents have lower odds, by factors of 0.9 and 0.7, respectively. Married respondents also have higher odds than never married respondents on being pretty happy vs not too happy, by a factor of 1.5, while widowed, divorced, and separated respondents have lower odds, by factors of 0.7, 0.8, and 0.5, respectively.

The poor fit of the independence model to the table—the model {M}{H} has $L^2 = 179.86$ with 8 df, P < .001—indicates a significant departure from

Table 3 Observed frequencies in the Two-Way Table in which general happiness is cross-classified by marital status, expected frequencies under various models fitted to them, and odds and odds ratios derived from them

| Marital status | Observed and expected frequencies-general happiness | | | | | | | |
	Very happy (VH)	Pretty happy (PH)	Not too happy (NTH)	Total	Odds on VH:PH	Odds ratio	Odds on PH:NTH	Odds ratio
Married	571	793	112	1476	0.72	2.3	7.08	1.5
	(560.2)	(814.6)	(101.2)		(0.69)	(2.0)	(8.05)	(2.0)
	[560.5]	[814.1]	[101.5]		[0.69]	[2.0]	[8.02]	[2.0]
Widowed	52	176	51	279	0.30	1.0	3.45	0.7
	(52.0)	(176.1)	(51.0)		(0.30)	(0.8)	(3.45)	(0.8)
	[49.2]	[175.9]	[54.0]		[0.28]	[0.8]	[3.26]	[0.8]
Divorced	74	279	76	429	0.27	0.9	3.67	0.8
	(78.1)	(270.7)	(80.1)		(0.29)	(0.8)	(3.38)	(0.8)
	[75.6]	[270.4]	[83.0]		[0.28]	[0.8]	[3.26]	[0.8]
Separated	13	59	26	98	0.22	0.7	2.27	0.5
	(12.3)	(60.4)	(25.3)		(0.20)	(0.6)	(2.38)	(0.6)
	[17.3]	[61.8]	[19.0]		[0.28]	[0.8]	[3.26]	[0.8]
Never married	118	375	81	574	0.31		4.62	
	(125.4)	(360.2)	(88.4)		(0.35)		(4.07)	
	[125.5]	[359.9]	[88.5]		[0.35]		[4.07]	
Total	828	1682	346	2856				

(Data are from the 1994 General Social Survey. Unenclosed numbers are the observed frequencies and the totals, and odds and odds ratios, derived from them. Numbers in parentheses and square brackets are expected frequencies, and odds and odds ratios derived from them, under a linear model and a partial linear association model, respectively. Expected frequencies under the independence model are not shown.)

L^2(Independence—{M}{H}) = 179.86 with 8 df, p < .001.
L^2(Linear model = {MH$_L$}) = 4.36 with 4 df, p = .359.
L^2(Partial linear association model = {M$_1$H$_L$}{M$_5$H$_i$}) = 8.41 with 6, df, p = .209.

independence in the population from which we drew our sample, though it would admittedly be a bit of a nuisance to have to describe the association using eight parameters. Here the linear happiness model, {MH$_L$}, is of substantial assistance, since the number of different odds ratios it requires to describe the association is cut in half, or reduced from eight to four. Table 3 shows, in parentheses, the expected frequencies and odds and odds ratios under this model, which indicate that while married respondents are twice as likely as never married respondents to report being very happy as opposed to pretty happy, and pretty happy as opposed to not too happy, the widowed, divorced, and separated respondents are less likely, by factors of 0.8, 0.8, and 0.6, respectively.

Given that the model {MH$_L$}, which has L^2 = 4.36, with 4 df, and P = .359, improves significantly upon the independence model and fits the data acceptably, we could easily select this model as preferred to describe the association in the population; or we might attempt, with partial linear association models, to simplify our model further. For example, given that the most pronounced difference suggested by the model {MH$_L$} is between married respondents and all others, we could fit a model, which can be designated {M$_1$H$_L$}, which constrains the linear association to involve only this first marital status category vs all others. Such a model (not shown in Table 3), which has L^2 = 14.48, with 7 degrees of freedom and P = .043, does improve significantly upon the independence model, but doesn't fit the data acceptably, and is improved upon significantly by the model {MH$_L$} (i.e. 14.48 − 4.36 = 10.12 with 7 − 4 = 3 df, p < .05). The model {M$_1$H$_L$} would, as a result, not be preferred over the model {MH$_L$} to describe the data, though it turns out that an alternative model that is hierarchical to both—model {M$_1$H$_L$} {M$_5$H$_L$}, which has L^2 = 8.41 with 6 df, and P = .209—does fit the data acceptably and is not improved upon significantly by model {MH$_L$} (i.e. 8.41 − 4.36 = 4.05 with 6 − 4 = 2 df, P > .10). This alternative model (shown in Table 3 in square brackets), having two degrees of freedom fewer than the model of independence, requires only two odds ratios, equal to 2.0 and 0.8, to describe the departure from independence in the table. The odds on being very happy as opposed to pretty happy, and pretty happy as opposed to not too happy, are higher for married respondents than for never married respondents, by a factor of 2.0, but lower for widowed, divorced, and separated respondents than for never married respondents, by a factor of 0.8.

The foregoing indicates that, in a two-way table having one ordered and one unordered polytomy, partitioning the association and constraining the ordered variable to have linear effects enable us to offer a simple description of it. Where a two-way table consists of two ordered variables, we can also employ a model that imposes a linear constraint on both variables—a model that has been referred to as a linear-by-linear association, or uniform association, model (see

Goodman 1979, Ishii-Kuntz 1994). In Table 4, we show the general happiness variable cross-classified by year, using data from the 1974, 1984, and 1994 General Social Surveys. Expected frequencies under the uniform association model are given in parentheses.

The uniform association model yields a single odds ratio of 0.9, which informs us that, between 1974 and 1984, and again between 1984 and 1994, both the odds on being very happy vs pretty happy and the odds on being pretty happy vs not too happy declined, by a factor of 0.9. While this trend appears to be a significant one, inasmuch as the uniform association model improves significantly upon the independence model—$L^2\{Y\}\{H\} - L^2\{Y_LH_L\} = 44.56 - 27.76 = 16.80$ with $4 - 3 = 2$ df, p $< .001$—the uniform association model does not provide an acceptable fit to the data and should not be used to describe the association present. The fact that the linear association model $\{Y_LH\}$, which relaxes the linear constraint on the general happiness variable, does fit the data acceptably (i.e. it has $L^2 = 0.93$, with 3 df, p $= .627$), and improves significantly upon $\{Y_LH_L\}$, informs us that the uniform association model fails to fit because the linear change in the odds on being very happy as opposed to pretty happy is unlike the linear change in the odds on being pretty happy as opposed to not too happy. The two odds ratios in square brackets, derived from the expected frequencies under model $\{Y_LH\}$ indicate that while the former odds declined by a factor of 0.8 between 1974 and 1984, and again between 1984 and 1994, the latter odds increased in each interval, by a factor of 1.1.

It turns out that in Table 4, as in Table 3, our simplest description of the association present is provided by a partial linear association model; in this case $\{Y_LH_2\}$, which constrains the linear change over time to involve a change in the odds on being in the second general happiness category, or the pretty happy category, versus the other two. Under this model, the expected frequencies for which are shown in curly brackets in the table, both the odds on very happy to pretty happy, and the odds on not too happy to pretty happy, declined by a factor of 0.8 over each interval. (In Table 4, having calculated the odds on pretty happy to not too happy rather than the reverse, the linear change is characterized by a ratio of 1.2, the reciprocal of 0.8). Given the L^2 of 4.42, with 3 df and P $= .219$, associated with this model, it would clearly be preferred, on the grounds of parsimony, over the linear association model $\{Y_LH\}$.

Three-Way Tables

One follows the same logic and procedures when analyzing data in multi-way tables. But the number of possible models that could describe the associations present in larger tables increases quite dramatically with additional variables or additional variable contrasts. Table 5 shows a simple 3-way table in which the general happiness item that we have been using is cross-classified

Table 4 Observed frequencies in the two-way table in which General Happiness is cross-classified by year, Expected frequencies under various models fitted to them, and odds and odds ratios derived from them

Year	Observed and expected frequencies-general happiness			Total	Odds on VH:PH	Odds ratio	Odds on PH:NTH	Odds ratio
	Very happy (VH)	Pretty happy (PH)	Not too happy (NTH)					
1974	557	724	192	1473	0.76		3.77	
	(527.7)	(787.0)	(158.3)		(0.67)		(4.97)	
	[563.5]	[716.5]	[193.0]		[0.79]		[3.71]	
	{546.5}	{716.6}	{209.9}		{0.76}		{3.41}	
1984	482	734	179	1395	0.66	0.9	4.10	1.1
	(463.3)	(762.5)	(169.2)		(0.61)	(0.9)	(4.50)	(0.9)
	[469.0]	[749.1]	[177.0]		[0.63]	[0.8]	[4.23]	[1.1]
	{466.9}	{748.8}	{179.3}		{0.62}	{0.8}	{4.18}	{1.2}
1994	828	1682	346	2856	0.49	0.7	4.86	1.3
	(875.9)	(1590.6)	(389.5)		(0.55)	(0.9)	(4.08)	(0.9)
	[834.5]	[1674.5]	[347.0]		[0.50]	[0.8]	[4.83]	[1.1]
	{853.6}	{1674.6}	{327.8}		{0.51}	{0.8}	{5.10}	{1.2}
Total	1867	3140	717	5724				

(Data are from the 1974, 1984, 1994 General Social Surveys. Unenclosed numbers are the observed frequencies and the totals, and odds and odds ratios, derived from them. Numbers in parentheses, square brackets, and curly brackets are expected frequencies, and odds and odds ratios derived from them, under a uniform association model, a linear model, and a partial linear association model, respectively. Expected frequencies under the independence model are not shown.)
L^2 (Independence—{Y}{H}) = 44.56 with 4 df, p < .001.
L^2 (Uniform association model—{$Y_L H_L$}) = 28.76 with 3 df, p < .001.
L^2 (Linear model—{$Y_L H$}) = 0.93 with 2 df, p = .627.
L^2 (Partial linear association model—{$Y_L H_i$}) = 4.42 with 3 df, p = .219.

simultaneously by year and marital status, the latter having been collapsed to contrast married and unmarried respondents. Models fit to these data are shown in Table 6. Because the table consists of a clearly defined dependent variable (happiness) and a pair of substantively interesting factors (year and marital status), we restrict our attention to logit-specified models.[15] That is, each model in Table 6 fits the two-way or joint {MY} marginal in Table 5, (or the six row totals in the table), to fit or allow whatever association exists between marital

---

[15]For additional substantive examples and a nontechnical discussion of logit-specified models, see Duncan & Duncan (1978, Appendix A), and Agresti (1990, Chapter 6). It should also be noted that, when the dependent variable is dichotomous, and the factors are categorical in nature, logistic regression models are equivalent to logit-specified log-linear models (see Aldrich & Nelson 1984, Morgan & Teachman 1988, Demaris 1992).

Table 5 Observed frequencies in the three-way table in which General Happiness is cross-classified by marital status and year, expected frequencies under the preferred model fitted to them, and odds and odds ratio derived from the observed and expected frequencies

| | | Observed and expected frequencies-general happiness | | | | | Odds ratios | | | Odds ratios | |
		Very happy (VH)	Pretty happy (PH)	Not too happy (NTH)	Total	Odds on VH:PH	Married unmarried	1984:1974 and 1994:1984	Odds on PH:NTH	Married unmarried	1984:1974 and 1994:1984
Year	Marital status										
1974	Married	473	493	93	1,059	0.96	2.7		5.30	2.3	
		479.0	**490.1**	**89.8**	**1,059**	**0.98**	**2.2**		**5.46**	**2.2**	
	Unmarried	84	231	99	414	0.36			2.33		
		99.0	**224.1**	**90.9**	**414**	**0.44**			**2.47**		
1984	Married	332	387	62	781	0.86	2.0	0.9	6.24	2.1	1.2
		325.0	**395.1**	**60.9**	**781**	**0.82**	**2.2**	**0.8**	**6.49**	**2.2**	**1.2**
	Unmarried	150	347	117	614	0.43		1.2	2.97		1.3
		133.2	**358.4**	**122.4**	**614**	**0.37**		**0.8**	**2.93**		**1.2**
1994	Married	571	793	112	1,476	0.72	2.5	0.8	7.08	1.9	1.1
		560.9	**809.9**	**105.2**	**1,476**	**0.69**	**2.2**	**0.8**	**7.70**	**2.2**	**1.2**
	Unmarried	257	889	234	1,380	0.29		0.7	3.80		1.3
		269.9	**862.3**	**247.8**	**1,380**	**0.31**		**0.8**	**3.48**		**1.2**
Total											

(Data are from the 1974, 1984, and 1994 General Social Surveys. Unbolded numbers are observed frequencies and the totals, and odds and odds ratios, derived from them. Bolded numbers are the expected frequencies and odds and odds ratios derived from them under the preferred model for the table $\{MY\}\{MH_L\}\{MH_L\}\{Y_L H_2\}$.)

Table 6   Model fitted to the observed data in Table 5

Model	Marginals fitted	df	L^2	P
(1)	{MY}{H}	10	387.31	<.001
(2)	{MY}{MH}	8	34.38	<.001
(3)	{MY}{YH}	6	342.76	<.001
(4)	{MY}{MH}{YH}	4	4.16	.385
(4a)	{MY}{MH$_L$}{YH}	5	5.81	.325
(4b)	{MY}{MH$_L$}{YH$_2$}	7	8.16	.318
(4c)	{MY}{MH$_L$}{Y$_L$H$_2$}	8	9.66	.290

M = Marital status, Y = Year; H = General Happiness. Subscripts denote associations that are constrained to be linear(L) or to involve the second (2) category of the general happiness variable—i.e., the pretty happy category—vs the other two.

status and year.[16] These models vary only in how they posit year and/or marital status are related to happiness.

The first model listed in Table 6 fits, in addition to the {MY} marginal, only the one-way happiness {H} marginal, and posits that happiness is independent of the joint categories of marital status and year.[17] That hypothesis can be easily rejected, given $L^2 = 387.31$, with 10 df and P < .001. Model (2), which fits the two two-way marginals {MY} and {MH}, but not the {YH} marginal, hypothesizes that within marital status categories, year and happiness are independent. Its poor fit to the data ($L^2 = 34.38$ with 8 df, P < .001) forces us to reject that hypothesis, while its significant improvement upon Model (1) ($L^2(1) - L^2(2)$ = 387.31 − 34.38 = 362.93 with 10 − 8 = 2 df, P < .001) indicates that the marital status/happiness association (which is excluded from the first model but included in the second) is highly significant.

Model (3) allows, unlike Model (1), year and happiness to be associated, but hypothesizes that within years, marital status and happiness are independent. Its poor fit to the data ($L^2 = 342.76$ with 6 df, p < .001) indicates that marital status and happiness are not independent, and its improvement upon Model (1) suggests the same about year and happiness. Because the comparison of Model

[16]While it is not revealed by a comparison of the models in Table 6 (since none exclude the {MY} marginal), it's worth noting that the marital status by year association, or the change in marital status over time, is pronounced and significant. We can estimate the change using the marginals in Table 5, which show that the odds on being married vs unmarried diminished from 1059/414 = 2.55 in 1974 to 781/614 = 1.27 in 1984 to 1476/1380 = 1.07 in 1994. They declined, over the whole of the 20-year period, by a factor of 1.07/2.55 = 0.41.

[17]The expected frequencies and odds and odds ratios under Model (1) are not shown in Table 5. The expected frequencies would yield odds on very happy to pretty happy and pretty happy to not too happy that are the same for married and unmarried respondents in all three years, and odds ratios contrasting year and marital status categories that equal 1.0.

(1) with Model (3) is testing the hypothesis of independence between year and happiness, the difference in L^2 values for the two models $((L^2(1) - L^2(3) = 387.31 - 342.76 = 44.55)$ is equivalent, apart from rounding, to the value of L^2 we obtained in testing the hypothesis of independence in Table 4.

Model (4) fits all three two-way marginals in the table and allows, in addition to the year by marital status association, direct effects of both year and marital status on happiness. It hypothesizes that there is no three-way interaction in the table (i.e. the change over time is the same for married and unmarried respondents, and the difference between married and unmarried respondents is the same in each year). The fact that Model (4) fits the data acceptably $(L^2 = 4.16$ with 4 df, $P = .385)$ and improves significantly upon Models (2) and (3) indicates that among the first four models in Table 6, Model (4) could easily be chosen as preferred.

Having $10 - 4 = 6$ degrees of freedom fewer than the logit-specified model of independence, Model (4) would require us to calculate six nonredundant odds ratios to describe the direct effects of year and marital status on happiness. The expected frequencies under the model (not shown in Table 5) would yield two different odds ratios to describe the effect of marital status on happiness, and four different odds ratios to describe the effect of year. Again, however, simplifying constraints can be placed on these associations. Model (4a) constrains happiness to be linear in its association with marital status, or the difference in the odds on being very happy as opposed to pretty happy across marital status categories to be the same as the difference in the odds on being pretty happy as opposed to not too happy. Model (4b) constrains the change in happiness over time to involve only a change in the odds on being pretty happy (as opposed to very happy or not too happy), while Model (4c) constrains that change to be linear; i.e. the same between 1984 and 1994 as between 1974 and 1984. The fact that the fit of model to data is not significantly eroded by placing these constraints on the associations suggests that all of them are consonant with the data at hand, and that Model (4c) can be chosen as the preferred model to describe them.

As Table 5 shows, odds and odds ratios derived from the expected frequencies under Model (4c) (in bold) indicate that while happiness has changed some-what over time, the effect of marital status on happiness has not. The $\{Y_L H_2\}$ component of the model gives rise to the odds ratio of 0.8, or its reciprocal $1.0/0.8 = 1.2$, which indicates that from 1974 to 1984, and again from 1984 to 1994, the odds on being very happy or not too happy as opposed to pretty happy have declined, by a factor of 0.8, or the odds on being pretty happy as opposed to very happy or not too happy have increased, by a factor of 1.2. The $\{MH_L\}$ component suggests that marital status is similarly and linearly related to happiness in each year. In each year, that is, married respondents are more than twice as likely as unmarried ones to report being very happy as opposed to pretty happy, and pretty happy as opposed to not too happy.

Larger Multi-way Tables

Space limitations preclude a full discussion of models for larger tables, though the methods used are the same, as is the logic employed in selecting a preferred model from among them. Taking our own example one step further, a four-way table constructed by cross-classifying happiness by race, marital status, and survey year simultaneously could be fit by a large number of models, including 18 logit-specified standard hierarchical models, and a much larger number of models that place constraints on the associations between the independent variables and dependent variable. Typically we need not fit all possible models, however, as a subset of the standard models will usually allow us to unequivocally establish which is preferred, and simplifying constraints can be imposed after the standard model is chosen.

In the four-way table just described, for example, the baseline model of independence, {RMY}{H}, yields an $L^2 = 502.05$ with 34 df, and P < .001. Most of the departure from independence is accounted for by a model which posits main effects of all three factors on happiness (a model, that is, which fits {RMY}{RH}{MH}{YH}, and has $L^2 = 34.73$ with 24 df, and P = .07). The main effects model improves significantly upon each of the three models that drop any one of those three effects (indicating we needn't consider any of the simpler models), but it is in turn improved upon significantly by one of the three models that includes a three-way interaction—model {RMY}{RMH}{YH}. Since that model is not improved upon significantly by models that include the other two interactions {RYH} and {MYH}, and since it fits the data acceptably, with $L^2 = 24.41$ with 20 df, and P = .225, we can easily choose it as the preferred model from among the standard ones.

We can simplify the model greatly by comparing it to a series of models that impose, one at a time, constraints on the effects of the three factors. Ultimately, we choose as preferred a model that can be denoted as {RMY}{RH}{$Y_L H_2$}{MH_L}{$RM_3 H_3$}. While it may, notationally, look somewhat more complex than the standard model chosen as preferred, it is in fact a good deal simpler. With an $L^2 = 36.74$ with 28 degrees of freedom, and P = .125, it fits the data acceptably and requires 8 fewer parameters (6 rather than 14) to describe the effects of the three factors. As before, we can calculate odds and odds ratios from the expected frequencies to estimate those effects. It can also be considerably helpful to plot the expected odds on a logarithmic scale, as in Figure 1.

As the {$Y_L H_2$} marginal notation implies, and as Figure 1 shows clearly, there was a linear year effect, or change, in the odds on being very happy vs pretty happy and not too happy vs pretty happy. Both of those odds declined by a factor of 0.84 from 1974 to 1984, and again from 1984 to 1994 (which implies that the odds on being pretty happy vs not too happy increased by a factor of $1/0.84 = 1.19$). Race and marital status have direct effects on the odds on very happy vs pretty happy (the {RH} and {MH$_L$} marginals imply those effects), but the effect of race and marital status interact in affecting the odds on pretty happy vs not too happy (as is implied by the {RM$_3$H$_3$} marginal). In each year, and in each marital status category, whites exhibited higher odds on being very happy vs pretty happy than blacks by a factor of 1.5. Whites were also more likely than blacks (again by a factor of 1.5) to be pretty happy as opposed to not too happy, among currently married and previously married (i.e. widowed, divorced, and separated) respondents, but among the never married respondents, whites were 3.4 times as likely to be pretty vs not too happy.

The fact that the race effect on the odds on being pretty happy vs not too happy varies by marital status implies that the effect of marital status on those odds varies by race. Among whites, currently married respondents are more likely than never married respondents, and previously married respondents are less likely than never married respondents, to be pretty happy as opposed to

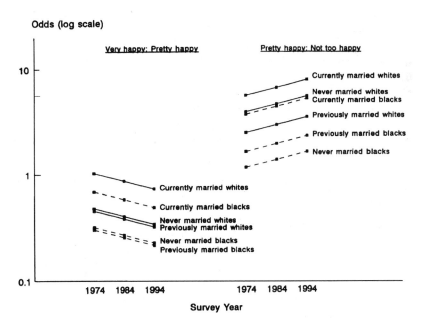

Figure 1   Expected odds on "very happy" vs "pretty happy" and "pretty happy" vs "not too happy" by Race, Marital Status, and Survey Year.

not too happy, by factors of 1.4 and 0.6, respectively. Among blacks, currently married and previously married respondents are both more likely than never married respondents to be pretty happy vs not too happy, by factors of 3.2 and 1.4. Finally, as regards the direct effect of marital status on the odds on being very happy vs pretty happy, the figure shows that, among blacks and whites in each year, currently married respondents are 2.2 times as likely as never married respondents to be very happy, while previously married respondents are somewhat less likely than never married respondents to be very happy, by a factor of 0.95. In these data, there is no evidence of any change in the marital status–happiness association.

Related Models and Methods

As we noted above, some of the most innovative and useful applications of log-linear models have occurred in the area of social mobility research. Given space limitations here, we have not covered models that involve such constraints as marginal homogeneity, symmetry, and quasi-symmetry, though the literatures cited above (see especially Sobel 1983, and Sobel, Hout & Duncan 1985) provide a useful starting point for researchers interested in them. Nor have we considered a wide range of related models that represent extensions of log-linear and logit modeling, including ordered logit and probit models that accommodate both categorical and continuous factors (Aldrich & Nelson 1984, Liao 1994), proportional hazard and event history models (Allison 1984), and latent class models (Goodman 1974, Clogg & Goodman 1984, Haberman 1988), which include models that allow the estimation of reciprocal and simultaneous effects (Mare & Winship 1991). We hope that our simple description of the general framework of log-linear modeling will facilitate an understanding of the relatedness and utility of these techniques.

Summary and Conclusion

Categorical data are ubiquitous in sociological work: Does a birth or death occur, do persons report that they are very happy or not so happy, do persons vote (and if so, for which candidate); are persons employed (and if so, full or part-time), etc. Log-linear models/methodology provide a powerful framework and the statistical tools to analyze categoric data. While the fundamental concepts and techniques were developed in the 1960s and 1970s, extensions and elaborations remain one of the most fertile areas in social statistics and social methodology. Understanding these more recent developments depends upon an understanding of the most basic concepts and techniques. Furthermore, these basic techniques remain an under-used and poorly understood methodology. Our review of them and references to nontechnical descriptions aim at encouraging their use and making this methodology more transparent.

The prime vehicle in this paper for illustrating key concepts and the basic analytic strategy involved in log-linear modeling was an extended substantive example involving variations in reported happiness by race, marital status, and year. Earlier we cited Davis's assertion (1994, p. 194): "Married people are distinctly happier than the nonmarried. And white people are distinctly happier than black people. But exactly why—and why is the marital status correlation declining?" Sociologist's can be expected to differ in their answers to these three important substantive question. But these techniques provide a framework for agreement on what are the "social facts" to be explained. Given data from the 1974, 1984, and 1994 General Social Survey, substantive explanation should focus on the first and second "facts"; these data provide no support for the often-made claim that the effect of marital status on reported happiness has weakened.

ACKNOWLEDGMENTS

Data used in this report were provided by the Inter-University Consortium for Political and Social Research (ICPSR), 426 Thompson Street, Ann Arbor, MI 48106-1248.

Literature Cited

Aldrich JH, Nelson FD. 1984. *Linear Probability, Logit and Probit Model.* Beverly hills, CA: Sage

Agresti A. 1984. *Analysis of Ordinal Categorical Data.* New York: John Wiley

Agresti A. 1989. Tutorial on modeling ordered categorical response data. *Psychol. Bull.* 105:290–301

Agresti A. 1990. *Categorical Data Analysis.* New York: John Wiley

Alba RD. 1987. Interpreting the parameters of log-linear models. *Sociol. Methods Res.* 16:45–77

Allison PD. 1980. Analyzing collapsed contingency tables without actually collapsing. *Am. Sociol. Rev.* 45:123–30

Allison PD. 1984. *Event History Analysis: Regression for Longitudinal Data.* Beverly Hills, CA: Sage

Bishop YMM, Fienberg SE, Holland PW. 1975. *Discrete Multivariate Analysis.* Cambridge, MA: MIT Press

Clogg CC. 1982a. Some models for the analysis of association in multi-way cross-classifications having ordered categories. *J. Am. Statist. Assoc.* 77:803–15

Clogg CC. 1982b. Using association models in sociological research: some examples. *Am. J. Sociol.* 88:114–34

Clogg CC, Eliason SR. 1987. Some common problems in log-linear analysis. *Sociol. Methods Res.* 16:8–44

Clogg CC, Goodman LA. 1984. Latent structure analysis of a set of multidimensional contingency tables. *J. Am. Stat. Assoc.* 79:762–71

Clogg CC, Shihadeh ES. 1994. *Statistical Models for Ordinal Variables.* Thousand Oaks, CA: Sage

Davis JA. 1974. Hierarchical models for significance tests in multivariate contingency tables. In *Sociological Methodology 1973–74*, ed. HL Costner, pp. 189–231. San Francisco, CA: Jossey-Bass

Davis JA. 1994. What's wrong with sociology? *Sociol. Forum* 9:179–97

Demaris A. 1992. *Logit Modeling: Practical Applications.* Newbury Park, CA: Sage

Duncan B, Duncan OD. 1978. *Sex Typing and*

Social Roles. New York: Academic

Duncan OD. 1975. Partitioning polytomous variables in multi-way contingency analysis. *Soc. Sci. Res.* 4:167–82

Duncan OD. 1979a. Constrained parameters in a model for categorical data. *Sociol. Methods Res.* 8:57–68

Duncan OD. 1979b. How destination depends on origin in the occupational mobility table. *Am. J. Sociol.* 84:793–803

Duncan OD, McRae JA. 1979. Multi-way contingency analysis with a scaled response. In *Sociological Methodology 1979,* ed. KF Schuessler, pp. 68–85. San Francisco, CA: Jossey-Bass

Feinberg SE. 1980. *The Analysis of Cross-Classified Categorical Data.* Cambridge, MA: MIT Press. 2nd ed.

Ganzeboom HBG, Treiman DJ, Ultee WC. 1991. Comparative intergenerational stratification research: three generations and beyond. *Annu. Rev. Sociol.* 17:277–302

Goodman LA. 1970. The multivariate analysis of qualitative data: interactions among multiple classification. *J. Am. Stat. Assoc.* 65:225–56

Goodman LA. 1971a. The analysis of multidimensional contingency tables: stepwise procedures and direct estimation methods for building models for multiple classification. *Technometrics* 13:33–61

Goodman LA. 1971b. Partitioning of chi-square, analysis of marginal contingency tables, and estimation of expected frequencies in multidimensional contingency tables. *J. Am. Stat. Assoc.* 66:339–92

Goodman LA. 1972. Some multiplicative models for the analysis of cross-classified data. In *Proc. 6th Berkeley Symp. Mathematical Statistics and Probability,* ed. J Neymann, pp. 649–96. Berkeley, CA: Univ. Calif. Press

Goodman LA. 1973a. Causal analysis of data from panel studies and other kinds of surveys. *Am. J. Sociol.* 78:1135–91

Goodman LA. 1973b. Guided and unguided methods for the selection of models for a set of T multidimensional contingency tables. *J. Am. Stat. Assoc.* 68:165–75

Goodman LA. 1974. The analysis of systems of qualitative variables when some of the variables are unobservable. I. A modified latent structure approach. *Am. J. Sociol.* 79:1179–259

Goodman LA. 1978. *Analyzing Qualitative/Categorical Data: Log-linear Models and Latent Structure Analysis.* Cambridge, MA: Abt Books

Goodman LA. 1979. Simple models for the analysis of association in cross-classifications having ordered categories. *J. Am. Stat. Assoc.*

74:537–52

Goodman LA. 1984. *The Analysis of Cross-Classified Data Having Ordered Categories.* Cambridge, MA: Harvard Univ. Press

Haberman SJ. 1974. *The Analysis of Frequency Data.* Chicago: Univ. Chicago Press

Haberman SJ. 1978. 1979. *Analysis of Qualitative Data,* Vols. 1, 2. New York: Academic

Haberman SJ. 1988. A stabilized Newton-Raphson algorithm for log-linear models for frequency tables derived from indirect observation. In *Sociological Methodology,* ed. CC Clogg, pp. 193–211. Washington, DC: Am. Sociol. Assoc.

Hagenaars JA. 1990. *Categorical Longitudinal Data.* Newbury Park, CA: Sage

Hauser RM. 1978. A structural model for the mobility table. *Soc. Forces* 56:919–53

Hauser RM. 1995. Better rules for better decisions. *Sociol. Methodol.* 25:175–83

Hout M. 1982. The association between husbands' and wives' occupations in two-earner families. *Am. J. Sociol.* 88:397–409

Hout M. 1983. *Mobility Tables.* New York: Sage

Hout M. 1984a. Occupational mobility of black men: 1962–1973. *Am. Sociol. Rev.* 49:308–22

Hout M. 1984b. Status autonomy, and training in occupational mobility. *Am. J. Sociol.* 89:1379–409

Hout M. 1988. More universalism, less structural mobility: the American occupational structure in the 1980s. *Am. J. Sociol.* 93:1358–1400

Ishii-Kuntz M. 1994. *Ordinal Log-Linear Models.* Beverly Hills, CA: Sage

Knoke D, Burke PJ. 1980. *Log-Linear Models.* Newbury Park, CA: Sage

Kurz K, Muller W. 1987. Class mobility in the industrial world. *Annu. Rev. Sociol.* 13:417–42

Lazarsfeld PF. 1955. Interpretation of statistical relations as research operation. In *The Language of Social Research,* ed. PF Lazarsfeld, M Rosenberg, pp. 115–25. New York: Free Press

Liao TF. 1994. *Interpreting Probability Models: Logit, Probit, and Other Generalized Linear Models.* Beverly Hills, CA: Sage

Mare RD, Winship C. 1991. Log-linear models for reciprocal and other simultaneous effects. In *Sociological Methodology 1988,* ed. PV Marsden, pp. 199–234. Washington, DC: Am. Sociol. Assoc.

Morgan SP, Teachman JD. 1988. Logistic regression: description, examples, and comparisons. *J. Marriage Fam.* 50:929–36

Raftery AE. 1986. Choosing models for cross-classifications. *Am. Sociol. Rev.* 51:145–46

Raftery AE. 1995. Bayesian model selection in social research. *Sociol. Methodol.* 25:111–63

Reynolds HT. 1984. *Analysis of Nominal Data.* Beverly Hills, CA: Sage

Rosenberg M. 1969. *The Logic of Survey Analysis.* New York: Basic Books

Sobel ME. 1983. Structural mobility, circulation, mobility, and the analysis of occupational mobility: a conceptual mismatch. *Am. Sociol. Rev.* 48:721–27

Sobel ME, Hout M, Duncan OD. 1985. Exchange, structure, and symmetry in occupational mobility. *Am. J. Sociol.* 91:39–72

Swafford M. 1980. Three parametric techniques for contingency table analysis: a nontechnical commentary. *Am. Sociol. Rev.* 45:664–90

Teachman JD, Paasch K, Carver KP. 1993.

Thirty years of demography. *Demography* 30:523–32

Wong RS-K. 1990. Understanding cross-national variation in occupational mobility. *Am. Sociol. Rev.* 55:560–73

Wong RS-K. 1992. Vertical and nonvertical effects in class mobility: cross-national variations. *Am. Sociol. Rev.* 57:396–410

Xie Y. 1992. The log-multiplicative layer effect model for comparing mobility tables. *Am. Sociol. Rev.* 57:380–95

Yamaguchi K. 1983. The structure of intergenerational occupational mobility: generality and specificity in resource channels, and barriers. *Am. J. Sociol.* 88:718–45

Yamaguchi K. 1987. Models for comparing mobility tables: toward parsimony and substance. *Am. Sociol. Rev.* 52:482–94

Annu. Rev. Sociol. 1996. 22:377–99

INNOVATIONS IN EXPERIMENTAL DESIGN IN ATTITUDE SURVEYS

Paul M. Sniderman

Department of Political Science, Stanford University, Stanford, California 94305

Douglas B. Grob

Department of Political Science, Stanford University, Stanford, California 94305

KEY WORDS: research design, experimental design, attitude survey, survey design, C.A.T.I.

ABSTRACT

In the last decade a revolution has occurred in the design of public opinion surveys. The principal breakthrough has been to combine the distinctive external validity advantages of the representative public opinion survey with the decisive internal validity strengths of the fully randomized, multifaceted experiment. The availability of computer-driven multifactorial, multivalent designs has encouraged a reorientation from narrowly methodological concerns to broader substantive issues. After a season in which the principal emphasis in survey-based experimentation was on standardization of measurement and methodological refinements, the emphasis now is on substantive discoveries and on innovation—new technology, new procedures, and new objectives. In this chapter, we survey the integration of experimental design and large-scale, representative, general population samples. After highlighting the limitations of the classic split-ballot experiment, we distinguish between nondirective and directive experimental variations, and, among the directive, between postdecisional and predecisional. We introduce a tripartite analytical scheme, sorting experimental variations as a function of whether they manipulate (i) the formulation of a choice, (ii) the context of choice, or (iii) the characteristics of the chooser. Finally we give an account of the experimental style now characteristic of general population attitude surveys, underlining its low emotional intensity and low cognitive demands, attributing both to features of (i) the interview site, (ii) the sample, (iii) the mode of interviewing, and (iv) considerations of ethics.

377

INTRODUCTION

The attitude survey has become a standard technique in social research, no more likely to excite comment, considered by itself, than an old and comfortable sweater on a fall afternoon. The initial glamour of large-scale survey research has long since faded, its promise of a genuinely scientific social science long since forgotten.[1]

Over the last thirty years the public opinion survey as a technique for social research has been institutionalized on a large scale. The General Social Survey (GSS) has been established in sociology, and the National Election Studies (NES) in political science, to produce standard data sets for their respective disciplines. Both have made possible fundamental contributions to survey-based social research, and each has promoted innovation, both methodological and conceptual, at the margin. Yet the chief obligation of the GSS and the NES is to extend a time series, requiring repetition of the same questions in the same way. Perhaps inevitably, given their primary missions, both have tended to promote the routinization of the public opinion survey as a method of social research.

In the last decade, however, the development, first of vignette analysis, and then of computer-assisted interviewing, has helped spur a revolution in the design of the public opinion survey. Although this revolution has been carried out on a number of fronts (for example, the use of computers to facilitate the so-called front-end of interview management), the principal breakthrough has been to combine the distinctive external validity advantages of the representative public opinion survey with the decisive internal validity strengths of the fully randomized, multifaceted experiment.

As with any revolution, when the terrain is closely examined, signs of earlier skirmishes can be spotted. Thus, experimentation has been deployed in attitude surveys for at least a generation. As we mean to make plain, however, the use of experimentation in public opinion surveys more recently has been transformed on two dimensions. The first has to do with form, the second with function. Computer-driven experimental designs are now capable of incorporating multiple factors, each capable of assuming multiple values. In turn, the availability of multifactorial, multivalent designs has encouraged a reorientation from narrowly methodological concerns to broader substantive issues.

Our focus is the integration of experimental design and large-scale, representative, general population samples.[2] We begin with the classic form of

---

[1] For something of the original glamour and promise, see McClosky 1967 and Glock 1967.

[2] We shall be only semi-scrupulous about this restriction, preferring to call attention to studies of merit even if, strictly, the sample is not representative of the general population. For more general discussions of experimentation, see Cook & Campbell 1979, Kinder & Palfrey 1993, McGraw 1994, and forthcoming 1996.

experimentation in attitude surveys, the split-ballot, then identify two developments especially, the vignette method and computer-assisted interviewing, that have transformed experimental design in general population surveys. To illustrate the variety of designs now on line, we distinguish between nondirective and directive experimental variations, and, among the directive, between postdecisional and predecisional. In addition, to bring order to the wide variety of specific manipulations now undertaken in attitude surveys, we introduce a tripartite analytical schema, sorting experimental variations as a function of whether they manipulate (i) the formulation of a choice, (ii) the context of a choice, or (iii) the characteristics of the chooser. Finally, we give an account of the experimental style now characteristic of general population attitude surveys, underlining its low emotional intensity and low cognitive demands, attributing both to features of (i) the interview site, (ii) the sample, (iii) the mode of interviewing, and (iv) considerations of ethics.

FORM AND FUNCTION: CONSTRAINTS OF THE SPLIT-BALLOT DESIGN

In architecture, function is supposed to define form. In public opinion research, form has defined function. The "split-ballot" experiment in particular has defined, and restricted, the nature and scope of experimental design in survey research for nearly a half century.[3]

Until the introduction of computer-assisted interviewing, whatever the mode of interviewing (whether face-to-face, over the telephone, or self-administered), public opinion questionnaires had to be printed in advance of being administered. Since separate printing of the whole questionnaire was necessary for each variation of the experimental variable, purely as a practical matter there tended to be only two forms of a questionnaire—the so-called split-ballot design.[4] The split-ballot was thus doubly circumscribed: An experiment could manipulate only a single factor, and the manipulated factor could assume only one of two values. Then, too, if multiple experiments were carried out in the same interview, one form of the questionnaire would contain one (of the two possible) versions of each experimental item. The consequence, little remarked, is that although the assignment of respondents to each condition of each experiment

---

[3] Two scholars, Howard Schuman and George Bishop, together with their colleagues, have made contributions notable both for scale and quality on a wide variety of subjects; see note 5.

[4] Examples of split-ballot designs occur that involve three values of the factor to be manipulated experimentally, but they are atypical and in any event involve variation of only one facet. In the overwhelming number of instances, the split ballot involves a single variation of a single factor. See also our discussion of Stoker 1995 in our section on predecisional directive designs, below.

is approximately random, their assignment to treatment conditions across experiments is perfectly correlated.

The requirement of having a fixed form, printed-in-advance questionnaire thus had the primary effect of favoring experimental designs of extreme simplicity. Moreover, by ruling out designs of an interesting degree of complexity, fixed and simple forms had the secondary effect of undercutting interest in the use of experimentation to assess substantive hypotheses. Instead, attention was concentrated on methodological problems. No logical necessity was at work here. But the occasional exception here and there notwithstanding, the predominant use of the split ballot design in survey research has been to identify method-driven variance.

On a wide array of topics, experimental studies of the consequences of variations in question ordering, wording, and context have contributed to enhanced reliability and, perhaps less conspicuously, to increased validity of measurement. Among the subjects on which important contributions have been made are the impact of question order; the differential strengths of open versus closed questions; the assessment of "don't knows" (or "no opinion") and particularly the role of "don't know" filters; the difference between the logic of "forbidding" and of "allowing;" the measurement of "middle" positions; the seminal problem of "nonattitudes"; and interviewer effects.[5] Survey research is an applied discipline as well as a scientific undertaking, and the split-ballot design has contributed to the acquisition of practical knowledge of the first order of importance in the design and interpretation of opinion measurement.[6]

Notable exceptions notwithstanding, the split-ballot research paradigm has four distinguishing features: (i) a single variation of a single facet is experimentally randomized; (ii) the stimulus for the experiment is an empirical anomaly or puzzle; (iii) the focus is on methodological problems rather than substantive theory; and (iv) the explanatory effort, insightful as it can be, is very much post hoc. By contrast, what marks the new wave of experimentation in survey research is the movement (i) from fixed to variable form, and (ii) from a predominantly methodological to a predominantly substantive focus.

[5]See, for example, Schuman 1986, Schuman & Bobo 1988a,b, Schuman & Scott 1989, Schuman et al 1986, Schuman & Presser 1981, Bishop 1987, 1990, Bishop et al 1986, Presser 1990a,b, Hippler & Schwarz 1986, Reese et al 1986.

[6]As a footnote to a proper sociology of knowledge, it is worth observing that survey research is one of the few research domains where analysts can be distinguished from practitioners, the latter having specialized competence in the techniques of study design and the conduct of interviews. As examples of experimental work in an applied vein, see Ayidiya & McClendon 1990, James & Bolstein 1990, 1992, Berry & Kanouse 1987, Kiesler & Sproull 1986, Leff et al 1986, Frey 1986, Willimack et al 1995, Krysan et al 1994, Singer et al 1995, Protess et al 1987, Poe et al 1988, Aquilino 1994, Schwarz et al 1991.

REMOVING CONSTRAINTS: THE VIGNETTE METHOD

Primary credit for bursting the seams of the split-ballot design should go to the development of the vignette method by Rossi and his colleagues.[7] To highlight both the distinctiveness of their factorial object approach and strategic issues of analysis it raises, we want to detail a specific application of the vignette method.

Consider a study by Thurman et al (1988) of popular conceptions of illness.[8] Their aim was to identify which aspects of individuals' behavior and self-presentation elicited judgments of mental illness. Accordingly, they generated an enormous number of descriptions of individuals, or vignettes. Each vignette described a (hypothetical but presented as real) person denominated by name, age, religion, education, marital and familial status. In addition, the vignettes factorially vary (i) a series of attributions, each potentially symptomatic of mental illness; (ii) the intensity or frequency of the attributed "symptom"; and (iii) the "bizarreness" and the visibility of deviant behavior. All respondents received a sample of 50 vignettes, randomly drawn from the universe of vignettes. For every vignette, respondents were asked to make the same judgment—namely, to rate the person's degree of mental illness. The vignette method thus centers on randomization and repeated applications.

As against the split-ballot, the vignette design offers an explosion of analytical possibilities. In the mental illness study, for example, instead of being confined to a single variation of a single factor, the impact of a dozen potential indicators of mental illness, taken individually and together, could be assessed—more than 7000 variations in all, opening up for exploration the multifaceted social construction of psychological illness. But vignettes also open up complex issues of design and analysis, three of which deserve particular mention. First, the vignette, not the respondent, is the unit of analysis. On this construction, the N in the mental illness experiment is the number of vignettes, over 7000, not the number of respondents, just over 140. Fairly clearly, the presumption that respondents are essentially substitutable for one another is not always justified, but given that the unit of analysis is the vignette, exactly when and how its validity can be rigorously demonstrated is by no means obvious.

The second problem exacerbates the first. It is perfectly true that each vignette is randomly composed. But the vignettes are also sequentially administered.

---

[7]See Rossi & Nock 1982, Warr 1990, Miller et al 1986, Rossi & Berk 1985, Thurman et al 1988, Shepelak & Alwin 1986. Specifically for a detailed discussion of the method, see Rossi & Anderson 1982.

[8]Strictly their study falls outside our purview since it employed a convenience sample of university undergraduates rather than a general population sample. We detail it anyway, because the specific application—to popular conceptions of mental illness—so vividly illustrates the richness of the vignette approach.

Considering the absolute number of serially repeated requests for an identical form of judgment based on a common vignette skeleton—in the mental illness experiment, 50 in a row—the risk of carryover effects from one vignette to another is surely high.[9] Large-scale serial repetitions threaten randomized factorial designs.

Finally, the opportunity costs of the vignette method are not trivial. Applied to any given domain, whether popular conceptions of mental illness or of justice (Miller et al 1986) or of criminal victimization (Warr 1990), a very large number of vignettes must be administered, consuming a relatively large amount of interview time. There is, it follows, a marked practical limit on the number of vignette experiments that can be executed in the course of any one study, with substantial costs; and even if only one is undertaken, there are nontrivial opportunities foregone to measure other attributes. These limitations notwithstanding, the vignette method helped break through the constraints of the split ballot design.

COMPUTER-ASSISTED INTERVIEWING AND COMPLEX EXPERIMENTAL DESIGNS

Through computer-assisted telephone interviewing (CATI), each experiment can have multiple facets, and each facet can take on multiple values. In a CATI[10] regime, the questionnaire becomes a computer program. Instead of requiring that for every experimental variation, an individual version of the questionnaire be physically produced in advance, the test item is "composed" at the moment of application. A specific operator is developed for every facet varied (whether of wording, ordering, or formatting). At the moment of application, the operator selects at random from among the values assignable to each facet. Yet, notwithstanding the complexity of experimental designs attainable, the actual manipulations are effortless for the interviewer and invisible to the respondent.

By way of illustration, consider the "laid-off worker" experiment. The purpose of this experiment, most broadly put, is to assess whether whites judge a claim for government assistance for African Americans the same as a claim for help for whites. But to put it this way obscures a central issue. To know that the race of a beneficiary evokes a distinctive reaction, important as this

[9]Moreover, it is by no means unreasonable to suspect that the carryover effects are highly susceptible to the kind of person-item interactions that the vignette design, by taking the vignette as the unit of analysis, is not well-positioned to estimate.

[10]We refer to CATI, since the bulk of practical applications to this point have been telephone interviews, but with the reduction in price for personal computers, the use of CAPI (computer-assisted personal interviewing) on a large scale is only a matter of time.

is to establish, is not enough. It is necessary to ask what it is about race as a social category that evokes a distinctive reaction.[11] Accordingly, in addition to race, other factors—gender, age, parental-marital status, and work history (whether reliable or unreliable)—are also varied. Since each attribute of the laid-off worker is varied independently of each other, and some are dichotomous but others polytomous, counting all combinations of characteristics, the experiment encompasses 96 variations.

In its profusion of configurations of characteristics, the spirit of Rossi's vignettes is manifest. The individual respondent not the vignette method is the unit of analysis. As a consequence, the main effects of the laid-off workers' attributes can be estimated, as can (a number of) interactions among attributes (e.g. what difference does it make to be African American *and* an unmarried mother?); so, too, can connections between characteristics of the laid-off worker and characteristics of the respondent (e.g. do liberals and conservatives react differently when assessing how much government help should be given an African American person who has not been a dependable worker?).[12]

Given that computer-assisted designs can be multifactorial and that the manipulated factors can be multivalent, experiments of substantial complexity can be carried out. No less important, many more than one experiment can be conducted in the course of just one interview, and since the randomization applies across, as well as within, measures, each experimental manipulation is orthogonal to every other. In addition to preventing experimental effects from cascading systematically through the interview, independence across treatment items opens up opportunities for innovation, an example of which is the development of a multitrait, multimethod, multigroup assessment of prejudice.

In the assessment of prejudice toward a group, a fundamental issue is the distinctiveness of hostility to particular groups as against the consistency of hostility across groups. Computer-assisted interviewing makes possible assessment of cross-group consistency experimentally. By way of example, consider a country experiencing two distinct streams of immigration, one black and the other white. (In real life, the country is Italy.) To assess intolerance toward

[11] Contrast this with a classic split-ballot formulation. Assessing responses to integration, Farley and his colleagues (Farley et al 1994) have manipulated experimentally the proportion of a neighborhood that is African American. Useful as this single factor variation is, it begs the question of what it is about the increasing concentration of African Americans in a neighborhood that evokes apprehension and hostility on the part of whites.

[12] The substantive finding emerging from the design, unanticipated at the time but since repeatedly validated, is this: when conservatives, who are more likely than liberals to categorize African American people in general as lazy, encounter a hard-working African American person, they are strikingly likely to favor government help. See M Peffley, J Hurwitz & P Sniderman (in press) for confirmatory analysis.

immigrants, two sets of measures of prejudice were developed, one centering on the ascription of undesirable personal characteristics (e.g. lazy, violent), the other on the attribution of responsibility for societal problems (e.g. causing crime to increase, jobs to decrease).[13] To see what difference being black makes (as opposed to being an immigrant whether black or white), both sets of measures were administered to every respondent, varying the race of the immigrant group. One half of the respondents were asked whether African immigrants tend to have undesirable personal characteristics, the other half whether Eastern European immigrants do; and the same, for the attribution of responsibility for social problems.

So far, the design is equivalent to a split-ballot, except in one critical respect. Unlike a split-ballot, respondents are randomly assigned not only to each set of measures but across the two sets of measures. Respondents are thus experimentally distributed across two conditions: in one, respondents assess the same group (whether Africans or East Europeans) throughout both series of prejudice measures; in the other, they assess one group for the first series, then switch to the other for the second (one half beginning with Africans then turning to East Europeans, the other half doing it just the other way round). Taking advantage of the randomization across measures, one can generate estimates of evaluative consistency for respondents making judgments of the same group for both series of measures and for those making judgments of one group for the first series and of a completely different group for the second. As it turns out, it is impossible to tell if respondents, midway through, have switched and begun evaluating an entirely different group. The multigroup, multimethod design thus offers evidence, of a kind previously unavailable, showing that prejudice entails a systematic tendency to respond to others negatively, not in virtue of their membership in a specific outgroup, but in consequence of their categorization as members of an outgroup.

NONDIRECTIVE DESIGNS

There is now a canonical account of the epistemic virtues of experimentation. The best rehearsed part of the account has to do with the power of randomization to rule out competing explanations (see McGraw 1996, McGraw & Hoekstra 1994). As Hacking (1983) in particular has driven home, part of an experiment's power to persuade on questions of causality has to do with the fact that in an experiment we intervene in the natural state of affairs and get to observe the

---

[13]The multiple methods of measurement are employed to overcome the limitations of any one method—a problem of general relevance, to be sure, but of special exigency in the assessment of prejudice, as the career of the concept of authoritarianism has notoriously demonstrated. See, for example, Christie & Jahoda 1954.

difference our intervention makes. Thus viewed, experimentation in attitude surveys is a method aimed at seeing the effect we produce when we manipulate an aspect of the interview, either by selectively exerting pressure on respondents, or by selectively distributing information, in an effort to induce respondents to give one rather than another response.

There is much to recommend this view of experimentation as centering on active intervention, but it privileges a narrow conception of the uses of experiments in attitude surveys. To expose a broader view, nondirective experimental designs need to be distinguished from directive. Directive designs correspond to the established conception of experimentation as active and deliberate intervention. By contrast, nondirective designs involve the randomized assignment of respondents to question form without an intent to sway, influence, or control the direction of their response.

Nondirective designs are easily the less familiar; so for illustrative purposes, we focus on the "list" experiment.[14] Common experience suggests that white Americans, to avoid the appearance of racism, will avoid expressing negative sentiments they hold about matters of race and may even express positive sentiments they do not hold. The list experiment procedure has been devised to get around this constraint. Although the designs of list experiments can be complex, the logic is straightforward. Suppose the task is to assess anger over affirmative action. Respondents are randomly assigned to a baseline or treatment condition. To each respondent in the baseline condition, the interviewer says: "I'm going to read you a list of some things that make some people angry. Tell me how many make you angry or upset. Don't tell me which ones. Just tell me how many." In the baseline condition, the list has four items, none racial in content (e.g. companies polluting the environment). In the other condition, everything is exactly the same, with respondents again instructed "Tell me how many make you angry or upset. Don't tell me which ones. Just tell me how many," except that there are now five items on the list; the fifth refers to affirmative action. Now, suppose that a particular respondent in the test condition is angry over pollution and upset over affirmative action. Asked how many items make her angry, she replies two, knowing with certainty that the interviewer cannot possibly figure out that one of the two refers to affirmative action. But although the interviewer can't tell,[15] the analyst, by contrasting the means of the baseline and treatment conditions, can (i) calculate the proportion of people

---

[14]The list experiment was conceived by James Kuklinski of the University of Illinois for the specific purpose of providing an unobtrusive measure of racial anger. See, for example, Kuklinski et al 1996.

[15]Unless, of course, the respondent says she is angry at all the items in the baseline condition, a possibility deliberately made remote by the writing of the items.

angry over affirmative action, and (ii) identify attributes of the individual that increase (or decrease) the likelihood of anger over affirmative action.

The list experiment is an illustration of a larger class of experimental variations that are nondirective, whether or not they are unobtrusive.[16] The experimental variations are not intended to influence, control, or manipulate the direction of responses. If, to take the example of affirmative action, whites reveal themselves to be angry over preferential treatment, that is a fact about their makeup that they have revealed, not an act that they have been persuaded or coerced into committing.

DIRECTIVE: POSTDECISIONAL AND PREDECISIONAL

Interventions characteristically occur before respondents answer the question put to them in public opinion surveys, precisely because their purpose is to influence the answers given. Not the least interesting development, however, has been the development of post- as against predecisional manipulations. The logic of a postdecisional intervention is easiest to see in a political context. Just because more people start off on one side of an issue does not mean that, if push comes to shove, they will stay there. Politics is about argument and counterargument: One side of an issue may start off with more supporters, but the other may enjoy more committed adherents. The result: the initial minority, after the rough and tumble of public argument, can wind up the winning majority.

One way of exploring the dynamics of political argument, then, is to begin with people after they have chosen a position on a public issue and present to each side a counterargument, to see whether one side can be talked out of its position more easily than the other. In the case of government programs to assist African Americans, for example, proponents and opponents are presented with counterarguments, each tailored to talk them out of the position they have just taken. As it happens, it appears easier to talk proponents of government assistance for African Americans out of their position than opponents out of theirs; indeed, so much so that when the effects on both sides are counted up, the initial majority in favor of government help for African Americans can turn into a clear majority in favor of African Americans having to rely on themselves (see Sniderman & Piazza 1993).

As outlined, the counterargument technique is only quasi-experimental. The counterargument that respondents encounter depends on the side of an issue they select, and those selecting one side of an issue, plainly enough, may differ systematically in any number of respects from those choosing the other. Then, too, given the logic of political argument, the strongest argument against

---

[16]For a definition and discussion of unobtrusive measurement, see Eugene Webb et al 1981.

government assistance for African Americans is unlikely to be the same as the strongest argument for it. An indeterminacy is thus built-in. Those on one side may change more than those on the other because, by virtue of being less committed, they are more susceptible to change. Alternatively, they may be more likely to change because the counterargument they heard was stronger. But how can these two possibilities be distinguished? To get leverage on this problem, so-called content-free[17] counterarguments have been developed. Taking advantage of computer-assisted interviewing, either a substantively relevant or content-free counterargument, is delivered. The proportion of respondents willing to give up a position on a public issue without having been presented with a substantively relevant reason for doing so can then be estimated. Moreover, since the content-free counterargument, by virtue of being content-free, applies symmetrically to both sides of an issue, the relative proportions on either side of an issue willing to abandon their view in the face of a counterargument can also be calculated, thus establishing whether those on one side of the issue are distinctively more susceptible to counterpressure.[18]

Postdecisional designs are a comparative rarity, however. Far and away the central focus is predecisional, the aim being to change a response about to be made rather than one already made. Given both the recency and volume of predecisional interventions in general population attitude surveys, it would be quite wrong to suggest that experimental work of this order is being undertaken under the direction of a single overarching theoretical perspective—or even of a small number of them. Not least because of the recency of substantively oriented experimentation in attitude surveys, research very much gives the impression of analysts starting off from a thousand different points and heading off in another thousand directions. To convey something of the variety and promise of this new wave of research, we shall impose an organizing schema of our own, classifying studies as a function of whether the experimental focus is on (i) the formulation of the choice, (ii) the context of the choice, or (iii) the characteristics of the chooser.

Formulation of the Choice

Arguably the most instructive, certainly the most prominent, research focus involving experimentation in attitude surveys, is the burgeoning research on "issue

---

[17] In a study of Italy, for example, respondents on both sides of the issue of regional autonomy were told: "Considering the complexity and the uncertainty of problems in Italy nowadays, are you still in favor of (or opposed to) autonomy for the regions, or would this make you change your mind?"

[18] Strictly, selection effects can still be at work, since respondents are self-assigned to opposing sides of an issue; although with identical counterarguments, the interpretation then favors substantive—i.e. the differences are part of the natural state of affairs—not artifactual factors.

framing." Under the heading of framing, two lines of work have developed. Their points of similarity notwithstanding, the two are worth distinguishing.

In the first line of research, framing effects refer to preference reversals evoked by alternatively formulated, but utility equivalent, choices. As Kahneman and his colleagues have shown in a classic series of laboratory-based studies,[19] contrary to the notion of rational choice, preferences are subject to reference point effects. (See, for example, Kahneman et al 1993, Kahneman & Knetsch 1992, and Green et al 1994.) Faced with two alternatives, each offering an opportunity to be better off, subjects have a strong propensity to favor the alternative promising the greater gain, even if it has the lower probability of occurring; however, faced with two alternatives, each involving a risk of being worse off, subjects have a strong propensity to favor the alternative entailing the lesser loss, even if it has the higher probability of occurring. This asymmetry—risk-taking in the domain of gains, risk-aversion in the domain of losses—is striking, just because the expected utility in the two cases is by construction the same (for a political example, see Quattrone & Tversky 1988). Or, to cite a second example, surgical treatment of lung cancer is significantly more likely to be elected if surgical outcomes are presented in terms of the probability of living rather than of dying—even though, from a statistical perspective, the information conveyed is exactly the same (Wilson et al 1987). The notion of framing, so conceived, is strict. Alternative formulations of a choice cash out just the same, from the point of view of expected utility. Indeed, precisely the point is to demonstrate that alternative formulations, even though exactly utility-equivalent, elicit preference reversals.

By contrast, in the second line of work, a frame is "a central organizing idea or story line that provides meaning to an unfolding strip of events, weaving a connection among them. The frame suggests what the controversy is about, the essence of the issue" (Gamson & Modigliani 1987, p. 143). From this perspective, people choose differently because they have been given a different choice to make.[20]

Applying this reasoning, Kinder & Sanders (1990) experimented with alternative formulations of affirmative action, varying objections to affirmative

---

[19]Characteristically, the work on framing conceived in Kahneman-Tversky terms has been conducted on nonrepresentative convenience samples, usually of undergraduates (e.g. Kahneman & Tversky 1979, 1984; Quattrone & Tversky 1988). We nonetheless include their work because of its obvious applicability to general population surveys, as Kahneman and his colleagues have themselves demonstrated in their studies of contingent valuation—see note 20.

[20]Framing, so construed, is by no means a new object of study. Classic question order and wording effects can also be construed as framing effects, in this second sense. The classic studies, however, have treated framing effects as measurement error, to be minimized, rather than as substantive variance, to be analyzed.

action, suggesting in one condition that it discriminates against whites, in the other that it gives an unfair advantage to African Americans. As they show, depending on whether the objections to affirmative action are phrased in terms of "reverse discrimination" or "unfair advantage," expressed preferences about affirmative action are differently related to positions on other racial policies, to deeper values such as equal opportunity, and to prejudice itself. Just so far as framing defines the meaning of a choice, these results suggest, how people choose—as opposed to what they choose—will vary.[21]

This conception of issue framing has recently been given a major extension. Again focusing on the public's reactions to the issue of affirmative action, Stoker (1995) has drawn a distinction between context-free and context-specific choices. Public opinion surveys, she points out, ask ordinary citizens their view of affirmative action either generalizing "over contexts in which affirmative action policies are implemented or making no reference to context whatsoever" (Stoker 1995, p. 4). In law, by contrast, judges confront the issue of discrimination in specific problem-contexts, each raising specific justifications for action. A finding of prior discrimination has, for example, emerged as a pivotal consideration in court-mandated affirmative action. Pursuing the intuition that context-specific and context-free judgments differ, Stoker designed an experiment distributing respondents across three conditions: a "baseline condition," in which no justificatory context for a judgment about affirmative action is supplied; a "representation" condition, in which the ground advanced for the policy is the need for a company's work force to approximate the general population; and a "discrimination" condition, in which the ground consists in a finding of prior discrimination. As it turns out, support for affirmative action is equivalently low in the first two conditions, but markedly higher in the third.

From a methodological point of view, it is worth underlining the benefit obtained from extending the standard split-ballot design by even one degree of freedom. If the experiment could have assumed only the standard two forms— say, in this instance, the baseline condition and the discrimination treatment— the finding would be systematically ambiguous. The increase observed in support for affirmative action could have been a function not of the particular reason given but merely of some reason, any reason, being given. But since support did not increase in the "representation" condition, even though it, too, presents a reason for supporting affirmative action, then the decisive factor must be the specific argument of prior discrimination, not argumentation per se. Thus, because they can be multivalent as well as multifaceted, computer-driven

---

[21]For a fascinating discussion of framing effects of racial policies in universalistic or group-particularistic terms, see Bobo & Kluegel 1993.

experiments can have an inferential power that the traditional split-ballot design cannot.

Context of the Choice

By the context of the choice we mean features of people's circumstances, apart from the specific terms in which the choice before them has been framed, that may guide the choice they make.

Both methodologically and causally, the notion of context can be given alternative (but not mutually exclusive) interpretations. Construed distally, the notion of context points to factors operating at some remove from the specific occasion of making a choice. In a pioneering research program, Iyengar and his colleagues have ingeniously manipulated one of the most prominent of the distal factors—namely, televised news.

Characteristically, they examine general population subjects (who are volunteers rather than random selections).[22] Varying their exposure to network news stories, Iyengar and his colleagues have uncovered agenda-setting effects, demonstrating that experimental subjects' judgments of the relative importance of various national problems covary with the relative emphasis the media places on them; and priming effects, showing that the evaluation standards that subjects rely upon when rating public figures or policies vary as a function of the problems and themes highlighted by television news (see especially Iyengar & Kinder 1987). More recently, this line of research has received a powerful extension in the studies of Ansolabehere & Iyengar (see Ansolabehere et al 1994 and, especially, Ansolabehere & Iyengar 1996). Focusing on the effects of political advertising, and embedding their manipulations in the context of actual campaigns (using real candidates competing in real elections), Ansolabehere, Iyengar, and their colleagues (1994) show that manipulating the character of political advertising—in particular the salience of attack advertising—can influence not only attitudes, by weakening a sense of political efficacy, but also political behavior, by undercutting the intention of voting.[23]

More often, however, the notion of context is construed proximally, the emphasis falling on features of the interview situation itself—the sequencing of questions, for example, or the terms of their introduction—intended to influence the direction or intensity of responses. A paradigmatic example of an immediate context effect is source influence. Thus, Smith & Squire (1990), studying the

---

[22]Purists might exclude their research on the grounds that the general population "samples" they typically analyze are not strictly randomized. In our view, this fails altogether to recognize the methodological innovativeness and the analytical power of their research program. See Iyengar 1987; Iyengar & Kinder 1987; Ansolabehere & Iyengar 1994, 1996.

[23]This result is relevant to our discussion, below, of ethics in experimentation with general population respondents.

effects of prestige names on support for state Supreme Court justices, show that both the likelihood of offering an opinion on whether or not a justice should be confirmed, and the direction of the opinion offered, is influenced by whether or not respondents are told the name of the governor who had appointed a particular justice. In weighing the alternatives put before them, however, respondents in public opinion surveys characteristically have to compensate for informational shortfalls; how they manage this can itself vary with the amount of information they have on hand.[24] Smith & Squire, accordingly, go on to show that the effect of the prestige name manipulation varies inversely with respondents' level of formal education, suggesting that those who are less well-informed tend especially to take advantage of the extra information supplied in the form of source endorsements in order to compensate for their lack of information. Methodologically, then, a major benefit of integrating experimentation with attitudes surveys is the ability to play off the steepness of gradients in both information on hand and skill in its utilization, analyzing the interactions of experimental treatments with individual characteristics, particularly levels of political awareness and sophistication, in the public taken as a whole.[25]

This type of source influence, in which the general public uses the source of an argument to evaluate its merits, has long seemed a paradigmatic example of irrational reasoning. However, illustrating the payoff in examining interactions of experimental manipulations and respondent attributes, Lupia (1995) examines the impact of media figure endorsements, varying the direction of the position attributed to them, on reactions to a contentious but second-rank issue: spending money to build more prisons. In an elegant analysis, he demonstrates that perceived political agreement with the source and judgments about the source's knowledge of policy—not mere liking of the source, nor even common interests with him—underlie persuasion "when the context within which the speaker and receiver interact itself supplies a basis for trust" (Lupia 1995, p. 13). From a methodological perspective, the point to underline is that Lupia's analysis, like Smith & Squire's, requires that respondent attributes take on the full range of values characteristic of a general population sample.

Characteristics of the Chooser

The last of the elements in our analytic schema—characteristics of the chooser as distinct from those either of the choice or its context—is systematically ambiguous. It most often refers to characteristics of experimental subjects, such

---

[24]For arguments on the interaction with political sophistication, see Sniderman et al 1991, ch. 1, 2.

[25]The steepness of awareness and political sophistication gradients in the general public sample has proven to be a theme of fundamental importance in the analysis of political and social belief. For a classic treatment, see Converse 1964; also see Luskin 1987.

as their level of formal education,[26] which typically tend to be enduring over time but which are in any case exogenous from the viewpoint of the experimental manipulation. But in addition to respondent characteristics that are (relatively) fixed, there are characteristics that are susceptible to manipulation, particularly mood, affective state, and cognitive orientation.[27]

There is a relative paucity of research on experimentally induced emotional states or cognitive orientations, partly for reasons we take up below in discussing the experimental style characteristic of attitude surveys. But, methodologically, the experimental manipulation of respondents' feelings and evaluative orientations in the course of a public opinion interview represents the opening of a new avenue of inquiry. To suggest the promise of this new avenue, we point to a pair of illustrations.

A premise whose truth frequently has been taken for granted is that citizens' judgments are more likely to be supportive of democratic rights if they are made in more deliberative and less emotional fashion. Kuklinski and his colleagues (1991, 1993) have excavated this taken-for-granted premise, and in the process strikingly demonstrated the power of a well-designed experiment to break new ground.[28] In their experiment on support for freedom of speech, respondents are assigned either to a deliberative instruction set, in which they are specifically asked to make up their mind after reflecting on the potential consequences of allowing a particular group to express its point of view, or to an emotion-arousing instruction set, in which they are specifically invited to make up their mind on the basis of their gut feelings. From the point of view of previous research, the conventional prediction is that the more thought respondents give the principle of free speech, the more likely they are to support it in the experimental test since they overwhelmingly support it in the abstract. Just because this prediction seems so obvious, the results of Kuklinski and his colleagues are the more striking. Respondents in the deliberative condition prove to be less, not more, politically tolerant than those in the emotion-arousing condition.

Similarly ingenious, Zaller (1992) has introduced the "stop-and-think" experiment. In the experiment, the intervention takes the form of presenting a question to a respondent on an issue, then, before he or she has a chance to

[26]See especially the programmatic research of Jon Krosnick and his colleagues, showing the impact of a number of variations in wording to be inversely related to education. See, for example, Krosnick 1987, Krosnick & Alwin 1987, Krosnick 1992, and Narayan & Krosnick 1995.

[27]For some pioneering research on the effects on the chooser of the mass media, political accounts, elite explanation, and third person effects, see Mutz 1994, McGraw 1991, McGraw et al 1995, and Cohen et al 1988.

[28]Technically, the Kuklinski study violates our emphasis on general population studies, but the exception is venial, since his results are so striking and his manipulation so readily importable to general public surveys.

respond, asking what kinds of thoughts come to mind. Analyzing their remarks, Zaller observes both the sizeable proportion—between one third and one half, depending on the issue—who expressed conflicting considerations and the decreased stability of issue positions in the "stop-and-think" condition, findings he takes to support his "top-of-the-head," non-attitudes model.

Finally, experiments in attitude surveys afford an opportunity to evoke evaluative orientations in the course of the interview. In a pioneering study, McGraw (1995) has examined the interplay of enduring and situationally evoked evaluative orientations. On the one hand, an opinion question, McGraw suggests, can be viewed as a persuasive communication. So conceived, it can be varied to present an argument on behalf of one or the other side of a political issue, a one-sided persuasive message, or on behalf of both, a two-sided message. On the other hand, choices on an issue assessed in an attitude survey may require individuals to take account of two values, as a choice about the death penalty in the United States can involve considerations of the importance of both retribution and racial equality; and these values, for any given individual, may or may not be in conflict. As McGraw shows, one-sided persuasive messages can indeed induce attitude change, but only when individuals hold incongruent values. This finding illustrates the special opportunity that experimentation in attitude surveys affords for uncovering the interaction of situational interventions and individual predispositions in general population samples.

EXPERIMENTAL STYLE IN ATTITUDE SURVEYS

By undertaking a gallery tour of recent studies, our aim has been to convey concretely the range, variety, and innovativeness of recent experimental design in attitude surveys. Having emphasized the diversity of current undertakings, we want to call attention to the commonalities in their experimental style.

Experimentation in attitude surveys tends to be characterized by: (i) interventions of deliberately low intensity, (ii) most often taking the form of manipulation of information rather than arousal of emotion, (iii) with the focus of experimentation falling primarily on variations in the framing of the choice presented to respondents and secondarily on variation in the immediate context of the choice as opposed to manipulation, whether by arousal or deception, of the chooser. These commonalities in experimental style, we shall suggest, reflect cumulative constraints in design manifest in survey-based experimentation—constraints, we argue, imposed by the interviewing (i) site; (ii) sample; (iii) mode and (iv) ethics.

Site

General population attitude surveys, whether conducted over the telephone, face-to-face, or self-administered, characteristically take place in the respondent's home, with both direct and indirect consequences for experimental design.

Directly, conducting an attitude survey in the respondent's home excludes manipulations requiring laboratory facilities, or indeed, assessments of variables utilizing specific spatial layouts.[29] The extension of computer-assisted personal interviewing, and in particular the exploitation of the computer screen for the manipulation of visual displays, may modestly relax the first constraint; it is less likely to relieve the second.

Indirectly, the typical site for attitude surveys raises compliance issues, just so far as the willingness of respondents to engage in experiments is reduced by virtue of the interview being conducted in their own home. It is one thing to induce adults to participate in an experimental protocol in an unfamiliar, perhaps even intimidating setting; quite another to do so in their own living room or kitchen. The problem of compliance, it should be observed, has two aspects. Globally, there is the problem of interview break-offs. Emotionally arousing or cognitively demanding manipulations tend to be ruled out for fear respondents will terminate the interview, the more so if they are in their own home and being interviewed over the telephone. Additionally, there is the problem of experimental exit, with respondents free to leave the field selectively, by refusing to complete an experiment, by selecting a "don't know, can't say" response, or making up a preference on the spot—the classic "non-attitudes" problem. Both complete break-off and selective exit, it should be obvious, raise potentially serious risks of self-selection effects.

Sample

The experimental subject of choice in the standard study, undergraduates, are distinguished not only by the insecurity of their social position, inducing them to comply and participate in studies, but as importantly, by the acuity of their cognitive faculties, favoring their intake of complex materials. (For an excellent discussion, see Sears 1986.) Moreover, both issues—what respondents are willing and what they are able to do—are aggravated by the extreme spread in levels of formal education, cognitive acuity, self-confidence, and intellectual sophistication. And this spread is important for experimental design. Tasks easily manageable, or willingly undertaken, by four fifths of a general

---

[29] As an example of an innovative technique barred by the site, see Fazio, Jackson, Dunton & Williams (1996, in press).

population sample can be quite outside the reach of the remaining fifth. Just so far as censorship of data, either through interview break-off or experimental exit, is tied to a dimension of respondent variation like education, the threat to validity is all too easily lethal. The result is an experimental style favoring both low emotional intensity and low cognitive demand manipulations.

Moreover, experimental subjects can be re-enrolled, not without difficulty to be sure, but feasibly all the same. By contrast, apart from the rare, and exceptionally funded, panel study, general population surveys are one-shot affairs. The conception of change they can examine is accordingly doubly foreshortened. On the one side, and most conspicuously, the examination of persistence of change tends to be out of bounds: whether changes evoked by experimental manipulations last a moment beyond the interview is not only unknown but unknowable. On the other side, and more subtly, the change evoked by an experimental intervention has to occur almost immediately. Respondents have to get the point of a manipulation virtually straightaway; hence a preference for immediately intelligible manipulations.

Mode

Face-to-face interviews open up opportunities for the presentation of information not available in telephone interviews. Visual aids, to mention an especially salient example, can readily be deployed in face-to-face, but not telephone, interviews (see e.g. Farley et al 1994). The unavailability of visual aids matters particularly because of the range of cognitive skills characteristic of a general population sample. Over the telephone, even metaphorically visual procedures (e.g. the familiar seven-point scales) are exceedingly risky, and a variety of adroit manipulations through variations in pictures are simply out of reach.[30] But if telephone interviewing narrows the range of manipulations, it strengthens their general control. With telephone interviewing, interviewers can be under direct monitoring, promoting standardization of their behavior. By contrast, in face-to-face home or work-sited interviews, the interview is conducted quite literally out of the sight of supervisors, and just so far as the behavior of the interviewer cannot be directly monitored, it cannot be strictly regimented. There are no rigorous studies of centralized vigilance of interviewer behavior, but given the greater complexity of instruments with experimental variation, it is not unreasonable to presume that there are gains in standardization of interviewer performance through centralized monitoring.

---

[30]For simple manipulations cleverly done with photographs, see Terkildsen 1993 and Sigelman et al 1995. By contrast, computer-driven interview schedules can assess other aspects of responses ordinarily overlooked, of which perhaps the most important is reaction time. See Bassili & Fletcher 1991.

Ethics

Although easily the least discussed, ethical constraints are arguably the most important parameter defining experimental style in general population attitude surveys. By way of at least limning the magnitude of the restrictions, let us set aside entirely the problem of harm and the issue of informed consent (see Diamond 1988) and consider only the question of deception.

A condition of making a variety of laboratory experimental manipulations work is presenting some respondents with information that is not strictly true, or alternatively misdirecting their attention. But either way they have been misled. A necessary, although not necessarily a sufficient, justification of deception surely is that everything is put right afterwards. Debriefing provides assurance that respondents are not treated merely as means to an end; that they leave the experimental setting as they entered it; even that entirely unanticipated misunderstandings are corrected. But it is difficult, purely as a practical matter, to guarantee debriefings in general population attitude surveys. Because of considerations of cost, it is usually not practical to contact respondents subsequent to an interview. Moreover, partly because of cost, partly because of the (usually low but never zero) risk of break-off, it is difficult to guarantee they can be debriefed at the end of it. The effect is that deception in general population attitude surveys is difficult to justify under current human subjects regulations.

Taking account of constraints imposed by interview site, sample, mode, and ethics, the net result is an experimental style in attitude surveys characterized by a trio of features: (i) interventions of deliberately low intensity, (ii) most taking the form of the manipulation of information rather than the arousal of emotion, (iii) with the focus of experimentation falling primarily on variations in the framing of the choice presented to respondents and secondarily on variation in the immediate context of the choice as opposed to manipulation, whether by arousal or deception, of the characteristics of the chooser.

REPRISE

After a season where the principal emphasis in survey-based experimentation was on standardization of measurement, with both the advantages and disadvantages this confers, the emphasis is now on substantive discoveries rather than methodological refinements, and on innovation—new technology, new procedures, new objectives. In order to bring some of these newer techniques more distinctly into view, we have distinguished between directive and nondirective designs, pre- and post-decisional interventions, and variations in the formulation of choice, the context of choice, and the characteristics of chooser. If this analytical scaffolding does its job of stimulating still newer techniques, it will properly be abandoned.

ACKNOWLEDGMENTS

For a close reading and a small mountain of helpful suggestions, we want to thank our colleagues at the Survey Research Center at the University of California at Berkeley, especially Laura Stoker, Michael Hout, Thomas Piazza, and James Wiley; and at Stanford University, especially Rui de Figueiredo.

Literature Cited

Ansolabehere S, Iyengar S. 1994. Riding the wave and claiming ownership over issues: the joint effects of advertising and news coverage in campaigns. *Public Opin. Q.* 58:335–57
Ansolabehere S, Iyengar S. 1996. *Going Negative.* In press
Ansolabehere S, Iyengar S, Simon A, Valentino N. 1994. Does attack advertising demobilize the electorate? *Am. Polit. Sci. Rev.* 88:829–38
Aquilino WS. 1994. Interview mode effects in surveys of drug and alcohol use: a field experiment. *Public Opin. Q.* 58:210–40
Ayidiya S, McKee A, McClendon J. 1990. Response effects in mail surveys. *Public Opin. Q.* 54:229–47
Bassili JN, Fletcher JF. 1991. Response-time measurement in survey research: a method for CATI and a new look at nonattitudes. *Public Opin. Q.* 55:330–44
Berry SH, Kanouse DE. 1987. Physician response to a mailed survey: an experiment in timing of payment. *Public Opin. Q.* 51:102–14
Bishop GF. 1987. Experiments with the middle response alternative in survey questions. *Public Opin. Q.* 51:220–32
Bishop GF. 1990. Issue involvement and response effects in public opinion surveys. *Public Opin. Q.* 54:209–18
Bishop GF, Tuchfarber AJ, Oldendick RW. 1986. Opinions of fictitious issues: the pressure to answer survey questions. *Public Opin. Q.* 50:240–50
Bobo L, Kluegel JR. 1993. Opposition to race-targeting: self-interest, stratification ideology, or racial attitudes? *Am. Sociol. Rev.* 58:443–64
Christie R, Jahoda M, eds. 1954. *Studies in the*

Scope and Method of "The Authoritarian Personality." Glencoe, IL: Free Press
Cohen J, Mutz D, Price V, Gunther A. 1988. Perceived impact of defamation: an experiment on third-person effects. *Public Opin. Q.* 52:161–73
Converse PE. 1964. The nature of belief systems in mass publics. In *Ideology and Discontent,* ed. DE Apter. New York: Free Press
Cook TD, Campbell DT. 1979. *Quasi-Experimentation: Design and Analysis Issues for Field Settings.* Chicago: Rand McNally
Diamond S. 1988. Informed consent and survey research: the FBI and the University of Michigan Survey Research Center. See O'Gorman 1988, pp. 72–99
Farley R, Steeh C, Krysan M, Jackson T, Reeves K. 1994. Stereotypes and segregation: neighborhoods in the Detroit area. *Am. J. Sociol.* 100(3):750–80
Fazio RH, Jackson JR, Dunton RC, Williams CJ. 1996. Variability in automatic activation as an unobtrusive measure of racial attitudes: a bona fide pipeline? *J. Pers. Soc. Psychol.* In press
Frey JH. 1986. An experiment with a confidentiality reminder in a telephone survey. *Public Opin. Q.* 50:267–69
Gamson WA, Modigliani A. 1987. The changing culture of affirmative action. *Res. Polit. Sociol.* 3:137–77
Glock CY. 1967. Survey design and analysis in sociology. In *Survey Research in the Social Sciences,* ed. CY Glock, pp. 1–62. New York: Russell Sage Found.
Green DP, Kahneman D, Kunreuther H. 1994. How the scope and method of public funding

affect willingness to pay for public goods. *Public Opin. Q.* 58:49–67

Hacking I. 1983. *Representing and Intervening.* New York: Cambridge Univ. Press

Hippler H-J, Schwarz N. 1986. Not forbidding isn't allowing: the cognitive basis of the forbid-allow asymmetry. *Public Opin. Q.* 50:87–96

Iyengar S. 1987. Television news and citizens' explanations of national affairs. *Am. Polit. Sci. Rev.* 81:815–31

Iyengar S, Kinder DR. 1987. *News That Matters.* Chicago: Univ. Chicago Press

James JM, Bolstein R. 1990. The effect of monetary incentives and follow-up mailings on the response rate and response quality in mail surveys. *Public Opin. Q.* 54:346–61

James JM, Bolstein R. 1992. Large monetary incentives and their effect on mail survey response rates. *Public Opin. Q.* 56:442–53

Kahneman D, Knetsch JL. 1992. Valuing public goods: the purchase of moral satisfaction. *J. Environ. Econ. Manage.* 22:57–70

Kahneman D, Ritov I, Jacowitz KE, Grant P. 1993. Stated willingness to pay for public goods: a psychological perspective. *Psychol. Sci.* 4(5):310–15

Kahneman D, Tversky A. 1979. Prospect theory: an analysis of decision under risk. *Econometrica* 47:263–91

Kahneman D, Tversky A. 1984. Choices, values, and frames. *Am. Psychol.* 39:341–50

Kiesler S, Sproull LS. 1986. Response effects in the electronic survey. *Public Opin. Q.* 50:402–13

Kinder DR, Palfrey TR. 1993. *Experimental Foundations of Political Science.* Ann Arbor: Univ. Mich. Press

Kinder DR, Sanders LM. 1990. Mimicking political debate with survey questions: the case of white opinion on affirmative action for blacks. *Soc. Cogn.* 8:73–103

Krosnick JA. 1992. The impact of cognitive sophistication and attitude importance on response-order and question-order effects. In *Context Effects in Social and Psychological Research*, ed. N Schwarz, S Sudman, pp. 203–18. New York: Springer-Verlag

Krosnick JA, Alwin DF. 1987. An evaluation of a cognitive theory of response-order effects in survey measurement. *Public Opin. Q.* 51:201–19

Krysan M, Schuman H, Scott LJ, Beatty P. 1994. Response rates and response content in mail versus face-to-face surveys. *Public Opin. Q.* 58:381–99

Kuklinski JH, Riggle E, Ottati V, Schwarz N, Wyer RS. 1991. The cognitive and affective bases of political tolerance judgments. *Am. J. Polit. Sci.* 35:1–27

Kuklinski JH, Riggle E, Ottati V, Schwarz N, Wyer RS Jr. 1993. Thinking about political tolerance, more or less, with more or less information. In *Reconsidering the Democratic Public*, ed. GE Marcus, RL Hanson, pp. 225–48. University Park, PA: Penn. State Univ. Press

Kuklinski JH, Sniderman PM, Knight K, Piazza T, Tetlock PE, et al. 1996. Racial prejudice and attitudes toward affirmative action. Unpublished ms

Leff DR, Protess DL, Brooks SC. 1986. Crusading journalism: changing public attitudes and policy-making agendas. *Public Opin. Q.* 50:300–15

Lupia A. 1995. *Who can persuade? Cognitive and strategic determinants of political credibility.* Presented at 12th Annu. Polit. Methodol. Summer Conf., Bloomington, Ind., July 27–30

Luskin RC. 1987. Measuring political sophistication. *Am. J. Polit. Sci.* 31:856–99

McClosky H. 1967. Survey research in political science. In *Survey Research in the Social Sciences*, pp. 63–144. New York: Russell Sage Found.

McGraw KM. 1991. Managing blame: an experimental test of the effects of political accounts. *Am. Polit. Sci. Rev.* 85:1133–57

McGraw KM. 1995. *Value conflict and susceptibility to persuasion: the impact of value-justified survey questions.* Presented at Meet. Am. Polit. Sci. Assoc., Chicago, Ill.

McGraw KM. 1996. Political methodology: experimental methods. In *A New Handbook of Political Science*, ed. R Goodin, H-D Klingemann. Oxford: Oxford Univ. Press. In press

McGraw KM, Best S, Timpone R. 1995. "What they say or what they do?": the impact of elite explanation and policy outcomes on public opinion. *Am. J. Polit. Sci.* 39:53–74

McGraw KM, Hoekstra V. 1994. Experimentation in political science: historical trends and future directions. *Res. Micropolitics* 4:3–29

Miller JL, Rossi PH, Simpson JE. 1986. Perceptions of justice: race and gender differences in judgments of appropriate prison sentences. *Law Soc. Rev.* 20(3):313–34

Mondak JJ. 1995. Media exposure and political discussion in US elections. *J. Polit.* 57:62–85

Mutz DC. 1994. Contextualizing personal experience: the role of mass media. *J. Polit.* 56:689–714

Narayan S, Krosnick JA. 1995. *Education moderates some response effects in attitude measurement.* MS. Ohio State Univ., Columbus

Peffley M, Hurwitz J, Sniderman PM. 1996. Racial stereotypes and political attitudes in contemporary white society. *Am. J. Polit. Sci.* In press

Poe GS, Seeman I, McLaughlin J, Mehl E, Dietz M. 1988. "Don't Know" boxes in factual questions in a mail questionnaire: effects on level and quality of response. *Public Opin. Q.* 52:212–22

Presser S. 1990a. Can changes in context reduce vote overreporting in surveys? *Public Opin. Q.* 54:586–93

Presser S. 1990b. Measurement issues in the study of social change. *Soc. Forces* 68(3):856–68

Protess DL, Cook FL, Curtin TR, Gordon MT, Leff DR, et al. 1987. The impact of investigative reporting on public opinion and policymaking: targeting toxic waste. *Public Opin. Q.* 51:166–85

O'Gorman HJ, ed. 1988. *Surveying Social Life: Papers in Honor of Herbert H. Hyman.* Middletown: Wesleyan Univ. Press

Quattrone GA, Tversky A. 1988. Contrasting rational and psychological analyses of political choice. *Am. Polit. Sci. Rev.* 82(3):720–36

Reese SD, Danielson WA, Shoemaker PJ, Chang T, Hsu H-L. 1986. Ethnicity-of-interviewer effects among Mexican-Americans and Anglos. *Public Opin. Q.* 50:563–72

Rossi PH, Anderson AB. 1982. The factorial survey approach: an introduction. See Rossi & Nock 1982, pp. 15–67

Rossi PH, Berk RA. 1985. Varieties of normative consensus. *Am. Sociol. Rev.* 50:333–47

Rossi PH, Nock SL, eds. 1982. *Measuring Social Judgments: The Factorial Survey Approach.* Beverly Hills: Sage

Schuman H. 1986. Ordinary questions, survey questions, and policy questions. *Public Opin. Q.* 50(3):433–42

Schuman H, Bobo L. 1988a. Survey-based experiments on white racial attitudes toward residential integration. *Am. J. Sociol.* 94:273–99

Schuman H, Bobo L. 1988b. An experimental approach to surveys of racial attitudes. See O'Gorman 1988, pp. 60–71

Schuman H, Ludwig J, Krosnick JA. 1986. The perceived threat of nuclear war, salience, and open questions. *Public Opin. Q.* 50:519–36

Schuman H, Presser S. 1981. *Questions and Answers in Attitude Surveys: Experiments on Question Form, Wording, and Content.* New York: Academic

Schuman H, Scott J. 1989. Response effects over time: two experiments. *Sociol. Methods Res.* 17:398–408

Schwarz N, Knauper B, Hippler H-J, Noelle-Neumann E, Clark L. 1991. Rating scales: numeric values may change the meaning of scale labels. *Public Opin. Q.* 55:570–82

Sears DO. 1986. College sophomores in the laboratory: influences of a narrow data base on psychology's view of human nature. *J. Pers. Soc. Psychol.* 51:515–30

Shepelak NJ, Alwin DF. 1986. Beliefs about inequality and perceptions of distributive justice. *Am. Sociol. Rev.* 51:30–46

Sigelman CK, Sigelman L, Walkosz BJ, Nitz M. 1995. Black candidates, white voters: understanding racial bias in political perceptions. *Am. J. Polit. Sci.* 39:243–65

Singer E, Von Thurn DR, Miller ER. 1995. Confidentiality assurances and response: a quantitative review of the experimental literature. *Public Opin. Q.* 59:66–77

Smith ERAN, Squire P. 1990. The effects of prestige names in question wording. *Public Opin. Q.* 54:97–116

Sniderman PM, Brody RA, Tetlock PE. 1991. *Reasoning and Choice: Explorations in Political Psychology.* Cambridge: Cambridge Univ. Press

Sniderman PM, Piazza T. 1993. *The Scar of Race.* Cambridge: Belknap/Harvard Univ. Press

Stoker L. 1995. Understanding whites' resistance to affirmative action: the role of principled commitments and racial prejudice. In *Perception and Prejudice: Race and Politics in the United States*, ed. J Hurwitz, M Peffley. New Haven: Yale Univ. Press

Terkildsen N. 1993. When white voters evaluate black candidates: the processing implications of candidate skin color, prejudice and self monitoring. *Am. J. Polit. Sci.* 37(4):1032–53

Thurman QC, Lam JA, Rossi PH. 1988. Sorting out the cuckoo's nest: a factorial survey approach to the study of popular conceptions of mental illness. *Sociol. Q.* 29:565–88

Warr M. 1990. Dangerous situations: social context and fear of victimization. *Soc. Forces* 68(3):891–907

Webb EJ, Campbell DT, Schwartz RD, Sechrest L, Grove JB. 1981. *Nonreactive Measures in the Social Sciences.* Boston: Houghton Mifflin. 2nd ed.

Willimack DK, Schuman H, Pennell B-E, Lepkowski JM. 1995. Effects of a prepaid nonmonetary incentive on response rates and response quality in a face-to-face survey. *Public Opin. Q.* 59:78–92

Wilson DK, Kaplan RM, Schneiderman LJ. 1987. Framing of decisions and selection of alternatives in health care. *Soc. Behav.* 2:51–59

Zaller JR. 1992. *The Nature and Origins of Mass Opinion.* Cambridge: Cambridge Univ. Press

Annu. Rev. Sociol. 1996. 22:401–35

MARKET TRANSITION AND SOCIETAL TRANSFORMATION IN REFORMING STATE SOCIALISM

Victor Nee and Rebecca Matthews

Department of Sociology, Cornell University, Ithaca, New York 14853

KEY WORDS: China, political economy, institutional change, stratification, inequality

ABSTRACT

The far-reaching institutional change and societal transformation occurring in former state-socialist societies have attracted new social science interest in transition economies. This chapter reviews recent research on China, highlighting the theoretical arguments and findings of general interest to social scientists. The paper argues that a paradigm shift is taking place within research on China, from state-centered analysis to a theoretical approach that locates causal forces within a macrosocietal framework. Within a macrosocietal framework, state socialism is viewed as a distinctive institutional arrangement in which society, economy, and the state are integrated through society-wide redistributive arrangements. Forces in economic and political change emanate not only from political actors but from economic and social actors as well. The chapter reviews work in which a macrosocietal approach is used to address stratification, societal transformation, and marketization in reforming Chinese state socialism.

INTRODUCTION

The far-reaching institutional change and societal transformation occurring in former state socialist societies have attracted new social science interest in these societies. In the past, research focused on them was relegated to the domain of area studies and set apart from mainstream social science. The new research on reforming state socialism has sought to move beyond reliance on weak research designs to the application of methods widely employed in modern social sci-

401

ences (Manion 1994). In place of assertions backed by weak evidence, the new research on societies in transition from state socialism (hereafter transition societies) is more apt to be theory-driven and reliant on systematic data collection. As more of the new scholarship moves beyond the confines of area studies, it has become increasingly comparative and cumulative in its aims. Studies of transition societies now address theoretical issues that trace back to the classical themes of modern social science. Indeed, studies of institutional change and market transition more often appear in disciplinary than in area studies journals. In this sense the market transition literature has led to the integration of research on state socialist societies into the mainstream of modern social science.

We focus on the Chinese transition experience in this article; other reforming state socialist societies include Vietnam, North Korea, and Cuba. Postcommunist societies in Eastern Europe and the former Soviet Union share important similarities with the Chinese case, stemming from their common set of economic and political institutions prior to reform. Although differences in trajectories of transitions across reforming state socialist and postcommunist societies have become more pronounced over time, path dependence is likely to result in structural similarities across transition societies (Nee & Stark 1989, Walder 1995b). All transition societies bear the institutional imprints of a long-lasting experience with state socialism, and they evolve into mixed economies characterized by hybrid organizational and property forms. The aim of this article is to review the recent research on China from the vantage point of the rapidly growing social science literature on transition societies, highlighting mainly the theoretical arguments and findings of general interest to social scientists.

In reviewing the literature we suggest that a paradigm shift is taking place within research on China, from state-centered analysis to a theoretical approach that locates causal forces within a macrosocietal framework. Analysts referring to state socialism as the "communist political order" emphasize the dominant role of the Leninist party, and they focus analytic attention on the state as a causal force. Such a state-centered approach assumes that both society and the economy are subordinated to the political order, as largely passive entities to be acted upon by the state. Although built by Leninist parties after they seized political power, state socialism was comprised of a matrix of society-wide institutions that joined society, the economy, and the state. The economy itself was and is embedded in social institutions shaped by custom, social norms, and local community and family relations. Thus, we argue, the sociological study of transition societies is advanced by research that brings societal institutions and structures more fully into explanations of the causes and effects of transformative change, rather than conferring causal priority to the political domain as does state-centered analysis.

The institutional changes that constitute market transition occur at national, regional, and local levels. At the national level, state policy in the implementing of economic reform has involved critical changes in legal-regulatory arrangements (i.e. decollectivization, fiscal decentralization, enterprise reform, legal and regulatory reform) and changes in the role of political institutions. Because prior economic development and state policy implementation differ widely in a country as large as China (or the former Soviet Union and Eastern Europe), regional variation in the rate and extent of institutional change must also be taken into account. At the local level, institutional change centers on alterations in the structure of social networks and institutional arrangements buttressing economic action. Departures from dependence on vertical connections with government officials are often accompanied by greater reliance on social networks linking economic actors within and across communities. Such changes involve shifts in social norms and customary practices, for example a greater reliance on network recruiting in low-level factory jobs as opposed to government assignment. In short, the emergence of a market society is not limited to the growth of markets conceived narrowly as a medium of economic exchange. Fundamentally, market transition entails a society-wide transformation involving interdependent changes in state policy and regulation, economic institutions (i.e. markets, property rights, and contracts), and informal norms and social networks that embed economic action.

This interdependence of politics, economics, and social organization suggests that the study of transition societies is best pursued as an interdisciplinary research program. Such a program has already crystallized around the new institutionalist paradigm (Cook & Levi 1990, Nee & Ingram 1997), influential in economics (North 1990), political science (Alt & Sheplse 1990), and economic sociology (many chapters in Smelser & Swedberg 1994). The integrating idea of the new institutionalist paradigm is the assumption that actors identify and pursue their interests in opportunity structures shaped by custom, cultural beliefs, social norms and networks, market structures, formal organizations, and the state. The new institutionalist paradigm is well-suited for studies of transition societies because it focuses analytical attention on institutional change, its causes, and effects. Moreover, unlike the neoclassical approach, the new institutionalist paradigm does not assume efficient markets nor governance structures.

A PARADIGM SHIFT FROM STATE-CENTERED TO NEW INSTITUTIONAL ANALYSIS

Although modern state socialism constituted a new type of political order, its pattern of economic integration was a familiar one. Polanyi [1957 (1944)] identified this as redistributive, a structure of social organization in which goods and services are distributed by central direction from lower level production units to a center and back again. Rather than direct exchange between buyer and seller as in a market economy, in a redistributive economy the fiat power of a chief or cadre mediates the exchange. Ancient redistributive societies (i.e. Egypt under the Pharaohs, Babylon, and Mayan civilization) were characterized by nonmarket trade of labor and goods; so too were modern state socialist societies. It is this common set of society-wide redistributive arrangements, not the domination of a single political party or level of economic development, which distinguished state socialism from market societies (Szelenyi 1978).

These redistributive mechanisms linked farm households and urban employees, rural communities and urban neighborhoods, and local and regional governments. Far from standing above society, at the lower and middle levels of the hierarchy agents of the redistributive state were also members of communities and neighborhoods where they engaged in ongoing social relations and were thus subject to the normative constraints of social groups (Parish & Whyte 1978, Madsen 1984, Whyte & Parish 1984, Nee 1989a, 1991a). Accordingly, the communist political order does not stand apart from society but is enmeshed in long-standing social connections that link the state to social groups and organizations. Thus causal forces within state socialism emanate not only from the political order, but also from social and economic arrangements not shaped by the state.

State-centered analysis has had a dominant influence in social science research on China. This reflects a realistic assessment of the importance of the state in a command economy. Although the totalitarian model did not have the same influence on the China field as it did in the study of the Soviet Union (Cohen 1980, Shue 1988), research nonetheless focused on the Communist party and the mechanisms through which it controlled the economy and society (Peck 1975). The party ruled through its control of the state, the imposition of its ideology, and the penetration of party-led mass organizations deep in society (Schurmann 1966, Vogel 1969, Whyte 1974, Walder 1986).

In the period of market reform, state-centered analysis emphasizes the persistent power of the administrative elite under conditions of rapid shift to market coordination. Market reform shifted responsibilities among different kinds of cadres. But although the nature of cadre power has changed, the state controls rural communities as in the past through clientelist politics (Oi 1989, 1990). The shift to markets in this view does not erode the institutional bases of cadre power because patron-client ties to cadres are still necessary for everyday economic transactions. State-centered analyses stress the continuing role of government in controlling both internal migration and job assignments in rural townships and small cities (Zweig 1992). Another theme in state-centered analysis is the role of political institutions in shaping the course of economic reforms in China.

Fiscal decentralization has altered incentives for political actors in local governments: officials seek to promote extensive economic growth as a means to increase government revenues (Wong 1992, Oi 1992). According to the state-centered approach, the strong economic performance of rural industry in the 1980s can be explained by the greater capacity of local governments to monitor township and village firms (Walder 1995b). Economic actors, dissident groups, and social movements are overlooked as causal forces. Instead, each phase of the reform cycle is interpreted through the lens of policy debates and power relations within the central state (Shirk 1993). The limits of reform thus are set by political actors.

At the level of the urban firm, state-centered analysis stresses the persistence of state controls despite deepening market reform. Building on Walder's (1992) analytical framework, Bian (1994) and Logan & Bian (1993) argue that the life chances of workers are still shaped by differential allocation of resources by the state to work units, according to the location of each firm in a segmented hierarchy. On a broader level, Putterman (1992, 1994) argues that the state impedes the shift to a market economy through its continued control over the allocation of agricultural products. The mandated quota sale of grain and other major agricultural products at fixed state prices perpetuates a long-standing policy of subsidizing the wages of urban workers. As in Oi (1989), Putterman's analysis emphasizes the persistent power of the supply bureaucracy, and the slow pace of the shift to reliance on market forces in the agricultural sector.

Thus, explaining societal transformation in the reform era, state-centered analysis places causal priority within the state system, rather than looking to societal sources of institutional change (Lieberthal & Lampton 1992, Walder 1995c). Although it is true that the state is often a decisive causal force in determining the timing and scope of reform measures, the state-centered approach provides a limited causal model of institutional change and societal transformation. Figure 1 schematically presents this implicit causal model. It shows political actors in the state domain as the causal agents of economic development and societal transformation. The economy is an appendage of the state, and economic agents are largely passive objects of manipulation and control by political actors in positions of administrative power. Society lacks autonomous bases from which social actors can resist the political order, or the capacity to impose limits on the power of political actors. The state-centered model outlined in Figure 1 most closely approximates the logic of the totalitarian image of state socialism (Friedrich 1954, Ulam 1963, Friedrich & Brzezinski 1965). However, pluralist and clientelist approaches to communist politics also assume the causal imagery sketched in Figure 1 (Skilling & Griffiths 1971; Walder 1986, 1992, 1994, 1995b; Oi 1989, 1992).

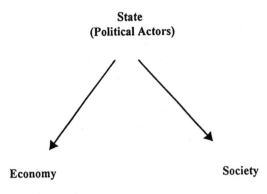

Figure 1   State-centered approach to societal transformation.

Even in unreformed state socialism, overlooking the possibility for autono-mous action on the part of societal actors forecloses attention to informal op-position to the terms imposed by the Leninist state. For example, field research in rural China prior to reform documents the extent to which peasants infor-mally resisted the imposition of collectivized agriculture and sought to limit the state's extraction of agricultural surplus by increasing fertility—the more children born, the more grain a household was allowed to retain—and diverting the most productive labor from collective tasks to the household's private plot. This and other social practices that resulted in low productivity and economic stagnation ultimately eroded the state's commitment to collectivized agricul-ture (Nee 1985, 1986, Nee & Su 1990). Other examples of informal resistance stemming from widespread discontent are detailed by Zhou (1993), who ob-serves that such resistance when mobilized can readily escalate into political challenges to communist rule.

In the era of market transition, bringing society back in is even more crucial. The limits of state-centered analysis are more apparent as a market society emerges in the wake of market reforms, and as horizontal linkages in soci-ety provide alternative social organizations for economic action. Rather than viewing society and economy as passive entities to be acted upon by the state and its agents, as in state-centered analysis, the new institutionalist paradigm points to the active role of social and economic actors. By seizing upon op-portunities opened up by economic reforms, the cumulative actions of social and economic actors impose decisive constraints on the power of the state, and these actions also work to erode the institutional foundations of redistributive state socialism, preceding and following regime change. Research on market transition finds that, under conditions of increasing market penetration, firms no longer can be viewed as mere appendages of the state (Qian & Xu 1993, Jefferson & Rawski 1994, Naughton 1995). Increasingly economic actors can coordinate their interests through market institutions and social networks by-passing the local party organization (Yan 1995), to some extent even within the state-owned sector of the economy (Su 1994). Furthermore, economic and societal actors may incrementally transform the state itself. Whether in Eastern Europe or China, party bureaucrats have not fared well relative to economic actors who take advantage of new opportunities in emerging capital, produc-tion, and labor markets, as professionals, managers, and entrepreneurs. This has created new structural incentives for opportunism and malfeasance, which in turn erode the effectiveness and legitimacy of the state (Nee & Lian 1994). From a societal perspective, actors in an emerging civil society may pressure the state for political changes more directly (Gold 1990b, Perry & Fuller 1991).

A rapidly changing opportunity structure for economic actors in the wake of expanding markets influences society in a number of ways. As ordinary citizens take advantage of opportunities afforded by emerging markets, they in turn incrementally change the economic field through their practical strategies for profit and advancement, by expanding production networks or niches, often beyond the reach of the state. Prior to economic reform, citizens who aspired to become entrepreneurs or merchants risked persecution by local officials. But in the reform economy, those who emerge as entrepreneurs, self-employed professionals, middlemen, merchants, peddlers, and workers in the private sec-tor incrementally alter the stratification order through their practical business strategies and socioeconomic advancement, diminishing thereby the relative power and advantages of the administrative elite—a point argued in market transition theory (Nee 1989b, 1996).

To be sure, the state has an important role in reconstructing a market society, as Polanyi [(1944) 1957] demonstrated in his discussion of the rise of market societies in the West. In the transitions from state socialism, continuous state interventions are critical to the emergence of a market society, from the creation of a new regulatory environment and changes in property rights, to building new market institutions (i.e. equity and commodity exchanges) and macroeconomic monetary and credit policies (Nee 1989a). The new institutionalist paradigm emphasizes the interdependent nature of interactions between the institutional domains of state, society, and economy. However, theories of transition pre-dict that in the course of market transition causal arrows emanating from and between the institutional domains of economy and society are likely to grow in significance, relative to causal arrows emanating from the state/political field (Szelenyi 1988, Nee 1996, Szelenyi & Kostello 1996).

Overlooking societal institutions and forces results in misspecified models of transformative change. Even state-centered analyses must increasingly include nonstate actors and institutions (Naughton 1995, Walder 1995c). However, state-centered analysis draws attention away from explanations that stress state-society interactions and societal forces as the motor of political change in China. What is emphasized instead is institutional change and economic development initiated directly by the state (Walder 1994). In this view changes within the state system, such as increasing elite divisions, are what create the conditions that allow for social movements to mount effective challenges to the political order. We agree in part with this extension of Skocpol's (1979) analysis of the causes of social revolution, but we point to the question left unaddressed in state-centered analysis, which is the ways in which the practical strategies and struggles of economic and social actors cumulatively give rise to institutional change. Moreover, we argue that a focus on departures from the central plan under state socialism masks the extent to which power—defined as control over resources—was not monopolized by central ministries but became dispersed across regional and local administrative centers. The departure from central planning occurred in China long before the market reforms initiated in 1978. Central planning was effectively dismantled during the Great Leap Forward launched by Maoists in 1958 (Schurmann 1966); it was never fully reinstituted in the aftermath of its failure, as evidenced in the high degree of autarchy and self-sufficiency that came to characterize Chinese counties during the late Maoist period (Shue 1988, Lyons 1990, Naughton 1990).

The arguments from market transition theory and state-centered analysis converge at points where the state-centered approach moves towards incorporating a greater role for markets. According to market transition theory, the shift to markets opens up alternative sources of rewards not controlled by the redistributive state, and this shift thereby reduces dependence on the state (Nee 1989b, 1991b). The idea that market reforms also open up alternative mobility channels for political actors and alter relations of dependence within the government hierarchy is formally modeled by Nee & Lian (1994) and was extended by Walder (1994) in his analysis of the decline of Communist power.[1] Both studies concur that the monitoring and sanctioning capacity of the party is weakened as a result of greater opportunism and malfeasance on the part of the party elite. Both conclude that market reforms weaken the party's capacity to monitor and sanction ordinary citizens and that as a result state control declines

---

[1] Nee & Lian's formal model explains the decline of political commitment within the administrative elite, and the increasing vulnerability to political challenge as a function of the erosion of political legitimacy. Walder (1995a,b) agrees because the model is consistent with his analysis of changing dynamics of principal-agent relations within the state system.

as a function of the shift to markets. This conclusion is consistent with market transition theory's hypothesis of the declining significance of redistributive power. Indeed, a tacit shift to a societal approach from within the state-centered perspective is apparent in Walder's (1995c) specifications of departures from central planning, which can be instigated by pressure for political change from economic actors in the second economy and from the practical strategies of ordinary citizens unable to satisfy their needs within a command economy. Indeed, because China after 1958 did not have much in the way of central planning (Naughton 1990, Qian & Xu 1993), Walder's arguments about departures from central planning are more accurately framed as transitions from state socialism.

THE EMERGENCE OF MARKET INSTITUTIONS

Rural Commercialization and Industrialization

In China markets first emerged in rural settings, where economic reforms led to early successes (Watson 1988). Decollectivization and the shift to the household responsibility system resulted in a 61% increase in productivity from 1978 to 1984, of which 78% can be accounted for by this change in incentive system (McMillan et al 1989). An analysis of rural decollectivization from a societal perspective highlights the importance of nonstate actors in the successful implementation of household-based agriculture. According to JY Lin (1988), it was farmers who provided the impetus to shift successfully out of collective agriculture, not state actors. Lin argues that there was no effective state monitoring of individual performance under collective agriculture, because of the decentralized nature of farm work. This was reflected in the egalitarian structure of work points. But monitoring is necessary in collective production for guaranteeing high work efforts on the part of peasants, who have little incentive to work efficiently if all shirking goes unpunished. By contrast, under the household responsibility system, no monitoring by the state is required, other than to ensure that households deliver the agreed-upon quota of grain to the state. In household production, incentives to work hard are already high because farmers obtain the full marginal returns to their labor (JY Lin 1988). Thus it was incentives at the societal level, rather than shifts in policy per se, which account for increases in agricultural productivity following decollectivization.

A societal perspective on rural reform also emphasizes that the well-being of rural households and communities is increasingly linked to rural markets rather than to the actions of state officials. Change in the social organization of agriculture was accompanied by rapid commercialization, as households sought to shift more of their production from the state sector (e.g. grain) to cash crops for the marketplace. With commercialization came increasing diversification and specialization, and the rapid expansion of rural-urban trade which bypassed the state supply and marketing distribution networks. Market forces became more decisive in shaping economic growth of rural communities, as evidenced in the increased significance of urban proximity and the quality of transportation linking villages to markets in towns and cities (Nee & Su 1990, Johnson 1994). Despite the efforts of local cadres, whether economic growth could be sustained beyond the initial gains accomplished by the shift to household production was determined by regional location and spatial proximity to urban markets and by the availability of low-cost transportation (Skinner 1994).

The most significant transformative change in rural areas, however, came not from the expansion of petty commodity production, but from the rise of market-oriented rural industry (Huang 1990, Parish 1994, Nee & Keister 1995). Byrd & Gelb (1990) show that market-oriented rural industrialization is advantageous both for rural communities as a whole and for the cadres who oversee them. First, salaries of local officials are closely tied to revenues generated from township and village enterprises. Cadres below the township level depend entirely on village enterprises for their salaries. Ironically, in localities where township and village enterprises are well-developed and profitable, local cadres have an incentive not to be promoted to higher, salaried positions in the state hierarchy because this would result in a reduction in their incomes. According to Byrd & Gelb, a close link exists between increasing per capita income in a community and the socially acceptable income for local cadres. Local cadres thus have an incentive to improve the general standard of living in their area through the development of rural industry. In this way, the relationship between local cadres and rural residents is itself becoming less vertical, as local cadres focus efforts on marketizing community production. Oi's (1992) state-centered analysis of the effect of fiscal reform on local government's incentive to promote market-oriented economic development complements the Byrd & Gelb analysis.

But analytical attention to state actors should not come at the expense of ignoring the crucial role in industrialization played by rural families themselves. The shift to the household responsibility system enabled households to allocate labor autonomously. Families did so in a flexible manner, shifting labor power from subsistence agriculture to industry, as nonfarm jobs opened up in township and village enterprises, and back into agriculture when demand slacked off. A flexible allocation of labor was beneficial to growth in rural industries and also meant that industrial growth was never achieved at the expense of agricultural production. Moreover, rural industries relied on the financial backing and entrepreneurial efforts of rural families, since state-owned urban firms were unable to provide them. Rural industrial growth in China could not have been so successful without the support of rural families in the reform environment.

When rural industrial growth was encouraged under Mao, labor and financial extraction were imposed on rural communities. Township and village enterprises responded to political pressures for extensive growth rather than to the profit motive and competition in a marketizing institutional environment. The result was both that agricultural production suffered and that rural industries were unsuccessful (Chang 1993).

Local Market Institutions

Rather than emphasizing the continued importance of vertical ties in the Chinese reform environment, a societal perspective looks to the market institutions emerging from increased horizontal transactions, and to the transformative effects that markets themselves may engender. The early market transition literature focused on the emergence and implications of product markets, as these were the first market institutions to develop. In product markets the terms of exchange between buyer and seller are negotiated rather than fixed by administrative fiat as in classical state socialism. The emergence of product or commodity markets not only encouraged the commercialization of agriculture and rural industrialization (Nee & Su 1990, Naughton 1994), but also stimulated product innovation in state-owned enterprises (Jefferson & Xu 1991). In the market transition literature, the extent of product markets is measured by the number of general and specialized marketplaces in a locality. Parpia (1994) for example shows that the extent of the product market corresponds to changes in dietary practices as peasants shift out of subsistence agriculture and obtain more of their food in local markets. Although an important dimension of marketization, product markets are only one of a number of market structures that make up a market economy.

The recent focus on the emergence of production markets stems from interest in examining the role of firms in creating a market environment (Nee 1996). It builds on White's (1981) theory of markets, which views the market as a social structure rather than as a mere medium of exchange. The neoclassical preoccupation with exchange markets, according to White, led economists to overlook the central feature of market institutions—that they are social structures reproduced through signaling and communication among participants. A production market, then, is a group of firms that view themselves as constituting a market and that are perceived as such by buyers. In White's definition, "markets are tangible cliques of producers watching each other" (1981:543). The production market can be viewed as a local business group in which producers communicate with each other, both to compete and to cooperate in gaining access to resources and securing larger market shares. As production networks, local nonstate firms work together against outside competitors, even while they compete internally for skilled workers, input material, and market share within the locality. Operationalized as the number of nonstate firms—private and collective—in a township, the production market variable specifies the population of firms that create a market environment. For example, if the locality has only one firm, whether large or small, then in effect there is no competition for product buyers, and hence, no production market. However, when there are many firms signaling to each other the prices paid for factor resources (e.g. labor) and products, a market environment is established. The larger the size of the production market, the more intense the competition between firms for resources and market share as well as the greater the probability of cooperation among cliques of producers, as in industrial districts in the Third Italy. In the market transition literature, the production market variable is neither a measure of economic growth nor a measure of economic development. No information is included on the size of the firm or the nature and volume of output and services. For example, the variable does not indicate the percentage of output contributed by industry; in many areas nonstate firms are small private businesses involved in commerce and construction. Economic development is measured instead as the level of per capita industrial and agricultural output, and economic growth is measured by the per capita increase in income.

The extent of the production market has been shown to have a significant effect on income mobility (Nee & Liedka 1995) and on the erosion of local cadre power. As local production markets grow in size, the administrative elite experiences a relative decline in their privilege and power (Nee 1996). This is explained by the effect of marketization in providing alternative mobility channels for economic actors: entrepreneurs in private firms, managers in township and village enterprises, and workers. The greater the extent of the production market, the more the income mobility of economic actors will tend to exceed that of the administrative elite.

Recent scholarship shows that labor markets are beginning to emerge in rural areas. Using national community-level data, Nee & Matthews (1995) model the determinants of labor markets, which they operationalize as the proportion of the village population working outside the village in nonfarm work. In their view, labor markets are an important focal point for studies of transitional societies, since a market for nonagricultural labor has implications for income mobility among rural households. When there is intense demand and competition for labor, as in a labor market, the bargaining power of workers improves and with this so do wages. Their regression results indicate that the extent of the local product and production market predicts the size of the labor market. Product and labor markets are linked because a market for commodities yields a more specialized division of labor, and thus an increase in demand for particular types of laborers. An increase in the size of the local production market means that there is both a growing demand for labor and increased competition for labor among firms, likewise leading to growth in local labor markets. The strength of network ties between relatives in country and in cities is equally crucial to the emergence of a rural labor market, since local firms must often rely upon imported labor from other areas. This finding is consistent with studies of labor migration in other developing societies that point to the importance of social networks in promoting and sustaining extra-local labor migration (Massey 1988).

Where rural labor markets have emerged, getting nonfarm jobs is based more on human capital attributes and household labor supply than on personal ties to the administrative elite (Nee 1996). The greater the extent of the labor market, the higher the returns on human capital (Parish et al 1995, Nee & Matthews 1995). Nee (1996) reports the surprising finding that, in the highly marketized southeastern coastal provinces of China, human capital has a significant negative effect on rural household income. It is difficult to reconcile these contradictory findings. However, the human capital referred to in Nee's study was that of the head of household, who was more likely to be engaged in agricultural than in nonfarm work. As Zhao (1993) points out, although the early reform period gave rise to a reduction in rural-urban inequality, by the mid-1980s agriculture products produced for the state were no longer profitable for farmers because the rural-urban price scissors once again worked to rural disadvantage. Notwithstanding, Nee's (1996) finding of negative returns on human capital for heads of households in rural Guangdong and Fujian remain anomalous. Using 1988 urban survey data, Xie & Hannum (1996) show that returns on human capital do not correspond with the rate of economic growth. Their study, however, operationalized economic growth as change in industrial output and did not distinguish between market and nonmarket sectors of the urban economy. Moreover, neither economic growth nor change in industrial output is an appropriate measure of marketization. More recently, researchers examining 1994 data find that returns on human capital are significantly higher in more marketized Guangzhou than in Shanghai, and they are the highest in the marketized sectors of both these cities (Nee & Cao 1995).

Some studies suggest that labor markets have yet to emerge in urban areas (Davis 1990, Xie & Hannum 1996). However, Groves et al (1994b) point to evidence of emerging labor markets for managers of state-owned firms. According to their analysis, the procedures for selecting new managers are increasingly sensitive to firm performance. Managers can be fired when firms are not performing well, and there is a significant turnover in managers within state-owned firms. When managers are selected in firms that have performed poorly, potential managers must submit detailed production proposals and provide a large security deposit. Large-scale internal migration of rural workers to cities also suggests the initial emergence of urban labor markets for temporary labor. By the mid-1990s nearly a quarter of urban residents in China were recent migrants from other areas, often finding jobs as household help, temporary workers in factories and construction sites, and day laborers. Likewise, the growing number of urban workers, technicians, and professionals who find secondary jobs consulting in state-owned firms and moonlighting in the second economy, or who work in private rather than publicly-owned firms, indicates that labor markets may be on the verge of emergence in many urban areas.

Research on the shift to markets has also sought to measure the extent of regional marketization. The idea is that while local market institutions encompass alternative mobility channels in the local arena, as internal migration grows in scale, regional markets become more important in shaping the life chances of ordinary citizens. Moreover, firms in local production markets not only compete within their locality, they also face increasing competition from distant firms as the regional market environment develops. Cluster analysis, in which provinces were grouped according to level of industrial output by state-owned, collective, and private firms, showed distinct regional differences in the predominance of these ownership types, and therefore in the regional shift to markets (Nee & Liedka 1995).

Although this regional measure of marketization has been criticized for merely reflecting the extent of rural industrialization, this is not the case. The cluster analysis examines the ratio of industrial output from private, collective, and state-owned enterprises. Private and collective firms rely primarily on markets and quasi-markets for their factor resources and distribution of output. Referring to the nation as a whole, Walder (1996:1064) points out that 68% of collective output was rural and 73% of rural output in 1989 derived from collective enterprises. But the statistics Walder cites overlook the considerable regional variation in the ratio of collective to private industrial outputs, relative to state output. In the less marketized inland region, not only is collective industrial output (27.2%) much smaller relative to state-owned output (65.9%) there, but private output (6.9%) is much smaller than private output in the relatively laissez-faire southeastern maritime provinces (19.4%), which in turn is much larger than the relative size of private output (7%) in the corporatist provinces, where collective-ownership forms (60.8%) dominate the industrial economy.

The Nee & Liedka cluster analysis was based on data from 1987 to 1989 and can also be viewed as a measure of the changing structure of property rights at the provincial level. During these years the rate of growth in output by private firms far exceeded that of both collective and state-owned firms. Thus what Walder's statistics also conceal is the dynamic growth of private relative to public ownership forms, and the growth of market-oriented firms (private and collective) relative to state-owned firms. Regional marketization and structure of property rights have significant positive effects on the erosion of relative cadre privilege and power, the rate of income mobility, the narrowing of the gender wage gap, the shift to commercialized agriculture, and the returns to private entrepreneurship (Griffin & Zhao 1993, Nee & Liedka 1995, Nee & Matthews 1995, Parish et al 1995, Nee 1996).

In sum, the market transition literature has specified a variety of local market institutions and has defined and operationalized them in a manner consistent with the sociological literature on markets as opportunity structures. The definitions of local and regional market institutions are conceptually and empirically distinct from the definition of redistributive power. In this way, tests of market transition theory, in which the income earnings of cadre and noncadre households are modeled across variation in the extent of local and regional marketization, are not tautological, as critics have claimed (Rona-Tas 1994, Lin 1995, Xie & Hannum 1996, Walder 1996:1063).

The Changing Structure of Property Rights

Unlike Eastern Europe and the former Soviet Union, China has resisted carrying out a formal program of privatization, and the dominant property form in China remains public ownership. This persistence in the underlying structure of property rights is a distinguishing feature of economic reforms in China, operating as a constraint on the extent of change in other institutional domains. Public ownership of productive assets, including land and buildings, provides a continuing economic base for the administrative elite. Nonetheless, significant changes have taken place in the structure of property rights, through the emergence of hybrid property forms and governance structures, extensive informal privatization of publicly owned assets, and a very high founding rate for private firms.

The downward devolution of public property rights instituted by fiscal reform altered incentives for political actors at the local level (Oi 1992). This institutional change paved the way for the rise of local corporatism, an institutional arrangement between plan and market, which emerged as a hybrid governance structure well-suited for China's partial reform (Oi 1990, 1992, Nee 1992, N Lin 1995). The significance of this institutional form is that local corporatist governments are wedded to community-level development. This orientation reflects a shift away from the role that local governments played as the lowest rung of a national redistributive mechanism rendering local communities dependent on superordinate state and government agencies. Rather than seeking to cultivate vertical ties with higher-level government officials as a means to secure a larger share of the redistributive pie, officials in corporatist arrangements focus their attention on building a coalition at the local level between political and economic actors to promote market-oriented economic development (Qian & Xu 1993, Wilson 1994, Nee & Su 1996).

Local corporatist arrangements are societal institutions rather than state organizations, because they incorporate political and economic actors in a community-owned multidivisional firm (Qian & Xu 1993). As a hybrid institutional form, local corporatism allows for a loose coupling between formal state rules and local adaptations based on the mutual interests of officials, community groups, and enterprise managers. Local corporatist arrangements enjoy a transaction costs advantage over alternative governance structures, in a rapidly changing institutional environment in which private property rights are poorly defined and weakly enforced, and in which state-owned enterprises face strong organizational inertia in their efforts to adapt to a marketizing environment (Nee 1992). By contrast to alternative governance structures, local corporatist arrangements facilitate opportunistic adaptation to a changing environment. Weitzman & Xu (1994) refer to the folk theorem to explain improved economic performance under local corporatist governance structures. In this view, local government, enterprise managers, and social groups cooperate on the basis of trust stemming from social capital accumulated in bounded communities. Frequent social interaction within bounded communities has been widely associated with conditions favorable to the accumulation of social capital (Homans 1974, Coleman 1990, Putnam 1993).

But the most significant source of change in the structure of property rights has come about through hidden privatization, in which rights over state assets are partitioned to open the way for private claims over the distribution of economic surplus, or they are simply stripped away by corrupt public employees. Although asset stripping by corrupt officials is a common form of privatization, it is best understood as a form of rent-seeking behavior widely viewed by ordinary citizens as illegitimate, and by the state as illegal (Krueger 1974). A socially legitimate form of privatization has been labeled informal privatization (Nee & Su 1996). In informal privatization, property rights over public assets are conferred and regulated by social norms. As in squatter's rights, the community recognizes the property rights of individuals based upon customary use and de facto possession. A common institutional means to privatize public assets is through lease arrangements that give long-term rights over economic surplus to the lease-holder. Although the lease agreement does not entitle the lease-holder to formal property rights, in effect this is viewed in the community as equivalent to private rights over property. The extensiveness of informal privatization demonstrates the utility of the new institutionalist paradigm because informal privatization results from the social appropriation of rights over communal assets.

To illustrate these processes, we refer to Christiansen's (1992) study of the informal privatization of agricultural land. Land in rural areas is legally owned by the collective and ultimately by the state. But during decollectivization, households were assigned cropping rights over specified plots of arable land. Although the land was initially assigned with term limits of 15 to 20 years, peasants no longer wishing to pursue agriculture soon began to transfer use-rights of the land to other peasants. According to Christiansen, the transfer of cropping rights is viewed by peasants as a legitimate means to transfer ownership of the land itself, which we interpret as indicating that land has been informally privatized. An aspect of informal privatization stressed by Nee & Su (1996) is that it is vulnerable to challenge, and for this reason those who have acquired informal rights over property have an incentive to maintain the stability of the corporatist network, which is viewed as critical to the continuing recognition of informal property claims.

PARTIAL REFORM IN CHINA'S MARKET TRANSITION

Economists advising the postcommunist governments of Eastern Europe and the Soviet Union argued that a big bang approach to instituting a market economy was critical for success (e.g. Sachs 1989). Rather than piecemeal incremental reform, the plan instead was to follow guidelines derived from textbook economics to dismantle the economic institutions of state socialism and replace them with a full set of market institutions in rapid order. Although in theory this approach was persuasive, in practice the big bang approach failed to realize its objectives, at least in the short run (Stark 1996). In contrast, the Chinese approach did not conform to textbook economics, and instead the timing and sequence of reform measures were shaped by the politics of a Communist elite still in command (Shirk 1993). Chinese reformers emphasized piecemeal incremental change, not by design, but by trial and error, resulting in an open-ended evolutionary process of institutional change (CZ Lin 1989).

The conditions confronting the urban transition in China closely approximate the institutional environments of Eastern Europe and the former Soviet Union. In urban China, state-owned enterprises still dominate the industrial economy. In the highly marketized city of Guangzhou, 30% of jobs are located in the marketized sectors of the municipal economy; the remaining jobs are in the public sectors (Nee & Cao 1995). Although the private economy remains small, a growing second economy flourishes in the interstices of the public sector, opening opportunities for secondary jobs from moonlighting to internal subcontracting. Hence, Chinese cities provide a strategic research site that allows analysts to study the effects of persistent partial reform. Economists like Kornai (1990) argued that partial reform was not likely to result in improved economic performance. But new instititutional analyses based on data from China pinpoint firm- and community-level processes that explain why partial reform in China has been more successful than might have been anticipated.

In the urban setting, reform of state-owned enterprises focused on changing incentives at the firm level by increasing firm autonomy. Groves et al (1994a) report findings, based on longitudinal data from 1980 to 1989, which support the view that partial reforms in state-owned firms have been successful in altering incentives for managers and workers. Managers have improved firm productivity through bonuses and by hiring workers increasingly on a contract basis, rather than on a permanent basis as in the past. One reason for improved productivity is that increased firm autonomy creates a shorter hierarchy between individuals who have useful information about the firm—managers—and individuals who make decisions about firms. Prior to enterprise reform, managers spent much of their time bargaining with superordinate state agencies, using information about the productive capacities of the firm as a bargaining chip. As a result, supervisory agencies often made planning decisions based on distorted firm information. When firms have more autonomy, managers no longer have the same incentive to bargain with and distort information, and, moreover, they are able to make more decisions about firm activities themselves. The fact that they can retain a portion of the profits also gives managers incentives to increase productivity.

Jefferson & Rawski (1994) likewise argue that institutional changes leading to increased managerial autonomy, the contract responsibility system, and dual pricing have altered incentives sufficiently to result in sustained improvements in productivity. The effect of these reforms has been that products are increasingly bought and sold on the market, both among and outside state-owned firms. There is an increased reliance on hard bank loans for investment capital. Retained profits are linked to firm performance, and poor performance is penalized. Based on their research employing data from large-scale surveys of industrial firms, Jefferson & Rawski argue against Walder's (1987) claim that managers are overly responsive to worker pressures to increase bonuses. Rather, the size of bonuses is closely linked with worker productivity. These findings suggest that productivity gains in state-owned enterprises may have passed the threshold where they are likely to be self-sustaining. This optimistic view of industrial reform is shared by Naughton (1995), whose concept of growing out of the plan captures both the incremental nature of partial reform and its successful implementation. However, continuing reports of persistent poor economic performance and high numbers of loss-making firms in the state-sector suggest the need to remain skeptical about overly optimistic assessments of the prospects for successful adaptation to a marketizing economy by large state-owned firms. The industrial heartland of Northeastern China, dominated by state-owned enterprises, is following the path of the state-owned firms in the former Soviet Union. In contrast, the nonstate sector of the industrial economy continues to outperform the state-owned sector by a wide margin.

With the advantage of hindsight, economists have begun to construct explanations for the unexpected success of partial reform in China. Rather than forcing reform to follow a predetermined plan, partial reform in China has absorbed lessons from small successes and failures. Reflecting back on the failure of the big bang approach in Eastern Europe, Murrell (1992a,b) argues that economic institutions are complex and intertwined with one another in a manner that requires gradual change to achieve success in improving economic performance. Knowledge tends to be limited to specific contexts, so that knowledge of particular kinds of institutions cannot be transferred if these institutions are destroyed or radically reformed. Gradual reform, he argues, would have been more appropriate in Eastern Europe, because it allows actors to apply context-specific knowledge of institutions to solve practical problems without destroying the relationships between institutions. When institutions are destroyed in big bang fashion, as in Eastern Europe and the former Soviet Union, a poor job of constructing new institutions is the likely outcome. This conclusion is consistent with Solinger's (1989) research on the persistence of relational contracting among Chinese industrial firms. Long-standing inter-firm trading relationships, by providing a basis for trust, smooth the shift to a market environment.

Qian & Xu (1993) develop a novel institutionalist argument to explain the success of partial reform in China. In contrast to the Soviet Union, China's economy has always been an M-form hierarchy rather than a U-form hierarchy. That is, the government is subdivided along regional rather than functional lines. Because regions are relatively autonomous, they have an incentive to increase local revenues, much of which they are allowed to retain. In addition, M-form hierarchies are more dependent on local revenues than the U-form hierarchy. Local areas can also experiment with institutional innovations, and the effects of failures are contained within the area. The effect of fiscal reforms after 1978 was to make regions and localities even more autonomous than before. The M-form hierarchy in China facilitated the rapid growth of the nonstate sector and the emergence of market institutions. The central state's grip over localities was weak prior to reform and even weaker following reform; as a result, institutional innovations and new programs did not have to go through many layers of bureaucracy to secure approval. Moreover, the ease of communication afforded by greater structural decentralization in the Chinese industrial economy provided a key ingredient for successful reform.

THE CONSEQUENCES OF MARKET TRANSITION FOR THE STRATIFICATION ORDER

The Declining Significance of Redistributive Power

Controversy has been generated over claims advanced by market transition theory, which argues that the shift to greater reliance on markets incrementally erodes the relative power and privileges of the administrative elite. In the view of state-centered analysts, in the absence of regime change the Leninist state and its cadres will continue to control the economy and society despite the penetration of market institutions. In their view, there is no intrinsic feature of markets that diminishes the power of officials in reforming state socialism. This is because the administrative elite can readily convert political capital into economic gain, even more so in a marketizing economy than in a nonmarket setting. State-centered analysts predict that, far from incurring an erosion of cadre power, the stratification order is not likely to be fundamentally altered by the shift to markets, and the former administrative elite will remain on top of the stratification order even after a change of regime (Rona-Tas 1994).

The controversy is in part the result of a misreading of market transition theory (Szelenyi & Kostello 1996). Empirical studies of market transition document that party members, cadre households, and cadre-entrepreneurs all have higher incomes and standards of living than do noncadre households (Nee 1989b, 1991b, 1996; Griffin & Zhao 1993; Nee & Liedka 1995). After controlling for human capital and household composition, what multivariate analyses of change in income show is that, in marketized regions of rural China, income returns to administrative positions are not statistically significant and are lower than those for entrepreneurs and nonfarm workers (Nee 1989b, 1996; Parish et al 1995). More importantly, even in the inland region where the income returns to cadre status are positive and significant, the relative size of this advantage is smaller than that obtained by entrepreneurs and many nonfarm workers (Nee 1996).[2] This finding indicates that, even in the less marketized inland region, many households that pursued market-oriented strategies of advancement—

---

[2]The effect of cadre status was negative and marginally significant in the preliminary test of market transition theory (Nee 1989b). Walder (1996) is correct that this finding was not replicated in analyses of the 1989–1990 survey. The important difference between the two surveys, overlooked by Walder, is that the 1985 survey was conducted in two peri-urban counties near the Special Economic Zone of Xiamen city, then among the most marketized areas of China. As a quasi-experiment, the purpose of the analysis was to test whether net income returns of the administrative elite grew at a lower rate than for ordinary households at the start of reform. The 1989–1990 survey by contrast was a national survey of townships, villages, and households and was much more representative of rural households and communities in China. Despite its nonrandom selection of rural counties, the villages and households in the sample were randomly selected.

small businesses or nonagricultural jobs—were better off than similar cadre households whose income comes from state employment. Hence, a significant negative income coefficient for cadres is not the required criterion of confirmation for market transition theory, as claimed by Walder (1996).

The declining significance of redistributive power hypothesis is confirmed if many economic actors from noncadre background experience a higher rate of income growth than do the administrative elite. This is true even where the redistributive power of cadres is augmented by economic reform, as is the case when cadres benefit from the rapid growth of rural industries—as long as the market power of many economic actors increases at a faster rate. Over time, this still leads to the incremental displacement of the administrative elite from the top income group. This change in the stratification order is reflected in the finding that only 30% of the cadre households in the 1989–1990 sample were in the top income quintile. Moreover, no income advantage was found in any region of China for any of the three variables measuring political capital: former cadre status, former cadre entrepreneurs, and households with cadre relatives (Nee 1996).

Based on their analysis of the Chinese Household Income Project (CHIP) survey of rural households conducted in 1988, Parish & Michelson (1996) report results "at variance with the Nee findings" showing that cadre advantage has increased in marketized regions of rural China relative to noncadre households. They describe their results as "preliminary," and indeed aspects of their model and variable specification are less than satisfactory.[3]

For Example Paris & Michelson also assert that it is necessary to differentiate occupations in the nonfarm worker category. This they do in their logistic analysis reported in their Table 2. However, in the analysis of relative income advantage (Table 3), they collapse all occupational groups—manager, technical worker, clerical worker, entrepreneur, and manual worker—into one group:

[3]Parish & Michelson report results of logistic regression analysis, based on a sample of 27,367 adult income earners, purporting to show cadre advantage in securing administrative positions. They could not have achieved statistically significant results, however, had they not included clerical workers in the "administrator" category (see their Table 2, row 2). Hence the findings they report in the coastal laissez-faire and corporatist regions point not to cadre advantage in securing administrative positions, but instead to possible cadre advantage in securing "run of the mill" clerical jobs.

The declining significance of the positional power hypothesis focuses on the fate of cadres or *ganbu* and not just the top administrators. As a status group, cadres comprised the elite of prereform China, representing the social group Djilas labeled the "new class" and Szelenyi's "redistributors." The ambitious cadre sought to advance through the bureaucracy, securing more power and privileges thereby. Relatively few cadres ever became top administrators; nonetheless cadres held power in the leading groups of local administrations and enjoyed privileges, albeit often small by contemporary standards (Madsen 1984, Oi 1989).

nonfarm laborer. In the nonfarm category they included farmers who listed seasonal off-farm work as a secondary job, biasing downward nonfarm income. Had Parish & Michelson compared the earnings return of cadres with managers, technical workers, and entrepreneurs, and differentiated these groups from manual and service workers, they would have obtained different results. Even if they had compared top administrators with the occupation groups differentiated in the nonfarm category, their results might still have been similar to Nee's findings. Instead they test the declining significance of redistributive power hypothesis by comparing only the top administrators (1.7%) with all nonfarm workers (16.4%). In no society, past or present, have all nonfarm workers earned more than the administrative elite.

According to market transition theory, the causes giving rise to a change in the mechanisms of stratification in reforming and postcommunist societies are linked inextricably to the expansion of market institutions. First, markets open up alternative mobility channels not controlled by the state, and this enables entrepreneurs to achieve greater wealth and power than do the administrative elite. (These entrepreneurs are simply households that started up small businesses after institutional change made self-employment legitimate. Prior to 1978, peasants with such capitalist leanings were likely to come under political attack in village struggle meetings organized by grass-root cadres.) Second, the emergence of labor and product markets enable nonfarm workers, and to a lesser extent farmers, to withdraw their goods and services until they are able to obtain more favorable terms of exchange and conditions of work than those available from the state-controlled economy. (The continued mandatory quota-sale of grain to the state imposed limits on the shift to markets in agriculture.)

Combined, these institutional changes alter the mechanisms determining the distribution of rewards in a manner that renders the relative power and privileges of the administrative elite open to challenges from below. These are not overt challenges as in social movements and political protests, but incremental, through countless acts of economic actors seeking profit and gain in labor and product markets. Such activity is not even perceived by the established elite because it takes place in economic institutions beyond the reach of the state. The theory assumes that the elite continue to derive power and privilege from position, and indeed empirical studies indicate that such power is augmented by marketization (Nee & Lian 1994). But relative to the gains made by many entrepreneurs and direct producers, the advantage of positional power is diminished as a function of the size of markets. Cadre-entrepreneurs gain exceptional windfall profits in the early stages of marketization through their control of public assets. But such advantages decline as markets thicken, and the redistributive power of cadre-entrepreneurs is eroded as the control of capital assets shifts to market coordination and private ownership. This is seen in the positive and significant income returns for cadre entrepreneurs and former cadre entrepreneurs in the 1985 survey, and the nonsignificant effect of cadre status and political capital on the income returns to entrepreneurs by 1989–1990 in rural China.

Another conceptual confusion has been the idea that because empirical tests of market transition theory used data from rural China, it must therefore be a theory bounded by rural society (Rona-Tas 1994, Xie & Hannum 1996), with its small-scale producers and small communities. A theory verified in this context, it is assumed, is not likely to apply to industrial societies, where large-scale complex organizations dominate the economic and political landscape, and the urban populations are more sophisticated and varied. Despite the differences in institutional context between rural and urban societies, market transition theory makes general claims that can be tested across the rural/urban divide and across former state socialist societies.[4]

Tests of market transition arguments in the urban context are at an early stage. Analyses of income returns in Tianjin from 1978 to 1993 report a persistence of cadre power in the redistributive sector and evidence of decline in income returns to party membership in the marketized sectors (Bian & Logan 1996). More recently, Nee & Cao (1995) report findings based on surveys (N = 3899) conducted in Shanghai and Guangzhou in 1994 that show no significant earnings advantage for party members, higher income returns for nonparty bureaucrats and professionals, substantially higher income returns for professionals and self-employed in the marketized sectors of the urban economy, and higher income returns to human capital in the marketized sectors. Whether the sources of structural change were domestic or international made no substantial difference in the emergent urban stratification order. This study provides the strongest confirmation of market transition theory to date. It indicates that the decline of cadre advantage has gone far beyond what Bian & Logan (1996) reported for Tianjin, the heavy industrial port city in North China.

As its analytical starting point, market transition theory points to the importance of change in the dominant mechanism of economic integration in bringing about transformative societal changes. Insofar as the institutional domain of markets has been long associated with the discipline of economics, market

---

[4]Rona-Tas (1994) does not mention the striking similarity empirical between urban findings reported in his study and those in the original test of market transition theory. Despite the technical sophistication Xie & Hannum's (1996) findings are inconclusive because they use the wrong exogenous variable: change in industrial output. This should be a control variable in tests of market transition theory (Nee 1996: 918–19), for under both Stalin and Mao extensive industrial growth occurred in the absence of markets. The appropriate causal variable to employ in tests of market transition theory is the extent of the shift to reliance on market institutions.

transition theory has been perceived as an economic rather than a sociological approach by its critics (Lin 1995). Yet as Polanyi [1957 (1944)] demonstrated in his pioneering work on the institutional foundation of modern market economies, sociological analyses of markets differ from those of neoclassical theory. Rather than viewing markets as simply medium or sites of exchange, the sociological approach has sought to examine markets as institutional and social structures (White 1981, Granovetter 1985, Swedberg 1994). This is the enduring intellectual legacy of Polanyi's concept of embeddedness. Another distinctive aspect of the sociological approach is to examine market transition as a societal transformation rather than simply a change in the coordinating mechanism of the economy. From the new institutionalist paradigm, the emergence of a market society entails changes at the national, regional, and local levels, from society-wide changes in the rules of the game to the interaction of market penetration with regional variation in the implementation of state policy and local differences in social structure and institutional context. In this view, for example, a history of out-migration prior to the Chinese revolution provides the network basis for a rapid incorporation into the global market economy and for rural-urban migration following market reform. State policy favoring earlier and more extensive market transitions in the southeastern maritime provinces stemmed in large part from reform leaders' recognition of the potential of such network ties to overseas Chinese capital and entrepreneurial talent (Lyons & Nee 1994).

The new institutionalist and public choice literatures have clearly shown that political markets are important in all societies (Buchanan 1968, Alt & Shepsle 1990). Surely overlooking political markets in the transitions from state socialism neglects an important dimension of new institutionalist analysis (Parish & Michelson 1996). But this is not an issue in the market transition literature, where the central state and local corporatist arrangements have been emphasized as important institutions in shaping the emerging market society (Nee 1989a, 1992). The issue instead is that in the absence of economic markets, the administrative elite monopolized power and privilege. In this situation, access to and control of political markets provided the only avenue for advancement. The shift to greater reliance on market institutions—labor, production, commodity and capital markets—opened alternative opportunity structures beyond the political markets controlled by the administrative elite. Insofar as economic markets grow more rapidly than political markets, market transition theory argues that this institutional change induces fundamental changes in the mechanisms of stratification.

The main empirical findings of the market transition literature, as this section has demonstrated, have focused on how institutional change centering on markets as a structure of opportunity is linked causally to transformative change. Although local social structures such as cliques of firms in local production markets, local corporatist arrangements in rural communities, kinship ties to the administrative elite, and the strength of urban network ties have been examined in causal models in the market transition literature, more research is needed to fill out the account of how features of local social structure and institutional contexts combine to both limit and facilitate the emergence of a market society. We agree with Lin (1995) that such careful specification of local social structure and institutional arrangements is likely to lead to improved multivariate models that can account for the enormous variation in modes of market transition at the local level. Why, for example, local corporatist arrangements appear to be dominant in the central maritime provinces Jiangsu and Zhejiang, and to a lesser extent Shandong, may well be accounted for by reference to enduring features of local social structure and prior economic development. Similarly, variation in local corporatist arrangements in these provinces, from corporatist arrangements that build on private enterprise as in the Wenzhou model to stable collective-ownership arrangements in the Sunan model, probably reflects preexisting differences in local institutional contexts and social structure.

No preconceived model of a market economy is assumed as the outcome of market transition (Nee 1989b, 1991b, 1992, 1996). The modern world economy has produced varieties of market economies, from the East Asian model to societal corporatist models in northwestern Europe. We speculate that the emerging postcommunist transition societies will similarly produce a variety of national and regional forms of market economies, which may well include stable patterns of local corporatist accommodations. In any case, mixed economies with various combinations of hybrid market forms are the likely outcome of market transition in reforming state socialism.

The Rise of Entrepreneurship

The rise of private entrepreneurship in China has opened up mobility channels both for entrepreneurs and for their employees, beyond the reach of the socialist state. Prior to market reform, private entrepreneurship, which had been actively suppressed by the state through the 1950s and especially during the Cultural Revolution, survived in rural areas, mainly in the private household economy that coexisted with collectivized agriculture. Peasants sought modest profit from marketing goods produced in their spare time. In cities private entrepreneurship had been all but eradicated by the late Maoist era (Whyte & Parish 1984).

Since 1978, the emergence of an entrepreneurial stratum has been closely intertwined with the expansion of markets and institutional environments favorable to private enterprise (Liu 1992). When local governments intervene through mobilizational methods commonly employed in the Maoist era, even to support market-oriented growth, the uncertainty this causes limits the entry of private entrepreneurs (Nee & Young 1991). By contrast, private entrepreneurs have flourished in southeastern China where local governments have adopted a laissez-faire policy and provided an environment in which credible commitment to market-oriented policies is backed by reliable administrative procedures. Private entrepreneurs are both the main catalyst behind market growth and the main beneficiaries of market penetration. They exploit new opportunities for profit and gain opened up by institutional change (e.g. new policies and laws) stemming from reform measures. Unintended growth in the population of entrepreneurs who seek to profit from producing for demand not met by the public sector exceeded the expectation of reformers (Gold 1990a). Cadre-entrepreneurs comprise a small percentage of the population of entrepreneurs, a proportion that declines as the population of entrepreneurs grows and draws on new groups in society. In the cities, for example, state employees and high school and college graduates increasingly seek jobs in emergent labor markets (*xiahai*) as they come to perceive that far greater opportunities for career advancement can be obtained in the growing market economy. According to market transition theory, the advantage of cadre status for entrepreneurial pursuits diminishes in the course of market transition because thicker markets reduce the strategic value of redistributive control over the movement of goods and services.

Competition between private and semi-private firms and public ownership forms, started early and intensified in the course of market transition. In the early stages the competitive exclusion of private enterprise by administrative elite developing rural collective enterprises imposed limitations on the growth of the private sector. But as markets thicken, the ability to restrict the market activities of entrepreneurs diminishes while the population of private firms attains the critical mass needed to enable direct competition to grow in intensity. The competitive advantage of the private property form is enhanced as informal privatization and joint-venture firms contribute to the legitimacy of private firms in the transition economy. As a result the growing out of the plan is increasingly accounted for by a greater market share of private and semi-private firms, a trend most pronounced in the highly marketized southeastern coastal provinces of Guangdong and Fujian.

The Dynamics of Income Inequality in Transition Economies

Market-driven economic development has long been associated with increasing inequality. That inequality increases in the early stages of capitalist economic development is not disputed in the social science literature on income inequality. Both economic liberals and Marxists concur that income is more equally distributed in agrarian economies and more broadly dispersed as the division of labor increases and as class differentiation grows. The market transition literature, however, has added a twist to the common wisdom about the effect of markets on the structure of inequality. Szelenyi (1978) speculated that if the main mechanism generating new inequalities in state socialism is redistribution, then access to market opportunities may operate as a corrective on inequalities. He developed this insight in a substantive analysis of urban housing in Hungary, where he showed that the administrative elite benefited the most from state subsidized housing. This insight was extended in studies of market transition in China and tested competitively with Kuznet's inverted-U shape hypothesis (Nee 1991b, Nee & Liedka 1995).

On the whole, empirical analyses of income inequality in transition economies provide a surprisingly consistent account. There is evidence consonant with the Szelenyi hypothesis of declining income inequality as markets are introduced to reforming state socialism (World Bank 1985; Nee 1991b, 1996). Most probably, the reduction in income inequality is the combined result of the effect of markets in reducing inequality between direct producers and redistributors, and of increases in state-purchasing price of grain and bonus payments to urban workers. In any case, the decline in income inequality was temporary. As markets thickened and income dispersion grew, especially as a result of differential returns to human capital and rates of economic growth across regions, income inequality increased. Without exception all empirical studies of income inequality in former state socialist societies show that over time markets have generated more inequality (Hsiung & Putterman 1989, Rozelle 1994, Rona-Tas 1994, Bian & Logan 1995, Nee & Liedka 1995). As predicted by the economics and Marxist literature, the effect of markets has been to create new inequalities greater than those under unreformed state socialism.

Studies of income mobility and inequality have produced new insights about the effects of markets, as well as confirmed long-standing beliefs. Progress in this area has derived mainly from better specifications of regional, sectoral, and institutional effects in models of income inequality. Rozelle (1994) analyzed regional income data to examine inequality among counties. He showed that rural industrialization is the principal cause of increasing inequality, and that agriculture is associated with reduced inequality. He reasons that barriers to trade in rural China increased the inequality caused by the shift from agriculture to industry, by limiting access to nonfarm jobs to residents of particular counties. As a result, income inequality within counties remained stable, while inter-regional inequality grew dramatically.

In another study, Nee & Liedka (1995) analyze data from a national survey of 138 Chinese rural communities and 7950 households. This study documents extensive income mobility from 1978 to 1989–1990, with distinct institutional effects and regional variations. Income mobility is most extensive in localities and regions where local corporatist governments play an active role in assigning nonfarm jobs, where market-driven economic growth occurs, and in more industrialized regions. In localities and regions where agriculture remains the main source of household income, income has stagnated. The findings on the effects of industrialization and economic growth conform to expectations stemming from the development economics literature. However, at the community level, local corporatist arrangements have an equalizing effect on the distribution of rewards. This finding documents the effect of social structure and institutions on constraining markets, which is consistent with the sociological literature (Smelser & Swedberg 1994).

Gender Inequality

As to the effect of market reform on gender inequality, the recent empirical literature reports mixed findings, with some scholarship showing that markets have disproportionately benefited men, and other reports providing a more optimistic account of the effect of markets on the life chances of women. Entwisle et al (1995) argue that rural women are being left behind in the rise of private entrepreneurship. Their study, based on data from eight provinces collected in 1989, shows that the odds of households starting up a private business are greater for families with more male than female labor. Among households who operate family businesses, male family members are also more likely to work in them. By implication, women in entrepreneurial households are relegated to work in subsistence agriculture.

Analyses focusing on the shift from agricultural work to nonfarm employment provide a more optimistic account of the effect of market transition on women. Parish et al (1995) assess the extent to which women are participating in emergent rural labor markets. Their data, drawn from ten rural counties in 1993, show that women are just 10% less likely to obtain nonfarm jobs than men. Moreover, women with nonfarm jobs make about 80% to 90% of male wages. Contributing to their optimism was the finding that women benefited from education, which increases their odds of obtaining nonfarm jobs and increases their prospects for higher wages. The Parish et al study was replicated by Nee & Matthews (1995) using a national rural survey of 7950 households in 69 counties, collected in 1989–1990. Their results confirm that the extent of the local labor market determines opportunities for nonfarm employment for both sexes. But their findings suggest that households obtain nonfarm employment for male family members first, before obtaining it for female family members. Employing regional analysis, Nee & Matthews also show that the gender wage gap narrows, the more extensive the shift to markets and the higher the rate of economic growth. Not only do wages improve for nonfarm workers when demand is high and supply of workers is taut, but the gender wage gap declines. As men begin to travel long distances to seek nonfarm employment, the women left at home derive an indirect benefit by assuming the role of head of household, which confers on them more decision-making power within the household. Women also benefit from the intervention of local corporatist governments. Where local governments play a key role in matching workers to jobs, women are more likely to obtain nonfarm employment.

PROSPECTS FOR SOCIETAL TRANSFORMATION

The Rebirth of Civil Society

The transition to a market economy has implications for societal transformation, going beyond changes in the stratification order. Some scholars argue that the expansion of autonomous bases for economic activities creates an environment in which a civil society can emerge. In this view, as market reforms continue to improve the life chances of citizens and societal autonomy expands, the desire for political change is also likely to find a broader base of expression (Gold 1990b, Perry & Fuller 1991). Wank (1995), however, argues against the view that the rise of a civil society implies that social groups will mobilize for political change. Based on his field research in Xiamen, he finds little evidence to support the view that entrepreneurs allied themselves to student protesters during the 1989 pro-democracy movement. In Xiamen, and presumably elsewhere, private entrepreneurs remain dependent on local officials, and as a result they have little incentive to join with students striving for political reforms.

Others have examined the appropriateness of the concept of civil society in China, a political culture lacking a tradition of individual rights and legal constraints protecting voluntary associations from arbitrary government interventions. In de Bary's (1991, 1995) view, something like a civil society existed in traditional China, in the form of local societies beyond the reach of the state and in associations of scholar-officials. To the extent that a civil society is emerging in China today, de Bary maintains it must be viewed as limited in nature and constrained by the threat of unbridled state power. Unger & Chan's (1995) analysis of the pattern of state intervention in China also reflects a more cautious assessment of the emergence of civil society in China. They suggest instead that China might be thought of as a corporatist society, in which the state assigns the right to represent segments of society to particular organizations. Such corporatism is not a trend of the reform era. Corporatist arrangements were prevalent during the Maoist era; for example, the ACFTU trade union was allowed monopoly representation of state sector workers. However, Chan

& Unger point to a significant difference in the nature of corporatist arrangements between the pre- and postreform eras. Whereas in prereform corporatist arrangements, representative organizations like the ACFTU were more or less mouthpieces for government policy, in the reform era they are increasingly responsive to the needs of their constituents.

The Vulnerability of the Communist Political Order to Erosion by Market Forces

Although a civil society need not accompany market transition, a formal model of dynamic changes in political commitment shows that market reforms alter the principal-agent relations between communist rulers and bureaucrats at the middle and lower levels of the state hierarchy (Nee & Lian 1994). The decline of political commitment among party members and economic bureaucrats is linked to the increasing relative payoff to opportunism and malfeasance in the market context, and to the diminished returns on political commitment to the party organization. Declining commitment in turn increases the cost of monitoring and enforcement by the party, even as its capacity to do so declines with erosion of political commitment among members. The exception to this rule is found in local corporatist communities. There, the monitoring and enforcement capacity of the party is reinforced, rather than weakened, by successful economic development. The model predicts the collapse of the communist political order when market transition fails to give rise to economic growth.

A complementary approach to party commitment is seen in Walder's (1994, 1995c) state-centered analysis of the erosion of the communist political order, which draws attention away from state-society struggle as the motor of political change in reforming state socialism. Instead, Walder argues that processes of economic change initiated by the state have implications for political change. Consequently, analysis of political decline need not take into account the implications of social movements and political protest by ordinary citizens in mounting political challenges to the state (Zhou 1993). Instead, changes within the state hierarchy are what created conditions that allow social movements and political protests to topple the Leninist state. The Nee & Lian (1994) model and Walder's work (1994) support the view that market reforms alter relations of dependence in the government hierarchy, greatly affecting the party's ability to monitor, sanction, and reward its members, and that this in turn reduces its capacity to govern, as both its legitimacy and its monitoring and enforcement capacity decline.

A convergence between state-centered analysis and market transition theory is apparent in recent scholarship (e.g. Walder 1995a). As pointed out earlier, this convergence comes from within the state-centered framework when these analysts bring into their implicit models societal actors and institutions. Because the economic rewards for political position are shallow, as the payoffs to participation in the market economy increasingly surpass the income returns to positional power, the incentive to defect from or not to seek political careers within the party increases. Instead, entering into the market (*xiahai*) becomes the preferred path for the bright and ambitious. In the long run the choices of these individuals, pursuing profit and gain in the market economy, hollow out the Leninist state, not only because talent is missing but because ordinary citizens can choose to ignore the party's exhortations and appeals to revitalizing the faith. At this point, state-centered analysis ceases to be state-centered and slips into a macrosocietal framework of analysis. Rather than assigning causal agency only to the political domain, new social and economic actors must be viewed as playing an increasingly important role in the politics of markets and of societal change.

CONCLUSION

The market transition literature has moved the study of transition societies to the center stage of Western social science. Rather than being viewed as a parochial area studies interest, analyses of the transitions from state socialism increasingly appear in leading disciplinary journals in the social sciences. The influence of this body of research is beginning to disseminate into the mainstream sociological literature (i.e. Breiger 1995, the recent "Market Transition Symposium" in the *American Journal of Sociology*), a process that may generate new theoretical and conceptual breakthroughs. Just as modern social theory grew out of the intellectual response to the rise of capitalism in the West, as reflected in the classical writings of Smith, Marx, Durkheim, Weber, and Polanyi, so the new work on the transitions from state socialism may revitalize social theory and theory-driven empirical research on societal transformation. Since the classical era of modern sociological thought, the conditions for research have improved considerably. The development of modern computing and progress in quantitative methods have made it possible to analyze societal transformation in progress in a manner unimagined by classical theorists.

Social science analysis of market transition is still at an early stage, but the results obtained both in theoretical development and cumulative empirical findings augur well for the future study of transition societies. We sense that a paradigm shift has already taken place, implicitly rather than explicitly, as scholarship has increasingly reached beyond the domain of the political order to encompass the actions of economic and social actors in explanations of institutional change and societal transformation. From the vantage point of a new institutionalist paradigm, the state comprises a formidable causal force. Yet to argue that processes within the state hierarchy are the only causal forces that matter in explaining institutional change is ultimately short-sighted and results in misspecification of causal models. For example, where do labor markets come from? They do not emerge from within the state hierarchy, as state-centered analysis would insist. Their emergence instead is linked to the rise of product and production markets. The emergence of labor markets in reforming state socialism is of fundamental importance in the explanation of changes in the stratification order. The new institutionalist paradigm takes the state fully into account in its causal imagery, but insists that the often unobserved action of economic and social actors in society must also be included in an adequate causal explanation of societal transformation.

Literature Cited

Alt J, Sheplse K. 1990. *Perspectives on Positive Political Economy.* Los Angeles: Univ. Calif. Press

Bian Y. 1994. *Work and Inequality in Urban China.* Albany: State Univ. NY Press

Bian Y, Logan JR. 1996. *Market transition and the persistence of power.* Am. Sociol. Rev. In press

Breiger R. 1995. Social structure and the phenomenology of attainment. *Annu. Rev. Sociol.* 21:115–36

Buchanan JM. 1968. *The Demand and Supply of Public Goods.* Chicago: Rand McNally

Byrd WA, Gelb A. 1990. Why industrialize? The incentives for rural community governments. In *China's Rural Industry,* ed. WA Byrd, Q Lin, pp. 358–87. New York: Oxford Univ. Press

Chang KS. 1993. The peasant family in the transition from Maoist to Lewisian rural industrialisation. *J. Dev. Stud.* 29(2):220–44

Christiansen F. 1992. Private land in China? Some aspects of the development of socialist land ownership in post-Mao China. *J. Communist Stud.* 3(1):55–70

Cohen S. 1980. *Rethinking the Soviet Experience.* New York: Oxford Univ. Press

Coleman JS. 1990. *Foundations of Social Theory.* Cambridge, MA: Harvard Univ. Press

Cook KS, Levi M, ed. 1990. *The Limits of Rationality.* Chicago: Univ. Chicago Press

Davis D. 1990. Urban job mobility. In *Chi-*

nese Society on the Eve of Tiananmen, ed. D Davis, EF Vogel, pp. 85–108. Cambridge, MA: Council East Asian Stud.

de Bary WT. 1991. *The Trouble with Confucianism.* New York: Columbia Univ. Press

de Bary WT. 1995. *Law and rites in Chinese constitutional and community compacts.* Presented at Conf. Confucianism Hum. Rights, Honolulu

Entwisle B, Henderson GE, Short SE, Bouma J, Zhai F. 1995. Gender and family businesses in rural China. *Am. Sociol. Rev.* 60:36–57

Friedrich CJ, ed. 1954. *Totalitarianism.* New York: Grosset & Dunlap

Friedrich CJ, Brzezinski ZK. 1965. *Totalitarian Dictatorship and Autocracy.* Cambridge, MA: Harvard Univ. Press. 2nd ed.

Gold TB. 1990a. Urban private business and China's reforms. In *Reform and Reaction in Post-Mao China,* ed. R Baum, pp. 84–103. New York: Routledge

Gold TB. 1990b. Urban private business and social change. See Davis 1990, pp. 157–77

Granovetter M. 1985. Economic action and social structure: the problem of embeddedness. *Am. J. Sociol.* 91:481–510

Griffin K, Zhao R, eds. 1993. *The Distribution of Income in China.* New York: St. Martin's

Groves T, Hong Y, McMillan J, Naughton B. 1994a. Autonomy and incentives in Chinese state enterprises. *Q. J. Econ.* 109(1):183–209

Groves T, Hong Y, McMillan J, Naughton B. 1995. China's evolving managerial labor market. *Journal of Political Economy* 103:873–92

Homans GC. 1974. *Social Behavior: Its Elementary Forms*. New York: Harcourt Brace Jovanovich

Hsiung B, Putterman L. 1989. Pre- and postreform income distribution in a Chinese commune. *J. Comp. Econ.* 13:406–45

Huang PC. 1990. *The Peasant Family and Rural Development in the Yangzi Delta, 1350–1988*. Stanford, CA: Stanford Univ. Press

Jefferson GH, Rawski TG. 1994. Enterprise reform in Chinese industry. *J. Econ. Perspect.* 8(2):47–70

Jefferson GH, Xu W. 1991. The impact of reform on socialist enterprises in transition: structure, conduct, and performance in Chinese industry. *J. Comp. Econ.* 15:45–64

Johnson GE. 1994. Open for business, open to the world: consequences of global incorporation in Guangdong and the Pearl River delta. In *The Economic Transformation of South China*, ed. TP Lyons, V Nee, pp. 55–87. Ithaca, NY: Cornell Univ. East Asia Prog.

Kornai J. 1990. *The Road to a Free Economy*. New York: Norton

Krueger A. 1974. The political economy of the rent-seeking society. *Am. Econ. Rev.* 64:291–303

Lieberthal KG, Lampton DM. 1992. *Bureaucracy, Politics, and Decision Making in Post-Mao China*. Berkeley: Univ. Calif. Press

Lin CZ. 1989. Open-ended economic reform in China. See Nee & Stark 1989, pp. 95–136

Lin JY. 1988. The household responsibility system in China's agricultural reform: a theoretical and empirical study. *Econ. Dev. Cult. Change* 36:S199–24

Lin N. 1995. Local market socialism: local corporatism in action in rural China. *Theory Soc.* 24(3):301–54

Liu YL. 1992. Reform from below: the private economy and local politics in the rural industrialization of Wenzhou. *China Q.* 130:293–316

Logan J, Bian Y. 1993. Inequalities in access to community resources in a Chinese city. *Soc. Forces* 72(2):555–76

Lyons T. 1990. Planning and interprovincial coordination in Maoist China. *China Q.* 121:36–60

Lyons T, Nee V, eds. 1994. *The Economic Transformation of Rural South China*. Cornell East Asia Ser., No. 70. Ithaca, NY: Cornell Univ., East Asia Prog.

Madsen R. 1984. *Morality and Power in a Chinese Village*. Berkeley: Univ. Calif. Press

Manion M. 1994. Survey research in the study of contemporary China: learning from local samples. *China Q.* 139:741–65

Massey DS. 1988. Economic development and international migration in comparative perspective. *Pop. Dev. Rev.* 14:383–413

McMillan J, Whalley J, Zhu L. 1989. The impact of China's economic reforms on agricultural productivity growth. *J. Polit. Econ.* 97(4):781–807

Murrell P. 1992a. Conservative political philosophy and the strategy of economic transition. *East Eur. Polit. Soc.* 6(1):3–16

Murrell P. 1992b. Evolutionary and radical approaches to economic reform. *Econ. Plan.* 25:79–95

Naughton B. 1990. China's experience with guidance planning. *J. Comp. Econ.* 14:743–67

Naughton B. 1994. Chinese institutional innovation and privatization from below. *Am. Econ. Rev.* 84:266–70

Naughton B. 1995. *Growing out of the Plan*. New York: Cambridge Univ. Press

Nee V. 1985. Peasant household individualism. In *Chinese Rural Development: The Great Transformation*, ed. WL Parish, pp. 164–90. Armonk, NY: Sharpe

Nee V. 1986. Peasant household economy and decollectivization in China. *J. Asian Afr. Stud.* 21:185–203

Nee V. 1989a. Peasant entrepreneurship and the politics of regulation in China. See Nee & Stark 1989, pp. 169–207

Nee V. 1989b. A theory of market transition: from redistribution to markets in state socialism. *Am. Sociol. Rev.* 54:663–81

Nee V. 1991a. *Social Exchange and Political Process in Maoist China*. New York: Garland

Nee V. 1991b. Social inequalities in reforming state socialism: between redistribution and markets in China. *Am. Sociol. Rev.* 56:267–82

Nee V. 1992. Organizational dynamics of market transition. *Admin. Sci. Q.* 37:1–27

Nee V. 1996. The emergence of a market society: changing mechanisms of stratification in China. *Am. J. Sociol.* In press

Nee V, Cao Y. 1995. *Testing market transition theory in the urban context*. Presented at Workshop Market Transition Debate, Univ. Calif. Los Angeles

Nee V, Ingram P. 1997. Embeddedness and beyond: institutions, exchange, and social structure. In *The New Institutionalism in Economic Sociology*, ed. V Nee, M Brinton, New York: Russell Sage. In press

Nee V, Keister LA. 1995. *Institutional change and agrarian transformation in China*. Presented at Workshop Market Transition Debate, Univ. Calif. Los Angeles

Nee V, Lian P. 1994. Sleeping with the enemy: a dynamic model of declining political commitment in state socialism. *Theory Soc.* 23:253–96

Nee V, Liedka RV. 1995. *Institutional effects on income mobility and inequality in reforming state socialism.* Presented at Annu. Meet. Am. Sociol. Assoc., 90th, Washington, DC

Nee V, Matthews R. 1995. *A fair day's wage: Why institutions matter in gender inequality.* Presented at Annu. Meet. Am. Sociol. Assoc., 90th, Washington, DC

Nee V, Stark D, eds. 1989. *Remaking the Economic Institutions of Socialism: China and Eastern Europe.* Stanford, CA: Stanford Univ. Press

Nee V, Su S. 1990. Institutional change and economic growth in China: the view from the villages. *J. Asian Stud.* 49(1):3–25

Nee V, Su S. 1996. Institutions, social ties and commitment in China's corporatist transformation. In *Remaking Asian Economies,* ed. J McMillan, B Naughton. Ann Arbor: Univ. Mich. Press. In press

Nee V, Young FW. 1991. Peasant entrepreneurs in China's "second economy": an institutional analysis. *Econ. Dev. Cult. Change* 39:293–310

North DC. 1990. *Institutions, Institutional Change and Economic Performance.* Cambridge: Cambridge Univ. Press

Oi JC. 1989. *State and Peasant in Contemporary China.* Berkeley: Univ. Calif. Press

Oi JC. 1990. The fate of the collective after the commune. See Davis 1990, pp. 13–36

Oi JC. 1992. Fiscal reform and the economic foundations of local state corporatism in China. *World Polit.* 45:99–126

Parish WL. 1994. Rural industrialization in Fujian and Taiwan. See Lyons & Nee 1994, pp. 119–40

Parish WL, Michelson E. 1996. Politics and markets: dual transformation. *Am. J. Sociol.* 101:1042–59

Parish WL, Whyte MK. 1978. *Village and Family in Contemporary China.* Chicago: Univ. Chicago Press

Parish WL, Zhe X, Li F. 1995. Nonfarm work and the marketization of the Chinese countryside. *China Q.* 143:1–29

Parpia B. 1994. *Social economic determinants of food and nutrient intakes in rural China.* PhD thesis. Cornell Univ.

Peck J. 1975. Revolution versus modernization and revisionism. In *China's Uninterrupted Revolution,* ed. V Nee, J Peck, pp. 57–217. New York: Pantheon

Perry EJ, Fuller EV. 1991. China's long march to democracy. *World Policy J.* 8(4):663–85

Polanyi K. (1944). 1957. *The Great Transfor-*mation. Boston: Beacon

Putnam RD. 1993. *Making Democracy Work: Civic Traditions in Modern Italy.* Princeton, NJ: Princeton Univ. Press

Putterman L. 1992. Dualism and reform in China. *Econ. Dev. Cult. Change* 40(3):467–93

Putterman L. 1994. Contradictions and progress: the state, agriculture, and 'third' sectors in China's economic reform. In *A Reformable Socialism?* ed. Y Gan, Z Cui. New York: Oxford Univ. Press. In press

Qian Y, Xu C. 1993. Why China's economic reforms differ: the M-form hierarchy and entry/expansion of the non-state sector. *Econ. Transit.* 1(2):135–70

Róna-Tas A. 1994. The first shall be last? Entrepreneurship and communist cadres in the transition from socialism. *Am. J. Sociol.* 100:40–69

Rozelle S. 1994. Rural industrialization and increasing inequality: emerging patterns in China's reforming economy. *J. Comp. Econ.* 19:362–91

Sachs J. 1989. My plan for Poland. *Int. Econ.* 3:24–29

Schurmann F. 1966. *Ideology and Organization in Communist China.* Berkeley: Univ. Calif. Press

Shirk SL. 1993. *The Political Logic of Economic Reform in China.* Berkeley: Univ. Calif. Press

Shue V. 1988. *The Reach of the State.* Stanford, CA: Stanford Univ. Press

Skilling HG, Griffiths F. 1971. *Interest Groups in Soviet Politics.* Princeton, NJ: Princeton Univ. Press

Skinner W. 1994. Differential development in Lingnan. See Johnson 1994, pp. 17–54

Skocpol T. 1979. *States and Social Revolutions.* New York: Cambridge Univ. Press

Smelser NJ, Swedberg R. 1994. *The Handbook of Economic Sociology.* Princeton, NJ: Princeton Univ. Press

Solinger DJ. 1989. Urban reform and relational contracting in Post-Mao China. *Stud. Comp. Communism* 22(2/3):171–85

Stark D. 1992. The great transformation? Social change in Eastern Europe. *Contemp. Sociol.* 21(3):299–304

Stark D. 1996. Recombinant property forms in Eastern European capitalism. *Am. J. Sociol.* 101:993–1027

Su S. 1994. *The dynamics of market-oriented growth of Chinese firms in Post-Maoist China.* PhD thesis. Cornell Univ.

Swedberg R. 1994. Markets as social structures. See Smelser & Swedberg 1994, pp. 255–82

Szelenyi I. 1978. Social inequalities in state socialist redistributive economies. *Int. J. Comp.*

Sociol. 1–2:63–87

Szelenyi I. 1988. *Socialist Entrepreneurs: Embourgeoisement in Rural Hungary.* Madison: Univ. Wis. Press

Szelenyi I, Kostello E. 1996. The market transition debate: Towards a synthesis? *Am. J. Sociol.* 101:1082–96

Ulam A. 1963. *The New Face of Soviet Totalitarianism.* Cambridge, MA: Harvard Univ. Press

Unger J. 1985. The decollectivization of the Chinese countryside: a survey of twenty-eight villages. *Pac. Aff.* 58:585–606

Unger J, Chan A. 1995. China, corporatism, and the East Asian model. *Aust. J. Chin. Aff.* 33:29–53

Vogel EF. 1969. *Canton under Communism.* Cambridge, MA: Harvard Univ. Press

Walder AG. 1986. *Communist Neo-Traditionalism: Work and Authority in Chinese Industry.* Berkeley: Univ. Calif. Press

Walder AG. 1987. Wage reform and the web of factory interests. *China Q.* 109:22–41

Walder AG. 1994. The decline of communist power: elements of a theory of institutional change. *Theory Soc.* 23:297–323

Walder AG. 1995a. Career mobility and the communist political order. *Am. Sociol. Rev.* 60:309–28

Walder AG. 1995b. Local governments as industrial firms: an organizational analysis of China's transitional economy. *Am. J. Sociol.* 101:263–301

Walder AG, ed. 1995c. *The Political Consequences of Departures from State Planning,* ed. AG Walder. Berkeley: Univ. Calif. Press

Walder AG. 1996. Markets and inequality in transitional economies: toward testable theories. *Am. J. Sociol.* 101:1060–73

Wank D. 1995. Private business, bureaucracy, and political alliance in a Chinese city. *Aust. J. Chin. Aff.* 33:55–71

Watson A. 1988. The reform of agricultural marketing in China since 1979. *China Q.* 119:448–80

Weitzman ML, Xu C. 1994. Chinese township-village enterprises as vaguely defined cooperatives. *J. Comp. Econ.* 18(2):121–45

White HC. 1981. Where do markets come from? *Am. J. Sociol.* 87:517–47

Whyte MK. 1974. *Small Groups and Political Rituals in China.* Berkeley: Univ. Calif. Press

Whyte MK, Parish WL. 1984. *Urban Life in Contemporary China.* Chicago: Univ. Chicago Press

Wilson S. 1994. *About face: social networks and prestige politics in contemporary Shanghai villages.* PhD thesis. Cornell Univ., Ithaca, NY

Wong C. 1992. Fiscal reform and local industrialization: the problematic sequencing of reform in post-Mao China. *Mod. China* 18:197–227

World Bank. 1985. *China: Long-Term Issues and Options.* Baltimore: Johns Hopkins Univ. Press

Xie Y, Hannum E. 1996. Regional variation in earnings inequality in reform-era urban China. *Am. J. Sociol.* 101:950–92

Yan YX. 1995. Changes in everyday power relations. See Walder 1995c, pp. 215–41

Zhao R. 1993. Three features of the distribution of income during the transition to reform. See Griffin & Zhao 1993, pp. 74–92

Zhou X. 1993. Unorganized interests and collective action in Communist China. *Am. Sociol. Rev.* 58(1):54–73

Zweig D. 1992. Urbanizing rural China: bureaucratic authority and local autonomy. See Lieberthal & Lampton 1992, pp. 334–63

Annu. Rev. Sociol. 1996. 22:437–58

FROM MARXISM TO POSTCOMMUNISM: Socialist Desires and East European Rejections

Michael D. Kennedy and Naomi Galtz

Department of Sociology, University of Michigan, Ann Arbor, Michigan, 48109

KEY WORDS: Russia, market economy, civil society, ideology and identity, class

ABSTRACT

In this review of the relationship between marxism and East European transformations since 1989, we consider why Eastern Europe is so important to marxism and how marxists have addressed its transformations. We also point to similar analyses of these transformations generated by nonmarxists, and we review exemplary East European interpretations of marxism to demonstrate that the principal challenge in developing marxism in Eastern Europe lies outside its traditional substantive foci and methodological practices. We propose that in order for marxism to maintain itself as an integrated project without ignoring or dismissing Eastern Europe, it must do more than address questions of class and capitalist formation, problems that can be analyzed in parallel fashion without commitment to the normative aspect of socialism. It must also address directly the region's experience with, and rejection of, "really existing socialism," rather than dismissing these and thereby allowing socialism to function as an ontologically absent but epistemologically structuring desire. In order for marxism to develop further in East European studies, we suggest it must find a way to rearticulate socialism's transcendent project within East European lifeworlds, a task grounded as much in discursive analyses of ideologies and identities as in the political economy of transformations.

INTRODUCTION

Marxism—as a theoretical system, political orientation, scholarly tradition, and capitalist counterculture (Bauman 1976, p. 47)—has had an extremely

437

complicated relationship to the communist-led societies of Eastern Europe.[1] In the wake of 1989, marxist thinkers have been drawn into intense discussion about what the old communist-led system was, why it collapsed so completely and rapidly across Eastern Europe and the former Soviet Union, and what this means for marxism and socialism. In this essay, we consider the burgeoning engagement with Eastern Europe by marxist scholars, as well as the challenges posed to marxism by East European social and theoretical transformations.

Our review is different from previous efforts in several respects.[2] First, we do not seek to contrast the "realities" of communist-led societies with core tenets of marxist theory (Hollander 1982, Lenski 1978, Connor 1979). We see marxism rather as a "knowledge culture" (MR Somers, forthcoming), with an implicit core and fuzzy boundaries, and as such impossible to verify or disprove in toto. Second, and in a related vein, we do not search recent events to find points of validation or invalidation for an existing marxist project. We assume that marxism is constantly being refashioned in the face of historical and intellectual challenges, and that its future will be determined in part by how marxists interpret 1989,[3] what questions they choose to take from it, and what questions they disregard. In this sense, we take up the challenge Michael Burawoy (1990) presents to consider the relationship between the internal history of marxist theory and the external history of the recent transformations in Eastern Europe. Unlike Burawoy, who is one of marxism's major proponents in sociology, we do not write from a marxist position; we attempt rather to be ridge-riders[4] between

---

[1] The organization of scholarship on communist-led societies, as reflected in journals and research centers throughout the Cold War, left a mixed geographical heritage. The Soviet Union and the juridically independent, communist-led East European states were linked in some circumstances (e.g. with the appropriation of federal monies to National Resource Centers for Russian and Eastern European Studies, or the journal *Soviet Studies*) and not in others (e.g. with a division made between the East European Committee, located in the American Council for Learned Societies, and the Soviet Union committee, located in the Social Science Research Council). In some circumstances all communist-led societies were thematized together (e.g. in journals such as *Problems of Communism* and *Studies in Comparative Communism*, or in Kornai 1991).

In this essay we focus solely on the European sites of communist collapse. For convenience, we use the term "East European" to indicate the European parts of the Former Soviet Union, as well as the conventional countries of reference. Of course, a case could be made that Eastern Europe and the Former Soviet Union (FSU) involve very different analytical problems, meriting their separate treatment, but given that these differences are minimized by marxists with their attention to modes of production and property relations, we provisionally treat this region as a relatively homogenous terrain.

[2] It does, however, build on Kennedy (1991), where pre-1989 marxist work on Soviet societies is discussed.

[3] Here, as at several other places in this chapter, we invoke 1989 as a shorthand for the systemic transformations that began before 1989 and continue through the present.

[4] As was Gouldner (1980), except his ridge was between marxism and sociology.

the social transformations of Eastern Europe and the intellectual transformations in marxism occasioned by them.

Our main thesis is that marxist sociologists may have to step outside their own tradition to interpret and adequately confront the challenge Eastern Europe represents to marxism. We ground this suggestion in a series of linked reviews of recent works, including: (a) marxist sociological responses to change in Eastern Europe emanating from sociology; (b) work on Eastern Europe by nonmarxists who appear to occupy a "marxist space" within sociology; and (c) the contributions of thinkers who incorporate elements of the marxist tradition but radically transform its framework.[5]

In recent theoretical work, marxist sociologists tend to locate Eastern Europe as a major threat to the marxist normative project, yet they seem to evade the topic of Eastern Europe when developing their justifications for continued socialist hopes. In their empirical explorations of change in East European societies, marxist scholars preserve their perspective by pursuing topics that lie in the mainstream of marxist research—especially those that might selectively reinforce lessons about the links between production and identity, class interests and legislation, etc—and by bringing to bear a methodological commitment to uncovering Real processes at work behind the Apparent or Ideological. However, while marxist thinkers produce a range of useful insights on institutions and politics in Eastern Europe through this approach, similar insights are generated by researchers who have parallel methodological and topical commitments, but who implicitly or explicitly work outside of a marxist normative framework. It is thus difficult to convince audiences outside the marxist tradition of the usefulness of a marxist framework for considering Eastern Europe.

The problem becomes more grave when one considers the overwhelming indifference to, and rejection of, marxist theory within Eastern Europe. Somewhat ironically, this rejection is itself often established and validated through an appeal to the Real (in this case "real" of "common sense") as opposed to the ideological (Kennedy 1994a: Introduction). Our intent here is not in any sense to reproduce a cold war standoff, with the "material-historical Real" of marxist theory juxtaposed to the "common-sense Real" of East European rejections of marxism. Rather, we suggest that there are social theorists who have transcended this divide by combining the normative commitment to radical democracy inherent in the contemporary Western marxist project with a willingness to push, topically and methodologically, beyond a traditional marxist approach.

---

[5]We must make the obvious apologies regarding the scope of this review. The marxist-linked sociological literature is vast, and a good portion of it, while not addressed to Eastern Europe in particular, has been inflected by a consideration of state socialism's collapse. Thus, we undoubtedly fail to treat certain works that others might have included in such a review.

RESPONDING THEORETICALLY TO 1989

We begin our consideration with attempts to redefine marxist boundaries after 1989 by two thinkers central to the elaboration of marxism within sociology. First, although Erik Olin Wright's work has not focused on Eastern Europe, his influential recent attempts to redefine and reconstruct the marxist project are in part direct responses to East European transformations. His "Class Analysis, History and Emancipation" represents a good point of departure (Wright 1993; see also Wright 1992).

Marxist thought, according to Wright, can be mapped by the relationship among three nodes: 1) class analysis, 2) historical trajectory, and 3) emancipatory potential. A marxist tenor, he argues, is achieved in any one node through the interpenetration of the other two. For instance, a distinctly marxist class analysis will not simply employ class descriptors; it will implicitly include an idea of historical trajectory (through class antagonism) and a commitment to the normative ideal of a classless society.

For Wright, marxism is currently challenged on two fronts. It is challenged from within by less totalizing visions of marxism and from without by world historical events (most notably the collapse of communism in Eastern Europe) that seem to question socialism's viability. Thus Wright does not specify the contemporary threat to marxism as wholly empirical or wholly theoretical; instead he suggests that there is an accumulated set of grievances that necessitate a corresponding reconstruction of marxist theory. In the main, this reconstruction is achieved through a loosening of analytical strictures within each of the nodes as classically conceived (and thus an implicit loosening of the interconnections among the three nodes). For instance, instead of being viewed as an inexorable drive through a series of materially necessitated stages, the historical trajectory can be examined through stages of social organization and property relations that interpenetrate, loop back, and move forward at variable rates in variable contexts (1993, pp. 24–25).

In contrast to Wright, who advocates to some extent a controlled disintegration within marxism's core, Michael Burawoy (1990) specifically reasserts the place of an integrated marxist project within sociology. Burawoy contends that each of marxism's core concepts has been tested through confrontation with anomalies, and that these challenges have yielded fruitful rethinkings from within the marxist tradition whenever a balance has been maintained between the internal (analytical) and external (historical) aspects of the problem (Burawoy 1990, p. 790). This is what allows him both to identify an expanding belt of live science (in Lakatos' understanding) (Burawoy 1990, pp. 777–78) within marxism, and to skillfully recast 1989 as marxism's greatest opportunity to grow as a science.[6]

The curiously undertreated point of both articles is the threat to marxism inherent specifically in the great changes of 1989. Both authors identify the collapse of communism in Eastern Europe as a significant challenge for marxists, even marxism's "most profound challenge" (Burawoy 1990, p. 790). In Wright it appears that the East European communist experience most directly threatens marxist projections of socialism's future, first by charting an uneven and unpredicted course of development, and second by casting doubt on the idea that a socialist state can foster efficient production. Similarly, in Burawoy, the events in Eastern Europe cast doubt specifically on the seventh of his core marxist propositions, the proposition that "the bourgeois relations of production are the last antagonistic form of the social process of production" [Marx (1859) in Burawoy (1990, p. 780)]. And yet both authors firmly wave away this threat to socialist potential through a familiar geographical move: "That socialism could never emerge in backward Russia without revolution in the West was a central tenet of all marxism from Marx to Kautsky and Luxemburg, from Plekhanov to Trotsky and Lenin" (Burawoy 1990, p. 791; echoed clearly in Wright 1993, p. 16).

Further, neither treats Eastern Europe in arguing for the continued viability of what Auerbach terms "socialist optimism" (Auerbach 1992). Wright recoups the viability of all three nodes through the analytic promise of class. Burawoy, meanwhile, engages in what Wright deems marxism's most basic move (Wright 1993, p. 22); he refocuses the debate on capitalist pessimism: "...Marxism still provides a fecund understanding of capitalism's inherent contradictions and dynamics... [Thus] the longevity of capitalism guarantees the longevity of Marxism" (Burawoy 1990, p. 792).

The reconstructions offered by Burawoy and Wright leave socialism and Eastern Europe in a curious place: The normative commitment to socialist objectives, and a concomitant faith in socialism's viability, are placed at the center of the marxist project, and Eastern Europe is posed as a challenge to that commitment. But in almost Lacanian fashion, our gaze at the central problem is diverted as marxists center on traditional problems of class and capitalism, leaving Eastern Europe's experience with socialism out of focus.

---

[6]Of course, Burawoy is writing just one year after the collapse. However, since 1984 he had been dealing with issues similar to those embedded in the collapse. This brings, of course, a different question to the surface: what makes the questions of 1989 particularly urgent? As Derrida (1994) notes, there is a certain "*toujours deja vu*" in the consideration of recent transformations. This must be the subject of another essay.

DEVELOPING MARXISM IN EAST EUROPEAN STUDIES

Perhaps not surprisingly, marxism has customarily approached Eastern Europe best when that area has been rent with strife.[7] It is clear that the tradition has been most interested in the region when there were crises, of either a progressive or a regressive kind. After the events of 1989, however, attention to Eastern Europe soared and has remained at a high level.[8]

The extensive discussion of the Yugoslav war of succession illustrates marxism's heightened concern for crisis in Eastern Europe, and Branka Magas's (1992) book on the destruction of Yugoslavia illustrates a marxist approach well. Distinguishing her perspective as marxist, she manages to preserve a sense of socialism's viability by identifying the particular contradiction between economic and political decentralization, on the one hand, and the absence of internal party democratization, on the other, as opening the space for a strong nationalist alternative (pp. 193–229). Bogdan Denitch's (1994) book carries forward many of the same themes as Magas's, but it also has the virtue of discussing Denitch's own democratic socialist politics in 1991 and suggesting the difficulty of organizing a democratic left alternative in this context (pp. 177–85).

The postcommunist economic transformations discussed by marxists also clearly articulate with the main forms of analysis and substantive concerns of the tradition. In this genre we find specific rebuttals of the success of privatization strategies as well as documentation of the social problems and growing inequalities associated with the transformation. At least if one looks at what is arguably the leading marxist journal in the English-speaking world, *New Left Review*, these are the ways marxists have entered the East European field over the last five years. A continuous leitmotif, especially in those journals more committed to developing marxist theory than to engaging East European transformations as a historical problem, is the diagnosis of "actually existing socialism" as a variation on the capitalist mode of production (see, e.g., Resnick & Wolff 1993).

Most of these studies are consonant with Wright's loosely coupled marxism: a marxism less distinct from other perspectives, and one politically more open to sacrileges of the past, particularly the necessity of the market (Nove 1991,

---

[7]Aronson (1995) suggests that communist Eastern Europe served to negatively stabilize the socialist referent: "The very immobility and ponderousness of the Soviet Union counted for something positive in our collective psychic space, allowing us to keep hope alive that a successful socialism might still emerge. It provided a backdrop against which alternatives could be thought about and discussed, including, for some, the hope that other versions of Marxism remained viable" (p. vii).

[8]Even still, it remains curiously absent from some of the most obvious places. Böröcz & Smith (1995, pp. 1–16) lament that they could not solicit any articles on changes in Eastern Europe, even though they are the central challenge to the theory. See Böröcz (1992) for one major challenge to the world systems theory that has not been seriously taken up.

Weisskopf 1992, Pierson 1995). But these innovations within marxism are not so compelling outside of it and thus are unlikely to appear important to those not already committed to the tradition. They don't illuminate East European transformations as much as they refine marxism in such a way as to reduce its distinction. Additionally, those innovations are not so apparently important for marxism in general, if Wright's list of reconstructive achievements is a good operationalization of innovation in the tradition. Thus, those interested in explaining East European social transformations or innovations in marxism might ask "why should marxism be developed in studies of Eastern Europe?" Michael Burawoy may make the best case.

Burawoy took a job in a champagne factory in Hungary in 1983, and he continues through the present to work in different Hungarian and Russian firms. Two major streams of collaboration have resulted from Burawoy's detailed work on the ground in East European industry. In the first, which culminated in a series of essays produced together with Hungarian sociologist Janos Lukacs (1992), Burawoy explains why the distinction between socialism and capitalism is not quite what the ideologues of the latter proclaim. In later collaborations with his Russian colleague Pavel Krotov (e.g. 1992, 1993, 1995), Burawoy has emphasized why the transition to capitalism in Russia is so erratic and directed more toward merchant than bourgeois capitalism.

In *The Radiant Past*, Burawoy and Lukacs construct an elegant ideal-type of state socialist enterprise. Due to shortages of equipment and materials and the importance of expansion and bargaining in managerial strategies and of employment security, workers generally have more organizational autonomy in state socialism than in capitalism, including considerable control over their immediate means of production. Exploitation (as defined in Konrad & Szelényi 1979) occurs through planners' appropriation of surplus. Critically for state socialism, this appropriation transpires visibly, at the point of production. Therefore, ideology acquires a more crucial role in state socialism than in capitalism—it is responsible for coordinating the efforts of workers (transparently) to engage in their own exploitation.

But participation in state socialism's collective ideological rituals—the daily practice of "painting socialism" (see Burawoy & Lukacs 1992, Ch. 5)—fools no one: The great unkept secret within socialist societies is that ideology and reality are worlds apart. And this distance generates the class consciousness that leads to the system's downfall—the very consciousness which, Burawoy argues, Marx mistakenly assumed to be at the heart of capitalist production. Capitalism does not collapse because, while it might engender a critical consciousness, interests generated within production relations lead to the manufacture of consent (see, of course, Burawoy 1979).

In Burawoy's subsequent work on the transformations of postcommunist capitalism in Russia, he and Krotov shift more directly to the critique of capitalism and away from the question of socialism's demise. The dominant features of the firm appear to be the same in postcommunist Russia as in communist Hungary: flexible working hours, autonomous work organization, and uneven technology. Middle-level management remains weak, and the successful entrepreneur is still one with good connections, albeit this time in a new organizational environment with a withered state and parastatal conglomerates wielding economic power (Burawoy 1992). Rather than fostering an ideal capitalist-type system based on "continual pressure to transform products and work organization in order to maintain profit in a competitive market" (p. 33), the postcommunist scene has actually amplified the control by workers over the shopfloor and enhanced the significance of managerial connections in determining corporate success (see also Clarke 1992).

According to Burawoy, this analysis of postcommunist relations in production serves to deflate capitalism's idealized sense of its own efficiency, but also provides a key to understanding historical change: Postcommunist capitalism is merchant capitalism, rather than bourgeois capitalism. The fate of this merchant capitalism depends, of course, on two kinds of forces—world capital and domestic proletarians. In their essay on a regional coal industry, Burawoy & Krotov (1993) address both. If we were to find the significance of Russian workers' mobilization, it would be in this sector (Crowley 1993), but to date, its only significance has been to generate greater state protectionism in alliance with its managers, rather than any significant transformative potential. (See Burawoy & Krotov 1995 for a further development of this argument.) This kind of protection is unlikely to lead to any kind of "dependent development," given the weakness of the state itself and given that Western capital is channeled through domestic conglomerates. This is all suggestive of the idea that merchant capital will simply continue to reproduce itself, leading to further dependency and underdevelopment.

This essay completes what becomes Burawoy's leitmotif: Reality is different than ideology and is to be discovered in the analysis of relations in and of production. (Or here, in specific, the celebration of commercial transformations is evidence only of merchant capitalism's development.) In a recent programmatic essay, Burawoy makes these points, but he also makes explicit what turns his case studies into something more powerful. He uses analogical comparisons with other epochal transitions to develop more theoretical arguments about the ideological conventions he seeks to critique, and how that critique might enable subsequently more refined comparisons among postcommunist sites (Burawoy 1995, Ch. 3).

We might note that Burawoy's move toward Russia and away from Hungary makes this argument more persuasive than it might otherwise be, for Russia's production relations are less transformed than are those of Hungarian and other East Central European firms. Thus Russia becomes the worst case scenario, allowing our capitalist utopian hopes to be dashed most effectively. But since Russia seems no more hospitable to socialist alternatives than other sites, perhaps the injunction to study capitalist alternatives is appropriate, and an institutional approach sensible.

FOUR ALTERNATIVES: STARK, KORNAI, STANISZKIS, SZELÉNYI

One might argue that institutional analysis is a perfectly good substitute for marxism, and certainly a good alternative to the neoclassical economics that sometimes dominates the analysis of postcommunism. Substantively speaking, at least, David Stark's work occupies much of the same space any marxist analysis would, with its focus on labor markets (Stark 1986), economic sociology (Stark 1989, 1992), and most recently property forms (Stark 1996). But Stark does not identify with marxism.

His institutional approach apparently accepts marxism's notion of colliding ordering principles, but he distinguishes his approach by arguing that tensions cannot be finally consolidated and released, as marxism implies; rather, they must continue in relatively localized stabilizations. He also argues that marxism's approach to complexity is "impoverished," maintaining that the public/private and socialism/capitalism distinctions are inadequate to understanding East European variety and that in general it is misleading to understand any system in terms of a single logic. Stark goes on to illustrate his general arguments with a plea to understand East European capitalism as distinctive, based on what he calls "recombinant property," something neither public nor private, characterized by a type of coordination that is neither market nor bureaucratic but designed to enhance flexibility in an environment so uncertain that assets and liabilities are hard to recognize.

Stark's general argument seems to be compatible with the kind of marxism that Wright (1993), at least, emphasizes. But by ridding the approach of any fundamental distinction between capitalism and socialism, Stark of necessity distances himself from marxism in this age where some elevation of socialism as a continuing problem and positive normative base remains one of marxism's distinctions.

Janos Kornai (1992) offers a different kind of critique of marxism from a neighboring position. It is interesting that of all the thinkers we consider here,

Kornai is probably closest to the mature Marx in the sense that he painstakingly argues from a standpoint of necessary historical developments (and devolutions) rather than from a standpoint of normative critique. According to Kornai, certain material necessities impel socialist societies along prototypical stages of development (allowing, of course, for feedback effects and historical variation). These developments are not historically mandated as such, but once communist power has been asserted within a state, these stages follow both from objective demands (including world-system constraints) and from the assertion and realization of natural self-interests and social desires by party leaders, bureaucrats, and workers.

In adopting this approach Kornai produces perhaps the definitive analysis of command-style economy and its decay, an analysis that can easily be appropriated by marxists themselves (e.g. Burawoy & Lukacs 1992; Clarke 1992, p. 9 ff). But Kornai's analysis is ultimately at odds with a marxist positionality. First and foremost, this is because he does not attempt to evade the "accident" of Russia; rather he treats it as a "recurrent regularity" (p. 373) that socialism has taken root only in the industrial "late arrivers" (p. 373). It is the very backwardness of these societies that allows the basic genetic program of socialism to begin to reproduce itself within their particular historical borders.

This idea, of course, both departs from classical marxist theory, which forecasts the growth of socialism in the developed economies, and sets the stage for another departure from more contemporary socialist hopes. For it is Kornai's overall conclusion that the power of "really existing communism" lies in the undivided, ideological party, which itself generates the dominant position of the state and quasi-state ownership, spawning institutional problems such as a surfeit of bureaucratic control, soft budget constraints, plan bargaining, and the chronic shortage economy. Because these occurrences are tightly linked, the superstructure cannot reform itself without incurring a revolution. Thus, although he is careful not to forecast too far into the future of transition, Kornai argues against the feasibility of socialist alternatives, including self-management; he finds that they reproduce the same problems of shortage and soft budget constraints as the old system did, but without the ideological dominance necessary to control dissent and maintain systemic coherence.

Jadwiga Staniszkis is another East European intellectual whose work occupies a space similar to marxism in her focus on the primacy of property relations and economic conditions and in her quest for the "reality" behind the "ideology" for the contradictions driving historical change. She is more oriented toward politics and national strategies of development than is either Stark or Kornai. In *The Ontology of Socialism* (1992), she develops a property-rights paradigm to argue that "Real socialism" tends toward crisis because of a lack of responsibility and accountability. The state, while aspiring to represent society and history, cannot rationalize crises, for it is itself ultimately particularist and subjectivist, interested in its own preservation and the extension of its prerogatives. While the state may inspire rebellion, it generates a nontransformative politics of identity, a morally-based rejection of political and economic authority that in fact reproduces the system and its redistributive politics. With no internally generated transcendent interests, communism had, according to Staniszkis, no immanent basis of change. Its end was the result of conjuncture and chance.

From Staniszkis (1991) the significance of the capitalist world order as the underlying mechanism of social change becomes obvious. In general, she argues that peripheries must continually adjust developmental strategies to their shifting locations in the world system; even communist-led societies experienced that imperative and devised COMECON as one strategy of development. A subsequent strategy, what she calls "political capitalism," is a means by which an opening to the West and real capitalism is made. "Postcommunist peripheral capitalism" depends on this institutional form to compete with global capitalism (Kennedy 1995).

Thus, for Staniszkis the conditions of politics are ultimately based on a national economic relationship to the global economy, and consequently her work suggests both methodological and epistemological affinities with world systems theory. But rather than follow the socialist foundations of Wallersteinian world systems analysis, she critiques socialism both as a political-economic and as a normative system, and thus she follows rather in a Listian tradition (see Szporluk 1988).

Ivan Szelényi is closest to Wright's marxist sociology (and most unlike the three figures mentioned above) in his steady focus on problems of stratification (here within socialist and postsocialist societies). Szelényi is clearly best known for his work with György Konrad on *Intellectuals on the Road to Class Power* (1979). In the mid-1980s, he recanted the central argument of that work (Szelényi 1987), finding instead that a class of socialist entrepreneurs or new petty bourgeoisie was developing within state socialism. This argument was developed most fully in a subsequent publication emphasizing the involutionary nature of change within state socialism, based on a middle-range theory of the Hungarian peasantry's "interrupted embourgeoisment" (Szelényi 1988).

After communism's collapse, Szelényi (& Martin 1991) continues to comment on various class theories of intellectuals, ultimately arguing that intellectuals came to power only to destroy the systemic base of their identity (Szelényi 1994, p. 7). Their rhetoric of privatization, argues Szonya Szelényi, W. Poster, and he, was dangerously distant from the real interests of the masses of workers, who continued to conceive of themselves as employees of the state and to hold to social democratic politics. This accounts for the return of the "left" to power in several states of Eastern Europe (Szelényi et al 1996).

Unlike the other thinkers noted above, Szelényi is firmly associated with the marxist tradition in the West. But why? His class analysis is based on Polanyi more than Marx. His accounts of historical transformation are notably Weberian, with their emphasis on cultural influences and value systems (Szelényi 1988) and dedication to multiplicity and conjuncture (Szelényi & Szelényi 1994). Szelényi implicitly engages the marxist tradition through his attention to inequality and class and their relationship to historical transformation. And this implicit connection appears all the more "self-evident" given Szelényi's reticence to explicitly mark his distance from marxism, and because most of the critique leveled against him is more culturally oriented than class-based (Frentzel-Zagórska & Zagórski 1989, Kennedy 1992). But Szelényi himself identifies with the populist tradition more than with the marxist one (Kennedy 1994b); his last written reference to socialism's normative desirability came probably in his call for a socialist civil society in 1979 (Szelényi 1979). But because populism is not a well-developed intellectual approach in North American sociology (Calhoun 1989), such a critical orientation can find its most suitable, and professionally appropriate, home in North America in marxism.

Our point in devoting such extensive attention to thinkers who are not themselves marxist but who fill a "marxist space" of inquiry is to illustrate that, when facing change in Eastern Europe, a marxissant methodology or topical concern is by no means an assurance of marxist commitments; sometimes, just the opposite. From the point of view of a marxist audience, the points of overlap between, for instance, Burawoy and Kornai, or Wallerstein and Staniszkis, might be taken merely as external validity checks. But for audiences interested in Eastern Europe and who lack a normative commitment to the marxist project, the question "why marxism?" is left oddly hanging, especially when one considers how marxism is regarded in contemporary Eastern Europe.

MARXISM'S APPEAL IN EASTERN EUROPE

It is difficult to see socialism as an empirical or positive reference, or marxism as a theoretical tradition, alive in East European intellectual debate today. Sometimes marxism is discussed by East European scholars to demonstrate its ideological rigidity and inflexibility (e.g. Mokrzycki 1992, Żybertowicz 1994). More often it is ignored.

Of course marxism is not ignored because East European thinkers don't understand it, or because they have not themselves contributed significantly to it. Portions of Polish sociology, for instance, were long informed by marxism and have since departed from it. Jacek Kuroń is embarrassed by his earlier flirtations with marxism (personal communication with Kuroń, 1994; see also Kuroń & Modzelewski 1966), even though his present politics is based on a critique of the concentration of wealth, as articulated in expressions such as "The Republic for All" against the "Republic of the Rich." While former marxist sociologist Włodzimierz Wesołowski (1979) remains motivated by a sympathy with the left, his continued work on inequality with its focus on elites is more informed by Weber and Habermas than by Marx (see, e.g., Wesołowski 1995a) and his critique of liberalism informed by communitarian thought (Wesotowski 1995b). Witold Morawski, whose early work on self-management (Hirszowicz & Morawski 1967) was clearly influenced by the young Marx, continues to study self-management but with no particular marxist affinity (1994). These intellectuals have no wish to engage marxism, seeing the affinity with the tradition clearly as something to move beyond rather than to debate, much less to embrace.

There are occasions when marxism is engaged, but these attempts often appear as part of a bygone era, when the Communist Party still mattered to marxism. Konrad Weiss felt obliged to address marxism only when asked to discuss the survival of utopias; and though he still identifies himself as a socialist, he believes marxism could only inevitably degenerate into dystopia (Weiss 1994). In Russia, specifically, which is so often located as both the heart of communism and the heart of communist failure, vibrant academic engagement with marxism is all but dead in any discipline, let alone the field of sociology, which is more pointedly engaged in the project of describing and easing a transition to market economy.

Boris Kagarlitsky, a political theorist celebrated in the West as an authentic Russian marxist is probably better known outside of Russia than within it.[9] In a fairly recent (1989) publication he makes reference to a new and growing circle of marxists in Russia, whom he believes will eventually serve as key interpreters and critics of the transition, allowing Russia to transcend its own provincialism, but he names no names. The historian Roy Medvedev—whose prosocialist framework made him somewhat anomalous among dissidents in the Soviet Union and continues to make him anomalous among "progressive" theorists in contemporary Russia—argued in the wake of the August coup that leftist parties would become crucial to the rebuilding of Russian politics

---

[9] In a similar vein, we suspect that Burawoy's collaborators, Lukacs and Krotov, are esteemed in their own countries more specifically for the strength of their sociology than for their marxism.

(1992).[10] But given the awkward positionality of communists in the Russian political scene, his prescriptions are necessarily more guarded now than in the 1970s and 1980s (see, e.g. 1981, pp. 203–93).

One important specific work to appear from Russia on the lessons for marxists embedded in the events of 1989 is Alexander Yakovlev's critical manifesto *The Fate of Marxism in Russia* (1993). Although produced by a long-time party theorist as well as one of Gorbachev's closest advisors, the book received virtually no treatment from specifically marxist journals. Reviews that did appear in the wider press tended to treat Yakovlev's theoretical work as a project of secondary importance and tended to criticize the book for its failure to shed insight on Kremlin intrigues under Gorbachev's tenure (Service 1993, Klinghoffer 1994).

Of course, there are easily understandable reasons for the lukewarm reception of Yakovlev's work among Western academics. He is inclined to employ unreflexive terminology and he takes a somewhat suspect political position, as a man who indeed critiqued Soviet marxism from the inside but critiqued it fairly late. The book's own introduction is apologetic vis á vis the lack of originality inherent in Yakovlev's rethinking of marxism (see "Prelude").

But this sense of a lack of newness is an important marker in and of itself: Much of what Yakovlev has to say resonates with a taken-for-granted critique of marxism that can be heard widely today in Russia. The central themes Yakovlev invokes include, first, the idea that marxism is ruthlessly future-oriented, and that in its zeal to break with the past, it disrupts basic processes of identity formation; second, that a return to and reconstruction of national history serves as a natural ground for positive identity formation; and third, that marxists mistakenly believed that, having understood history, they could then control it.

Perhaps Yakovlev's most fundamental theme, and one that resonates widely within Russian society,[11] is the idea that the 1917 revolution represented a break with Russia's path, a "disruption of the evolution of the natural progress of

---

[10]Given the success of communist parties in post-communist Russia, Hungary, Poland, and Lithuania, some might be inclined to think Medvedev is right. However, we believe it is very important to avoid conflating—as Medvedev himself would, undoubtedly, also avoid—the return of these parties to political power with the return of the Left, or of marxism, per se. It must be understood that these parties represent deep networks of political actors, forged pre-1989, that are currently promising to soften the transition to market economies for vulnerable populations, especially for constituencies in heavy industry. Surely the transformation of political identities and parties in Eastern Europe is profound, and all analysts would do well to recognize the lability of identity formation in the region, rather than jump to the conclusion that labels are self-evident (Harsanyi & Kennedy 1994). Nevertheless, all of these transformations engage in some way the rejection of marxism, even when they represent the attempted reassertion of social relations á la "really existing socialism."

[11]A widely circulated Russian anecdote runs, "Why is the battleship Avrora considered the most dangerous weapon in all of history?" "Because it fired one salvo that caused 70 years of devastation."

history [that] escalated into a Russian calamity" (p. 7). In this sense, Yakovlev's critique intersects at a certain historical and geographical moment with that of Western marxists who also locate Bolshevik Russia as the site of an evolutionary disruption. But where the idea of disruption allows Western marxists to jettison Russia in order to restore or maintain socialist hope (e.g. Burawoy 1990), for Yakovlev the lesson moves in the opposite direction. He cannot jettison Russia. The lesson for him, as for so many other Russians, is that there must be an abandonment of socialist hope, that this is the way of returning to a state of freedom and "normalcy." Or, as Hollander writes:

> Most importantly intellectuals in communist and formerly communist states have fewer illusions about the perfectibility of the social world and human beings than their Western counterparts; they are also freer of an oppressive sense of meaninglessness that often translates into the current forms of political alienation in the West and they are less likely to confuse and conflate the personal and the social realm. Above all, intellectuals in the East are immune to the seductions of political utopias and the temptations of secular religion; this may enable them to pursue an attainable agenda of human improvement and liberation, something that no longer animates many of their Western counterparts (1992, p. 308).

Our suggestion here is not that a moral or sentimental prerogative should be granted to Yakovlev for having felt socialism "on the skin." However we do suggest that there is a problem, virtually untouched by marxists, of the link between the collapse of socialist hope in Eastern Europe and something "in marxism's bones." At the very least, important, and overlooked, lessons are embedded in Eastern Europe around identity, the role of discourse in shaping experience, and the constitutive power of ideology in socialism (and in the rejection of socialism). Here specifically we mean to indicate socialism as a presence, even when rejected, and not—as marxism often understands socialism—as an absence, unrealized but desired.

Like Yakovlev, Polish intellectual historian Andrej Walicki "knows" the essence of marxism. Its utopia, he argues (1995) in stark contrast to Wright, "involved the abolition of commodity production and monetary exchange. In other words, it was a vision of a totally marketless economy" (p. 90). Walicki further argues that an inherent tension exists between the marxian conceptions of historical necessity and of freedom, a tension that opens the space for a drive to direct all human economic activities, leading to control by one minority that claims the knowledge and right to steer others (pp. 88–89). This, of course, sounds like any theory of elites, from Mosca to Michels. But through a detailed intellectual history, Walicki makes a convincing case that the notions of freedom embedded in marxist thought are themselves culpable for the crisis that was Eastern Europe. While marxists might dismiss his work as hopelessly antimarxist,[12] Walicki's critique should contribute to marxism's reconstruction, especially if the problem of the normative is to be placed at center stage.

THE NORMATIVE AND POLITICAL

One of the most important engagements of marxism, as Wright, Aronson, and others note, is with rethinking the normative. Analytical marxism, and John Roemer's work in particular, are cited by Wright as exceptionally innovative and important contributions to the emancipatory node of marxism (Wright 1993). But although Roemer has made linkages between his own reformulations and the collapse of communism, and although he asserts that the opportunity costs of shifting to market socialism are lowest in postcommunist economies (1994, pp. 126–27), much of Roemer's work has developed independently of analysis of Eastern Europe. Unfortunately for Roemer's analytical marxism, Michael Burawoy's (1994) critique of his proposal for market socialism illustrates that without simultaneous work on the empirical/political levels, this kind of normative rethinking is unlikely to produce much that is helpful in East European studies.

The other marxism notably concerned with the normative is critical theory, contemporarily represented most prominently by Jürgen Habermas. But as in Roemer's work, Eastern Europe has not figured much in his approach. Polish public intellectual Adam Michnik recently challenged Habermas, saying that he had not engaged Stalinism theoretically (Habermas & Michnik 1994), something Habermas acknowledged (p. 10). Indeed, Michnik criticizes much of the left tradition for failing to consider the East European experience more seriously. Nevertheless, the events of 1989 did push Habermas to comment on the transformation and its implications for socialist thought (1990).

After reviewing the range of responses to the transformation and its relationship to socialism, Habermas (1990) argues explicitly against the notion that marxism as critique is as exhausted as actual socialism has been. Instead, he affirms that what needs to be jettisoned are the mistakes in marxism that actually made Stalin's codification of the tradition possible: 1) the focus on labor; 2) the holistic conception of society; 3) an over-concrete conception of conflict and social agencies; 4) the restricted and functionalist analysis of constitutional democracy; and 5) the essentialization of history. Habermas argues against socialism's transformation into an idea or an ethic, however, and reproduces his argument about popular sovereignty based on procedural justice embedded

---

[12]And it would be hard to dismiss him as "simply" antimarxist. He writes for instance: "I treat Marxist communism as an ideology that has compromised itself but that nevertheless deserves to be seen as the most important, however exaggerated and, ultimately, tragically mistaken, reaction to the multiple shortcomings of capitalist societies and the liberal tradition" (1995, p. 9).

in communicative rationality. And with that, Habermas demonstrates that his prior transformation of the critical perspective anticipated the challenge posed by communism's collapse. But is this Habermasian perspective useful for doing more than establishing the basis for a dialogue between respected critical intellectuals? Can it guide the analysis of East European transformations?

DEMOCRACY'S EMANCIPATION AND DISCOURSE'S POWER

The clearest way in which Habermasian problems were introduced into Eastern Europe was through the discourse around civil society. "Civil society" was not, however, introduced as a marxist, or even postmarxist, term: Gouldner (1980) and Jean Cohen (1982) remind us just how simply Marx conceived the term. And in fact, many East Europeans were invoking civil society in its Lockean sense, reliant mostly on the celebration of private property and the contract, rather than on the more democratic potentials of the tradition associated with Montesquieu (Taylor 1990).[13]

Independent of Taylor, Andrew Arato's work in the early 1980s was among the most important to link civil society and critical theory in East European studies. His subsequent work with Jean Cohen (1992), *Civil Society and Political Theory*, is itself inspired by East European transformations. One of the most important subsequent empirical developments in this body of thought is an interpretation of the revolution of 1989 itself and how this transformation broke with previous understandings of revolution (Arato 1994). Arato points out that those who have led the transformation of Eastern Europe have actively resisted the revolutionary tradition that gave birth to the system against which they have initiated their attempts toward system change. The vision that emerges from this kind of antirevolutionary revolutionary practice is a utopia of the Rechtstaat, of a state and society ruled by law.

With this, Arato enables us to see civil society as discourse. He demonstrates that its political focus contributed to the demobilization of civil society after the parliamentary elections in Hungary and to the loss of civil society's emancipatory potential. Indeed, the contradictory expectations of a nonrevolutionary revolution lay the foundation for a kind of radical right reaction.

Such an undertaking resembles the marxist project in profound ways, for it is both a social analysis and a critical one, based on a sense of historical transformation and emancipatory commitment. It nonetheless suffers from two profound weaknesses: (*a*) its continued underdevelopment of the political-

---

[13]This distinction could in fact be used to characterize critical intellectuality in the 1980s era and to anticipate its withering away in the postcommunist one (Kennedy 1990).

economic foundations of democracy's possibility; and (b) its almost utopian view of subject formation. The first point is familiar in marxist critiques, while the latter is rather nicely developed in the so-called "Slovenian Lacanian School" (Laclau 1989).

Slavoj Žižek and Renata Salecl illustrate rather powerfully how this "radical contemporary version of the Enlightenment" (Žižek 1989, p. 7) can both supplement and contradict marxist and civil society approaches. For instance, Žižek depends heavily on marxist conceptions of labor power for imagining the central blindspot, or lack, in ideological notions of freedom (p. 22). But in direct contrast to most marxist assumptions, he departs from the notion that ideology is somehow apart from, and a distortion of, the Real. Instead, for this school, ideology constitutes reality, by filling the lack with something that enables action. The Real of Desire is thus not apart from ideology, but in fact ideology constitutes it. According to this principle, socialism, and its embodiment in a concrete actor like the party, can become itself a source of oppression as it assumes the role of the object of desire, whose mastery of history and society resolves all contradiction. In contrast, democracy, as an emancipatory alternative, treats the place of Power as necessarily empty (1989, p. 147); democracy is, in other words, immanent in the constant struggle to maintain a distance between ideology and its surmise (Salecl 1994a, p. 141).

While this approach shares with the civil society literature a commitment to radical democracy, it also is much more skeptical of what the Rechtstaat can accomplish and of its underlying ideological motifs. In Salecl's analysis of the end to Yugoslavia (Salecl 1994b, chapter 4), for instance, the significance of any oppositional movement depends on its linkage to other ideological elements. Civil society was a powerful opponent to the subordination of the political to the social in self-management ideology because it could exploit admissions of the plurality of self-management interests. But once the possibility of free elections opened up, the significance and meaning of any oppositional movement came to be inscribed in their location in a differently politicized ideological space. The prospects of any movement were determined by their articulation with nationalist politics.

Salecl is careful in her analysis of the Yugoslav War not to indict the East as having an exclusive claim on the politics of intolerance (Salecl 1994b). On the one hand, appeals to the civilized character of Western civil societies deny the "metaracism" underlying their constitution; and on the other, it also distances the Yugoslav conflict into one of enduring tribal hatreds for which the West has no responsibility. This emphasis on ideology also allows us to begin to approach rape as an integral part of the war's character, destroying the fantasy structure and identity of the Bosnian nation and of its individual women.

This kind of attack, Salecl argues, is designed to obliterate one identity—a multinational Yugoslav one—to replace it with another—a Bosnian Muslim fundamentalism—which might then "justify" the originating assault.

While this form of critique might be associated with the marxist tradition, its claim to centrality in it, or connection with Burawoy's or Wright's marxisms, is weak at best, for here there is a refusal to elevate the "Real" in any recognizably marxist form above ideology and desire. To introduce Žižek and Salecl here in marxist East European studies is thus to recall those debates in the mid-1980s about Laclau and Mouffe's post-marxist challenge to marxism (Laclau & Mouffe 1985, Mouzelis 1990).

We would only propose here that it may be even more important in the field of East European studies than elsewhere for a dialogue to occur between approaches rooted in the reality of class and production, and ones that emphasize discourse, ideology, and identity in constituting that reality. For in order to reaffirm and maintain itself as an integrated project without dismissing or ignoring Eastern Europe, marxism must adequately confront Eastern Europe's experience with, and rejection of, "really existing socialism." If we can elevate the discursive and the ideological to at least a potentially constitutive moment in the making of historical transformations and class relations, then perhaps we can begin to analyze the possibilities of socialism in the places where it was understood as experienced and real, not as desired in its absence.

CONCLUSIONS

Marxism's emphasis on the reality of class relations in capitalism has traditionally meant that socialism itself is bracketed as an eventual alternative, something not articulated, but desired. Under communist rule, Eastern Europe might have been considered the fulfillment of that desire, but its conflicts and contradictions made real socialism into another alternative—this time, of course, something undesirable to most Western marxists. Thus, communism's collapse in Eastern Europe enables marxists to return socialism to its ontologically absent, if epistemologically structuring, position.

This strategy might reproduce marxism in a Western-centered community, especially if East European rejections of marxism are dismissed as false consciousness or the reflection of a particular and therefore limited politics. But with this treatment, not only is the particularism of Western marxism heightened, but the potential for an East European marxist revival is put at risk. After all, it is possible for East Europeans and nonmarxist sociologists to recoup marxism's methodological and analytic insights, and to recreate its methodologies, while abandoning its normative and political commitments as hopelessly naive.

While the political economy and historical sociology of Eastern European transformations are clearly important to marxism, and while marxism can and does contribute to their explanation, the principal challenge for marxists in Eastern Europe lies elsewhere. For marxism to develop as a perspective, it must find a way to articulate socialism's transcendent project with the life-worlds of Eastern Europe, a task which is, we suggest, grounded as much in discursive analyses of ideologies and identities as in the political economy of transformation. Thus, a trek through this somewhat methodologically and epistemologically estranged terrain may in fact be the route to marxism's recovery of itself in Eastern Europe as an integrated project.

Any *Annual Review* chapter, as well as any article cited in an *Annual Review* chapter, may be purchased from the Annual Reviews Preprints and Reprints service.
1-800-347-8007; 415-259-5017; email: arpr@class.org

Literature Cited

Arato A. 1994. Revolution, restoration, and legitimation: ideological problems of the transition from state socialism. See Kennedy 1994a, pp. 180–246

Aronson R. 1995. *After Socialism.* New York: Guilford

Auerbach P. 1992. Socialist optimism. *New Left Rev.* 192:5–35

Bauman Z. 1976. *Socialism: The Active Utopia.* London: Allen & Unwin

Böröcz J. 1992. Dual dependency and property vacuum: social change on the state socialist semiperiphery. *Theory Soc.* 21/1:77–104

Böröcz J, Smith DA. 1995 Introduction: Late twentieth century challenges for world system analysis. In *A New World Order? Global Transformations in the Late Twentieth Century,* ed. J Böröcz, DA Smith, pp. 1–16. Westport, CT: Praeger

Burawoy M. 1979. *Manufacturing Consent: Changes in the Labor Process Under Monopoly Capitalism.* Chicago: Univ. Chicago Press

Burawoy M. 1990. Marxism as science: historical challenges and theoretical growth. *Am. Sociol. Rev.* 55:775–93

Burawoy M. 1994. Why coupon socialism never stood a chance in Russia: the political conditions of economic transition. *Polit. Soc.* 22:585–94

Burawoy M. 1995. From Sovietology to comparative political economy. In *Beyond Soviet Studies,* ed. D Orlovsky, pp. 72–102. Baltimore: Johns Hopkins

Burawoy M, Krotov P. 1992. The Soviet transition from socialism to capitalism: worker control and economic bargaining in the wood industry. *Am. Sociol. Rev.* 57:16–38

Burawoy M, Krotov P. 1993. The economic basis of Russia's political crisis. *New Left Rev.* 198:49–69

Burawoy M, Krotov P. 1995. Russian miners bow to the angel of history. *Antipode* 27:115–36

Burawoy M, Lukacs J. 1992. *The Radiant Past: Ideology and Reality in Hungary's Road to Capitalism.* Chicago: Univ. Chicago Press

Calhoun C. 1989. Classical social theory and the French Revolution of 1848. *Sociol. Theory* 7/2:210–25

Clarke S. 1992. Privatization and the development of capitalism in Russia. *New Left Rev.* 196:3–27

Cohen JL. 1982. *Class and Civil Society: The Limits of Marxian Critical Theory.* Amherst: Univ. Mass. Press

Cohen JL, Arato A. 1992. *Civil Society and Political Theory.* Cambridge, MA: MIT Press

Connor WD. 1979. *Socialism, Politics and Inequality: Hierarchy and Change in Eastern Europe and the USSR.* New York: Columbia Univ. Press

Crowley S. 1993. *From coal to steel: the formation of an independent workers movement in the Soviet Union, 1989–91.* PhD thesis. Univ. Mich., Ann Arbor, Mich.

Denitch BD. 1994. *Ethnic Nationalism: The Tragic Death of Yugoslavia.* Minneapolis: Univ. Minn. Press

Derrida J. 1994. Spectres of Marx. *New Left Rev.*

205:31–57

Frentzel-Zagórska J, Zagórski K. 1989. East European intellectuals on the road of dissent. *Polit. Soc.* 17(1989):89–113

Gouldner AW. 1980. *The Two Marxisms: Contradictions and Anomalies in the Development of Theory.* New York: Seabury

Habermas J. 1990. What does socialism mean today?: the rectifying revolution and the need for new thinking on the left. *New Left Rev.* 183:3–21

Habermas J, Michnik A. 1994. Overcoming the past (interview/discussion). *New Left Rev.* 203:3–16

Harsanyi N, Kennedy MD. 1994. Between utopia and dystopia: the liabilities of nationalism in Eastern Europe. See Kennedy 1994a, pp. 149–80

Hirszowicz M, Morawski W, eds. 1967. Z Badań nad społecznym uczestnictwem w organizacjii przemysłowej. Warszawa: Książka i Wiedza

Hollander P. 1982. Research on marxist societies: the relationship between theory and practice. *Annu. Rev. Sociol.* 8:319–51

Hollander P. 1992. *Decline and Discontent: Communism and the West Today.* New Brunswick: Transaction

Kagarlitsky B. 1989. The importance of being Marxist. *New Left Rev.* 177:29–36

Kennedy MD. 1990. The constitution of critical intellectuals: Polish physicians, peace activists and democratic civil society. *Stud. Comp. Commun.* 23:281–303

Kennedy MD. 1991. *Professionals, Power and Solidarity in Poland: A Critical Sociology of Soviet-Type Society.* Cambridge: Cambridge Univ. Press

Kennedy MD. 1992. The intelligentsia in the constitution of civil societies and postcommunist regimes in Hungary and Poland. *Theory Soc.* 21:29–76

Kennedy MD, ed. 1994a. *Envisioning Eastern Europe: Postcommunist Cultural Studies,* Ann Arbor: Univ. Mich. Press

Kennedy MD. 1994b. An introduction to East European ideology and identity in transformation. See Kennedy 1994a, pp. 1–45

Kennedy MD. 1994c. Interview with I. Szelényi, November 4 (for video series, *The Cold War and its Aftermath*). Adv. Stud. Cent., Int. Inst., Univ. Mich, Ann Arbor

Kennedy MD. 1995. On the end of the cold war and on postcommunist peripheral capitalism: interview with Jadwiga Staniszkis. *Periphery: J. Polish Affairs* 1/1:19–21

Klinghoffer AJ. 1994. Review of *The Fate of Marxism in Russia* by Alexander Yakovlev. *Russ. Rev.* 53:602–3

Konrad G, Szelényi I. 1979. *Intellectuals on the Road to Class Power.* New York: Harcourt Brace Jovanovich

Kornai J. 1992. *The Socialist System: The Political Economy of Communism.* Princeton, NJ: Princeton Univ. Press

Kuroń J. 1994. Rzeczpospolita dla Każdego: Mysli o programie dzialania. (The Republic for all: some considerations concerning the Program of Action). *Zycie Gospodarcze.* May 22, 1994.

Kuroń J, Modzelewski K. 1966. *An Open Letter to the Party.* Prague: Prazskeho Studentskeho Parlamentu

Laclau E. 1989. Preface in Žižek S. *The Sublime Object of Ideology.* London: Verso

Laclau E, Mouffe C. 1985. *Hegemony and Socialist Strategy: Towards a Radical Democratic Politics.* London: Verso

Lenski G. 1978. Marxist experiments in destratification: an appraisal. *Soc. Forces* 57:364–83

Magas B. 1992. *The Destruction of Yugoslavia.* London: Verso

Medvedev RA. 1981. *Leninism and Western Socialism.* Transl. ADP Briggs. London: Verso

Medvedev RA. 1992. After the communist collapse: new political tendencies in Russia. *Dissent* 39:489–97

Mokrzycki E. 1992. The legacy of real socialism, group interests and the search for a new utopia. In *The Polish Road from Socialism: The Economics, Sociology, and Politics of Transition,* ed. W Connor, P Ploszajski. Armonk: ME Sharpe

Morawski W, ed. 1994. *Zmierzch Socjalizmu Państwowego: Szkice Z Socjologii Ekonomi cznej.* Warszawa: PWN

Mouzelis NP. 1990. *Post Marxist Alternatives: The Construction of Social Orders.* Basingstoke: Macmillan

Nove A. 1991. *The Economics of Feasible Socialism Revisited.* London: Unwin Hyman

Pierson C. 1995. *Socialism After Communism: The New Market Socialism.* Univ. Park: Penn. State Univ. Press

Resnick S, Wolff R. 1993. State capitalism in the USSR: a high stakes debate. *Rethinking Marxism* 6 (Summer):46–68

Roemer JE. 1994. *A Future for Socialism.* Cambridge: Harvard Univ. Press

Salecl R. 1994a. The ideology of the mother nation in the Yugoslav conflict. See Kennedy 1994a, pp. 87–101

Salecl R. 1994b. *The Spoils of Freedom: Psychoanalysis and Feminism after the Fall of Socialism.* London: Routledge

Service R. 1993. Review of *Lenin's Gravedigger: The Fate of Marxism in Russia* by Alexander Yakovlev. *New Statesman & Soc.* 6:45

Somers MR. 1996. Where is sociology after the historic turn? Knowledge, cultures, narrativity, and historical epistemologies. In *The Historic Turn in the Human Sciences,* ed. TJ. MacDonald. Ann Arbor: Univ. Mich. Press. In press

Staniszkis J. 1991. *The Dynamics of Breakthrough in Eastern Europe: The Case of Poland.* Berkeley: Univ. Calif. Press

Staniszkis J. 1992. *The Ontology of Socialism.* New york: Oxford Univ. Press

Stark D. 1986. Rethinking internal labor markets: new insights from a comparative perspective. *Am. Sociol. Rev.* 51:492–504

Stark D. 1989. Coexisting organizational forms in Hungary's emerging mixed economy. In *Remaking the Economic Institutions of Socialism: China and Eastern Europe,* ed. V Nee, D Stark. Stanford: Stanford Univ. Press

Stark D. 1992. Path dependence and privatization strategies in East Central Europe. *East Eur. Polit. Soc.* 6:17–51

Stark D. 1996. Recombinant property in East European capitalism. *Am. J. Sociol.* 101:993–1027

Szelényi I. 1979. Socialist opposition in Eastern Europe: dilemmas and prospects. In *Opposition in Eastern Europe,* ed. R Tokes. Baltimore: Johns Hopkins Univ. Press

Szelényi I. 1987. Prospects and limits of the East European new class project. *Polit. Soc.* 15–16(2):103–44

Szelényi I. 1988. *Socialist Entrepeneurs: Embourgeoisement in Rural Hungary.* Madison, WI: Univ. Wisc. Press

Szelényi I. 1994. Socialist entrepreneurs revisited. *Adv. Stud. Cent. Work. Pap. Ser. No. 4.* Int. Inst., Univ. Mich., Ann Arbor

Szelényi I, Martin B. 1991. The three waves of new class theories and a postscript. In *Intellectuals and Politics: Social Theory in a Changing World,* ed. C Lemert. Newbury Park, CA: Sage

Szelényi I, Szelényi B. 1994. Why socialism failed: toward a theory of system breakdown—causes of disintegration of East European state socialism. *Theory Soc.* 23/2:211–32

Szelényi S, Szelényi I, Poster W. 1996. Interests and symbols in post-communist political culture: the case of Hungary. *Am. Sociol. Rev..* In press

Szporluk R. 1988. *Communism vs. Nationalism: Marx and List.* Oxford: Oxford Univ. Press

Taylor C. 1990. Modes of civil society. *Public Culture* 3/1:95–188

Walicki A. 1995. *Marxism and the Leap to the Kingdom of Freedom: The Rise and Fall of the Communist Utopia.* Stanford: Stanford Univ. Press

Weiss K. 1994. On the power and frailty of Utopias. See Kennedy 1994, pp. 46–54

Weisskopf TE. 1992. Challenges to market socialism: a response to critics. *Dissent* Spring:250–61

Wesołowski W. 1979. *Classes, Strata, and Power.* Transl. G. Kolankiewicz. Boston: Routledge & K. Paul

Wesołowski W. 1990. Transition from authoritarianism to democracy. *Soc. Res.* 57(2):435–61

Wesołowski W. 1995a. Rozumienie polityki wśród politikòw. The understanding of politics among politicians. In *Świat Elity Politycznej,* (The World of Political Elites), ed. W Wesołowski, I Panków, pp. 111–68. Warszawa: IFiS PAN

Wesołowski W. 1995b. The nature of social ties and the future of postcommunist society: Poland after Solidarity. In *Civil Society: Theory, History, and Comparison,* ed. JA Hall, pp. 110–35. Cambridge: Polity Press

Wright EO. 1992. *Reconstructing Marxism: Essays in Explanation and the Theory of History.* London: Verso

Wright EO. 1993. Class analysis, history and emancipation. *New Left Rev.* 292:15–35

Zybertowicz A. 1994. Three deaths of an ideology: the withering away of marxism and the collapse of communism, the case of Poland. *Poznań Stud. Philos. Sci. Humanities* 36:121–35

Annu. Rev. Sociol. 1996. 22:459–87

GENDER AND CRIME: Toward a Gendered Theory of Female Offending

Darrell Steffensmeier

Department of Sociology, Pennsylvania State University, University Park, Pennsylvania 16802

Emilie Allan

Department of Behavioral Sciences, St Francis College, Loretto, Pennsylvania 15940

KEY WORDS: gender, feminism, crime theories and research, women and crime, crime patterns

ABSTRACT

Criminologists agree that the gender gap in crime is universal: Women are always and everywhere less likely than men to commit criminal acts. The experts disagree, however, on a number of key issues: Is the gender gap stable or variant over time and across space? If there is variance, how may it best be explained? Are the causes of female crime distinct from or similar to those of male crime? Can traditional sociological theories of crime explain female crime and the gender gap in crime? Do gender-neutral or gender-specific theories hold the most explanatory promise? In this chapter we first examine patterns of female offending and the gender gap. Second, we review the "gender equality hypothesis" as well as several recent developments in theorizing about gender differences in crime. Third, we expand on a gendered paradigm for explaining female crime first sketched elsewhere. We conclude with recommendations for future work.

INTRODUCTION

The principal goal of this article is to advance theory and research by reviewing selected issues in the gender and crime literature; by advancing a gendered paradigm of female offending which builds on existing theory and on the growing body of work on gender; and by proposing a series of recommendations for further research.

459

No single article can do justice to the vast literature on gender and crime, to both the old and especially the new writings. If criminologists were ever indifferent to female crime, it is certainly the case no longer. Although profound questions remain, more is known about gender and crime than is known about age and crime or about race and crime.

Sociologists may also welcome the solid evidence that confirms the utility of traditional sociological theories of crime in explaining crime by women as well as by men, and in explaining gender differences in crime—at least for the minor crimes that dominate both official and unofficial data on crime. Much of what we still need to learn has to do with the profound gender differences in patterns of serious offending, rather than the less consequential differences in patterns of minor crime.

We first assess similarities and differences between female and male patterns of offending. Next we briefly review explanations of those patterns and of the gender gap, particularly the so-called "gender equality" hypothesis that gender differences in crime converge as male and female roles become more similar. We then seek to advance theory and research in the field by expanding on a "gendered" paradigm begun elsewhere (Steffensmeier & Allan 1995) that can illuminate the critical relationship between gender and crime and by setting forth a number of recommendations for future work.

FEMALE AND MALE PATTERNS OF OFFENDING

Patterns of offending by men and by women are notable both for their similarities and for their differences. Both men and women are more heavily involved in minor property and substance abuse offenses than in serious crimes like robbery or murder. However, men offend at much higher rates than women for all crime categories except prostitution. This gender gap in crime is greatest for serious crime and least for mild forms of lawbreaking such as minor property crimes.

Many sources provide data that permit comparison of male and female offending. We review FBI arrest statistics (US Department of Justice 1990) for men and women, and we draw also upon offender information from the National Crime Victimization Survey, and on findings from surveys on self-reported crime, from studies of criminal careers and delinquent gangs, and from case studies that provide a wealth of qualitative data on the differing contexts of male and female offending.

Table 1 summarizes a variety of information drawn from male and female arrest data for all FBI offense categories except rape (a male crime) and runaway and curfew (juvenile offenses): trends in male and female arrests rates per 100,000 population (columns 1–6), trends in the female percent of arrests (columns 7–9), and the offending profile of males and females (columns

Table 1 Male and female arrest rates/100,000, male and female arrest profiles, and female percentage of arrests. (1960–1990, uniform crime reports)

Offenses	Male Rates			Female Rates			Offender-Profile Percentage				Female Percentage (of arrests)		
							Males		Females				
	1960	1975	1990	1960	1975	1990	1960	1990	1960	1990	1960	1975	1990
	(1)	(2)	(3)	(4)	(5)	(6)	(7)	(8)	(9)	(10)	(11)	(12)	(13)
Against Persons													
Homicide	9	16	16	2	3	2	.1	.2	.2	.1	17	14	11
Aggravated assault	101	200	317	16	28	50	1	3	2	2	14	13	13
Weapons	69	137	165	4	11	14	1	2	.5	.7	4	8	7
Simple assault	265	354	662	29	54	129	4	6	4	5	10	13	15
Major Property													
Robbery	65	131	124	4	10	12	1	1	.5	.5	5	7	8
Burglary	274	477	319	9	27	32	4	3	1	1	3	5	8
Stolen Property	21	103	121	2	12	17	.3	1	.2	.5	8	10	11
Minor Property													
Larceny-Theft	391	749	859	74	321	402	6	10	9	20	17	30	30
Fraud	70	114	157	12	59	133	1	2	2	7	15	34	43
Forgery	44	46	51	8	18	28	.5	.5	1	1	16	28	34
Embezzlement	—	7	8	—	3	5	—	.2	—	.1	—	28	37
Melicious Mischief													
Auto theft	121	128	158	5	9	18	2	1	1	1	4	7	9
Vandalism	—	187	224	—	16	28	—	2	—	1	—	8	10
Arson	—	15	13	—	2	2	—	.3	—	.1	—	11	14
Drinking/Drugs													
Public drunkenness	2573	1201	624	212	87	71	36	8	25	4	8	7	9
DUI	344	971	1193	21	81	176	5	15	3	9	6	5	11
Liquor laws	183	276	428	28	43	102	3	5	4	5	13	14	17
Drug abuse	49	523	815	8	79	166	1	7	1	6	15	13	14
Sex/Sex Related													
Prostitution	15	18	30	37	45	62	.2	.4	4	3	73	73	65
Sex offenses	81	55	78	17	5	7	1	1	2	.3	17	8	8
Disorderly conduct	749	597	499	115	116	119	11	5	14	6	13	17	18
Vagrancy	265	45	26	23	7	4	4	.3	3	.2	8	14	12
Suspicion	222	31	13	28	5	3	3	.1	3	.1	11	13	15
Miscellaneous													
Against family	90	57	51	8	7	12	1	.5	1	.5	8	10	16
Gambling	202	60	14	19	6	2	3	.2	2	.2	8	9	15
Other Exc. traffic		871	1139	2109	150	197	430	13	23	19	20	15	15
Total	7070	7850	9211	831	1383	2122					11	15	19

10–13). All calculations in Table 1 adjust for the sex composition in the population as a whole and are based on ages 10–64 (i.e. the population most at risk for criminal behavior).

Arrest Rates, 1960, 1975, 1990

For both males and females, arrest rates are higher for less serious offenses, and both male and female rates trended upward during both periods (1960–1975, 1975–1990) for many offense categories. Large increases are found mainly for petty property crimes like larceny and fraud, for substance abuse (DUI, drugs, and liquor law violations), and for assault. A number of the public order offense categories trended downward, especially public drunkenness, gambling, and many of the sex-related offenses. The similarity in male and female trends suggests that the rates of both sexes are influenced by similar social and legal forces, independent of any condition unique to women or men.

Arrest Profiles

The similarities are even more evident in the profiles of male and female arrest patterns displayed in columns 10–13. These profiles reflect the percentage of total male and total female arrests represented by each crime category for 1960 and 1990. The homicide figures of 0.2 for men in 1990 and 0.1 for women mean, respectively, that only two tenths of 1% of all male arrests were for homicide, and only one tenth of 1% of all female arrests were for homicide.

For both men and women, the three most common arrest categories in 1990 are DUI, larceny-theft, and "other except traffic"—a residual category that includes mostly criminal mischief, public disorder, local ordinance violations, and assorted minor crimes. Together, these three offense categories account for 48% of all male arrests and 49% of all female arrests. Note, however, that larceny arrests are the most numerous category (20% in 1990) for females; but that for males, DUI arrests are more important (15%). Arrests for murder, arson, and embezzlement are relatively rare for men and women alike, while arrests for offenses such as liquor law violations (mostly underage drinking), simple assault, and disorderly conduct represent "middling ranks" for both sexes.

The most important gender differences in arrest profiles involve the proportionately greater female involvement in minor property crimes (collectively, about 28% of female arrests in 1990, compared to 13% of male arrests), and the relatively greater involvement of males in crimes against persons and major property crimes (17% of male arrests, but only 11% of female arrests). Ironically, men and women were slightly closer in their profiles in these more "masculine" categories in 1960, when they represented 11.4% of male arrests and 8.4% of female arrests.

Female Percentage of Arrests

Although some authors profess to see major changes over time in the female percentage of arrests (e.g. Adler 1975, Simon 1975), the numbers for 1960, 1975, and 1990 are perhaps more remarkable for their similarity than for their differences. For all three periods, the female share of arrests for most categories was 15% or less and was typically smallest for the most serious offenses. Major change is found principally for the female share of arrests for minor property crimes such as larceny and fraud, which averaged between 15% and 17% in 1960, but jumped to between 30% and 43% by 1990.

National Crime Victimization Survey (NCVS)

The relatively low female participation in serious offending is corroborated by data from the NCVS (Bureau of Justice Statistics 1992). In NCVS interviews, victims are asked the sex of offender, and totals turn out to be quite close to those found in UCR data. In 1990, for example, women are reported to be responsible for about 7% of robberies, 12% of aggravated assaults, 15% of simple assaults, 5% of burglaries, and 5% of motor vehicle thefts reported by victims. These percentages have held unchanged since the NCVS began in the mid-1970s.

Self-Report Studies

The pattern of a higher female share of offending for mild forms of lawbreaking and a much lower share for serious offenses is confirmed by the numerous surveys in which persons (generally juveniles) have been asked to report on their own offenses (Canter 1982). This holds both for prevalence of offending (the percent of the male and female samples that report any offending) and especially for the frequency of offending (the number of crimes an active offender commits in a given period). However, gender differences are less for self-report data than for official data (Jensen & Eve 1976, Smith & Visher 1980), and gender differences are smaller still for self-report prevalence data on minor offenses such as shoplifting and minor drug use (Canter 1982).

Gang Participation

Girls have long been members of gangs (Thrasher 1927), and some girls to-day continue to solve their problems of gender, race, and class through gang membership. At issue is not their presence but the extent and form of their participation. Early studies, based on information from male gang informants, depicted female gang members as playing secondary roles as cheerleaders or camp followers, and ignored girls' occasionally violent behavior.

Recent studies, which rely more on female gang informants, indicate that girls' roles in gangs have been considerably more varied than early stereotypes would have it. Although female gang members continue to be dependent on male gangs, the girls' status is determined as much or even more so by her female peers (Campbell 1984). Also, relative to the past, girls in gangs appear to be fighting in more arenas and even using many of the same weapons as males (Quicker 1974), and the gang context may be an important source of initiating females into patterns of violent offending (Fagan 1990). The aggressive rhetoric of some female gang members notwithstanding, their actual behavior continues to display considerable deference to male gang members, avoidance of excessive violence, and adherence to traditional gender-scripted behaviors (Campbell 1990, Chesney-Lind & Shelden 1992, Swart 1991). Ganging is still a predominantly male phenomenon (roughly 90%). The most common form of female gang involvement has remained as auxiliaries or branches of male gangs (Miller 1980, Swart 1991), and girls are excluded from most of the economic criminal activity (Bowker et al 1980).

Criminal Careers

The study of individual careers in crime—the longitudinal sequence of crimes committed by an individual offender—has become an increasing focus of criminology. The research comparing male and female criminal careers is limited to violent career offenders and has found substantial gender variation: (i) Although violent offenses comprise only a small percentage of all the offenses committed by offenders in any population, females participate in substantially less violent crime than males during the course of their criminal careers; (ii) the careers of violent females both begin and peak a little earlier than those of males; (iii) females are far less likely than males to repeat their violent offenses; and (iv) females are far more likely to desist from further violence (see reviews in Denno 1994, Kruttschnitt 1994, Weiner 1989).

Case studies and interviews, even with serious female offenders, indicate no strong commitment to criminal behavior (Arnold 1989, Bottcher 1986, Miller 1986). This finding stands in sharp contrast to the commitment and self-identification with crime and the criminal lifestyle that is often found among male offenders (Sutherland 1937, Prus & Sharper 1977, Steffensmeier 1986, Commonwealth of Pennsylvania 1991).

APPLYING TRADITIONAL THEORY TO THE EXPLANATION OF GENDERED CRIME PATTERNS

A long-standing issue concerns whether female crime can be explained by theories developed mainly by male criminologists to explain male crime. Do the macro social conditions producing male crime also produce female crime? Are the pathways or processes leading to crime similar or distinct across the sexes? A variety of evidence suggests that there is considerable overlap in the "causes" of male and female crime, and that both traditional and more recent theoretical perspectives can help explain both female offending patterns and gender differences for less serious crime. The explanation of serious female crime and of gender differences in serious crime is more problematic.

Similarity in Social Backgrounds

The social backgrounds of female offenders tend to be quite similar to those of male offenders (see reviews in Chesney-Lind & Shelden 1994, Denno 1994, Steffensmeier & Allan 1995). Like male offenders, female offenders (especially the more serious ones) are typically of low socioeconomic status, poorly educated, under- or unemployed, and disproportionately from minority groups. The main difference in their social profile is the greater presence of dependent children among female offenders.

Regression of Female Rates on Male Rates

The extent to which male rates can predict female rates provides indirect evidence of similarity in the etiology of female and male crime (Steffensmeier & Allan 1988, Steffensmeier et al 1989). Groups or societies that have high male rates of crime also have high female rates, whereas groups or societies that have low male rates also have low female rates. Over time, when the male rate rises, declines, or holds steady across a specific historical period, the female rate behaves in a similar fashion. Statistically, when the female rates for a given group are regressed on the male rates for the same group, across time or across crime categories, the results for most comparisons do not differ significantly from a prediction of no difference (Steffensmeier & Allan 1988, Steffensmeier & Streifel 1992). Such findings suggest that female rates respond to the same social and legal forces as male rates, independent of any condition unique to women or to men (Bortitch & Hagan 1990, Steffensmeier 1980, Steffensmeier & Streifel 1992).

Aggregate Analysis

In an aggregate study of structural correlates of female crime rates, Steffensmeier & Streifel (1993) report findings similar to those for comparable aggregate studies of male rates. For example, rates of female crime tend to be higher in cities with high levels of economic inequality and poverty. There is a major need for further macro-aggregate studies of female offending.

Theory Testing with Self-Report Data

Theory testing with individual-level self-report data has identified causal factors for female offending that are quite consistent with those suggested by traditional theories of crime such as anomie, social control, and differential association (Akers et al 1979, Giordano et al 1986, Hagan 1989, Jensen & Eve 1976, Paternoster & Triplett 1988, Rankin 1980, Smith 1979, Smith & Paternoster 1987, Tittle 1980). Measures of bonds, associations, learning, parental controls, perceptions of risk, and so forth have comparable effects across the genders.

However, such findings apply mainly to minor offending; available self-report data sets do not lend themselves to the study of serious offending— either male or female—due to limited sample size, question content and format, and other problems. Aggregate methodology is perhaps even less adapted to the study of gender differences in criminal career paths and in the context of offending.

SHORTCOMINGS OF TRADITIONAL THEORIES   The traditional theories are helpful in explaining overall patterns of female and male offending, and they shed some light on why female levels of offending are lower than for males. These approaches are less enlightening when seeking answers for a variety of both subtle and profound differences in female and male offending patterns.

For example:

Why are serious crimes against property and against persons so much less a feature of female offending? Male criminal participation in serious crime greatly exceeds female involvement, regardless of data source, crime type, level of involvement, or measure of participation (Kruttschnitt 1994, Steffensmeier 1983, Steffensmeier & Allan 1995). Women are far less likely to be involved in serious offenses, and the monetary value of female thefts, property damage, drugs, injuries, is typically smaller than that for similar offenses committed by men.

Why are female offenders less likely to participate in or lead criminal groups? Females are also more likely than males to be solo perpetrators, or to be part of small, relatively nonpermanent crime groups. When female offenders are involved with others, particularly in more lucrative thefts or other criminal enterprises, they typically act as accomplices to males who both organize and lead the execution of the crime (see Steffensmeier 1983, for a review). Perhaps the most significant gender difference is the overwhelming dominance of males in more organized and highly lucrative crimes, whether based in the underworld or the "upperworld" (Steffensmeier 1983, Daly 1989, Commonwealth of Pennsylvania 1991).

Why do women seem to need a higher level of provocation before turning to crime, especially serious crime? For example, in comparison to male offenders, female offenders are more likely to also be victims as children or adults (Chesney-Lind & Shelden 1992, Daly 1994, Gilfus 1992, Widom 1989). In her analysis of the Philadelphia cohort data, Denno (1994) reports that, although many factors are as predictive of female as male criminality, female offenders are more likely to have had records of neurological and other biological or psychological abnormalities. Likewise, Daly (1994) reports that female offenders (in comparison to male offenders) in a New Haven felony court had greater childhood and adult exposure to abuse, but that the female felons were nevertheless more conventional than the males in having greater responsibilities for children, commitment to education, and legitimate sources of income.

Why does female offending often involve relational concerns? Situational pressures such as threatened loss of valued relationships may play a greater role in female offending. Although the saying, "She did it all for love" is sometimes overplayed in reference to female criminality, the role of men in initiating women into crime—especially serious crime—is a consistent finding across research (Gilfus 1992, Miller 1986, Pettiway 1987, Steffensmeier 1983, Steffensmeier & Terry 1986). Such findings also suggest that women are not uniformly less amenable to risk, but rather that their risk-taking is less violative of the law and more protective of relationships and emotional commitments.

These and other questions often involve subtle issues of context that are not addressed by most traditional and contemporary theories, and which tend to be invisible (or nearly so) to quantitative analyses. Fortunately, as we discuss later, contextual issues are illuminated by a wealth of qualitative information to be found both in the traditional criminological literature (Elliott 1952,Reitman 1937) and in the profusion of qualitative research produced by feminist criminologists in recent years.

THE GENDER GAP AND CRIME

The gender gap in crime—the low level of female offending in relation to that of males—is universally recognized by criminologists. Almost as universal is the assumption that the gender gap varies significantly by age, race, geographic area, and time. In fact, Sutherland and other early criminologists cited variations in the ratio of female to male arrests to demonstrate the superiority of sociological explanations of crime over biological explanations (see the review in Steffensmeier & Clark 1980): If the gender gap had a biological basis, it would not vary, as it does, across time and space.

The Gender Equality Hypothesis

It also was assumed that variations could be best explained by differences in gender equality over time and among social groups (Sutherland 1924, see review in Steffensmeier & Clark 1980b). This interpretation is depicted in Figure 1.

Specifically, the assertion was that the gender gap in crime is less in social settings where female roles and statuses presumably differ less from those of

Gender Equality ---------------▸ Masculinity &
                                  Taste for risk ---------------▸ Higher Female
                                                                    Share of Crime

Figure 1   Gender equality and crime.

men: that is, in developed nations, compared to developing countries; in urban, compared to rural settings; among blacks, compared to whites; among people of older ages, compared to younger; and in time of war, compared to peacetime.

This early explication of the gender equality and crime hypothesis became the standard sociological explanation for the gender gap in crime, but it never attracted widespread public attention until the 1970s when several feminist criminologists suggested that increases in the female share of arrests could be attributed to gains in gender equality as a result of the women's movement (Adler 1975, Simon 1975). The media enthusiastically embraced this interpretation of the "dark side" of female liberation.

The gender equality hypothesis continues to influence theories of gender and crime, as exemplified in the power-control approach developed by Hagan and his colleagues (1993). According to power-control theory, the gender gap in "common delinquency" is minimized for girls raised in "egalitarian" families (families headed by women and families in which the mother works in a position of authority equal to or greater than that of the father). As with the earliest statements of the gender-equality hypothesis, greater gender equality is assumed to lead to higher rates of female crime (although the precise mechanisms are more complex).

Recent challenges to the assumptions of the gender equality hypothesis have questioned (i) whether the gender gap in crime varies as much as previously believed; (ii) whether women in fact have experienced greater social equality in the specified groups and times; (iii) whether the gender gap in crime is in fact less in the specified groups and times; and (iv) whether the gender equality approach fares better than alternative hypotheses for explaining whatever time-space variations in the gender gap do in fact exist.

The evidence for time-space variations is meager and often statistically flawed. Variation in the gender gap is sometimes found for this or that offense, mainly for less serious forms of lawbreaking. But across most offenses, the more systematic analyses of self-report data and official arrest statistics reveal that the gender effect is far more stable than variant across race, age, social class, rural-urban comparisons, and in comparisons of less-developed and developed nations (Cantor 1982, Steffensmeier & Allan 1988, Tittle 1980, Steffensmeier et al 1989). Even the apparent narrowing of the gender gap during war largely disappears when controls are included for the wartime absence of young men most at risk for crime (Steffensmeier et al 1980). Further, structural factors other than gender equality appear to better explain those instances where the gender gap is not stable across societies or population subgroups.

Recent Trends in Female Crime and the Women's Movement

It also is questionable whether the women's movement has led to a significant narrowing of the gender gap in crime over recent decades. Looking again at UCR data on the female percentage of arrests for the periods 1960, 1975, and 1990 (columns 7–9 in Table 1), significant increases across both periods are found mainly for minor property crimes (larceny, fraud, forgery, and embezzlement); women averaged around 15% in 1960 and between 30% to 40% of arrestees for these crimes in 1990. The largest increases (12% to 19%) in the female share of arrests for these categories occurred between 1960 and 1975, before the women's movement had gained much momentum. Consistent but small increases (1% to 3% for each period) are found for major property crimes and malicious mischief offenses. However, no clear trends are found for the categories of crimes against persons, drinking and drugs, and the sex-related crimes. For all three periods, the female share of arrests for most offense categories was 15% or less, and was typically smallest for the most serious offenses.

It is plausible to argue that greater freedom has increased female participation in the public sphere (work, shopping, banking, driving, and the like), and this could help account for some of the increases in the female share of arrests for petty property offenses like larceny (shoplifting, employee theft), fraud (misuse of credit cards), or forgery (writing bad checks). But do such behaviors as shopping, banking, or working in shops really reflect female emancipation? Such offense categories do not reflect white collar crimes, as Simon argued, but petty offenses committed by economically marginal women (Chesney-Lind 1986, Daly 1989, Steffensmeier 1980, 1993).

Alternative Explanations for Gender Gap Differences and Trends

Of course, for many offense categories, trends in the female share of offending are inconsistent with the gender equality hypothesis. However, a variety of alternative explanations provide more plausible and more parsimonious accounts for those increases in the female percent of arrests that did occur.

GENDER INEQUALITY Some feminists (and others) espouse a position diametrically opposed to that of Adler & Simon (Chesney-Lind 1989, Daly 1989, Miller 1986, Richie 1995). They point to the peculiarity of considering "a hypothesis that assumed improving girls' and women's economic conditions would lead to an increase in female crime when almost all the existing criminological literature stresses the role played by discrimination and poverty (and unemployment or underemployment) in the creation of crime" (Chesney-Lind & Shelden 1992:77; see also Steffensmeier 1980).

Patriarchal power relations shape gender differences in crime, pushing women into crime through victimization, role entrapment, economic marginality, and survival needs. Nowhere is the gender ratio more skewed than in the great disparity of males as offenders and females as victims of sexual and domestic abuse. The logic of the gender inequality (or marginality) approach, depicted in Figure 2, suggests that greater gender equality would lead to a lower female share of crime.

The role of inequality may be seen in career paths of female teens who drift into criminality as a consequence of running away from sexual and physical abuse at home. The struggle to survive on the streets may then lead to other status offenses and crimes (Gilfus 1992, Chesney-Lind 1989), including prostitution and drug dealing (English 1993). Especially when drug abuse is involved, other criminal involvements are likely to escalate (Anglin & Hser 1987, Inciardi et al 1993). Other feminist researchers have chronicled how female vulnerability to male violence may drive women into illegal activities (Miller 1986, Richie 1995). Despite histories of victimization or economic hardship, many of these women display considerable innovation and independence in their "survival strategies" (Mann 1984).

The gender inequality argument is also supported by Steffensmeier (1993), who points out that increases in petty property crimes are less likely to result from workforce gains than from the economic pressures on women that have been aggravated by heightened rates of divorce, illegitimacy, and female-headed households, coupled with greater responsibility for children. In addition to increased economic pressures, Steffensmeier (1993) goes on to enumerate several other factors that can help explain increases in the female percentage of arrests for property offenses, including the increased formalization of law enforcement, increased opportunities for "female" types of crime, and trends in female drug dependency.

INCREASED FORMALIZATION OF LAW ENFORCEMENT   Steffensmeier (1993) enumerates a number of other alternative explanations for increases in the female

Gender Inequality - - - - - - - - - - → Victimization &   - - - - - - - - - - - - - - → Higher Female
                                            Econ. Marginality   Share of Crime

                                            or

Gender Equality - - - - - - - - - - → Less Victimization & - - - - - - - - - - - - - → Lower Female
                                          Grtr Econ. Well-Being   Share of Crime

Figure 2   Gender inequality and crime.

percent of arrest for some categories. For example, some increases in female arrests may have been an artifact of improved records processing that provided more complete tabulation of female arrests for some categories of arrest, particularly during the 1960s.

INCREASED OPPORTUNITIES FOR "FEMALE" TYPES OF CRIME   The increased percentage of arrests of women for petty property crimes reflects not only economic marginalization, but also an increase in opportunities for these crime categories (Steffensmeier 1993). Largely excluded from lucrative forms of crime (Steffensmeier 1983), women have increased their share of arrests for economically motivated crimes largely in those categories that (i) require little or no criminal "skill"; (ii) have expanded due to changes in merchandising and credit; (iii) are easily accessible to women in their roles as consumers and heads of families. Together, growing economic adversity among large subgroups of women has increased the pressure to commit consumer-based crimes, which are likewise expanding, such as shoplifting, check fraud, theft of services, and welfare fraud.

TRENDS IN FEMALE DRUG DEPENDENCY   Rising levels of illicit drug use by women appear to have had a major impact on female crime trends, even though female drug arrests have not outpaced male arrests since 1960. Drug dependency amplifies income-generating crimes of both sexes, but more so for women because they face greater constraints against crime and need a greater motivational push to deviate (Anglin et al 1987, Inciardi et al 1993). Female involvement in burglary and robbery, in particular, typically occurs after addiction and is likely to be abandoned when drug use ceases (Anglin et al 1987).

Drug use is also more likely to initiate females into the underworld and criminal subcultures and to connect them to drug-dependent males who use them as crime accomplices or exploit them as "old ladies" to support their addiction (Miller 1986, Pettiway 1987, Steffensmeier & Terry 1986). The drug trends also help explain the small rise in the female percentage of incarcerated felons, from about 3% in the 1960s to 6% in the 1990s (but compare to 6% in the 1920s).

Other Criticisms of the Gender Equality Hypothesis

Several criticisms of the gender equality hypothesis have focused on power-control theory, on contradictory evidence such as the traditional gender-role definitions commonly found among female offenders, or on the manner in which gender gap trends in specific crimes are at odds with the gender equality hypothesis. Perhaps the most telling criticism is that theory development has been suppressed by the popularity of the gender equality hypothesis.

CRITICISMS OF POWER CONTROL   The power-control version of the gender equality approach has been challenged for its uncritical acceptance of the gender equality hypothesis (Morash & Chesney-Lind 1991) and for adding little or nothing to the explanatory power of control theory (Jensen 1993). Empirical challenges have come from several studies that report findings at odds with power-control assertions (Jensen 1993, Morash & Chesney-Lind 1991, Singer & Levine 1988, but see Grasmick, Bursik & Sims 1993). However, these studies employed somewhat different operationalizations of the independent variables.

TRADITIONAL GENDER-ROLE DEFINITIONS OF FEMALE OFFENDERS   The gender equality hypothesis is further undermined by the prevalence of traditional gender-role definitions assumed by most male and female offenders (Bottcher 1995). A few studies report a relationship between nontraditional or masculine gender role attitudes and female delinquency on a given item but not on other items (Heimer 1995, Shover et al 1979, Simpson & Ellis 1995). The bulk of studies, however, report that traditional rather than nontraditional views are associated with greater delinquency (see reviews in Chesney-Lind & Shelden 1992, Pollock-Byrne 1990, Steffensmeier & Allan 1995).

HOMICIDE AND BURGLARY TRENDS   The basic irrelevance of the gender equality hypothesis to trends in the female share of arrests can be seen by looking in greater depth at the patterns for homicide (for which the female percent of arrests declined) and burglary (for which the female percent of arrests increased). In the case of murder, the decline in the female share of arrests (from 17% in 1960 to 10% in 1990) is accounted for not by any sharp drop in female arrests for murder, but by the great increases in male arrests for felony murders connected with the drug trade and the increased availability of guns.

Similarly, much of the increase (from 5% to 8%) in the female share of arrests for burglary between 1975 and 1990 resulted from drops in recorded male arrests, partly because of a shift from burglary to drug dealing on the part of male offenders, and partly because of increased police compliance with UCR reporting recommendations that theft from cars be reported as larceny rather than burglary (Steffensmeier 1993).

SUPPRESSION OF THEORY DEVELOPMENT   Over-reliance on the gender equality hypothesis has retarded sociological efforts to develop a multivariate framework for explain gender differences in crime. In a sense, reliance on the gender equality hypothesis can be seen as another example of seeking unique explanations where female crime is at issue.

Application of Traditional Theory to Explanation of the Gender Gap

It is perhaps premature to abandon traditional criminological theories without fully exploiting their insights, which would suggest that females offend less than males: because they are less subject than males to the cultural emphasis on material success (anomie); because they are less exposed to influence from delinquent peers (differential association and/or social learning); because they have stronger social bonds and are subjected to greater supervision (social control); and because they are less likely to become involved in gangs (cultural transmission).

Findings from a number of self-report studies support the ability of traditional criminological theories to partially account for the gender gap in crime. These studies show that the relationship between gender and delinquency is significantly reduced when controls are included for friends who support delinquency (Simons et al 1980), parental controls (Hagan 1989), and social bonds (Jensen & Eve 1976). However, as with power-control theory (but framed explicitly in terms of "common delinquency"), the significance of the traditional theories for explaining the gender gap is limited by the fact that these studies have been confined to minor (mainly male) delinquencies. As already noted, they also lack sensitivity to the manner in which the criminal behavior of women differs from that of men in terms of paths to crime (e.g. prior experience as victims) and in terms of context.

The critical need is for an approach that can explain not just minor but serious female offending, and one that can explain the gender gap not just where it is least, but where it is greatest. Gender differences are most robust in both the prevalence and incidence of serious offending, yet robust theoretical tests for these differences are notable for their absence. Until such tests can be carried out, the relevance of traditional theories will remain unknown with regard to that domain of criminality where gender differences are greatest and where statistical variation is sufficient for theory testing.

TOWARD A GENDERED THEORY

No satisfactorily unified theoretical framework has yet been developed for explaining female criminality and gender differences in crime. Criminologists disagree as to whether gender-neutral (i.e. traditional theories derived from male samples) or gender-specific theories (i.e. recent approaches derived from female samples and positing unique causal paths for female as compared to male criminality) are better suited to these tasks. We take the position that the traditional gender-neutral theories provide reasonable explanations of less serious forms of female and male criminality, and for gender differences in such crime categories. Their principal shortcoming is that they are not very informative about the specific ways in which differences in the lives of men and women contribute to gender differences in type, frequency, and context of criminal behavior. Gender-specific theories are likely to be even less adequate if they require separate explanations for female crime and male crime.

Here we build on a framework for a "gendered" approach begun elsewhere (Steffensmeier & Allan 1995). This approach is compatible with the traditional, gender-neutral theories. The broad social forces suggested by traditional theories exert general causal influences on both male and female crime. But it is gender that mediates the manner in which those forces play out into sex differences in types, frequency, and contexts of crime involvements.

Key Elements of a Gendered Approach

A gendered approach should include at least four key elements. First, the perspective should help explain not only female criminality but male criminality as well, by revealing how the organization of gender deters or shapes delinquency by females but encourages it by males. We use the term "organization of gender" to refer broadly to things gendered—norms, identities, arrangements, institutions, and relations by which human sexual dichotomy is transformed into something physically and socially different.

Second, a gendered perspective should account not only for gender differences in type and frequency of crime, but also for differences in the context of offending. Even when men and women commit the same statutory offense, the "gestalt" of their offending is frequently quite different. Because the gender differences in context are small for trivial or mild forms of lawbreaking, but large for violent and other serious forms of crime, contextual analysis can shed light on the gender differences for serious offenses—hitherto the most difficult to explain.

Third, compared to theories based on male crime, we need to consider several key ways in which women's routes to crime (especially serious crime) may differ from those of men. Building on the work of Daly (1994) and Steffensmeier (1983, 1993), such differences include: (a) the more blurred boundaries between victim and victimization in women's than men's case histories; (b) women's exclusion from most lucrative crime opportunities; (c) women's ability to exploit sex as an illegal money-making service; (d) consequences (real or anticipated) of motherhood and child care; (e) the centrality of greater relational concerns among women, and the manner in which these both shape and allow women to be pulled into criminal involvements by men in their lives; (f) the greater need of street women for protection from predatory or exploitative males.

Fourth, the perspective should explore the extent to which gender differences in crime derive not only from complex social, historical, and cultural factors, but from biological and reproductive differences as well (Kruttschnitt 1995, Udry 1995).

Figure 3 summarizes a gendered paradigm of offending that takes into account the four criteria enunciated above. We sketch here key features of this

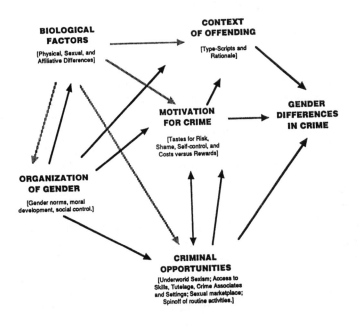

Figure 3 Gendered model of female offending and gender diiferences in crime. *Broken line* indicates weak effect; *solid line* signifies strong effect.

paradigm that affect men and women differently in terms of willingness and ability to commit crime.

The Organization of Gender

The organization of gender together with sex differences in physical/sexual characteristics contributes to male and female differences in several types of relatively enduring characteristics that increase the probability of prosocial and altruistic response on the part of females but antisocial and predatory response on the part of males.

In the discussion that follows we elaborate briefly on five areas of life that inhibit female crime but encourage male crime: gender norms, moral development and affiliative concerns, social control, physical strength and aggression, and sexuality. Gender differences in these areas condition gender differences in patterns of motivation and access to criminal opportunities, as well as gender differences in the type, frequency, and context of offending. These areas are not discrete, but rather they overlap and mutually reinforce one another.

GENDER NORMS   The greater taboos against female crime stem largely from two powerful focal concerns ascribed to women: (i) nurturant role obligations and (ii) female beauty and sexual virtue. In varied settings or situations, these concerns shape the constraints and opportunities of girls' and women's illicit activities.

Women are rewarded for their ability to establish and maintain relationships and to accept family obligations, and their identity tends to be derived from key males in their lives (e.g. father, husband). Derivative identity constrains deviance on the part of women involved with conventional males but encourages the criminal involvements of those who become accomplices of husbands or boyfriends. Greater child-rearing responsibilities further constrain female criminality.

Femininity stereotypes (e.g. weakness, submission, domestication, nurturance, and "ladylike" behavior) are basically incompatible with qualities valued in the criminal underworld (Steffensmeier 1986). The cleavage between what is considered feminine and what is criminal is sharp, while the dividing line between what is considered masculine and what is criminal is often thin. Crime is almost always stigmatizing for females, and its potential cost to life chances is much greater than for males.

Expectations regarding sexuality and physical appearance reinforce greater female dependency as well as greater surveillance by parents and husbands. These expectations also shape the deviant roles available to women (e.g. sexual media or service roles). Moreover, fear of sexual victimization diverts women from crime-likely locations (bars, nighttime streets) and reduces their opportunities to commit crimes (McCarthy & Hagan 1992, Steffensmeier 1983).

MORAL DEVELOPMENT AND AMENABILITY TO AFFILIATION   Gender differences in moral development (Gilligan 1982) and an apparent greater inherent readiness of women to learn parenting and nurturing (Beutel & Marini 1995, Brody 1985, Rossi 1984) predispose women toward an "ethic of care" that restrains women from violence and other criminal behavior injurious to others. Women are socialized not only to be more responsive to the needs of others but also to fear the threat of separation from loved ones. Such complex concerns inhibit women from undertaking criminal activities that might cause hurt to others and shape the "gestalt" of their criminality when they do offend.

In contrast, men who are conditioned toward status-seeking, yet marginalized from the world of work, may develop an amoral world view in which the "takers" gain superior status at the expense of the "givers." Such a moral stance obviously increases the likelihood of aggressive criminal behavior on the part of those who become "convinced that people are at each other's throats increasingly in a game of life that has no moral rules" (Messerschmidt 1986, p. 66).

SOCIAL CONTROL   Social control powerfully shapes women's relative willingness and ability to commit crime. Female misbehavior is more stringently monitored and corrected through negative stereotypes and sanctions (Simmons & Blyth 1987). The greater supervision and control reduces female risk-taking and increases attachment to parents, teachers, and conventional friends, which in turn reduces influence by delinquent peers (Giordano et al 1986). Encapsulation within the family and the production of "moral culture" restricts the freedom even of adult women to explore the temptations of the world (Collins 1992).

PHYSICAL STRENGTH AND AGGRESSION   The demands of the crime environment for physical power and violence help account for the less serious nature and less frequent incidence of crimes by women compared to those by men. Women may lack the power, or may be perceived by themselves or by others as lacking the violent potential, for successful completion of certain types of crime or for protection of a major "score." Hustling small amounts of money or property protects female criminals against predators who might be attracted by larger amounts. Real or perceived vulnerability can also help account for female restriction to solo roles, or to roles as subordinate partners or accomplices in crime groups. This can be seen in a variety of female offense patterns, including the exigencies of the dependent prostitute-pimp relationship (James 1977). Together, physical prowess and muscle are useful for committing crimes, for protection, for enforcing contracts, and for recruiting and managing reliable associates.

SEXUALITY   Reproductive-sexual differences (especially when combined with sexual taboos and titillations of the society as a whole) contribute to the far greater sexual deviance and infidelity among males. Women, on the other hand, have expanded opportunities for financial gain through prostitution and related illicit sexual roles. The possibilities in this arena reduce the need to commit the serious property crimes that so disproportionately involve males.

Although female offenders may use their sexuality to gain entry into male criminal organizations, such exploitation of male stereotypes is likely to limit their criminal opportunities within the group to roles organized around female attributes. The sexual dimension may also heighten the potential for sexual tension which can be resolved only if the female aligns herself with one man sexually, becoming "his woman."

Even prostitution—often considered a female crime—is essentially a male-dominated or -controlled criminal enterprise. Police, pimps, businessmen who employ prostitutes, and clients—virtually all of whom are male—control, in various ways, the conditions under which the prostitute works.

Access to Criminal Opportunity

The factors above—gender norms, social control, and the like—restrict female access to criminal opportunity, which in turn both limits and shapes female participation in crime. Women are also less likely than men to have access to crime opportunities as a spin-off of legitimate roles and routine activities. Women are less likely to hold jobs as truck driver, dockworker, or carpenter that would provide opportunities for theft, drug dealing, fencing, and other illegitimate activities. In contrast, women have considerable opportunity for commission, and thus for surveillance and arrest for petty forms of fraud and embezzlement.

Females are most restricted in terms of access to underworld crimes that are organized and lucrative. Institutional sexism in the underworld severely limits female involvement in crime groups, ranging from syndicates to loosely structured groups (Steffensmeier 1983, Commonwealth of Pennsylvania 1991). As in the upperworld, females in the underworld are disadvantaged in terms of selection and recruitment, in the range of career paths and access to them, and in opportunities for tutelage, skill development, and rewards.

Motivation

Gender norms, social control, lack of physical strength, and moral and relational concerns also limit female willingness to participate in crime at the subjective level—by contributing to gender differences in tastes for risk, likelihood of shame or embarrassment, self-control, and assessment of costs versus rewards of crime. Motivation is distinct from opportunity, but the two often intertwine, as when opportunity enhances temptation. As in legitimate enterprise, being able tends to make one more willing, just as being willing increases the prospects for being able. Like male offenders, female offenders gravitate to those activities that are easily available, are within their skills, provide a satisfactory return, and carry the fewest risks.

Criminal motivations and involvements are also shaped by gender differences in risk preferences and in styles of risk-taking (Hagan 1989, Steffensmeier 1980, Steffensmeier & Allan 1995). For example, women take greater risks to sustain valued relationships, whereas males take greater risks for reasons of status or competitive advantage. Criminal motivation is suppressed by the female ability to foresee threats to life chances and by the relative unavailability of type scripts that could channel females in unapproved behaviors.

Context of Offending

Many of the most profound differences between the offenses committed by men and women involve the context of offending, a point neglected by quantitative studies based on aggregate and survey data. "Context" refers to the characteristics of a particular offense, including both the circumstances and the nature of the act (Triplett & Myers 1995). Contextual characteristics include, for example, the setting, whether the offense was committed with others, the offender's role in initiating and committing the offense, the type of victim, the victim-offender relationship, whether a weapon was used, the extent of injury, the value or type of property destroyed or stolen, and the purpose of the offense. Even when males and females participate in the same types of crimes, the "gestalt" of their actions may differ markedly (Daly 1994, Steffensmeier 1983, 1993). Moreover, the more serious the offense, the greater the contextual differences by gender.

A powerful example of the importance of contextual considerations is found in the case of spousal murders, for which the female share of offending is quite high—at least one third, and perhaps as much as one half. Starting with Wolfgang's classic study of homicide, a number of writers propose that husbands and wives have equal potential for violence (Steinmetz & Lucca 1988, Straus & Gelles 1990). However, Dobash et al (1992) point out that the context of spousal violence is dramatically different for men and women. Compared to men, women are far more likely to kill only after a prolonged period of abuse, when they are in fear for their lives and have exhausted all alternatives. A number of patterns of wife-killing by husbands are rarely if ever found when wives kill husbands: murder-suicides, family massacres, stalking, and murder in response to spouse infidelity.

In common delinquency, female prevalence approaches that of males in simple forms of delinquency like hitting others or stealing from stores or schools, but girls are far less likely to use a weapon or to intend serious injury to their victims (Kruttschnitt 1994), to steal things they cannot use (Cohen 1966), and to steal from building sites or break into buildings (Mawby 1980).

Similarly, when females commit traditional male crimes like burglary, they are less likely to be solitary (Decker et al 1993), more likely to serve as an accomplice (e.g. drop-off driver), and less likely to receive an equal share of proceeds (Steffensmeier & Terry 1986). Also, female burglaries involve less planning and are more spontaneous, and they are more likely to occur in daytime in residences where no one is at home and with which they have prior familiarity as an acquaintance, maid, or the like (Steffensmeier 1986, 1993).

Application of Gendered Perspective to Patterns of Female Crime

The utility of a gendered perspective can be seen in its ability to explain both female and male patterns of criminal involvement as well as gender differences in crime. The perspective predicts, and finds, that female participation is highest for those crimes most consistent with traditional norms and for which females have the most opportunity, and lowest for those crimes that diverge the most from traditional gender norms and for which females have little opportunity.

Let us briefly review some examples of property, violent, and public order offending patterns that can be better understood from a gendered perspective.

In the area of property crimes we have already noted that the percentage of female arrests is highest for the minor offenses like small thefts, shoplifting and passing bad checks—offenses compatible with traditional female roles in making family purchases. The high share of arrests for embezzlement reflects female employment segregation: women constitute about 90% of lower level bookkeepers and bank tellers (those most likely to be arrested for embezzlement), but slightly less than half of all accountants or auditors. Further, women tend to embezzle to protect their families or valued relationships, while men tend to embezzle to protect their status (Zeitz 1981).

Despite Simon's (1975) claim that female involvement in white collar crime was on the increase, in fact it is almost nonexistent in more serious occupational and/or business crimes, like insider trading, price-fixing, restraint of trade, toxic waste dumping, fraudulent product commerce, bribery, and official corruption, as well as large-scale governmental crimes (for example, the Iran-Contra affair and the Greylord scandal). Even when similar on-the-job opportunities for theft exist, women are still less likely to commit crime (Steffensmeier 1980).

The lowest percentage of female involvement is found for serious property crimes whether committed on the "street" such as burglary and robbery or in the "suite" such as insider trading or price-fixing (Steffensmeier & Allan 1995). These sorts of offenses are very much at odds with traditional feminine stereotypes, and ones to which women have very limited access. When women act as solo perpetrators, the typical robbery is a "wallet-sized" theft by a prostitute or addict (James 1977, see also Covington 1985, Pettiway 1987). However, females frequently become involved in such crimes as accomplices to males, particularly in roles that at once exploit women's sexuality and reinforce their traditional subordination to men (American Correctional Association 1983, Miller 1986, Steffensmeier & Terry 1986).

Female violence, although apparently at odds with female gender norms of gentleness and passivity, is also closely tied to the organization of gender. Unlike males, females rarely kill or assault strangers or acquaintances; instead, the female's victim tends to be a male intimate or a child, the offense generally takes place within the home, the victim is frequently drunk, and self-defense or extreme depression is often a motive (Dobash et al 1992). For women to kill, they generally must see their situation as life-threatening, as affecting the physical or emotional well-being of themselves or their children.

The linkage between female crime and the gendered paradigm of Figure 3 is perhaps most evident in the case of certain public order offenses with a high percentage of female involvement, particularly the sex-related categories of prostitution and juvenile runaways—the only offense categories where female arrest rates exceed those of males. The high percentage of female arrests in these two categories reflects both gender differences in marketability of sexual services and the continuing patriarchal sexual double standard. Although customers must obviously outnumber prostitutes, they are less likely to be sanctioned. Similarly, although self-report studies show male rates of runaways to be as high as female rates, suspicion of sexual involvement makes female runaways more likely to be arrested (Chesney-Lind & Shelden 1992).

Female substance abuse (as with other patterns of female crime) often stems from relational concerns or involvements, beginning in the context of teenage dating or following introduction to drugs by husbands or boyfriends (Inciardi et al 1993, Pettiway 1987). Women tend to be less involved in heavy drinking or hard drug use—those drugs most intimately tied to drug subcultures and the underworld more generally (Department of Health & Human Services 1984). Female addicts are less likely to have other criminal involvements prior to addiction, so the amplification of income-oriented crime is greater for female drug users. Female addict crimes are mainly prostitution, reselling narcotics or assisting male drug dealers, and property crimes such as shoplifting, forgery, and burglary (Anglin & Hser 1987).

Advantages of Paradigm

A gendered approach helps to clarify the gendered nature of both female and male offending patterns. For women, "doing gender" preempts criminal involvement or directs it into scripted paths. For example, prostitution draws on and affirms femininity, while violence draws on and affirms masculinity.

At present it is unclear whether nontraditional roles for women will contribute to higher or lower rates of female offending. Traditional roles constrain most women from crime but may expose others to greater risks for criminal involvement. Wives playing traditional roles in patriarchal relationships appear to be at greatest risk both for victimization and for committing spousal homicide. Similarly, women emotionally dependent on criminal men are more easily persuaded to "do it all for love." (Note, nevertheless, that men are also more easily persuaded by other men.) Cross-cultural differences complicate the issue further. For example, among gypsies, traditional gender roles prevail and male dominance is absolute. Yet, because gypsy women do practically all the work and earn most of the money, their culture dictates a large female-to-male involvement in thievery (Maas 1973).

A gendered approach can also help explain both stability and variability in the gender effect. A growing body of historical research indicates that the gender differences in quality and quantity of crime described here closely parallel those that have prevailed since at least the thirteenth century (Beattie 1975, Hanawalt

1979). Even where variability does exist across time, the evidence suggests that changes in the female percentage of offending (i) are limited mainly to minor property crimes or mild forms of delinquency (Hagan & Simpson 1993, Steffensmeier 1980) and (ii) are due to structural changes other than more equalitarian gender roles such as shifts in economic marginality of women, expanded availability of female-type crime opportunities, and greater formalization of social control (Beattie 1995, Steffensmeier 1993). The considerable stability in the gender gap for offending can be explained in part by historical durability of the organization of gender (Walby 1990). Certainly for recent decades, research suggests that the core elements of gender roles and relationships have changed little, if at all (for a review, see Steffensmeier & Allan 1995, see also Beutel & Marini 1995). Underlying physical/sexual differences (whether actual or perceived) may also play a part. Human groups, for all their cultural variation, follow basic human forms.

SUMMARY AND RECOMMENDATIONS

An examination of gender patterns in crime reveals that there are both similarities and differences in female and male patterns of offending. Traditional criminological theories deserve more credit than they have received in recent writings in terms of their ability to provide general explanations both of female and male offending patterns and of the gender gap in crime. Certainly this is the case with minor acts of crime and delinquency which have been frequent objects of quantitative analysis. Likewise, the manner in which female and male rates of offending parallel one another across differences in time, race, class, and geography suggests that they are responding to similar social forces. Such findings suggest that there is no need for gender-specific theories.

On the other hand, explanation of serious crimes by males and females is more problematic, partly because the lower frequencies of offending complicate the task of quantitative analyses. Qualitative studies reveal major gender differences in the context and nature of offending. Traditional theories have not adequately explored such gender differences. Our gendered paradigm seeks a middle road that acknowledges both the utility of traditional theory and the need to describe how the organization of gender (and biological/physical differences) specifies the impact of social forces suggested by traditional theory. Space limitations prevent us from broaching some of the most important areas related to female criminality, such as patterns of female victimization (Price & Sokoloff 1995) and gender differences in criminal justice processing (for a review, see Steffensmeier et al 1993). Even our coverage of patterns and etiology of female offending is selective and cursory. Nevertheless, some recommendations emerge from this review that could improve the yield of future theory and research.

We need to examine more closely whether various criminogenic factors (e.g. family, peers, schooling) vary by gender either in the magnitude or the direction of effects. Factors generally seen as uniquely relevant to the explanation of female crime (e.g. childhood abuse, personal maladjustment, victimization) should be explored in relation to male crime (Bjerregaard & Smith 1993).

Conventional theories were never designed to tap the encompassing structure and repetitive process of gender as it affects the criminal involvements of either women or men. Therefore we need to operationalize and test variables drawn from gendered approaches, particularly in relation to the explanation of serious and habitual criminal behavior.

Both theory development and research need to look more closely at the intersection of gender with other dimensions of stratification (Hill & Crawford). Do gender-specific effects of causal variables also vary by race, class, or ethnicity? Care must be taken to avoid confusing gender effects with other subgroup effects, however. Identification of gender effects must entail female-male comparisons within the same population subgroup. For example, the fact that arrest rates for black females exceed arrest rates for white males for some offenses tells us something about race effects but nothing about gender effects (Heimer 1995, Simpson & Ellis 1995, Sommers 1992).

So far, the study of criminal careers has centered almost exclusively on male offenders. As Gilfus (1992:64) notes, "Little attention has been paid to questions such as whether there is such a thing as a female 'criminal career' pattern and, if so, how that career begins and what shapes its contours." In-depth studies of serious female offenders need to focus on career dimensions such as onset, frequency, duration, seriousness, and specialization.

Such studies need to examine both the immediate context of the offense and the larger social setting of serious or habitual offending, following the fine examples set by Miller's (1986) study of street women, Campbell's (1984) research on girls and gangs, Steffensmeier & Terry's (1986) research on institutional sexism in the underworld, and Bottcher's (1995) study of high-risk male and female youths, and their siblings. Such studies reveal the extent to which the lives of delinquent girls and women continue to be powerfully influenced by gender-related conditions of life.

Some of the most profound contributions to our knowledge concerning gender and crime (including the studies cited in the previous paragraph) have come from criminologists who have exploited theory and research from other sociological specialities (e.g. family, organization, network analysis) in the study of female criminality. Also needed is application of a life course perspective to female offending, as Sampson & Laub (1993) have done so effectively in their study of male offending.

We need a clearer understanding of the specific behaviors involved in particular crimes committed by women and men, the nature of their criminal roles, the circumstances leading to criminal involvement, the motivations for committing crimes, and the vocabularies used to justify their crimes. The same statutory charge applied to women and men may reflect very different behaviors and circumstances, as illustrated in the research on spousal homicide described above (reviewed by Dobash et al 1992).

Criminal opportunity has many dimensions that vary dramatically by gender. We need to understand how crime opportunities are shaped by legitimate opportunities, by the structure of the underworld, and by changes in productive and routine activities (Steffensmeier 1983, 1993). As already noted, women have little access to either upperworld or underworld opportunities for lucrative white collar or organized crime. Professional crime, traditionally dominated by white males, is on the decline.

Over the last three decades, the largest gains in female arrests relative to male arrests were for nonviolent economic crimes such as fraud and forgery—crimes now within the reach of virtually every American citizen. Changes in female motivation as well as in the social or economic position of females are likely to be less important than the nature of societal crime opportunities in shaping patterns of female offending and variations in the gender gap. This is a neglected area of research in criminology, and is one where sociologists with their expertise in broad societal trends can make a major contribution to the study not only of female criminality but also to crime more generally.

If significant differences in the gender gap are found, all plausible explanations should be explored. Tests of the gender equality hypothesis should attempt more suitable operationalization than assumed group differences in equality (such as age, race, urban residence). On the other hand, an interesting inquiry into the sociology of knowledge could address the longevity of the gender equality hypothesis in the face of so much contrary evidence.

Our knowledge about fundamental issues in the study of gender and crime has expanded greatly with the proliferation of studies over the past several decades, although significant gaps still exist. Given the relatively low frequency and less serious nature of female crime, expanding research on female offending may seem hard to justify. But research on the gendered nature of crime contributes to the understanding of male as well as female crime. Furthermore, the study of gender and crime is a productive arena for exploring the nature of gender stratification and the organization of gender more generally.

Literature Cited

Adler F. 1975. *Sisters in Crime.* New York: McGraw-Hill

Akers R, Krohn M, Lanza-Kaduce L, Radosevich M. 1979. Social learning and deviant behavior: a specific test of a general theory. *Am. Sociol. Rev.* 44:298–310

American Correctional Association. 1983. *Female Inmate Classification: An Examination of the Issues.* Natl. Inst. Correct. Washington, DC: US Gov. Print. Off.

Anglin D, Hser Y. 1987. Addicted women and crime. *Criminology* 25:359–97

Arnold R. 1989. Processes of criminalization from girlhood to womanhood. In *Women of Color in American Society,* ed. M Zinn, B Dill. Philadelphia: Temple Univ. Press

Beattie J. 1975. The criminality of women in eighteenth century England. In *Women and the Law: A Social Historical Perspective,* ed. DK Weisberg. Cambridge, MA: Schenkman

Beattie J. 1995. Crime and inequality in 18th century London. In *Crime and Inequality,* ed. J Hagan, R Peterson. Stanford, CA: Stanford Univ. Press

Berger R. 1990. Female delinquency in the Emancipation era: a review of the literature. *Sex Roles* 21:375–99

Beutel A, Marini M. 1995. Gender and values. *Am. Sociol. Rev.* 60:436–48

Bjerregaard B, Smith C. 1993. Gender differences in gang participation, delinquency, and substance use. *J. Quant. Criminol.* 9:329–56

Boritch H, Hagan J. 1990. A century of crime in Toronto: gender, class and patterns of social control, 1859–1955. *Criminology* 28:601–26

Bottcher J. 1986. *Risky Lives: Female Versions of Common Delinquent Life Patterns.* Sacramento: Calif. Youth Authority

Bottcher J. 1995. Gender as social control: a qualitative study of incarcerated youths and their siblings in greater Sacramento. *Justice Q.* 12:33–57

Bowker L, Gross H, Klein M. 1980. Female participation in delinquent gang activities. In *Women and Crime in America,* ed. L Bowker, pp. 158–79. New York: Macmillan

Brody LR. 1985. Gender differences in emotional development: a review of theories and research. *J. Pers.* 14:102–49

Bureau of Justice Statistics. 1973–1992. *Criminal Victimization In The United States, 1991.* Washington, DC: Dept. Justice

Campbell A. 1984. *The Girls in the Gang.* Oxford: Basil Blackwell

Campbell A. 1990. Female participation in gangs. In *Gangs in America,* ed. C Huff. Newbury Park, CA: Sage

Canter R. 1982. Sex differences in delinquency. *Criminology* 20:373–98

Chesney-Lind M. 1986. Women and crime: the female offender. *Signs* 12:78–96

Chesney-Lind M. 1989. Girls' crime and woman's place: toward a feminist model of female delinquency. *Crime Delinq.* 35:5–29

Chesney-Lind M, Shelden R. 1992. *Girls, Delinquency, and Juvenile Justice.* Pacific Grove, CA: Brooks/Cole

Cohen A. 1966. *Deviance and Control.* Englewood Cliffs, NJ:Prentice-Hall

Collins R. 1992. Women and the production of status cultures. In *Cultivating Differences,* ed. M Lamont, M Fournier. Chicago: Univ. Chicago Press

Commonwealth of Pennsylvania. 1991. *Organized Crime in Pennsylvania, The 1990 Report.* Conshohocken, PA: Penn. Crime Comm.

Covington J. 1985. Gender differences in criminality among heroin users. *J. Res. Crime Delinq.* 22:329–53

Daly K. 1989. Gender and varieties of white-collar crime. *Criminology* 27:769–94

Daly K. 1994. *Gender, Crime and Punishment.* New Haven, CT: Yale Univ. Press

Daly K, Chesney-Lind M. 1988. Feminism and criminology. *Justice Q.* 5:497–538

Decker S, Wright R, Refern A, Smith D. 1993. A woman's place is in the home: females and residential burglary. *Justice Q.* 10:1–16

Deisite A. 1989. Maced greeter gives police key evidence. *The Patriot* p. B1

Denno D. 1994. Gender, crime, and the criminal law defenses. *J. Crim. Law Criminol.* 85(1):80–180

Department of Health and Human Services. 1984. *Drug Abuse and Drug Abuse Research.* Rockville, MD: Natl. Inst. Drug Abuse

Dobash R, Dobash RE, Wilson M, Daly M. 1992. The myth of sexual symmetry in marital violence. *Soc. Probl.* 39:71–91

Elliott M. 1952. *Crime in a Modern Society.* New York: Harper & Brothers

English K. 1993. Self-reported crime rates of women prisoners. *J. Quant. Crimol.* 9:357–82

Fagan J. 1990. Social processes of delinquency and drug use among urban gangs. In *Gangs in America*, ed. C Huff. Newbury Park: CA: Sage

Gilfus M. 1992. From victims to survivors to offenders: women's routes of entry and immersion into street crime. *Women Crim. Justice* 4:63–89

Gilligan C. 1982. *In a Different Voice: Psychological Theory and Women's Development.* Cambridge, MA: Harvard Univ. Press

Giordano P, Cernkovich S, Pugh M. 1986. Friendships and delinquency. *Am. J. Sociol.* 91:1170–203

Grasmick H, Bursik R, Sims B. 1993. Changes in the sex patterning of perceived threats of sanctions. *Law Soc. Rev.* 27:679–705

Hagan J. 1989. *Structural Criminology.* New Brunswick, NJ: Rutgers Univ. Press

Hagan J, Gillis A, Simpson J. 1993. The power of control in sociological theories of delinquency. In *Advances in Criminological Theory*, Vol. 4, ed. F Adler, W Laufer. New Brunswick, NJ: Transaction

Hanawalt B. 1979. *Crime and Conflict in English Communities, 1300–1348.* Cambridge: Harvard Univ. Press

Heimer K. 1995. Gender, race, and the pathways to delinquency: an interactionist explanation. In *Crime and Inequality*, ed. J Hagan, R Peterson. Stanford, CA: Stanford Univ. Press

Hill G, Crawford E. 1990. Women, race, and crime. *Criminology* 28:601–26

Inciardi J, Lockwood D, Pottieger A. 1993. *Women and Crack-Cocaine.* New York: Macmillan

James J. 1977. Prostitutes and prostitution. In *Deviants: Voluntary Action in a Hostile World*, ed. E Sagarin, F Montanino. New York: Scott, Foresman

Jensen G. 1993. Power-control vs social-control theories of common delinquency: a comparative analysis. In *Advances in Criminological Theory*, Vol. 4, ed. F Adler, W Laufer. New Brunswick, NJ: Transaction

Jensen G, Eve R. 1976. Sex differences in delinquency. *Criminology* 13:427–48

Kruttschnitt C. 1994. Gender and interpersonal violence. In *Understanding and Preventing Violence: Social Influences*, ed. J Roth, A Reiss, 3:295–378. Washington, DC: Natl. Acad. Sci.

Maas P. 1973. *King of the Gypsies.* New York: Bantam

Mann C. 1984. *Female Crime and Delinquency.* Birmingham: Univ. Alabama Press

Mawby R. 1980. Sex and crime: the results of

a self-report study. *Br. J. Sociol.* 31:525–43

McCarthy B, Hagan J. 1992. Mean streets: the theoretical significance of situational delinquency and homeless youths. *Am. J. Sociol.* 98:597–627

Messerschmidt J. 1986. *Capitalism, Patriarchy, and Crime: Toward a Socialist Feminist Criminology.* Totowa, NJ: Rowman & Littlefield

Miller E. 1986. *Street Women.* Philadelphia: Temple Univ. Press

Miller W. 1980. The molls. In *Women, Crime, and Justice*, ed. S Datesman, F Scarpitti. New York: Oxford Univ. Press

Morash M, Chesney-Lind M. 1991. A reformulation and partial test of the power control theory of delinquency. *Justice Q.* 8:347–76

Pettiway L. 1987. Participation in crime partnerships by female drug users. *Criminology* 25:741–67

Pollock-Byrne J. 1990. *Women, Prison, and Crime.* Belmont, CA: Brooks/Cole

Price B, Sokoloff N. 1995. *The Criminal Justice System and Women.* New York: McGraw-Hill

Prus R, Sharper CRD. 1977. *Road Hustler.* Lexington, MA: Lexington

Quicker J. 1983. *Homegirls: Characterizing Chicano Gangs.* San Pedro, CA: Int. Univ. Press

Reitman B. 1937. *Sister of the Road: The Autobiography of Box-Car Bertha.* New York: Macauley

Richie B. 1995. *The Gendered Entrapment of Battered, Black Women.* London: Rutledge

Rossi A. 1984. Gender and parenthood. *Am. Sociol. Rev.* 49:1–19

Sampson R, Laub J. 1993. *Crime in the Making.* Cambridge, MA: Harvard Univ. Press

Shover N, Norland S, James J, Thorton W. 1979. Gender roles and delinquency. *Soc. Forces* 58:162–75

Simmons R, Blyth D. 1987. *Moving Into Adolescence.* New York: Aldine

Simon R. 1975. *The Contemporary Woman and Crime.* Washington, DC: Natl. Inst. Mental Health

Simons R, Miller M, Aignor S. 1980. Contemporary theories of deviance and female delinquency. *J. Res. Criminol. Delinq.* 17:42–57

Simpson S, Ellis L. 1995. Doing gender: sorting out the caste and crime conundrum. *Criminology* 33:47–77

Singer S, Levine M. 1988. Power-control theory, gender and delinquency. *Criminology* 26:627–48

Smith D. 1979. Sex and deviance: an assessment of major sociological variables. *Sociol.*

Q. 20:183–95

Smith D, Paternoster R. 1987. The gender gap in theories of deviance: issues and evidence. *Criminology* 24:140–72

Smith D, Visher C. 1980. Sex and involvement in deviance/crime: a quantitative review of the empirical literature. *Am. Sociol. Rev.* 65:767–82

Sommers I, Baskin D. 1992. Sex, race, age, and violent offending. *Violence Vict.* 7:191–201

Steffensmeier D. 1980. A review and assessment of sex differences in adult crime, 1965–77. *Soc. Forces* 58:1080–1108

Steffensmeier D. 1983. Sex-segregation in the underworld: building a sociological explanation of sex differences in crime. *Soc. Forces* 61:1010–32

Steffensmeier D. 1986. *The Fence: In the Shadow of Two Worlds.* Totowa, NJ: Rowman & Littlefield

Steffensmeier D. 1993. National trends in female arrests, 1960–1990: assessment and recommendations for research. *J. Quant. Criminol.* 9:413–41

Steffensmeier D, Allan E. 1988. Sex disparities in crime by population subgroup: residence, race, and age. *Justice Q.* 5:53–80

Steffensmeier D, Allan E. 1995. Gender, age, and crime. In *Handbook of Contemporary Criminology,* ed. J Sheley. New York: Wadsworth

Steffensmeier D, Allan E, Streifel C. 1989. Modernization and female crime: a cross-national test of alternative explanations. *Soc. Forces* 68:262–83

Steffensmeier D, Clark R. 1980. Sociocultural vs. biological/sexist explanations of sex differences in crime: a survey of American criminology textbooks, 1919–1965. *Am. Sociol.* 15:246–55

Steffensmeier D, Kramer J, Streifel C. 1993. Gender and imprisonment decisions. *Criminology* 31:411–46

Steffensmeier D, Rosenthal A, Shehan C. 1980. World War II and its effects on the sex differential in arrests: an empirical test of the sex-role equality and crime proposition. *Sociol. Q.* 21:246–55

Steffensmeier D, Streifel C. 1992. Time-series analysis of female-to-male arrests for property crimes, 1960–1985: a test of alternative explanations. *Justice Q.* 9:78–103

Steffensmeier D, Streifel C. 1993. *Structural covariates of female as compared to male violence rates.* Presented at Annu. Meet. Am. Sociol. Crim., Phoenix, AZ

Steffensmeier D, Terry R. 1986. Institutional sexism in the underworld: a view from the inside. *Sociol. Inq.* 56:304–23

Steinmetz S, Lucca J. 1988. Husband beating. In *Handbook of Family Violence,* ed. R Hassselt, A Morrison, S Bellack, M Hersen, pp. 233–46. New York: Plenum

Straus M, Gelles R. 1990. *Physical Violence in American Families.* New Brunswick, NJ: Transaction

Sutherland E. 1924. *Criminology.* Philadelphia: Lippincott

Swart W. 1991. Female gang delinquency: a search for "acceptably deviant behavior." *Mid-Am. Rev. Sociol.* 15:43–52

Thrasher F. 1927. *The Gang.* Chicago: Univ. Chicago Press

Tittle C. 1980. *Social Sanctions and Social Deviance.* New York: Praeger

Triplett R, Myers L. 1995. Evaluating contextual patterns of delinquency: gender-based differences. *Justice Q.* 12:59–79

Udry JR. 1995. Sociology and biology: What biology do sociologists need to know? *Soc. Forces* 73:1267–78

US Department of Justice. 1960–1993. *Uniform Crime Reports.* Fed. Bur. Invest. Washington, DC: US Gov. Print. Off.

Walby S. 1990. *Theorizing Patriarchy.* Cambridge, MA: Basil Blackwell

Weiner N. 1989. Violent criminal careers and "violent career criminals." In *Violent Crime, Violent Criminals,* ed. N Weiner, M Wolfgang, pp. 35–138. Newbury Park, CA: Sage

Widom C. 1989. Child abuse, neglect and violent criminal behavior. *Criminology* 27:251–71

Zeitz D. 1981. *Women Who Embezzle or Defraud.* New York: Praeger

SUBJECT INDEX

CUMULATIVE INDEXES

CONTRIBUTING AUTHORS, VOLUMES 1–22

CHAPTER TITLES, VOLUMES 1–22

SOCIAL PROCESSES

Ordering Information

Annual Reviews publications may be ordered directly from our office; through authorized stockists; through booksellers and subscription agents; and through participating professional societies. Prices are subject to change without notice.

- **Individuals:** Prepayment required on new accounts in US funds, checks drawn on a US bank or charge to VISA, MasterCard, or American Express.

- **Institutional buyers:** Please include Purchase order.
  - Calif. Corp. #161041   ARI Fed. #94-1156476.

- **Students / Recent Graduate Discount: 30% off retail price. 1.** Must be a degree candidate at, or graduate in the past three years from, an accredited institution; **2.** Present proof of status; **3.** Order direct from Annual Reviews; **4.** Prepay. Discount does not apply to Handling Charges, Index on Diskette, Standing Orders, Annual Reviews Preprints and Reprints, or Institutional Buyers.

- **California orders** add applicable sales tax.

- **Canadian orders** add 7% GST. Registration **# 121449029 RT.**

- **HANDLING CHARGE: $3 per volume.** Handling charge is not subject to discount.

- **Standard Postage paid by Annual Reviews** (4th class bookrate/surface mail). **Optional Services: UPS ground $3.00** extra per book in the contiguous 48 states only. **UPS Air** or **US Airmail** to anywhere in the world is available at cost. UPS requires a street address. P. O. Box, APO, FPO, not acceptable.

- **Standing Orders: Save 10%** with your prepaid standing order. Receive the new volume each year upon publication. Save 10% each year by payment of prerelease invoices sent prior to the publication date.

- **Prepublication orders:** Advance orders may be placed for any volume. **Your credit card will be charged upon receipt of order. Volumes not yet published will be shipped during the month of publication indicated.**

- **Back Volumes** are available. For prices and availability: **http://www.annurev.org**

Individual articles from any *Annual Review* are available, as are all articles cited in any *Annual Review.* Call **Annual Reviews Preprints and Reprints: 1.800.347.8007** from USA or Canada. Call **1.415.259.5017** from elsewhere. Base price: $13.50 per article.

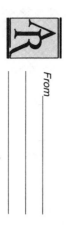

From

ANNUAL REVIEWS INC
4139 EL CAMINO WAY
P O BOX 10139
PALO ALTO   CA   94303-0139